The 4th Michigan Infantry in the Civil War

The 4th Michigan Infantry in the Civil War

Martin N. Bertera *and* Kim Crawford

Michigan State University Press · *East Lansing*

♾ The paper used in this publication meets the minimum requirements
of ANSI/NISO Z39.48-1992 (R 1997) (Permanence of Paper).

Michigan State University Press
East Lansing, Michigan 48823-5245

Printed and bound in the United States of America.
16 15 14 13 12 11 10 1 2 3 4 5 6 7 8 9 10

LIBRARY OF CONGRESS CATALOGING-IN-PUBLICATION DATA
Bertera, Martin N.
The 4th Michigan Infantry in the Civil War / Martin N. Bertera and Kim Crawford.
p. cm.
Includes bibliographical references and index.
ISBN 978-0-87013-973-4 (cloth : alk. paper) 1. United States. Army. Michigan Infantry Regiment, 4th (1861–1864) 2. Michigan—History—Civil War, 1861–1865—Regimental histories. 3. United States—History—Civil War, 1861–1865—Regimental histories. I. Crawford, Kim, 1957– II. Title.
E514.54th B475 2010
973.7'474—dc22
2010003509

Jacket design by Robert Tombs
Book design by Charlie Sharp, Sharp Des!gns, Lansing, Michigan
Cover photograph is of Jonas Richardson and is used courtesy of the Bentley Historical Library, University of Michigan.

green press INITIATIVE

Michigan State University Press is a member of the Green Press Initiative and is committed to developing and encouraging ecologically responsible publishing practices. For more information about the Green Press Initiative and the use of recycled paper in book publishing, please visit *www.greenpressinitiative.org*.

Visit Michigan State University Press on the World Wide Web at *www.msupress.msu.edu*

Contents

Preface

A narrative that attempts to show the Civil War as it was experienced by soldiers in one of Michigan's most distinguished combat regiments requires first-person accounts, and this true story of the 4th Michigan Infantry contains many voices of the men who served in it. These mainly come from soldiers' letters to their friends and families, many published in their hometown newspapers, but also from their diaries, reports, and reminiscences.

This is not the complete story of any one of these individual soldiers, of course. But from their experiences—and those of the people who served with them, commanded them, reported on them, and fought them—we attempted to construct a history of the 4th Michigan that was more than a recitation of marches and maneuvers and positions on battlefields, but one that was human and personal. We hope the picture that will emerge from these pages is not of marble statue heroes or nameless men in sepia portraits, but one of real people who walked the streets of your hometown 150 years ago, or farmed the fields where your neighborhood now stands—men who volunteered, got sick, suffered, died, did heroic things, and who were afraid and lonely. We hope the narrative informs their role in some of the most important battles of the war—sometimes when they were in the very thick of the fighting, and sometimes when they weren't. Yet we have tried not to always view them under a microscope, isolating them from the rest of the war, but to put them in context of events. And we tried to present this regiment's story accurately, avoiding sentimental and romantic excesses that sometimes characterized Civil War era journalism and historical writing. We have retained the sometimes irregular spelling, punctuation, and grammar of the original documents.

Acknowledgments

We are indebted to many descendants of the 4th Michigan's soldiers and Civil War collectors who shared unpublished sources. Jeff Phelps provided us with transcripts of the letters of Charles Phelps, while Robert Walkowiak permitted us to quote from the diary of his ancestor, Irvin Miner. A collector who asked not to be identified provided us with copies and transcripts of the letters and diary of Silas Sadler, the diary of Charles Doolittle, the letters of Charles J. Fox, and other items. Glen McQueen allowed the use of the George Millens diary.

Steve Roberts permitted us the use of the first two diaries of his relative, Henry S. Seage, while another family member, John DeVinney, kindly allowed us to quote from Henry's third diary. Thomas Spain let us quote Edgar Noble's diary. Craig and Ann Emery and Hal Flynn provided the memoir of Harrison Daniels. Edgar A. Luce Jr. let us draw from the memoir written by his grandfather, Moses Luce, as well as copies of biographical materials and articles about him. Nancy Findley provided transcripts of letters by Lemuel Allen, while Lynn Bryant provided letters by Noah Cressey. Steve Bucher and Rose Miller shared transcripts of letters of David Webster. Kenneth D. Andrews provided us a copy and transcript of a remarkable letter written by Albert Westgate.

Special thanks go to Hazel Pray Monahan, curator of the Hudson Museum in Michigan; to the late William F. Heckert of Kokomo, Indiana, who, long before we undertook this project, had for years researched the 4th Michigan Infantry; and to our friends Bob Coch and Dale Niesen, who have helped so many authors and researchers into Michigan's Civil War past and who have once again helped us. And we acknowledge the assistance of John Heiser of the Gettysburg National Military Park; Kerry Chartkoff, expert on Michigan's regimental Civil War flags; Robert Krick, historian of the Richmond National Battlefield Park, and Donald Pfanz, historian of the Fredericksburg and Spotsylvania National Military Park; John Gibney, David C. Ingall, and Chris Kull of the Monroe County (Michigan) Historical Museum; Mark Patrick, formerly of the Detroit Public Library; and Don Harvey and Ed and Lois Russell of "Michigan in the War" web site. We also thank Trevor K. Plante of the National Archives; Terry Reimer of the National Museum of Civil War Medicine; and Joyce Hicks of Auburn University for their assistance with our research questions.

In Michigan, we thank Karen Jania of the Bentley Historical Library, Kim Leese, Lee Lewis, Ray Lennard, Janine Delcamp, Dave Prince, Dan Eleson, Greg and Patty Martin, Roxie Lee Halloway, Cary Russo, Steve Lutz, Butch Miller, Gary Holmes, Bob Elliott, William Jerdan, Bill "Haversack" Hanusik, Charlie Middleton, Gregory Mahar, Timothy Twiss, William P. Watson, Bessie Boise Haight, Herb E. Hochraldel, Larry Houghton, Norma McAllister, Al Coe, Larry Cymbola, Ken Oberholtzer, Tom Hout, Brian Benson, Dan Flynn, George Dupuie, Steve Magina, Doug Truitt, Jim Zuieski of the Ella Sharp Museum in Jackson, Linda Kronberg, Julia Smith, Wesley E. Powers Jr., Timothy Curtis, Ruth A. Merriweather, Leonard Overmyer III, Karen and Daniel Pardee, Bob Windon, Juliet Smith, Gary Neil Sexton, Rick Rice, Patrick Freeman, Gary Drake, Bill Carr, and Bill Christen.

We must also acknowledge the assistance of Dee Seadler, Jim Green, and Jon Deiss in Maryland; Ed Wenzel, Deborah Petite, Elmer Woodward, Brian Pohanka, Dr. John T. Daily, and Thomas P. Lowry in Virginia; Alex Dalgleish and Brent Vossberg in New York; Bob Minton and Peter J. D'Onofril in Ohio; Nancy Curtis, Sue Peterson, Corky Reed, Anita Crabtree, and Donnalyn Bancroft Yates in California; Bill Clark and family, Pennsylvania; Dolores Jones in Tennessee; Cecile Vreeland and Sharon Mershon in Oregon; Robert Vreeland and Linda Dahle in Washington state; Kathryn Harris Aragon in New Mexico; Jackie Wood in Oklahoma; Gene E. Salecker, Illinois; Diane Farnsworth, Texas; Peggy Munoz, Montana; Patricia Davidson-Peters, Arizona; and William C. Floyd, Maryland.

Finally, we thank our wives, Kathy Bertera and Kelly Kolhagen-Crawford, for their patience and support.

CHAPTER 1

We Will Strive to Do Our Duty as American Soldiers

He was only a small-town hotel proprietor and an officer in the local militia, but even before the Civil War's first shots were fired, Dwight Woodbury was ready to serve his country. "[We] tender to the Governor of the state and to the government of the United States, our services in case of any contingency which may require such service," he wrote in January 1861. From the south-central Michigan town of Adrian, Woodbury sent those words in a letter to his state's new governor, Austin Blair, writing not only for himself but also on behalf of the officers who served under him in the state's 3rd Militia Regiment.[1]

Across the South the secession movement roiled, its proponents convinced that the election of Abraham Lincoln meant the abolition of slavery in the United States. The nation was lurching toward war with itself as those states broke away. While many dreaded the breakup of the country and some welcomed it, Woodbury would stand by the U.S. government. He was 36 years old, a businessman, husband, and father, well liked in his community. He stood at about average in height and build, with dark hair and beard, and had the habit of biting his lower lip, which a friend said indicated Woodbury's "earnestness of purpose." Politically he was a Jacksonian Democrat, a stripe that would soon be called "War Democrat." These Northern Democrats agreed with Lincoln and Republicans that military force should be used to stop the Southern states from seceding, though they didn't believe the abolition of slavery should be a primary goal of the federal government.

Woodbury had been born in upstate New York and come of age in Michigan and Ohio. Like many young men, he followed the Gold Rush to California to try to win his fortune. When he returned, he worked as a conductor on the Michigan Southern Railroad and married a businessman's daughter; he ran the Brackett House, a hotel in Adrian. More significantly, he had long been involved with the state militia and was colonel of volunteers from Michigan's Lenawee, Washtenaw, and Jackson counties. While many militia officers proved to be less than professional soldiers, Woodbury would prove to the commanders of the Union army that he was an effective military man—one who understood orders and could be counted on to do his duty.[2]

Only six months before his letter to the governor, in July 1860, Woodbury and his militiamen played host to a dashing young fellow named Elmer Ellsworth, a New Yorker who was a friend of then–presidential candidate Abraham Lincoln. Ellsworth had been touring with his Zouaves, an exotically uniformed, precision march-and-drill outfit that thrilled audiences with their performances, and it was said that Woodbury and Ellsworth became friends. Soon both men led regiments from their states into the Civil War. Colonel Ellsworth would become a national martyr after May 24, 1861, shot by an angry secessionist innkeeper after cutting down a Confederate flag flying from the man's roof in Alexandria, Virginia.[3]

That was still some months off as Woodbury wrote to Governor Blair early in 1861. While historians have tended to believe that the Michigan militia was not a competent military force, Woodbury was confident that his was the only organized militia regiment in Michigan ready in the event the federal government called for soldiers. The U.S. government, still under President James Buchanan, was making no such move that January. But when news of the Rebel attack on Fort Sumter reached Michigan in mid-April, Woodbury quickly reminded Blair that he and his men had volunteered months earlier. "Now that the honor of our flag has been assailed, the law set at defiance and civil war inaugurated, the third regiment renews its offer," he wrote.[4]

Like many other would-be military commanders, Woodbury hoped he would be asked to lead the first group of Michigan volunteers to fight for the United States, since Lincoln's administration now asked the governors of the Northern states to raise troops. Though Woodbury wouldn't get the command of the new 1st Michigan Infantry Regiment, he was on the governor's short list for a state command. He was quickly authorized to open a recruiting office in Adrian.[5] Within a month's time, Woodbury was commissioned to lead state soldiers in a volunteer regiment enrolled as the 4th Michigan Infantry. He was their first colonel, but he would not be their last; in the course of the next three years, he was among nearly 200 men of his regiment killed or mortally wounded in the Civil War.

In the wake of the surrender of Fort Sumter community meetings were convened around Michigan to raise troops and money to pay for them. Companies of volunteers that included farmers, store clerks, schoolteachers, carpenters, mechanics, and laborers formed under the auspices of local leaders, often men who served in militia units. In the town of Monroe in the state's southeastern corner, a company called the Smith Guards was named for a resident veteran of the Mexican War, Col. Joseph R. Smith. Soon the volunteers began to drill under Smith's direction. They elected as captain a local land agent named Constant Luce. "We have about 70 old Flint Lock Guns," Luce wrote to the state's new adjutant general, John Robertson, "which we would be pleased to exchange for Rifles as soon as you get them." This would take longer than Luce might have expected. Only in early in 1862 would the men comprising the 4th Michigan get rifles. The more immediate development was that the Smith Guards became Company A in the 4th Michigan. One of the company's men was an 18-year-old originally from Albany, N.Y., then working as a drug store clerk in Detroit. His name was George W. M. Yates and he'd recently returned to Michigan, where his mother had lived for several years. Yates tried his hand at trading horses in Texas, but wasn't successful. But he would prove a good soldier and become friends with a daring and ambitious young officer named George Armstrong Custer. That friendship would shape Yates's Civil War career and ultimately determine his fate.[6]

In Adrian, the town where Woodbury lived, two companies had quickly formed after the news of Fort Sumter. Now a third organized, its men calling themselves the Adrian Volunteers, or more dramatically, the Lenawee Tigers. Their captain was James H. Cole, an acquaintance of Woodbury who also active in the militia. But after so many men from the Adrian area had already enlisted, Cole came up short of what he needed for a full company. Years later he recalled that Woodbury was concerned this shortage of men might cause the state to delay the organization of his regiment. "If we do not get another company in a few days, the boys in the northern part of the state will sidetrack us," Woodbury said, according to Cole's memory of the conversation. "Can't you scare up some more recruits and then we will be ready to be sworn in on time?" In response, Cole took a train 50 miles west to the town of Coldwater, rented a horse and buggy, and drove another 20 miles south across the state line to Angola, Indiana. There he talked to some men who wanted to join regiments from the Hoosier state, but hadn't been chosen for Indiana's initial federal quota of 6,000 recruits.

These men from Angola and Steuben County were part of a company formed under a Mexican War veteran named Baldwin J. Crosswait. Given the chance to join a Michigan regiment that was almost certainly going into federal service, 40 of them signed on with Cole. Shortly before these men left on the trip to Adrian late in May, however, they were in a confrontation with the sheriff in Angola. One of their number, store clerk Frederick W. Meech, was arrested for selling illegal whiskey and beer. The volunteers decided they weren't leaving without him. Before they departed for Michigan, they surrounded the sheriff's house and "rescued" Meech, 24, into their ranks. Together the Indiana enlistees and the Adrian men under Cole became Company B of the 4th Michigan.[7]

Thirty miles or so beyond Coldwater and Angola to the west, in the southern Michigan town of Sturgis, a company formed called the Peninsula Guard. These men would become the 4th Michigan's Company C. One of the recruits was 21-year-old Eli Starr from nearby Centreville. Starr may have been influenced by his friend Daniel Knipple, who joined the 2nd Michigan Infantry Regiment. Knipple was sure the war would be short. "Bring a blanket, a good undershirt, 2 if you wish, a good pair of drawers," he wrote Starr from a new camp set up in Detroit. "Leave your best clothes at home—I don't think the war will last six months." Starr's parents asked him not to go to Detroit to enlist yet, so Eli promised to wait and join men from their area. It didn't take long. Starr signed up with the local company that soon went into the 4th Michigan. Of course, his friend Dan, like so many others who believed the conventional wisdom about the war, was wrong about how short it would be.[8]

In the town of Ann Arbor, the ex-mayor, lawyer Robert J. Barry, recruited a company that bore his name, though he soon resigned as its captain, "not being able to leave his business for so long a term." In his place, members of the company elected John M. Randolph to be their new captain. These enlistees began training at the local fairgrounds. They became the 4th Michigan's Company D.[9] One of the volunteer-officers was a young man from Adams Center, New York, who reportedly was passing through the Ann Arbor area when he decided to join up. His name was Jairus W. Hall, and he would ultimately take the role of a commander of the "reorganized" or reconstituted 4th Michigan late in the war. Another young man who soon signed on with the company was Charles W. Phelps, from Washtenaw County. In May, Phelps, 21, was traveling around southeastern Michigan, trying to join a company that was going to be accepted into a new regiment, or if he failed at that, to find employment. But on the 22nd Phelps found out the company he'd joined in Oakland County, called the Pontiac Light Guards, was disbanding since someone in authority decided they weren't needed.

"I guess I shall go to Detroit and join the second Regiment," he wrote to his brother. "If I don't go off in the army I will come out that way. . . . I'll be d——d if I will stay here anyway." Phelps looked for work in Pontiac's three tin shops, but they had all the employees they needed. He soon learned that the 2nd Michigan Infantry had left Detroit. He began to wonder if he was going to get in the war at all. "[The] second regiment is gone to Washington so there is not much danger," he wrote. "Who cares anyway?" But Phelps did want to serve, and a month later he signed on with the Barry Guards Company, which by then was part of the 4th Michigan.[10] In just over two years time, young Phelps and scores of his comrades would find themselves in battle at the edge of a field of grain belonging to a man named John Rose, who lived outside of a small Pennsylvania college town called Gettysburg.

Men from the small southern-central Michigan towns of Hillsdale and Jonesville in Hillsdale County, just west of Adrian, soon became the regiment's Companies E and H, recruited by their respective captains, George W. Lumbard, a Hillsdale attorney, and Moses A. Funk, a businessman and carpenter. Funk's volunteers, from the Jonesville area and the northern part of the county, called themselves the Grosvenor Guard after a state political figure. Lumbard's men were known as the Hillsdale Volunteers. "I think I can say that if called [to service], we will not disgrace the state," Lumbard wrote to Adjutant General Robertson. "Don't forget us." Lumbard would play an important and sometimes controversial role in the regiment's leadership. Within less than a month after writing that letter, Lumbard's company was accepted into the 4th Michigan Infantry.[11]

About a dozen of Lumbard's volunteers were students at Hillsdale College, and one of them, sophomore Moses A. Luce, had just turned 19. "Together with twelve fellow students, I enlisted in Company E, 4th Michigan Infantry," Luce wrote years later. He was six feet tall but slim enough that people thought of him slight in build, the son of an abolitionist pastor. In time, he would receive the Medal of Honor from Congress for running through enemy fire near Spotsylvania Court House, Virginia, to rescue one of his comrades.[12]

Volunteers from around Hudson, about 15 miles west of Adrian, formed a company known as the Lenawee Guards or alternately, the Hudson Volunteers. These men would become Company

F in the 4th Michigan. They selected as their captain Samuel DeGolyer, a local politician and partner in a company that manufactured wagons and parts. DeGolyer wanted to make sure state military officials didn't forget them. "We wish to urge our claims in every honorable way with a view to our acceptance at an early day," he wrote to the state adjutant general. "We drill every Night. . . . Please advise me as to our future prospects."[13]

In the Lenawee County town of Tecumseh, a few miles northeast of Adrian, the Tecumseh Volunteers organized under their captain, Deputy Sheriff David D. Marshall. They became Company G in the 4th Michigan. Marshall resigned his post from the sheriff's office shortly before the company left to rendezvous with other volunteer companies in Adrian. One of the first recruits for the company was a 24-year-old named Harrison Daniels. "Being the second man to enlist in the Township of Franklin, I walked to Tecumseh, nine miles from home, and was soon drilling," he remembered. Daniels said Tecumseh residents "took good care of us and furnished us a very neat uniform which consisted of a red cap, blue jacket and red pants, so that with clean faces and blackened shoes, we made a very good appearance."[14] Soon that colorful uniform would be given up for one of gray—the color all the men of the 4th Michigan would wear until later that summer.

In the village of Trenton, a few miles south of Detroit on the Detroit River, some men formed a company organized under David A. Granger, though he would not go off to war with them. Since Granger's group didn't have enough for a regulation company (roughly 100 men), they traveled to Detroit on May 7 to join enlistees from the Continental Fire Company No. 8. This combined group was quartered in the Continentals' engine house. A Detroit newspaper called this company the Continental Rifles, but they were also known as the Trenton Volunteers. They became Company I in the 4th Michigan. William Vreeland from Wayne County was allowed to sign up with the company, though he was only 17. "You look young," Granger said to him, according to an account Vreeland later gave. But Vreeland's cousin, the company's first lieutenant, Marshall W. Chapin, intervened on his behalf. "He is all right, Captain," Chapin assured Granger. "I know him."[15]

A young schoolteacher from upstate New York, Edward H. C. Taylor, had been working on Grosse Ile in the Detroit River, but his relationship with his boss wasn't going smoothly. He joined the company as a lieutenant. "The pay is good—$100 a month and rations," he wrote about his new post. A Democrat from a Democratic family, Taylor was put off when his sister was saddened to hear he joined the army. "I am sorry that my volunteering has caused any sorrow, but this is a time when anyone with the least spark of patriotism ought to come forward," he wrote. He added that "several gentlemen of education and wealth" joined as privates right along "hard working men," and that he would have done the same. "The people of this city—Detroit—are very kind in fitting out the men," he wrote.[16]

Like many if not most regiments in the Civil War, there was no Company J in the 4th Michigan. The regiment's Company K was comprised mostly of men from in and around Dexter, a small Washtenaw County town a few miles northwest of Ann Arbor. Their captain was a 44-year-old attorney, Alexander D. Crane, who held the rank of major general in the state militia. Like most organizers of volunteer companies, Crane asked the state for "arms of any kind" so his men could drill. These Dexter Union Guards were soon joined by about 30 men from Howell, a town in nearby Livingston County, who figured that they ought to sign on with a company going into a regiment certain to be mustered into federal service. Dexter residents, like others sending off their sons, brothers, and husbands, presented the company with a flag, waterproof capes, sewing kits, and other necessities.[17]

One of the company's lieutenants was Harrison H. Jeffords, about 24 and living in the Washtenaw County township of Lima, some 12 miles or so west of Ann Arbor. A recent graduate of the University of Michigan's law school and owner of a brick-making business, Jeffords would become one of Michigan's Civil War heroes. Whether he had a premonition or was just being prudent, on May 22 he made out his will, instructing that 70 acres of land be divided up between his mother and father in the event of his death, and bequeathing to his sisters an undetermined number of bricks and his two-horse buggy.[18]

Almost nothing was certain, in those days of late April and early May, about whether these men and thousands like them would get into a regiment. Michigan had more volunteers and companies than places for them. The state's first infantry regiment to form was a "90-day" unit, meaning the volunteers' hitch was over in three months. In May, the federal government directed that the term of enlistment for the men of subsequently forming regiments must be three years. Yet even with the long-term enlistments, there were questions about how many regiments were needed, and whether new ones would be accepted into the service of the federal government. Thousands of men who wanted to become soldiers were told to "hold themselves in readiness" and wait for their companies to be called. Some wondered whether they had a better chance to get into the service by joining a different company or even enlisting in another state. "If you have no encouragement of [our] being accepted by our own state *soon*, we shall go in with the Ohio volunteers at Toledo," an anxious Samuel DeGolyer wrote to Michigan's adjutant general less than a week after his company organized.[19]

A newspaper reflected the jealousy and competition between companies in Lenawee County when the Adrian Volunteers got accepted into the 4th Michigan while the men from Tecumseh initially were left hanging. The men of the Tecumseh company, the local editor complained, "enlisted not for effect, but for service. They feel a little sore and just so we think, that they should have been entirely overlooked and left out of the organization of the Fourth Regiment, while a third company from Adrian, under Capt. Cole, not fairly commenced and without, at the time, a dozen bona fide volunteers, should have been given precedence over them."[20]

As men waited for their companies to be called, there was also the matter of who was going to pay for their supplies and housing until the governor and his advisors decided if they were needed. Many towns raised money to support the men and boys from their company until they were accepted, but some did not. Enlisting at this point posed a problem for a man who'd left his farm or his job intending to fight for his country, only to wait around the county seat, the fairgrounds, or some other encampment. Eli Starr, who signed up for the Peninsula Guards, wrote a sardonic letter expressing his disgust with this. Starr apparently quit his job expecting he'd ship out right away, but then found out he was going nowhere just yet. In mid-May, a company officer told the recruits from Centreville that they had orders from the state adjutant general to meet at Sturgis in preparation for the rendezvous, or gathering, for the formation of their regiment. Starr made the dusty 10-mile march with the other men from their hometown. But when they got to Sturgis, the men found there were no such orders to assemble. "They didn't want us as they had expected," Starr groused about his officers, "and after very generously permitting us to pay our own bills [for food and other expenses, they] informed us that they could give no definite information as to when they would want us to return."[21]

Starr told the officers he'd had enough of this—he was quitting the company. Immediately his captain offered him noncommissioned rank as an enticement. "I have already explained to you the sudden termination of my military career," Eli wrote a friend. "Well, they found out that my disgust was complete and not wishing to lose me, they [rode] over offering me the office of Sergeant, this I now have under consideration."[22] Starr stayed with the company. A few days later they got the order to board an eastbound train and join the 4th Michigan at Adrian.

Because of these initial uncertainties, the identities of the companies making up the 4th Michigan changed as plans for the regiment formed in the weeks after Fort Sumter. Preliminary state military orders published early in May indicated that companies from the towns of Paw Paw, St. Joseph, and Dowagiac in western Michigan would be part of the regiment, but this placement did not happen. The companies from Hillsdale, Jonesville, and Tecumseh, closer to Adrian, soon took their places. By the first week in May, it was clear from newspaper reports (likely reflecting Woodbury's discussions with state officials) that a fourth regiment of infantry was going to be formed with the companies from Adrian, Hudson, Monroe, Sturgis, Trenton, Ann Arbor, and Dexter. Within another week or so, the final lineup of companies was settled.

The rendezvous was planned for Colonel Woodbury's hometown, his appointment as the 4th Michigan's commander becoming official on May 16. "Col. Woodbury returned from Detroit last night," a local newspaper reported. "The Fourth Regiment has been formally accepted by the Governor and ordered to rendezvous at Adrian." The new regiment's quarters and camp was the north wing of Adrian College, on a hill at the edge of town. Woodbury called this temporary home Camp Williams in honor of Brig. Gen. Alpheus S. Williams, one of Michigan's most experienced military men.[23]

Woodbury's lieutenant colonel was William W. Duffield, member of a prominent Detroit family and agent for a bank across the Detroit River in Windsor, Canada. Duffield, who reportedly served as an officer with volunteers from Tennessee in the Mexican War, remained with the 4th Michigan for a few months, eventually resigning to take command of the 9th Michigan Infantry. The regiment's major was Jonathan W. Childs, 28. He had attended high school and taught college in Ypsilanti before studying civil engineering, then teaching and working on government surveys in Minnesota. The chaplain for the regiment was the Reverend Dr. Henry Strong, Woodbury's Episcopal Church pastor and friend.

Dr. David P. Chamberlain, a 37-year-old medical doctor and native of New York state who lived with his wife and child on Hudson's Main Street, later said that he believed he was going to be made the surgeon of the 4th Michigan, but had to settle for the post of assistant surgeon since Governor Blair's own physician, Dr. Joseph Tunnicliff Jr., 42, of Jackson, was given the job. Tunnicliff, however, would not remain long with the regiment, while Chamberlain became one of its most respected figures.[24]

Now the state's military board began to take bids for contracts to feed, clothe, and equip its new soldiers, while sheds were built behind the Adrian College student dormitory for the regiment's kitchen and mess. In the meantime the men spent their days in their communities with drill and exercise, listening to speeches and lectures from local politicians and preachers, and sometimes attending fund-raising events and entertainments put on for them. At last the captains of the companies got word from Woodbury that Camp Williams was ready. Other than volunteers from Adrian, the first to arrive at the campus on May 24 were the Indiana men who had joined the local Lenawee Tigers, soon to be Company B. These men took a four-hour ride in carriages and wagons to Coldwater and boarded an eastbound train to Adrian, joining the local men.[25]

Two days later, on the 26th, a Sunday evening, the members of the Detroit's First Presbyterian Church presented the Trenton Volunteers, including the contingent of Continental firemen, with Bibles. That week a dark-haired, dark-eyed 23-year-old packed his possessions and left them with a friend, with instructions for his things to be sent east in the event something happened to him. This was John M. Bancroft, a draftsman educated at Dartmouth College, who had been living and working in Detroit. "Placed my trunk and bookcase labeled for home, 'Reading, Mass.,' in the second story of Mr. Hinchman's store," Bancroft wrote in his diary. A short time later, the men of his company got on the train for the trip that took them to the regiment's rendezvous. "Leave Detroit for Adrian at 7:30 o'clock," he noted. "Stopped in Trenton for a reception of the company." They reached Adrian later that night.[26]

That same day the Smith Guards also boarded the train leaving Monroe, but not before local firemen bought them ale and cigars, a final parting gift. Over the course of the previous week these Monroe men received donations of gray uniforms, a company flag, and other items from the townspeople. Monroe's firemen made the trip with the company to Adrian, joining in the parade escorting the volunteers from the depot to Camp Williams. Residents were thrilled to see the men streaming into Adrian, making the mile-and-a-half walk to the campus. "As the companies marched through the streets yesterday and today on their way to the camp, they were cheered by our citizens all along the route," the local paper reported.[27]

The moving of the companies continued. On the morning of May 27, the Hillsdale Volunteers assembled as a crowd of area residents watched. The men drilled and were presented with flannel overshirts and other items. They took a break for lunch and the company reassembled at the fire hall for patriotic speeches and the march to the train. The volunteers picked up three would-be enlistees who decided to join on the spot when they saw all the excitement. One young man handed the reins of his wagon's team to a boy standing nearby, with instructions to tell his father that he'd gone with the volunteers. Two other lads had come to town for groceries, but when told that the company was leaving, they went, too, giving their purchases to another fellow to carry home. The company boarded the cars and as the train left for Adrian, "men waved their caps and handkerchiefs, making the air ring with their cheers."[28]

The companies from Jonesville, Hudson, and Tecumseh left home the next day. It was a rainy, but that didn't stop a large crowd from gathering in Tecumseh that afternoon. "They made a beautiful and imposing spectacle in their Blue and Red," bragged the local paper. The men were accompanied by a local cornet band on the march to the train.[29] At Jonesville friends and relatives of the Grosvenor Union Guard also flooded into the town to watch their company leave. "It was not the women and the children alone whose eyes were full of tears, or who were loudly sobbing at the thought of the parting," their paper reported, "for scores of manly faces were moist, and handkerchiefs were generally displayed." The volunteers "wore very serious faces, and many of them could not restrain their regret at the separation from home. . . . Generally, however, they mastered their feelings, and the last handshakes were strong and firm." Just a few days earlier, their captain, Moses Funk, who was not a man of means, sought a loan so that he could buy his uniform. In response the village council voted to buy him a sword. When local gadflies complained about the expenditure, the local paper dismissed them as "grumblers" and "lazy loungers."[30]

In Hudson the Lenawee Guards began the day drilling from 8:00 A.M. to 10:00 A.M. while a crowd gathered. By early afternoon, a procession that included a band, the local fire company, and a company of "cadets" (militia boys too young to enlist) formed on Main Street and marched with the volunteers to a lot near the fairgrounds. There were speeches and parting gifts, and the friends of Captain DeGolyer presented with him with a new revolver. Then the parade reformed and marched to the station to board the eastbound train, where they found the men from Jonesville already on board.[31]

Again some of the young cadets and musicians were too excited to stay behind, so they went, too. One was Albert H. Boies, then 16. "How well I remember our position as we marched through the streets of Adrian and up to the college building, headquarters of the Fourth regiment," he wrote years later. Boies played his fife, as did a teen named Will Carleton, who would go on to be a famous Michigan poet. Accompanied by a bass drummer and a snare drummer, the boys could only play one march, a tune called "Dandy Jim," someone remembered. In the months ahead Boies would join the 4th Michigan, but for now he was proud just to tramp along to see the new camp.[32]

The Dexter company received their parting gifts on May 29, cheering the local women and boarding the train for Adrian, and so did the Barry Guards in Ann Arbor. The Guards marched from their camp at the local fairgrounds that morning to the courthouse square, accompanied by young men in cadet companies from the University of Michigan. Each man was presented a Bible and "housewife," or sewing kit, donated by the women of the city. After remarks by a local clergyman and one of company's lieutenants, the men marched to the railroad depot, accompanied by a crowd. "There were many tearful eyes and swelling hearts," a correspondent reported, " and we felt sad, too, when the husband kissed the wife, saying, 'Good bye Francis, God bless you.'"[33]

Quarters at Adrian College were spartan but adequate. "Immediately on our arrival in camp, each man was furnished with a blanket," wrote Lt. Richard DePuy, a lawyer from Ann Arbor. "The boys . . . fell hastily to work filling the ticks [mattress bags] assigned the company with straw for beds." Some men simply bedded down on hard floors, and some complained that there wasn't enough water for washing. John Bancroft, who'd been living in a Detroit fire hall, recorded his first night at Camp Williams: "Slept last night on a bed of loose straw in two small rooms with 15 others in the College at Adrian. . . . Awoke to a frosty morning and to find very little chance of soap and water." Jonas D. Richardson, 21, from Washtenaw County, thought the arrangements were fine. "We are quartered in the College Buildings and everything is fixed up as nice as one could wish," he wrote. A soldier's letter to his local paper suggested that the enlistees from Monroe may have stayed in tents, perhaps because they'd come to camp well equipped; he wrote that the Monroe company men "are quartered in between the buildings."[34]

With the regiment's companies assembled, Sgt. Eli Starr wrote, the men started a "systematic drill." A typical day began with reveille at 5:00 A.M., breakfast at 6:30. There was drill from 9:00 to 11:30 A.M. with the midday meal at 12:30 P.M. Drill resumed at 2:00 P.M. and ended with a dress parade at 5:00 P.M. The men headed for supper at 6:30 P.M. and it was lights out at 9:30. "Our provisions are abundant," Starr wrote, "fresh beef every day, beans, hams, pork, bread, butter, sugar, milk, potatoes & various other things not drawn in the regular Army rations." As for drinking with comrades when they were off duty, Starr found out that "if I drank with one I must drink with all so I stopped entirely." Abstinence was also urged by the regiment's chaplain and like-minded temperance officials. Starr managed to room with friends, but there were more than a few arguments and fights between the new soldiers. "We have some pretty hard cases here as must be expected," Starr explained. "There have been 8 fights since I commenced writing this[. T]he belligerents are at once marched to the guard house."[35]

As did many proud volunteers, Jonas Richardson bragged that his company, D, was the best in camp and so were his officers. John Bancroft, however, came to a different conclusion about the officers of Company I when there was trouble a few days later involving Lt. Edward Taylor and Captain Granger. "Granger is a rascal and Taylor is not competent," the young soldier declared. A soldier who enlisted at Trenton, James G. Tuttle, confirmed this. " [B]efore the regiment was mustered into the United States service, a number of us had some difficulty with our officers, and we left the company," he wrote. "I joined the Hudson company."[36]

Whatever happened, Edward Taylor felt he had been abused by Granger. "I have resigned in Co. I as lieut[enant] on account of disagreement with my Captain who treated me in a scrubby manner and in consequence, he, when the matter was properly laid before the Governor, lost his position as Captain," he wrote that month. Taylor, nicknamed "Ned," was temporarily attached to Company A, but he came to regret resigning his commission. Granger later joined a Massachusetts regiment as a private, worked his way through the ranks to captain, and ultimately died of wounds in the fall of 1864.[37]

There were other troubles in Camp Williams, filled as it was with raw recruits. A few men were drummed out of the regiment for serious offenses, one for striking an officer. Another fellow got abused on his way out of camp after it was recognized he had been joining different companies and then deserting once he got food and clothing. Yet another was discovered trying to form a "secret society" within the Hillsdale company and he, too, was ejected.

A brawl involving many of the volunteers erupted after a detail of men who'd been the relief guard came off duty on the evening of June 11. They went to get their supper, only to find the mess sheds closed. A sympathetic officer got the mess attendants to fix them a cold meal, but others, for reasons that aren't clear, objected. They showed up at the mess hall and disrupted the meal, knocking over food and tables and starting a large fight. The officer of the day, whose job it was to keep order, rounded up enough guards to arrest the combatants, but then the friends of those put in the guardhouse also got involved. "[They] laid siege to the lock up and compelled an evacuation [of those arrested]," the local paper said. "The affair created considerable excitement for a time." How Colonel Woodbury restored order and discipline is unknown, but the matter quickly faded from the newspaper.

A few men were dismissed by federal officers during inspections because they failed to measure up or were considered too young, but 21-year-old Charles Barlow of Company K told a friend the examination was perfunctory. "[T]he surgeon felt our hands[,] hit us a few light taps on the breast[,] asked us our age & passed on to the next," he wrote. William Vreeland, the teenager who joined up at a word from his cousin, said he didn't get that much of an exam. "I was not stripped, I was not looked over at all," he remembered years later. "We were taken by companies and marched single file past some 3 or 4 men who only looked at [us] as we marched past. . . . That was all the examination I recollect."

A few men who backed out of service faced humiliation, run out on rails. "When we were mustered in, there was one that refused to take the oath and when we were through the Captain told us that we might break ranks for a few minutes," Stiles H. Wirts, an 18-year-old in Company F, wrote about one such incident. "We took the hint and caught him and elevated him on a rail and let him ride around until the guards took him away from us and put him in the guard house."[38]

The fact that so many of men in the regiment had friends and family members a short train ride away meant there was still socializing. "I can come home any time that I wish, and as often," bragged Jonas Richardson, "but don't want to come before I get my uniform." Friends visited John Bancroft once drill was over on his first Saturday in camp, and his diary and Adrian newspapers reflect that soldiers often went to town. Of course, that sometimes led to trouble. At least two men from camp were arrested and jailed for getting drunk and using foul language, businessman Charles Cleveland complained. The thrill of having soldiers in town soon wore off, since many of them were "mischievously-disposed fellows, calling for articles such as tobacco, cigars and drinkables at stores and after coolly order it to be charged to Uncle Sam," Cleveland wrote.[39]

One 4th Michigan officer, a religious man who had worked in a banking office and taught Sunday school, tried to influence men to be civil. "I was officer of the Guard Tuesday & one of the sentries got his back up & rather insulted me for reproving him for swearing," wrote Lt. George Monteith, 21, from Adrian. "I immediately put him in the guard tent & kept him till he seemed penitent & released him to return to guard duty with friend advice about profanity. Since then how pleasant & kind he has been to me."[40]

Most men adapted to army life as June days passed. "The daily routine of camp discipline has been strictly enforced, and the effect is plainly visible to any one who saw them when they were raw recruits," reported the *Detroit Free Press*. This suited some soldiers. "I am getting as tough as a pine knot," Corporal Richardson wrote. "I like military life first rate. All the boys are well and in fact the whole Regiment, our field officers, can't be beat." He also learned that rank had its privileges. "All lights are put out at nine o'clock and every man has to Retire. I can go out and in whenever I chose," he bragged. "All Officers Both Commissioned and noncommissioned have the password as soon as [it is] issued."[41]

Uniforms arrived from a Detroit contractor, "West Point gray" in color. This was not unusual, for many U.S. troops had gray uniforms at this time. A shipment of more than 300 Springfield muskets also arrived, bringing cheers from the men. "The whole redgiment have got their United States dress, it is of gray & over coats of the same with capes on them," Colonel Woodbury wrote. Many thought the uniforms were sturdy and good-looking, but others soon concluded the quality was poor. "Some of the men are now of the opinion that as long as the contractors get their pay for making them properly they should make them so that they will not rip and tear before they have been worn 24 hours," complained a soldier to a Detroit newspaper. "Many of the uniforms have been made of the poorest kind of satinment [satinet, a cotton-wool cloth]. We did not volunteer for purpose of complaining but we do think it a shame to put on uniforms that do not wear a month, [whereas] they should wear a year. These will wear out soon and then we will have to replace them ourselves [or] go without." This soldier, who initialed his letter "S.P.S.," was probably Stephen P. Savery, 20, from Washtenaw County, a musician in Company K.[42]

In the meantime, because most of the companies hadn't managed to enlist a full complement of 100 men, recruiters from the 4th Michigan went out into nearby communities to drum up more volunteers. In addition, a respected, 15-piece musical ensemble from Cleveland, Ohio, called Hecker's Band or the Hecker Band and led by John Van Olker, signed on with the 4th Michigan. These musicians were German, or men of German descent. "Our band . . . is hard to beat," S.P.S. wrote in their praise. "The way they play 'Dixie' and the 'Girl I left behind' put us in a quiver."[43]

Yet some drill, the arrival of uniforms, and a band did not make the 4th Michigan quite ready to go off to war. Not all the men had weapons, and after preparing three other regiments for war, the State of Michigan was scratching around for more. "I fear I cannot furnish you with respectable arms for your regiment," wrote Jabez Fountain, quartermaster general of the state's military department, to Woodbury. "I am having the state ransacked for arms, but I find but very few that are fit for service." By mid-June, only about half of the companies had been issued weapons, described as a combination of "minnie [Minié] muskets" and "marine muskets."[44] While the companies used these weapons in drill, ultimately they were left behind when the regiment headed east. What the soldiers would soon find out was that the firearms they would receive at Washington, D.C., weren't much better.

Perhaps the 4th Michigan's most poignant moments in Adrian came after two Indiana men in Company B asked Woodbury for permission to marry their sweethearts, and the colonel consented. One of the grooms was Frederick W. Meech, the clerk from Angola who might have still been in jail had his friends not broken him out. His bride was Helen Darrow. Also tying the wedding knot were George E. Young and his bride Elizabeth Freygang. On the evening of June 19, the regiment, on dress parade, formed in a hollow square. Into the center marched the couples and friends and family members from Angola, accompanied by the chaplain, the Reverend Strong. "The Damsels were as blooming as Western roses, and their head dresses were composed of red, white and blue ribbons, intended to convey the idea that they were not only in favor of union—to a man—but also in favor of that other union, quite as glorious," a Detroit paper reported. The hometown paper of the young couples didn't spare sentimentality or hyperbole, declaring the ceremony "one of the most romantic scenes that will ever be recorded in history."

The men of the regiment kneeled so that a large crowd of visitors could view the service. The band played and the regiment gave the couples three cheers as they left for a honeymoon of a few days. Young's parents sent a wedding cake, which he shared with his comrades in

Company B. "We hope that he will as faithfully discharge his duty as a soldier, as he did as a lover, which will be highly appreciated by both his parents and youthful bride," the editor of the *Angola Republican* wrote, undoubtedly with a sly grin. If anyone questioned the wisdom of the young lovers marrying on the eve of the departure of the regiment for war, it did not appear in the papers. "I should think it would [not?] be pleasant for them to leave their new wives behind," wrote Lieutenant Monteith.[45]

The next day, June 20, a telegram arrived in Michigan for Gov. Austin Blair from Simon Cameron, President Lincoln's secretary of war. "Send on your fourth (4th) regiment by Elmira and Harrisburg," the message read. "They can be furnished with arms etc. here or if necessary at Harrisburg." That same day, the 4th Michigan formally mustered into the service of the United States. The new regiment's time in Michigan was drawing to an end.[46] Now the women of Adrian who had sponsored the making of a regimental flag for the 4th Michigan finalized arrangements for its presentation the next day. On the morning of June 21, people from around the area poured into the town in overloaded coaches from the east and west and by horse and wagon and on foot from all points. The Michigan South Shore Railroad cut fare in half for passengers headed for Adrian. "The town swarmed with people," said one local journal. "The excursion trains poured a tide of humanity through our streets, while the surrounding county towns emptied themselves of their population. . . . Our streets too were thronged with a busy crowd; our shopmen were voluble and busy." From Detroit came Michigan VIPs, Senator Zachariah Chandler, Gen. Alpheus Williams, and state adjutant general John Robertson, accompanied by their wives. As the sun rose higher, so did the temperature—a typical hot Michigan summer's day.[47]

The ceremonies were scheduled for the mid-afternoon and as the time drew near people streamed toward the college and the field used as the regiment's parade ground. At 2:30 P.M. the men of the regiment, about half of them carrying muskets, marched out and formed a hollow square around a platform. The crowd was estimated to be in the thousands, so a few men from each company acted as crowd control to keep people back. Inside the regiment's square were the officers, state officials and their wives, and newspaper correspondents. About 3:00 P.M., a carriage containing the regiment's color sergeant and four women pulled through the crowd, and the ranks of the square opened to admit them. The ladies took their places on the platform and 4th Michigan's new flag was unfurled. A *Detroit Free Press* correspondent, writing about the banner in advance of the presentation, claimed the flag was made of heavy silk, emblazoned with the state coat of arms on one side, the U.S. "stars and stripes" on the other, but this was incorrect. Reports from correspondents from Hudson and Adrian papers who attended the ceremony described it as a U.S. flag with the words "The Ladies of Adrian to the / Fourth Regiment Michigan Infantry / Defend It," stitched in gilt letters on three stripes. Holding the flag in her hands, Mrs. Josephine S. Wilcox stepped forward.[48]

"In behalf of the ladies of Adrian, allow me to present to you this, our National flag, and we trust a few words from us in expression of our feelings on this occasion may be kindly received," she said. "When you follow this standard in your line of march, or onto the field of battle, and see it waving in lines of beauty and gleams of brightness, remember the trust we have placed in your hands, and we will follow you in our hearts, with all our hopes and our prayers." It was a proud and patriotic occasion, and Dwight Woodbury answered with a short speech. "In accepting this beautiful banner at your hands, from those you represent," he said, "I have but few words to offer save those expressions of my own gratitude, and that of the body of men committed to my command. . . . We will strive to do our duty as American soldiers. It [the flag] has defended us; it will defend. To no inferior force shall it ever be surrendered, and sooner than be trailed to treason it shall become pall of the regiment." He concluded his speech assuring the women that as the regiment followed the flag into battle, the soldiers would remember them.

Politicians followed, including Senator Chandler, with more speeches, and the men joined in the crowd's cheers. Then the soldiers fell into line for inspection by the military officials, and the band played marches and patriotic tunes. The regiment paraded for two hours in the muggy heat. Finally the men were dismissed and the crowd slowly drifted away from Camp Williams for home.[49]

The time for speeches was over. The next day the state's military department issued orders that the regiment move out in three days, leaving Adrian on June 25 for Toledo—the first step in a long journey to Washington, D.C. While plans for the route changed over the next 48 hours, the order nevertheless meant the men had a chance to visit home. "Most of the boys are gone home to see their friends. I go this afternoon to see the Raymonds at Raisin," John Bancroft noted, referring to a family who probably lived on the River Raisin in the Monroe area or in Raisin Township in Lenawee County. Of course, that also meant there was an opportunity to get in trouble in Adrian. "A little row occurred at Wahl's Saloon on Main Street last night between a soldier and several Germans," a newspaper reported. "Two or three knockdowns took place." The sheriff and a deputy arrived and stopped the brawl.

Officers and men prepared for the regiment's departure. Woodbury announced that his regiment wasn't going to take minors into the service, at least not without written permission of their parents, and now came four petitions from families who said their sons weren't of legal age. At least one would-be soldier was dismissed when it was proved he wasn't 18, but other teens remained in the regiment because they had permission or were not pressed too closely about their real age. William Vreeland, who was 17, said later that although Woodbury noticed him, the colonel merely changed his job and allowed him to stay. "You are pretty young to carry a musket," Woodbury said, according to Vreeland's account. "Would you like to take care of my horses?" The teenager said he would. But young Vreeland served only briefly with the regiment, for he was discharged later in the summer for an injury.[50]

Woodbury issued detailed orders for last company inspections and roll calls on the morning of June 25—the men were to be on the parade ground with their knapsacks packed and a day's rations in their haversacks, and then they would march to the depot. "Packing up to leave for Wash[ington]," wrote Bancroft on June 24. "No drill." Since David Granger was no longer captain of Company I, Lt. Jeremiah D. Slocum of Adrian was commissioned by the governor to take his place. Bancroft went to town that evening for his last night out in Adrian.[51]

"We are all packing up our traps, getting ready for a start," jotted Dr. Chamberlain, the regiment's assistant surgeon, as officers shouted orders and men hurried about the next morning. "The boys are busy at the pumps, filling their canteens with water for the day. . . . Some are saying goodbye to friends and all feel in good spirits." Chamberlain agreed to send accounts to his local newspaper, and this dispatch was the first of many.[52] As wagoners moved equipment and baggage from the college, crowds began to gather. Around 9:00 A.M. the regiment marched out of Camp Williams, leaving the campus. The day was turning warm, the soldiers' packs were heavy and the road dusty, but people cheered them. The 4th Michigan was accompanied by local firefighters as they tramped to the station. The sun was over the trees as the march was ending. Near downtown Adrian, the companies changed from columns of four into two single-file lines so they could board the cars. "There is a great crowd of people here, some saying 'good bye' some crying, some with 'stiff upper lips,' wrote Dr. Chamberlain. "We shall be off soon." It took more than an hour for the 1,040 men and officers to get on the train.

Colonel Woodbury stood on the rear platform at the end of the train as well-wishers waved flags and cheered. While others tried to remain upbeat and positive for the sake of the departing soldiers, a man named William A. Whitney, who knew Woodbury, made a solemn vow to the colonel as they shook hands. "I promised him that in case he fell on the battlefield, I would come after his remains and bring them to Adrian," Whitney wrote. How Woodbury responded to this promise Whitney did not say.[53]

It was time. At about 11:30 A.M., the regiment's train slowly pulled out of Adrian, taking along assorted correspondents and some friends and relatives of officers who were allowed to accompany them on the first leg of the trip. "The last hurried words of parting were uttered and amid the cheers of the assembled thousands," a reporter wrote, "the train moved away." The whistles of other locomotives in the nearby yard and roundhouse also sounded, joining the tumult in a noisy good-bye to the 4th Michigan.[54]

"There were many who did shed tears and more who could [have,] but for our sakes did not," John Bancroft wrote as the train rattled to the southeast. "And for the cause for which we go, they bid us God speed and hope for the best. . . . Good bye, friends, you have been very kind to me."[55]

CHAPTER 2

The Loss Is Great, the Confusion Greater

THE TRAIN BEARING THE 4TH MICHIGAN ROLLED INTO TOLEDO BETWEEN NOON and 1:00 P.M. Dr. Chamberlain said there was "a great crowd of people to receive us." After a pause of two or three hours, the regiment boarded two eastbound trains, arriving in Cleveland that evening for "supper and some good hot coffee," wrote a man who initialed his dispatch "W." The soldier noted that "we were cheered at every station and bid God speed by everyone." Sgt. Eli Starr of Company C described the trip as "one continuous ovation" with women and children throwing flowers; other accounts told of people waving flags and bringing "eatables," pitchers of water, and bouquets to the soldiers at points where the train stopped for water and wood. The men were well fed in part because the regiment's quartermaster, Henry A. Grannis, traveled ahead to make the arrangements.[1]

Orvey S. Barrett, a Lenawee County man who was then 26 and a sergeant in Company B, remembered that Cleveland was where he was first issued his "hardtack," the infamous thick, unleavened bread or cracker that soldiers came to joke about and depend upon. "They were round," he wrote, "and as large as an elephant's foot, and as tough as a prohibitionist's conscience." Barrett said some of the men, awestruck by the seemingly indestructible crackers, stood on the platforms of the cars, seeing how far they could sail them, while others were "trying to pulverize them" with coupling pins. The musicians of the Hecker Band from Cleveland probably had a better time, since they were allowed off the train for about three hours to visit friends and family.[2]

The 4th Michigan transferred to another eastbound train that night and left for Erie, Pennsylvania, driving on through the early morning hours of June 26. Sgt. John Bancroft of Company I wrote that the citizens of Erie gave the men coffee and cake and other treats. The correspondent who signed his dispatches to the *Detroit Free Press* "Hamilton" wrote that the citizens waited all night for the regiment's arrival, which came about 4:00 A.M. Then the train continued along the Lake Erie coast another 45 miles or so, crossing the state line into New York. "At Dunkirk stopped and went to Lake Erie to bathe," Bancroft noted. "This was a great treat indeed." A soldier who attracted the concern of a Dunkirk woman seems to have been John B. Warren, 40, of Company H, who had been injured in Adrian the day before when a heavy trunk fell on him as the train was being loaded, badly bruising his leg. The *Dunkirk Union* reported that the lady saw a limping Michigan soldier, led him to her home, and bandaged the injury. The soldier was visibly moved, the journal noted, telling her, "You done it just as my sister would."[3]

The men changed trains at Dunkirk, boarding the New York & Erie Railroad that morning. It took them southeast across New York to the town of Olean, to Hornellville, and on east to Elmira near the Pennsylvania state line. Citizens continued to bring them coffee and snacks at their brief stops before they arrived for several hours rest at about three-thirty in the afternoon. Many Michigan families came from the state of New York, and the diaries and letters of some soldiers mention that they saw old friends, neighbors, and relatives along the way. The regiment left the cars and marched to the camp of the 23rd New York and "partook of a hearty supper prepared by the ladies of Elmyra," wrote "W." At 11:30 P.M., the 4th Michigan boarded freight cars of a train taking them south. The men thought it funny that they were loaded onto cars used for livestock; James H. Cole, the captain of Company B, remembered that the soldiers brayed, neighed, barked, mooed, crowed, oinked, cackled, and meowed as the train pulled out. Orvey Barrett wrote that some pranksters pulled a coupling pin and detached three or four cars until officers got the train backed up and reconnected them.

The men tried to sleep as the train clattered through the Susquehanna Mountains. Now it was June 27, and there were two or three more stops before they reached Pennsylvania's capital. At Williamsport the men left the freight cars for more comfortable passenger cars, and again women from the town came through the train with food and water. As the train rolled on, a soldier named John Rouse of Company K suffered a head injury when he fell from a platform. He was left behind and worked on by a surgeon, and caught up with his regiment after a brief recuperation. By mid-afternoon of the 27th, the train carrying the 4th Michigan reached Harrisburg.[4]

The regiment got a respite from traveling and Sgt. Eli Starr was relieved they were done with the longest part of their trek. "I haven't slept two hours since starting, being on guard all the time day & night," he complained. "This was for the purpose of seeing that not a man was left at any station." The regiment was issued more equipment, first tents and then muskets. Shortly after they got off the train at Harrisburg, according to John Bancroft, "We got tents and set ourselves to work to set them, and then have a chance to wash in the canal. We got coffee, etc. late in the evening." The place was called Camp Cameron, a temporary stopping point set up for Union soldiers headed for Washington, D.C. As did many, Sgt. Jonas Richardson went for a walk the next day with his friend Jim Clark. He declared the state capitol "the handsomest place I think that I ever saw."[5]

For the first time, many of the soldiers of the regiment cooked for themselves. Sergeant Bancroft expressed confidence. "We are now ready for a soldiers life, fare and privations," he wrote. "Rations of salt pork and ham, Hard biscuit are given out once a day and coffee twice." The 4th Michigan's assistant surgeon wasn't so sure the men were ready to cook their own food since so many of them had been fed by their mothers, wives, and sisters. "It is a little amusing to see the boys cooking their 'grub,'" Dr. Chamberlain wrote. "It is dealt out to them in the crude state, except bread." The doctor admitted he had an easier time, since he and the regiment's surgeon, Dr. Joseph Tunnicliff Jr., "messed"—made their eating arrangements—together. Doctors had to pay for their own food, so Tunnicliff hired an aide or servant named John Livermore who'd spent several years in the Rocky Mountains and was familiar with camp life and cooking. The doctors and their helpers were able to "get up a first rate meal," Chamberlain wrote.[6]

Muskets for the men arrived in boxes. Orvey Barrett described them as "old buck and ball" weapons, while Jim Tuttle called them "old-fashioned flintlock muskets transformed into [percussion] cap locks." The soldier who signed his letters "W" wrote that they were "very much disappointed" with these old weapons, since they thought they were getting Enfield rifles, far better, more accurate firearms. Some reports said Col. Woodbury was angry that his men had again been issued outdated weapons, but that Secretary of War Simon Cameron assured him via telegraph that the regiment's use of these muskets was strictly temporary and they would get better firearms when they reached Washington. With the regiment in camp for the last two days in June, officers ordered the resumption of drill with the expectation that they might face mobs and street fighting with Confederate sympathizers in Baltimore. On July 1, the men were awakened at 4:00 A.M., struck their tents, had breakfast, and again boarded cattle cars. The train stopped at York, and Sergeant Bancroft had a close call when it started without him. He managed to catch up and cling to some part of a car, perhaps a ladder or a rear platform. "Rode across a bridge some 200 ft. in length, hanging by my arms," he noted. Whether he climbed to safety or was pulled in by comrades, he made it aboard.[7]

The train crossed into Maryland and slowed to a halt several miles outside of Baltimore. The regiment debarked, formed up, loaded their weapons, and marched to the depot for the rail line to Washington. Back in April when the first Union volunteers were on their way to Washington, there had been a riot by a secessionist mob as they passed through Baltimore. A number of soldiers from that regiment, the 6th Massachusetts Infantry, and civilians were killed in the disturbance. Rumors swirled that other Union troops moving through the city would be attacked. Sgt. Thomas Jones of Company B wrote that "the Colonel [Woodbury] says he will have us burn the town if they try to stop us." Now crowds watched the troops march through and there was indeed at least one Confederate sympathizer who wanted trouble. This "crank of a Rebel" pointed a revolver at the regiment's flag bearer, Orvey Barrett said. As a "file-closer"—a soldier responsible for keeping gaps from forming in the ranks—Barrett was at the rear of that particular platoon and in a position to see the gunman. Barrett claimed he raised his musket at the secessionist "in less time than it would take to pull a trigger." But the Detroit correspondent "Hamilton" said the gunman was knocked down and subdued by law officers before the Michigan soldiers could react. Eli Starr and Dr. Chamberlain gave similar accounts of the incident. "Had that pistol been discharged, the result would have been a terrible indiscriminate slaughter," Barrett wrote. "W.," the 4th Michigan soldier writing to the *Detroit Free Press*, didn't see this incident. He wrote that the people of Baltimore had been "perfectly kind" to the 4th Michigan. Apparently jeered and cheered by the crowd—there were reports of both—the regiment marched on to the depot for another train and boarded the cars that evening as rain began to fall.[8]

Jim Tuttle of Company F remembered that because the men didn't yet have cartridge boxes for their ammunition or scabbards for their bayonets, the soldiers put their bullets and powder charges in their pockets and hooked their bayonets over the barrels of their muskets, but in a reverse position so the long blades didn't poke into the ceiling of the railcars. But bayonets weren't designed to be put on this way, so part of the upside down-mounted blades protruded over the business end of the muskets, Tuttle wrote. This would prove embarrassing for some of the new soldiers. At a point called the Relay House or "Halfway House" on the trip to Washington, D.C., the regiment again stopped to change trains. Again the rumor swept through the 4th Michigan that they were going to be attacked by Confederate guerillas. Jim Tuttle later claimed that as the men waited to get out, some excited Union soldiers ran up to the train, glad to see the arrival of more Northern troops; some of them fired revolvers in the air in a celebratory salute. "Our boys supposing they were guerillas blazed away and 'buck and ball' went flying fast and furious for a few seconds when the officers succeeded in stopping the firing," Tuttle wrote. Since the men had hooked their bayonets upside down on their muskets, these also went flying, he insisted. "No one wanted to admit they had fired, but every man that fired a shot had blown his bayonet away, so they were easily detected," Tuttle claimed. A news account by "Hamilton" stated that Massachusetts soldiers ran up and cheered the 4th Michigan as its train rumbled by. He wrote that some of the Michigan men fired into the air in return. Orvey Barrett didn't write of these particulars, saying only that the report of a Rebel attack at the Relay House "was a false alarm."[9]

A hard rain kept falling as the men boarded cars for the final miles from the Relay Station to Washington, where they arrived after midnight on the morning of July 2. An officer met the regiment and led them through quiet city streets to a large, empty brick building on Pennsylvania Avenue, where the men slept on the floor, using their knapsacks for pillows. Later that morning the men ate a late breakfast of hard crackers and cheese and marched in the afternoon to the city's arsenal, where they were issued slightly better muskets, and then returned to their temporary quarters for the night. The regiment marched to Meridian Hill on July 3, the grounds of a mansion once occupied by ex-president John Quincy Adams, less than two miles northwest of Washington's center. Here they set up their new camp. "From our elevated position we can see moving hither and thither tens of thousands of soldiers and on every hand the landscape is dotted with tents," wrote Lt. Richard DePuy of Ann Arbor. They called the place Camp Mansfield after a Union general. Some of the regiment's men complained they hadn't been properly supplied with provisions since they'd left for Washington. Sgt. Eli Starr said there was a kind of protest about the food shortage by Company C on the night of July 5, but the men settled down after being admonished by Colonel Woodbury. James Spence of Company E groused that "provisions have been short ever since we left Adrian," but he admitted that within a few days after arriving at Meridian Hill they had "received better fare with the promise of that improving."[10]

Union artillery roared to mark the Fourth of July and the men saw President Abraham Lincoln, General Winfield Scott, Secretary of State William Seward, and other VIPs when a review was held. Sergeant Bancroft heard a rumor that Scott "said today that those of us who were living"—presumably after a great battle or campaign against the Confederacy—"would dine at home at Christmas." Their camp on Meridian Hill was close enough to the White House that Lemuel Allen of Company G told his family that "with a spy glass we can see the president sometimes standing in the door" about a mile-and-a-half away." Not long afterward Allen toured the White House and other buildings "and had the honor of shaking hands with 'HONEST OLD ABE,'" he wrote. Stranger still was that two of his comrades from Company G, Harrison Daniels and William C. Pierson, got passes and strolled down to the White House when they were excused for duty because they were sick. "After being admitted, we were shown a waiting room," Daniels later wrote. "Presently a door opened and President Lincoln entered, followed by his cabinet and others of military rank." Daniels thought the president "truly the homeliest man that I had ever seen," but Lincoln warmly greeted him and Pierson when they rose and saluted him. Hundreds of other soldiers from the 4th Michigan and other regiments also went to town and took in the sights—the White House, the Washington Monument, the Patent Office, the museums. "I could not tell everything we seen if I should write a month," wrote Charles H. Barlow, a Livingston County man in Company K. But now that he'd traveled across several states to Virginia, Barlow came to some conclusions about his Wolverine State. "I like Michigan better than all . . . not that I am homesick, far from it. But it looks like the air seems cooler, freer & the girls are better looking," he wrote.[11]

The weather was mild for July, though as the month wore on there were days of more typical summer heat. The men enjoyed reasonably good health, given 19th-century medicine and health practices—only one man had died of illness while the regiment was in Adrian, with another dying there shortly after they left. But now they began to experience more sickness. Soon a 43-year-old man from St. Joseph County, Alexus B. Parsons, died of illness. Dr. Chamberlain said that some of the men's common affliction was their own fault. "Almost all are trouble more or less with the Diarrhaea," he wrote, "but they are very imprudent in eating a great deal of fruit. . . . The water is soft, which is good enough after we get used to it."[12] Of course, many soldiers, North and South, suffered and died from typhoid fever and dysentery, not because of eating too much fruit but because of contaminated drinking water, poor hygiene, and bad food. Those who survived it or could afford to joke about diarrhea sometimes called it "the Virginia two-step," but disease would take more lives during the Civil War than battle.

The regiment resumed drilling, but the question of what lay ahead for this new and growing Union army was on many minds. "General Scott is old and feeble," wrote Washington W. Carpenter, one of the Indiana men in Company B. "I do not believe Lincoln knows Scott's policy. He has seventy-five thousand men in and around Washington that he can bring into line of battle in two hours." Carpenter seemed disgusted that Virginian secessionists fired at Union pickets and were not made to pay for these attacks, but he'd heard rumors that the Union army would soon be moving south against Confederate positions at Fairfax. "There will undoubtedly be some fun there," he wrote with the bravado of a soldier who hadn't yet been in combat. Dr. Chamberlain, though presumably more sophisticated in understanding what would happen to men hit by flying lead, echoed the men's naive enthusiasm for battle. "We have just received orders to pack our traps to move to Alexandria [Va.] in the morning," he wrote on July 13, referring to the town that served as a jumping-off point from Washington to Virginia. "The boys are elated with the idea of getting where there is a chance for some fun." His notion about war as "fun" would soon change.[13]

For the next few days thousands of Union troops were on the move, some boarding steamers on the Potomac River for transport to Alexandria. This army was under the commander of Brig. Gen. Irwin McDowell. The 4th Michigan was part of its Third Division, commanded by Col. Samuel P. Heintzelman. Specifically, they served in this division's Second Brigade under Col. Orlando Willcox, a native Detroiter and West Point graduate. Willcox's first Civil War command, the 90-day 1st Michigan Infantry, served in this brigade, as did two New York regiments.[14]

The 4th Michigan moved from Meridian Hill on July 14, marching through Washington's cheering crowds to the Potomac wharfs and the waiting steamships. It was a short trip to Alexandria and they arrived in the early afternoon. Sgt. Eli Starr said the soldiers removed their hats and caps as they marched by the house where Colonel Ellsworth had been shot and killed. Then they continued into the countryside to Cloud's Mill in Virginia's Fairfax County. "When we arrived our tents had not come, so we went to picking blackberries, there being plenty on the ground where we were to be quartered," wrote Henry L. Case of Hillsdale County. "It was funny to see the boys stooping over picking, for they were on low bushes or vines." Dr. Chamberlain said this area was "the heart of the enemy's country," with many abandoned houses.

The regiment was here briefly, marching west with their division on July 16. The Second Brigade was ordered to nearby Fairfax Station. They were instructed to leave behind their tents, each man taking only a blanket and hardtack along with his weapon and ammunition. But men did not live by hardtack alone. George Young of Company B said that the soldiers quickly learned "a trick" from the 11th New York, a regiment of "Fire Zouaves"—to raid the local Virginia farms for livestock and produce, a practice soldiers euphemistically called "foraging." "The boys are coming in with hogs, geese, chickens, fresh bacon, sugar rice and flour, find them secreted in the woods," he reported. But the night was cold and damp and the men had only blankets or overcoats for shelter. "The boys begin to think this was campaigning in earnest," Dr. Chamberlain wrote. He came up with some historical booty when one of the raiding Zouaves threw away a portrait of George Washington taken from a Virginia plantation. The doctor packed it up and sent it home.[15]

Their brigade moved out the next morning and soon came across felled trees and debris across the road and nearby railroad tracks—obstacles left by the Confederates to block their way. But they reached abandoned Rebel trenches, capturing a few enemy troops in the process. At the order of their division commander, four companies of the 4th Michigan under Major Childs remained to guard the train dépot at Fairfax Station while the rest of the regiment proceeded to Fairfax Court House. The men watched as thousands of Union soldiers, cavalry, and artillery marched on to the southwest toward Manassas Junction and the Confederate positions. But at Fairfax Station, the men continued pilfering nearby farms for food. "As soon as they boys had stacked arms the chickens & pigs (rather numerous) had to suffer," wrote Lt. George Monteith of Company G. Orvey Barrett tried to kill an old sow, but six shots from his small-caliber pistol had no effect on the animal. However, Washington W. Carpenter, the smallest man in Company B, easily dispatched a pig with a shot from an old Colt revolver.

On the morning of July 18 and on into the next day, the soldiers heard cannonading in the distance. The fact that they weren't at the scene of this fighting, preliminaries for what would be called battle of Bull Run, was disappointing. "Our company, B, is detailed to stay out," complained George E. Young, one of the Indiana men. "I do not like that." Some were put to work clearing the rail line of trees and piles of earth left by Rebels, while some guarded the railroad depot and others acted as a reserve at Fairfax Court House.[16] Jim Tuttle of Company F got in trouble when he had "a little argument" with company officers, Capt. Sam DeGolyer and Lt. Simon B. Preston, on the morning of July 20. Unfortunately for him, since his part of the regiment was then posted at Fairfax Court House, the officers had a jail cell at their disposal. Tuttle was locked up. "I had not yet got the hang of strict military discipline," he admitted later. Now he faced court-martial, for he had, by his own words, "talked pretty bad to the Captain."[17]

Sunday, July 21, dawned clear and mild and again cannon pounded in the distance. "Today the guns are firing at Bulls Run in the direction of Manassas Gap," Sergeant Bancroft wrote. "The firing has been going on for two hours." He realized that men were fighting and dying. Later he noted, "All day long we have listened to the guns." Sgt. William Limbarker, 26, of Company F, also wrote in his diary as the hours passed. "It's a pleasant day," he wrote; "the Cannonading commenced this morning at half past Nine o'Clock this morning and be[e]n heavy very heavy all day up to fore."

Bull Run

It was frustrating to hear the battle but not be able to pitch in, wrote Charles Barlow of Company K. "I tell you Charley you don't know how it makes one feel to get as news as that (7 miles to a battle) & then be tied up. but we had to obey orders & could not help our boys in the fight."[18] Dr. Chamberlain was taking care of sick men at Fairfax Station as soldiers from the 4th Michigan finished clearing the railroad tracks, allowing Union troops to be brought up by train. "It was lively times all day at the Station," the doctor said. "Couriers were arriving hourly from the field with dispatches for Headquarters, and to hurry up the reserve." The regiment's companies at Fairfax Court House saw the smoke drifting into the sky from the battlefield, and soon they saw the physical results of the fighting as ambulances brought casualties back that afternoon. "A great many of the wounded were brought to the Court House," wrote Second Lieutenant William McConnell of Company H. "It was indeed a sad scene—some with an arm or a leg shot off."

Sgt. Ransom Bush, 37, of Company K had been put to work with a detail of men gathering food and livestock, but he also listened with his comrades, noting developments in a letter to his wife. "They are gitting at it purty hot By the firing of the guns they have Ben firing about one [h]our and it gets hotter all the while," he wrote. By afternoon he added the bitter development: "The news is that they have Drove our men Back to Centervill [*sic*]."[19]

That news was correct—the Union army was defeated in the first major battle of the war, which Confederates would call the first Battle of Manassas. As cannon fire echoed over the landscape that morning, Capt. Sam DeGolyer hadn't been able to stand the waiting—he and some other officers and men headed toward the sound of the battle "to see the fight," Dr. Chamberlain wrote. Other accounts said that DeGolyer volunteered to carry orders and messages from his generals to commanders in the field. Ultimately this question about DeGolyer's going into the battle would become a point of controversy among the top officers of the regiment.

Sgt. William F. Robinson of Company H, from Jackson, who'd been a dentist in civilian life and was about 24 or 25, said he was "off on a scout" that day. He was among the officers who went toward the battlefield and came within about a mile of it. "I could see the flash of the cannon, and volumes of smoke rise," he wrote. Knowing his regiment could be ordered to move at any moment, he hurried back to Fairfax Station. But DeGolyer continued on into harm's way. Whether he was carrying messages or just trying to help in the confusion of crumbling Union lines, DeGolyer and the regiment's adjutant, Lt. Francis S. Earle, 24, of Grand Rapids, rode into Confederate lines. The fact that they and some other Union troops were dressed in gray uniforms meant it was impossible for the two sides to tell each other apart at times. "They saw two armed men carrying a wounded man on a litter," Dr. Chamberlain wrote about what he'd heard of DeGolyer's and Earle's adventure. "They asked DeGolyer where the hospital was. He asked them what regiment they belong to. They said South Carolina First. He drew his revolver and ordered them to give up their arms." Earle decided it was time to get back to Union lines, but DeGolyer pressed on and was captured. One report said that DeGolyer was last seen "telling the Captain of one of the Artillery Companies where to point his guns." Another officer of the 4th Michigan, Lt. Simon B. Preston from Hudson, of Company F, was reportedly carrying dispatches that day to General McDowell. He was also captured.[20]

That afternoon or evening the two parts of the 4th Michigan reunited at Fairfax Court House to await developments as the defeated Union troops streamed back toward them. "I saw men who were so frightened that they threw away their blankets, guns and everything, to aid them in their flight," said Dr. Chamberlain. Orvey Barrett wrote that part of the 4th Michigan was positioned along the road that led from the battlefield to Fairfax Court House, "ordered to stop all stragglers," referring to men who were retreating without orders. "Talk of stopping a cyclone; it was impossible. The rush of soldiers, congressmen, and other civilians, from Washington, literally forced us from the highway."[21]

Edward H. C. Taylor agreed. "I had the honor if arresting the flight of a Colonel of Pennsylvania troops, who left his Reg. and fled from the field of Battle," he wrote. "Late in the afternoon when I had returned to Fairfax thinking all was going well with our troops on the advance I was suddenly startled by the order to 'fall in.' We took our places in rank and marched out a mile towards Bull's Run and halted for the purpose of stopping the flight of our men. Among the first we stopped was this Col. whom I stopped with my bayonet on his breast in spite of his drawn pistol which he vainly tried in his excitement to fire, but as he forgot to cock his pistol, I could afford to laugh at him." The Company A man said they were able to hold the retreating men for a while, but "the crowd became so dense that we were forced to give way to their pressure."[22]

Fred Meech of Company B said the 4th Michigan's men lay on their arms, expecting to be sent in to take up the fight as thousands of Union soldiers retreated. But when his regiment was finally ordered to get to their feet and march (late that night or early in the morning of July 22), he was disgusted to see that they, too, were heading back toward Washington. Sgt. William E. Limbarker of Company F called it "shameful" and "a disgraceful retreat," a widely held opinion. "We could not have marched it any quicker if h-e-l-l had been right at our feet," Meech complained. Sergeant Bush was also angry and disappointed and he blamed his superiors. "Wee have got a corrages [courageous] lot officers," he wrote with sarcasm. "As [soon] as the battle was over they ordered us to retreat to Washington." Lieutenant DePuy insisted that Colonel Woodbury and the other officers were as outraged as their men that they hadn't been allowed to fight, "but as soldiers we must obey orders."[23] As it turned out later, Woodbury privately blamed his own lieutenant colonel, William Duffield, for claiming that orders arrived to start the regiment retreating, when in reality no such order was received.

Some men posted out in the darkness as pickets were angry to find the 4th Michigan marched off without telling them. "Well there we stood till 3 o'clock when we found out our regiment had retreated 3 hours before," a peeved Charles Barlow wrote. They quickly picked up their packs and joined the great tide of soldiers, moving like so many refugees. "The sight was painful to behold, waggon loads of wounded men came pounding along over the rough roads," Barlow continued, "& their groans sound in my ears yet." Dr. Chamberlain, his assistant, and sick men who could walk also retreated from Fairfax Station, moving along the railroad line toward Alexandria. "Piles of ammunition, guns, and all kinds of stores were left for the enemy," the doctor wrote. He was among many Union men able to board the train that shuttled back and forth from Alexandria along the line of the retreat, evacuating soldiers throughout the early morning hours of July 22.

Sergeant Robinson described the retreat along the road as "one moving body of panic stricken men, horses and wagons, some of the horses dashing madly through the crowd, without any riders." "The loss is great," wrote Bancroft in his diary, "the confusion greater." At five in the morning it began to rain on the downhearted and angry men of his regiment. "When we got within about a mile of Washington we halted and camped under the shed of a brick kiln which sheltered us from some of the rain, and rested there that day and night and then [the next day] marched to our old camp on Meridian Hill where we are now," Fred Meech said of the aftermath. Lieutenant Monteith was less negative than some. "Crossing Penn[sylvani]a. Ave. we rec[eive]d 3 cheers for retreating in good order while other Reg[imen]ts were completely scattered," he wrote.[24]

Fortunately for these men the Confederate generals didn't follow up on their victory. Back in Washington, the Union army was now under the command of Gen. George McClellan, and Dr. Chamberlain soon felt that things were now going "a little more 'ship shape'" as McClellan imposed order and discipline on the shaken troops. No one was yet sure whether the missing Captain DeGolyer and Lieutenant Preston had been killed or captured, but they were missed. "We all feel their loss severely," the doctor wrote of the officers. "They were both respected and loved by the entire Regiment." Chamberlain noted that DeGolyer had led by his strength and courage, uncomplaining about hardships and setting a fine example for his men; Preston had been an officer always ready to assist his men and try to see to their care and comfort. "Poor fellows! They were too rash and venturesome for their safety," he wrote.[25]

The fact that DeGolyer and Preston were missing was good news, ironically, for one man—Pvt. Jim Tuttle. Because the officers who had him arrested for insubordination were now prisoners, Tuttle no longer faced court-martial. "No one else caring to prefer charges against me,

I was released in time to help cover the retreat of the demoralized army," he claimed. But the larger questions about how the war should be prosecuted, and how and why the army had been beaten so badly, weighed on the minds of many. Lieutenant Monteith, a religious man, saw it in religious terms: "What causes the most anxiety on my part is the wickedness of our own people," he wrote. "I can see it in the army more than before, coming from all parts of the country & so generally demoralized that it seems if God would visit his wrath upon us. But then, ten righteous in Sodom would have saved it from his vengeance & this gives me strong hope that he will help us and we will come off conquerors." Edward H. C. Taylor, a Democrat, saw the Confederate victory as a matter of "too many traitors at home" and what he felt was the weak administration of President Lincoln. Taylor thought the government should compromise with the South, and that the administration was filled with incompetent and politically ambitious men. He hoped McClellan would be given a free hand to fight the war as he saw fit, calling him "the salvation of the nation in this crisis."[26]

Dr. Chamberlain felt he could explain Bull Run more objectively and analytically, now that he spoke with some Southerners and realized the war was not going to be "some fun.": "We have underrated our enemy very much," he wrote to his hometown newspaper. "They firmly believe they are in the right in this controversy; they are a brave people. . . . Now these people are fighting as they believe, to protect their hearth stones, their wives and children, and their property from the ruthless band of a hireling soldiery. Can we convince them of their error? Not by the destruction of private property."[27]

He continued his thoughts on the battle's impact a few days later. Bull Run had shown the new soldiers, as well as himself, what really happened to men hit by gunfire. "I have numerous applications for discharges from those who have all at once discovered some old scars or injuries, which they affirmed at the time of their enlistment [had] never given them any inconvenience," the assistant surgeon wrote. Recruiters, he noted, should be more particular about selecting men for service. "I would rather have 500 men of the right stripe that 1,000 of these fellows who make great promises at home. These same men are generally grumbling about their rations, finding fault and making others discontented who would otherwise be satisfied." He advised community leaders back home to make sure that the families of the volunteers weren't reduced to poverty because their husbands and fathers joined the army. If women back home truly wanted to help, they could send jellies, preserves, and wine for the sick and old clothes, sheets, and other textile products that could be turned into cloths for medical uses.

The doctor also felt that the Bull Run defeat was not so much the fault of the soldiers as of the officers, and that there was anxiety on the part of officers now they were going to be tested on their knowledge of tactics. "That is a move in the right direction," Chamberlain wrote. "Men who were made Major Generals on account of political influence were found not be the material for warriors. It was also found to be bad policy to learn them military tactics in the teeth of batteries, which were mowing down our men at such a fearful rate." The doctor later claimed his letters about Bull Run enraged some people at home.[28]

But many men still wanted the chance to fight, to avenge those killed at Bull Run and defeat the Confederacy. One was David C. Laird, a 19-year-old Hillsdale County man in Company A, who heard grumbling from men who felt they shouldn't have to stay for their full three-year hitch. This idea came as a result of goings-on in the 1st Michigan Infantry, a "90-day" regiment. Before the battle, officers of the 1st Michigan had talked to their men about swearing an oath to fulfill a three-year hitch, but many of them refused, saying they wanted to return home first. On July 25, just four days after that regiment suffered at Bull Run, its men left for Detroit. Some members of the 4th Michigan—it is not clear how many—went with them, apparently having had their fill of army life.

Col. Dwight Woodbury wrote to state military authorities about the fact certain members of his regiment traveled home with the 1st Michigan—some with permission, some without. Two men from Company C who had never sworn into the service of the U.S. were allowed to go home, and the colonel had granted furlough to a soldier from Company F—but that was all. "All others are deserters," Woodbury wrote, advising they should be arrested. Soldiers like young David Laird had no patience for the complainers and deserters. "I will not return [to Michigan] (if my life is spared) until the rebels are dispersed," he vowed, though he understood now that the war was not going to be a short one. "I think the war will last three years, at least," he wrote.[29]

The 4th Michigan returned to the routine of drill and work, or fatigue, on Meridian Hill, where they built a fort that was part of chain of defenses for Washington. Company I's Sgt. Michael J. Vreeland, 22, of Brownstown Township in Wayne County, said the regiment's discipline was strict and that the soldiers "were not allowed to leave the camp for any purpose whatsoever, so that for all the good it does, we are just as far from Washington as ever." But 18-year-old Pvt. Stiles H. Wirts didn't let orders and guards stop him from having a good time. He bragged that he routinely sneaked out of camp to visit a couple of nearby families who happened to have charming daughters. Of course, Vreeland would ultimately leave the service of his country with the brevet (honorary) rank of a brigadier general, while Wirts soon became a prisoner of war, his military career ending much sooner. Officers and noncommissioned officers were allowed to leave camp, however. Sergeant Limbarker of Company F took a day to tour the Patent Office and the White House with one of his company's lieutenants. "Old [Abe] did not ask us to Drink or Dine with Him[,] the old Sucker," Limbarker joked. The sergeant added that "he has pleasant place."

The regiment didn't stay long on Meridian Hill. On August 8 the men marched with their brigade in the heat to Arlington Heights in the hilly, wooded Virginia countryside. Some described this as a few miles from Washington on the road to Fairfax Court House, or two or three miles out on the way to Fall's Church, where there were Confederate positions. They called this place Camp Union. Pickets here regularly traded fire with Confederates, initially, and there was the periodic false alarm. Sgt. John Bancroft noted that "Capt. S," probably Jeremiah Slocum of Company I, fell into a regimental latrine or cesspool, a kind of a ditch, when the 4th Michigan was called out on a rainy night just days after they arrived. But the weather turned surprisingly cool for August and the men received some of their pay. The regiment's new brigade was briefly under the command of Brig. Gen. William T. Sherman. Sergeant Bancroft wrote to a Detroit newspaper that Sherman was "a plain, quiet sort of a man, but very prompt and business like in his actions." Of course, Sherman would go on to be one of the war's great generals.[30]

Each morning, Lt. William McConnell told friends, one company from the 4th Michigan went on guard duty around the immediate vicinity of the camp while another went out on picket. Picket duty involved the posting of squads in advanced positions as frontline sentries, taking the men further into the countryside. Lt. George Monteith described one of the first picket assignments on August 9. Moving with 40 men, a few lieutenants, and three dragoons for carrying dispatches, he reached a crossroads about a mile and a half from Camp Union. When Confederates fired at his men and they fired back, the entire regiment hurried out in line of battle, though nothing came of this incident.[31]

This sort of disturbance would eventually prompt soldiers to realize that unless there was truly a threat of attack by the other side, picket firing served no good purpose except to risk injury or death to men who weren't in battle, but merely on routine duty. Such shooting also deprived of sleep the pickets' reserves and their comrades back in camp. In other words, most men would come to the conclusion that picket firing was a dangerous and pointless waste of everyone's time.

By the middle of the month, the 4th Michigan and their brigade were pulled back a mile or more toward the Potomac—the men could see Washington and Georgetown from this place—and the troops again built fortifications. The regiment proudly named their particular spot Fort Woodbury. A renewed confidence returned to troops dispirited over Bull Run. "If they attack us at this point, that is Arlington Heights, we are preparing to give them a warm reception," wrote Washington W. Carpenter. "I tell you I begin to feel good at the prospects of an engagement."

Other changes took place in late July and early August—in uniforms, weapons, and personnel. "We have been furnished with a blue uniform in place of the grey one, which bore too close a resemblance to that of the Secessionists," wrote Private James Redfield of Company A, referring to the fact that soldiers hadn't been able to tell from friend from foe at Bull Run. The 4th Michigan's new clothing was described by another soldier as a "semi-Zouave" uniform with a fez, dark blue pants, and white or tan gaiters. Of course, the exotic head wear would also turn out to be temporary, for soldiers quickly learned that a fez simply couldn't keep the rain off a man's face as well as a forage cap with a visor or a slouch hat with a brim. More importantly, a soldier writing to a Detroit newspaper stated that Companies A and B (the regiment's "flanking companies," received rifles that fired Minié balls (or "minnie balls," as the soldiers called them). These rifles were far more accurate and had longer range than muskets. But not all the men got the better rifles. Many were given more "buck and ball" muskets, just like the ones they had been issued earlier.[32]

Sgt. Orvey S. Barrett of Company B later wrote that men weren't happy about these weapons, and some soldiers formed a noisy, mock "funeral procession" for the old muskets they turned in, accompanying the boxes to the quartermaster's depot, firing a "salute" over them, and attracting a lot of attention. Noticing that this spectacle drew a crowd, some of them formed a plan: When they went back to camp, 40 men from Company B engaged in more noisy shenanigans. Some strapped muskets onto their backs and got down on their hands and knees so that the barrel stuck out over their heads; others pulled the triggers with strings, firing off blanks. While this loud and distracting silliness was going on, another group of soldiers engaged the sutler (a licensed, traveling merchant) with the nearby 14th New York Infantry in conversation. But as the sutler was engaged and musket blanks were going off, a barrel of whiskey disappeared from his tent. "It was never found," Barrett joked, "but you could buy a canteen full for $5 of one who knew where it was." A detail was sent out to look for the missing whiskey, he noted with deadpan humor, but its members were quite drunk when they came back to camp.[33]

Ft. Woodbury, drawn by Lt. Charles Gruner.

These sorts of high jinks were an exception. Jonas Richardson noted that "we practice at target shooting every morning." Shortly after the 4th Michigan was moved back toward the Potomac in mid-August, Sergeant Richardson said that "the orders have been given not to fire on the Rebble [*sic*] pickets unless they fired on us first." Capt. Alexander Crane of Company K, who had hurt his foot some weeks previously, was pressured by Governor Blair to resign; Crane did so. Capt. James Cole of Company B accidentally shot himself in the thigh with his revolver on August 18 and was removed back to a Washington area hospital. Moses Funk of Company H resigned, reportedly when a new federal law went into effect that no man over the age of 40 could be a captain, though some thought he hadn't been able to pass the new tactics examination.[34]

Dr. Joseph Tunnicliff Jr., the regiment's surgeon, resigned to become surgeon of the newly reorganized 1st Michigan Infantry, its new soldiers now required to serve a three-year hitch. Major Jonathan W. Childs wrote that the officers of the 4th Michigan had gotten along with each other well with the exception of Tunnicliff, whom Governor Blair had wanted to go into the regiment. Tunnicliff apparently was not satisfied with life as a military surgeon and spent much of his time away from the regiment, often attending Congress and not returning to camp for days. This was unacceptable to Colonel Woodbury, who asked the doctor to spend more time in camp, Childs said; Tunnicliff was unhappy with this request and went back to Michigan to get a different appointment. Another version of Tunnicliff's leaving (published in the hometown newspaper of Dr. Chamberlain and perhaps written by him) claimed that Tunnicliff hadn't been able to pass an examination by medical authorities. Whatever the reason for Tunnicliff's departure, Chamberlain believed he was going to be appointed to the post of regimental surgeon. But a number of people back in Michigan complained to Governor Blair about Chamberlain's published assessment of what was wrong with the Union army and the Lincoln administration's war effort—they thought the doctor unpatriotic. Chamberlain later wrote that Blair, in order to curry favor with those who wanted him punished, found another doctor to serve in the role of surgeon, leaving Chamberlain as assistant surgeon.

Lt. George Monteith got a desirable new assignment when Colonel Woodbury asked him if he would serve as adjutant for Sherman's brigade. This turned out to be the first in a series of jobs as staff officer or aide that would sometimes take young Monteith out of the regiment and get him better pay, food, and living arrangements. "Friday last I went out with Capt. Cole & Co. B on picket, he being destitute of suits, it was very wet & rainy, but my quarters were [are now] in a chapel," he wrote from the headquarters of his brigade at Fort Corcoran. Monteith's letters show he was happy to be at division headquarters, though he still got assignments that took him to the picket line and, eventually, into battle.[35]

Back in camp with the 4th Michigan, Major Childs wrote that the officers of the regiment were downright angry with the *Detroit Free Press* correspondent who signed his dispatches "Hamilton" or "H." The man's name was actually H. H. Finley, Childs said, and his reports had been unfair and inaccurate, "the blackest of bare faced lies," stating that the officers had been quarrelsome, uncaring, and corrupt. "He is careful to keep without our lines," the major wrote about Finley. "Should he enter them, the men would tar and feather him." Edward Taylor also said press accounts of officers abusing or mistreating men were not true.[36] As did many Civil War soldiers, Ned Taylor expressed anger at sutlers, the mobile merchants who sold goods at high prices to soldiers, who usually had nowhere else to shop. "It is a shame the way the Sutler (the authorized pedlar to the Reg.) charges," he complained. "Gingerbread for which one cent in Geneva [N.Y.] would have been almost too much, he sells at *five*. Butter which could be bought, so the papers tell, in Michigan for seven he sells for *fifty* cents about. . . . He gets his price for he has no opposition." In the meantime the soldiers of the regiment built fortifications and drilled, waiting for the day when they took the offensive. "Inform all enquiring friends that I am well and like my trade first rate," wrote Sgt. Jonas Richardson to family.[37]

As the Union army drilled and worked on those August days, two men from the 4th Michigan figured in incidents and situations that made national headlines. First, in an odd piece of poetic justice, James Tuttle—the soldier who escaped court-martial after Capt. Sam DeGolyer was captured at Bull Run—also fell into Confederate hands. This happened when Company F was out on picket on August 10. "A considerable boddy of the enemy cavalry charged down on us and we made for the woods," Tuttle wrote. But he and Pvt. Stiles H. Wirts—who previously enjoyed sneaking past the camp guard near Washington to go flirt with girls and pass worthless old Michigan banknotes—got separated from the rest of the company. They found themselves surrounded when they emerged from the woods. Over the next couple of days, the prisoners were marched to Centerville and then transported to a place Tuttle identified as Lynchburg. Here they were held in a vermin-infested jail in which they fought rats all night. Then they were taken to Richmond and placed in one of the tobacco warehouses now overflowing with Union prisoners. Perhaps even more ironic was that by the time Tuttle arrived in Richmond, Captain DeGolyer was no longer there—he had just escaped from Rebel prison and soon became a national hero to the North. Worse still for Tuttle, he now faced an even starker fate than court-martial: He was, he claimed, chosen as one of 151 Union prisoners who, in the lengthening summer of 1861, faced the prospect of being hanged by the Confederate States of America.[38]

CHAPTER 3

McClellan Moves Slow but Sure

THE DAY AFTER PRIVATES TUTTLE AND WIRTS WERE CAPTURED, GOOD NEWS REACHED THE 4TH Michigan—Capt. Sam DeGolyer was alive. On August 11, Colonel Woodbury stood before the regiment, reading aloud a letter from the captain. He and Lt. Simon B. Preston were prisoners in Richmond, hoping to be exchanged soon. No one had been sure up to this point whether they had been killed at Bull Run. "Cheer after cheer resounded through the air," wrote Sgt. William F. Robinson, "and it seemed as though the boys of his Company could not restrain themselves, so filled were they with joy."[1]

DeGolyer and Preston, reportedly captured near the stone bridge over the creek, were among a thousand or so prisoners. By foot and by train, they were brought to the Rebel capital and initially housed in the Liggon & Co.'s tobacco factory. Within a day or so some were shifted into an adjacent building. The Union men were allowed to see local newspapers, and DeGolyer was concerned about reports that the prisoners would soon be put to work on Rebel fortifications or moved to North Carolina. Neither prospect appealed to him; he told Lieutenant Preston that he was going to try to escape. Preston thought this too risky, but Quartermaster Sgt. Henry C. Jencks of the 2nd Rhode Island Infantry was willing. While prisoners still had some money and valuables in their possession, they could purchase and send out for items. DeGolyer obtained some dark-colored clothing and got an old slouch hat from the chaplain of a Connecticut regiment. They also got 10 cents' worth of soda crackers and a loaf of bread. But perhaps most important of all, DeGolyer and Jencks got help from unnamed friends in Richmond. On the night of August 13, they made their move, taking advantage of the system that was set up for prisoners' messes, cooking arrangements, for groups of men sharing food rations.

"We saved our cold meat and bread, cut it up, put in seasoning and made a stew," the captain later explained, "the officer of the guard permitting one of us [from each mess] to go into the yards to the fire to cook it." He and Jencks got permission and went down to the yard. Though neither man revealed details that might compromise those who aided them, DeGolyer's vaguely worded account suggested they may have crept into a drain or ditch, or perhaps under a wagon, possibly when a distraction was staged to draw attention away from them. However they did it, he and Jencks got away from the prison undetected.

"By the aid of friends yet in Richmond, of whom it would not be policy to speak," he wrote, "we stepped in between the outer guard and a small barn, between two brick buildings. We were fastened in here. When the Negroes and cooks left we were left in there alone. By starting off a board, we crawled through and dropped down into a ravine and made our way down near the [James] River.[2]

Who helped the men? History shows that Union sympathizer and spy Elizabeth Van Lew and her black servants, dedicated secret agents, helped many prisoners escape from Richmond. But there was also the suggestion that Jencks's family owned a factory in Richmond and may have had connections willing and able to aid the escapees. For the record, the tobacco building was near the river.

The night was cloudy and the men waited in a ravine, listening for an alarm. None came. They made their way northeast and reached some fortifications outside of town. Here they remained still for some three hours before deciding no soldiers were posted there. The escapees removed their shoes and passed through quietly, and reached a bridge from which the planks or treads had been removed. They edged their way across the narrow beams over what was probably the Chickahominy River.

The men took to the woods and underbrush, crawling through briars and thickets in the rain, trying to move north. Unfortunately, they found when the sun came up they'd made a large circle and come back to that same bridge they crossed hours before. The men hurried into a muddy ditch near the woods when an overseer arrived that morning with slaves who spent the day cutting timber close by. "We felt relieved when night came," DeGolyer wrote.[3]

For the next several days, with the weather remaining rainy, Jencks and DeGolyer traveled at night and hid by day. With no stars to guide them they sometimes moved in the wrong direction. At times Confederate troopers rode by. DeGolyer said they had a close call at the town of Bowling Green, where dogs barked at them and a railroad agent came to his door to investigate. Their bread and crackers lasted five days, but they were still far from safety and had to live on what raw wheat and green corn they could find. Covered with bites of mosquitoes and ticks, it took them eight nights and seven days of hardship to reach the Rappahannock at a point downriver from Fredericksburg. Some slaves told them about a man living nearby, "Uncle Jim," who would take them across in his skiff for 10 cents, and the two escapees may have crossed in that manner.

Then they made their way across the peninsula formed by the Rappahannock and the Potomac. By the next night, August 21, they had reached the wide river, "their clothes nearly torn off and themselves almost exhausted for want of food."[4]

Gathering pieces of downed tree limbs, cast-off poles, branches, and driftwood on the shore, the pair used what remained of their ragged clothing to tie this debris together into a makeshift raft. "We found it would hardly hold one of us, but it was the best we could do," the captain said, the Potomac "looking like a sea before us." They pushed out into the water. If Jencks's later estimate of the area of their crossing point was accurate, the river was about two miles wide. They took turns, with one lying in the nearly submerged tangle of logs and branches while the other held onto a piece wood at the rear of their ramshackle raft, kicking his legs. "Before we got half across," the captain wrote, "our strength appeared entirely exhausted."

The wind and the current worked against them and it seemed they were making little progress. "Our limbs were nearly frozen and quite stiff," Jencks wrote. They were slowly crossing the big river, but within a half mile of the Maryland shore, the raft was coming apart. The men were sure that they would drown, and they prayed, trying to stay afloat. Suddenly they felt the river bottom below their feet. "As grey morn began to appear in the East, we struck the shore," DeGolyer wrote. "We hardly realized it." The trip across the Potomac had taken them seven hours, and no one had seen them. They were chilled, nearly naked, and hungry, but DeGolyer and Jencks wept for joy. They rested.[5]

A news report featuring Jencks's account had the two of them being plucked from the river by a passing schooner called the *Catherine Jane* before they reached the Maryland shore, but DeGolyer's detailed account stated the pair crossed the Potomac on their own. He said that the captain of a schooner saw them on the shore and provided them blankets and food. After this rest they continued on foot up the riverside to find the U.S. Navy, since they knew the Union forces had blockaded the Potomac. The pair walked as much as several miles along the Maryland side and flagged a patrol ship. The navy vessel U.S.S. *Union* picked them up across from the point where Potomac Creek enters the river on that afternoon of August 22. "At 1 P.M. observed two men making signal to us from the beach," an officer recorded in the ship's log. "Sent the cutter off. Proved to be two officers who had been captured at Manassas and escaped."[6]

"We signaled her with a pocket handkerchief," DeGolyer said about the *Union*. "They sent a boat off, and after satisfying themselves that we were what we represented, took as aboard, gave us provisions and every comfort in their power. We shall never forget Captain Goldsborough and the steamer Union." The steamer *Josephine* came up that evening and DeGolyer and Jencks transferred over as the sailors cheered. By the next day the escapees were back in Washington, and their story was quickly in the newspapers. As perhaps the first Union officers to escape from Confederate prison, they were national news and heroes to boot. "We were sent to General [Winfield] Scott, then to President Lincoln. We were furnished with money, papers and a carriage to our Regiment," DeGolyer wrote. "The cheering of the different companies and the congratulating was too much."[7]

Not long after his captain became a national hero, Jim Tuttle was in a far different fix. He was one of a number of prisoners, officers and men alike, loaded on a train to South Carolina. Among his fellow prisoners was Col. Orlando Willcox of the 1st Michigan, who noted that the journey began on September 10, 1861. It had turned out that a number of Rebel privateers captured at sea were facing trial and possible execution by the United States on charges of piracy, since the Lincoln administration initially maintained that these men were criminals and not entitled to be treated as prisoners of war. The Confederate government warned that if the U.S. executed those sailors, they would respond in kind. "So the Rebels selected the same number of us to correspond in rank," Tuttle wrote, "to send to Charleston, S.C. as hostages." Tuttle was also being harangued by Lt. Simon Preston, the other officer from his company who'd been captured at Bull Run. Preston wanted him to serve as his orderly, but the soldier wasn't interested in being an officer's servant.[8]

Eventually the United States decided to hold Rebel captives of questionable status as prisoners of war so as not to start an endless round of tit-for-tat executions. Tuttle wrote that after a couple of weeks in the Charleston jail (and in the shadow of its gallows), the prisoners were moved to Castle Pinckney, an old fort on a small island in the harbor. He showed his disregard for authority again early in October when he refused the guards' order to pile wood and clean up the fort's parade ground. "We [Tuttle and another prisoner] conferred together and agreed that it would be giving aid and comfort to the enemy (or words to that effect) and agreed not to do it," he wrote. Tuttle was taken before the commander, who had him locked in "an old bomb proof magazine utterly devoid of light and almost [devoid] of air," until "I came to my senses," he wrote. For three days he was kept in what was probably a box of stone and wood, given a pint of water and a hardtack each day. By the third day he couldn't stand because of the stagnant air. He was dragged back before the commander, who seemed concerned for Tuttle's health, but who asked him if he was willing to do his duty. "I said, Yes, I am willing now to do my duty as I see it, but, I said, Captain, I will die before I will clean up a Drill ground for the enemys of my country." The Rebel prison commander ordered Tuttle taken back to his quarters, saying, "He is the most stubborn man I ever saw." Tuttle's story is confirmed by the 1861 diary of another prisoner, Capt. William Withington of the 1st Michigan. "Oct. 8–Tuttle of the 4th Michigan released from three or four days solitary confinement in the dark magazine for refusal to work," Withington wrote.[9]

Tuttle had had enough—he had to try to escape. Guards were lenient about allowing prisoners out of the fort to bathe. After all, there was nowhere for the prisoners to go, given the distance to shore. But that gave him the opportunity he needed. Over the course of the next three weeks, he built a raft from boards from an old outhouse with the help of two other prisoners, but they backed out when it came time to attempt an escape. Tuttle said he then used a couple of posts from the palisade, or outer fence, to make a one-man raft and that he actually experimented with it in the water. He even made himself paddles to strap to his hands so he could row away from the island.

But he never got the chance to try. Tuttle said he had shared his plan with his friend Wirts and word got around. Another prisoner helped himself to Tuttle's raft, tried to escape, and failed. As a result the prisoners of Castle Pinckney were shifted back to the Charleston jail. According to Colonel Willcox's prison diary, the transfer back to the jail occurred on October 30. On New Year's Day, 1862, the prisoners were put on trains and sent to Columbia, where they were placed in the local jail and what Tuttle described as a "long shanty barracks."[10]

It was time for another escape bid. Though the barracks were walled off into several sections like cell blocks or dormitories, the men learned to loosen boards in the partitions, allowing them to unbolt doors and move through the barracks to talk with fellow prisoners. "One dark rainy night I took the axe in our room when we were locked up and as soon as we were all locked in I told the boys to strike up the Anvil Chorus, a noise that was characteristic of its name," Tuttle wrote. As the men sang the famous operatic song, Tuttle struck the floor on the pounding backbeat, though he gave no explanation about why prisoners were allowed to have an axe in a prison barracks. Tuttle said he split the boards so that they could be repositioned over the hole he created. Then they started to dig, making a passage back under the shanty and a board fence into a narrow lane or alley just beyond the barracks. How long this digging took he did not say.[11]

It was a Saturday night when Tuttle, Wirts, and another prisoner, John Archer of the 1st Michigan, made their break. Tuttle made a reconnaissance, emerging from the tunnel into the alley, which was fenced on both sides, then returning to the prison. On the side away from the prison was a gated yard, and beyond it, a Columbia street. The three men emerged from the tunnel, climbed the fence, and dropped into the yard, which was closed off from the street by a tall board fence. The men were wearing their Union blue uniforms and caps, but these were partially covered by brown overcoats they received from the Sanitary Commission, a body organized to help provide necessities to U.S. soldiers. "A tight double gate" separated the enclosed property from the street. As Tuttle tried to look through a crack or a hole to see what was happening beyond it, the gate suddenly swung open. A man standing outside demanded to know what they were doing.

Tuttle didn't miss a beat. "Playing 'I Spy,'" he replied sarcastically.

"You had better find some other place to play it," the man warned.

"All right," Tuttle answered, and walked confidently out, his partners following. While people in the street watched them curiously, no one challenged them. The three Michigan soldiers strode into the South Carolina darkness. Hundreds of miles from Union lines, they hoped they could reach eastern Tennessee, where they'd heard were people with strong pro-Union feelings. As DeGolyer had done before them, the men traveled at night and hid by day. With the exception of a meal provided by slaves running a plantation in the absence of their departed masters in the Confederate army, and a meal of "cow peas" and mice found in an abandoned shanty, the three men lived on corn. "I don't feel that I can recommend them [mice] as a popular diet," Tuttle wrote.[12]

It was cold, rough going. Two weeks into their escape, Archer injured his foot, so they halted for a week while he mended. Then they pressed on, camping off the road by day, creating a fire when they could to cook and to dry their socks and warm their feet. But Wirts got sick, probably with an infection, perhaps pneumonia, that robbed him of his strength. On the 31st night of their bid for freedom, the young soldier collapsed; he urged Tuttle and Archer to continue, but they refused, stepping off the road to build a fire and shelter him. "It was raining, and was quite cold and uncomfortable. . . . When it got light enough to see, I found our position was untenable," Tuttle said. He knew they needed a better place to camp and hide, but shortly after they took to the road they ran into a squad of 15 men searching for escapees. "Of course, there was nothing for us to do but surrender," Tuttle wrote.[13]

In the time Tuttle and his comrades traveled at night after their escape, they had covered about 60 miles. They were well treated by the leader of the squad, fed, and taken by horseback about 30 miles to the town of Winnsboro, where they were turned over to the local sheriff. He allowed them a parole, so they could move about the town until 9:00 P.M. "The people of the town treated us very nicely, according us perfect freedom," Tuttle recalled. But then it was back on the train to Columbia and prison. Again Tuttle and his comrades found themselves in separate cells and on bread and water for eight days when they refused to clean up the place, but then they were put on a train to Richmond and rejoined their comrades in the Libby tobacco warehouse.

By now it was the spring of 1862. Tuttle again was pondering escape when hundreds of the enlisted men were given parole. "We were taken down the river [under] two flags of truce [on] boats." They passed the now famous ironclad *Monitor,* and transferred to a Union transport. On May 20, "we were discharged [from] the United States service." Tuttle had been in the army just shy of a year. He went back to Michigan and married his sweetheart, but soon joined another regiment, ultimately surviving the war and, just after the turn of the 20th century, writing down a narrative of his experiences with the 4th Michigan and as a prisoner of war.[14]

While Tuttle experienced captivity, his regiment soldiered on in the Virginia countryside. After the return of Captain DeGolyer to the 4th Michigan late in August 1861, the regiment's newly appointed surgeon, Dr. William E. Clark, arrived. He was 42 and from Dowagiac, a dedicated abolitionist Republican. Dr. David Chamberlain, the regiment's assistant surgeon, wrote later that he didn't think much of Clark's abilities as a surgeon, but then there were strong personal and political differences between the two. Lt. Colonel William Duffield had been sick and hospitalized but was said to be improving. He was soon appointed colonel of the new 9th Michigan Infantry. The captain of Company E, George Lumbard from Hillsdale County, had been so sick that some didn't expect him to live, but he too made a slow recovery.[15]

Colonel Woodbury was proud of comments President Lincoln had made about his regiment during a visit to the Union army's camps and forts in Virginia that week. This was especially important since word reached the colonel that Governor Blair expressed doubt about him. Many U.S. military officers held conservative Democratic views, most notably General George McClellan and those associated with him, such as General Fitz John Porter. They were regarded with suspicion by "Radical Republican" political leaders like Blair, who were growing more insistent that the war must have as a main goal the abolition of slavery. They also suspected Northern Democrats wanted a compromise to end the war without addressing the issue. Blair wanted Lincoln to take an aggressive, uncompromising stand against the Confederacy. Woodbury knew he must impress upon Blair that he was ready to fight, and wanted him to know that Washington VIPs were impressed with the 4th Michigan, part of the newly created Army of the Potomac.

"In our review on Monday by Gen'l McClellan, in presence of the President & Mr. [Secretary of State] Seward, the President publicly admitted that the 4th was *superior in every* respect to either the other seven regiments on the grounds," Woodbury boasted. "I hope my dear Governor that before the War closes I shall by my actions with the 4th be able to give you, and the people of Michigan, or a portion of the state at least, more confidence in men than I learn from my friends you now have." The stronghold his men built was named Fort Woodbury because of the good impression his regiment made on the brass. Sgt. Michael Vreeland (cousin of teenager William Vreeland, who went home on disability) bragged to his sister that this performance had gotten the men of the regiment free, for the moment, from fatigue duty.[16]

There are many ways tragedy can befall a young soldier, and almost all of them occurred as the regiment performed picket duty. Typically these happened when Confederates met them with gunfire and ambush, but there were also accidents. A private in Company F, George Lawson from Hudson, died late in August when, just after returning to camp from picket duty, Corporal Lucius Hammond bumped his gun against a tree and it discharged, striking Lawson. Captain DeGolyer had Lawson's body sent home. Union and Confederate pickets maintained aggressive postures. On the night of August 29–30, Privates Adelbert Benson of Company A and James Livingston, a St. Joseph County teen in Company C, were captured when they went to scout Rebel positions. Like the other men from their regiment who were taken prisoner early in the war, they would eventually be exchanged. Livingston would be discharged for medical reasons early in 1863, while Benson would die in battle at Gettysburg.

Days later on September 3 Corporal Levi J. Courtright, 37, from the town of Reading in Hillsdale County and serving in Company E, was shot while on picket and died a short time afterward. Seemingly the first of the 4th Michigan to be killed by enemy fire, he left a wife and several children. Vengeance may have been on the minds of three Company H men who went on reconnaissance three days later; they shot down two Confederate soldiers "who were skulking around to shoot our pickets," wrote Lt. Simon B. Hadley. The avenging soldiers were Alvin Dodge from Hillsdale County and John Boyles of Lenawee County, while the third, "Bennet," was probably George Bennett or Alexander Bennett. The Bennetts were Indiana men in Company H. "The major of the New York 14th was with them," Hadley proudly wrote. "He said the boys were as cool as though they had been shooting squirrels."

Sgt. Jonas Richardson described how the "Ann Arbor boys" of Company D exchanged gunfire with Rebels when they were on picket, standing in a field, days later. "Fred Wilkenson [*sic*] came very close to the end of the rope, a ball passed through the top of his hat, just scrapeing his head enough to make it bleed. . . . Fred is going to send his old cap home." In the meantime, as many as a third of some companies from the regiment were sick, and some of these men died. One was the Hudson company's George Brockway, who expired at a Georgetown hospital of typhoid fever.[17]

By the second week in September, the ring of trenches and forts protecting Washington was growing stronger. A network of new roads allowed the movement of Union troops, equipment, and supplies to these forts. In front of them, troops cut down thousands of trees for clear fields of fire. The Confederates made a threatening demonstration on September 13, advancing troops and opening artillery fire that sent Union pickets retreating. The Michigan men and other nearby regiments turned out at the alarm, but the Rebels merely burned down some farms and buildings and withdrew after skirmish firing.

Letters and diaries from members of the 4th Michigan show that Confederates kept up hostilities into September. Lt. George Monteith, now an aide-de-camp to the new division commander, General Fitz John Porter, told of a close call. "I had a party of 8 officers to look about a new line of picket I was trying to station, we rec[eive]d two volleys of musketry from the enemy & in our retreat, two men of my number were taken prisoners, none of us shot," he wrote.[18]

Edward Taylor was on two patrols from the 4th Michigan in confrontations with Rebels. In the second instance, Taylor said, "when we summoned them to surrender, the rascals fired upon us and cut and ran, leaving blankets, guns, haversacks and knapsacks behind." One Confederate clapped his hands to his buttocks when the Michigan patrol opened fire and apparently hit him, but he "didn't run any slower on that account," Taylor wrote. "I fired at one and didn't aim quite sure, but hit his cartridge box, which exploded (we were quite near at the time)."[19]

Lt. Harrison H. Jeffords of Company K, from the Dexter area, wrote home to friends that month that he'd been stabbed in the hand in another encounter. "You must excuse if you find any difficulty in reading as my hand is not quite well from a thrust by a bayonet through the hand that I received in a small skirmish," he wrote. "Do not worry yourself about it as it is almost well and will not bother me." While there had been picket fire that month, this report of a bayonet wound is striking, since men's accounts and other historical evidence show that bayonet fighting was not common. Though Jeffords apologized for his penmanship, his handwriting in this letter is no worse than other examples of his script. Jeffords didn't describe how he was wounded, but related a fight he described as "fun." "I went out the other day with about 70 men as pickets[,] I guess we fired 50 shots," he wrote. The Confederates came to within "40 rods" (more than 200 yards) in order to burn down a house. The Michigan men opened fire and ran to cut off the Rebels' retreat, "but their legs was to [*sic*] long, they made remarkable good time to the rear."[20] The fact Jeffords was wounded in hand-to-hand fighting with a Rebel wielding a bayonet in September 1861 foreshadowed terrible things.

Away from the picket line, life in camp was routine, satisfactory, and even musical. Capt Richard DePuy of Ann Arbor, now commanding Company K, noted that the men got paid for the months of July and August on September 19. "The boys have plenty of money and enough to eat and wear," he wrote. "These three essentials make an army enthusiastic and efficient." He wished the editor of a local paper back home could witness "the happiness of our regiment" on a typical evening. "You would think it was a grand orchestra," DePuy insisted. "Lute, horn, cymbal and harp, commingled with sweet toned singers, make the air vibrate with harmonious joy." Lieutenant Jeffords agreed. There was "dancing, singing, prayer meetings—foot races[,] music from 10 or 12 brass bands with a host of listeners," he wrote. Sergeant Richardson of Company D thought the military life fine. "Soldiering is not so awfle after one gets initiated, hard crackers, and coffee makes a good meal[;] for a change Pork and Beans *we* consider a luxury." They also had fresh beef three times a week, bread from the oven each night—it was, he said, "all that we could wish for." He said he enjoyed trading picket fire, writing that his company, acting as a reserve while the rest of the regiment was out on picket, ran to join them after the major rode into camp at full speed to get them. "We killed one Secessionist and got all his traps, napsack, etc," he wrote about the mid-September clash. "It was fun to stand behind the trees and shoot at the rascles." But later that same month, a policy of "don't shoot unless shot at" became the order for pickets.[21]

A photographer visited the camp during this time, either the famous Matthew Brady or one of his studio's team. Many pictures were taken of the officers and men of the 4th Michigan, and some these photographs remain on file with the National Archives. Sergeant Richardson of Company D had his picture made, though he wasn't pleased with the result. "I send you the photograph which was taken a few days ago. It is not a very good one," he explained to relatives. "The picture is of those that belong in our tent. I also send you one of a small group of men with the Captain and Lieutenant on the right and left."[22]

Capt. Sam DeGolyer returned to Michigan early in September to recruit more men. He was also promoted to the rank of major later that month when Lt. Col. William Duffield left to take command of a new regiment. Major Childs was promoted to replace Duffield. A strong, hearty man, DeGolyer had come through his escape from Richmond in reasonably good shape and recovered quickly. He was given a hero's welcome in Hudson and returned to the regiment in about a month's time with nearly 100 new recruits. One was Albert H. Boies, a small, dark-haired, dark-eyed farm boy who recently turned 17 and who had been one of the local cadets; his parents allowed him to go with DeGolyer on the condition that Albert not serve in the ranks. "I had never been away from home more than a day at a time before," Boies wrote later, "and now I was in for over a thousand days."[23]

The promotions of DeGolyer and Childs had been made by Gov. Austin Blair—without Colonel Woodbury's input. The colonel complained to Blair that neither he nor his men approved of the promotion of DeGolyer. "I am sorry to say it has produced much bad feeling in the regiment which at first was directed toward me, as it naturally thought the appointment would not have been made without consulting at least the Field Officers of the regiment," the colonel wrote. Furthermore, Woodbury said, the officers of the regiment intended to ask DeGolyer to resign. Why the bad feelings toward DeGolyer? "DeGolyer has done nothing to entitle him to promotion," the colonel charged; "he went to Bull Run that day of the battle *without being sent as he represented as courier,* & out of mere curiosity to look upon the battle, was taken prisoner, and therefore lost three months drill which has well prepared his *ranking captains* Cole, Wood, Randolph & Lumbard, either of them for the promotion."[24]

Woodbury's letter to Blair was revealing. Not only was the colonel critical of DeGolyer, he also charged that his former lieutenant colonel, William Duffield, had been lying about Woodbury's conduct at Bull Run. "I hear he has mentioned frequently at home that I went off to Bull run & left the regiment without saying anything to him in regard to it," Woodbury complained. "The facts are these—The night before the battle Duffield expressed a wish to go & I desired he should, & supposed until noon on the day of the battle that he was going." But Duffield did not go, and instead urged Woodbury to do so. "I did so, & was not absent from camp *four hours,* and this by his advice."

As retreating Union soldiers hurried past Fairfax Court House, it was Duffield who wanted the 4th Michigan to pull out, the colonel insisted. "I would not consent until I rec'd orders from [Gen. Irvin] McDowell and we then went to sleep until 2 A.M. when I was awakened by Duffield who said that McD had sent an Orderly directing us to fall back to Washington which we did. I now learn that Gen'l McDowell *never sent any such order* and that Duffield fabricated the whole thing," Woodbury complained. This had cost his regiment the chance to make "a reputation in being the last to leave the field."[25]

There were complaints and problems among some of the officers. Lieutenant Jeffords of Company K wrote that Capt. Richard DePuy had been drinking on duty but escaped serious consequences. "DePuy has turned out rather poor by so much so that the Colonel is sorry he made the appointment," Jeffords claimed; "he was very Drunk on 'Duty' but got discharged. I sh[o]uld get the appo[in]t[men]t before long." Edward Taylor, who'd gone from being a lieutenant to a private after resigning his commission, complained to family and to state military authorities, though nothing came of these efforts. "Col. Woodbury promised me when I resigned my place as Lieut. in Co. I that he would give me the first vacancy," Taylor groused to a relative. "Two have occurred but are already temporarily filled." Taylor claimed he was more familiar with drill and better able to command than some of the regiment's captains.

Apart from these jealousies, the largest military movement in which the 4th Michigan had been involved since Bull Run came on the night of September 28. Elements of the Army of the Potomac marched out of camp to seize more Virginia ground, and the Confederates pulled back. Soldiers thought this was a great victory, but it really amounted to an expansion of Union lines outside of Washington. "The Rebels all left on our approach," wrote Sgt. Lemuel Allen, a Tecumseh man in Company G, "and both places were taken without firing a shot." The men bivouacked in the woods near Fall's Church, though some gave the nearest landmark as Hall's Hill.[26]

The move would have been unremarkable as far as the 4th Michigan was concerned, except for a tragic case of mistaken identity in the darkness that some blamed on the regiment's pickets. This occurred as thousands of Union troops moved during that night march, with the 71st Pennsylvania Infantry coming down the road to where the men of the 4th Michigan had been moved into the woods. These Pennsylvanians were called "the California regiment" because their commander, Col. Edward Baker, a U.S. senator and old friend of Abraham Lincoln, won his fortune on the West Coast. Baker's second-in-command, Lt. Col. Isaac J. Wistar, was in charge of the 71st Pennsylvania as it marched with its brigade that night. Wistar had no idea other Union regiments were so far out in advance of his own—he'd been ordered to throw out skirmishers after passing what he thought was the last crossroads held by Union soldiers. He was surprised, therefore, to find pickets from a New York regiment at the junction. But as his column marched on, all hell broke loose.

"At the first turn to the right, which occurred within a quarter of a mile after the deployment of my skirmishers, they began to come in collision with picket guards, who said they belonged to the Fourth Michigan," Wistar reported. Suddenly a volley of shots ripped from the woods beyond a fence on the left side of the road, striking the second and third companies of the 71st Pennsylvania. There was "considerable confusion" and Wistar, on horseback, shouted for everyone to cease firing, since he was understood the shooting from the trees was by Union troops. By the time firing ended, several of his men were killed and many more were wounded.[27]

Members of the 4th Michigan denied they had anything to do with this tragic error. Charles W. Phelps of Company D, one of the pickets that night, claimed that a regiment of "Californians" became convinced they were being charged by Confederate cavalry and opened fire on other Union troops ahead of them, and that this happened just as they were marching by the Michigan pickets. Phelps claimed that when these Union soldiers shot back, the so-called Californians "throwed there [*sic*] musket, run like the devil and said the Michigan 4th fired first. I told them they were d——m liars for we belong to that reg't."[28]

Reports showed that some Union soldiers on the road that night did have a brush with mounted men thought to have been Confederates, but not those Pennsylvania soldiers. In any event, Colonel Woodbury joined in the denials that his men were involved in the "friendly fire" tragedy when the matter appeared in the *New York Times*. "The pickets of the Michigan 4th extended to the road on which the California and other regiments were passing and were between the two fires of the two regiments," he insisted, "but, knowing that there was a mistake being made, used every effort to prevent the panic-stricken soldiers from firing upon each other." The Michigan soldiers, he claimed, had not fired a shot.[29]

But one member of the 4th Michigan said that they did fire. In a reminiscence written later, Moses Luce, a sergeant in Company E, stated he was on picket that night and heard the tramp of soldiers in the distance. He saw troops coming over the ridge towards him. "I was in the yard of somebody's house," he wrote. "I had a loaded musket. I set the bayonet and ordered the advancing horseman to halt, which he did, but back of him came a swarm of men, *evidently Confederates* [emphasis added], and I fired my musket at the frontage of the line." His shot opened a lively round of firing. "Bullets whizzed past my ears," he wrote. Luce claimed the commander of the 71st Pennsylvania, Colonel Baker, that night turned his men and the 4th Michigan to successfully "beat back" an enemy attack. In truth, there was no Rebel attack; Union officers who were present didn't believe there had been any Confederates—only inexperienced young soldiers firing at each other in the night.[30]

Within days of this advance into the countryside, the men of the 4th Michigan, like hundreds if not thousands of other soldiers, cleared trees for fields of fire. "Michigan boys know woodcraft to perfection," Sgt. John Bancroft noted. "Never was land cleared quicker save by hurricane." The troops also burned the trees and anything else that obstructed the guns. The fires made a quite a spectacle as he stood picket on the night of October 1. "The country is being devastated crops destroyed and wasted, grains stacks scattered, fences broken down, houses burned, forests cut to open range for our artillery, etc." he wrote. Jonas Richardson agreed. "Look in any direction and you can see hundreds of trees falling at a time," he wrote.[31]

The bivouac of the regiment shifted early that month with their division, eventually moving two miles on October 11 to a location called Minor's Hill. Though many soldiers thought they might be marching out on a new offensive, this would be their camp for the winter of 1861–62, and soon Union encampments covered the area. "The country around here is rolling—in some places quite hilly," wrote Martin A. Blowers, a 24-year-old farmer from Hillsdale County who had come with DeGolyer's new enlistees. "Our camp is on an elevated piece of ground, giving us a fine view of the countryside around."

A soldier whose letter was signed "Y" explained the situation faced by pickets. "The rebels are now occupying another range of hills about two miles west of us," he wrote, "and with the aid of glass, occasionally a rebel may be seen to emerge from the woods into a corn field, secret himself behind a shock of corn, and fire upon our pickets and then seek cover again in the woods." Pvt. William H. Marsh of Company H, from Hillsdale County, wrote that their pickets now extended two miles beyond Fall's Church, with Union artillery shelling Rebels building breastworks. "I was out scouting yesterday, all day; was fired at twice," he wrote. "The rebels don't know how to shoot, for they didn't hit me."[32]

Not all were so fortunate. Sgt. George W. Jeffers from Coldwater, in Company H, was hit in the right hand by gunfire by a hidden Confederate sharpshooter on October 17 and lost his ring and middle fingers. "In all probability he will go home and I will have to do about double work until I get another sergeant broke to the harness," complained Sgt. William F. Robinson. But those who knew about Jeffers's situation were more sympathetic. A writer from the regiment who signed his dispatch "J.B.V." talked with Jeffers, who sadly related that his one-year-old child at home had died only three weeks earlier and his wife was seriously ill. A report in the *New York World* stated the suspect sharpshooter was a "Mr. Williams, of Alexandria," who was once held by the U.S. but since become a scout for the Confederates. "[I]n the event of his capture, he is to be hung forthwith," the paper reported. Jeffers soon mustered out of the army, but he eventually joined another regiment.[33]

The young soldiers continued to sometimes endanger themselves. In mid-October some men from Company E decided to try to set off an artillery shell they'd found. They succeeded. "The pieces flew in every direction, but fortunately no one was hurt," Martin Blowers wrote about the explosion, though Henry Seage, a new recruit from Hudson recently turned 17, noted that one of the boys suffered a cut on the head. Not long afterward Blowers wrote that Sgt. Darwin Van Allen of Company H accidentally shot himself in the foot with his revolver. On November 23, Lewis Ritter of Company D was wounded in the hip by a shot fired by one of his own comrades, James Murphy, who was drunk. Murphy was arrested and so was Sgt. William Limbarker of Company F, who was accused of inducing Murphy "to drink ardent spirits with him." Ritter recovered, returning to duty early in 1862, while Murphy was sentenced by a court-martial to spend a month in jail and lose two months' pay. It was a light sentence, but Murphy was considered a good soldier. Limbarker was eventually acquitted on the charges that he'd given Murphy alcohol.[34]

There were moments of pride, humor, and goodwill, especially when the army was visited that month by Abraham Lincoln in a review of the troops with General McClellan. Lieutenant Jeffords wrote from Minor's Hill of the humorous sight of the president attempting to keep his hat on his head while riding by the Union soldiers. "McClellan rode so fast on his [illegible] horse that old Abe could hardly keep up with him and had a great deal of trouble with his 'plug' hat," Jeffords wrote of the scene. "As he rode along, cheer after cheer met him from the thousands. Of course he had to take his hat off, and the fun was to see him get it on again with his high rate of speed until[,] getting desperate[,] he would give it a jam down over his eyes. I had to laugh till I cried." The reviews by McClellan made the men realize they were a part of a huge army of tens of thousands, and this helped to instill confidence in them and trust in their general. "As McClellan, accompanied by his guests, staff and body guards, rode along in front of each Division, each Soldier took off his cap and gave cheer after cheer," wrote Sgt. Jonas Richardson. "I think it was the grandest sight that I ever beheld," agreed Sgt. William Robinson.[35]

Virginia nights were sometimes chilly in October, and men were issued winter clothing and new tents before the month ended. Off-duty soldiers could walk the camps to visit friends in other Michigan regiments. Rumors continued to circulate about a new advance on Richmond, and some Northern newspapers were clamoring for McClellan to launch an offensive. But some recognized they weren't going anywhere soon. "Nothing indication [*sic*] of a forward movement presents itself," Sergeant Richardson agreed. "I think that if it were the intention of our Army to attack the enemy in front of the Capitol, they would have done so long before this." Like many in the Army of the Potomac, he was confident in their commander. "McClellan moves slow but shure," he had written two weeks earlier, "and when we do get at them we will mow them down [like] the dew before the morning sun." Joel H. Barnes, from Kalamazoo County, had tobacco on his mind. "I wish I had some of the Michigan tobacco here," he wrote his parents; "here what we get is not worth a dam and costs at least a dollar a pound at that."[36]

Not all soldiers approved of McClellan's caution. In a remarkable letter to his brother, a soldier from Company G wrote that several women had managed to join the 4th Michigan—and that they had no patience with their general and no mercy for the Rebels. "Several of the soldiers with me on picket are women," wrote Albert Westgate, a hired farmhand from Adrian in his early 20s. "They are all from the town were Uncle Silas used to live. They are very patriotic to destroy this infernal rebellion by what ever it takes. They say M'Clellan has been a shit-ass for sitting around all the time when he should be driving rebs back to Richmond." He continued: "The gals say that is the only way the Union can win this thing and I tend to agree with them. Also they don't believe in taking any prisoners—just shoot 'em dead and let the buzzards have a feast. They are good soldiers and take their share of the duty and they are also fair shots, too."[37]

Westgate wrote that his sergeant knew these women were present, "but as long as he says nothing to the Lieutenant everything will be all right for them. The danger that we face daily makes us all work well together." That was all Westgate said on the matter of the women in the regiment. Were they discovered, quietly removed, and sent home? Did these women make it through the war without being discovered? The answers are unknown, and Westgate did not survive the war to reveal anything more about them.

Since late in August, the soldiers of the 4th Michigan and the rest of the army had often seen a sight that probably few others had witnessed—men rising into the sky in a balloon. This tethered lighter-than-air device was operated by Professor Thaddeus Lowe as an aerial platform from which Union officers could observe enemy movements and positions. Sgt. William Limbarker commented on it. "There was a balloon sent up from our Fort Thursday," he noted, "and he reports a hundred and fifty thousand [men] within nine miles of our camp." As October ended, Sgt. John Bancroft of Company I was one of several men ordered to report to their division commander, Gen. Fitz John Porter. He gave them their new assignment: They were to report to Professor Lowe at the Columbian Armory in Washington, D.C.

This service took Bancroft away from duty with the 4th Michigan for some months, though his diary reflects that he was generally stationed in Washington and often operating near his division and sometimes visited with his friends. But he learned the technical preparations for launching the balloons and went up himself. Being associated with Lowe and the balloon *Intrepid* would bring him into contact with notables such as Gen. Dan Sickles and various reporters and artists from publications like the *Philadelphia Inquirer* and *Frank Leslie's Illustrated Newspaper*. Though the men of the 4th Michigan had seen one or another of Lowe's balloons for weeks, they still enjoyed watching them. "The latest 'new thing' we have is large balloon which is anchored a little north of us," Martin Blowers wrote from the camp on Minor's Hill. "It is a splendid affair, some forty feet in diameter. On one side is painted a large eagle with the likeness of Gen. McClellan."[38]

Fall gave way to winter, but men told of mild nights and delightful Indian summer days. By late November, nights were sometime cold enough that Edward H. C. Taylor had to put down his pen every few minutes to warm his fingers over the candle. He was delighted when a parcel containing apples and treats from his sister had arrived, and he enjoyed them with a few friends.

"Your cakes were excellent and have given me quite a distaste for bacon, beans, hard bread and 'Jimmie's' cooking," Taylor joked.[39]

Life in camp was now truly routine. General McClellan vowed there would be "no more Bull Runs"—the soldiers had to be well drilled, well supplied, and completely prepared before they went on the offensive again. "Time hangs heavily upon us while waiting for something to transpire and relieve the monotony of camp," wrote Dr. Chamberlain. Union soldiers were referring to slaves as "contrabands" now, and while the Lincoln administration continued to wrestle with the abolition of slavery as an aim of the war, many slaves understood that to reach Union lines was to escape their status as chattel of plantation owners. Though some editors and politicians didn't acknowledge that the conflict was about slavery, Chamberlain told of a young slave who came to the 4th Michigan to get away from his owners.

"Our regiment was out on picket duty two days of last week," wrote the assistant surgeon, "and while there, a young contraband about ten years old came into our lines, who is learning Yankee style very fast." The boy made his escape as his mistress was preparing to travel to join her Confederate officer husband. The Michigan men took an immediate liking to the child, but they did tease him: Wasn't he afraid that they might sell him off to Cuba, back into slavery? "No," the boy replied confidently. "'Cause if you would, what's all dis muss about?"[40]

Not all the Michigan men agreed with the idea that slavery was the central issue of the war, and some were harshly unsympathetic to the plight of the slaves. Racist views were not uncommon. "I cannot say that I exactly like the idea of freeing all of the Negroes," Sergeant Richardson wrote as the year wound down. "If you had seen as many of them as I have, you would probably be impressed with the same opinion. I go in for cleaning out the Rebels first and the Negroes afterwards."[41]

New enlistees had been coming into the 4th Michigan since early fall, and soldiers' letters and diaries indicate that they were put through the regimen of drill before they went out on picket. Green soldiers sometimes provided amusement for their comrades. "Last night one of Co. B's new recruits who was standing on post thought he saw a secesh and blared away," William F. D. McCarty of Hillsdale County wrote. "This morning some of us went to the place and found that he had shot into a chestnut tree. He was on picket for the first time and I suppose he was a little excited after a day or so of picket duty. He will do better. The boys of our regiment all feel in good spirits and want to fight." The diary of young Henry Seage indicates it took about three weeks before he and some of the other newcomers cooked their own meals, and about a month before they went out on picket.

As the weather grew colder the men of the 4th Michigan, like all troops, built winter quarters. Some cut down timber and stole or otherwise gathered lumber from local houses and barns, and built platforms with floors raised off the ground. Often soldiers built log or lumber sides, using their tents as the upper portion and roofs of their quarters. Capt. John Randolph of Company D wrote that some men did away with their tents entirely, having made roofs of tree limbs, branches, and earth. These log houses were "just as good houses as anyone could wish to live in," the captain insisted. An account by an officer who signed his letter "Y" noted that the regiment built Colonel Woodbury a small but comfortable cabin, "cozy and elaborately set off with patriotic and war emblems." At some point that winter, the colonel's wife, like the spouses of other regimental commanders in the division, joined her husband in camp. Winter quarters or no, however, men continued to get sick. Mifflin W. Hall from Monroe County, a hospital steward from Company A, estimated that on average, the regiment had about 15 men a day in the hospital. Typically some men were coming in as others got well enough to return to duty.[42]

Perhaps it was because of the boredom, but practical jokes, often involving gunpowder, were perpetrated that winter, according to Orvey Barrett. When a soldier from Company B got in trouble for leaving camp to forage in the country, an officer ordered that he stand on a barrel for two hours as punishment. His comrades dug a hole under the barrel before the man began his sentence, placing a pile of blank cartridges under it. As the man stood on the barrel, his comrades set off the charge, blasting the barrel off the ground and the surprised soldier with it. Barrett was annoyed by an acquaintance who constantly asked to borrow his pipe, so Barrett taught him a hard lesson by placing some gunpowder in his pipe bowl. The pipe, of course, exploded when the borrower lit up. "His heels went up, and he [went] over backwards," Barrett recalled with satisfaction. On another occasion a trickster from Company B blew the chimney barrels off the top of their large winter cabin during a barbeque to which they'd invited officers, filling the quarters with smoke.

But the general rule was duty and drill. Sgt. Jonas Richardson, writing as he almost always did on a Sunday evening, told of the grandeur of "sham battles" or combat exercises in which the men of their division participated, firing unloaded muskets and artillery that produced plenty of smoke but no casualties. Yet there was disappointment that after six months, the 4th Michigan had "had no real engagement with the enemy yet," and the men truly were "anxious to display our military skill on the field." Although no formal order stated that the Union army was going into winter camp, it had done so. "It is the general impression," Martin Blowers wrote, "that we shall remain here some time."[43]

Blowers was correct. It would be spring before the Army of the Potomac went on the offensive. In the coming year, the 4th Michigan would get its turn in battle.

CHAPTER 4

We Shall Go into the Storm of Battle with Brave Hearts

OFFICERS OF THE 4TH MICHIGAN TREATED THE MEN TO A FEAST ON WHAT WAS UNDOUBTEDLY FOR many their first Christmas away from home. Turkey, chicken, and oysters were main dishes, and Silas Sadler of Company G called the meal "Jolly good." The day was clear and mild, and Sgt. Jonas Richardson said tables were set outside in the streets of the regiment's camp. He and others had been busy "making wreaths, globes, letters and stars to decorate Co. D's street." The camp was a grand sight to see, for "each company built a large arch over the front of their street." Henry Seage of Company E also noted the raising of the evergreen arches and that some got into the holiday spirit with drink along with the good food. "Company C tight," he recorded. "Oysters for Christmas Dinner one Pint to each Man."

The diary of Sgt. William Limbarker of Company F reflected the homesickness many felt. Though he was allowed to go to Washington on Christmas, where he enjoyed comfortable lodgings and a concert by the Christy Minstrels, he nonetheless wrote that he missed his ex-wife and daughter. "O God don't I wish I would see my famley this winter," he noted. "I would give all I have to do so." By now Colonel Woodbury and other regimental commanders had brought their wives into winter camp. "[H]er cheerful and refining presence adds an attractive picture of comfort," an anonymous officer wrote about Mrs. Woodbury. The effect "takes off the rough edge of campaign life."

Sadler's parents sent him a box of food that arrived on January 3. "I have been eating Jell[y] and buck wheat cakes ever since," he wrote. Still, there was duty to attend. "New Years we was out on picket, we watched the old year out and the new year in." William F. D. McCarty of Company E said it was an eventful duty, with the 4th Michigan's pickets bringing "in thirteen rebel prisoners." Many officers were allowed leave back to Michigan, but Woodbury and Adjutant Earle remained in camp during the holidays. Both received presents of swords from the officers. Lt. George Monteith, assigned to the division headquarters at nearby Hall's Hill, witnessed the comic mock drill and dress parade put on by the officers and men of the 44th New York for the holiday, calling it "the most ludicrous affair I ever saw."[1]

Changes came with the New Year. Major Samuel DeGolyer resigned and left the regiment, reportedly to join the staff of another Union general in the west, though soon he would get authorization from Michigan adjutant general John Robertson to lead a new artillery battery. But there was an unhappier and political subtext. Not only had Colonel Woodbury expressed dissatisfaction with DeGolyer after Bull Run, the major had been arrested before Christmas for allegedly taking lumber from a nearby civilian's cabin. For this he was brought up on charges. "Our Major has Got in to a fix and I think he will be Dismisst from the Armey for snaring lumber[—]they would call it stealing in Michigan[—]and he has been ordered before a board of examiners and it will be a killer on him to leave to go home now," Sergeant Limbarker wrote.[2]

What is ironic about his recording of this news is that Limbarker himself had "been out a snairing some doores and window's for a long cabin" a week earlier. But as far as Michigan officials were concerned, DeGolyer, now an abolitionist after his experience as a prisoner, was a heroic leader, and he would prove himself an able artillerist in the Union Army of the Tennessee. In DeGolyer's place, Capt. James H. Cole of Company B, recovered from the wound he received when he'd accidentally shot himself, was the new major. Capt. Charles Doolittle of Company H agreed with Cole's promotion. "A very satisfactory appointment," he noted. Sergeant Limbarker was even more emphatic in his feelings about the former major: "Sam DeGolier has gone and I am damnd glad of it," he wrote, "for he was a fool in military maters." Historians have disagreed. Author Edward Bearss called DeGolyer "one of the best artillery officers" in the Union army during the fighting at Vicksburg.

Another change came in mid-January when Capt. John M. Oliver of Company F, a Monroe man who'd started out as a lieutenant, was commissioned colonel of the new 15th Michigan Infantry Regiment. "He is a good one," Limbarker wrote of Oliver, "and I am sorry he left this Company for there will be some Damnd fool in his place." These and other resignations and vacancies triggered a series of promotions and movements between some of the companies' commissioned and noncommissioned officers. Lt. Simon B. Preston, the other officer from Company F who'd been captured at Bull Run, was exchanged and released from Confederate prison late in January, one of at least four 4th Michigan prisoners freed that month. He went home. Others returning to Michigan early in 1862 included Capt. George Lumbard, who recruited for the regiment in Adrian, and Captain Doolittle of Hillsdale. Doolittle had started his service as a lieutenant in Company E, but was promoted late in the summer; he spent several days with his wife and children. "How pleasant to be with those we love," he noted. The diary of Enoch Davis, the Ohio farmer who'd enlisted with the Indiana men, reflected dramatic changes in the Virginia winter during the early weeks of 1862, when it sometimes turned bitterly cold and snowy. The regiment could be inactive one day because of mud and rain, but busy drilling the next.[3]

But perhaps the most important change for the 4th Michigan came when new Springfield rifles arrived on January 11, replacing the obsolete muskets, some of which dated back to the 1840s. "It would have done your soul good to have seen the happy faces in our regiment when our *rifles* were distributed," Sgt. Eli Starr of Company C wrote; "they are of the Springfield pattern with elevated sights. Our *shots* [i.e., marksmen] Geo. W. Akers etc. will strike the size of a man's hand with ease at 100 yards. With such guns and such a cause we would be less than men were we to give the Old Peninsula cause to blush. . . . We are satisfied now, and shall go down into the storm of battle with brave, strong hearts."[4]

Sgt. Jonas Richardson of Company D agreed—the rifles were far more accurate than the muskets, and the impact on the men's morale was great. The secessionists, he warned, "had better prepare themselves for the long road." Corporal Irvin S. Miner, 23, from Hillsdale County, was one of the men who could handle the weapons with some skill. "Shot at target I hit the bulls eye at one hundred yds off hand," the Company F man noted two days after the new rifles arrived. A few days later, he wrote that he was making even longer shots. "Shot at target off hand at 250 yds. I hit two inches below bulls eye." In the weeks that followed, Miner would record that he hit targets at greater distances.

Men like Eli Starr were impatient to go on the offensive, but Sergeant Major James Clark, who became a lieutenant in the coming months, wrote that muddy road conditions would prevent them from going anywhere soon, especially with artillery. By now deaths from illness had declined somewhat and occasional mild days graced January and February, but snow and rain predominated. Silas Sadler of Company G said standing with the advance guard on the Leesburg Turnpike was awful on the night of January 23. "Had the worst time on picket we ever Had," he noted in his diary, "rained and Hailed all the time."[5]

Though Sgt. Bill Limbarker's marriage had ended some years previously, his thoughts that winter often were about his ex-wife Harriet. He expressed in his diary his worries and prayers about her and their daughter Eva, who'd been sick with diphtheria. But his more immediate concern as a soldier was that he facing court-martial, charged with providing alcohol to a soldier on guard duty back in November. Typically Limbarker noted the usual camp life details—target practice, picket duty, inspection, and dress parade. One of his more unusual entries that season was when the chaplain, the Reverend Dr. Henry Strong, paid him a visit in order to learn to handle a rifle. "I told him he aught to shoot with spiritual balls in Sted of lead," the sergeant noted, "but he says they are not so good for Sesesh [secessionists] as lead ones now[.] Bully for him."

On February 24, a cold day, high winds knocked over a nearby sutler's shanty. Soldiers made the most of the confusion, grabbing items that would have otherwise cost plenty. "My diary records that I had stole a cheese from the sutler," Albert H. Boies wrote, tongue-in-cheek, nearly 25 years later, "but I think that must have been a mistake." Boies admitted there were men who remembered that morning and wondered who left a quarter section of cheese outside their tent. Sgt. Orvey Barrett of Company B also profited from the sutler's disaster, snatching two boxes of cigars, some figs, a jackknife, and other items. The angry merchant stalked off to complain to Colonel Woodbury that soldiers were stealing him blind. Of course, the soldiers thought the sutler had been doing the same thing to them for months.[6]

For some time since their last brigade commander, William Tecumseh Sherman, had been sent west, the 4th Michigan was part of a brigade under Brig. Gen. George W. Morell. The regiment served with the 9th Massachusetts (a Boston-Irish regiment), the 62nd Pennsylvania, and the 14th New York. One soldier in the 9th Massachusetts, Irish-born Timothy Regan, sometimes mentioned the 4th Michigan in his diary.[7]

Together these regiments comprised the Second Brigade of Brig. Gen. Fitz John Porter's division. By early March, President Lincoln ordered the organization of the army into several large corps, so their division was part of the Third Corps commanded by Gen. Samuel P. Heintzelman. But pressure was building on Lincoln's administration to show progress in putting down the rebellion. The president demanded action from McClellan, and even common soldiers knew that as the weather improved, they would be on the march. "I expect, Mr. Editor, to date my next [letter] somewhere near Manassas," Martin Blowers wrote early in March to a newspaper.[8]

Elements of the Army of the Potomac began to move out a few days later. McClellan planned to advance his forces in a manner that would force the Confederates to abandon their positions and open the road to Richmond, but incur minimal bloodshed. On the morning of March 9, the 4th Michigan was sent several miles to the town of Vienna, a few miles from Fairfax Court House, to guard and work on repairs to the railroad to Alexandria. That same evening, Confederate forces under Gen. Joseph Johnston, who held Manassas and Centreville, gave up their positions and began to withdraw. Early the next morning, the Union army began to move forward.

The 4th Michigan was ordered back from the bivouac at Vienna to Minor's Hill, where the men quickly picked up their gear. Then they marched back out again to rejoin their division, which advanced toward Fairfax. The road was very bad, wrote the regimental correspondent who signed his dispatches "Y," in "many places the mud was knee deep." It was a long, weary day, and they halted two or three miles from Fairfax Court House. The men bivouacked in a pine thicket, sleeping on what one soldier called "our couch of boughs" and joined their brigade and division the next morning near Fairfax. "The report is this morning that Centerville is in our hands & also that the rebels are deserting their works at & retreating from Manassas," wrote Company B's George W. Millens, 22, from Lenawee County. But what caught the attention of reporters was the revelation that abandoned Rebel "cannon" were actually logs painted and propped up to look like artillery. That suggested McClellan had been held fooled, kept in place for months by the mere illusion of Confederate strength. Lincoln responded to this embarrassing news by taking away McClellan's authority as general-in-chief of all Union forces, leaving him in command of just the Army of the Potomac.[9]

Officers and men who were sympathetic to McClellan believed that taking Confederate positions without loss of life was proof his tactics worked. "[T]he wisdom of McClellan's long delay becomes apparent in that without sacrifice of life or treasure, he now is nearer Richmond than by another path," wrote Edward Taylor of Company A. For the next few mid-March days, the 4th Michigan remained with its division at Fairfax, drilling and undergoing a review by McClellan. "Provisions are scarce and [prices] very high," complained the soldier who signed

MARTIN N. BERTERA

The 4th Michigan stands at attention outside of its camp on Minor's Hill as the band plays, ushering in the New Year, January 1, 1862. The drawing, from a lithograph, was by Lt. Charles Gruner.

his letters "Y." Tea cost $5 per pound; coffee, $1.25, while butter was running between 40 and 50 cents and sugar from 30 to 40 cents.

Mistakes continued to cause casualties. On March 12, Pvt. Samuel Tyler of Company H, only about 25, was "accidentally shot through both legs" by a cavalry trooper there at Fairfax. William F. Robinson, by now promoted to lieutenant, wrote that Tyler (whose last name was also given as Taylor) was taken to a hospital in Washington, but he died less than six weeks later, leaving his wife Mary a widow. "[H]e was a fine fellow, well loved by all his mates, and also by all of his Officers," Robinson wrote. That same day Tyler was shot, McClellan rode by Porter's division, and the men cheered him enthusiastically. While they were aware that Republican leaders weren't happy with their commander, they appreciated McClellan's concern for them. "The men love him as one man & would die for him if necessary," Millens wrote. More importantly, McClellan now adapted his plans: He would load his men onto ships and sail down the river to Chesapeake Bay, moving the army south to the tip of the Virginia peninsula formed by the York and the James rivers. A large Union stronghold on the coast, called Fortress Monroe, was located here, not far from the town of Hampton. From this secure place, with mountains of supplies and big guns, the Army of the Potomac would advance on Richmond. By divisions and brigades, thousands of Union soldiers were shifted toward Alexandria for the journey.[10]

The wet, muddy march of the 4th Michigan to the port began on March 15, with the men moving some 14 miles to the town of Cloud's Mill. Here they moved into a comfortable camp of tents equipped with stoves, previously occupied by a New York regiment. Within another day or so, they shifted to a hillside called Camp California within three miles of Alexandria. The town was thronging with thousands of troops, and the loading of so many men onto ships took time. As did many soldiers, a number of 4th Michigan men had thrown away coats, ponchos, rubber gum blankets, and other gear thought to be unnecessary on the long march from Fairfax—the weather had been mild then. But now a cold front blew in, bringing rain and discomfort. Writings of Henry S. Seage of Company E and musician Noah Cressey of Company F reflect their misery, since there weren't enough tents or sufficient shelter. Silas Sadler noted that the men were issued "rations of Bitters"—whiskey—to take their minds off the sodden chill.

After marching all day with heavy packs from Cloud's Mill to Camp California in the rain, Cressey told his brother, the men, soaked, had to try to lie down "and Sleep all Dripping in water." He called it one of the hardest things he'd ever experienced. The next day Henry Seage wrote that men who tried to leave camp to get out of the weather "were tied up." Officers tried to keep the men busy with drill. Finally, after delays and standing in the rain and mud for hours, the men boarded the steamer *Daniel Webster* on March 21. One of a flotilla of transports, it was also the flagship of their division commander, Gen. Fitz John Porter. Colonel Woodbury and his officers considered it an honor to accompany him. The *Webster* pulled away from the docks and anchored in Chesapeake Bay that night, as did others, waiting for the completion of the boarding of the troops. The next day this fleet of steamers, schooners, and tugboats got underway as ladies on shore waved their handkerchiefs and men cheered.[11]

The transports moved down the Potomac, sailing by George Washington's historic farm, Mt. Vernon, and old gun emplacements once held by the Confederates. Union gunboats escorted the ships when they reached Chesapeake Bay. "The passage of 25 steamers tugs & schooners down the river & especially their appearance at night exceeds anything in Grandeur I ever beheld," wrote Lt. George Monteith. Cpl. Charles Phelps of Company D noted that there were "ducks enough to patch Hell a mile" and he enjoyed watching the porpoises "jump up in the water." But another man in his company, David Webster, about 26, said that "the boys amused themselves a shooting" at those porpoises. Martin Blowers wrote that "a thousand or more passengers made our boat rather crowded for comfort, but the pleasant weather and fine prospects . . . conspired to keep us in good spirits and make the trip agreeable."

The flotilla arrived at Fortress Monroe on Sunday, March 23, and the men saw the famous ironclad the *Monitor,* which earlier in the month battled the Rebel ironclad, the *Merrimac* (renamed the *Virginia* by the Confederates). "It is the queerest looking craft that I ever saw," wrote Sgt. Jonas D. Richardson to his brother. "She is only about two or three feet above, and about ten feet below the surface of the water, being constructed apparently more for service than for ornament." While many described the ship's turret as "a cheese box," it reminded Richardson of a revolving tanning vat. The soldiers were also impressed by the big cannon of the massive Fortress Monroe.[12]

The ships offloaded the thousands of soldiers, and the 4th Michigan with its division marched that afternoon through the burned-out town of Hampton into the country to camp in a clover field. The weather was fine initially but with spring fickleness changed to rain and cold over the next few days as the Union army gathered, probed, and advanced. McClellan prepared to move northwest up the narrow peninsula against the Confederate defenses that blocked the way. This Rebel line stretched from Yorktown on the York River across those few miles of land to the James River. Yorktown, of course, was a historic place, where the Continental Army and allies from the French army and navy forced the British army under Cornwallis to surrender 80 years earlier.

The men of the 4th Michigan shifted their bivouac, standing guard and trying to find things to eat until supply lines were established. Harrison Daniels of Company G remembered that

Soldiers of the 4th Michigan, like other Union troops, dig earthworks while on fatigue duty at Yorktown, Va., during the first days of May, 1862. Drawing by Lt. Charles Gruner.

by March 26, the only thing soldiers had left in their haversacks was some coffee—everything else had been eaten and no rations were yet available. "The third day we got desperate and dug muscles [mussels], boiled them and drank some of the broth," Daniels wrote. Two days later, the regiment was part of a force making an advance toward Confederate positions at the town of Big Bethel. The Confederates pulled back on that hot spring day as Union troops approached up the road from Hampton. "We did not get a chance to see a Rebel, but there has been a large number of them there," George Millens wrote after returning to camp on March 28. In the heat of that day's march men threw away whatever extra clothing, coats, and blankets they had left, and slaves seeking protection came in large numbers to the Union camps.[13]

The regiment had a few days of quiet. Edward H.C. "Ned" Taylor, Democrat and McClellan supporter, was convinced the general's approach to the Confederate capital would end the rebellion. "Very soon we will [go] 'on to Richmond,' turning their position by moving from east and south. . . . Success can hardly fail to attend our advance and soon victory will end the war," he predicted. Two days later McClellan ordered his army to move on Yorktown. The 4th Michigan and its brigade led their division, the troops rising before dawn and marching beyond Big Bethel toward another set of Rebel positions. As the soldiers of Morell's brigade reached Howard's Bridge over the Poquoson River, skirmishers went out and Confederates opened fire from their trenches. According to Morell, General Porter ordered the 4th Michigan to extend the brigade's line of battle to the river. As they did, Union artillery opened up on the Rebels, who fled. It appears that the men of the 4th Michigan might not have fired a shot in their first confrontation with the Confederates on the peninsula, though Henry Seage wrote that they "took two prisoners."[14]

Their brigade marched on. As they moved by the abandoned Rebel positions near Howard's Bridge at a place called Cocklestown, the soldiers discovered barrels of peanuts and molasses hidden by the Confederates. Albert H. Boies later wrote some of these treats were hidden in an outhouse, while others simply recorded they were found the barrels in area buildings. Men from the 14th New York were among the troops who joined the Michigan men in the enjoyment of the peanuts and molasses. Boies said the two regiments kidded each other about it afterward. When the Michigan soldiers marched by the 14th New York, someone invariably would call out, "Hello there, who got the peanuts?" New York soldiers yelled back, "Who stole the molasses?" Henry Seage made note of the day's treat in his diary: "Molasses had to suffer." Their brigade advanced another three miles toward Yorktown, with the 4th Michigan camping that night in the woods.[15]

Porter's division rose the next morning, April 5, at daybreak, marching into a heavy rainstorm and deep mud. Dr. Chamberlain wrote that the 4th Michigan led this march to Yorktown, which anchored the line of Confederate forts, breastworks, and trenches across the peninsula. "We came in right of the rebel works about ten o'clock in the forenoon," he wrote. "When we were within about a mile of them, w-h-i-z came a shell over our heads, making most of the men dodge their heads, involuntarily. The next instant all were cheering. The dance was about to open." The regiment's assignment was to support Capt. Charles Griffin's battery, part of their brigade's artillery, and soon these and other Union guns were firing back from a hill off the road. The Michigan men took positions to the right of the batteries, partially screened from the Rebel gunners by some pine woods and brush. Dr. Chamberlain wrote there were remnants of trenches here, dug back in the American Revolution. The men of the regiment quickly began to improve, extend, and enlarge these old works as the artillery blasted. "Pieces of shell were flying in every direction," the doctor wrote. Edward Taylor said that Griffin's gunners silenced a battery of three Rebel cannon. "Every shell he [Griffin] threw exploded within their works," he wrote.

The firing continued for two hours, lulled, and resumed sporadically. Major James Cole cracked a joke when his hat was blown off his head by the impact of an exploding shell. Another soldier felt something smack nearby and fall into his shirt—a small but spent iron ball, canister shot from a Confederate gun, dropping down his collar. He reached back, removed it from this shirt, and dropped it into his pocket, a souvenir of Yorktown. Some men realized there was nothing for them to do until their commanders called on them, so they lay down in their earthworks to rest. Others were so interested in the projectiles fired at them that they jumped out of their trenches and ran to retrieve expended Rebel cannon balls and shells that plunged into the ground without exploding.[16]

Capt. Charles Doolittle wrote that the Confederate gunners "have the range of our gun pretty well and strike pretty close to our men drawn up in line in [the] rear of Griffin's gun." Several Union artillerymen were hit and sharpshooters also fired at the Rebel gunners. But for all the lead that was flying, the men of the 4th Michigan escaped injury until sunset, when a private whose name was given as "Joseph W. Thomskins" of Company C was wounded by a shell that exploded near the center of their line. Fragments struck him in the neck, shoulder, head, and groin. These wounds soon ended his service with the regiment. The 4th Michigan went on picket that night, moving quietly forward to what George Millens called "a short distance of their breastworks"—close enough that he could sometimes hear the voices of Confederates. Sharpshooter firing periodically cracked across the fields, and Rebel artillery fired three shots in the darkness toward the Michigan men. Finally they were allowed to bed down with their weapons close at hand. The regiment remained there the next day under sporadic cannon and picket fire. Dr. Chamberlain explained that there'd been talk of storming a nearby Confederate fort during these first days at Yorktown, and there was pride throughout the regiment when an artillery commander said he would choose the 4th Michigan to do the job.[17]

Though the men were convinced a large battle was about to be fought, there would be no storming these Confederate forts. Other than periodically trading picket fire, the soldiers worked, digging and extending trenches. General McClellan didn't order his army to attack; instead he ordered a siege, believing that there were tens of thousands of Confederate troops in the Yorktown defenses. For the next four weeks, the Army of the Potomac dug trenches, built roads, and erected bridges to bring up big guns to blast the Confederates out. The commander of the division of which the 4th Michigan was part, General Fitz John Porter, was McClellan's point man for the siege preparations. The regiment remained on the front with its brigade at Yorktown for the next few days, bivouacking in rain and cold. Most of the soldiers still had no tents. Often exposed to shelling, they came through it with only a couple of minor wounds. They were still short on food, since the army's supply system hadn't quite been finished, and they could build no fires at night. Brigadier General Morell expressed pride in his men for their conduct on April 5 and the way they bore up over the next several days. "They were raw troops, for their first time under fire," he wrote, "and yet I doubt if their patience and coolness could have been surpassed by veterans."[18]

Irvin Miner, who had recorded excellent target shooting in his diary, now put his skill to deadly use. "I was detailed as a sharpshooter to pick off the enemy's gunners. Was shot at five times. I hit one reb at 1100 yds," he wrote. Early the next morning, April 8, Capt. George Spalding of Company B was wounded in the arm while he was out "on a scout" of the ground between the Union lines and the Rebel works, attempting to determine the number of heavy Confederate guns, but he recovered quickly. That same day, the 4th Michigan got praise from Gen. Samuel Heintzelman when their pickets "rustled" 19 or 20 cattle intended for Rebel sustenance. The cows were grazing near a Confederate fort, and it seems the Rebels inside were distracted when a carriage pulled up and they cheered the visitor. Capt. Charles Doolittle wrote that Lt. John Gordon of Detroit and 20 men drove off the cattle, "laying out 2 of the rebels" in the process. "It was handsomely done," the general noted approvingly.

Their brigade was pulled back the next day, shifting about a mile to the right, or east, to camp with Porter's division in a peach orchard on an old farm near the York River. The soldiers again went to work digging new trenches. Henry Seage of Company E wrote that a Confederate sharpshooter fired at the men from a hiding place high in a chimney of a burned-out house at the time, but the brigade's artillery commander, Charles Griffin, brought out a gun "and soon made a ruin of the chimney, reb and all." The weather continued fair and foul, but at last new tents arrived.[19]

A new routine was soon established as big Union guns were brought up and thousands more soldiers arrived. The men of the 4th Michigan, like other troops, would leave their camp to stand picket, sometimes at night in the shrinking no man's land between the lines. Or they went on fatigue details, working on roads, gun emplacements, and earthworks. Of course, some soldiers have always tried to get out of work, and Dr. Chamberlain remembered an Indiana man named Orville Carver as notable in this regard. In order to dodge fatigue, Carver tied a piece of bandage around one of his toes to indicate he'd been injured. This worked for a while, since officers and the assistant surgeon himself assumed a man with a bandaged foot was unable to work. Unfortunately for Carver, it soon dawned on Dr. Chamberlain that he didn't remember bandaging the soldier's foot, so he asked to see Carver's "injured" toe. Of course, Carver was soon back digging trenches. But the weather improved and men could sometimes hunt for oysters down on the York River when they were off duty, or they could buy them from local residents. Once there was an established work-and-picket routine, officers quickly resumed inspections, drill, and dress parades.[20]

But the artillery roared as gunners dueled, sometimes trading shots at night, and squads of soldiers clashed in the darkness as they conducted reconnaissance between the lines. The men saw Union gunboats firing their cannon from the York River. On the night of April 17 came heavy firing from the Rebel entrenchments and forts. "Firing all night, on guard, hott as thunder," Enoch Davis noted. A history of the 5th New York states that the 4th Michigan "took three hundred prisoners" that night when Confederates came out of their forts to attack the new Yankee trenches, but military records and reports and soldiers' accounts make no mention of such a significant capture by Woodbury's men—only sharp skirmishing. His regiment came through these scraps with barely a scratch.

But that kind of luck could not hold. Captain Abram R. Wood of Company C, about 35, had been sick when the Union army shipped out from Alexandria, but he improved and joined his regiment in mid-April. Wood became the regiment's first fatality at Yorktown when he walked out beyond his picket line on the night of April 18 and was shot by a soldier about 22 years old from his own company. That soldier—an odd fellow named Luke Barnes who didn't fit in well with others, according to family letters—thought Wood was a Confederate. "In posting pickets Friday evening he passed outside of our lines a few rods and was shot by one of his own men," Martin Blowers wrote of Wood, who had a wife and children back home. "He survived but a few hours." George W. Owen of Company A wrote that before Wood died, he stressed that his wounding was not the picket's fault. This case of mistaken identity was the regiment's only fatality at Yorktown. In the wake of Wood's death Lt. Harrison H. Jeffords was promoted to take his place. Luke Barnes may have paid an emotional price for his mistake, as his words would seem to indicate in the months ahead. Another member who suffered a terrible blow that month was the chaplain, the Reverend Henry Strong; he was notified that two of his children had died back at home.[21]

Though the morale of the regiment was high, an exception was Dr. William E. Clark, the surgeon. Clark was angry about his treatment by Colonel Woodbury, and he let Governor Austin Blair know it. "On reaching the regt. every obstacle was thrown in my way as my assuming my duties," Clark complained. The problem appears to have been one of politics as well as personality, for Clark, like the governor, was an abolitionist and Republican, while Woodbury was a War Democrat. "I have been aware that his [Woodbury's] influence was against me from the first,"

Clark complained. He had confronted Woodbury, but the colonel replied that he was satisfied with Clark as doctor and surgeon. But this didn't end the matter, and Clark and his brother Joseph B. Clark of Dowagiac, charged in subsequent letters that Woodbury spoke insultingly of Republicans and hoped to pressure Dr. Clark to resign. As a result, Clark wanted the governor to place him in another Michigan regiment. He would eventually get his wish, though he would prove to be even more unpopular there.

Was Dr. Clark treated as badly as he claimed? Had there been a kind of conspiracy among Democratic officers to make things difficult for him? Albert H. Boies, then a high-spirited teenager from Hudson, wrote years later that Dr. David Chamberlain suggested to Clark that he needed a helper to do chores. Chamberlain recommended Boies. In the three months Boies had the job, he drove Dr. Clark to distraction and cursing. Boies failed to salute the doctor when he was in the presence of a general. Asked by Clark to see if a pot of clean water was hot, Boies stuck his finger in it to check. Boies admitted that he and his friend Fred Duryee, Dr. Chamberlain's young assistant, enjoyed aggravating the high-strung Dr. Clark. "Fred and I practiced some amusing things upon the surgeon, who by the way, was very eccentric and absent-minded," Boies wrote.[22]

The weather turned rainy. Nights were still sometimes very cold, while days could be hot and humid. Several men of the 4th Michigan had close calls as they dug rifle pits within range of the Confederate guns, sometimes directly in front of their forts, as soldiers extended trenches and roads for the artillery. Lt. William F. Robinson of Company H wrote his parents that "our boys look up and laugh and sing out 'put him in the Guard House' every time a shell bursts over their heads." On the morning of April 29, shells dropped in among soldiers "working in full view of the enemies fortification distant about one half mile," wrote George Millens. "The rebels threw shells at us all the forenoon striking the dirt & burying themselves in the sand & then explode [—] one shell cut a mans shovel handle off." The Confederates were excellent shots, he noted, but none of them were injured. Edward Taylor said that the Rebel shells were so unreliable that Union soldiers generally had only to worry about being physically struck by the projectiles.

April turned to May and the rate of Confederate shelling increased. Officers like Lieutenant Robinson believed that the battle for Yorktown would soon begin, with the Union army having to fight as many as 100,000 Rebel defenders they believed were inside. "It will take some hard fighting to take the Rebel forts," wrote Silas Sadler. "They are pretty strongly fortified but God will be with the right. . . . I am in hopes God will spare me through the great battle that is so close at hand."[23]

There were nothing like those huge numbers of Confederate troops at Yorktown. When the Union army arrived in early April there had only been about 11,000 Rebel troops present, and they had been reinforced over the weeks that followed. But as McClellan prepared to open fire with his masses of artillery a month later, the Confederate commander, Gen. Joseph Johnston, ordered his men to evacuate their positions, covering the withdrawal to the northwest with the artillery bombardment that began on May 1.

As this shelling continued, Col. Dwight Woodbury made up his mind to confront Gov. Austin Blair about a subject that was very important to him—promotion. Woodbury started by saying he was surprised that a couple of officers in other outfits had been promoted to colonel. He had some very good officers in his regiment; why had they not been considered? Then Woodbury pointed out that he was Michigan's most senior colonel—he had served for a year and run a good regiment. Yet there was no sign he was going to be promoted to brigadier general.

Of course, Woodbury needed Blair to approve of such a promotion because the War Department consulted with important state politicians on the question of generalships. These weren't just matters of military leadership and experience, they were also matters of politics. Woodbury believed he had the support of Michigan's congressional delegation, yet no promotion had come. That had to mean that Blair wasn't interested in seeing him become a general, and Woodbury wanted to know why. How Blair answered Woodbury is unknown—office copies of the governor's outgoing correspondence were destroyed by a fire in later decades—but Woodbury never got his brigadier general's star.[24]

The Confederate artillery kept firing into the early morning hours of May 4—and suddenly stopped. Sergeants Jonas Richardson and Irvin Miner were assigned to a detail digging trenches near Rebel positions that morning when the Union soldiers realized the Confederates were gone. "Was detailed to work on outer parallel, but came back to camp after visiting deserted fortifications," Miner noted. "Yorktown evacuated." Richardson was leading a fatigue duty detail to Union forts numbered 10, 12, and 13 when the discovery was made. "The firing had been so incessant during the night that we were expecting considerable hindrance," he wrote, "but what was our surprise when upon clearing the breastwork to find our Pickets and sharpshooters almost under the shade of the Rebel fortifications at Yorktown. Soon one or more are seen to climb the walls and for [a] moment strain his eyes in all directions to see if it were possible to catch a glimpse of the enemy, but no, all is gone." Pvt. Blowers of Company F wrote that "there was much rejoicing among the troops" over what he and others called "a bloodless victory." Elements of the Union army moved out in pursuit, but Porter's division remained at Yorktown. Later they heard cannonading in the distance.

There was still danger at Yorktown, for the Confederates had left land mines or booby traps called "torpedoes," made of artillery shells, planted around the works. As a sergeant and some men from another regiment were walking to Yorktown's fort, Charles Phelps wrote, "one of them struck something attached [to] or stept on one of those torpedoes which you have heard of." The device exploded, "wounding 5 or 6 pretty bad," he wrote. Dr. Chamberlain treated the wounded men.[25]

There was fierce fighting the next day near Williamsburg, where Confederates under Gen. James Longstreet fought a rearguard action against the pursuing Union troops, but the 4th Michigan remained with its division and others at Yorktown for another three days. On the night of May 7 the regiment packed and marched to Yorktown to spend the night in the abandoned works. The next day around noon they headed to the town's wharf, boarding the steamer *Vanderbilt*. The ship headed up the York River with other transports about 25 miles through the moonlit night to the town of West Point, Virginia.

The next day, May 9, the soldiers climbed into pontoon boats that took them ashore, where they camped on the grounds of a plantation. Here their division joined that portion of the Union army that had gone after the Rebels from Yorktown. The Michigan men watched the burial of troops who'd been killed in the fighting and witnessed the hanging of a black man accused of cutting the throats of wounded soldiers who hadn't been able to protect themselves. They cheered when General McClellan rode by their camp on May 11 but remained near West Point for two more days, when the next phase of McClellan's advance on Richmond began. The Union army rose before dawn, and having been issued three days' worth of rations per soldier, slowly got started as brigade after brigade moved out, wagons and caissons rattling along. The men of the 4th Michigan tramped on in the rising heat, some men falling out from exhaustion. The dusty road to the west took them through woods, and they covered 12 miles or more before stopping to bivouac in a field at Cumberland. Capt. Charles Doolittle complained that they had taken a wrong road that day and so had marched additional miles because of the error.[26]

Stopping, starting, waiting, and marching in rain and mud and heat, the regiment and thousands of other soldiers slowly moved over the next four days. On May 16 they marched only five miles on the muddy road, stopping that night at a place called White House Landing on the Pamunkey River. They camped in a clover field for two days, and here the men of the 4th Michigan learned on the 18th they were now part of a new army corps that had been created by General McClellan. This was the Fifth Corps, and it was commanded Gen. Fitz John Porter. In Porter's place, Brig. Gen. George W. Morell was put in charge of their division. Col. James McQuade of the 14th New York would command their brigade. Thus the regiment was part of the Second Brigade, First Division, Fifth Corps of the Army of the Potomac.

As the lead elements of the army reached the Chickahominy River, Confederate troops pulled back to the edge of Richmond, destroying area bridges. The Chickahominy, running from the northwest to the southeast, provided a natural obstacle to McClellan's men. In the days that followed, the army moved up for what soldiers assumed was going to be the siege of the Rebel capital. On May 19 the 4th Michigan slowly moved out from White House Landing with its brigade in rain and mud, marching several miles and reaching Turnstall's Station on the Richmond & York River Railroad.[27]

Again the brigade of which the 4th Michigan was part alternately marched, stopped, and waited as the army pulled itself along like a giant caterpillar. The soldiers were in camp one hot day, moved a few miles the next, and then were sent out, briefly, without their knapsacks on a march that seemed to promise a brush with the enemy. But this movement on May 22 was ordered to a quick halt. The men went back for their packs and continued on, marching about six more miles in a hard rain. The Confederate capital was only several miles away to the west. "We are now within twenty miles of Richmond," wrote George W. Owen of Company A, "and will probably be in Richmond before next Saturday night."[28]

They camped in a field surrounded by woods that night, not far from the town of Old Cold Harbor, a few miles east of the Chickahominy. They remained in their bivouac the next day and heard gunfire ahead, where Union columns were pushing on. But for the Michigan regiment the officers ordered a dress parade, and one soldier from Company B, Homer E. Fisher, an Indiana man, was court-martialed for fighting with Major Cole while they'd been on the march. Colonel Woodbury, who lived for a time in Ohio when he was a young man, was believed by some be the writer of a letter back to a small-town newspaper, using the pseudonym "Volunteer." Volunteer confidently predicted that the men of the Union army "soon expect to be in the capital of the Bogus Government." The writer mocked the Confederate generals for hurrying their forces back

Wading the Chickahominy River on a reconnaissance in force, the 4th Michigan engages Confederate pickets in a skirmish near New Bridge on May 24, 1862. Though Union commanders and government officials were pleased by the regiment's aggressive performance, it ultimately did not matter, given McClellan's withdrawal of the Army of the Potomac a month later from the Richmond area. Drawing by Lt. Charles Gruner.

to Richmond from Williamsburg, rather than fighting. "[I]t is the wish of all the officers and men that they would make a stand," he wrote, "for we feel confident that we could soon close the rebellion if the only give us fight."[29]

The 4th Michigan's first real clash with the enemy was coming on May 24. Their mission was a simple reconnaissance, and the clash would be considered a skirmish, but it gained them national attention and praise.

As the Union army reached the Chickahominy, its left wing, on the south, was able to cross the river to the side where Richmond lay a short distance away. But further north, the right wing of McClellan's force, including the Fifth Corps, almost due east of Richmond, hadn't crossed. The general's staff needed information about the disposition of the Rebels and needed to know where crossings could be made. As the 4th Michigan bivouacked near Cold Harbor on May 23, a group of engineers and officers, aides to McClellan and other commanders, were sent to investigate. One, a young cavalry lieutenant who lived in Michigan, was George Armstrong Custer. The Chickahominy was 40 or 50 feet wide and swollen with rain, but Custer successfully waded the river.

Now he was ordered to make another reconnaissance, further upstream to the northwest. This time, it was a reconnaissance in force. Custer would go accompanied by the 4th Michigan and a squadron of U.S. Army cavalry. On the rainy morning of May 24, the regiment awoke before dawn and soon marched on the main road that led from Cold Harbor to a Chickahominy crossing called New Bridge. This was one of the structures that had been destroyed by the Confederates. Hiram B. Fountain, a private from Company F who had enlisted from Hudson a year earlier at age 19, wrote that they were only to take their rifles and canteens. After moving about two miles from camp, the column stopped when they reached a house being used as General Porter's headquarters, and there Colonel Woodbury received his orders. The men thought they were going on picket duty, perhaps to work on the damaged bridges or fix roads, Fountain said.[30]

But instead of marching directly to the river, the men of the 4th Michigan turned off to the right, or northwest, moving on a road through the woods past the last Union pickets. The men left the road, moving into the trees that bordered the river. As they reached an opening in these woods—Sgt. Jonas D. Richardson described it as a wheat field—some of them saw Confederate pickets across the river, leaving open ground and disappearing into the trees.

By now the regiment had marched about a half-mile up the Chickahominy from New Bridge, the place where Lieutenant Custer decided the first troops would ford. He led the way, with Colonel Woodbury sending some 30 men from Company A with him. Many of these men were from Monroe and they recognized Custer as a neighbor. "Why, that's Armstrong Custer," said one of the soldiers. "Hello, Autie," said another. But there was no time for socializing. These soldiers, the First Platoon of Company A, were led by Capt. A. Morell Rose, 30. They emerged from the woods, waded into the water, and according to Colonel Woodbury, "crossed without difficulty at double-quick."

Rain was still falling. The skirmishers, now on the Richmond side of the river, found no enemy infantry, though they saw some Rebel cavalry pickets on a hill in the distance. The First Platoon from Company A formed a line perpendicular to the Chickahominy and advanced through the woods, moving toward New Bridge. The other part of the company, Second Platoon, stayed on the opposite riverbank, moving in concert with their comrades and acting as a reserve. The rest of Woodbury's men stayed a short distance behind in the woods, marching on a parallel course back down the river on the Union-held side. For some minutes, the First Platoon skirmishers went undetected on the Rebel side of the Chickahominy.[31]

"The skirmishers approached within about 400 yards of the bridge," Woodbury reported, "when they came upon the camp of the enemy, who were apparently unaware of our presence, being gathered in squads through the camp." This was the bivouac of the 5th Louisiana Infantry Regiment, detailed to guard New Bridge. Part of a brigade under Brig. Gen. Paul J. Semmes, these Louisianans had three companies out on picket that morning, yet none detected the approach of the 4th Michigan. Now two of these companies were stunned to hear gunfire and look up to see Union troops—the 30 men from the regiment's Company A—firing at them from the woods.

Lt. Nicolas Bowen, a U.S. Army topographical engineer and one of the officers leading the reconnaissance, described that meeting tersely: "[W]e found the enemy and charged them." He also said that Custer was "the first to open fire upon the enemy." But though the Louisiana men were initially stunned and dropped back, their officers quickly reformed them and brought up their reserves. Another Confederate company on picket a fraction of a mile away hurried to the scene. In short order the Confederates came right back, engaging the 4th Michigan skirmishers. Woodbury, like some of the other officers, was on horseback, though Lt. William F. Robinson said the colonel got as wet as any of the men when he forded the Chickahominy. As the firing increased, the colonel committed more men to the fight, and it was Custer who rode back across the river to get them.

At the sound of the opening gunfire, Company A's Second Platoon, under Lt. William C. Brown of Monroe, broke into a run along the edge of the river toward New Bridge, where strong Rebel pickets were posted. Brown's men opened fire on them. When the rest of the regiment heard the skirmish fire, the officers halted and formed a line of battle in the woods at the river's edge. "[We] loaded our guns, fixed bayonets and were ready for the contest," wrote Leister T. Scholfield, a 23-year-old soldier in Company H.[32]

Company B was ordered forward to cross the river, keeping to the left, toward New Bridge, while two other companies were sent across to the right to aid Company A's First Platoon. There are conflicting suggestions that these first reinforcing companies on the right were G and K or F and D; Jonas Richardson said they were Companies C, D, F, and I. Whatever the order of their arrival on the southern side, the men from Company B, wading the Chickahominy near the wrecked bridge, were most exposed to musketry of Confederate pickets. Richardson said the men gave a tremendous shout as they ran out of the woods into the river. "Our men crossed under a severe fire, the water in places being up to their armpits, obliging them to take off their cartridge boxes and hold them above their heads," reported Lieutenant Bowen, the engineer, whose horse was shot from underneath him. Irvin S. Miner of Company F wrote that "we plunged waist deep in water with a shower of lead in our faces." Charles W. Phelps of Company D noted the crossing was made in a hard rain and confirmed that the water was so deep in places that men had to swim, even while trying to keep their ammunition dry.

But the first three companies made it across to join Company A's First Platoon skirmishers, slogging out of the river into the belt of woods where their comrades were trading fire with the Confederates at their encampment. A short distance to the southeast, Company B reached the trees to establish the left of the Michigan line. Abel M. D. Piper, 25, a big man from Lenawee County nicknamed "Elephant," was killed and several others were wounded, Cpl. George W. Millens wrote. But the company, under Capt. George Spalding, kept up a steady fire. Along with the other Michigan soldiers who had crossed, they pushed the Louisianans back by reason of their superior rifles and protection in the trees. Orvey Barrett wrote that Custer cheered them, shouting, "Go in, Wolverines, give them hell!"

They did. "The enemy on the opposite side of the river cooperating with their forces on our flank, effected a crossing and drove our troops back about 400 yards," Col. T. G. Hunt of the 5th Louisiana wrote. By now the 4th Michigan had four companies across the Chickahominy in a line of battle. "The fight continued from behind trees for a while in which the Rebels got far the worst of it, for our shots told every time," George Millens bragged.[33]

Not only had these 4th Michigan companies established a strong line, they also cut off some of the Confederates and made them prisoners. Captain Spalding, whose left arm was still in a sling from his wound at Yorktown, said later that a Confederate officer indicated he was surrendering.

But only 10 feet away from Spalding, the Rebel raised his musket and fired. The bullet ripped away the captain's pistol belt, causing him pain, but no serious injury. One of the heroes of the action in this vicinity, it was claimed, was Homer Fisher of Company B, who had been arrested and court-martialed in a "drumhead" trial the night before for his fight with Major Cole. Fisher begged his officers not to be left behind that morning, so he was allowed to go with his company. But he got separated from them as they forded the river, and he emerged from the water closer to New Bridge. Alone, he came across a five Rebels in the woods, reportedly "destroying" their picket post, according to an account published later, by killing, wounding, and capturing the lot. For his actions, Fisher's court-martial was commuted.[34]

At the skirmish line, Woodbury would write, the Louisianans were reinforced by two additional regiments, though Confederate reports state that the 5th Louisiana was in fact bolstered by three companies of the 10th Georgia Infantry. The Georgians advanced, but their smooth-bore muskets didn't have the range of the Union rifles; three of them immediately fell wounded. Colonel Hunt ordered his men to charge, and he claimed in his report this action forced the Union troops to pull back across the Chickahominy. Other accounts say the Confederate attack was repulsed and that the Georgians and Louisianans retreated to a safe distance, hundreds of yards away in the brush-covered ground. Pushing up from the woods along the river, the Michigan soldiers formed along an old fence that rose above a drainage ditch or channel from the river to a nearby field. The 4th Michigan's side of this fence, the ditch, was a swampy mess, though it provided some cover. Here, Leister Scholfield wrote, "we fought hard for two hours, in mud and water up to our waists." Some soldiers stood in shallower sections. "The water was knee deep in this," wrote Charles Phelps, "and right on the back was a fence which made a good breast work."

The clash now reached its climax. Woodbury ordered most of the rest of his men across, leaving only one company on the northern side of the river as a reserve. Millens claimed that some Rebels on the other side "began to run & we all plunged in." The accounts of soldiers and officers from the regiment indicate companies like H and D crossed the river late in the skirmish. "We commenced firing on them at this [ditch]" Phelps wrote; "the reg't all came across and opened on them[.] we kept up for about half an hour when the rebels run like the devil." The 4th Michigan had been on its own in this day's fighting—the squadron of U.S. cavalry troopers, for whatever reason, did not ford the river and join in. But at last the Rebels brought up an artillery piece and opened fire on the Michigan men. This was probably the point at which the regiment withdrew across the Chickahominy.[35]

"The enemy, strongly re-enforced, advanced upon us, but we held him in check till our ammunition gave out," Lieutenant Bowen reported. There was no reason to stay any longer. The soldiers of the 4th Michigan were running out of cartridges and they had shown infantry could ford the rain-swollen river. Woodbury said his regiment withdrew in good order, removing their wounded and 10 or 12 of the wounded Confederates. "We took some 37 prisoners, including 1 officer," he reported. The 4th Michigan's officers believed they had killed 100 or more of the enemy, though a more conservative count by Confederate officers put their dead at 18 with another 26 men wounded and 34 or more missing. Rebel fatalities may have been higher than this; John Bancroft noted that 4th Michigan men found the bodies of eight more Confederate

MARTIN N. BERTERA

The 4th Michigan returns to camp, greeted by Gen. George McClellan and his staff, after the regiment's skirmish at New Bridge. Though the fight wasn't a significant one in a historical sense, it was considered a victory and gained for the regiment national publicity. Drawing by Lt. Charles Gruner.

soldiers in the Chickahominy in that same vicinity three weeks later. That could mean that at least 26 Confederates were killed in the New Bridge skirmish.

Back on the north side of the Chickahominy, one of the Confederate prisoners spoke to Woodbury now that the clash was over. "I might have shot you half a dozen times," the Rebel claimed.

"Why didn't you?" Woodbury asked.

"I took you for some damned common orderly," the prisoner answered. If the colonel or any of the officers or men who heard that explanation laughed out loud, the record does not show it. News accounts and men's letters said that McClellan and Porter personally congratulated Woodbury and his regiment. Lieutenant Bowen, who reported on the mission to his superiors, was also impressed. "Too much praise cannot be given to Colonel Woodbury and his command," he wrote. Writing back to an Ohio newspaper, Woodbury called the skirmish "a brilliant affair for us."[36]

Incredibly, for all the gunfire exchanged, only two of the 4th Michigan's men had lost their lives at New Bridge. In addition to Pvt. Piper, a Lenawee County man, Franklin Drake, 20, of Company B was mortally wounded and died a short time later. Several more men were injured less severely. The mission had only been a reconnaissance and, as far as history was concerned, a mere skirmish. But it brought the name of George Custer to the attention of the press and the commanders of the Union army. "Lieut. Custer deserves praise for his coolness and bravery," wrote a member of Company A. "It will do his friends in Monroe good to hear that he is already making his mark so soon after graduating [from West Point]."

This had been the 4th Michigan's first real fight as a regiment. They had pushed into Confederate-held ground, thrown the defenders back, and held their position with discipline. They had withdrawn in good order. Colonel Woodbury was proud of his regiment, and so were Generals McClellan and Porter. McClellan himself would transmit the news of their success on to President Lincoln and Secretary of War Edwin Stanton. "The conduct of my own officers was, without exception, faultless, and both officers and men gave conclusive evidence of their coolness under fire," Woodbury wrote.

General Porter warmly congratulated Lt. Col. Jonathan Childs as he turned his prisoners over for questioning that day, shaking Childs's hand. "The 4th Michigan is covered in glory," Porter said proudly. "Covered with mud and water, too," Childs joked.

Perhaps the only discouraging word about the skirmish seemed to have come from the brother of Dr. William Clark, the regiment's unhappy surgeon—and this was aimed squarely at Woodbury. Dr. Clark had gone across the river with the men of the 4th Michigan that day and had received kudos in the press for treating wounded men while under fire. Clark's brother, Joseph, claimed in a letter to Governor Blair that Woodbury hadn't really crossed the Chickahominy with the men who did the fighting, but was taking credit for having done so. Given the other statements that place the colonel with the skirmishers, this criticism of Woodbury cannot be taken seriously.[37]

For the other officers and men of the regiment, New Bridge was a great victory. Henry Seage of Company E, 17, recorded the skirmish in his journal in the typical brief style of a young Civil War diarist, but his pride was obvious in the last sentence of his entry for Saturday, May 24: "McClellan met us & said Boys you done nobly today."[38]

CHAPTER 5

A Whirlwind of Bullets, Yells, and Shrieks

THE DAY AFTER THE CLASH AT NEW BRIDGE THE 4TH MICHIGAN HELD A FUNERAL FOR THE TWO men killed. "We buried our comrades today (Piper and Drake)," noted George Millens of Company B, "with artillery honor & all due respect." Their entire brigade attended. But that afternoon it was back to the routine of inspection and dress parade. The men learned that in honor of their victory, the brigade commander, Col. James McQuade, renamed their bivouac "Camp Michigan." The next day the brigade and division rose before dawn and marched two miles closer to New Bridge. They set up their camp in the rain in a field near a mill owned by a local physician, a certain outspoken secessionist named Dr. Gaines.[1]

On May 27 the regiment was involved in another mission into Confederate-held ground. Their First Division, accompanied by two federal cavalry regiments and additional artillery, was ordered to deal with a Rebel force at Hanover Court House. McClellan felt these Confederates were a threat on his army's right flank and rear as he was "quietly closing in" on Richmond. Eliminating the threat would clear the way for reinforcements that McClellan hoped would join him from the north. "Left camp early in the morning in a drenching rain & marched," Millens wrote. The road leading from New Bridge to Mechanicsville and on to Hanover Court House was bad, the going slow. Many troops straggled as the column moved through the thick mud, but the rain stopped around nine o'clock. The sun came out and the day became hotter. The Second Brigade halted around noon in some woods a few miles from a place called Peake's Station when the sound of gunfire reached them. Up ahead, elements of their division were in a fight.[2]

Millens wrote that the regiment had covered about 10 miles by that point, but "the fighting in front of us ca[u]sed us to hurry along. We did, coming to the place where the fight first commenced & the rebels were retreating." Ahead of them, another Union brigade attacked the Confederate position blocking the road two or three of miles from Hanover Court House. After an hour or more of fighting, the Rebels retreated. By the time McQuade's brigade got to the scene, this skirmish was over. Some of the Union troops pursued the Confederates while most of Gen. George W. Morell's division, including the 4th Michigan, marched on in the afternoon heat along the railroad track to Hanover Court House. But then a larger force of Rebels, waiting in woods not far from the scene of the initial fighting, sprang an attack on the division's First Brigade. These soldiers, under Brig. Gen. John Martindale, were at the end of the First Division's column. "We passed about a mile when heavy discharges of Musketry gave us to understand that we were attacked in the rear," Millens recorded.[3]

The 4th Michigan and other regiments turned and rushed back toward the fighting, and those closest quickly became engaged. Morell's men routed the attackers, a brigade of inexperienced soldiers from North Carolina, in a fierce firefight. The Rebels suffered heavy casualties. Lt. George Monteith, serving on the staff of General Porter, was one of the aides credited for carrying orders under fire, riding "fearlessly back and forth amid the showers of the enemy's bullets." But the 4th Michigan, at the head of their brigade as it marched that afternoon, was at the rear when it turned to join this fracas. Therefore, Millens noted, "we did not get into the fight." The 4th Michigan "was held in reserve in the wheatfield" not far from the battlefield, according to Colonel McQuade. "The fierce and irresistible attack of the other regiments routed the enemy so completely that it was not necessary to bring the Fourth into action."

The Michigan men marched and ran for many exhausting miles that day, and more than 50 of their comrades from other regiments were killed. But some in the regiment weren't happy they didn't get in the fight. "Our Regt. was not in the battle, we were nothing but spectators," wrote Lt. William F. Robinson. "The other Regts. cleaned them out with calling on the reserve. I was not at all sorry, though our boys thought it hard not to be allowed to pitch in, but we get just as much praise as though we were in it and had 50 or 100 killed." The 4th Michigan and others of their division camped in the field, and the men "slept on our arms all night."[4]

"This morning we buried the dead & went over the Battle field," Millens wrote the next day. Charles W. Phelps said they also cared for wounded men. Others did picket duty and marveled at the numbers of prisoners. But the high point came when General McClellan rode through, congratulating their division on the victory. "Little Mc passed and was vociferously cheered," Miner wrote. Sgt. Jonas Richardson said that the soldiers crowded around their beloved general, who told them, "Boys, you have done just what I expected of you." Lieutenant Robinson wrote his father on "secesh" stationery he found or confiscated, expressing confidence the Union army would soon take the Rebel capital and he could come home. "When we get to Richmond I will try to get a furlough for a few days," he wrote. Late in the afternoon of the next day the order came to march back to their camp near New Bridge, and they arrived early on the morning of May 30, "a good deal fatigued," wrote Dr. David Chamberlain."[5]

Perhaps they would have arrived earlier had not someone carried out a memorable prank on the regiment. Orvey Barrett wrote that as the 4th Michigan made the tiring march back to camp, Company B acted as the column's "flankers," point men who moved through the countryside off the road, to make sure there were no traps or ambushes. Once the regiment was close to their camp, it halted on the road at a place where there were thick trees and brush on one side and a steep bank on the other. Here Company B rejoined the column. Though it was dark, "some mischievous fellow in the rear" noticed Union-strung telegraph wires drooping low from the overhanging tree limbs. Reaching up with his rifle, this soldier proceeded to strike the wires with the gun barrel. Knocking the wires back and forth immediately created a crackling electrical resonance in the night—a sound that rattled loudly down the cables as the soldiers waited to resume the march. This pounding, clattering noise from the telegraph lines sounded very much like a runaway team of mules stampeding out of control.

Officers and men alike thought they were about to be trampled, so they cleared the roadway "in two seconds," jumping for their lives. Barrett tumbled 20 feet down the embankment. "I saw the colonel['s] and the adjutant's horses leap a ditch fence on the north side of the road," he remembered. Albert Boies described the panic as "men pitching right and left, falling over each other and scrambling into the brush, in order to get out of the road." He said he never did find out the cause of the noise. "If I could have known the fellow who caused the stampede, I think I could have mauled him," Barrett complained.[6]

After dusting themselves off and trying to find their caps, they got back to camp and resumed picket along the Chickahominy. A fierce storm opened over the countryside, flooding the river on the night of May 30. Silas Sadler of Company G called it "the Hardest thunder Storm I ever seen[,] got wet through." But other events were in motion that now brought the Union and Confederate armies into combat again. A day or so before the 4th Michigan had gone with its division to Hanover Court House, two Union army corps crossed the Chickahominy south of New Bridge, increasing the pressure on Richmond. This caused Confederate commander Gen. Joseph Johnston to strike at McClellan's forces on the south side of the river, in the vicinity of places called Seven Pines and Fair Oaks.

The attack began around noon on May 31, smashing into Union positions and sending thousands of Northern soldiers fleeing. Although the flooding from the previous night's rain swept away some of the bridges that they had rebuilt, Union reinforcements hurried over a surviving bridge and stopped the Confederate advance. Near New Bridge, the men of the 4th Michigan and others from the Fifth Corps heard the sound of this fighting and prepared to go into battle: "[In] the afternoon the roar of cannon & musket have been incessant," George Millens noted. "We have been in readiness but not called upon." Sgt. Jonas Richardson wrote that the men had been issued 60 rounds of ammunition and prepared to go in. But then they waited hours, not moving until early on the morning of June 1. The men only marched about a half a mile and halted by the side of the road, near the banks of the river.

The men soon learned that the bridges in their vicinity had been swept away or damaged badly enough to prevent crossing. The Confederates renewed their attack but again were stopped in bloody fighting. Orvey Barrett said that the men of the 4th Michigan wanted to get into the fight, but couldn't. "We could see the flash of bursting shells and vomiting cannon," he wrote. "The excitement among the men of the regiment was very manifest." Dr. Chamberlain agreed that "the treacherous little stream kept rising so rapidly as to baffle all attempts to construct a pontoon bridge to take us over." They listened to the roar of battle, "and I fear some were doing some tall cursing and swearing because we could not get over," he wrote. But the firing ended late that afternoon or early that evening.

Over the course of May 31 and June 1, over 5,000 Union men were killed, wounded, or captured, while the Rebels suffered more than 6,100 casualties. The battle of Seven Pines–Fair Oaks was over and Gen. Fitz John Porter's corps had no part in it. "We started to help," Irvin Miner wrote that day, but "our boys can not cross the river so we return to camp at night."[7]

A period of relative quiet descended along the Chickahominy, though illness spread and the muggy heat and mosquitoes seemed unbearable. Soldiers were put to work on fatigue as McClellan moved to bring more men and guns to the gates of Richmond, just as he had at Yorktown. Jonas Richardson wrote a letter as he sat on the riverbank, sure that McClellan's plan would soon have them in Richmond. "Pontoon bridges are being built all along the stream and we will soon be able to cross and drive the enemy inside his chane [chain] of fortifications [and] doubtless make one more stand," he wrote. "But whatever may be their intentions, past events prove to us that their cause is a hopeless one."

Richardson spoke to Rebels with differing views of the conflict. A soldier from North Carolina, wounded and captured at Hanover Court House, was pleasantly surprised that he hadn't been killed outright when he fell into Union hands. Not only had he been told that Yankees would show no mercy, the soldier also learned he didn't have a very accurate picture about the battles fought so far. "He now says that he is in hopes that old Jeff [Davis] will be caught and torn to pieces inch by inch," Richardson wrote. But Dr. Gaines, the local plantation owner who served in the Confederate Congress, remained angry and hostile. Richardson said the doctor had vowed that he would eventually dig up the graves of Union soldiers buried on his property and feed their remains to his hogs. "It is rather tough to be compelled to protect such a man's property," the sergeant wrote.[8]

The pickets at New Bridge also talked with their Rebel counterparts. Richardson told a friend that the soldiers exchanged newspapers, and the orderly sergeant of Company K, named William Ihrig, went out into the no man's land between the lines to speak to a Confederate who turned his gun upside down and stuck it bayonet first into the ground before walking over to meet him. The rebel asked Ihrig what regiment he belonged to. "The one that whipped the Louisiana Tigers so like hell," the sergeant replied, referring to the New Bridge skirmish. "We know you," the Reb reportedly answered. "You belong to the Michigan 4th; you took good care of our wounded and we are much obliged to you for it." Charles W. Phelps of Company D heard a different version of that conversation. When the Rebel learned that the sergeant was from the 4th Michigan, he was said to have answered: "There is some goddam bully boys in [that] regiment."[9]

Picket at night on the Chickahominy was nerve-wracking and exhausting for young Albert Boies of Company F. His sergeant warned him the swamp was full of Rebel guerillas. After a tense couple of hours watching shadows, Boies wrote that he couldn't sleep when he was relieved for a break. Thus when it was time for him to go back on picket at 2:00 A.M., he knew he was bound to nod off. Of course, it was a serious offense for a picket to fall asleep. Officers who noticed a picket guard dozing sometimes tried to approach him and grab the rifle out of his hands, proving beyond doubt the picket had been sleeping. Boies knew this. "Therefore I took off one of my suspenders, and tied it around my gun, and then to my wrist." Sure enough, Boies drifted off to sleep. Shortly before daylight, the officer of the guard came up and tried to grab his rifle. But with the stock tied securely to Boies's wrist, the officer couldn't pull it away. Boies insisted he hadn't dozed off. "I made him think I was just musing, not asleep at all," Boies wrote.[10]

Within the regiment, there were more changes. Edward H. C. Taylor wrote that Major James H. Cole had "went crazy from coup de soleil," or sunstroke, something Capt. Charles Doolittle said occurred on June 3. In his resignation letter, Cole admitted that he'd been "sun-struck for the *second* time" and was no longer able to perform his duties. John Randolph, the senior captain, became major in the weeks ahead. "No officer is more capable than cap," Sergeant Richardson wrote about Randolph. "Altho' we would hate to part with him we would like to see him gain a better position." As for the men, William McCarty of Company E wrote that they were "anxious to try our hands once more" against the Rebels after their success at New Bridge, though the regiment was experiencing "considerable sickness" they attributed to the damp weather rather than bacteria-laden water and disease-carrying insects. "Many of our boys are very sick with the Typhoid fever," he wrote.[11]

Of course, it was Dr. William Clark, the regimental surgeon, who was in charge of care for the sick. But Clark continued to chafe at Colonel Woodbury's treatment of him. Clark admitted that the colonel had been pleasant and kind for a time that spring while Woodbury was still hoping he would be made a brigadier general. But now Woodbury, having "relinquished all hopes of being made a Brigadier, has resumed his former insulting treatment of me," the doctor complained. He asked the governor to move him into "a regiment commanded by a gentleman."[12]

Despite Clark's ill feeling toward Woodbury, it seems that most personnel of the 4th Michigan trusted and respected the colonel, just as most soldiers of the Army of the Potomac seemed to have faith in Gen. George B. McClellan. Edward "Ned" Taylor resented the fact that Republican leaders, their press, and the Lincoln administration were angry and impatient with McClellan for not having opened his attack on Richmond. "We are confident of success with McClellan at our head, let his enemies and abolitionists say what they please," Taylor wrote late in May. He was so confident the Union army was about to take the Confederate capital that he wondered if the Rebels might wage a guerilla war once Richmond fell.

His pro-McClellan, anti-abolitionist views were typical of comments made by Michigan soldiers and officers who were Democrats, who felt they were fighting to restore the Union rather than to bring an end to slavery. Taylor was outraged by legislation introduced in the U.S. Senate to enlist blacks as soldiers. "Now I speak not only for myself but for nineteen out of twenty in this Co. or Reg. or Army when I say that if that became law we would sooner lay down arms than fight. . . . When we cease to fight for the Union and begin to fight for Negro equality I am ready to lay down arms and will [do so]." In time, Taylor and many other Northern Democrats would change their minds about this.[13]

The weather was sometimes rainy and almost always hot as the men stood picket or worked on roads and bridges for the artillery. The colonel supervised the work on one of those crossings, so it naturally became known as "Woodbury's bridge," a New York regiment recorded. Irvin Miner wrote that picket duty brought the men in plain view of the Confederates, but that they'd worked out an accommodation: "The lines are in sight of each other and they agree not to shoot except at officers." Sgt. John Bancroft of Company I, after being temporarily assigned to the balloon service, returned to the 4th Michigan on June 7. He was warmly greeted by his old comrades, and he could still visit with friends he made while serving with Professor Lowe's aeronauts, since a team of balloonists was posted practically next door to the Gaines farm.

Despite the work and picket details, soldiers sometimes got their hands on liquor. "Gut [got] pretty tite," Enoch Davis of Company B noted after a day of chopping trees near the river. Men could also go for a dip in the Chickahominy or in Gaines's millpond. George Millens, who'd been sick that month with fever, chills, and weakness, spent a brief period in a regimental hospital but soon returned to duty, though his symptoms periodically came back. It was also during this time that General McClellan shifted more of his army across to the south side of the Chickahominy, leaving the Fifth Corps, commanded by his most trusted lieutenant, Gen. Fitz John Porter, on the north side, reinforced by an additional division.[14]

Sgt. Eli Starr wrote a note home to Michigan, sending back $20 and stating he'd been experiencing "tough living, hard fighting and plenty of it." "I shall either be in my grave or else home by the 4th of July if things prosper as they have," he wrote. "I am now Orderly [sergeant] of Co. C. Write soon." Perhaps the most unusual event came a week later when soldiers on picket found several bodies of Confederates in the river where they had fought New Bridge skirmish. In a case of macabre souvenir collecting, some men from Company K "divide[d] a rebel jaw-bone to send the teeth to the rural districts," Bancroft noted.[15]

But the most significant development in front of Richmond was one the men knew nothing about. Confederate General Joseph Johnston had been wounded during the battle of May 31, and Jefferson Davis replaced Johnston with his own military advisor, Robert E. Lee. By mid-June, Lee was making plans to go on the offensive. Lee intended to bring "Stonewall" Jackson and his three divisions down to join the Army of Northern Virginia; he would take most of his own men from the defenses of Richmond and move them northeast toward Mechanicsville. He would launch his attack directly on the Fifth Corps.

Soldiers heard the sound of periodic but distant shelling and skirmish fire during the hot June days, but the 4th Michigan wasn't affected. On June 20, however, Confederate shells fell into the camp for hours as gunners let fly. None of the Michigan men were injured, and over the course of the following days Rebel cannon again fired a few shots when they went on picket near New Bridge. Union siege guns were now in place and began firing. George W. Millens of Company B noted on June 25 that it was exactly one year ago that the regiment had left Adrian for Washington. He also wrote with satisfaction that the Confederates "have had a little taste of our siege guns, many of our shots passing through their works." In the meantime Sergeant Bancroft got sick and noted he was variously treated with morphine, tincture of sulfuric acid, mercury, and whiskey; he also wrote that the big Union batteries were firing.

That same day, General McClellan received reports that Stonewall Jackson's command was less than 20 miles away—Jackson had brought his men on a wearying march from the north—and he knew a fight was coming. The 4th Michigan, as part of Porter's Fifth Corps, was ordered to be ready to move north to meet the Confederates. "We fell out with three days rations in haversacks to march," Miner wrote, "but did not go." The next day Sergeant Bancroft, still sick, was told to report to the hospital. On the way he met Colonel Woodbury, who asked him if he was interested in working as a draftsman for General McClellan. Bancroft replied that he was.[16]

Mechanicsville or Beaver Dam Creek

But there would be no new posting for the sergeant. That morning, the men of the 4th Michigan were again told to be ready to march, Dr. Chamberlain wrote. In the afternoon, about three miles to the northwest near the town of Mechanicsville, Lee's attack on the Fifth Corps began, and this was the start of what became known as the Seven Days. At New Bridge, the men of the 4th Michigan and the other regiments of their division heard the gunfire as Confederate soldiers opened the assault. The Second Brigade of which the 4th Michigan was part, now commanded by the gruff Brig. Gen. Charles Griffin, previously their brigade's artillery commander, was put in motion toward Beaver Dam Creek.

"At three o'clock P.M. we got the orders to go to Mechanicsville in light marching order, where we arrived about two hours before sundown, found our force engaged with a superior force of the enemy," the assistant surgeon wrote. The Union troops fighting here were from a division called the Pennsylvania Reserves under Gen. George McCall. This division, recently sent to reinforce the Fifth Corps, was supported by artillery and dug in on high ground behind Beaver Dam Creek at the point where it joined the Chickahominy River.[17]

Much of the Rebel infantry of Gen. Ambrose P. Hill's division had to cross fields and swamp to attack the Union positions, and scores of them were cut down by cannon and rifle fire. Stonewall Jackson hadn't entered the fight as ordered, probably he was suffering from a kind of nervous and physical exhaustion. But other Rebel troops under generals James Longstreet, A. P. Hill, and Harvey Hill did attack. The fight was well under way by late afternoon when the 4th Michigan reached the Union lines east of Mechanicsville.

Capt. Marshall W. Chapin of Company F, 31, from Detroit, said the regiment halted for a few minutes on the road, probably the old Church Road leading to the town. "McCall's division were having it hot & heavy just to the left of us," he wrote. The 4th Michigan's brigade got its orders and marched over fields on the right of the Union line, where Rebel troops were trying to force a crossing of the creek in some woods. McCall asked the newly arrived troops to go in at that place, one of the most vulnerable spots in his position. The 4th Michigan and the 14th New York tramped in as the sound of the fighting raged. Although the Michigan men got there shortly before the battle subsided, they relieved a regiment, the 5th Pennsylvania Reserves, that had used up its ammunition. "Our regiment was passed along the entire length of the line of battle, and finally formed on the right where they had a position facing a piece of thick woods and underbrush," Dr. Chamberlain wrote. "They were ordered to lie down, all but one company (I) which were deployed as skirmishers."[18]

This company entered the woods, to "see what was there," the assistant surgeon said. These skirmishers got about 50 yards into the woods when Confederate troops in the underbrush opened fire. "Our boys soon fell back, it being so dark in the woods that they were unable to distinguish friend from foe," wrote Chamberlain. Other accounts indicate the entire regiment quickly became involved in a fierce but brief firefight. Captain Chapin wrote that the 4th Michigan relieved some of the Pennsylvanians just as Confederates attacked their line. "When we commenced the Rebells were advancing but we soon drove them back killing any quantity of them & losing very few our selves, but soon it got to dark to see to fight," he wrote. Brig. Gen. Charles Griffin reported that "the Fourth Michigan was scarcely in position when it was attacked by two regiments of the enemy, which were repulsed in the handsomest manner, the regiment firing about 15 rounds per man."

"Several were killed on the spot and some taken prisoners," Dr. Chamberlain wrote of his regiment's casualties. "Our loss was about twenty killed, wounded and missing." More specifically, General Griffin reported that the regiment suffered three men killed, 22 wounded, and four missing. Company B's Enoch Davis noted that the Union troops had "hild [held] the enemy at bay." Lt. George Monteith, serving as an aide to Porter, was again among the staff credited by the general for gallantry in "carrying orders, conducting reinforcements, directing batteries and rallying troops." While the 4th Michigan's came into the battle late on the far right of the Union line, the U.S. Army officer commanding one of the Pennsylvania brigades appreciated it. "[H]ere the Fourth Michigan . . . (Griffin's brigade) were engaged and rendered important service," wrote Brig. Gen. Truman Seymour. Of course, things might have turned out worse for the Michigan soldiers had Stonewall Jackson attacked that part of the Union line as Lee ordered. In that case the 4th Michigan could have paid a much higher price at Mechanicsville.[19]

Darkness brought a close to the fighting and Union soldiers lay down with their rifles close at hand in the trees and fields south of the creek. The Confederates suffered casualties of nearly 1,400 men, while Union casualties were under 400. Yet that night, Gen. George McClellan made his controversial decision: He pulled Fitz John Porter's Fifth Corps back to defensive positions on the high ground near Gaines' Mill. McClellan had already given the order for his army to move its wagons, the sick and the wounded, and the big guns to points south of the Chickahominy River. As historian Jeffry Wert described it, the commander of the Army of the Potomac "had lost the strategic initiative to Lee." Lee correctly gambled that an attack on McClellan's right would cause him to halt his offensive.[20]

The men of the 4th Michigan, like most of the Union troops who fought at Mechanicsville, rested and waited until orders came to withdraw early the next morning, June 27. Captain Chapin wrote that he found a blanket among the dead on the battlefield, wrapped himself in it, and "was soon asleep." At about three o'clock in the morning, the order came for the men to withdraw, Capt. John Randolph reported. The men were on the march with their Fifth Corps before daybreak, back to Gaines' Mill. Now they were the rear guard of the Union army. "We could not understand it for we had driven the enemy back with very little loss," Captain Chapin wrote of McClellan's decision. Capt. Charles Doolittle agreed. He didn't understand the withdrawal either, but he "presume[d] it is all right."

"Our route led us through our old camp, where we arrived about 7 o'clock in the morning,"

Dr. Chamberlain wrote. Though he had expected to find that the regiment's baggage and hospital had been packed and evacuated when they returned to camp, "we found our hospital tents still standing, filled with the sick, and everything as we had left it, the rebels only two miles in our rear." The doctor managed to load the sick men on passing ammunition wagons, but he still had plenty of tents, medicine, books, clothes, and bedding. Choosing about 75 pounds worth of items, he then made a pile of the rest of the supplies, splashed them with turpentine, and set them ablaze. "I went to Col. Woodbury, told him what I had done, and asked if I had done right," Chamberlain wrote. "He laughed and said he thought I would not be court martialed, as there was no possible chance to save anything more from the camp." Sgt. John Bancroft helped the assistant surgeon and went to work putting the torch to supplies. "Move and burn stores and send wagons to the rear over the Chickahominy," he noted. "Go back about one-and-one-half miles and form in line to check the enemy."[21]

Gaines' Mill

The Fifth Corps dropped back, south of the two crossroads communities called New Cold Harbor and Old Cold Harbor, an area that was a short distance south of Gaines' Mill. Charles Griffin, the 4th Michigan's brigade commander, reported that this position was on the east side of "Gaines' Creek," but more correctly it was just south and east of Boatswain's Creek, one of the many small runs that wound through the valleys into the Chickahominy. That river now lay behind the Fifth Corps, posted on high ground in a curving line of battle facing west, northwest, and north. Griffin's men got their orders after 9:00 A.M., moving about a mile or so south from the site of their old camp to a large hill or ridge with their brigade. The men stacked their knapsacks in the rear of their lines and built defensive positions. Then they waited. Orvey Barrett later claimed that the advancing Rebels "took possession of our deserted camp, rioted awhile on what was left—whiskey, hard-tack and other commodities."

The First Division, to which the 4th Michigan belonged, held the left, or the western section of the Fifth Corps's line. This was a strong defensive position, stretching east through some woods and along high, rolling ground and farmland above Boatswain's Swamp. Some accounts called this high ground Turkey Hill. Captain Randolph characterized the regiment's position as being on "the left center" of the Union line. Specifically, the 4th Michigan's Second Brigade held the right of their division's line, while the regiment was itself on the left of its brigade. This was a point about 1,000 yards south of the town of New Cold Harbor and a stone's throw from a farm occupied by a family named Watt. To the regiment's right the line of troops and artillery continued along the hilltops for more than a mile. "Our Regt was in the woods facing a ravine[,] Captain Chapin wrote of this position; "we built up brest works of logs rails [and] 7 bales of hay, Co. A & F had a first rate one of bales of hay. Here we lay untill about three PM when . . . the ball opened on the right & left of us & kept up some time without attacking us." Albert H. Boies of Company F later said he suggested the men cover the hay with earth so they wouldn't catch fire.[22]

Another of the regiments in their brigade was given the task of delaying the attacking

Confederates, from the direction of Gaines' Mill. These Union troops were forced back late that morning as the Rebels came on. Lee ordered his forces forward, but the Rebel attacks took place in a piecemeal fashion. The fighting started for other Union troops much earlier than it did for the 4th Michigan. Gen. George W. Morell, First Division commander, wrote that "the enemy approached through the woods from the direction of New Cold Harbor, and made their first serious attack about 12 o'clock upon the right, which was handsomely repulsed by Griffin's brigade."

The regiment helped to blunt this and other assaults that followed at 2:30 and 5:30 P.M., attacks that extended along the division's front. Private Millens of Company B said that he and his comrades also fought behind a temporary breastwork of rails. "They made an attack & were repulsed & ran in every direction leaving the colors on the field but soon they came up & were repulsed & a third time came up[,] one Regt after another in line of battle to our one[.] we pored in a discharge of musketry piling their dead in heaps," Captain Chapin wrote. "At last they came down on us & we gave it to them in good style. At this time the musketry was terrific but we held them right to it & our brest works did good service." Emerging from the woods on the other side of Boatswain's Swamp, scores of men under A. P. Hill were hit by Union rifle fire and artillery as they tried to cross. Some of those who made it across the creek faced being shot down as they tried to climb the high banks. In front of the 4th Michigan, Rebels who survived this fire had to charge up the ravine toward the strong Union defenses.[23]

Just as they held a good position at Beaver Dam Creek, the soldiers of the Fifth Corps again had the advantage of high ground and good cover. They also had excellent artillery and accurate rifles. Hundreds of Confederate soldiers were killed and wounded by late afternoon as Robert E. Lee again waited for Stonewall Jackson to strike the right flank of Porter's position. Finally, by 5:30 or 6:00 P.M. the Confederates had a coordinated assault hitting the entire Union line in fighting the likes of which soldiers hadn't seen before. Some Union reinforcements arrived on the field, but regiments that had been fighting for hours were running out of ammunition.

A Union commander who witnessed the battle in the vicinity of the 4th Michigan late that afternoon was Col. H. G. Sickel of the 3rd Pennsylvania Reserves. His regiment was ordered to support one of the Union batteries on the hill. Sickel reported his men came under terrible fire when they were shifted to help the 4th Michigan as the regiment attempted to cover a gap in the Union line: "Soon after the attack by the enemy on the center of the line[,] we were ordered to support the Fourth Michigan, which soon shifted to the left, under a galling fire from the enemy's guns." Another officer who saw this heavy fire was Capt. Edwin Bishop of the 2nd New Jersey Infantry, sent to relieve the 4th Michigan by Gen. Fitz John Porter.

Now the last two veteran Confederate brigades available to Lee joined in the attack on Porter's men. One was Gen. John Bell Hood's famous Texas Brigade, thought to contain the best combat troops in the South. As this wave of soldiers stormed up the slope toward Morell's First Division, men from the brigade to the left of the 4th Michigan broke, running back over the hill. Confederates poured through the gap and hit the remaining Union troops, including the 4th Michigan, with fire from the side or flank as well as from the front—a deadly and untenable situation for soldiers. "At the fourth and last [attack], about 6:30 o'clock, they came in irresistible force, and throwing themselves chiefly against the center and left, swept us from the ground by overwhelming numbers and compelled us to retire," General Morell wrote. It was a critical moment. "Just at the time that we were about being relieved by another Reg't"—probably the 2nd New Jersey—"the Regts on the left of us gave way & the Rebells commenced to flank us," Captain Chapin wrote.[24]

Capt. John Randolph of Company D reported that "the regiment held its ground until its ammunition was nearly expended, when it was relieved and fell back, contesting every foot of the ground, and formed our line of battle in the rear of the reserves." He stated that as the action came to a close that evening, "we held the ground where we had fought against such fearful odds." Yet reports by Union commanders described this action as the 4th Michigan and its brigade being driven back. Though the regiment fought well, the breaking of the First Division's First Brigade set off a chain reaction of panicking men, with Confederates troops delivering cross fire at close range. Col. Dwight Woodbury did his best to keep his men fighting, as did another colonel from their Second Brigade, and for that their commander gave them credit. "The left wing of the brigade, consisting of the Fourth Michigan and the left wing of the Fourteenth New York, under command of Colonel McQuade, held its position until late in the evening, but was forced to retire after the troops on the left of the line gave way," General Griffin wrote.

The soldiers retreated into the woods. Woodbury had been sick that day, Captain Randolph wrote, and so was Lt. Col. Jonathan Childs, but both were courageous and conspicuous on the field. But then Childs was hit, reportedly wounded in groin, and carried from the battlefield. Woodbury wasn't ready to give up the fight as Union soldiers retreated from the trees. The colonel, on horseback, rode back to a point where he could re-form his regiment as soldiers streamed toward the Chickahominy. "Col. Woodbury seeing how it was going[,] planted our colors in the . . . open field in the rear at right angles to the position we had formerly held & shouted to rally on the collors [*sic*]," Captain Chapin wrote. "Each captain lead [*sic*] his co. out of the woods at the order & formed the new line."[25]

> I lead [*sic*] mine out & in doing so lost one Lieutenant Joseph Smith & several men. I made my men as all the rest did lay down & fire laying [down] & thus avoid as much as possible as shell & sollid shot that flew around us for we were in a perfect crossfire the enemy being on three sides of us. Col. Woodbury, Capt. [George W.] Spalding, Lieut. [Simon B.] Preston, & Lieut. [Charles] N. Marvin were in the immediate vicinity . . . & we did all we could to rally the men of other Regts into our ranks. . . .
>
> We succeeded in rallying a good many of them to lay down & fire with our men. After the men of our side had about all got in & Col. Woodbury & Spalding & Marvin had gone to their posts I called Lt. Preston to my side & told him to lay down, that I could take care of the Co. & there was no use exposing both of us to such a fire[.] he stopped a moment at my side & asked for Lieut. Smith[.] I told him he was shot. At that moment he jumped round & said my God Capt. I have lost an arm. I looked & sure enough a ball had passed through his arm near the shoulder & into his side.[26]

Chapin used his handkerchief to tie a tourniquet around Preston's arm above the wound and directed two men to twist the ends of the cloth to a stick, tightening the cloth to stem the bleeding. They took Preston to the field hospital, which Albert Boies described as a log house to the rear. But within minutes one of the soldiers returned with bad news—the surgeons had left the hospital, and he was sure that Preston was bleeding to death. "The hospital was afterwards taken by the Rebells & I lost both Lieut. Preston & the man that staid with him," Chapin wrote. Preston, then about 36 and previously captured at the first Bull Run, survived three days. The man who took him to the hospital, Hiram B. Fountain, was initially listed as missing in action, but he had been captured and would eventually be released in a prisoner exchange.

The fighting on the hillsides and fields above the swamp raged as the sun went down behind the trees. A young soldier named Converse (probably Orrin Converse) later said he witnessed the death of Capt. Richard DePuy, the Ann Arbor man who commanded Company K. DePuy, 31, just halted his company on one of the fallback moves; he had put his sword back in his scabbard when a bullet struck him in the head, killing him instantly. Converse believed the same bullet that had killed DePuy also struck him in the hand.[27]

The situation for the men of Porter's Fifth Corps was going from bad to worse. Millens, like others, observed that the Union line broke on the right as well as the left, so that the 4th Michigan was hit with the cross fire. "[We] were compelled to fall back which we did," he wrote, "halting three times & forming & delivered our volleys to the enemies ranks." Albert Boies saw Corporal Charlie DuPont of Company K fall to the ground, struck in the head by a gunshot. Charles Barlow, 22, saw it, too. They thought DuPont was dead, but he survived with the loss of an eye. "[O]ur Captain killed, First Lieutenant, killed, First Sergeant killed . . . a whirlwind of bullets, yells and shrieks. Was it so or was it a bad dream?" Barlow later asked DuPont.

The regiment was ordered to fall back again. Captain Chapin said the men did this quickly, moving "20 or 30 rods," or roughly 400 feet. But then the order came to double-quick, or run, as Confederate forces flooded across the battlefield, nearly surrounding them. The men had left their knapsacks at the rear in piles, said Edward H. C. Taylor of Company A, but as the Rebels threatened to overwhelm them, someone ordered them to be burned. Now it was just a matter of escape. Other Union troops were also retreating, some of them crossing paths with the 4th Michigan, breaking their ranks and mixing in. "[I]t looked as if the army was panic stricken," Albert Boies remembered, "masses surging to the rear, officers striving to check them and form them into a line, riderless horses galloping about, dead and dying on every hand, wounded being carried to the rear, and then the sharp musketry fire, and belching of a hundred cannons, all made it seem as though pandemonium reigned supreme."

"I myself got astray & followed the wrong collors [*sic*] for some distance," Chapin wrote of the retreat. "When I discovered my mistake, I found I had but six of my men with me but saw others striding along [—] none could tell where our collors were." As soldiers headed for the Chickahominy, where Union forces held the south side of the river, some tried to find their regiments. Chapin made up his mind to stop and gather them up: "I began to shout *fall in 4th Mich[.,] fall in 4th Mich* & my boys took up the cry."[28]

Men from the 14th New York joined them and Chapin soon rounded up 200 soldiers. He was joined by Lieutenant Marvin and Sgt. Maj. William H. Loveland of Company D. They blocked the road, only allowing wounded soldiers to pass, and ordered others into their line. In short order he had as many as 500 men from various outfits, but General Porter decided that men should return to their own regiments. After this, Captain Chapin was left with about 250 men from his brigade—not enough for the counterattack he had in mind. He resumed a tired march to the rear. By the time he found the rest of their brigade, it was clear the fight was over. "I tell you I was very tired & hoarse from haloring [hollering]," Chapin wrote.

George Millens, who managed to stay with the main part of the regiment in the retreat, said that the men had been nearly out of ammunition after the third time the 4th Michigan fell back and reformed: "We retreated about one mile & met some reinforcements & halted & formed. As they passed us on double quick the Rebels broke & run in turn. we were soon supplied with ammunition & were ready to go in again but were not needed." The diary of Henry Seage of Company E, though brief, didn't reflect as much order in the retreat as Millens and Chapin did. "[F]ell back fighting," he noted that night; "commenced about 1 o'clock. Had to fall back. Am wounded in leg. Lost knapsacks. We were routed & retreated in bad order."[29]

According to Millens, those reinforcements regained possession of the battlefield, but historians say the fresh Union troops pushed the Confederates back so that they could withdraw. Though Lee's army incurred high casualties, it succeeded in breaking the confidence of George McClellan. He moved the Union army to the south toward the James River. Richmond was no longer in danger from the Army of the Potomac. Though the battles continued for a few more days, McClellan's offensive was over.

The men of the 4th Michigan who hadn't been captured or killed rested briefly near the Chickahominy with no food, supplies, or blankets. Edward H. C. Taylor wrote that thousands of other survivors of the battle had already crossed or were then crossing the river, where the rest of the Union army was standing guard or moving toward the James. Charles Barlow remembered "lying on the ground that night, completely exhausted by the fearful fighting, dazed by the terrible and shocking sights that had met my gaze but a few hours before." A soldier named George Crogan was next to him.

"George," Barlow said. "The captain is killed?"

"Yes," Crogan answered. "It's so."

Barlow asked about Lt. Jeptha Beers.

"Yes," Crogan replied. "He's dead."

Barlow said he went on naming comrades, "one after another," with Crogan confirming the terrible truth, though in reality, Lieutenant Beers was mortally wounded and in Confederate hands.[30]

Other survivors rested. "Sleep on the sand without any blanket," wrote Sgt. John Bancroft in his diary. "Woke up about 1 o'clock [the morning of June 28] and crossed the river." Captain Chapin said the regiment moved before daybreak, joining the rest of the army on the south side of the Chickahominy. The movement across the bridge south of the battlefield was "one of those awful marches, night marches where we move 150 or 100 feet to rest ten minutes or one-half hour," Bancroft wrote. Dr. Chamberlain said the night was cold and that the men were silent as they slowly trooped over a causeway and bridge through the swamp and over the river. When they finally got across before the sun came up, they slept in a field.

The 4th Michigan lost 15 men and officers killed in action in the fighting on Turkey Hill and the woods and fields above Boatswain's Swamp, with another 41 wounded and 32 missing. The regiment's death toll rose to 23 as eight of those seriously wounded died in the days after the battle. In addition to Lieutenant Beers, 41, from Tecumseh, Lt. Thomas D. Jones, 24, had been mortally wounded. Beers, who'd been reassigned from Company G to Company K, died in a Confederate field hospital. Jones, from Coldwater, survived less than a month, dying on a hospital ship in New York Harbor. Dr. William E. Clark, the regiment's surgeon, was at the field hospital that was captured and it seems he chose to remain behind to take care of wounded men. He would stay at Gaines' Mill for several days before he was released by the Rebels, by then seriously ill himself.

Among of the 4th Michigan's dead at Gaines' Mill was Sgt. Frederick W. Meech, 25, of Company B, from Indiana—the man rescued from the sheriff in Angola more than a year before by his friends so he could join the regiment with them, and who had married his sweetheart at Adrian. Meech had proved to be a good man—Sergeant Major Loveland called him "as true and brave a soldier as ever took up arms" and "a hero on the battlefield," one of a few soldiers he recognized in his report. Irvin Miner from Company F was one of the men unable to get away with the regiment as they retreated. He spent the next 40 days as a prisoner before gaining his release on parole in prisoner exchanges.[31]

One 4th Michigan soldier captured at Gaines' Mill was fortunate to recognize and be acknowledged the next day by his old U.S. Army commander from the Mexican War—General John Bankhead Magruder of the Confederate army. The soldier, 36-year-old John Sanders, a Washtenaw County man in Company D, was with a group of prisoners brought to Magruder's headquarters. According to an account published years later, Sanders thought he might get better treatment if he could demonstrate he had a connection with the Rebel division commander. "Hello, General Magruder," Sanders greeted his old commander from the last war. "How have you been these past 20 years?"

Magruder was shocked that a Union solider recognized him. "Who the devil are you?" he demanded.

Sanders gave his name and said he'd been in the 4th U.S. Infantry Regiment in the Mexican War.

"Who was your colonel?" Magruder asked sharply.

"You were," Sanders replied.

"Your captain?"

"Anderson."

"Your first lieutenant?"

"Roberts."

Magruder was delighted at this coincidence, according to the account. "Gentlemen," he said, turning to his staff, "he was thar. This fellow was in my regiment in the Mexican War. W-e-l-l, well. Gentlemen, what can we do for one of my old boys who has happened to get on the wrong side this time?" Magruder's aides laughed and Sanders was removed from the prisoners, who were sent on to Richmond. Sanders reportedly was escorted under a white flag to Union lines and turned over to Union pickets. There is no mention in the state summary of his service record that he was ever a prisoner of war.[32]

But while Sanders came out of the battle of Gaines' Mill with a fine story, more than 6,800 Union soldiers were killed, wounded, or missing. For Lee's army, it was even worse, with 8,700 casualties. For the next few days, the Army of the Potomac, though strong and intact, retreated. The 4th Michigan Infantry would face an even worse fight.

CHAPTER 6

At It We Went Tooth and Nail

On the morning of June 28 men of the 4th Michigan and other regiments who fought and escaped the battle of Gaines' Mill with their lives were roused from their sleep on the south side of the Chickahominy. Henry Seage, who had been wounded slightly and separated from his company, found his outfit. Discipline and order were still expected, no matter the losses and the retreat, so soldiers cleaned their rifles and stood inspection. There was a good chance Porter's Fifth Corps would have to soon fight again as the Army of the Potomac withdrew toward the James River. This was some 13 miles as the crow flew, but for soldiers and wagons the route led across swamps, through woods and over confusing country roads.

Dr. Chamberlain spent the morning working on the "walking wounded" like Seage, soldiers who had been hit, but not so badly that they couldn't march. Around noon their regiment was on the move with the division for a place less than a few miles away called Savage's Station, where some 2,500 sick and wounded Union soldiers were gathered. Chamberlain called it "nothing but a farm house with a place [for passing trains] to [obtain] wood and water, but now had the appearance of quite a town." Because McClellan was abandoning the supply line that stretched back to the east, this railroad would soon be cut off by pursuing Confederates. Those sick and wounded who couldn't accompany the army as it retreated south, or who couldn't be placed on wagons pulling east, were left to become prisoners, at least temporarily. Some doctors and hospital aides stayed with them. Chamberlain wrote that there "was no time to look up friends" at the station, but Capt. Marshall Chapin of Company F saw Lt. Joseph L. Smith of Hudson, wounded the night before. Smith, about 32, "had just had his leg amputated but was doing well," Chapin said. He survived.[1]

The regiment marched on with the First Division, moving about eight miles as other troops fought a rearguard action to the north. The men of the 4th Michigan rested in the rain that night on the banks of the White Oak Swamp. Some mules broke loose that night, causing an alarm that caused soldiers to think for a moment that Rebel cavalry was attacking. Dr. Chamberlain said the men laughed at each other's reactions when they realized what happened, and went back to sleep. The next day, June 29, the men worked on a corduroy road or causeway through the swamp, wrote Sgt. John Bancroft of Company I. There were long periods of waiting in the suffocating heat, and they moved only a mile and a half. Some said officers moved the column slowly to make sure they didn't walk into any ambushes. While other regiments bivouacked in the woods that night, the 4th Michigan and the 14th New York kept going, finding the way along the roads, sometimes hearing shots off to their left, sometimes hearing hoofbeats in the distance. "The night was spent in our tramp through roads with the underbrush coming down close to it nearly all the way," Dr. Chamberlain wrote.

He said the soldiers knew the Confederates were pressing close, but in reality Lee was disappointed his generals weren't making a more aggressive pursuit. The doctor claimed there was never any confusion during this march, but George Millens wrote that they took some wrong turns through the forests, ravines, and hills and did some backtracking. It was exhausting. "May you never experience how tired we were," Bancroft complained. As light came into the sky on June 30, the men of the 4th Michigan rested. About noon, the rest of their division joined them. The march south resumed.[2]

After moving another few miles on a route called the Quaker Road, their division passed a large hill or ridge and came within sight of the James River at a place known as Turkey Island Bridge. Here Union gunboats could bring their protective firepower to bear. The soldiers of the 4th Michigan cooked their coffee and ate hardtack for breakfast in a grove of pines on the river. By afternoon they could hear firing as Confederate troops attacked the Union army rear guard to the north. Sergeant Bancroft had been getting sick again, bad enough that the doctor excused him from duty. But when word came that they were moving out, going back to the heights they had passed earlier, he got to his feet. "Orders came to sling knapsacks and retrace our steps which we did for about a mile," Dr. Chamberlain wrote, "which brought us back to Malvern Hill." John Bancroft went, too, though ill and exhausted: "I cannot bear to leave the regt., so I go along up the hill."

Here the Union army gathered, on another excellent defensive position. Less than a half-mile north of the sharp turn in the James River called Turkey Bend, Malvern Hill rose from ravines, low fields, and riverbeds to a height of 150 feet. Uneven in shape and bounded by creeks, this hill was more of a wide ridge or rising plateau that was made up of farms and meadows, patches of woods, and rolling ground. This battlefield would be more than a mile long and nearly a mile across at its widest point, toward the southern end. North of Malvern Hill, in the meantime, fighting raged. But here Union artillery went into position on the high ground, dominating the routes that Lee's men would use to attack. With its brigade, the 4th Michigan reached an open area that afternoon on a crest called Crew's Hill, about two-thirds of the way along the length of the ridge. The regiment "took a position the large field and lay down on their arms to await events," Chamberlain wrote. Pvt. Millens called this "a nice battle ground."[3]

Suddenly cannon balls and shell began to fall, strike, and bounce into their ranks as Confederate guns fired on them from the left, or west. Sgt. Ambrose J. Easton of Company K was killed. For about three minutes, shot and shell came at them "like a hail storm." Capt. John Randolph of Company D said the regiment "soon changed our position under shelter of a piece woods" nearby. Union artillery and gunboats on the James began firing back. After being pounded by the superior Yankee guns, Millens wrote, the Rebels "bug out." When the guns fell silent, a party of pioneers was sent to check the woods where Rebels fired. They found an abandoned Confederate field artillery battery surrounded by dead gun crew members, horses, and infantrymen. Other members of the 4th Michigan said that large numbers of Rebel prisoners were brought in.

Union officers spent the rest of the day posting divisions and brigades and batteries, while soldiers who'd been fighting to the north retreated, joining them at Malvern Hill. The 4th Michigan buried Easton—"a true soldier & a brave man," Capt. Harrison Jeffords of Company C wrote. "We had the opportunity to do for him what we could not do for many others. We buried him in a beautiful spot in the shade of a tree that can be identified at any further time." The regiment stayed in the woods that night and slept on their arms on that western part of the hill with their brigade. Morell's division held the curving left portion of the new front line, again facing north. The 4th Michigan would be in the thick of the fight here.[4]

While combat went on in places near Malvern Hill that last day of June, about 12 miles away at the impromptu hospital near Gaines' Mill, the peevish surgeon of the 4th Michigan, Dr. William E. Clark, again wrote to Governor Blair, complaining of ill treatment not by the Confederates, but by his commanding officer, Col. Dwight Woodbury. Clark was a prisoner of the Rebels, though he had certain freedom of movement, and he knew he was soon to be released. Again he asked that the governor place him in another Michigan regiment. Clark wrote that shortly before these Seven Days battles began, he'd been treated better by Woodbury. The colonel had apologized for his previous treatment, Clark wrote; Woodbury told the doctor he never really wanted Clark to resign from the regiment, but that Dr. Chamberlain and some officers did. Of course, Clark was outraged at this and spoke with some of them, ultimately deciding that Woodbury lied to him. Clark's brother, adding his two cents to the doctor's complaint to Governor Blair, said it appeared Woodbury had read Dr. Clark's mail. These complaints were enough for the governor, who in weeks ahead would assign Clark to the 19th Michigan Infantry. But before the unhappy surgeon got his wish, the 4th Michigan was in the most costly battle of its service.[5]

Malvern Hill

Early on the morning of July 1, the soldiers of the 4th Michigan rose and moved out of the woods on Crew's Hill, marching a short distance into the fields west of the Quaker Road near the home

The 4th Michigan fires volleys at the advancing Confederates during the battle of Malvern Hill, its costliest battle, on July 1, 1862. Drawn by Lt. Charles Gruner.

of Dr. J. H. Mellert. Malvern Hill rose behind them; here one of many Union batteries was posted, looking north down the slope to where the ground leveled off and then rose slightly into thick woods. Confederates attacking from these trees would have to cross a wide field to reach Union positions. The regiment's assignment was to support this battery on the left, relieving the 83rd Pennsylvania Infantry that had spent the night here. Sgt. John Bancroft noted that their position shifted several times, but Private Millens of Company B wrote that they were ultimately posted "in a ravine." Capt. John Randolph called it a knoll. Both were referring to a valley or depression between the rising, rolling pieces of ground making up Malvern Hill. Other Union regiments extended the line to the right, or east. The guns fired periodically and skirmishers were sent out as the sun rose, watching and waiting for the Confederates. Robert E. Lee had been trying for days to destroy McClellan's army and again ordered his generals to attack.

"On Tuesday, July 1st, we were ordered to march out to support a battery," Captain Chapin wrote. "The battery kept up an occasional fire all day." To their right another Union division was attacked at around ten in the morning, but the Confederates were repelled by artillery fire. By early afternoon, as the summer sun beat down, Rebel troops twice appeared on the ground in front of Griffin's men, probing but not pressing attacks when the Union batteries opened fire. Two guns on the hill above the 4th Michigan blasted at Rebel infantrymen who came out of the woods in the first probe around noon, and they quickly retreated. Capt. George W. Lumbard of Company E said that around two o'clock, "we could see great clouds of dust rising, which warned us that the rebels were advancing in great force." This Rebel probing action came farther to the right, but it met the same artillery response "and back they went, limping and howling to the woods," Lumbard wrote. But these were preliminaries. The Confederates were working their way down from the north in preparation for a large-scale attack, positioning their guns and troops.[6]

The field fell quiet in the afternoon heat—it was so hot that Sgt. John Bancroft covered himself with hay to try to keep the sun off, and so quiet that some of his comrades were able to kill and butcher a pig and cook dinner. But the quiet ended at 5:30 P.M. when the Confederate guns opened fire again. "Such cannonading I never heard but our position just under the brow of a hill protected us perfectly although some of the Battery men suffered severely," Chapin wrote. Millens agreed that the regiment's position in the ravine sheltered them, with shells from both sides passing overhead. The Confederate barrage lasted about 30 minutes and the Union batteries answered. Rebel troops were spotted stealthily approaching through the valley of the creek to the left of Griffin's division, trying to flank them. Griffin ordered regiments over to the left of the 4th Michigan to stop them, but no sooner had he done so than more Confederates troops came out of the trees before them and all across the Union front. Charles W. Phelps of Company D wrote that "we heard them coming out of the woods a-hollering like the devil."

Out in a wheat field that lay just north of where the regiment was posted—between the Michigan soldiers and the oncoming Confederates—U.S. Sharpshooters had been skirmishing. They fell back and joined the 4th Michigan. As the gray-and-butternut-clad troops came within range, the Union guns again opened fire. "[T]he whizzing, whirring and whistling of every species of projectile was perfectly bewildering," Dr. Chamberlain wrote. "Still that mass of human beings came rushing on in the face of such terrible fire for a full half mile." Col. Dwight Woodbury prepared his regiment to meet them. "On they came with a shout that made the woods ring, and confident of an easy victory, they still rushed on in spite of the grape and canister from our batteries, which mowed them down by the hundreds," Captain Lumbard wrote. Since Lt. Col. Jonathan Childs had been sick, wounded, and transported away, Capt. John Randolph was in command of the left wing of the regiment.[7]

The 4th Michigan moved up to the edge of their hill, waiting for the moment to fire as the Rebels drew closer. The regiment waited in the standard line of battle, its companies side by side, each company in two ranks or parallel rows of men, one behind the other. The front line seems to have been in a kneeling position or prone on the ground, while the second rank stood or knelt behind them. "We took our position in plain sight of the Rebells," Captain Chapin said. "It was a grand sight to see the Rebells come up & know that they came on to sure death. Colonel Woodbury did not give the order to fire untill they were at easy range." When the Confederates were about 110 yards away, the colonel gave his instructions.

"Fire by rank! Battalion ready!" he shouted. His orders were probably echoed down the line, repeated by company officers. "Rear rank, aim, fire!" At the shattering crack of their rifles billows of smoke rolled away over the hillside and hung in the thick air. Woodbury's orders continued: "Load!" Then Woodbury ordered the front rank to fire and another volley blasted. As his soldiers prepared to fire again, he shouted encouragement. "Now boys, give them three cheers, and hold your ground!" The men did cheer, for their firing into the Confederate troops, already devastated by artillery, sent them back to the cover of the woods. But only for a time. "[S]uch volley as were pored into them nothing could stand," Captain Chapin wrote. "Those who escaped broke & fell back but they were soon reinforced & the fire became steady on both sides."[8]

Private Phelps said that 4th Michigan fired less than a dozen volleys when the first Confederate regiment broke, but he agreed that they were soon replaced by another. "We held them[,] mowing them down like wheat," he wrote, while the battery posted near the 4th Michigan also blasted canister into the Rebel lines. Captain Chapin said the 4th Michigan's men were ordered to keep down, and he believed this saved the lives of many of the soldiers. George Millens said his regiment "gave it to them by file & kept them in check untill our cartridges were gone." Orvey S. Barrett, describing the battle years later, wrote that "the thunder of the cannon was awful; clash of arms, shouts of combatants, was deafening." Albert Boies claimed that the first to die in Company F was 20-year-old William Murphy of Wyandotte. Murphy had had a feeling that he wouldn't survive if he went into battle that day, as he told his officers. But there was no excuse from the battle line. Murphy was struck in the head and killed instantly.

By Lumbard's estimate, this rifle fight raged for 30 minutes when, to their right, the 9th Massachusetts Infantry charged the Rebel line. Some said this charge failed and the Massachusetts men turned and ran toward the 4th Michigan; others thought the charge initially succeeded, but turned chaotic when about half the 9th Massachusetts didn't hear the order to halt, causing a confused retreat. Some of the Irish soldiers were shot down by mistake on the smoke-blanketed hillside, according to James F. Gilmore of the 4th Michigan. Officers yelled for their men to hold their fire. Some of the survivors of the 9th Massachusetts dropped to their hands and knees and crawled through the regiment's line, but Companies A and F were disrupted by the fleeing troops. "We were obliged to cease firing in order not to kill them," wrote Chapin, who was on the right of the regiment's line, commanding Company F. "Now came the grandest [scene] of all [—] the Rebells charged back on the 9th, following them in to our lines."[9]

Colonel Woodbury knew his battle line could be broken as the Massachusetts men ran through the 4th Michigan's ranks with Confederates close behind. He tried to halt and reorganize the fleeing soldiers—and shouting, he hurried out in front of his line. But in doing so, the colonel became an obvious target. "It was in trying to rally the 9th [Massachusetts] men as they came through A & F that Col. Woodbury was killed," Chapin said. Cap in one hand, sword in the other, the Adrian militia commander who had organized and led the regiment since its inception was struck in the head by a bullet. Though some newspaper accounts said he gave patriotic and dramatic last words of encouragement and a good-bye to his men, Dr. Chamberlain wrote that Woodbury fell back, killed instantly. He was 38 and left a wife and young daughter. Just a moment later, Capt. A. Morell Rose of Company A was also killed.

Other men from Company A were struck down—Charles Austin was the first, and his friend Frank Gale asked Sgt. Richard R. Lassey of Monroe if he should take Austin off the field. "I told him to wait a minute or two," Lassey wrote. But no sooner had he spoken when Gale suddenly clapped his hand to his chest and fell, killed by musket fire. The angry Michigan men waited until the Massachusetts soldiers were clear and then fired. The Confederates could hardly have been closer. "[A]s soon as the 9th were out of the way we poured in such a volley that there was very few left of them on our end of the line to run, but what there was made tracks in double quick," Captain Chapin continued. "We were so close that I gave them a couple of shots from my revolver & it did its duty."

Chapin stated that the Michigan men held their ground, and it appears that they and their brigade helped blunt this phase of the Confederate attack along with blazing Union artillery. According to a letter written after the battle by J. Q. Adams—a man identified as Woodbury's brother-in-law—a group of men from Company A recovered the colonel's body and carried it back to some woods about 500 feet away during this lull. These woods were probably near the

Mellert House, just south, or to the rear of the regiment's position. But the fighting again raged as more brigades of Rebel troops marched out of the trees to the north and up the hill, attacking relentlessly. Chapin wrote that with the Massachusetts men gone, the Confederate infantry "came up shouting & in great force. . . . our Regt. did not flinch not even a man . . . at it we went tooth & nail. My boys fired away their sixty rounds & then I set my sergeants to cutting off the cartr[id]ge boxes from the dead & wounded & passed them around."[10]

As the fighting intensified other officers of the 4th Michigan were hit. Capt. George W. Spalding, 25, who'd risen up through the ranks of Company A from sergeant, was struck in the neck, but not fatally. As he was taken off the battlefield, he asked that Sergeant-Major William H. Loveland take over command of his company, since he didn't think there were any commissioned officers left. Lt. John A. Gordon of Company I, was struck in the arm but wouldn't leave, while Adjutant Francis S. Earle of Grand Rapids was hit in the knee. He was fortunate, for the wound wasn't serious.

Noncommissioned officers pitched in, picking up rifles, closing gaps in the line, and shouting orders. Sgt. Richard Watson Seage of White Pigeon, not quite 25 and older brother of Henry Seage, shot a weapon until it was fouled by his repeated firing, Captain Lumbard wrote. "Then, amid the tempest of a leaden storm, [he] went to work and cleaned his gun, and then again went to firing." The captain sent Sergeant Seage to find the regiment's color bearer and have him wave the flag so that the men could give it three cheers.[11]

Seage carried out his assignment and the color bearer waved the flag, Lumbard wrote; Seage went back to firing a rifle until he was hit in the head by a nearly spent musket ball. Seage dropped to the ground, but he was incredibly lucky—though his skull was dented and he'd been knocked unconscious, he survived. Richard Watson Seage was taken to the nearby field hospital, which would soon be captured by the Confederates when the Union army left the field. He, like hundreds of other Union soldiers, spent time as a prisoner that summer. Albert Boies from Hudson was knocked head-over-heels backward by a bullet that struck him high on the left side of his torso. But the teenager wasn't dead either, for the ball had ripped through the diary in his pocket, sending a shock through his body that left him senseless but alive.

James Harroun of Hillsdale, a private in Company E, was so swept up by the emotion of the fight that his shouts of encouragement to his comrades turned into a running speech. He jumped to his feet, hat in one hand, rifle in the other, and carried on for 10 minutes before Captain Lumbard told him he could do as much good firing as he could making speeches. Harroun resumed shooting at the Rebels. But there were growing gaps in the line, and one noncombatant, the company's cook, Frank Forncrook, decided to take a place there. Forncrook had brought a kettle of food up from the rear that afternoon, up the southern slope of Crew's Hill. As the battle raged, Forncrook ran to his company, picked up a rifle and cartridges from the dead and wounded, and began firing. But after only several minutes, he was shot and killed. Though officers often used phrases as "not a man flinched" to describe the courage of their men under fire, there were exceptions. William F. D. McCarty, a young noncommissioned officer in Company E, was later accused of leaving in the face of the enemy.[12]

Lumbard wrote that the 4th Michigan was alone on the left of the battle line as other Union regiments were relieved and the artillery batteries ran out of ammunition. This may have occurred near the end of the regiment's fighting that night, as other outfits moved up to replace those that had been fighting since the battle started. Although reports by Union commanders don't state that the regiment was on its own, Edward "Ned" Taylor proudly wrote that soon after the battle, "Gen. Fitz John Porter said, 'the fourth saved the Army on the 1st of July.'" That was high praise from the commander of the Fifth Corps.

The accounts by Lumbard and Chapin reflect the regiment's desperate situation. Lumbard said his men fired 80 rounds, a statement indicating his men were forced to scavenge more ammunition. They were out of cartridges and would have to retreat while other Union troops from their division, waiting in reserve, moved up to take their place, Brig Gen. Charles Griffin reported. Colonel Woodbury's brother-in-law, who seems to have been in close contact with officers of the 4th Michigan, also wrote of this. After the colonel's body was moved into the woods at the edge of the battlefield, "the 4th were forced to retreat in a different direction." Another regiment from their brigade, the 14th New York, had moved to a point to the 4th Michigan's left during the fighting, and they, too, retreated. Their route took them through the woods where the Michigan men had placed the body of their colonel. Major Davis from that New York regiment took the rings off Woodbury's fingers as well as his revolver, shoulder straps, letters, and ambrotype portraits of his wife and daughter. At least his family would get these items back.[13]

By this point the men of the 4th Michigan were no longer in a position to retrieve Woodbury. The sun was going down and the 4th Michigan could carry on the fight no longer. Whoever was in command of the regiment at this point—perhaps Lumbard or Randolph—asked Lt. Col. W. Y. Ripley of the U.S. Sharpshooters to go back and bring up reinforcements. Ripley did so, and soon two New York regiments were on their way to the front. "My men were now nearly all out of cartr[id]ges when a movement was made all along the line to fall back[,] that is[,] in our regiment up to [Companies] A & F," Captain Chapin wrote. "But as I had received no orders I did not understand what it ment & supposed that the Rebell were forcing the left." He proudly claimed he kept those two companies standing in place, some of the men with empty guns. Chapin indicated that the Confederates weren't in his immediate front as the 4th Michigan's companies to his left pulled out, but other accounts say there was still fighting going on.

"Before the enemy got up to us the order came to me to retire that we were being relieved & we fell back at a walk past through the new Regts' line & formed on the colors and marched off in good shape," Chapin wrote. Capt. John Randolph of Company D, said to be the regiment's most senior captain, wrote that he brought the regiment off the field. Randolph reported that the New York regiment marched up under a murderous fire to relieve the 4th Michigan, though official reports indicate their division's Third Brigade relieved the Second Brigade. "[T]aking the position held by us, they gave the rebels such a check that in confusion they fell back," Randolph wrote of the New York men.[14]

Though the shooting would go on until nightfall, the battle was over for the 4th Michigan. The fighting had been worse than Gaines' Mill. At Malvern Hill, the regiment suffered 41 men and officers killed in action, with some 100 men wounded and 32 missing. One of the dead was Sgt. Eli Starr of Company C, the young man from Centreville who had joined the Peninsula Guard company in Sturgis, and who'd been given the rank of sergeant as an enticement to stay. Starr was probably 22 years old. As some of the 4th Michigan's wounded men died over the next weeks, the regiment's death toll from Malvern Hill would rise to 54 killed or mortally wounded, proving to be the regiment's single most costly battle. Brig. Gen. Charles Griffin credited the regiment for its performance. "The handsome manner in which the Fourth Michigan stood its ground and the good order in which it retired from the field was the subject of comment among all who witnessed it," he wrote. Griffin had seen for himself how fierce the battle was that evening, with his horse shot dead under him.[15]

It was dark when the regiment reached a large house or plantation at the southern end of Malvern Hill, not far from the James River, which was being used as a hospital, signal station, and headquarters. Sgt. John Bancroft was tired and sore, and he could still hear the sound of musketry and artillery behind them about a mile or so away—"we did not mind it much," he wrote. Men lay down in the dust. The hospital was overwhelmed with critically wounded men, so those whose wounds weren't immediately life-threatening had to wait. One was Bancroft's lieutenant from Company I, John Gordon, who had stayed with the regiment during the fight although he was hit. Bancroft tied Gordon's handkerchief around his arm. As the exhausted, smoke-grimed soldiers rested, the firing died away after 9:00 P.M.

Almost everyone in the regiment had lost friends by this time in prior battles and skirmishes, but not on this scale. Their colonel was gone, too. With the exception of the querulous Dr. Clark, Dwight Woodbury had been respected and trusted by his men and officers, some of whom had known him as a neighbor, all who knew him as their leader. "He was as good and brave an officer as ever drew a sword in defense of the Union," wrote Sgt. James W. Vesey of Company C. "We all loved him and would have lost our right arm for him." Capt. Charles Doolittle, from Hillsdale, took out his diary. "Our Colonel was killed and our regt badly cut up," he noted; "the loss in my Co. [H] being from 18 to 20. God has been good to me." Enoch Davis of Company B also briefly summed up the terrible day before joining his comrades in brief rest. "Another hard fight fot [fought] today," he wrote, "& we whiped the Enemy bad[.] This battle was fot near Malverns Hill."[16]

Davis was only partially correct. The Union army had handed Lee a loss of thousands of men killed and wounded, but it was the Union army retreating from the battlefield that night. The 4th Michigan marched away with the rest of McClellan's force on an exhausting, all-night trek several miles through the rain to a plantation on the James River, called Harrison's Landing. Captain Doolittle said they arrived "wet tired and disgusted," though his own faith in McClellan "was strong as ever," he noted. "It was long after daylight when we reached the open field and then in the midst of a shower, with rebel artillery behind us, we waded through the mud and sought to erect some shelter," John Bancroft wrote. He and Michael J. Vreeland of Brownstown Township in Wayne County, a sergeant from Company I who was being promoted to lieutenant, made themselves a "house" of fence rails and wheat stalks and spent the balance of July 2 resting.

As the Union army left Malvern Hill on the long march to Harrison's Landing in the early morning hours of July 2, young Albert Boies regained consciousness at the Malvern House field hospital. Boies gave different accounts about his experience in the years that followed, but the version he shared with other veterans was that his comrades dragged him off the battlefield after he'd been wounded. Feeling like he'd been hit with a sledgehammer, Boies walked with thousands of other troops along the James River, trudging on even after the thick mud pulled his shoes off his feet. He was taken by ship to a Washington, D.C., hospital, where, he later said in another version of his story, he shook hands with President Lincoln and was comforted by the First Lady.

Like Boies, others who were sick, lightly wounded, or lucky enough to be moved or transported to Harrison's Landing and City Point, Virginia, were taken by ship to hospitals and camps with medical departments. One was David Webster from Company D. "The last battle we was in was a hard one," he told his mother, "for the bullets flew around us like hales [hail] and for my part I do not want to go into any more places like that." Orderly Sgt. Richard Lassey, 29, of Company A, had been slightly wounded in the arm; he sent a letter back to his wife, listing the company's casualties throughout the Seven Days. "We fell back about twenty miles and fought them all the way and any of the time we could have whipped them," he wrote. "What it means I can't say." Lassey was not long at City Point; he soon returned to the camp of the 4th Michigan at Harrison's Landing.

Dr. Chamberlain, the assistant surgeon of the regiment, hadn't left Malvern Hill. The battlefield was virtually covered with thousands of wounded men, and Union and Confederate parties worked through the night of July 1–2, carrying them to field hospitals. Chamberlain worked on the wounded there on the field until dawn. The wounded, like Sgt. Richard Watson Seage, had to stay behind. Chamberlain was among the doctors who volunteered to tend them. He also located Woodbury's body, burying it in a place where it could be recovered. With the aid of stragglers, he gathered up and worked on the suffering, though the Confederates took charge of the hospital the day after the battle.

Officially, Chamberlain was a prisoner, but the reality was that he was allowed to move around, spending nearly two weeks at Malvern Hill, trying to care for wounded men who died by the score in the days after the battle. Many other injured men were shipped to Richmond. On July 14, sick after the nearly endless work, and hampered by the loss of medical supplies and instruments stolen by Confederate soldiers, Chamberlain and two other army surgeons were released on parole along with nearly 60 wounded men and prisoners, including Richard W. Seage. They were picked up by the steamboat *Vanderbilt*.

"No one knows how to appreciate kindred, friends and country until he has been deprived of them," the doctor wrote. As Chamberlain returned to the 4th Michigan's camp that night, he met young Henry Seage and told the young soldier that his older brother was back at the landing. Henry hurried down the next morning to bring his brother into camp, and Richard Seage cooked what must have been a celebratory dinner for Henry and his friends in Company E.[17]

In the meantime the Union army remained in camp by the James in the rain. The Rebels quietly positioned some guns across the river from the camps and fired on them one night in early July. Union gunboats and artillery quickly returned the fire, forcing them to leave. "The shells flew around here pretty thick for about three quarters of an hour," wrote Pvt. Charles W. Phelps; "one shot struck within about a rod of where I was standing and throwed dirt all over me and into the tents." The shell grazed a man's back, and he was the regiment's only casualty.

The next day, the 4th Michigan was one of the regiments sent across the river to try to prevent reoccurrences of such an attack by cutting down trees and burning down buildings of the plantations to punish the locals and deprive the Confederates of cover. The men, of course, ransacked the places, helping themselves to "any amount of geese, turkeys, chickens, pigs," Phelps wrote; "such things suffer when we find them. You can bet on that." Moses Luce believed, as did other soldiers, that one of the plantations destroyed belonged to an ardent secessionist said to have fired the first Rebel gun at Fort Sumter in the spring of 1861. Luce identified this man as "Runyon," though he meant Edmund Ruffin. Other historical accounts, though, say that Ruffin's estate wasn't among the ones destroyed.

Far worse than that Rebel shelling incident for soldiers was the fierce and muggy heat and debilitating illness. "We are so completely worn out that most all the boys are nearly sick," wrote George Millens of Company B. Sgt. John Bancroft spent a few days in the hospital at Harrison's Landing being treated with opium. Scores of other sick and wounded Union soldiers and officers continued to move away by barges and steamships to hospitals in Washington and elsewhere in the North, and some didn't survive. Dr. William E. Clark, suffering from chronic diarrhea, was taken to New York. Within a month's time or less, he would be back recuperating in Michigan and finally get his wish to join a new outfit, the 19th Michigan Infantry. On July 8, President Lincoln arrived at Harrison's Landing, and though it was oppressively hot, Millens felt that "things are beginning to look more cheerful."[18]

One day before the president's visit, Capt. Harrison Jeffords wrote to a friend back home, telling of the death of Ambrose Easton and his own luck. "I have escaped so far with [a] slight wound on the hand[,] two holes in my boot & sword scabbard cut in [two] & have lost 22 of my co.," he wrote. "Our colors was shot almost to ribbons." But for the 500-some men and officers of regiment who remained unwounded and healthy enough to attend their duties, there was the question of would be their new commander. With Woodbury dead, command would have ordinarily devolved to the regiment's lieutenant colonel, Jonathan W. Childs. But Childs, sick and wounded, was back at Fortress Monroe. Nor did the 4th Michigan have a major at that time—the man who'd held that position, James Cole, had been forced out because of his health. This meant that Capt. John Randolph of Ann Arbor, the regiment's senior captain, was in charge of the regiment through mid-July.

But it was Capt. George Lumbard who ended up promoted past Randolph by order of Fifth Corps commander Gen. Fitz John Porter and the recommendation of Gen. Charles Griffin, commander of the corps's First Division. Subject to Governor Blair's approval, this made Lumbard lieutenant colonel, his commission dated from July 1. This was just what Jonathan Childs wanted—he would be promoted to colonel, with Lumbard commissioned as his second-in-command. These moves put Lumbard in charge of the 4th Michigan until Childs returned to the regiment on August 1. George Millens, however, didn't approve when Lumbard conducted battalion drill on July 23, a hot day: "Lumbard puts on style," he grumbled disapprovingly. "I wish Col. Childs would come back."

Ironically, it would turn out that Childs soon came to regret he recommended that Lumbard be his lieutenant colonel. In less than three months' time, Childs would be forced to resign from the regiment or face charges that appear to have been brought about by Lumbard. In addition to the promotions of Childs and Lumbard that summer, Captain Randolph was commissioned as major. By the end of the July, Randolph returned to Michigan with Sgt. Jonas Richardson to recruit for the regiment.

Another change was the resignation of the regiment's chaplain, the Reverend Henry N. Strong, who'd been a friend of Colonel Woodbury. Harrison C. Daniels, a veteran of the 4th Michigan who wrote a memoir of his experiences nearly 50 years later, claimed that Strong had been dismissed by Woodbury after it came to his attention that the chaplain had been caught coming back to camp from Washington drunk sometime during the winter of 1861–62, and that Strong had been playing poker (and winning) against the officers. Yet this claim can't have been strictly accurate, for Strong's resignation wasn't processed by the Fifth Corps's assistant adjutant general until nearly three weeks after Woodbury was killed. While the regiment's letter writers and diarists reflect nothing as harsh as Daniel's allegations, they do suggest some were dissatisfied with Strong and his infrequent sermons and services. His replacement, the Reverend John Seage of White Pigeon, the English-born father of Richard Watson Seage and Henry Seage, would prove a popular and heroic chaplain for the 4th Michigan.[19]

Despite the rain and heat, inspection, drill, reviews, and dress parades were soon resumed. Soldiers were re-equipped as shipments of supplies arrived and replaced the tents and packs that were lost at Gaines' Mill and the clothes and equipment that had been worn out and damaged during the campaign. The camp of the regiment shifted from a muddy field to a wooded area and then back into a field near Harrison's Landing. The men washed their clothes and bathed in the James.

The regiment's assistant surgeon, Dr. Chamberlain, who rejoined the regiment from Malvern Hill in mid-July, was allowed to go home, exhausted and sick. In his place, a Dr. M. I. Mead of Albany, N.Y. took temporary charge of the regimental hospital, wrote George Owens from Company A. He and Private Millens also said parties from the regiment returned to the battlefield under flags of truce on July 17, 18, and 20 in attempts to recover Colonel Woodbury's body, but these were unsuccessful since Dr. Chamberlain had already buried his remains. Back in Michigan less than a week later, Chamberlain told his hometown newspaper that he had "found Col. Woodbury's body and had it decently interred, and the spot is marked so the remains can be recovered in the future."

Aside from the large numbers of men who were suffering from illnesses like malaria, dysentery, and heatstroke, this was a time of routine camp life. There was an exception when the Confederates managed to again fire on the Union camps from the south side of the James on the night of July 31–August 1, and men from the 4th Michigan crossed on August 2, carrying out patrols and capturing one prisoner.[20]

Stories circulated about where their division would be sent next. "Various rumors are afloat about our camp in regard as to what will be done with Morell's division," wrote Sgt. James W. Vesey of Sturgis. Would they be sent back to Fortress Monroe on the Virginia coast? Back to Washington for military police duty? Or Baltimore? Vesey wondered if the regiment would go back in a new campaign against Richmond. As those first muggy and sometime rainy days of August slowly passed, Sgt. John Bancroft recorded in his diary a typical daily schedule:

- Reveille
- Policing of streets
- Breakfast

- One hour's drill by Company
- Guard mounting
- Working and Policing parties fatigue
- Cook, eat and sleep 'til 3 o'clock
- Drill, Dress Parade, Rations
- Supper, bathing, washing of clothes
- Cleaning of muskets, writing rolls, letters,
- Reading papers, etc.[21]

A member of the 4th Michigan who got into trouble at Harrison's Landing was a regimental musician, and this appears to have been the drum major, Isaac Duffenbaugh, an Ohio man about 26 years old. According to a story later told by a New York soldier, the 4th Michigan's drum major called on some officers of the 5th New York Infantry, hoping to find a fellow he had heard was a professional drummer.

The New York officer in question and his comrades invited the drum major of the 4th Michigan (unnamed in the account) into their tent to share a meal. No, the officer said, he was not a drummer. "But," he said, "I can appreciate good drumming when I hear it, and if you have no objections I should be very much pleased to hear what you can do with the drum-sticks!"

"All right," the Michigan drummer said. "What shall I play?"

"Let us have the long roll," the New York officer suggested innocently.

Of course, in 19th-century military practice, "the long roll of the drum" was an alarm—when a drummer "beat" or sounded the long roll, it was to warn of emergency, a call for soldiers to immediately assemble with their guns. Without thinking, the 4th Michigan's drum major pounded out that warning call-to-arms. The New York officers, having successfully set up the drum major to commit a serious breach of order, dashed out of their tent and disappeared, probably stifling guffaws of laughter as the men of the 5th New York rushed out with their rifles.

The officer of the day, whose job it was to see things ran smoothly in a regiment, hurried over and found out it was a false alarm. He had the Michigan drum major arrested on the spot. "He tried to explain, but it was of no use. He was sent to the guard house," Alfred Davenport would write, telling the story years later. The drum major spent some time in jail before the 5th New York's colonel looked into the matter and released him.[22]

But it could not have been long. In any event the days of Union regimental bands came to an end in August. The Hecker Band from Cleveland, like all such bands, was mustered out of the service by order of the War Department. Musicians who had formally enlisted as soldiers were ordered back to their companies, while those who had signed on strictly as band members were allowed to transfer to brigade bands, if that met with the approval of their commanders. Of course, those who wished to stay on as soldiers were welcome to do so. Duffenbaugh, for one, went back home to Ohio.[23]

Now the men who had been captured during the Seven Days battles began returning to the Union army after being paroled by the Confederates, and one was Irvin S. Miner of Company F. Taken prisoner at Gaines' Mill, he had spent 40 days in Rebel hands. During this time, he'd first been housed in an old tobacco warehouse in Richmond, then moved to a camp of tents on Belle

Isle in the James River, and then again to another island camp near the locomotive works. He saw hundreds of Union prisoners of the Rebels brought in, one prisoner shot and two bayoneted to death by the guards; he'd been hungry to the point of being faint.

Miner managed to hold onto some money after his capture, so he was able to sometimes buy bread and milk and keep up his strength. He spent many days and nights in the rain, carving rings out of the bones from the soup the prisoners were served, until finally on August 4, he and a group of his fellow prisoners were marched 20 miles from Richmond to a place called Aiken's Landing. They collapsed in a wheat field that night, exhausted and hungry. But the next day at 10:00 A.M., they too were loaded on a transport that took them back down to the camps of the Union army at Harrison's Landing, arriving about five in the afternoon.[24]

These men rejoined their outfits in time for a new action—a move by the Union army back to the east and away from the Confederate capital. On August 10 marching orders arrived, requiring the soldiers be prepared to leave quickly. The men of the 4th Michigan put their new knapsacks on wagons while the officers loaded whatever baggage they'd managed to replace on river transports. For the next few days they remained under marching orders until they finally began, on foot, on the night of August 14, going only a fraction of a mile and then lying down in the dust to rest.

The march resumed in earnest the next day with the men moving along the road through woods just north of the James River, all day and through the night, until nearly dawn on the morning of the August 16, passing the town of Charles City Court House along the way. They crossed the place where the Chickahominy entered the James on a long pontoon bridge that day and enjoyed "a glorious bath," Sergeant Bancroft wrote. That night, their brigade reached Williamsburg. It had been an exhausting march, but along the way, the men purchased or otherwise relieved local farmers of chicken, eggs, peaches, pies, biscuits, and ears of corn.[25]

On the 17th the march continued. The 4th Michigan reached Yorktown in the afternoon and found that its entire division was there. The next day the soldiers made a considerably longer all-day march of some 25 miles to Hampton. On the 19th the soldiers rose, bathed in salt water, and trudged the last few miles to board ships that took them past Fortress Monroe. Now the Union army truly left the York-James peninsula, going back the way they had come in March. The 4th Michigan sailed on the *Belvidere*.

The next morning the soldiers awoke to find they were steaming up the Potomac River. The transports landed them at Aquia Creek on the Virginia side, and they encamped at the Potomac Bridge, a few miles away. Their division and corps had orders to join the Union Army of Virginia under Gen. John Pope in northern Virginia, and they would do some marching to get there. This army had been created by the War Department late in June to keep Washington safe. By early August, George McClellan, a commander with an uncertain future, was ordered to bring his Army of the Potomac to that vicinity. Lee, anticipating that the Union forces on the peninsula were being withdrawn, had quickly given orders for attacks on Pope. Now new battles began, though the 4th Michigan's division and corps weren't yet involved.

On August 21 the regiment and the Second Brigade of which it was part rose and moved several miles west in the heat to the town of Fredericksburg on the Rappahannock River. Henry Seage and Charles Phelps complained that the rest of the brigade got to move by train while the Michigan men marched. One who didn't make it to Fredericksburg was Moses Luce of Company F. Afflicted with sunstroke, he collapsed and was placed in an ambulance. Luce was sent to an army hospital in Alexandria. Even though he recovered quickly, he would spend the next six months there, often doing guard duty, until January of 1863. But for the others in the 4th Michigan, August 22 brought a march of 25 miles along the river to the northwest to Ellis Ford in hot, dusty weather that turned rainy. The men could hear cannon firing in the distance and they bivouacked without tents, some soldiers acting as pickets to keep an eye on the river ford in case of a crossing by Confederate forces. Men went out foraging for food and Irvin Miner shot a hog; he noted on the 25th that he "commenced cooking for the officers today." The men expected to be marching again, but the order didn't come until August 27, when they moved 20 miles or so north to Warrenton Junction.[26]

This urgent march in the blazing sun was made in response to some very bad news. Robert E. Lee's top lieutenants had been bringing their forces together to fight John Pope, and one day earlier Stonewall Jackson's corps had made a daring and unexpected march around Pope's right, striking the Union supply line, the Orange & Alexandria Railroad, near Manassas Junction. Troops under Pope pursued Jackson and thousands of soldiers, North and South, closed in on the site of the first big battle of the Civil War—Bull Run.

On August 28 the 4th Michigan's men were awakened hours before daylight. They cooked some breakfast and moved a short distance only to have to stop and wait for a few hours. Finally the regiment was able to march with its corps and division, heading northeast toward Manassas Junction and going into bivouac after a march of 18 miles. The soldiers could hear the firing several miles to the north as the preliminaries got under way: Jackson's men, who had been concealed in thick woods, attacked Union troops near the town of Groveton, drawing Pope into what would turn out to be an effective and deadly trap.

The next day the men of the 4th Michigan marched with their First Division of the Fifth Corps the remaining few miles toward Bull Run. The men saw the wreckage of Union rail cars and supply depots destroyed by Jackson's men at Manassas Junction. Pope ordered the Fifth Corps early that morning to go to the town of Centreville, miles farther to the north, but then changed his mind and issued orders sending them west toward the town of Gainesville. These indecisive orders sent Fitz John Porter's men marching many miles uselessly back and forth through the countryside. But at last they were heading in the right direction, to where James E. Longstreet's Confederate corps, with Robert E. Lee, was joining Stonewall Jackson in the wooded countryside.

By early afternoon of August 29, Porter's men had marched three or four miles west of Manassas Junction along the Manassas Gap Railroad. The 4th Michigan and its brigade did picket duty in the hills at a point between the towns of Gainesville, which was now behind Confederate lines, and Manassas Junction. General Porter awaited instructions as his shorthanded Fifth Corps acted as the left wing of the Union army. The soldiers saw dust clouds rising as Rebel troops under Longstreet marched toward them, coming out of the west through a pass in the mountains called Thoroughfare Gap. Longstreet's artillery got into position and fired some rounds toward Porter's men before falling silent, waiting. In the meantime, just two or three miles north near Groveton, Pope began sending his men forward in piecemeal attacks that were easily repulsed by Jackson. "Firing toward the mountains," Sgt. John Bancroft wrote in his diary. "Battle going on. Under the shell today."

Pope was sure that he had Jackson on the ropes. He ordered Porter to launch a flank attack against the Confederate general, envisioning a devastating drive by the Fifth Corps up from the south. But Porter's officers, including his division commander, Gen. George W. Morell, urged him not do so. To follow Pope's order would be suicidal—the Fifth Corps would open itself to a destructive flank attack by Longstreet, whose men waited quietly for their opportunity to strike. Porter believed it best not to move his men in this risky manner, so they waited. They were hungry since they had not been resupplied, so the soldiers foraged when possible. Pvt. Henry Seage's comrades found an old woman living in a valley by a railroad bridge that day and helped themselves to her geese.[27]

Second Bull Run

But other than coming briefly under fire from Rebel guns in the hills south of Groveton, the 4th Michigan and the Second Brigade didn't get into any fighting on the 29th. The men lay on their arms, waiting into the night. Early the next morning, the 4th Michigan withdrew. Along with the rest of their division and corps, their brigade was ordered to join Pope's army near Groveton. But night marches were risky and confusing affairs, and the 4th Michigan was part of two brigades that became separated from the rest of Fifth Corps. They marched past Bull Run several miles east toward the town of Centreville. At dawn, out of provisions, the men gathered up farmers' corn and apples as they continued in the wrong direction through the rolling countryside.

Near Centreville the men halted and were able to draw some rations and have breakfast. Meanwhile, to the west, General Pope was furious that Porter hadn't attacked Rebel positions as he had ordered the day before. Gunfire sounded all that day, August 30, as Union troops marched west past the 4th Michigan on their way into battle. But by afternoon, the men of the regiment saw soldiers limping back from the front—the walking wounded. These men were comparatively lucky. One Union brigade after another was driven back that day as they attacked Stonewall Jackson's strongly entrenched positions, and many soldiers were killed.

Sergeant Bancroft wrote the word "countermarch" in his diary, meaning that the 4th Michigan was finally being sent back to where the battle was going on. But it was too late for them to have a role. While some of the Fifth Corps' troops were sent into the fight, the Second Brigade of the First Division wasn't there. "Porter's Corps engaged except our brigade," Bancroft wrote.[28]

This was actually a stroke of luck for the 4th Michigan, which had lost so many men during the Seven Days. The fact that they weren't present at Groveton meant they weren't foolishly sacrificed in the Second Battle of Bull Run, as so many other troops were. "I am very glad we did not get in it," Charles Phelps wrote about the battle, "for it seems to me it was a bad conducted thing." Not only were the Union troops battered when Pope sent them to attack Stonewall Jackson's strong positions, those soldiers on the Union left were hit by a powerful flank attack that afternoon by Longstreet's corps. These Union soldiers, under Gen. Irvin McDowell, broke and ran. Bancroft recorded the bad news in his diary: "Left wing [of the Union army] turned. Slight panic. After dark [our] army all come back onto Centreville Heights."

Though responsibility for the disaster at the Second Battle of Bull Run lay with General Pope, he blamed it on Fitz John Porter, commander of the Fifth Corps. Radical Republicans were happy to accept Pope's accusations, since Porter was a Democrat and associated with George McClellan. Though the troops thought Porter was a good commander, he was soon cashiered as a result of Pope's charges. "Under him [Pope] any army of the size of ours would seem demoralized," wrote Edward H. C. Taylor of the 4th Michigan, "for to keep up the tone of an army requires more genius and head than he possessed. . . . He was outwitted and befooled and was unable to mass or deploy the forces at his command." An officer from the 4th Michigan who had been on detached service as an aide to Porter, Lt. George Monteith, would soon give testimony at Porter's court-martial. It would take Porter the rest of his life to get official vindication.[29]

As it turned out, one member of the 4th Michigan did go into action near Bull Run. This was James Henry of Company H, about 26, from Hillsdale County. Henry hadn't been able to keep up with his regiment on the marches of August 28 because of his badly blistered feet; he'd fallen out four or five times. He couldn't find his regiment once night fell and on morning of the 29th found himself with the 11th Massachusetts Infantry. When they were ordered into action hours later, Henry went with them and was wounded by musket fire. He was sent to a hospital in Washington, D.C. For him, the war was over. In less than six months, he would be discharged.

The night of August 30 was a long one for the 4th Michigan, whose brigade now acted as part of the reserve and rear guard as thousands of Union soldiers streamed back from Bull Run. The regiment bivouacked near Centreville and the next day expected to see battle when victorious Confederates pursued the retreating Union army. But this didn't happen. Rain fell and the men of the regiment stood in line of battle in front of a section of fortifications before open fields.

Dr. Chamberlain, now the regiment's surgeon, arrived back at the 4th Michigan that day along with the regiment's new assistant surgeon, Dr. Luther C. French, 42, of Hudson. Though Governor Blair previously refused to make Chamberlain the regiment's chief surgeon, he had a change of heart late that summer, possibly because the doctor had strong support in the regiment and from people back home. Arriving about the same time as Chamberlain was the rumor that Gen. George B. McClellan had been restored as the commander of the Union army. The rumor was true; accounts state that thousands of soldiers cheered the news.[30]

The weather turned cold. For the next two days, the men of regiment, weary and hungry, kept watch in the rain, finally moving out with the others of its brigade and division early in the morning of September 2. It was a long march of 30 miles and it finally brought them that night to Langley, Virginia, outside of Washington near the Chain Bridge. The soldiers built fires of fence rails, roasted corn, and bivouacked in a field. The next morning they marched on to Minor's Hill—the place where they had encamped over the winter; it was the place they had left back in March on the spring offensive that was supposed to take Richmond.

Though men were happy that McClellan was back in command of the army, it was still depressing for Dr. Chamberlain to return to this place and think of all the men who'd been lost. The 4th Michigan was much smaller now, with scores of men missing because of illness and wounds, men killed in battle or by disease, men captured. For the survivors who returned to this camp where the regiment had spent the winter months, Minor's Hill was now "a dismal, lonesome place," the surgeon wrote.

What Chamberlain did not write in his letter, but what every man knew, was that virtually nothing had been accomplished in terms of vanquishing the Confederacy, in spite of the thousands of casualties, the misery and suffering, all the millions of dollars spent and the hundreds of miles marched. Certainly those thoughts occurred to Sergeant Bancroft, now back on Minor's Hill. "Many a brave fellow gone to his long home," he wrote in his diary that night. "Many broken bones. Many weary, aching miles."[31]

There would be many more graves and broken bones and aching miles yet to come.

CHAPTER 7

The Sight Was Horrible and One I Hope I Never See Again

THE 4TH MICHIGAN REMAINED ON MINOR'S HILL FOR THREE DAYS, AT TIMES ON GUARD FOR A Confederate attack. But this threat turned out to be a reconnaissance by Rebel cavalry. On September 6 the men marched to nearby Upton Hill near Fall's Church, where they and other elements of their corps alternately went on picket and stood ready for battle. That week Capt. Charles Doolittle from Hillsdale resigned his commission to become colonel of the 18th Michigan Infantry. But the important development for the troops was that the Confederate Army of Northern Virginia was on the march. In the wake of Pope's defeat at Bull Run, Lee decided it was an opportune moment to invade the North. By September 4, McClellan and the War Department were aware the Rebels were coming. Over the next several days and by different routes, the Union army moved out to meet Lee.

The men of the regiment, who remained on picket outside of Washington, heard rumors about this and read developments in the papers. "The report is the rebels are in Maryland," George Millens of Company B wrote on September 8. The men had been without their knapsacks since they left Harrison's Landing in August, but the next day these important carry-all packs finally caught up with them. At last on the morning of September 12 they began to march. The regiment initially headed back into Washington and got on the road to Rockville, Maryland, on another terribly hot day. Sgt. John Bancroft of Company I thought it was beautiful country, but Irvin Miner of Company F observed that the heat during the 20-mile march was dangerous. "Very warm," he noted in his diary. "Several men fell dead with sunstroke on the march."[1]

The next morning the men moved out on the road to Frederick and got to within a day's march of the town. On the way they could hear the sound of gunfire ahead to the northwest. Residents of the towns of Rockville and Leesburg lined the streets as the soldiers tramped through, offering them milk, bread, coffee, and cold ham, Henry Seage noted. They reached Frederick on the 14th, but serious fighting was already taking place as Union forces attacked Confederate positions ahead on South Mountain, a broad ridge running north and south, where Rebels held key passes. The Southerners managed to hold on through the day but suffered high casualties, and they pulled back that night to the west. Lee formed his forces, about 40,000 men, on the high ground near Antietam Creek, near the small town of Sharpsburg.

As the Rebels took their positions the Union army moved forward. The 4th Michigan, with its brigade and division, drew rations and marched from Frederick on September 15 to join the rest of the Union army converging on Sharpsburg. They reached the village of Middletown, covering about 15 miles and approaching South Mountain, where they saw dead and captured Confederates from the prior battle and Union wagon trains rolling up into the hills. Much of the army, ahead of the Fifth Corps, was just a day's march or less away from Sharpsburg. By the 16th, the first Union troops began to arrive there.

At the bivouac of the 4th Michigan near Middletown, Henry Seage noted that it was his 18th birthday. As the regiment passed through Turner's Gap on South Mountain, they again heard cannon fire to the west when Confederates opened up on Union infantry at Antietam Creek. The 4th Michigan's brigade reached the town of Keedysville and marched through that evening, joining elements of two other corps. Now they were on the doorstep of the coming battle, a mile or so from the ground where it would be fought. "Fair prospects for a fight tomorrow as they are surrounded," wrote Miner in his diary that night.[2]

Antietam

The next day, September 17, began the bloodiest single day's battle in American history. Miner's assessment was very nearly correct—Lee's Confederates were in a dangerous position, though not completely surrounded. Henry Seage noted it started at daylight with the opening of the big guns, but for the 4th Michigan, posted with the rest of their corps as a reserve near the center-left of the Union lines, there was no fighting. As the shooting intensified the 4th Michigan was moved toward Antietam Creek with its division, but then these troops were ordered to halt and wait. The men sat down, some of them watching from a hill on the east side of the creek. Sgt. John Bancroft wrote that he was sent forward, probably with his company, to support Union batteries of Parrott guns; so was Silas Sadler's Company G. "Get some glimpses of the smoke and the changes of the lines from the hill," Bancroft wrote. Irvin Miner may have had a better vantage point. "I had a fair view of the fight all day as we were posted on a high hill," he wrote.

HUDSON MUSEUM

Under fire from Confederate pickets on the opposite side of the Potomac River, the 4th Michigan crosses at the Shepherdstown Ford and captures a battery on Sept. 19, 1862, after the Battle of Antietam. Drawn by Lt. Charles Gruner.

"Result not decided." Pvt. Charles Phelps of Company D also told his brother that he witnessed the action: "We were where we had a good view of the field . . . it was a hard battle."

Dr. Chamberlain said that for a regiment that had been in so much fighting, "it was something of a novelty to be near a battle & not be in the front rank." He, too, said the topography was such that "we had a fair view of part of the battlefield, could see the masses of troops rushing to the encounter, with the falling ones making the fields speckled with their prostrate forms. The Rebs had a fine position, & we had to assail them to a great disadvantage to ourselves." To his hometown newspaper, he wrote that "all day long the battle raged; the incessant roar of artillery and musketry was deafening." The men saw their comrades drive deep into the center of Rebel positions, but ultimately McClellan declined to send in his reserves to smash what remained of the thinned Confederate lines. Many of the exhausted Southern soldiers were out of ammunition. Had McClellan ordered a last attack with his Fifth Corps, Lee had no reserves to meet them.[3]

Brig. Gen. Charles Griffin, commander of the Second Brigade, later reported that an order came at 4:00 P.M. from Fifth Corps commander Gen. Fitz John Porter, moving the Second and Third brigades of their division a half-mile to the right, or north, to support another corps's attack, but the soldiers weren't sent in. By evening, they were sent back to where they bivouacked the previous night, a mile or so away. There had been bitter, terrible fighting and some regiments involved that day were truly shattered. Though the Union army had won in terms of stopping the Confederate invasion and killing and wounding a slightly higher number of Rebels than they themselves suffered, McClellan missed the chance to destroy Lee's army. The conclusion Irvin Miner had written in his journal was correct—thousands of men had been killed or crippled, but the essential issue had *not* been decided.

The next day, the regiment moved forward again, this time to the southern portion of the now-still battlefield where Union Gen. Ambrose Burnside's forces had fought. They helped bury some of the thousands of dead and remove the wounded. "Very quiet today," Henry Seage wrote in his journal. "No firing, only pickets." The men drew rations, had baked squash for their dinner, and got orders to march south about a mile and a half to where Antietam Creek flowed into the Potomac River. The men bedded down on the ground as rain fell that night. Though some men by now declared the battle was a Union victory because the Confederates had pulled away, they knew a terrible price had been paid. "Our loss is heavy," George Millens wrote. "The rebels are thought to be in tite place."[4]

The soldier's observation was correct. Lee had pulled his weakened army back around Sharpsburg and the Union army was there in strength, including tens of thousands of men who hadn't been involved in the battle of Antietam. But McClellan didn't order a renewal of the attack on the Confederates. Over the course of that night and into the early morning hours of September 19, Lee's men withdrew across the Potomac. At last the order was given for the Fifth Corps to press forward. The men of the 4th Michigan, now led by Col. Jonathan Childs, rose at 5:00 A.M. and prepared to move out. Soon they marched through Sharpsburg, which had been heavily damaged in the fighting. "Nearly every house struck with solid shot or shell," Sgt. John Bancroft wrote. "Things look rough." Sharpsburg's residents emerged from their cellars and shelters as the troops went by. The people of this town at the edge of Maryland's border with Virginia were as divided as the nation itself. Bancroft said a woman pointed out the house of Confederate sympathizers as the soldiers marched past, and children vowed to get their revenge on them. But the regiment's more important mission came after they moved beyond town.

Shepherdstown Ford

The boundary here between North and South was the Potomac River, and the Rebels had posted artillery and infantry on a high bluff to prevent pursuit. The aggressive Fifth Corps commander, Fitz John Porter, decided these obstacles must be cleared away—he ordered his men and guns forward to engage them. Soon artillery was firing from either side of the river. As the 4th Michigan neared the Potomac, the men formed in line of battle. "Two companies are ordered out as sharpshooters," Bancroft wrote. These men joined other skirmishers trading fire with the Rebels on the south bank. According to Sgt. James W. Vesey of Company C, the two companies were I and A. Capt. John Gordon of Detroit, who had come up through the ranks of Company I, was wounded during this skirmishing. He had only been captain for about two weeks and he'd been previously wounded at Malvern Hill.

By late afternoon the rest of the regiment was ordered forward to support the skirmishers. "As we were marching by the flank down a ravine in the woods," Vesey wrote, "a shot from a rebel battery on the opposite bank fell in our number." It killed a man from Company C.

Sergeant Bancroft was standing behind the unfortunate soldier, Luman Buck. "While going down to the river a fragment of a shell strikes the man in front of me taking off the top of his head and killing him instantly," Bancroft wrote. But the men moved into position and opened fire. "We acted as good sharp shooters and were sent out on skirmishes and had significant firing at them across the river," wrote Charles W. Phelps. Now their assignment changed. "We had only been out but a short time when Gen. Griffin rode down and ordered Col. Childs to cross the river with his regiment and take the artillery on the other side," Vesey wrote. The brigade commander called the 4th Michigan to attention. "Men," Griffin said, "we are ordered to ford the river, and dismount those pieces over there. Are you willing to go?" The soldiers cheered. Robert H. Campbell from Hillsdale, who had just been made first lieutenant and quartermaster about two weeks earlier, remembered that Childs asked his regiment to make the crossing on a strictly voluntary basis—that those who didn't want to make the crossing did not have to. Only two men stepped out of the ranks, he claimed. Campbell also wrote that Childs began to make a speech, but that "a shell at that moment bursted over them," cutting it short.[5]

The attack commenced. At about 5:30 P.M. some 60 men from the 1st U.S. Sharpshooters Regiment led the way across, first through a drained canal that ran parallel to the river and then into the Potomac itself. "While we were crossing, the Fourth Regiment Michigan Volunteers rendered us efficient support by firing volleys over our heads," wrote Capt. John B. Isler of the U.S. Sharpshooters. "My men as they crossed also fired several volleys. After we had crossed, the Fourth Michigan followed us, and when on the other side we jointly advanced up the bluff in front." Vesey claimed it was dark and nearly quiet except for the occasional hum of a bullet whizzing through the night as the regiment started down the bank to the canal's towing path, but other accounts say it was evening and there was more than enough light to see across the river.

Captain Isler said the Confederate musket fire was "sharp" as his men crossed; he lost four of his sharpshooters. As Michigan troops reached the south side of the canal, they fixed bayonets and officers drew their swords. Vesey said Colonel Childs called out: "Battalion, forward double quick—march!" Yelling and cheering, the troops plunged into the river. This place was called Shepherdstown Ford; at some points, the water was said to be little more than knee deep, but at others it was up to a man's chin. The Potomac was cold and variously estimated to be between 500 and 900 feet wide. A few more men were wounded in the crossing. Those in deep water could only try to keep their rifles from getting wet, so there was no way for them to return fire. "Yet on the boys went struggling thro' the water over the uneven bottom and charging up the opposite steep [and] drove the enemy and captured a fine battery of brass twelve pounders," wrote a proud Edward H. C. Taylor of Company A. The river "was deep, ran swift and the 'Rebs' were thick on the other. . . . I never expected to come out alive." Dr. Chamberlain wrote that the soldiers, once across, "started up the bank with one of the yells peculiar to the 4th Michigan at a bayonet charge."[6]

The Confederates on the bluff didn't wait around for a close-quarters fight. "Imagine our agreeable surprise," wrote Henry Magee of Company F, "[when] the rebels after a faint, very faint resistance fled, leaving their battery along the river in our possession." Vesey agreed. "On our arrival across, no rebels could be seen, save a few wounded and sick ones," he wrote. The Rebel commander at the bluff, Gen. William Pendleton, decided to pull back, abandoning his artillery, much to the disgust of Robert E. Lee and Stonewall Jackson. The Michigan soldiers found some cannon hidden, and the Rebel gunners seem to have dumped at least two pieces over the bluff before retreating. Vesey said the soldiers "dismounted five pieces of artillery, two ten-pound rifled parrot guns and three brass twelve-pounders." One or two of the guns turned out to be Union pieces captured at the first battle of Bull Run, part of a federal battery that had been under Griffin's command back when he'd been an artillery captain. They also took several prisoners. "Whenever there is a river to cross they always seem to call on our regiment," Pvt. Silas Sadler of Company G wrote. "When we left Michigan we had Eleven hundred and forty men now we have only got 300 [—] that is using them up pretty fast."[7] Although the Confederates fled, General Fitz John Porter, commander of the Fifth Corps, considered this river crossing a dangerous assignment, and he was impressed that Colonel Childs had volunteered his regiment for the job; he felt that Childs should be nominated for "a medal of honor."[8]

The regiment returned to the Maryland side of the river to camp, drying themselves by their fires and cooking coffee. On the morning of the 20th, they again went back to the Confederate side, this time unopposed. The men captured a few more Rebels and foraged in the countryside, helping themselves to Virginia geese, turkeys, and flour. Relieved by their division's First Brigade that day, the 4th Michigan waded back to their bivouac. "We were hardly settled in Camp before we were roused by a heavy firing in the direction of the River," Edward Taylor wrote. The men fell in and marched toward the Potomac to pitch in to this new fighting. It turned out that after the 4th Michigan was relieved, the Confederates suddenly struck hard at the troops on their side of the river. Hurrying to the Potomac, the Michigan men came across their comrades who'd been hammered in this skirmish—bedraggled, rookie soldiers of the 118th Pennsylvania Infantry Regiment.

Untried in combat, these Pennsylvanians had gone across with their First Brigade and marched into the countryside, where they'd run into the troops of Gen. A. P. Hill, rushing to protect the Confederate rear. The experienced Rebel combat division opened a heavy fire on the green Union soldiers, who'd been given defective and obsolete weapons. Many broke and ran, pursued by Confederates all the way to the river. While other regiments of their brigade got back safely to the Maryland side, many men from the 118th Pennsylvania were captured and wounded. The Second Brigade, of which the 4th Michigan was part, once again was sent to get control of the situation. "We are brought up in battle and remain all day wet and weary," Sergeant Bancroft wrote. Edward Taylor agreed: "They were again obliged to call up this (Griffin's) Brigade to stem the tide and *now* we repossess the opposite bank and the river." Others concurred with Silas Sadler—that it was becoming the general's habit to send them for such work: "I dont know how it is but when they have got any river to charge across they take the [4th Michigan]," Charles Phelps wrote.[9]

A period of relative quiet followed for the 4th Michigan and much of the Army of the Potomac as McClellan declined to pursue Lee's army. Not all the men had tents, but more supplies arrived and the regiment set up a new camp. When Dr. Chamberlain tended wounded and captured Rebel troops, he found some with whom he had dealt at Malvern Hill. "Our men treat them with the utmost kindness," he said of the Confederates. "The poor fellows say they have had more kindness shown to them by their captors than by their comrades. All express themselves as sick and tired of the war and anxious to have it closed."

Though the days in late September and early October were warm, nights were becoming colder. Sgt. John M. Bancroft received his lieutenant's commission on September 28—he was being shifted to Company K—and Henry Seage noted on September 25 that it had been one year since he'd left home. Two days later he learned from his captain that his father, the Reverend John Seage, who had come from England decades earlier, was going to be the regiment's new chaplain. John Seage was an Episcopal minister who had raised his family as they traveled from Canada, New York, and Vermont before coming to Michigan, and he settled in White Pigeon, in St. Joseph County. Harrison Daniels of Company G would remember Reverend Seage as a homely preacher, but one who cared deeply about the men and their spiritual welfare. He felt Chaplain Seage was a dramatic improvement over the regiment's first chaplain.[10]

President Lincoln came to review Gen. Fitz John Porter's Fifth Corps on October 3, and George Millens thought the president looked "care worn." Moses Luce of Company E remembered (as Harrison Jeffords had written in the fall of 1861) Lincoln trying to keep his hat on his head as he rode along the lines. "Holding his lines in his left hand he would throw out his right arm about his stovepipe hat and then the soldiers would yell in approval," Luce wrote. "They loved this homely man because he was so human, and yet was firm in the principles he believed necessary to the salvation of the Union." Several new recruits from Michigan joined the regiment that same day. And when the Reverend John Seage preached his first sermon for the regiment on Sunday, October 12, the men who'd been missing services since the departure of the regiment's first chaplain were happy. "Our new chaplain preached today," Millens wrote in his diary. "We were much pleased with him." Captain Jeffords agreed; he called the next week's service "a good sermon," saying that it "seems more like Sunday than it has for a long time." Reverend Seage would soon mark his 53rd birthday.

Edward H. C. Taylor was pleased to be detailed to his Second Brigade's headquarters as a clerk. "My duties here are tolerably easy at times tho' sometimes I shall have my hands full." Taylor had been hoping for promotion since resigning his lieutenant's commission in the spring of 1861. He sometimes told his relatives about his friends and acquaintances serving in the army, and he mentioned a 23-year-old from Detroit who'd also been in Company A. "George Yates is Quarter Master Sergeant of the Regiment," Taylor wrote. "He is well—There is something strange about the boy—He has been wandering over the South for some years . . . holding no communication with his friends—He is tolerably steady but a little 'fast.'" Actually Yates had been promoted to lieutenant and adjutant of the regiment, and he would soon advance to higher staff assignments.[11]

While Union soldiers enjoyed the quiet of camp life during these October days, the Lincoln administration was chafing over the lack of a pursuit of Lee by McClellan, despite the fact the president had ordered him to do so. Republicans in Congress wanted McClellan dismissed, while Democrats defending the general were angry about Lincoln's coming Emancipation Proclamation that would make the abolition of slavery a war aim. Then in mid-October, Confederate cavalry under Gen. J. E. B. Stuart made a raid into Pennsylvania that further embarrassed McClellan. As a result of this raid, the brigade of which the 4th Michigan was part was awakened early on October 16 and sent across the Potomac on a reconnaissance a few miles into Virginia, pushing back a small Confederate force. Rain set in and Union troops spent a miserable night in bivouac, continuing their advance for a few more miles to the town of Martinsburg the next day. "Had quite a skirmish[,] took some prisoners," Silas Sadler wrote about these clashes. But that afternoon orders came for them to return to their old camp near Sharpsburg, and they got back late that night.

Harrison Jeffords wrote that the people of the area "seem to be all *secesh*" and that the soldiers saw women decorating a burial ground for Confederate soldiers just outside of town. "As we were returning quite a number of Ladies had assembled at the graveyard with beautiful bouquets & as we passed would lay them on the graves of the dead Rebs and then take them up and lay them down again as others passed, all to be seen & make us feel bad, I suppose," he wrote.[12]

According to a letter by Charles W. Phelps of Company D, 13 men from Company K left the regiment and transferred into "Griffin's battery," part of the artillery assigned to their division. Others from his company joined a federal cavalry regiment. Phelps himself was thinking about transferring to the navy, but ended up staying with the 4th Michigan. As the men of 4th Michigan went through the rituals of camp life, Col. Jonathan Childs wrote to Gov. Austin Blair, forwarding to him a list of names of officers and men whom he wished to promote and who would therefore need commissions from the governor. "The men whom I have recommended are competent and very worthy," the colonel wrote. "They have nobly done their duty throughout the campaigns and bravely earned their promotions upon the field of battle." He said that many in the 4th Michigan had proved themselves brave, and he added a cautionary note: "[I]n many instances it has been difficult to determine whom to recommend."[13]

Some winter clothes and equipment began to reach the soldiers, and late in October the Army of the Potomac started moving out in a too-late pursuit of Lee. The Michigan soldiers waited, getting the order to march late on October 30 and moving towards Harper's Ferry with their corps, bivouacking in the cold. The marches were sometimes long and the days hot over the course of the next week as they moved south into the Shenandoah Mountains after the Confederate army, but the diaries of the 4th Michigan show there were days when the regiment didn't move at all. The men at times heard firing in the distance and the soldiers foraged sheep and apples and other produce from the local farmers. "Plenty meat to eat," Irvin Miner of Company F noted on November 2, "but it was stolen from the citizens by our boys." By November 7, it was snowing hard as the men marched to a town called White Plains. But the pursuit of the Rebels was effectively over. Within two more days the Union army was gathering in camps around the town of Warrenton.[14]

Now the soldiers began to hear what much of the officer corps had just been told: McClellan had been relieved of command. Lincoln believed he'd given McClellan every chance and all necessary support to take the war to the Confederates, but the general refused and Lee's army had withdrawn across the Rappahannock without being seriously challenged. Miner learned of the general's removal when he was on guard duty near his colonel's tent. "The report is that McClellan is removed from his command," he wrote in his diary. "Great indignation is shown on account." Word of the dismissal spread through the camps. The next day there was large review as McClellan said good-bye to his men, some who alternately shed tears and then cheered him. Many officers and men of the Fifth Corps were particularly angry about McClellan's replacement with Gen. George Burnside. George Millens called that move "ridiculous." Sergeant Bancroft noted the officers were deeply affected when they said good-bye to their beloved commander on November 11: "Officers of Porter's Corps meet to shake hands with Gen. McClellan. Never were they so disheartened with the aspect of affairs." Edward Taylor, a Democrat, agreed, writing "the blow struck consternation among us all."

"Many a poor soldier of the old Army cried at the announcement and when he rode along the lines looking even more splendid than ever, tho' sad, very sad," Taylor continued. He was furious with the Radical Republicans who called McClellan "slow and inactive" and demanded a winter campaign against the Confederacy. Such an offensive would mean misery and death from exposure, and Taylor, like other Democratic soldiers, questioned why the Fifth Corps—Fitz John Porter's corps—hadn't been given the all winter clothing, tents and supplies they all needed. "One could wish the Army turned loose upon the North," he wrote bitterly, "for there are our worst enemies."

If the men of the Fifth Corps were angry about the dismissal of McClellan, they were no happier when their corps commander, Fitz John Porter, left them the next day. Porter had also been removed and was going back to Washington to face charges by the failed Gen. John Pope in connection with the Second Battle of Bull Run. Because Porter was so closely connected with McClellan, his army career would soon be destroyed. Gen. Joseph Hooker, a critic of McClellan, now took over the Fifth Corps, though this would turn out to be a temporary command when Burnside's new organization of the army went into effect. "Our corps is pretty down about their taking Porter away," Millens wrote. "No Porter, no McClellan [—] we fear the results." Irvin Miner wrote that the atmosphere in the army had been gloomy at McClellan's removal, but that "the gloom thickens" with the dismissal of Porter.[15]

Lt. William F. Robinson's thoughts on the removal of McClellan and Porter reflected the sentiment of many soldiers—while they were concerned the Radical Republicans were "politicizing" the war, most soldiers were generally willing to give their new commanders a chance. "I may be mistaken but I am sadly afraid that Father Abraham has lost his wits but time will tell," the officer wrote. "[I]t may be for the best but we cannot see it. We are willing to give him [Burnside] a trial and abide by what he says as long as he makes no blunders. I had the honor of personally shaking hands with Geo. B. McClellan and bidding him 'good bye,['] it seemed more like attending a funeral of some dearly beloved friend than anything else that I can compare it to."[16]

It turned out these Union soldiers were right to be concerned, for Burnside was perhaps the worst general to lead them in the Civil War. Even then, he was planning to move his army southeast to the town Fredericksburg. There, the general proposed, he would cross the Rappahannock River and force Lee's army to fight.

Within the 4th Michigan, a problem between the top officers now reached a surprising juncture. Early in November, Col. Jonathan Childs quietly turned in his resignation to his superior officers, citing "unexpected and urgent circumstances of a private nature having transpired within a few days." What these circumstances were he didn't say, but Brig. Gen. Charles Griffin, forwarding Childs's resignation, urged his commanders to accept it on the grounds it was "absolutely necessary for the interest and harmony of the regiment." Hardly had the regiment arrived in Warrenton a few days later when Childs notified Gov. Austin Blair of his resignation. Childs said he was resigning because of what he described as "strong suspicions [and] dissatisfaction manifested on the part of several officers as to my course in recommending for your approval several persons for promotions."

Childs left much unsaid in what was likely a surprising letter to the governor. The Union army, he explained, would soon be engaging in a major battle, and it was essential that there be harmony within the 4th Michigan. "And to establish that in this Regiment," the colonel wrote, "it is evident *one* of *two* officers should resign. And it is from the purest motive that I am willing to make the sacrifice."

Why did the commander of his regiment believe he had to resign in this disagreement with one of his officers? Probably because it was this particular unnamed officer, and not Childs, who held the upper hand. Officers and men who commented on this matter over the course of the next two or three weeks would say Childs was facing a court-martial, so he had no choice but to resign. Though the nature of this controversy remains obscure, it appears as though Lt. Col. George Lumbard instigated a court-martial against Childs, the man who had requested that Lumbard be his second in command.

While Childs was leaving rather than face military trial, he may have got a measure of satisfaction when, in the weeks ahead, Capt. Harrison H. Jeffords of the Dexter area was commissioned the next colonel of the 4th Michigan—not Lumbard. It was a matter of several weeks before Jeffords took command of the regiment, and it may be that Childs recommended him for command. Jeffords's commission as colonel would date from Childs's resignation late in November, and he would be promoted "over" Lumbard. But what caused Childs to resign? Childs spoke of disputes and dissatisfaction over his choices for promotion within the regiment. But a War Department official would write years later that there was evidence that Childs had been drinking heavily during the fall of 1862, and affidavits by men who served with him said he'd been sick and in pain. The threat of a facing an embarrassing court-martial for this may have been enough for Childs to leave. An ex-soldier from the regiment, Jerome Allen of Elkhart, Indiana, later stated that Jonathan Childs "was asked to resign, [but he was] a good officer otherwise."[17]

General Burnside quickly reorganized the Union army into a system of "grand divisions," each made up to two army corps. The Fifth Corps was placed in what was called "the Center Grand Division" along with the Sixth Corps, and this huge unit was commanded by Gen. Joseph Hooker. Gen. Daniel Butterfield, senior division commander in the Fifth Corps, became the new corps commander. Because Gen. George W. Morell of the First Division of this corps was transferred in this reorganization, Gen. Charles Griffin, the tough artillerist and brigade commander, now became commander of the Fifth Corps' First Division.

The men of the regiment sometimes did guard duty in the town of Warrenton, and often passed off worthless, old, locally issued Michigan banknotes to sutlers, local merchants, and farmers who had livestock, food, and goods to sell, but who didn't want federal "greenback" dollars. The soldiers called these valueless notes "spooney," wrote Dr. Chamberlain. They were happy to use these authentic-looking bills to purchase food, tobacco, and other items since it had been months since they'd been paid. Miner used spooney to buy his dinner. "Had turkey for dinner that I bought with Erie & Kalamazoo," he wrote at Warrenton, probably with a smile. Lieutenant Robinson wrote that the soldiers were also passing off "facsimiles of Southern scrip, which they can get in Philadelphia for 25 cts a hat full." While it might not look good for soldiers to do this, he admitted, Union generals "do not bother themselves much to find out whether good or bad money is passed, and I say it is not wrong when they [Virginia residents] refuse to take Uncle Sams paper, to let them have something that they will take."

The soldiers stripped local barns and houses of wood and bricks, incorrectly figuring that the Army of the Potomac was soon going into winter camp and they would need these materials to build weatherproof quarters. But then the Union army was ordered to begin a march toward Fredericksburg, about 25 miles away as Burnside's plan was put into effect. Two days later, November 17, the 4th Michigan with its corps rose and broke camp at about 3:00 A.M. and started on the march. There was a heavy mist that soaked the men's blankets and packs, and in the afternoon it rained. Lt. John Bancroft was sick, but pressed on anyway. They covered slightly more than 10 miles and bivouacked in the woods. The march resumed the next morning in a drizzling rain that made the road slippery, Irvin Miner complained.[18]

The road ahead was so jammed with troops and equipment that the regiment had to wait in the rain all morning on November 19, and at least some of the men served as rear guard as the column trudged through the mud toward Fredericksburg. The 4th Michigan moved only a few miles and camped in the cold, wet countryside. "I don't see how we are a-going to advance after the rain commences," complained George Millens. This slow march continued in the rain through woods, hills, and swamps until the entire army was gathered near Falmouth on November 23. Here they formed new encampments. Supplies ran low, so there were times when the men didn't even have enough hard crackers to keep hunger at bay on nights when the temperature dropped. "Awful cold last night," Miner wrote that night. "I never suffered so much with the cold in my life." He, too, fell ill.[19]

The men of the regiment, like other soldiers, did picket and guard duty and got their camp in order. The slow, sodden move down from Warrenton was proof, they felt, that the season for marching and fighting was over. Yet General Burnside intended to launch a new offensive across the Rappahannock, and diaries and letters suggest that many officers at the regimental level understood this. The change in the leadership of the 4th Michigan now took place with the resignation of Col. Jonathan W. Childs, who had started out as the regiment's major and become its commander after the death of Woodbury. He went around the camp and bid his men goodbye on November 28 and departed the next day. Childs led boldly in the short time he'd had charge of the regiment—his command and example had been confident and brave when the regiment had crossed the Potomac at the Shepherdstown Ford under fire. But the colonel had done something that left him vulnerable to charges of some sort. Lt. William F. Robinson knew that Childs was going to resign a good two weeks before the colonel actually left the regiment. Robinson mentioned this matter to his father.

"I shall not resign at present[,]" Robinson wrote, "the reason why is to be a secret between us, so here goes[:] Charges have been preferred against Col. Childs and rather than stand a Court Martial he is going to resign and when we get a head to our regt. Things will be regulated[.] Now do not mention this to a live person as I would do nothing to injure him and none need ever know that charges were preferred against him." Other soldiers knew what happened, but said nothing of the details. Edward H. C. Taylor mentioned Childs in passing in a letter sent early in

1863 to his mother: "He has resigned and gone home," Taylor wrote. "He was not liked as well as Woodbury."[20]

For the record, Childs's widow years later got a statement about her husband's health from Dr. John Watts, an Adrian physician who joined the 4th Michigan late in the summer of 1862 as "second assistant surgeon." Watts wrote that Childs had been bedridden with a severe case of pleurisy on October 1, yet a few days later the colonel had gone with the regiment "on a forward movement in a weak & debilitated condition." Watts recalled that in December 1862, near Fredericksburg, "I was informed Col. J.W. Childs had resigned on acct. of physical disability." But in fact Childs made no reference to his health in his explanation to Governor Blair. Men who served under him later gave statements that Childs had indeed been sick with a kidney ailment and pleurisy and troubled by back pain during the fall of 1862, but there were also statements given that, as one War Department official later put it, Childs "drank to a considerable degree at this period and went on occasional sprees." In any event, Childs's resignation from the 4th Michigan didn't end his military service. He later became a captain in the 2nd U.S. Colored Troop Regiment and served until early in 1866. Whatever Childs had done, even enlisted men in the 4th Michigan were aware he had no choice but to leave. George Millens of Company B noted in his diary that there were charges pending against the colonel that would have been heard had he not resigned. This left Lt. Col. George Lumbard from Hillsdale County in charge of the regiment, for the time being.[21]

Union supply lines were not all worked out by the point the army had reached the Falmouth area. Provisions would now come by way of the Potomac River to the Aquia Creek landing and then overland, by train on the Richmond, Fredericksburg & Potomac line. There were days when the soldiers went hungry, with only a hardtack or two to eat. Even on Thanksgiving Day, men complained about not having enough, though it seems that those attached to the First Division headquarters staff got coffee, soup, and fresh beef. Dr. Chamberlain wrote that hungry soldiers shouted "hardtack!" when a quartermaster passed by the regiment. Writing home, he also addressed the issue of the soldiers' feeling about the removal of their top generals. "The question is frequently asked, 'How do you like the removal of McClellan?'" the doctor said. "The answer has as often been given; We did not like it. But what of that? Suppose we do not like it? We are not fighting for Gen. McClellan or any other man. We are fighting for our county, and the maintenance of its laws, authority and institutions. Because we could not have the man we like best for a commander is no reason why we should lay down our arms."[22]

The nights were bitter and fair days fewer as November turned to December. Adequate food shipments and winter clothing and supplies began arriving, and the men of the 4th Michigan did picket duty at a place called Stoneman's Switch or Stoneman's Station on the railroad, where a Union supply depot was growing. The men suffered in the cold rain and snow; some soldiers on picket built shelters and got huge bonfires going to keep from freezing. The night of December 7 was so cold that a wagon's wheels froze solidly to the ground, Irvin Miner insisted, and the cold and illness took lives.

It was by now common knowledge among the men that Confederate forces were gathered on the west side of the Rappahannock at the old town of Fredericksburg. Charles W. Phelps wrote his brother, summing up the situation. "We are in camp at present pretty near Fredricksburg but the [Rebels] hold the place[.] I don't know whether we are a going to try to cross here[.] There is a large army." Phelps, perhaps thinking of the miserable conditions he and his comrades faced, warned his brother not to join the service. But there was worse to come. By December 8 and 9, word began to spread among the soldiers that they would soon be on the march. Men were dismayed that they would be leaving the camp where they'd fixed up their tents with off-the-ground foundations and floors and fireplaces, but on December 10, the 4th Michigan got its marching orders along with the brigade and division.[23]

These orders specified the men have three days' rations in their haversacks and be ready to march. The soldiers were allowed to retire to their tents until 3:30 A.M. the next morning. The men of the 4th Michigan ate a hurried breakfast and were soon on the muddy road to the Rappahannock with thousands of others. In short order they heard cannon fire in the distance, and the sun slowly rose over the trees. After a few hours their part of the column arrived near Falmouth on the river. Across the water lay Fredericksburg.

Burnside's plan had been for the Union army to march down from Warrenton and quickly surprise Lee by crossing the river on pontoon bridges. But the bridges hadn't arrived in anything like a timely fashion. As a result, the Confederates knew for days that the Army of the Potomac was on the east side of the river. On the morning of December 11, many Union engineering personnel were killed and wounded as they attempted to build the bridges, shot by Rebel rifleman firing from the buildings of Fredericksburg. Union guns opened up on the town, smashing buildings and setting them on fire, but still the Confederate soldiers kept firing from hiding places in the wreckage. Soldiers from a New York regiment and the 7th Michigan Infantry climbed into boats and crossed the river to drive the Confederates out. They and other Union troops did so in fierce house-to-house fighting, allowing the engineers to complete their bridges over the Rappahannock. Soldiers quickly began crossing into Fredericksburg from the eastern bank, and they ransacked the town.[24]

But only part of Union army got across before nightfall. "Our division went into camp on this [the eastern] side of the river, and the night passed off without anything worthy of note," wrote Major Randolph of the 4th Michigan. The regiment bivouacked with its division in the fields near a place where the generals made their headquarters called the Phillips House.[25]

On the Confederate side of the Rappahannock outside of Fredericksburg, Lee's entire army was digging in or already positioned on high ground, forming a strong defensive line with scores of cannon, waiting for Burnside's attack. A sunken road that lay at the base of the ridge called Marye's Heights, just west of town, provided Rebel infantry with a perfect trench. Above the road on the hills, Confederate gunners could see the approach from Fredericksburg. Their defenses stretched for miles in a rough semicircle, north to south, around the town.

The next morning, December 12, the brigade and division of which the 4th Michigan was part shifted closer to the Rappahannock. Their Second Brigade was under the command of Col. Jacob B. Sweitzer, a Pennsylvanian. Thousands of soldiers began crossing the river on the bridges into Fredericksburg. "Our troops have been crossing all day," George Millens wrote in his diary. "We have not crossed yet but are ready." Company F's Irvin Miner agreed that the men were set to go over a pontoon bridge, but Rebel shelling caused officers to have them lie down near the cover of ruins of a nearby railroad trestle. The cannon sounded all day, the soldiers waiting as Burnside finalized his plans. That night the 4th Michigan fell back about a half-mile and bivouacked in a cold, muddy field. Henry Seage shared blankets with his father, Chaplain John Seage, trying to keep warm. Lt. John Bancroft noted that the moon shone down that night as the guns roared.[26]

Fredericksburg

The men of the regiment were awakened at 4:00 A.M. on December 13, a day that would turn out to be one of the worst in the history of the Army of the Potomac. A friend of Henry Seage's in Company E, Artemus C. Todd, 20, had died of disease two days before at hospital that had been set up a short distance away at Falmouth. Now in the chill of the morning, Seage's father sold off Todd's possessions. By the time the sun was rising over the hills around eight o'clock, the cannon resumed firing. "The Rebels have not left yet, but are back some ways from the river," George Millens noted. The colonels of the Second Brigade of the First Division, Fifth Corps, were called to Colonel Sweitzer's tent about nine o'clock for their orders: Their regiments had to be ready to get across the bridge, move into Fredericksburg, and be in line of battle, all within 40 minutes of the command to move out.[27]

The soldiers waited for that order as the Union artillery continued to pound Rebel positions. From high ground on the east side of the Rappahannock, many saw what was going on. At 11:30 A.M., troops of the Second Corps marched west out of Fredericksburg, driving off Confederate skirmishers and heading across the open ground that slowly inclined to the hills about a half-mile from town. Scores of these Union soldiers fell dead and wounded as Rebel gunners on Marye's Heights opened up. As the surviving men pressed on and reached the base of the hill, Confederate infantry behind the Stone Wall at the sunken road let loose with volley after volley, killing and wounding scores more. "Our brigade on this side of the river could distinctly see all the movements on the opposite side, and it was awfully grand, but terrible," wrote Major Randolph.

Now it was time for the 4th Michigan's division and corps to cross into the town. "About 1 P.M. the order came for our division to fall in," Randolph continued. "In a few minutes we were ready. Our regiment led—Lieut. Col. G[eorge] W. Lumbard commanding, and in less time than I can write it, we were on our way." The soldiers filed down to the river, waited, and moved forward, marching across the pontoon bridge. All the while shot and shell from Union guns "screamed through the air like so many demons" over their heads. Some said the crossing by the elements of their Fifth Corps began after 1:00 P.M., with some soldiers not getting over to Fredericksburg until much later in the afternoon. Edward H. C. Taylor wrote a quick note to his mother. "A battle is going on and our Div. is just going in," he wrote. "Our troops are in Fredericksburg. . . . We have lost heavily and have a hard position to gain. We hope for the best. I never felt less like a fight than now." Yet Taylor was sure that his division would take the Rebel positions—if not this day, then the next.[28]

Around the same time that the regiment was crossing with Sweitzer's Second Brigade into Fredericksburg and Union soldiers were fighting and dying in the fields, a second part of General Burnside's plan was under way less than three miles downriver. There a division of Union soldiers marched forward to engage the Confederates. Hundreds of them were hit by Rebel cannon and

HUDSON MUSEUM

Marching toward Confederate positions along the Sunken Road just outside of Fredericksburg on Dec, 13, 1862, the 4th Michigan comes under fire from infantry and artillery. Drawing by Lt. Charles Gruner.

infantry fire, but they pushed forward and engaged them in a close-quarters rifle battle. These Union troops would soon be driven back in terrible fighting.

Back in Fredericksburg, the men of the 4th Michigan's First Division and others from their corps filled the streets, waiting for the order to advance. An account by Henry Seage suggested the men had time to poke through the buildings, most of which had been hit by artillery. "Not a house escapes the prying eyes of our soldiers," he wrote. "Costly pianos were used to cook our coffee. Beautiful oil paintings were hung on the line of stacked arms." Soldiers dragged furniture outside, took a seat, and looked at pilfered books. Dr. Chamberlain said Fredericksburg had been "an aristocratic and wealthy town," its dwellings built with more taste and comfort than any town he'd seen in the South. But the impact of the shelling was amazing. "When I saw the destruction of Sharpsburg, Md., I thought that was complete," he wrote. "But it was only child's play compared to this." An order came for men to clear out several houses for use as hospitals; Chamberlain said that everything in these residences was smashed to pieces.[29]

There was also time for a mistake that sent the some of the soldiers of the 4th Michigan back to the east side of the Rappahannock River. Henry Seage, after noting in his diary the regiment had crossed over to Fredericksburg about 2:00 P.M., then stated: "came back again & countermarched again." Years later, in a small history of Company E, Seage explained that he and others returned to the Falmouth side of the river because of "mistaken orders." How many soldiers this involved is not clear. But Seage wrote that an aide to the division commander, a Lieutenant Ross, galloped after the wayward soldiers, calling them "damned cowards." Seage's father, though a practicing minister, was furious at this insult, calling Ross a "drunken liar." These soldiers of the 4th Michigan went back over the bridge to Fredericksburg, rejoining their command.[30]

The order came for their First Division to move forward to a position just outside of town.

To the troops, it seemed as if the artillery opened up on them as they became visible to Rebel gunners on the heights. The 4th Michigan filed around an old brickyard followed by the 9th Massachusetts, the 62nd Pennsylvania, the 32nd Massachusetts, and the 14th New York. Here was a brook or a "mill race," and as the men lay down to escape the artillery fire, they filled their canteens, Major Randolph wrote. Lieutenant Colonel Lumbard, impatient to advance, walked over and asked Colonel Sweitzer three times over the course of several minutes for permission to go into battle. A soldier from the 118th Pennsylvania, thinking that Lumbard was leaving because he was afraid to make the attack, started to draw his pistol on the lieutenant colonel, but some men from the 4th Michigan grabbed this soldier, handling him roughly until officers intervened.[31]

About 3:00 P.M. the First Brigade of their division moved out to support and relieve other Union outfits that were being beaten back by Rebel artillery and infantry. Major Randolph wrote that he saw hundreds of Union troops advance, only to be shot down. "[T]he brave fellows fell by scores in almost every rod of the road," Randolph wrote. "The sight was horrible and one I hope I may never see again." The soldiers of the 4th Michigan waited, crouching or flat on the ground. About an hour after the First Brigade advanced into the fight, the division commander, General Griffin, received orders to send the rest of his men forward to carry the Rebel works. Griffin reported that a brigade from another division would go with them. Colonel Sweitzer was on horseback, as were his aides. One of them was Lt. George Yates of the 4th Michigan. Sweitzer took off his hat and waved it above his head. "Second Brigade, forward—double quick—march!" he shouted. The soldiers cheered and hustled up a small hill and into the open. Immediately men began to fall, hit by gunfire, along their brigade's line.[32]

Major Randolph, the acting lieutenant colonel of the 4th Michigan, commanded the right wing of the regiment, while Capt. Harrison Jeffords, who had been in charge of Company C since May, commanded the left. Henry Seage later wrote that as other troops advanced and fought up ahead near the Stone Wall, the Second Brigade reached a little ravine or depression that afforded them some protection from the Rebel guns. Sweitzer's men lay down. But there was no way for Union soldiers in front of them to fight in the open for very long while exposed to the heavy fire. Finally these men turned and retreated. Seage wrote that General Griffin was on the field and saw what was happening, ordering the Second Brigade to remain in place and not let the retreating soldiers disrupt them. "Lie still, boys, and let them pass through," he ordered, according to Seage's Fredericksburg account, and the fleeing soldiers jumped over the rows of prone men, heading back to town. Now it was the Second Brigade's turn to attack. By some reports, it was 4:00 P.M. or later.

Colonel Sweitzer rode to the front of his brigade and ordered the charge. Captain Robinson said Sweitzer swung his sword in the air, shouting, "Come on, boys, there is nothing here that will hurt us!" The men rose to their feet, again cheering, and moved quickly up the slight ascent. This land was open until it reached to a kind of embankment or berm—the sort that struck Randolph as typical of the crests or elevated mounds on which Virginia fences were built, while Seage and others described it as an unfinished railroad ditch and embankment and even an old canal. Another 500 feet or so beyond this berm was the sunken, stone-lined road where the Confederate infantry was firing.[33]

"As we reached the crest of the hill, the leaden and iron ball was awful and many a brave one fell," Maj. Randolph wrote. "But quickly closing up our broken ranks, we marched into that terrible fire." Henry Seage agreed that the troops advanced over bloody ground. "[W]hat a sight! Over the bodies of headless, armless, legless, disfigured men we pass," he wrote in a memoir of the battle. "To the right and to the left are the lifeless forms of the slain! Oh! What a sacrifice! . . . But on we go, with a yell." The winter sun was dropping behind the hills and there was much smoke drifting over the field, but as their line pressed on toward the base of Marye's Heights, the Confederate gunners saw them and redoubled their fire. Seage wrote that as the soldiers reached the embankment, they found a ditch filled with water. "If we succeed in crossing the ditch, then the stone wall must be scaled, then the batteries above must be taken at the point of the bayonet," he said in his memoir of the battle. "All this flashes through our minds and we know that with our terribly thinned ranks and without support this is impossible."[34]

The soldiers therefore flattened themselves on this low ground, he wrote in his account of the battle, "and refuse to make further useless effort." In his Company E history, based largely on his diary, he gave a similar description. "[We] went into fight in the 'horse shoe;' got as far as old canal and laid down. Kept up constant fire all day." His words "old canal" apparently referred to the ditch created by the berm, something he also referred to as the unfinished railroad in his paper on the battle. Major Randolph also described the men throwing themselves down behind the berm running parallel to the Stone Wall.[35]

Though most of the men of the 4th Michigan were on the ground, firing at the Confederate infantry, Randolph wrote that some soldiers stood up to take their best shots. "In a short time we were ordered to relieve the regiment on our front," he said. "As they fell back, our men took their places and we opened fire on the enemy. And the men were ordered to keep down as much as they could. But as they became more and more excited they would get up and take deliberate aim as though they were shooting squirrel." Officers were also exposed. Lieutenant Yates suffered multiple wounds when a shell exploded in the stomach of his horse, throwing him to the ground. "The rebels have got a very strong fortification here," wrote Charles Phelps about the fight at the Sunken Road; "when we went in we were under a heavy fire of both musketry and artillery." This was the climax for the battle for the 4th Michigan and their brigade. Though darkness was falling, the Confederates could see the flashes of the Union rifles. The 4th Michigan's new acting adjutant, Lt. James Clark, from the Ann Arbor area, walked over to his comrades in Company D, urging them to keep their front rank filled. "One of the boys told him to keep down, or he would be hit," Randolph said. "The words were hardly out of his mouth when a musket ball struck poor Jimmy on the third button of his overcoat, glanced to the left and went directly through him."

Another Ann Arbor soldier, Corporal Fred Wildt, was also hit and killed instantly. Edward H. C. Taylor of Company A described the Confederate fire as "murderous." Walter C. White, 28, his friend and tent mate from Hudson, died as he lay on the ground. A bullet or projectile struck him in the top of his head. Others had close calls. Lt. Michael Vreeland of Company I, who been promoted from sergeant earlier in the fall, had his forage cap blown off his head. When he picked it back up, there was a jagged tear of a projectile through the top.[36]

The firing tailed off. Though the fighting was over, the men of the 4th Michigan and other regiments of their division, spread across the field, were not withdrawn. Exhausted, they would spend the night, literally holding the ground in the bitter cold. "Into the smoke and dust of battle," Lt. John Bancroft wrote. "Words cannot tell. We lost but few men but there are many on the field dead and dying." Bancroft was correct. Regimental losses were reported at nine killed, 41 wounded, and one missing, but the death toll would rise in the days after that battle as men who'd been severely wounded died. In all, 14 men from the 4th Michigan would be tabulated as killed or mortally wounded. This was low compared the casualties suffered by regiments that had attacked the Confederates in broad daylight—the 4th Michigan, though having taken part in a disastrous battle, was fortunate to be among the last soldiers sent in, as evening and darkness settled over the smoky field. More than 7,000 Union soldiers had been killed or wounded or were missing.

A bad night was now in store for those who survived. The soldiers, who had to leave their knapsacks behind, spent the night without tents or campfires or blankets on that spot in the bloody field below Marye's Heights. "The living laid down with the dead," Randolph wrote, "and thus they slept." Lieutenant Bancroft said sleep wasn't possible: "Lay all night on the cold damp ground, hearing the groans and calls of the wounded. Too cold to sleep." George W. Millens noted that they spent the night lying in mud.[37]

Lt. William F. Robinson said some of the corpses on the battlefield were covered with blankets after night fell. But since the surviving soldiers didn't have their packs with them, some shared the dead men's blankets. Others warmed their cold hands and their ears by pressing them against the still-warm carcasses of horses. But if that seemed macabre, he wrote, it was nothing compared "the groans of the wounded and the dying"—men calling for water and for help.

The 4th Michigan, like other regiments that spent the night on the field, was resupplied with ammunition for what some figured would be the terrible continuation of the battle the next day, but thankfully that did not happen. As the sun came up across the river behind them, thousands of men, both dead and alive, still covered the field. There was some periodic sharpshooter firing and skirmish fire, but if the Union soldiers did not get up, they were reasonably safe. "We were protected by a little rise of ground," Phelps wrote of their situation, "if we laid down we had to lay flat all day until dark." Perhaps no man's diary expressed that day, December 14, as succinctly as Lieutenant Bancroft's. "Sunday 14th 1862," he wrote. "Battle of Fredericksburg. Sharpshooting all day. Lay low all day. Almost every man who stood up is shot. How would you like it? five regiments lying close to the ground and have to lay there all day long—waiting—for what—thinking of what? on that bright December day—home and church and friends. Nothing to eat save what we have. No coffee or meat. No orders all day."[38]

"Sunday morning [Dec. 14] dawned upon us," wrote Maj. Randolph. "The rebels during the night had dug some pits for their sharpshooters, and if one of our men showed his head a dozen bullets would be after him." The men wondered whether they would be ordered to get up and resume the attack on the Confederate position, which would result in even greater numbers of casualties. But General Burnside had been dissuaded from making a further assault on the heights. George Millens of Company B wrote that "we are still upon the front skirmishing," but strictly from a prone position. "We lay flat on our faces." Irvin Miner of Company F said that they kept up the skirmish "fire all day." The hours passed slowly by, the men unable to get up. Finally, the sun began to set, and the men began to understand that they would live for at least another night. They were not going to be sent in again to attack the strong Rebel defenses. As night fell, the soldiers noticed a peculiar curtain of light in the sky, a "splendid Aurora Borealis in the evening," John Bancroft noted. Still they waited. George Millens wrote in his diary that it was 10:00 P.M.—Henry Seage said 11:00 P.M.—when other troops came up to relieve them in front of the Stone Wall. The 4th Michigan men moved out, back down the sloping fields into Fredericksburg. With the rest of their brigade and division, the hungry soldiers drew rations in the darkness, and some men made their way through the town to try to get their knapsacks. Someone in the command structure of the Union army had the sense to provide a ration of whiskey to these men. "Lay down," Lieutenant Bancroft wrote in his journal that night of December 14, "and sleep in the streets near the railroad."[39]

Though gunfire would continue through the next day, the battle of Fredericksburg was over.

CHAPTER 8

Three Cheers for Colonel Jeffords

THE BATTLE HAD BEEN A DISASTER FOR THE UNION ARMY. "I SHOULD NOT BE SURPRISED IF THEY (the Confederacy) was recognized," Charles Phelps of Company D wrote his brother after Fredericksburg. "[T]hey ought to have their independence for they have worked hard enough for it." Like other soldiers, Phelps expressed a diminishing faith in his government and leaders. Was the sacrifice of so many men worth it, what with the poor leadership that had been inflicted on them? "Our leading men are the biggest rascals we have," he wrote. "They dont care a d——m as long as they can get a big name and their pockets lined. I am not going to worry my self about the things. [The Union] may go to Hell if I get out all right and that is the general feeling among the men."

Edward H. C. Taylor, Democrat and McClellan supporter, called Gen. Ambrose Burnside a "poor weak-minded fool" who sent the Union army in to be slaughtered. Taylor had begun to think that the army's defeats under Pope and Burnside were intentional—that Radical Republicans who influenced Lincoln's administration wanted the conflict to drag on until they could make the abolition of slavery the policy and goal of the U.S. government. Lincoln's Emancipation Proclamation, a critical first step in the ending of slavery, fueled the conspiratorial view held by

Taylor. He ascribed the earlier defeats of McClellan not to the general's failures, but to interference by the Lincoln administration.[1]

On December 15, a day after their withdrawal from the battlefield, soldiers of the 4th Michigan like George Millens and Henry Seage said the men "laid around" Fredericksburg. Irvin Miner wondered if they would be ordered to resume the attack, but instead Union soldiers continued ransacking the town. Confederate artillery fired into Fredericksburg that night and Seage later wrote that several brick structures were knocked down, injuring many men. But at some point that evening the regiment moved toward the river, with the troops trying to find relatively undamaged rooms. It was the first time that Lieutenant Bancroft had slept in a house since June 1, when he'd left Washington after duty with the balloon service. For the average soldier in the regiment, it had been even longer since he had a real roof over his head.

That night the Army of the Potomac began the withdrawal. Early on the morning of December 16, the 4th Michigan crossed one of the pontoon bridges to the eastern side of the Rappahannock. Rain began to fall and there was an order to halt and bivouac at the place where they'd spent the night before the battle, but soon came the order to return to their old camp near Stoneman's Switch. They packed up their tents once more and marched several miles on through the mud with thousands of other soldiers. When they arrived, the men found their old winter quarters had been stripped, while they were gone, of all the boards and beams.[2]

Quickly the soldiers set about building new quarters, cutting more wood, gathering stone, and putting up fireplaces. This work continued for the next few days as more bitter cold descended. Yet there were still periodic days of warm weather that turned camp streets and the parade ground into acres of mud. One of the more curious events was that in Company E—the company that had gone astray back across the Rappahannock before going into battle at Fredericksburg—a "court of inquiry" was held by noncommissioned officers on a charge of cowardice against Sgt. Charles J. Fletcher of Hillsdale County, who, records show, had been wounded in action in the battle. According to Henry Seage's diary, these sergeants and corporals found Fletcher guilty and reduced him in rank, though he would regain his stripes in the spring of 1864.

Lieutenant Bancroft, who'd been assigned to Company K, was now reassigned to his old company, I. On Christmas Day he noted that the camp had been "trimmed up," and Dr. Chamberlain joked that instead of just having "pork and hardtack" they would instead have "hardtack and pork." But accounts of the 4th Michigan's fare for the holiday suggest it wasn't really that bad. Edward H. C. Taylor felt that "Christmas dinner was a sumptuous one for a soldier"—roast beef, baked beans, potatoes, jam, biscuits, and pie. But good food wasn't enough to lift George Millens's spirits—he felt that it was "a lonesome Christmas." Nothing was going on, he wrote, except "the officers are having a tight [drinking party] upon Uncle Sams whiskey."[3]

The routine of winter camp was less than two weeks old and the year was coming to a close when the division of which the 4th Michigan was part went on a reconnaissance to try to intercept Confederate cavalry raiders. On the afternoon of December 30 the First Division of the Fifth Corps and other Union forces marched 10 or more miles northwest to a place called Hartwood Church near the Rappahannock River. The Second Brigade marched even further—these soldiers and an artillery battery continued on to a point on the river called Deep Creek. The men of the 4th Michigan recorded that this was a march of somewhere between 15 and 18 miles. They halted for the night at 10:00 P.M., the soldiers on guard or otherwise bivouacking in the mud. Henry Seage hadn't been well, and he fell out, exhausted. He and soldiers Tip Burnett and Philip Stanback shared a tent about a mile away from the rest of the regiment.

The next day elements of the First Division clashed with Confederate troopers at some of the river fords, but the 4th Michigan and the Second Brigade did not. They continued marching before daylight, with no breakfast, and moved several more miles up the river. Here they got orders to return to their old winter camp. It was late on the last night of the year when they got back, having marched nearly 50 miles in a little over 24 hours, with only six hours rest. Irvin Miner complained that they were "tired, hungry and sore." The point of the mission had been to cut off the retreat of a cavalry incursion by J. E. B. Stuart, but they'd been 24 hours too late. "And thus ends the year, '62," Miner continued. "May we be more successful in the next." One of Henry Seage's friends, a soldier named Burt, happened to have a bottle of Jamaican rum ("which tasted bully," Seage wrote), so the men had their supper and celebrated the coming of 1863.[4]

The New Year began for some of the Michigan officers and men as a continuation of the drinking that had gone on the night before. The day was relatively warm and fine and the soldiers underwent inspection and drill. Miner, his half-brother Austin, and a friend named Henry Beal from Company C cooked up dinner for Company F. There was still alcohol around. "Several of the company got quite mellow over the contents of three canteens of whisky," he wrote. Henry Seage, who had been promoted to corporal after Fredericksburg, recorded that many men in his company also did more tippling. "Boys most all tyght [*sic*] in Co.," he wrote.

Lincoln's Emancipation Proclamation, granting freedom to all people held as slaves in Confederate states and territories, went into effect that day, and diaries and letters from men of the 4th Michigan reflected their feelings on the issue. Edward Taylor, a Democrat who maintained he and most Union soldiers were fighting for the restoration of the country and not for abolition, expressed anger about the proclamation. He was furious that the loyalty of Democratic soldiers was questioned by Radical Republicans, even though they'd been fighting for the United States since the outset of the war. "Still[,] because the Negro is not our God we are no patriots," he complained, sarcastically, of the Radical Republican view, but "almost as 'bad as the traitors of the south.'" Many soldiers thought slavery was morally wrong and understood that it was the cause of the war, but racial prejudice caused them to believe that blacks shouldn't be treated as equals. Yet accounts of the Union army show that while the proclamation wasn't popular, most soldiers accepted it, thought it just, and hoped it would help the war effort. Luke Barnes of Company C, probably 22 years old from St. Joseph County, reflected this attitude: "[A]s for President Lincolns Proclamation, I don't like it very much but maybe it is all right [—] may God grant it so to be."[5]

Barnes, writing to a brother at home, said he was reasonably healthy, though he admitted he was suffering from "a bad diahrea which keeps me on the trot a good share of my time." That was common. "The shits is something that a soldier is seldom rid of and a great many die of it," he explained. Barnes was also feeling very blue, perhaps from what would today be called depression or even post-traumatic stress. Barnes had shot and killed one of his own officers, Capt. Abram R. Wood, by mistake while on picket near Yorktown. Though Barnes said nothing about this incident in his letter, he was troubled. On one hand he tried to live a Christian life, yet he said he had been "wicked" and "prone to sin." He expressed concern about his older brother Joel in Company K. Luke was feeling so badly that he had even hoped for death on the battlefield, though he knew it was wrong to feel that way. The fatal bullet had not come, and now he felt gloomy, listless, and restless—uninterested in relaxing, sleeping, reading, or even talking with fellow soldiers. But he tried not to give up hope entirely, for he knew it would make his mother happy if he survived. "[M]aybe I can do some good in the cause which all true Christians ought to strive to do," he wrote.[6]

No matter how men were feeling about the conduct of the war, the flag was still an important symbol, even for men disgusted by the failure of the Union generals. A civilian from Michigan visiting the regiment wrote that the 4th Michigan needed new colors, for the U.S. flag presented to them back in Adrian was "a complete wreck, pierced by innumerable bullets, battered and torn and no longer capable of being unfurled." That visitor, J. Q. Disbrow, sent back a suggestion to Adrian. "Do not these gallant men deserve another flag to replace it?" In fact, Adrian firefighters were already thinking about a new flag and planning a fund-raiser, with patriotic residents joining in. Whether they ultimately paid for a banner to replace that original flag is not certain, but a new one was soon brought from Washington to the 4th Michigan by its quartermaster.[7]

In camp, the officers of the regiment kept up drill while the weather fluctuated. The men hadn't been paid for several months, so the appearance of the paymaster was a highlight, but low points were standing for hours in the cold, waiting for General Burnside to review their corps, and standing picket in the rain. One of the most interesting distractions for the soldiers was the chance to purchase, enjoy, and discuss a lithograph of scenes depicting the 4th Michigan's experiences so far in war—pictures drawn by the regiment's unofficial artist, Lt. Charles Gruner. Produced by a New York printing company as a poster-like souvenir, the lithograph featured combat scenes of the New Bridge skirmish and the battle of Malvern Hill, as well as the regiment on dress parade at Minor's Hill. It contained a view of Fort Woodbury, and the men at work at Yorktown. Also featured were portraits of its first two commanders, Dwight Woodbury and Jonathan Childs. Luke Barnes bought two copies of the lithograph to send home. He called them "very nice for they are true pictures" that showed "some of my adventures and hardships." Others who got copies of the lithograph included Luke's brother Joel and Edward Taylor, who sent one to his mother, describing the scenes for her. "If we had the fording of the Potomac at Shepherdstown and the battle of Fredericksburg in some way mentioned—the thing would be complete," he wrote. In fact, a later edition of the lithograph, produced late in 1863 or early 1864, would include scenes of Fredericksburg and two battles in which the regiment would soon take part—Chancellorsville and Gettysburg.[8]

By the middle of January, on a cold, rainy Thursday, the men knew that the commander of the Union army was up to something. "Our sick were all moved today," George Millens wrote, "indications of a move." Then an order came, confirming they had to be ready to march at any moment. General Burnside issued an address to his men—they were about to land "a fatal blow to the Rebellion." He gave no specifics, so rumors were rampant, Irvin Miner noted. The temperature plunged to freezing and the order to depart camp was delayed.

The "Mud March"

Finally, it came on January 20—the start for the Fifth Corps of what became known as Burnside's infamous Mud March. The general's plan was to move the Union army to the northwest, beyond Fredericksburg, and cross the Rappahannock to force the Army of Northern Virginia into a fight. But the winter weather wasn't cooperating. "Strike camp after a week of preparation," wrote Lt. John Bancroft, "and go about two miles. Begins raining. Soon changes to snow." It was late afternoon when they moved out, going only two miles in the rain and mud.[9]

"This morning we are stuck in the mud," Millens wrote the next day, "but managed to march about 4 miles. It rained all day & tonight it still rains horrible." Others recorded the miserable conditions. "Mud awful deep," wrote Henry Seage. "Could hardly get along." It took all day to move those three or four miles, Irvin Miner recorded; "the mire was about impassable. . . . I saw lots of artillery stuck in the mud and also the ammunition and subsistence trains." Hillsdale County's Sgt. John W. Hewitt of Company E, then about 21, called it "tough marching[,] mud 6 inches deep." Edward Taylor noted the deaths of exhausted animals, that "horses and mules died by the score all along the road." It was an impossible situation, Lt. Michael Vreeland agreed. "[I]t took twelve span of mules to haul our one light field piece & five & six or eight to draw an empty wagon," he wrote. "We were obliged to burn our pontoons where they were stuck in the mud."

The men again bivouacked in the wet and cold. The next day some men of the 4th Michigan were among those sent into the woods to cut down trees and "corduroy" the roads in an attempt to move the artillery. In fact, the offensive was declared over, but still the guns had to be dragged back to where they'd started. Seage wrote that two men were hurt by a falling tree. Other soldiers waited in the rain in the dripping woods, and some built huge bonfires.[10]

From the other side of the Rappahannock, the Confederates enjoyed watching this miserable "advance" of the Union army. "Rebels over the river laugh at us," Bancroft wrote. By January 23, there was simply no doubt that Burnside had sent them on another useless, foolhardy mission. "The movement is an entire failure and we are falling back to our old camp," Miner wrote. "Burnside, I predict is played out. . . . I saw forty horses stuck in the mud with one caisson. Winter campaigning will not work in Virginia." The next day the men were ordered back to camp. As was usual, they found that many of their camp's wooden structures and buildings had been stripped, but the prospect of having to rebuild these was probably made more palatable by the appearance of the paymaster with some four months' back wages. The next day, the 25th, they set to work rebuilding their winter quarters.

To the surprise of no one, Burnside was removed as commander of the Union army. In his place came Gen. Joseph Hooker, who'd been a vocal critic of Burnside. While many historical accounts of the Army of the Potomac speak of the Mud March as a low point for the morale of the troops, Lt. Michael Vreeland denied it. "As regard the demoralization of the troops, it is an absurd lie," Vreeland insisted. "I do not attach any blame to anyone for the failure of the enterprise and I think our generals showed good sense in abandoning the project. . . . I hope the howlers for a winter campaign are satisfied."[11]

The weather continued snowy and rainy and the men were allowed a day or two without drill once back in winter camp. Since the resignation of Colonel Childs back in late November, Lt. Col. George Lumbard had been in command of the 4th Michigan. By now it was usually the case in a Michigan outfit that if its major died or was promoted to another post, then the senior captain would be commissioned as the new major. Or if a regiment's lieutenant colonel was killed or wounded or was sick to the point of disability, the major would almost certainly replace him, receiving a new commission at the higher position. There were examples where this kind of automatic promotion based on seniority did not happen, but such exceptions proved the general rule. Soldiers in the 4th Michigan like Charles W. Phelps therefore expected that Lieutenant Colonel Lumbard would become the new colonel.

The promotion of Capt. Harrison H. Jeffords to colonel, therefore, was unexpected. How and why was Jeffords promoted over Lumbard? A biography of Childs said he was a Republican, so his opinion on who should be commissioned to replace him probably carried weight with the governor, who may have been unhappy about Childs being forced to resign. Childs also had an uncle who served for years in the state legislature who almost certainly knew Blair, as he participated in political affairs. Jeffords also had the endorsement of Col. Charles Doolittle, formerly of 4th Michigan, now commander of the 18th Michigan. While it was the governor's prerogative to commission officers for Michigan's military units, Blair wished to talk to Jeffords face-to-face before announcing his promotion.

By the third week in January Jeffords knew he was being considered for promotion in the regiment, though it is not clear if he knew he was going to commissioned colonel. "I hereby ask for a leave of absence for fifteen days to go to the State of Michigan," he wrote on February 1 to his superiors in the Grand Division, of which the regiment was part. He noted his visit was regimental business. "I have never been absent from the Regiment since its organization." Jeffords's request was approved.[12]

As Jeffords left for his meeting with Blair, Lt. John M. Bancroft expressed what could be called the conventional wisdom—that Lumbard would be commissioned colonel, while Jeffords would be promoted the post of lieutenant colonel. Bancroft wrote to a friend in Detroit that he and others in the regiment had more confidence in Jeffords than they had in other officers, a comment that seems to have been a swipe at Lumbard and Major Randolph. "Capt. J is recommended for lt. col. and most of us think he is the *best man here* by all eclats [*éclat,* acclaim]," Bancroft wrote.

Austin Blair acted. On February 12, the governor instructed Michigan adjutant general John Robertson to issue a commission to Jeffords, making him colonel of the 4th Michigan. Two days later, the news appeared in the *Detroit Free Press.* There are no specific accounts about how this news was greeted in the regiment or how it was received by Lumbard. But when Jeffords got back to the regiment on March 10, there was no doubt how the soldiers felt: The men cheered him. "Col. Jeffords has arrived and was treated with a public gathering, a thing unusual here," Lieutenant Bancroft wrote. "He spoke a few words which were well received by the men, who proposed three cheers for Col. Jeffords. The men and most of the officers was well pleased." Irvin Miner of Company F agreed: "Col. Jefries [*sic*] returned to the regt. and was enthusiastically cheered by the boys." This unusual demonstration by the men, like Bancroft's comment that most of the regiment felt that Jeffords was the "best man," is evidence of the respect they had for him.[13]

While Harrison Jeffords had been back in Michigan, the men of the regiment dealt with snowstorms, work details, rain, and deep mud near Falmouth. They had their pictures taken, chopped and loaded wood onto wagons, underwent inspection and dress parade, and stood picket. Irvin Miner was delighted to have a visit from his father in mid-February, though he wondered what his father was up to when Miner senior went off one day to ride along the Confederate line. "I suppose he has some project a-foot for moving the army," Miner wrote in his diary. "He has just returned having scouted the whole country from Falmouth to opposite Fredericksburg without finding anything but their pickets." Yet Miner was sad the next day when, through the falling snow, he saw his father off to the train. "I went to the cars to bid him goodbye," Miner wrote in his diary. "It seemed hard but I concealed my feelings and emotions."

There were periodic thaws, heavy snows, and complaints as the men had to travel farther from camp to get firewood, since they cut down everything in the immediate neighborhood. While Miner's journal mentioned the typical duties, weather, and conditions in camp, two of the more unusual entries came in early March when he and Albert Boies discovered a cave and explored it on their own time for a couple of days. "It was a dangerous adventure and full of peril," Miner wrote. Young Luke Barnes continued to be dispirited, clashing with his lieutenant and comrades, feeling depressed and persecuted, and thinking of desertion. "Oh mother if I could only die and leave this wicked and unfriendly world," he wrote, "what a relief it would be to my poor weary soul but God has seen fit to let me live."

Lt. John Bancroft wrote that the new army commander, Joe Hooker, made a favorable impression by "looking [going] after the deserters and skulkers" and by limiting the numbers of officers and men who could be away on leave. Sgt. John Hewitt of Company E noted in early February that for the first time nearly six months their brigade drew soft bread, rather than hardtack. Within a few weeks' time, Corporal Charles Phelps would declare, "We live better now that we ever have before in the army." Potatoes, onions, beans, salt, fresh meat, bread, coffee, tea, and sugar—all these items and others besides the soldiers now had in abundance, he said. These, too, were part of Hooker's improvements for the Union army.[14]

Within the regiment, Capt. Charles B. Parson, about 27, who began as a second lieutenant in Company E, resigned, honorably discharged for disability in early March. About two weeks later, Dr. David P. Chamberlain went home seriously ill. Lt. John Bancroft was transferred to Company H. It was also time to retire the 4th Michigan's first flag. Lt. Robert H. Campbell, the regiment's quartermaster, wrote years later that this U.S. flag was bullet-riddled and torn, its staff broken. It was sent home to Michigan, he wrote. A letter written by Edward Taylor later in the spring agreed. "You should have seen the old flag of the 4th Mich.," he told his sister. "It has been sent home for safe keeping, as it was so torn and cut from shot and shell that it could not be carried. We have a new one now, but I think more of the old soiled flag we fought under on the Peninsula and in every battle till the last." Lieutenant Campbell went to Washington, D.C., and picked out another U.S. flag to replace it.[15]

In the meantime the soldiers landscaped their camp. By March 12 fair weather permitted the 4th Michigan to play baseball with the 44th New York from their division's Third Brigade. St. Patrick's Day celebrations centered in the all-Irish 9th Massachusetts. "The amusements began at 9 A.M. with a fantastic dress parade in which the officers, even to the Colonel, were in

Before the resumption of campaigning and battle in the spring of 1863, the return of mild weather allowed for ball games at the camp of the 4th Michigan near Falmouth, Virginia.

the ranks with muskets," wrote Cpl. Irvin Miner. The comic parade went off with considerable laughs, "after which their self-elected Colonel was presented with a huge wooden sword," he continued. Officers took part in horse races, and men vainly attempted to climb greased poles to try to win a prize of 10 dollars, a gallon of whiskey, and a furlough. Men ran races while tied up in huge sacks, and companies vied to catch a hog that had been shaved and covered in grease. But the good times came to a halt when the horses of a lieutenant of the 9th Massachusetts and of a surgeon from the 62nd Pennsylvania collided while racing, killing the lieutenant. The sound of cannonading could be heard in the distance, Miner noted—a clash of Union and Confederate cavalry miles to the northwest. But the men of the 4th Michigan and their comrades were not involved.[16]

With the appointment of Hooker came the end of Burnside's previous "grand division" organization of the Army of the Potomac. The 4th Michigan was still part of the Fifth Army Corps, now under the command of Gen. George G. Meade. In addition to improving the soldiers' food and medical care, Hooker put into effect the use of emblems or badges that soldiers would wear to identify them by corps and division. This allowed officers and men, whether in the confusion of battle or while on a long march, to easily find or identify their comrades with a glance at the badge all would wear. The Fifth Corps emblem was already a Maltese cross, but now the different divisions would wear crosses of different colors. The First Division's cross would be red. Edward H. C. Taylor, who expressed no faith in the new commander, was cynical about the new emblems. "An order has just come down directing this Division to wear as a distinctive badge a red woolen maltese cross on the front of the cap," he told his sister. "Hooker is bound to put his mark on his sheep before he takes them to slaughter."[17]

But most of the soldiers approved of Hooker's measures, and for the first time in months affairs seemed to be looking up. There were always exceptions, however, and now came what must have been an embarrassing distraction for the 4th Michigan's new colonel. No record, letter, or account of the regiment suggested that Harrison Jeffords was anything but a good soldier, well respected by his men. But now that Jeffords was colonel, the man who had expected to have that job, Lt. Col. George Lumbard, instigated a charge that Jeffords had overstayed his 15-day leave back to Michigan. After all, Lumbard had apparently succeeded in forcing Jonathan Childs to resign back in the fall; perhaps he could derail Jeffords's new command. Ten days after Jeffords returned to his regiment in camp near Falmouth, a charge of "conduct to the prejudice of good order and military discipline" was issued against him. Lumbard signed the complaint as "witness." The complaint alleged Jeffords, as a captain, had been granted a 15-day leave of absence on February 10, but that he hadn't returned until March 10. Though Jeffords had been named colonel, he had been gone twice as long as his commanders authorized.[18]

Jeffords had to take this charge seriously. He wrote to the ranking U.S. Army officer in Michigan, Lt. Col. Joseph R. Smith, the old veteran who had helped drill and organize Company A when it was a collection of green volunteers from Monroe. Jeffords reminded Smith that he hadn't overstayed his leave by choice, but because Smith ordered him to do so. "Since my return to the Regt. I have been requested to appear before a Commission and answer charges of absence without leave," Jeffords wrote. "Immediately on my return I made an explanation in writing to the commander of the Brigade, stating that I reported to you before the expiration of my 'leave of absence.' " Smith had ordered him to take a detachment of men who would be leaving Detroit for regiments in the Union army in Virginia.

But a railroad accident prevented Jeffords from getting to Detroit in time to join those men when they departed, so Smith instructed Jeffords to wait and take another group of men. This ended up being a delay of more than a week. "This explanation was considered satisfactory to the com[man]d[in]g officer of the Brigade," Jeffords wrote Smith. "And he recommended that no further action be taken. I took command of the Regt. and was mustered into the service [as colonel], after which time I was *cited* before the Commission, and they decided that you had no authority to retain an officer and recommended further action. I shall have to defend myself before a Court Martial. . . . I had no intention of violating any orders."[19]

Jeffords asked for delays in the start of the proceeding in order to produce certain witnesses, and the court-martial, which included Lumbard, Lt. Col. Norval Welch of the 16th Michigan, and Lt. Col. Joshua Chamberlain of the 20th Maine, granted them. When Jeffords and his counsel, Col. Jacob Sweitzer, were ready to proceed, Lumbard recused himself from the panel. Jeffords was so confident in his defense that he hadn't even asked for the removal of Lumbard, who had filed the complaint against him.

The Court-Martial of Harrison Jeffords

On April 6, the court-martial convened, meeting in a large tent near the First Division headquarters. Col. Strong Vincent of the 83rd Pennsylvania was added to the panel, as was the lieutenant colonel of the 2nd Maine. Vincent, an attorney by profession, was made president of the court-martial. The charges against Jeffords were read, and to the surprise of the court, Jeffords pleaded "guilty" to the specific allegation that he had been absent beyond his 15-day leave, but "not guilty" to the charge. This threw the panel into a quandary. They cleared the room to consider the question. Jeffords offered a letter from Lieutenant Col. Smith, the federal commander in Michigan, to show that Smith ordered him to remain there beyond his leave. But the judge advocate wasn't ready to accept it as evidence yet. The officers decided the trial would proceed.[20]

Lt. Col. Edward Sherlock of the 5th Michigan testified that he had been sent back to Michigan to recruit troops in the summer of 1862, by order of his corps commander and the U.S. secretary of war. Sherlock's direct order was to report to Lieutenant Col. Smith, who assigned him to the Detroit Barracks. "During the time I was there he [Smith] exercised the authority of detaining officers for the purpose of bringing detachments down to the Army of the Potomac and the Southwestern Army," Sherlock testified; this happened regularly. He further explained that "Lt. Col. Smith informed me that he had detained Colonel Jeffords to take command of a detachment to go to the Army of the Potomac, and he wished me to remain to assist Col. Jeffords."[21]

"Col. Jeffords came down to Washington with the detachment as fast as the trains would permit," he continued. Not only that, the men Jeffords brought back weren't exactly the cream of the crop, so he had his hands full. Of more than 100 recruits sent to the Union army, "a good many of them ran away," Sherlock said. Two Michigan civilians who had been part of conversations with Smith and Governor Blair agreed with Sherlock, testifying that the highest governmental and military authorities in Michigan wanted Jeffords to take new men back with him.

In sum, Jeffords presented a powerful case that he had been required to stay beyond his leave. It showed that Jeffords's intention was to replace some of the many soldiers the regiment lost in battle and to sickness. In addition, both Lt. Col. George Lumbard and Col. James McQuade testified that Jeffords's character had been "good" and "excellent" respectively.[22]

Jeffords submitted a statement to the court, and Colonel Sweitzer read it into the record: "I offer the following statements to how that if I am guilty of the charge, it was through misapprehension of the facts, and that I had every reason to believe I was strictly discharging my duty, and obeying my superior," the statement read.[23]

Other military men agreed with this, Jeffords noted. "I was detained by the order of an officer that I had every reason to believe I was in duty bound to obey," Jeffords' statement continued. "If [Smith's authority was] doubtful, the safest rule is obedience . . . the principle is clearly recognized by the War Department, that an officer acting in good faith is not liable to punishment." Jeffords cited War Department General Order No. 16, 1863. "I did act in good faith," he insisted. "I was acting on the advice of the Governor of the State to take the men with me when I returned, and if guilty of the charge against me, the guilt does not rest in any intention, which always constitute[s] a part of the offense," he argued.[24]

The court-martial now met in private to deliberate. Reconvening, the panel found Jeffords guilty of both the charge and the specification. How Jeffords was expected to defy Lieutenant Col. Smith was never explained. Yet the officers of the court-martial appear to have understood that to push the matter much further was to risk the wrath of Austin Blair, an important Republican leader. It could create political embarrassment, if not a political problem, for the army and the War Department. The court-martial quickly added that Jeffords's sentence should be a reprimand by his commanding general. "The court is thus lenient because they believe the accused acted in good faith and believed at the time he was obeying a legitimate order," Col. Strong Vincent wrote. Gen. Charles Griffin, commander of the division of which the 4th Michigan was part, approved the court-martial's finding.[25]

While a reprimand was considered a blot on an officer's record, it appears that most of Jeffords's men were pulling for him, understanding that he was in an impossible situation. "I think he shall come out all right," wrote Lt. George L. Maltz to a friend early in April. "It was not his fault." Maltz, who had risen through the ranks in Company I and was now second lieutenant of Company E, wrote that Jeffords "is well liked by his officers and men. We hope he may be soon released [from arrest]." Lt. John Bancroft was even stronger in his words about the Jeffords court-martial, blaming it on Lumbard. "We all hope he [Jeffords] will soon be in command of the regiment for the Lt. Col. has lost rather than gained friends by his actions since Jeffords' Promotion. In Brigade drill he [Lumbard] has showed his ignorance of tactics and is quite irritable generally," Bancroft wrote.[26]

Jeffords accepted his reprimand with a kind of let's-get-on-with-it attitude. It appears that no reports of the court-martial appeared in Michigan newspapers. After he had been returned to duty, Jeffords wrote a confident letter home to a local newspaper, showing he was in charge of the regiment. He stressed the soldiers were sure of success in the coming season and not interested in reports of compromise and peace talks. Jeffords probably had his recent troubles in mind when he wrote these sentences, possibly with wry humor, emphasizing certain words. "The *legal* profession is well represented here," Jeffords noted. "I think a majority of the field officers are lawyers." (Both Strong Vincent and Norval Welch, officers who served on the court-martial, were attorneys, as was George Lumbard.) He continued: "Sometimes I meet members of our *old Class,* all *retained* on the same *side.* I am now finely domesticated, and endeavoring to sustain the former good reputation of the Regiment. Its present condition is everything I could wish, and I know that when the order is again given to *move* (and it soon will be) we shall not be left behind."

Lieutenant Colonel Lumbard, having failed to stop Jeffords from taking command of the regiment, made peace with his new colonel. "I did have to make a explanation as to what made me stay beyond my time and that was all settled satisfactory," Jeffords wrote to friends about his court-martial. "I was not punished, am in command of the Regt & intent to stay so. . . . Col. Lumbard is not going to resign & is very friendly to me."[27]

As the Jeffords case had played out, regimental camp life went on and the weather slowly but unevenly moderated. While the soldiers hadn't been able to finish a ball game with the 14th New York because of the rain and cold, within days there was weather Irvin Miner called "beautiful and warm." Yet on the night of April 4–5, there was a snowstorm. There were resignations by officers, perhaps the most significant being that of Dr. Chamberlain. The surgeon who had written so many letters to the *Hudson Gazette* had gotten a leave in January to return home, but the doctor hadn't completely recovered from his severe illness in the summer of 1862. On March 13, 1863, he resigned and was honorably discharged. "The regiment were very sorry to lose Dr. Chamberlain," Lt. John Bancroft wrote. To replace Chamberlain, Jeffords would recommend the assistant surgeon, Dr. Luther French of Hudson. French had joined the regiment back in August 1862. Dr. John S. Watts of Adrian, who also joined in the late summer as second assistant surgeon, moved up to take French's former spot. George Monteith, now a captain and back with the regiment, replaced Charles Marvin of Hillsdale, who resigned late in January.[28]

The family of Edward H. C. Taylor was probably surprised to hear of his change in opinion about the army accepting black soldiers. For some time, Republican Party and abolitionist leaders had argued that blacks should be allowed to join the Union army, an idea that some Northerners thought objectionable. Taylor previously was against blacks in the service, but now he had a change of mind, though not a change of heart. "I must say I begin to think differently," wrote Taylor. "Not that I love the negro more but I do believe they are more fit to be *used* than I once thought. I would have little objection to seeing them put into regiments with white officers but kept *by themselves*." Taylor had seen Confederates using black soldiers doing picket duty across the Rappahannock, so why couldn't the Union army also utilize them?[29]

Just a week earlier, Irvin Miner of Company F wrote to relatives, suggesting that the war had gone so badly for the Union because many people in the North weren't committed to defeating the Confederacy. "There are too many traitors right at home among us," he wrote. "It is these wolves in sheep's clothing that clog the wheels of Government, and in a great measure help to turn our victories into defeat." He accepted that Lincoln and the military leaders had to move slowly and carefully, but there was more loyal men in the North could do. "While some are periling their lives on the battlefield and undergoing the hardships and privations incident to a soldier's life," he wrote, "those at home should give their united support to the Government in every way thought best to further the one end—that of ending this unhappy strife, and consequently the shedding of more blood."[30]

Men also commented on the draft. Sgt. Jonas D. Richardson of Company D, a Washtenaw County man writing to a friend, said most soldiers backed the new conscription law and wanted to see strong measures to back it up. "The government should enforce the draft if necessary," Richardson wrote, "and if men of the North would offer the slightest opposition, let the hemp [rope] be the cure."[31]

There were periodic alarms in March and April when the men were suddenly issued plenty of ammunition and told to be ready to march, but nothing came of these. A number of new recruits, many of them drafted men brought into the regiment by Jeffords and other officers, began to learn the elements of drill. On March 26, two days after the 4th Michigan's quartermaster brought a new U.S. flag from Washington, Gen. George Gordon Meade, Fifth Corps commander, held a review of their division. Robert Campbell would later write that Colonel Jeffords was "much pleased" with this new flag, vowing "to be its special guardian and defender."

Sgt. John Hewitt of Company E was the victim of a joke that generated "considerable amusement" when someone tricked him into thinking a bit of soap was actually cheese on April Fool's Day, while Lt. Michael Vreeland wrote a letter home on a more serious matter, strongly urging his brother not to enlist. "Alpheus what ever you do never enlist in the Army as a private soldier,"

Vreeland wrote; "if you were old enough to get a commission it might do but as a private soldier now I have no time to write you all I would like to but will tell you some other time . . . it would kill you in one month[;] take my word it is a perfect Hell for any ones spirit at all."

President Lincoln arrived on another visit to the army on April 7, reviewing the 4th Michigan's brigade that day and thousands more soldiers the next. Lieutenant Bancroft said that the 12th New York, which apparently hadn't been paid in sometime, wasn't impressed. When an officer called for "three cheers for the President Lincoln," instead the men of that regiment called out "Paymaster, paymaster," instead. When the grand review was held, according to Bancroft, "there was no cheering." Other witnesses from other regiments and brigades in the same First Division of the Fifth Corps disagreed, however, and said Lincoln was cheered.[32]

A surprise came three days later when a corporal on picket for a New York regiment gave birth, Irvin Miner recorded. "The said corporal proved to be a female who has been through all the battles," he wrote. Colonel Jeffords was released from arrest that week following the court-martial, and on April 12 he resumed his command of the 4th Michigan. But the portentous development came on April 14—marching orders that told the soldiers to carry with them eight days' worth of rations and plenty of cartridges. The men were so pleased that they held a dance in streets of their camp, the music provided by their brigade's band. But the skies opened up the next day and heavy rains stopped the army from going anywhere for the moment. It meant a delay in the resumption of the war.

"We have layed [*sic*] still about long enough," wrote Phelps, summing up the feeling of many soldiers, "and it is time to expect a move." He had no doubt that Joe Hooker was going to take the war to the Confederates, and his comrade Sgt. Jonas D. Richardson agreed. "The men have confidence in General Hooker," Richardson wrote days before the Army of the Potomac moved out. "We believe him able to lead us on to victory when the time comes, to strike. . . . But one feeling exists among us and that is that the only way sure and safe road to peace is to fight it out and not yield an inch until this rebellion is put down."[33]

CHAPTER 9

Christ How the Canister Flew

COLD, WET WEATHER DESCENDED ON NORTHERN VIRGINIA IN MID-APRIL, BUT THE MEN OF THE 4th Michigan set up a baseball match—officers versus privates, final score unknown—when the storm front passed on the 22nd. Chaplain John Seage, who left on sick leave after the Mud March, returned to the regiment, bringing tobacco for his son Henry in Company E. About the same time more conscripts arrived from the Detroit barracks. These men were divided up among the Michigan regiments; the 4th Michigan's Company K got five of them. One was Pvt. James Houghton, from Cohoctah in Livingston County, drafted in early February, who would leave a journal/memoir of his experiences. Houghton told of an old Detroit washerwoman who smuggled canteens of whiskey in laundry baskets to the conscripts until the officers figured it out and arrested her. He related that his comrades broke into the cargo on the ship that took them from Detroit to Cleveland, stealing boots and candy, but that they'd thrown up the stolen sweets when a Lake Erie storm tossed the ship, making them seasick. Once in camp with his new regiment, Houghton and his comrades were given a kind of "dugout" tent, six or seven feet square and pitched over a hole in the ground, probably the site of a cabin where soldiers previously built raised bunks and floors. It made for uncomfortable living. "This we didn't have to endure for about a week," Houghton wrote. His hitch as a draftee was only for nine months, but he would be at two of the bloodiest battles of the Civil War.[1]

Corporal Irvin Miner from Company F had taken a couple of lessons in fencing that month, and on April 25 he had instruction of the artistic sort. Miner sketched the nearby Potomac Creek Bridge and surrounding country, possibly at the direction of the talented Lt. Charles Gruner of Company C. The next day, the 4th Michigan left camp with the other regiments of their Second Brigade for picket duty. Miner complained that he'd suddenly taken lame in the foot and was "barely able to walk."

But now that the weather was clearing, the new offensive by Gen. Joseph Hooker was about to begin. On April 27, the Fifth Corps and two others in the Army of the Potomac, the Eleventh and the Twelfth Corps, began to move out, marching along the Rappahannock River past Fredericksburg. The Fifth Corps was the last to go. The 4th Michigan came back from picket and broke camp, hoisting what Henry Seage called "heavy knapsacks" and starting the march with their division toward a river ford about 20 miles away. Again soldiers threw away extra clothing and blankets and items thought to be too heavy to carry. Houghton said the road was strewn with these, quickly scooped up by the local poor people. The troops only moved several miles that afternoon before they stopped and bivouacked in a field near Hartwood Church. Lt. John Bancroft of Company H found himself "aching and tired."[2]

Hooker's plan called for two corps to cross the Rappahannock River near Fredericksburg to focus the attention of Lee's forces there, while the Fifth Corps and others moved quietly to northwest, where they would cross the river and head south on the Confederate side, back toward Fredericksburg. He planned to catch and smash Lee's army between these wings of the Union army without incurring the terrible casualties from head-on attacks that the men suffered in December. The Fifth Corps's crossing point was Kelly's Ford. Late on the morning of April 28, the 4th Michigan continued on as the skies opened up. It was a long, wet, and tedious march, but they reached the ford and bivouacked in the woods that night. The soldiers crossed the Rappahannock on a pontoon bridge the next day, with the 4th Michigan going over at about eleven o'clock, marching a few miles south to wade a creek and pressing on. They reached the Rapidan River about sundown, fording this river, too, holding their ammunition and haversacks up out of the water. Lieutenant Bancroft said the water was "deep, rapid and cold" and the rain set in again. "[A]11 of the yelping and yelling mingled in with some horid oaths, anyone would think that the devels School was out for noon," Houghton wrote about the cursing. The lead elements of their force ran into some Rebels posted in the area as guards and took them prisoner. The men of the 4th Michigan camped that night in their wet clothes on a hill near the crossing, called Ely's Ford, with thousands of other Union troops.[3]

The next day the men started another slow, careful march by 6:30 A.M. on the ford road to a place called Chancellorsville. This was not a village, but a single large brick house several miles west of Fredericksburg. The house served as an inn for travelers on the pike, who could stop at this opening in the rough, forested countryside called the Wilderness. The 4th Michigan arrived at Chancellorsville around noon; Henry Seage said they passed a small line of now-empty Rebel fortifications along the way. The soldiers of their brigade gathered in a field and probably had a rest and some coffee until orders came about four o'clock from their corps commander, Gen.

George G. Meade. Another brigade had run into some Confederates just three miles east of Chancellorsville, so their Second Brigade was ordered to quickly head that way.

Seage said the regiment moved out with the brigade on the road to Fredericksburg. The men could see empty Confederate works up ahead and it appeared the Rebels had quickly pulled back. Corporal Miner indicated that the 4th Michigan moved east a few miles that evening to a point near Banks' Ford, a Rappahannock crossing three miles west of Fredericksburg. Others indicated they didn't go that far. Sgt. Edgar Noble of Company K thought that they marched about two miles. Lt. John Bancroft wrote that some Rebels were taken prisoner, but the regiment didn't become involved in any fighting. Whether they marched five miles or two that evening, Gen. George Griffin, their division commander, ordered their brigade to return to Chancellorsville. The weather stayed rainy, but the men had fresh beef for their dinner when they camped in the woods near the house at about 11:00 P.M. "The prospect is a big fight tomorrow," Miner wrote in his diary.[4]

Chancellorsville

Robert E. Lee had by now received reports about the Union troop movements and figured correctly that the main attack on his forces, which were outnumbered more than two to one, was coming from Chancellorsville. Leaving a division and a brigade at Fredericksburg to fight the Union troops there, Lee and Stonewall Jackson marched less than 44,000 men west to face Hooker. Now the battle would begin in earnest. On May 1, Joe Hooker's advance began again, but only briefly. The 4th Michigan's Second Brigade led their First Division out that morning, moving east on a country road that ran toward the Rappahannock River crossings north and west of Fredericksburg. As they marched, other Union troops heading directly east toward Fredericksburg met Confederates again and the shooting began. But by early afternoon, General Hooker made a surprising decision: He ordered troops who had been advancing to halt, pull back, and take up defensive positions near Chancellorsville.

"We went about 2 miles near the 'U. States Ford' and faced about and came back as far as the Rebel camp in the woods and formed 'Line of Battle,'" Corporal Seage recorded. Col. McQuade's report on the Second Brigade stated that his regiments were headed toward Banks' Ford, farther east on the Rappahannock, and came back late in the afternoon to where they had encamped the previous night. Here, he wrote, the brigade formed in line of battle in support of another division that was trading fire with the enemy troops posted east of Chancellorsville.

But the movement of the 4th Michigan was complicated and more dangerous than McQuade's report indicated. Col. Harrison Jeffords had been given orders by his division commander to "open communication with the left [wing of the Union forces] next the Rappahannock." In other words, his assignment was to link up with troops who were supposed to cross the river near Fredericksburg. But this effort by the 4th Michigan to reach the other wing of the Union army did not succeed, since events were overtaking Hooker's plan. Some men from the 4th Michigan who probably didn't know about Jeffords's order wrote that their brigade became separated from the rest of the First Division as evening fell—they believed that they had lost their way in the

The 4th Michigan charges into woods northwest of Chancellorsville on the afternoon of May 4 to determine the Confederates' position, but Rebel artillery opens a heavy fire that quickly sent the regiment and their brigade back in a hurried retreat. Drawing by Lt. Charles Gruner.

wooded countryside. Seage recorded that after the 4th Michigan sent out skirmishers, they found that the Rebels were "directly in front." This began an all-night-long "backward and forward" movement. Lieutenant Bancroft recorded similar movements, writing that on a reconnaissance toward the Rappahannock, he and his men had moved so far east that they actually came within sight of Fredericksburg. "On our return the Brigade is cut off by the advance of the rebels and [we] have to return by a new route. March and countermarch all night."[5]

"The night was spent in sending out scouting parties to learn the Rebels position," James Houghton wrote. Like Bancroft, he said that his company traveled eight miles toward Fredericksburg. "We had orders not to speak above a whisper," he continued. Soon it was understood Confederates were coming toward them, and they pulled back. Others told of this harrowing all-night march back to the safety of Union positions. "Our Brigade was cut off & marched and counter marched from 6 o'c[lock] till 4 o'c[lock] the next morning," wrote John Hewitt of Company E. Lieutenant George Maltz of Detroit, now assigned to Company E, told of this tense night shifting through the woods, dodging the enemy: "Our Brigade was at one time cut off, this was in the night, and we kept moving, and countermarching."

Henry Seage later wrote that their brigade was on guard, front and rear, the soldiers concerned that the Rebels were all around them, until enough light came into the sky to see on the morning of May 2. "At last we took the Ford road to the left [west] and went till we joined [Andrew A.] Humphrey's Division and then laid down for an hour," Seage wrote in his diary. Soon they were sent back to Chancellorsville, marching on a road through the woods. They rejoined their First Division around daylight. The 4th Michigan had been given an important mission, and though they hadn't been able to reach the left wing of the Union army, they had made the attempt and come back without losing a man. Colonel Jeffords was proud of the trust the army brass had in his regiment.[6]

Fortunately for the soldiers of the 4th Michigan, their division and corps would not become heavily involved in the battle that was now shaping up around Chancellorsville. The regiment was allowed some sleep, had breakfast, and went to work building defensive positions with logs, brush, and dirt about a mile east of the big brick house, along a road that led northeast to the river. The positions of other Union corps extended farther into the woods and fields south and west of Chancellorsville. But the Confederates were on the move that day. Gen. Stonewall Jackson was then marching with his force of about 27,000 men south of the Union positions, circling around to strike them from the west. It was a dangerous but daring move for Lee to divide his force, but it worked even though some Union officers noticed the movement of Jackson's troops and reported them massing west of Chancellorsville. The poor leadership of some Union generals meant that almost nothing was done to prepare for the coming Rebel attack.

The men of the 4th Michigan could hear skirmish fire during the day as they worked cutting trees and brush and digging trenches, but the only danger confronting them was when a Rebel patrol fired on their picket line around six in the evening and then pulled out, James Houghton wrote. Then came the attack of Stonewall Jackson's infantry, striking the Union line two or three miles to the west, late in the afternoon. The brunt of the assault fell on the Eleventh Corps, which was composed largely of German immigrants. Many of these men ran toward Chancellorsville. Though some of the better-led regiments within this corps fought stubbornly and slowed the Rebels, American-born soldiers didn't think much of them. "The fighting continued all night," Miner wrote that night. "The 11th Corps run disgracefully at the first approach of the enemy." Lieutenant Maltz repeated the joke that the Eleventh Corps was "composed of Lager Beer, principally" and Edward Taylor complained that these soldiers "have always played the cowards." But the men of the 4th Michigan only had to listen to the gunfire. By nightfall, they received orders to be ready to march toward the fighting at the center and right of the Union lines near Chancellorsville. "We have to be on the move and under arms all night," Lieutenant Bancroft wrote.[7]

That move came at about 4:30 A.M. on May 3. The Eleventh Corps, reorganized after the shattering attack by Jackson, shifted into a position east-northeast of Chancellorsville where the Fifth Corps had been, while the Fifth Corps moved to the Union right, along the Ely's Ford Road about a half-mile north of the big inn. Hooker's critics would charge that he had the manpower and the opportunity to attack and destroy the still-divided Confederate forces. Instead he consolidated his army into a contracting loop around Chancellorsville while also protecting the routes back to the river crossings.

Henry Seage suggested in a later history of the 4th Michigan's Company E that their regiment hurried to stop the attack of Stonewall Jackson's infantry on the morning of May 3 with guns blazing, but other accounts, including his own diary entry for that day, aren't so dramatic. Historians note that Jackson's attack had hours earlier become disorganized, slowed, and ground to a halt. Though it was initially successful, other Union troops entered the fighting on the night of May 2 and formed new defensive lines. After the shooting ended, Confederate units rested and reorganized in the darkness.[8]

Still, there was danger on the morning of May 3 as the men of the 4th Michigan and their brigade and division established their lines north of Chancellorsville. According to a newspaper account, Capt. Jairus W. Hall, who had started out in the regiment as a lieutenant, was ordered to lead his Company D in a skirmish line to find the Confederate positions. Hall, then about 23, was enough of a veteran to understand that officers were targets, so he took off his officer's coat and hat and put on a private's.

One member of the company was Henry W. Newton, 21, who joined at the formation of the regiment in the spring of 1861 but who'd been sick for almost two years. As a result, he had never been in battle. Hall, knowing of Newton's fragile health, asked him to stay behind and guard the company's knapsacks, but Newtown pleaded to go on the patrol. Hall relented. The company moved into the woods northwest of Chancellorsville. As they advanced, a Confederate officer suddenly stepped out from behind a tree, and so did two or three of his men. Hall realized there were other Rebel soldiers behind nearby trees, leveling their muskets at his patrol. "Surrender, you damned Yankee," one yelled. "Surrender be damned," Hall shouted, jumping behind a tree as he pulled his revolver. The woods erupted in gunfire and the Confederates soon fled, but not before one of Hall's men was struck and fatally wounded. It was Newton. His father, Thomas Newton, about 45 years old and a member of the regiment then on duty with the quartermaster at the United States Ford, soon got the terrible news. Tom Newton was given his son's watch and pocketbook. "I would rather hear that he had been killed than to hear that he had turned his back to the enemy," the father reportedly said when told how Henry had died. As he turned away with his son's effects, tears streamed down his face, the regiment's quartermaster wrote.[9]

In the meantime the 4th Michigan and its brigade took their places along Ely's Ford Road, on a hill across from the woods where Hall had taken his patrol. The Second Brigade took control of a section of the road not far from a local landmark called "the white house," less than a mile north of Chancellorsville. Here Union guns were posted, with three of regiments of their brigade lying down nearby, facing the west and forming a defensive position to the left of the battery. Then came more guns and then the 4th Michigan, posted in support of the 16th Michigan Infantry from their division's Third Brigade. A Detroiter in that regiment, Lt. Charles H. Salter, wrote of the pride the men of the 4th and 16th Michigan regiments had when their division commander, Gen. Charles Griffin, placed them on the hill, facing the Confederates that morning. Soon the Union guns were firing.

"Whilst the ball was going, Gen. Hooker came where we were and sat down amongst us for about an hour," Salter wrote from the battlefield. "He told Gen. Griffin that our position must be held at all hazards; and that everything depended on our being able to hold this place. Gen. Griffin told him that he had two of his best regiments here, and could hold it against all the devils in hell, and that the rebels had not men enough in the Southern Confederacy to take it." The anecdote would be proudly remembered and retold, with variations, for years by men of both Michigan regiments.[10]

Out in front of the Michigan troops, the men of the 32nd Massachusetts were deployed as skirmishers. Beyond their line were woods that hid the Confederates until they launched a renewed attack at about 7:00 A.M. "[Our batteries] Give them grape and canister," Bancroft wrote when the Rebels came out of the Wilderness. "Woods on fire where there are many wounded. We take many prisoners." The Confederates charged the Union lines in that vicinity over the next few hours, but their advances were stopped by the batteries, throwing out what Private Houghton called "a wall of fire." Lieutenant Salter of the 16th Michigan said he'd never seen anything so "terribly grand" as when the Rebels charged, only to be shattered by the artillery. "I saw one officer, ahead of the rest, waving his sword, when a discharge of grape took him and cut him all to pieces; and we could see them destroyed in every possible manner," Salter wrote.

All day long the men of the 4th Michigan lay on the ground by the guns. There was sharpshooter firing and periodic shelling from the Confederates, and at some point the woods on the other side of the ford road caught fire. Some wounded soldiers in the forest who hadn't been removed or weren't able to crawl to safety died in the flames. Henry Seage would remember years later that the cries of wounded men could be heard as the smoke and fire reached them. So did James Houghton: "We could plainly hear the poor fellows scream and yell," he wrote. The drifting smoke from the fire was so thick by the afternoon that the sun was obscured, Seage wrote in his diary. The Massachusetts men were pulled back from their skirmish line, seemingly replaced by pickets from the various regiments along the road.[11]

The 4th Michigan suffered casualties from hidden Rebel marksmen. At least two men were killed by sharpshooters, one of them being Corporal Theodore Haberfelder of Company A. Haberfelder had been wounded at Fredericksburg, but recovered. According to an account in his hometown newspaper, he was on picket that day when he was shot by a Confederate who had climbed a tree in the woods across from where the 4th Michigan was posted. This report said Haberfelder's comrades were able to kill this sharpshooter, though Houghton wrote that it was Union gunners who brought a small rifled cannon to bear on a tree where the puff of smoke had been seen. After the artillery piece fired into the tree, he wrote, no more sharpshooter fire came from it. Lt. John Bancroft was also hit by a Rebel sharpshooter, but remarkably it was a spent bullet that smacked him on the back of his right hand. It did no damage other than a bruise.

There was little rest for the men of the regiment that night, for two or three times there were alarms that brought them awake and ready for battle.[12] The worst scenes of the fighting that day were further to the south, closer to Chancellorsville, where thousands of soldiers, North and South, were killed and wounded in terrible artillery barrages and infantry attacks. By comparison to the casualties suffered by the regiments involved in this combat, the soldiers of the 4th Michigan and their brigade and division had an easy time.

The morning and early afternoon of May 4 were quiet in the salient northwest of Chancellorsville, with only some picket fire. At 4:00 P.M., however, an order came from Gen. Charles Griffin ordering the Second Brigade to make a reconnaissance toward the Confederate position, to see whether they had pulled out. The 4th Michigan would act as skirmishers, leading a fast-moving probing action into the smoking forest. "We had to advance through a piece of woods which was a filled with 'Rebs' watching our movements," wrote Lt. George Maltz. "They were taken by some surprise. And the first thing, we were rushing in there in double quick style, and they [Confederate pickets] had to skedadle to their main force." Some Michigan men stopped to fire when they spotted Rebel riflemen. As they charged in ahead of their brigade, Orvey S. Barrett of Company B saw a Rebel sharpshooter with a telescopic rifle and an old plug hat tumble "some sixty feet" from a tree, shot down by one of his comrades. "We took 8 prisoners and killed and wounded several," Lieutenant Maltz said.

There were nightmarish sights in those burned-out woods as the 4th Michigan charged in—the bodies of men who'd been left, dead or wounded, in the woods that burned the day before. "[We] see soldiers crisped, burned and cracked open," Lieutenant Bancroft noted. "Horrible site." Pvt. Houghton agreed—the dead had swollen and charred in fire, beyond any recognition. A drafted soldier who had come in at the same time as Houghton, John S. Conant, 26, in Company H, concurred. "It was a hard sight to see those that were killed two or three days ago nearly burned up," he wrote, "for the rebels set the woods on fire and it run through and doubtless killed some that were wounded." But there was no time to stare.

They chased on after the Rebel pickets, part of A. P. Hill's division. As these retreating Confederates reached the safety of their defenses made of log breastworks and trenches in the woods about a mile west of Chancellorsville, their gunners opened on the 4th Michigan with a fury. "We drove the pickets about ½ mile when we came upon the entrenchments and received a murderous volley," Irvin Miner wrote. This wasn't just musketry, but also grapeshot and canister. Bancroft wrote that the smoke and flying lead "looks like a storm." As the Confederate guns fired, Col. James McQuade, the commander of the brigade, was thrown from his horse and the Michigan soldiers dropped to the ground. "Christ how the canister flew in to us," wrote Charles Phelps. "I never had balls fly around much thicker." Barrett and Houghton said that ground in front of the Confederate defenses was low, so some of the artillery blasts passed over them. Still, they were in a terrible position. General Griffin, satisfied that the Rebels hadn't left, gave the order for his men to withdraw.[13]

"Our bugle sounded the 'recall,'" Orvey Barrett said, "and then we proceeded to 'git.'" Though he considered himself a fast runner, he "could not gain an inch" on the man in front of him. "I put a big tree between me and them mighty quick," Phelps agreed about this retreat. "We found out they had not gone so we fell back where we came from," he wrote. The Confederates fired after the 4th Michigan and then their infantry left the defenses, chasing the Union soldiers back through the woods. Barrett said that the men of the 9th Massachusetts had followed the 4th Michigan into the trees when they went in, but they had been ordered to stay low and await developments. Now as the Michigan men ran past them on the way out, the Massachusetts troops rose and fired into the Confederates, discouraging further pursuit.

The skirmish was over. Six of the 4th Michigan troops had been killed and 12 others wounded that afternoon. Phelps thought his Company D had come out of the business rather fortunately—none of them had been killed. In Irvin Miner's Company F, three men were wounded and one was missing, though it would turn out that the wounds of one of those men, Henry L. Lawrence of Hudson, then about 23, were fatal. Worse for Miner personally was that his younger half-brother, Corporal Austin D. Miner, probably 22 years old, was the missing man. In time the Union army would determine that Austin Miner was killed in action. The regiments of the Second Brigade went back to their positions near Ely's Ford Road. Lieutenant Maltz wrote that other Union regiments cheered them when they returned from their mission, but that reconnaissance wasn't enough for his captain. Henry Seage noted that Company E had to undergo an inspection that evening. Still, the brigade commander was pleased about their mission. "I feel it my duty to make especial mention of the conduct of the Fourth Michigan Volunteers, deployed as skirmishers during the reconnaissance on the 4th," Colonel McQuade reported. "Their advance was so rapid and determined that the skirmishers of the enemy were driven to their works without being afforded an opportunity to return our fire effectively. To this I attribute the slight loss sustained during the skirmish."[14]

That night the Union generals met with General Hooker to discuss whether they should withdraw back across the Rappahannock or continue the offensive against Lee. The Fifth Corps's commander, Gen. George G. Meade, argued that they should attack, and most of his colleagues agreed. But Hooker, who had suffered a concussion a day earlier, ruled otherwise. Within hours, elements of the Union army began their retreat.

There were more alarms through the night and early morning of May 4–5, Lieutenant Bancroft noted, and the regiment's pickets may have sounded some of these warnings. Harrison Daniels later wrote that his Company G was on picket, and that suddenly he saw a small light in the darkness ahead of him. Daniels was willing to investigate, so Lt. Jerome Allen warned the pickets that Daniels was venturing out beyond the line. Daniels said he carefully stepped forward and then dropped onto his hands and knees, crawling until he was about 150 feet from the light; it was a small fire in the woods. "I saw plainly the cause of the light[,] . . . a Confederate soldier who was trying to draw our fire." Of course, if Union pickets shot at that firelight, they would give away their positions to Rebel sharpshooters. Daniels watched as the soldier dropped twigs and leaves into the fire; he raised his rifle, aimed at the Rebel and fired. "The light went out," Daniels wrote. Had the Confederate collapsed and smothered the small fire? Had Daniels wounded him or even missed, allowing him to kick away the burning sticks? Daniels couldn't tell. He went back to his own lines.[15]

When the sun rose on May 5, the situation was relatively calm for the men of the 4th Michigan and their brigade—"Very quiet along the lines," John Hewitt wrote, "no fighting except for the sharp shooters." The men heard firing to the south, where Lee was hoping to step up the attacks on the Union positions, but the attack was repulsed, according to Bancroft. By the afternoon, the men knew they were leaving. Rain beat down and orders came for them be ready to move out at 8:00 P.M. They packed their gear and waited for hours as the rain came harder. Finally, the order to move came about 3:00 A.M. on May 6. The Fifth Corps acted as the rear guard during those early morning hours while the Union army quietly pulled out of Chancellorsville in the rain. The soldiers trudged northeast through the mud and woods to the U.S. Ford, where engineers had made pontoon bridges across the Rappahannock. "Hooker commenced a retreat," Hewitt continued in his diary when he had a moment. "[V]ery bad roads."

Bancroft wrote that the 4th Michigan marched and countermarched with its brigade, probably reflecting their brigade's shifting movement while covering the retreat. Private Houghton said that Union telegraph wires cut down along the roads tripped many a soldier in the darkness, sending them sprawling in the mud. "There was Swear words heard over the matter," he wrote. Houghton jokingly asked one friend who fell "what he was doing down there[.] His reply was that He was just getting ready for inspection." The 4th Michigan made the crossing at about 6:00 A.M. "No Rebels in sight," Bancroft noted. Charles Phelps claimed they were the second-to-last Union regiment to go back over the river. The regiment stopped to make coffee after the all-night work. Then the 4th Michigan marched back down the river toward Falmouth.

It was about 10 miles or so from the ford to the encampment that they'd left in late April, and it rained all day. Hewitt said the roads were in "horrid" shape; Colonel Jeffords described it as "mud [as] deep as I ever saw it." No one disagreed. "I was mud all over," Phelps wrote. "We were the worst looking seeds you ever see." The regiment reached the site of its old camp at about 3:00 P.M. Lieutenant Bancroft said that his comrades built a fire in a hospital tent; he took a bath (likely in a nearby Potomac Creek) and someone gave him a swig of whiskey. He wrote that he "slept soundly" after the rigors of the retreat.[16]

Some records state that eight men from the 4th Michigan had been killed or fatally wounded during Hooker's failed, nine-day offensive, but the number may have been higher given that at least one of the missing men would in time be classified as killed in action. At least another dozen had been wounded.[17] Compared to regiments that had been involved in fierce fighting or subject to artillery barrages near Chancellorsville, their casualties were light. "Our Regt. has been very fortunate during all the engagements and I have escaped as usual unhurt," Jeffords wrote.

Many histories speak of the disappointment and frustration the Union soldiers felt after turning away from Chancellorsville, and Edward Taylor of the 4th Michigan certainly felt that way. "Hooker has failed entirely in this move—has been outwitted, in fact," he wrote. A few days later, he conceded that "we did whip them in actual battle, but as a *whole* we did not gain our end. . . . Our men are brave but no advantage was made of our actual gain and our valor was wasted by poor generalship." Taylor's prior letters had shown him to be a McClellan man, yet he insisted that he and the rest of the Union army "don't so love McClellan that we would be unwilling to fight under any *good* General whom the government would favor and support." Taylor wrote that he had had doubts about Hooker for months. "Most of the winter I have lived within ten rods of his quarters and know him to be a *whiskey* 'bloat'—one of the most profane men I ever knew and a terrible braggadocio. Still when he took command particularly just as this move began I was willing to give all support in word and deed, for I thought there must be something beneath his exterior." That had turned out to be a false hope. Now with the Union army back in camp, Taylor complained, Hooker didn't want the soldiers to see critical comment in the press. "Now no papers are permitted to be sold within the lines unless they contain laudations of Hooker and the Administration. All others are prohibited. Is he afraid the soldiers will see their own opinion in print?"[18]

Not all soldiers felt that way. Lt. George Maltz said that the men had had faith in the general and his plans, and had cheered him on the battlefields at Chancellorsville. "We are now waiting patiently for what the future brings forth," he wrote to a friend back in Detroit. "The army is *not in any way demoralized.*" Lt. Michael J. Vreeland of Company I, from Brownstown Township in Wayne County, then sick and in a division hospital, agreed. "You all seem to think the Army has suffered a serious defeat," he wrote home, "but be assured such is not the case[. T]he Army never was in better spirits."

Vreeland insisted the Rebels hadn't been victorious—they had suffered "a severe blow," the worst they experienced so far. It was just that the Union army couldn't follow up on the losses they'd inflicted on Lee. Vreeland, then about 24, explained that the Union Army of the Potomac always had be make sure that Washington was safe, and so couldn't risk offensive movements that might allow Lee to strike it. "I wish the people could understand this," he wrote. Writing late that month, Lt. John Bancroft agreed with Vreeland that the soldiers trusted their commander. "Gen. Hooker has gained the confidence of the army and they want no interference," he wrote in an apparent reference to reports that General-in-Chief Henry W. Halleck wanted to replace Hooker.[19]

Perhaps some of the most positive comments to come out of the 4th Michigan were from Col. Harrison H. Jeffords. He was proud of his regiment and of the confidence that his superiors had in it during the battle. The brass asked the 4th Michigan four different times "to perform some duty requiring the utmost skill and bravery and I am happy to tell that every time they have done it to the entire satisfaction of the Generals and received their warmest thanks," Jeffords bragged.

In the meantime, the Union army was under orders to be prepared once again to move out from its encampments near Falmouth, but no such movement materialized. They heard that the great Confederate general Stonewall Jackson had died after being shot by his own men at Chancellorsville. As mid-May brought out fine weather and the greening of the countryside, it occurred to men like Bancroft that it was now the second anniversary the creation of the 4th Michigan. And though he'd only been their commander for a brief time, the enlisted men of the regiment presented Colonel Jeffords with what some of them called "a splendid horse," complete with saddle and bridle. The presentation on May 11 was made with a speech by Sergeant Major Richard Watson Seage, who was soon to be promoted to the rank of second lieutenant in Company I. Clearly, the troops of the 4th Michigan trusted and respected their commander. Jeffords was delighted and proud; the horse, he said, was "magnificent." "I wish you could see him," he wrote friends. "He is such a splendid fellow, the best horse in the Corps. So you see I am all right, and my good qualities are appreciated." At the same time, the commander of the brigade of which the 4th Michigan was part, Col. James McQuade, wrote a glowing endorsement of Capt. Jairus Hall to the governor of Michigan. "He is not only a gallant officer, but one of the very best disciplinarians that I know," McQuade wrote, recommending a promotion for Hall. This soon happened.[20]

There was disconcerting news in the army. Some regiments formed for only two years back in the spring of 1861 had now served out the term of their enlistments; so had regiments that formed for nine months, back during the summer of 1862. "9 mo[nth] and 2 yrs. troops are leaving every day," Lt. George Maltz told a friend. "We had one div[ision] commanded by Gen. Humphrey leave since our return, beside many other N.Y. Regts of our corps. The 14th N.Y. of our Brigade left today." The army needed thousands of more men, Maltz wrote. "Every man in the South is a Soldier and when we attack, these men rally to fight, leave their work, and go in with a will," he continued. "I think the North will learn in course of time what has to be done. Give us enough men and we can see the thing through and we can save the Union—Draft—Conscript, or anything else, I want to see it out now."[21]

On May 22, Major John M. Randolph, 36, of Ann Arbor, who'd started out his service with the 4th Michigan as the captain of Company D, was discharged for disability by a War Department order. Lt. John Bancroft hoped the major's post would be filled by Capt. Jairus Hall, who'd started out the war as a second lieutenant but who'd been leading Company D since late in the summer of 1862. "We hope to have him for Major in place of Randolph," Bancroft wrote. "[Capt. David D.] Marshall [of Company G] expects it but will not get three votes if left to the [officers of] the line." Bancroft had nothing to worry about. Harrison Jeffords had a good sense of the sentiments of his officers and men, and he recommended to Gov. Austin Blair that Jairus Hall be commissioned major.

But in the wake of Chancellorsville and the mustering out of thousands of soldiers, it didn't seem to men like Charles Phelps that the Union army was going anywhere soon, for the brigade commissary had recently moved ovens up to Kelly's Ford. "That looks like [we are] staying here," he wrote. Two years had passed since he'd joined the outfit that became Company D in the 4th Michigan. "I am on my last year now," Phelps wrote. "One year from the 16th of this month. The time will soon pass I hope[.] I don't think we will see more than one Battle if that (no knowing though)," he added.[22]

Many of the regiments of the First Division of the Fifth Corps cleaned up their camp or shifted into a new site, since it was thought this would improve their health. As the weather turned hot and muggy, the men put their quarters "in summer trim" on May 25 and 26, and a visit by Austin Blair to their camp and those of the nearby 7th and 16th Michigan regiments made for a pleasing distraction. "Gov. Blair made a speech here yesterday and it being the 1st one the men had heard for a long time, he tried several times to get a laugh or cheer," Lieutenant Bancroft wrote. "But when he told them he thought they would have been more successful [at Chancellorsville] had they been 100 miles farther from Washington, that succeeded." Yes, the men found that line funny, since many in the army believed government interference was its biggest problem.

It was, Bancroft said, "a gala day." The governor reviewed their brigade that afternoon before making his speech to the 4th Michigan, and the lieutenant was impressed that Blair, a Radical Republican, didn't use the opportunity to make critical comments about the Union army's favorite former commander, George McClellan. But Blair was an experienced politician and he was aware of his audience. "The boys were better satisfied than they expected as many of them curse the Republican for continuing the war etc., making it a negro war," Bancroft wrote about the speech. The governor had spoken of home and of the friends who prayed for the soldiers. The men liked that, and they were pleased to see that Blair brought along his wife and his niece. "The presence of the ladies was an unusual and pleasant thing," Bancroft said. Corporal Irvin Miner was among the men pleased with the governor's words. He wrote that Blair's speech was "enthusiastically received."[23]

The paymaster came the next day and the men were naturally pleased to see him. But hardly had they finished rebuilding their tent-covered shanties and their discussions of the governor's visit when they were ordered to pull up stakes and start on the march for Kelly's Ford, miles upriver to the northwest. Doubtless there was grumbling about the army's commanders and their knack for untimely decision-making. Again the soldiers broke down their tents and that afternoon marched 10 miles to Hartwood Church and bivouacked for the night. Their division and corps were on the move, heading for positions along the Rappahannock to guard the fords. The next day, the 4th Michigan marched on to Kelly's Ford along with a battery and another regiment, while another part of their Second Brigade took up positions at Ellis Ford a few miles away. Bancroft noted that the Fifth Corps commander, Gen. George G. Meade, came to look over his soldiers and their placement along the river.

Union soldiers, including companies from the 4th Michigan, were quickly put to work digging rifle pits. There were open fields at this location, mountains in the distance, and attractive women in the neighborhood, Lieutenant Bancroft said. Harrison Daniels of Company G remembered being smitten by a dark-eyed girl named Julia Reese who lived with her mother near Kelly's Ford. Daniels had stopped at the house to fill his canteen and shared sips of water from a gourd with Miss Reese. "Now I never would have believed that I, a Union soldier, could have fallen in love with a black eyed rebel, but when I had gone away, I found that to be a fact." Daniels visited her several times and managed to spend a few "happy hours" with her over the next three or four weeks.

The soldiers of the 4th Michigan could also see Confederates across the river. The men of the regiment did picket and underwent inspection, but they could also go fishing and swimming when they were off duty. One soldier, writing to a newspaper in Monroe, said it was a much more pleasant place than their last camp, where trees had been cut for miles around and where the grass had been trampled into the mud or dust. "Here we have plenty of shade and the fields are green with grass," wrote the man, who signed his letter "W." John Hewitt noted that Colonel Jeffords was put in charge of the forces guarding the ford near them on June 4, but one of the regiment's new soldiers, James Houghton of Company K, had a much more personally important matter to complain about—he'd been the victim of theft. "To day I got 37 dollars of my money stole," he complained.

The next day, Corporal Irvin Miner, like Harrison Daniels, became enamored of a girl of about 18 who was among a group of women he escorted into camp to trade. "I nearly lost my heart," he wrote, to this young lady who he decided was "good looking, accomplished, agreeable and rich though rather inclined to be rebellious." (Whether this young woman was the lovely Miss Reese, with whom Daniels was so taken, is unknown). The men could hear gunfire in the distance on June 6 as Union and Confederate cavalry clashed up the river, and the men expected to be moving out at any moment. Yet there were meetings between the two sides that weren't so hostile. Three days later, a sergeant from Company D swam over to the Rebel side of the Rappahannock while a Confederate soldier came over to the 4th Michigan's side. They exchanged newspapers. "Lieut. [Edwin] Gilbert [of Ann Arbor] commanding our company gave him a drink of whiskey," Charles Phelps wrote of the hospitality shown the visiting Reb. "That is the way it goes [—] one day on good terms and the next a Battle."[24]

But it was the regiment's chaplain who had the most dangerous experience of any member of the regiment in those early June days—the Reverend John Seage, father of Henry Seage and Lt. Richard Watson Seage. Chaplains routinely did duty as regimental mail carriers or took on other responsibilities, and on June 8, the English-born John Seage, 53, had an even more important job. At 4:00 P.M., he rode out of the 4th Michigan's camp at Kelly's Ford on a good horse, with

$6,000 or more from the men of the regiment and a few broken watches in his haversack. The chaplain was on his way to Washington, D.C., to forward the money on to men's families and to get the watches repaired.

Reverend Seage had made himself a reputation as a caring but tough, no-nonsense preacher. When a Union officer insultingly questioned the courage of 4th Michigan soldiers separated by mistake from the regiment at Fredericksburg, John Seage, enraged, called the officer "a drunken liar." Nor did the chaplain sit back and watch as others went into combat. Colonel Jeffords noted that during battle, Seage "fights or prays & don't care which." After Chancellorsville, Jeffords wrote, Reverend Seage had come across a man burying dead soldiers, but one had been a tall fellow in life and his corpse wasn't going to fit in the grave dug for him. When the chaplain saw that the gravedigger was about to cut the dead soldier's legs off rather than dig a proper grave, John Seage dealt him a severe lesson in respect for the dead. "The Chaplain knocked him down & kicked [him] after he was down [and] licked him handsomely," Jeffords wrote with satisfaction.

This was the picture of the Reverend Seage as he rode into the late afternoon, carrying the thousands of dollars entrusted to him by his regiment. Lt. Robert Campbell later wrote that Seage spoke of riding into a thicket of woods, with a ravine on one side of the road. "I was alone & on horseback When 12 miles from the Camp near Deep Run Mill I was halted by a party of men who ordered me to halt & surrender," Seage reported. "I asked by what authority? The leader replied ['I]n the name of Mosby's Cavalry.['] I replied, 'I don't recognize that authority & shan't surrender.[']"

In one account of this incident, John Seage said there were five horsemen confronting him that evening, armed with revolvers. Three of them fired as Seage wheeled his horse, "or rather the horse turned," Seage wrote. A bullet ripped through the chaplain's right wrist, tearing the artery and smashing bone, lodging in his ribs. His horse jumped across the ditch as the gunmen fired. Seage was hit in the back, the bullet going through his left shoulder and breaking his clavicle as it exited. A third bullet cut his left ankle and a fourth, he said, "made a flesh wound in my thigh."[25]

But even as he was hit, his horse plunged on through the trees. The crippling wounds to his wrist and shoulder left Reverend Seage's hands useless, and he was bleeding heavily, but he was fortunate in one important regard: he had the best horse. Seage's mount quickly outpaced the pursuing Rebels as they galloped after him. He was barely conscious, but he stayed in the saddle. "Our Division train & Commissary was about a mile back, thither my horse took me," he wrote. In the meantime, some men from the 4th Michigan were detailed to guard that supply train, and they heard the gunshots. When they saw a rider approaching a short time later, they ran to see who it was. "My God!" someone shouted. "It's our chaplain." Seage, having lost so much blood his vision was failing, was taken to doctors there with the wagon train. Word was carried back to the regiment's camp, and his sons and two other men hurried over to see him that night. By the time his sons returned the next day, "we found Father doin well," Henry Seage wrote in his journal.

The Reverend John Seage survived. He hadn't lost any of the five watches, 26 letters, and thousands of dollars that officers and men of the regiment entrusted him to transmit to their families. As it turned out, John Seage only had a few days to rest there with the Union army before it marched north on the start of what would become known as the Gettysburg campaign.

By ambulance, train, and boat, Henry Seage took his father to a Washington hospital, his wrist in splints and both arms in slings. His wounds were restitched and rebandaged, and a medical man John Seage identified as the surgeon-in-chief of the army, a Dr. Clymer, sent him home for two months to recover. Though the Reverend Seage was partially disabled by his wounds for the rest of his life, he would return to his regiment.

Over the course of the war, Mosby's raiders and other guerillas would interrupt, waylay, rob, capture, or destroy hundreds of Union wagons and wagoners, expresses, trains, messengers, and dispatch riders. But the Reverend John Seage was one who got away.[26]

There were bigger, more momentous events in the works, and even newspaper correspondents recognized it. "Mysterious Movements of Rebel Troops," one headline read late in May. "Believed they are Preparing to Make a Demonstration." Union balloonists could plainly see columns of Confederates marching, dust rising. But why, the papers asked. Was it simply a ruse? A distraction so that J. E. B. Stuart's cavalry could conduct a deep raid into the North? How would the Union Army of the Potomac respond? None of the soldiers knew. But by early June Union generals had reports that the Army of Northern Virginia was marching north. The 4th Michigan remained at Kelly's Ford, the men walking picket, swimming in the river, and enjoying the first crop of cherries and mulberries. But persimmons were not ripe, at least not yet; Lt. Orvey S. Barrett of Company B experienced a close call when he separated himself from his fellow pickets on the river to get some of this fruit.

Temporarily posted at the Mountain Run Ford, about three miles from Kelly's Ford, Barrett wrote, his company patrolled the river, watching for Rebel cavalry and keeping their eye on the house of a rabid anti-Union man named Atkinson. One morning, Barrett said, he climbed a persimmon tree on the bank of the river to pick some fruit while his comrades moved on. Suddenly a squad of Rebel cavalry appeared across the river, their carbines aimed at him. "Yank, come over," one ordered. Barrett replied that he couldn't swim, but they weren't interested in his excuse. As Barrett dropped down from the tree, one of the troopers fired over his head to impress upon him the need to obey. But rather than comply, Barrett rolled and scrambled to cover as the Rebels fired at him. The shots brought his patrol and the reserve pickets on the run and the troopers rode off. Only Barrett's pride was hurt, and it turned out the persimmons he picked weren't ripe, but horribly bitter.[27]

Finally on June 10, proof of the much-talked of movement came into the 4th Michigan's camp—orders for their brigade to be ready to march with three days' worth of rations. They did not leave just yet, though, and that week heard cannons in the distance as the cavalry clashed upriver and they watched as two other Union corps marched by. The companies of the 4th Michigan underwent inspection, waiting for word to move out. As the soldiers stood watch along the river or swam or did washing, they continued to trade items and sometimes insults with Confederates. Barrett said one wag from the 4th Michigan called over to a raggedly dressed soldier on the opposite bank: "I say, Johnny Reb, why don't you wear better clothes?" The Rebel didn't miss a beat. "We-uns don't wear our best clothes when we go to kill hogs," he replied.[28]

Edward H. C. Taylor, who had been working as clerk at the First Division, wrote to his relatives that he was now back with the 4th Michigan and promoted to sergeant major. "It will not be so easy as my clerkship," he wrote, "but chances are good for the future." That same night

Irvin Miner and other soldiers bathed in the Rappahannock and noticed that two Confederate officers were watching them, but a thunderstorm blew in bringing a hard rain. The next day, June 13, was warm, and new clothing was issued to some of the troops—another seemingly routine day. But then the order came around 4:00 P.M. and the men of the 4th Michigan struck their tents. In the evening they marched, moving only six miles to the town of Morrisville. Though they did not know it, the lead elements of the Army of Northern Virginia were as far as 100 miles north on the other side of the Blue Ridge Mountains in Maryland, on their way into Pennsylvania.

The regiment reunited with their Second Brigade, First Division, and Fifth Corps. Their job guarding the fords along the Rappahannock was over, and they marched from the river on a route that headed north-northeast, in the direction of Washington, D.C., with most of the rest of the Army of the Potomac. Over the next two days, they moved about 20 miles, first to Catlett Station and then to Manassas Junction in the rising heat, the army on its guard. The regiment remained at the junction with its division and corps on June 16 but was shifted to the west a few miles that night into the Thoroughfare Gap, to picket along the railroad line at this passage through the Bull Run or Catoctin Mountains. The march resumed the next day, about 15 miles through Centreville and on to Gum Springs. It was so hot that a man dropped out of the ranks from exhaustion every few moments that afternoon, Lieutenant Bancroft wrote. The men learned that Lee's army was invading Pennsylvania.

The 4th Michigan, with its division, remained in bivouac under a blazing sun there on June 18 and most of the next day, and they could hear the sound of gunfire as the cavalry clashed at the mountain passes. They marched at 4:00 P.M., covering a few miles to the town of Aldie, situated on the edge of mountains where the Confederate cavalry was screening the northward movement of Lee's army in the Shenandoah Valley to the west. A hard rain set in that night, and again the regiment got a rainy day of rest when their brigade stayed in bivouac on June 20.[29]

The next day they awoke before dawn and marched west with a force of cavalry and infantry from their division, through the pass to the town of Middleburg, where other Union troops pushed the Confederate cavalry back. The 4th Michigan, acting as a support or reserve, wasn't involved in the fighting, and soldiers used the opportunity to forage chicken, mutton, fruit, and milk in the countryside. They bivouacked in the field and came back to Aldie on June 22, remaining for four days. Jim Houghton said the soldiers of the regiment were the victims of fraud when they stopped at a mill on the return to Aldie at dusk. The men crowded in to get flour, which was a rare thing for soldiers on the march. But it wasn't until they were leaving that the realized they'd gotten plaster of Paris instead. In revenge, some of the soldiers went back to the mill and stole a beehive full of honey, while others helped themselves to the milk of local dairy cows; some butchered a calf. The men were in good spirits, Lieutenant Bancroft wrote, though they would be glad of the chance to get clean clothes and food that was more than hardtack, boiled beef, and coffee. The next day was June 24, and Corporal Henry Seage, who had escorted his wounded father to Washington and put him on a train home, returned to the regiment.

There was one more day in camp at Aldie—the men heard the news that tens of thousands of Confederate soldiers were marching toward Harrisburg. Their own march north continued early in the afternoon of June 26 and into the night, going about 15 miles through Leesburg, across the

Potomac at Edwards Ferry over a pontoon bridge into Maryland. It was around this time that the soldiers of the 4th Michigan went through the property of a northern Virginia plantation owner who'd become an officer in the Confederate army. Though Houghton didn't give a specific date, this incident occurred while the army was on the march out of northern Virginia. The place had many cherry trees that were full of fruit. But they didn't just pick the cherries—they chopped off all the trees' branches and limbs. "Other trees were served in the same way till the Boys got all they wanted," he wrote.

The regiment's diarists noted it rained on the 26th, and Lieutenant Bancroft, who had been sick, called their travel that day "one of the most tiresome marches of the war." Luke Barnes of Company C, now about 23, was unable to keep up and was captured that day by Confederates. But exhaustion and foraging aside, the men understood what was at stake. The Army of Northern Virginia was now strung out in long columns as it invaded Pennsylvania, and this could be the opportunity the Union army needed to trap and destroy it. In four days, their corps, too, would be in Pennsylvania, joining most of the rest of the Army of the Potomac. "It is thought throughout the army that he [Lee] is getting himself into a trap of his own setting by going so far north, and that he had better remain on his own 'sacred soil,'" a soldier from the 4th Michigan wrote to his hometown newspaper. "Should he with his army get captured up there, it would be a gigantic death blow to the rebellion."[30]

The soldiers of the 4th Michigan marched seven miles into Maryland, having moved about 15 miles that day with their corps. The Union army continued north by different roads and routes, staying between the Confederate army and Washington. Irvin Miner of Company F said the country they'd left behind was "the most beautiful" he'd seen in Virginia. The next day, June 27, they marched at 6:00 A.M., their brigade reaching the Monocacy River around noon. But the horses couldn't cross at this point, so the troops continued up the river to a ford and crossed about five in the afternoon Some soldiers like Henry Seage fell out, exhausted, while their comrades tramped on. Their brigade paused for dinner and then continued into the night, finally stopping near Frederick. Sgt. John Hewitt, also of Company E and one of the regiment's farm boys, marveled at the scenic countryside, the picturesque farms, and the good crops.

The regiment stayed in bivouac on June 28 and walked picket that evening, guarding the nearby railroad. That day word spread that their corps commander, Gen. George Gordon Meade, had been made commander of the Army of the Potomac—Joe Hooker had resigned in an angry feud over the movement and placement of forces with the general-in-chief at the War Department, Henry Halleck. The promotion of Meade to command of the army resulted in the promotion of Gen. George Sykes, a career army officer, to command of the Fifth Corps. There had also been a temporary change in the command the corps's First Division—just after Chancellorsville, Brig. Gen. Charles Griffin went on sick leave, so the senior brigade commander in the division, Brig. Gen. James Barnes, took his place.

The next day the men of the 4th Michigan returned to their bivouac from picket, packed up, and marched to the northeast, covering some 20 miles. Two of Cpl. Henry Seage's Company E comrades, Frank Waller and George Walker, got into a fight along the way, and their company commander, Lt. George L. Maltz of Detroit, "parted them by knocking Waller down with his sword." But Waller apparently got the last shot in, throwing a punch that left Walker with a gash under his eye. It was well past sundown when their division stopped for the night a couple miles beyond the town of Liberty. A summer rain soaked the landscape and the troops.

The men broke camp at 3:00 A.M. on June 30 and began their march without breakfast. It continued a rainy day as they trooped east and north, their packs heavier with the soaking. They passed through the tiny town of Unionville, Maryland, where residents turned out to cheer, wave flags, and sing patriotic songs, James Houghton remembered. "This made us forget our tired limbs and sore feet for a while," he wrote. As their brigade reached the town of Union Mills that night, they learned that thousands of Rebel troopers, J. E. B. Stuart's cavalry division, had ridden through that very morning. Henry Seage said the Union officers decided to send out skirmishers two miles ahead before they camped, tired and hungry. The men washed off the days' sweat and grime and mud in Pipe Creek.[31]

In the meantime General Meade organized his new staff and received reports about the strength and location of the Confederate army, some 80,000 troops under Lee. Moving along scores of miles of Pennsylvania roads from Chambersburg to York and Carlisle, they were in a dangerous situation. When Lee learned the Union army was much closer than he'd thought, he ordered his generals to pull their divisions together. By the night of June 30, they had almost all done so. The confrontation between the armies would begin the next day as both converged on a small crossroads town called Gettysburg.

CHAPTER 10

They Were Soon on All Sides of Us

THE MEN OF THE 4TH MICHIGAN ROSE AND DREW RATIONS WITH THEIR BRIGADE EARLY ON THE morning of July 1, but the march didn't start until around nine o'clock. Lt. Robert Campbell, the quartermaster, wrote that Col. Harrison Jeffords came to him that morning, concerned that many of the soldiers of the regiment had taken to wearing hats with brims rather than regulation forage caps. Jeffords, about 26, understood that a hat was better for keeping the hot sun off a man's head and neck, but the regiment would soon be marching into Pennsylvania—a good Union state. Hats just weren't "soldier-like" in appearance, Jeffords felt. "I want you to draw caps for those men, so that all may look alike," the colonel said, according to Campbell.

The two men had gone to high school together, but Campbell had to tell the colonel that it would take requisitions by all the company commanders for him to get the caps. Jeffords wasn't interested in waiting. "Then I order you to get a cap for every man in the regiment who hasn't one," he said. Campbell smiled at this. "All right, Colonel," he replied, "but you must give me a written order to that effect." The two officers went on about their business. When he saw Jeffords minutes later, Campbell thought the colonel would give him the order for the caps. Instead, Jeffords handed his revolver to Campbell and told him to never mind about the caps. "I was at the first Bull Run, on the Peninsula Seven Days' fighting, second Bull Run, Antietam, Fredericksburg and Chancellorsville," Jeffords said, turning over the pistol. "In all these campaigns, I have never needed to use it, and it has been a heavy load to carry."

Supply officers like Campbell were often with the wagon trains, vulnerable to raids like one Stuart's cavalry had just made. "You as quartermaster are liable to be mixed up with the guerillas and have much more need of it than I have," Jeffords continued. "Besides, you have better means of transportation for heavy artillery than I have." Campbell said he considered the colonel's remarks only half-serious, but he accepted Jeffords's sidearm. "Within a few minutes the bugle sounded," Campbell remembered. Time to move out. The 4th Michigan began the long day's march with its brigade, division, and corps.[1]

The 4th Michigan's part of the column reached the state line in the afternoon. James Houghton of Company K wrote that Jeffords ordered the regiment to a halt after they crossed into the Keystone State. "Men," he said, "you are now standing on free soil once more. Now give three cheers for the free states." The soldiers roared their approval and continued on the road to Hanover, several miles away. The troops were hailed as heroes and given sandwiches and drinks of cold water as they marched through small Pennsylvania communities. "A glorious reception was given by the ladies in all the towns we passed through," Sergeant Hewitt noted. By around 5:00 P.M. their division reached Hanover. The column turned off the road about a mile from town, the soldiers figuring this was their bivouac. They had seen dead horses in the area and other signs of the recent fight between Stuart's troopers and Michigan cavalrymen, now under the command of the young brigadier, George Custer, with whom they'd crossed the Chickahominy at New Bridge. Lt. John Bancroft of Company H and Assistant Surgeon John Watts stopped to dine with a local woman Bancroft described as an authoress, while the soldiers made their meals. But just 90 minutes after halting, they were told there would be no bivouac here—the march must go on. "While eating our supper at Hanover we had heard the heavy guns to the westward," John Bancroft wrote years later.

The men of the Fifth Corps fell in, tramping toward Gettysburg, where other Union troops had for hours been engaged in bloody battle. Evening came on, then twilight and then moonlit night, but the march continued. A rumor that George McClellan had once been more made their commander—false but heartening—swept through the ranks, Lt. Orvey S. Barrett of Company B wrote, and officers repeated it, boosting the men's spirits. "An Aide-de-camp came riding along, saying: 'Boys, keep good courage, McClellan is command of the army again,'" Barrett wrote. He said that he knew this was false, as did Lieutenant Campbell. But the soldiers cheered and threw their hats in the air.

It was around midnight when the tired soldiers halted and the regiment's diarists got their chance to record the events of July 1; their corps had covered over 20 miles. Irvin Miner of Company F wrote that they were within five miles of Gettysburg, "tired sore and nearly played out." The soldiers moved off the road, ate cold salt pork and hardtack, and lay down in some woods to sleep. "We were well aware," Houghton wrote later, "that the next day would be a day of bloodshed."[2]

Gettysburg

"Rose at 4 A.M.," Henry Seage wrote about the morning of July 2, "had inspection [of] arms." Before daylight, the march of the final few miles to Gettysburg began. The regiment, with its brigade, division, and corps, turned off the Hanover Road as they neared the Confederate-held town, going left, or south, and then west on country roads that took them to the Union army's position on the hills south of town. Lieutenant Bancroft wrote that the regiment advanced, probably with others from their brigade and division, back north toward the Hanover Road, but they were recalled before 8:00 A.M. Their brigade's commander, Col. Jacob B. Sweitzer, reported that their division was initially placed by a farm on what he understood was the Union right. This was near Wolf's Hill, high ground east of Rock Creek and south of the Hanover Road. A regiment from their brigade, the 9th Massachusetts, was chosen here for picket duty and detached, leaving the 4th Michigan, 62nd Pennsylvania, and 32nd Massachusetts to comprise Sweitzer's command.

Soon the brigade was shifted with the rest of the First Division and Fifth Corps from the right of the Union line toward the center and left. Sweitzer reported his Second Brigade was "moved a considerable distance to the left." This was about a mile to the southwest, the point where Rock Creek passed under the road to Baltimore; soon it was moved further west. Bancroft also noted this shifting movement in account he wrote in his diary shortly after the battle. "[W]e formed in Mass and moved southward to the Baltimore and Gettysburg Pike up which we moved over a small creek and lay in the sun upon the hillside until about three[-thirty] P.M.," he wrote. This high ground was called Powers Hill, and some accounts say the men rested in an orchard. "There we remained until late in the afternoon (the precise time I do not remember), and the command had a few hours' quiet and rest," Sweitzer wrote. This wasn't quiet in the conventional sense; it was just that his men weren't under fire at that moment as cannon periodically sounded. The day was warm and partly cloudy; Bancroft noted the 4th Michigan moved into an open field, where the men lay down. As the sun rose higher in the lengthening afternoon, their brigade commander wondered if they would become engaged in battle at all.[3]

Across the woods and fields a mile or more west of where the Fifth Corps rested, two Confederate divisions moved into position parallel to and across the Emmitsburg Road, which ran south-southwest from Gettysburg. These Rebels would launch Lee's second day attack on the left of the Army of the Potomac. On the first day of the battle, July 1, attacking Confederates badly hurt the army's First Corps and sent it and the Eleventh Corps retreating through Gettysburg to Cemetery Hill, a prominent height just south of town. More Union forces arrived through the night. As a result, this high ground—a natural defensive position, was held in the early morning hours of July 2 by four strong Union corps as well as the Eleventh and the damaged First corps, their line stretching nearly two miles. The Fifth Corps now waited in reserve near the center of this line. At the same time the Sixth Corps was marching north up the Baltimore Pike to join them.

Gen. George Meade's forces should have been in a good position to defend against another attack. But early in the afternoon the commander on the Union left, a politically connected appointee, Gen. Dan Sickles of New York, ignored Meade's orders and shifted his Third Corps from that north-south ridge line anchored by a rocky hill called Little Round Top. He moved his corps as much as three-quarters of a mile forward through the landscape of boulders and ridges, oddly shaped farm fields and woodlots. This created gaps in a now-uneven line, the Union army's left wing hanging, thin and vulnerable.

At about 3:00 P.M. Meade ordered the Fifth Corps to march to the left to support Sickles. When the order reached the First Division, officers shouted, bugles and drums sounded, and the soldiers shouldered their rifles and packs in the afternoon heat. The 4th Michigan's James Houghton wrote that the men were issued 20 extra cartridges, "which we put in our haversacks where we could get them handy." The brigades of their division—the Third, the Second, and the First—marched west from Powers Hill on a lane called the Granite School House Road about three-quarters of a mile to the Taneytown Road. "We then proceeded to the front and left by a small by-road," Bancroft wrote of this movement, "passed the ammunition train on our left[,] just as they were drawing off, the rebels having begun to shell them." His reference to the Confederate barrage meant it was about 4:00 P.M.[4]

Other accounts indicate the First Division column marched south on the Taneytown Road for a short distance and turned right, moving west across country and through some woods. They were greeted by the familiar punch and roar of Confederate artillery on hills to the west and the reply of Union guns. The 4th Michigan was probably near the center of the column as it briefly halted its march to join the left wing of the Union army. The zigzag line ahead of them was held by three brigades from Sickles's Third Corps and bolstered by artillery batteries. It covered about a thousand yards, jutting southeast to northwest from a strange glacial pile of gigantic boulders called Devil's Den, to their left, over sometimes broken ground variously covered by trees, fields, scrub growth, and stone fences to the Emmitsburg Road. As artillery echoed over this landscape, Rebel infantry emerged from the woods to the south and west.[5]

Two brigades of Confederate troops, including some of the South's finest fighting men in the division of Gen. John Bell Hood, led the assault, advancing east over the farms in front of a large, tree-covered hill called Round Top, which lay just south of Little Round Top. Their assignment was to smash and turn the Union left. Less than an hour earlier, Meade's chief engineer, Gen. Gouverneur Warren, found out that Sickles had left Little Round Top undefended. He was stunned, for it was clear that a major attack by Rebel infantry was about to begin. He immediately sent aides to find a brigade to hold that hill. Those aides rode hurriedly down to find Fifth Corps officers who could provide troops, and it was about this point that the head of the First Division of the Fifth Corps stopped on the low ground northwest of Little Round Top, the men waiting for officers to determine where they would take their positions.[6]

Warren's urgent message had reached General Sykes, the Fifth Corps commander, and he sent an aide riding up to the First Division's column, looking for Brig. Gen. James Barnes. The aide was intercepted by Col. Strong Vincent, commander of the division's Third Brigade. When told that troops were needed to hold Little Round Top, Vincent turned his brigade and made for the hill, arriving there just ahead of Hood's men. That left Barnes's division with only two brigades to help Sickles—the First Brigade, under Col. William S. Tilton, and the short-handed Second Brigade, which included the 4th Michigan with its 316 enlisted men and 26 officers. They moved forward on the Millerstown Road, soon to be known as the Wheatfield Road, to join the Third Corps.

As the Second Brigade marched on, Colonel Sweitzer reported, they skirted some woods. This was likely a triangular-shaped parcel of trees called Trostle's Woods that lay just north of the wheat field owned by farmer John Rose. There was also a larger woodlot nearby on undulating land to the south, called Rose's Woods. This lot was roughly five hundred yards wide with a strip of trees at its western end, extending north toward the Wheatfield Road. The Wheatfield, estimated by different historians to have been between 11 and 20 acres in size, stood directly east of this band of trees and north of the main portion of Rose's Woods. In addition to the trees bordering the Wheatfield, there were stone fences enclosing it along the southern and eastern sides. The Wheatfield Road ran at an angle along the northern edge of the field.

As the guns pounded and the 4th Michigan marched with its brigade by the yellow field of grain, the next wave of Confederates in two more brigades came from the west, heading toward Devil's Den and Rose's Woods. Some of the soldiers the 4th Michigan would soon face were among these attackers—Georgians under Brig. Gen. George "Tige" Anderson. The Georgians had a terrible march across the fields as Union artillery fired. The 4th Michigan filed into position in the woods on the western end of the Wheatfield, a stand of trees about 500 feet wide. "There was also a battery planted there that was feeding the Rebbels with grape and canister as fast as they could," James Houghton wrote. Possibly he was referring to guns positioned along the Wheatfield Road just west of where the Michigan men waited, but he may have meant a New York battery there in the Wheatfield.

The wooded strip where the 4th Michigan and its brigade took their position stood in part on a wide rocky ledge the soldiers later called Stony Hill and also on some low ground slightly west and south of the Wheatfield, below the hill. Some of this low ground was open and wet but some was covered by the trees and brush of Rose's Woods. The Stony Hill wasn't a commanding height like the Round Tops, but a rise of ground like a wide rocky shelf above the field, reaching a height of several feet. Their brigade occupied this area, with the 4th Michigan on the Stony Hill at the far right of their line, facing west-northwest. Those who had a view from the trees saw rolling land stretching west toward the Peach Orchard and the Emmitsburg Road. Their comrades from Tilton's First Brigade connected in Rose's Woods on their left, at an angle. Tilton's troops faced south.

A few hundred yards further south, Sickles's men on the extreme left of this jagged line became involved in firefights with attacking Rebels. These Union soldiers near Devil's Den and the southeastern portion of Rose's Woods were under the command of Brig. Gen. J. H. Hobart Ward. Other troops, mostly under the command of Col. Philippe Regis de Trobriand, were posted along the southern edge of the Wheatfield, linking with Tilton's brigade. Volleys of rifle fire spread down their line as Anderson's Georgians and other Confederate troops came on. The shooting intensified and at least two Union regiments fighting in the trees southeast of the 4th Michigan's position retreated north across the Wheatfield when they were hit by Confederate fire from the front and flank.[7]

The arrival of Tilton's and Sweitzer's brigades allowed other Third Corps regiments on or near the Stony Hill to join the fighting near Devil's Den and in Rose's Woods, where they were soon needed. "We . . . marched near to where the Third Corps was fighting," Houghton recalled. "The regiment that we was to relieve was stationed in the north end of a narrow strip of woods that lies directly west of the Wheatfield." But with no Confederates in front of the 4th Michigan or the regiment to their left, the 62nd Pennsylvania, Colonel Sweitzer ordered them to change positions, turning to the south to support the one regiment of their brigade, the 32nd Massachusetts, that became involved in the fighting on the lower, southern portion of the wooded hill. The 4th Michigan continued waiting.

An anonymous account of the battle in a letter by an officer of the 4th Michigan (probably Lt. John Bancroft), published in Detroit a month after the battle, echoed these preliminaries. "[W]e formed, in the edge of a wood, facing *west,* a battery in open ground on our right, and part of [the] Third Corps on our left, facing *south,* and engaged with the enemy in the woods to our left," the officer wrote. Bancroft's diary and postwar Gettysburg account, in substantially similar language, agreed. Though the 4th Michigan wasn't in the front line, bullets were "whizzing, buz[z]ing and spatting all around us," Houghton remembered. "We were ordered to [lie] down as we could do no firing while there was other troops in front of us." Soon the walking wounded, soldiers on their way to find medical attention, began to limp by. Houghton said that those who could do so shouted at the waiting Michigan soldiers, "Go in and give them hell!" The 4th Michigan hadn't yet fired a shot.[8]

Unable to break the Union line in Rose's Woods, General Anderson pulled his brigade back and the firing died away. It was about 5:00 P.M., possibly later. But this lull didn't last long; Anderson's troops attacked again as more Confederates came into the fight—about 1,800 South Carolinians under Brig. Gen. Joseph Kershaw, followed by another brigade under Brig. Gen. Paul Semmes. Kershaw's target was the Stony Hill and the guns that stood nearby along the Wheatfield Road. Again Union artillery cut down scores of Rebels as they advanced. Late afternoon was turning to evening and Union soldiers in the woods on the southern part of the Stony Hill traded rifle fire with some of Kershaw's and Anderson's troops.

As the Confederates' renewed attack commenced on the Stony Hill and toward the Wheatfield Road to the northwest, a surprising order from General Barnes came to Colonel Sweitzer: When it came time to pull out, his brigade should fall back to the cover of Trostle's Woods. That order upset the commander of the 32nd Massachusetts, whose men had been more involved in the fighting than any other regiment in the Second Brigade so far. Prepare to retreat? But why? Yet Sweitzer soon learned that Tilton's First Brigade, to his left, was indeed pulling out. Soon Barnes ordered Sweitzer to withdraw his troops, too, concerned his men were about to be flanked by the Rebels attacking across the fields to the west. Barnes thought his two brigades should fall back and form a new line, since there was only a line of Union artillery to his right—guns that were vulnerable because they were unsupported by infantry. He was also concerned about the large gap between those batteries and his men's position on Stony Hill.

Much to the surprise of Colonel de Trobriand, Barnes's First and Second brigades, including the 4th Michigan, dropped back. And to the surprise of Confederate General Kershaw, the Union forces on the Stony Hill "seemed to melt away." The 4th Michigan, along with its fellow regiments, withdrew to the north, across the Wheatfield Road into Trostle's Woods. Now the remaining regiments of the Third Corps near Devil's Den and the Wheatfield, some fighting stubbornly and incurring high casualties, were driven back. Nearly two hours had gone by since the Confederate attack began, and so far the 4th Michigan had played no role in the fighting.

As their brigade marched to Trostle's Woods across from the Wheatfield, more Confederate infantry was heading their way.[9]

The Wheatfield

About the same time the 4th Michigan was pulled off Stony Hill with its brigade, a critical message reached Maj. Gen. Winfield Hancock, commander of the Second Corps, near the center of the Union line: Reinforcements were needed on the Union left. Hancock ordered a division under Gen. John C. Caldwell into the fight and soon Caldwell's four brigades were forming in or near Trostle's Woods. As Sweitzer's and Tilton's brigades waited in the western part of those woods, Caldwell's brigades marched out, one after another, across the Wheatfield Road into combat in Rose's Woods and on the Stony Hill. In the meantime, Sickles's vulnerable positions were hit hard and driven back by advancing Confederates. Caldwell's fresh troops confronted Anderson's and Kershaw's brigades, forcing most of these Rebel soldiers to retreat. It appeared that the Union reinforcements halted the Confederate assault and regained lost ground. The Rebel troops had fought hard and suffered serious losses even before Caldwell's division drove them off the Stony Hill and out of the Wheatfield. Most retreated into Rose's Woods.[10]

As the 4th Michigan waited with its brigade in Trostle's Woods, their part in this bloody battle began to unfold. Colonel Sweitzer initially reported that his men had been in those trees for 15 minutes (though in a supplemental report he admitted he couldn't say how long it was) when General Caldwell rode up to him. "[He] said his brigade was driving the enemy like hell over yonder in the woods, pointing at the same time beyond the wheat field, and asked if I would give him the support of my brigade," Sweitzer reported. "I referred him to General Barnes, who was not far off." Caldwell quickly consulted with Barnes, who gave his consent. The 4th Michigan and the other two regiments of Sweitzer's brigade, about 1,000 soldiers and officers in all, were called to attention and Barnes made brief, patriotic remarks. The soldiers responded with a cheer, "and we started off across the wheat-field in a line parallel to the road, our right flank resting on the woods," Sweitzer wrote in his initial report. That "right flank" of his brigade was the 4th Michigan, at the western edge of the field.

In the moments before they advanced, it is likely that Colonel Jeffords gave commands to his regiment, with the color guard, bearing the U.S. flag Lieutenant Campbell picked out back in March, stepping out six paces ahead of their line. Officers of the three regiments of Sweitzer's brigade would have barked orders down the lines: "Regiment, shoulder arms—forward, march!" The Michigan troops, along with the Pennsylvania and Massachusetts regiments, moved south over the Wheatfield. James Houghton recalled that "we moved up in line of battle to the South end of this narrow strip of woods that lies west of the Wheat field." The brigade commander noted that the 4th Michigan headed into low ground covered by brush and trees, the area where the 32nd Massachusetts had been posted earlier.[11]

But all was not going well for the Union soldiers in the woods up ahead. Houghton said that in the minutes before they'd moved out, he saw other Union outfits—"the battery and Infantry that was in front of us"—stop firing and move in the direction of Little Round Top. They were retreating, pulling back to the east. The guns he mentioned were Capt. George Winslow's Battery D, 1st New York Light Artillery, which had been posted in the Wheatfield. Other Union troops in Rose's Woods were fiercely engaged by Rebel troops, and Union batteries to the northwest at the Peach Orchard were about to come under attack by the brigades of Confederate generals William Wofford and William Barksdale. Lieutenant Bancroft saw wounded Union troops streaming back, and he also figured they were from the Third Corps, though certainly many of these soldiers were from Caldwell's division of the Second Corps. Other witnesses indicated some of the retreating soldiers soon included the 4th Michigan's own comrades in the First Brigade. "The 3rd Corps were badly cut up in the woods and wounded men were coming back through our ranks when we were ordered forward," Bancroft wrote. Houghton said that the 4th Michigan "moved up and occupied their position." Now it was after 6:00 P.M.[12]

There was good reason for these Union soldiers to retreat. Though Rebel troops from the brigades of Anderson, Kershaw, and Semmes had been driven out of those trees earlier when Caldwell's division hit them, they refused to quit. Along with Wofford's men coming from the west, they reformed and advanced. In fighting that was sometime hand-to-hand, these Confederates engaged and enveloped the Union troops and drove them back. With some Northern soldiers running out of ammunition and others seeing their positions being turned, Caldwell's men, like the Union soldiers who'd been out near the Emmitsburg Road, retreated. Many were killed and wounded. Some accounts say that it was at this point that Caldwell turned to General Barnes for additional troops—he needed these men because his own brigades were hard pressed. The Union line from Rose's Woods to the Peach Orchard and beyond was giving way.[13]

Though the sound of fighting raged that evening, James Houghton wrote, there seemed to be a lull just before the 4th Michigan marched across the Wheatfield with the other two regiments of their brigade. Col. Sweitzer reported his troops advanced to the stone fence in the trees south of the field, the 4th Michigan on the far right. He believed his men were going to support "our friends in the woods in front," and that Tilton's First Brigade was going to connect with his Michigan troops in the trees up ahead. In reality, the only friends in the woods up ahead were retreating. In the letter extract published in Detroit a month later, the unnamed 4th Michigan officer wrote that his regiment had skirmishers out in those woods before the brigade advanced, but these skirmishers came back and rejoined the regiment—a point made by Lieutenant Bancroft in both his July 2 diary entry and in an account he would send to the Michigan adjutant general years later.

Even as the 4th Michigan marched south, Rebels they couldn't yet see were advancing fast on their right, heading for the trees on the Stony Hill. These were Wofford's men, helping silence the batteries at the Peach Orchard and Wheatfield Road along with Barksdale's troops. With Kershaw's men they soon reached the Stony Hill west and northwest of the 4th Michigan's position. At the same time to the south and southwest, the brigades of Anderson and Semmes again advanced into Rose's Woods.

"We moved across the wheatfield and opened fire in response to the stray shots that were coming from the rebels in our front," Bancroft wrote. Those shots, fired from points south of the 4th Michigan line, were probably from Anderson's men. The unnamed officer from the 4th Michigan whose account was published after the battle stated that Company A was on the far right of the regiment's line as it marched to its position—a distance he estimated was about 500 feet—and some of its men saw Rebels coming from the west. Word was sent to Col. Jeffords about these Confederates on their right, the officer wrote. The regiment came to a halt as the firing commenced with the Rebels in the trees directly before them. Now the 4th Michigan and the other two regiments from their brigade would discover they had marched into a deadly situation.[14]

It was a hot evening in Rose's Woods. Houghton said he and his comrades opened fire "in good earnest" at "the Rebs that was south of us." These included Capt. George Hillyer's 9th Georgia Infantry Regiment, part of Tige Anderson's brigade. Because this regiment had lost so many officers, Hillyer was in command. The 9th Georgia had been fighting since shortly after 4:00 P.M. Hillyer wrote that he and his men were in line with their brigade near a branch of Plum Run that flowed through Rose's Woods. The Georgians took cover in the bed of the creek, in the low ground near the southwest corner of the Wheatfield, their rifles resting on the top of the bank. Through the trees they had watched Union troops cross the Wheatfield.

While Hillyer didn't know the identity of these Northern men, historian Harry P. Pfanz believed they must have been from the 4th Michigan. Hillyer saw a Yankee color-bearer marching proudly, a handsome man carrying a fresh-looking flag, several feet in advance of his regiment's line, which halted in the woods. This soldier waved the flag, seeming to flaunt it at the Confederates, before he stepped back into position. Hillyer said this line of Union troops opened fire at about 40 yards from the Georgians, but the volley passed over his men, protected by the creek embankment. He ordered his men to fire and they did so rapidly. Soon through the smoke he could only see the legs of the Union soldiers—and then the smoke was so thick that he couldn't see anything.[15]

But as the men in the 4th Michigan's line traded fire with these Georgians, some heard "a rattling of canteens and a heavy tread of Infantry" coming from behind them, Houghton said. It was the sound of Confederate troops coming through the trees over the Stony Hill. One old soldier from the 4th Michigan's Company E later said that the wood and bushes where they stood were such a thick tangle that the men couldn't see what was happening on their flank: "[W]e entered an underbrush so dense we were unable to see through to defend ourselves," recalled Jacob H. Perine. Both his brigade commander and a historian of the 32nd Massachusetts, which had been engaged with the Rebels here earlier, gave similar descriptions of this low ground on which the 4th Michigan stood, facing south.[16]

The account of the officer published in Detroit stated that Lieutenant Colonel Lumbard, on the right, tried to turn that portion of the regiment to face the new threat, but it was too late. With the attention of most of the 4th Michigan focused on the Confederates before them, this Rebel attack hit the right and rear of the regiment with effective, deadly surprise and force. Lt. Michael Vreeland of Company I, part of the regiment's right wing, would tell his son that the first he realized that Confederates were on their flank was when a bullet struck him in the back. It tore through his lung and smashed into his ribs. According to his grandson's account of this experience, Vreeland staggered and tried to shout a warning to his men, but quickly felt blood rising in his throat. As he raised his sword to point to the enemy on their flank, another bullet struck his right hand, knocking him down. Two of the company's sergeants, William H. Jackson of Detroit and John H. Kydd, were both hit and were among the soldiers who fell dead or dying in the woods.[17]

Vreeland's small company was essentially wiped out in the moments that followed. In an undated statement made after the battle, Vreeland described to the War Department the dire circumstances to explain how his men lost 22 Springfield rifled muskets and other equipment. "The Right Wing of the Regiment to which my Company belonged was surrounded by the Enemy," Vreeland wrote. "Of my Company five (5) men were killed, ten (10) wounded and the remainder taken prisoners." Corporals Charles H. Ladd, about 25, and David Laird, 19, both of Company A and also part of the regiment's right wing, were among many others hit. Ladd was killed, and Laird fatally wounded in the back. Lieutenant Bancroft of Company H agreed with Vreeland's description of the attack. "[T]hey were soon on all sides of us," he wrote of the Rebels.[18]

In the meantime the Second Brigade's commander, Colonel Sweitzer, saw Union regiments retreating from the woods just beyond the 4th Michigan, but he thought these troops were being relieved by other Union infantry protecting the Michigan soldiers' right flank. "I observed also that there was considerable firing diagonally toward our rear from these woods, which I thought were shots from our troops aimed over us at the enemy in the woods beyond and falling short," he wrote. Yet there were so many bullets ripping from the trees west of the Wheatfield—how could all these shots be accidental? The soldier carrying the brigade colors, Ed Martin, seems to have realized the truth first. "Colonel," he said, "I'll be damned if I don't think we are faced the wrong way; the rebs are up there in the woods behind us." As Confederate gunfire crackled from the trees and their flank attack struck the 4th Michigan, urgent messages reached Sweitzer: The enemy was enveloping the 4th Michigan and the 62nd Pennsylvania, to its left. The colonel ordered the regiments "to change front," to turn to face these Rebels. As he gave the order, the firing around them became "rapid and severe."[19]

Those men of the 4th Michigan who hadn't been killed or wounded in the volleys coming from the right and rear turned to see soldiers charging out of trees behind them. "[W]e saw that they wore the gray uniform and was not over 10 rods [165 feet] distant," Houghton wrote; "they were on [the] double quick passing through the woods out into the Wheat Field east of us." Jacob Perine said the Rebels pressed their attack, coming closer, and he scrambled to get away. As he and his comrades fell back, a bullet grazed his elbow and another stung his side. He'd been struck in the hip, but not seriously. A third bullet cut a button on his shirt, just above his belt. "We came out of the brush and mixed with the confederates," Perine said of this moment. They were as close as 10 or twelve feet. Though his arm was paralyzed temporarily, he was determined to escape. "And I've never run so fast in all my life," he said. Scores of his comrades were captured. Kershaw's and Wofford's brigades pursued the escaping troops into the Wheatfield, yelling as they came.[20]

As the Rebel musketry exploded from the woods west of the Wheatfield, Colonel Sweitzer saw his short-handed brigade had no protection from this attack. He sent an aide, Lt. John Seitz, riding back to find General Barnes across the road in Trostle's Woods. But then Barnes and his staff saw the Rebels streaming into the Wheatfield and enveloping Sweitzer's men, and they knew they had to leave quickly. Barnes's aide, Lt. Charles Ross, told the general that "he might bid goodbye to the Second Brigade, as he did not think he would see any of them come out again." By the time Seitz reached Trostle's Woods, Barnes was gone and Confederates were coming down the Wheatfield Road. They shot Seitz's horse from under him, so he ran back to Sweitzer with the news that was already dreadfully obvious—the brigade was nearly surrounded "and in damned bad shape." Confederate musketry was hitting the Second Brigade's line from three different directions, cutting men down. There was no help coming; Sweitzer ordered his men to retreat. "Our good Old Regiment was now in a criticle Situation," James Houghton wrote; "there was Rebels South west, North and Northeast of us. There was now only two things for us to do[,] that was to Surrender or pass directly in front of their lines and receive the contents of their well loaded rifels."[21]

John Bancroft, writing in his diary account, and Henry Seage, writing years later, agreed that Colonel Jeffords and Lieutenant Colonel Lumbard gave orders to turn the 4th Michigan to face the Rebel attack from the right and rear, so that the regiment could retreat fighting. But was there time and room to effectively execute such maneuvers while under fire at close range, as they were nearly surrounded? Some accounts said they did, but others said the situation was chaotic, with scores of Michigan men captured. The anonymous 4th Michigan officer's published account told of the regiment falling rapidly "back toward the east, in tolerable order." But other witnesses and survivors indicated little or no order. Seage wrote to a Gettysburg historian that the regiment was executing Jeffords's order when "we became mixed up with the Rebs. Of course, it was 'every man for himself.'" In his diary Bancroft wrote that the regiment "fell back slowly," but years he later told the state adjutant general: "We broke crossing the Wheatfield, many of the men never left the woods and were taken prisoner."[22]

John S. Conant of Company H gave a simple description of what happened, writing to his family three days later. "Just before night my regiment went into the fight," he wrote, "we were flanked by the enemy and lost a good many men[;] we had to break and run." John Coxe, a private in the 2nd South Carolina Infantry, later wrote the Union retreat was indeed disordered. Part of Kershaw's brigade, he witnessed this when his comrades and Wofford's brigade charged into the trees at the west end of the Wheatfield, driving the Yankees out. "It became a regular rout," Coxe wrote later, "and while the panic-stricken enemy fell by the scores and hundreds, Wofford lost only a few men. . . . Emerging from the woods on the other side, we drove the enemy across a wheat field." A soldier-historian of the 32nd Massachusetts, on the left of the brigade line, wrote that the Confederate attack struck before Jeffords could turn his regiment. He described the attack on their brigade's right and rear, specifically on the 4th Michigan, as "curling it and the 62nd Pennsylvania up like a worm at the touch of fire, and throwing them in the greatest confusion."[23]

The Michigan soldiers were hit by what William Tolford, 32, of Company F called "a severe cross fire," but James Houghton of Company K indicated later there was order in the retreat. "Soon the order came to about face double quick march," Houghton wrote, "and in less than two minutes our Regiment was passing out acrost the wheat field directly in front the Rebels[. I]t was here that the crash came[,] a storm of lead swept through our ranks like hail." As the smoke lifted from the woods between Plum Run and the southwestern corner of the Wheatfield, Captain Hillyer's Georgians stepped up the banks of the creek, for the rifle fire coming at them had died away. Hillyer walked forward, expecting to find that proud Yankee flag carrier dead or wounded, but it was as if the man had disappeared. For by the time the smoke cleared, the line of Union troops was gone, broken and pushed back by his Confederate comrades, Wofford's and Kershaw's men. The 4th Michigan's retreat was under way, moving east across the bloody Wheatfield with Sweitzer's other two regiments. Hillyer's men joined in the pursuit.[24]

As the Second Brigade's line broke and men fell back, there was close-quarters fighting, "personal combat," and firing at point-blank range. Colonel Sweitzer reported that the 4th Michigan and the 62nd Pennsylvania had "become mixed up with the enemy, and many hand-to-hand conflicts occurred." One was the struggle for the 4th Michigan's U.S. flag. A military unit's colors were a tempting prize for the enemy, and the regiment's national banner could hardly have been more vulnerable than it was at this moment. The unnamed officer whose account appeared in the *Detroit Free Press* explained that while the 4th Michigan's right wing was broken up and "mostly taken prisoners," the men from the regiment's left wing followed the flag of the 62nd Pennsylvania as they hurriedly retreated. That left only "a very small squad near our colors," the officer wrote, when a bloody melee for the 4th Michigan's flag occurred.[25]

A regiment's flag (or flags, if a regiment had a national banner and a blue regimental flag) was carried at the center of their line of battle, where it would be the most visible, and this officer's description indicated that the 4th Michigan's U.S. flag and color guard was where it was supposed to be. But with the regiment's right broken and the left retreating, the color guard paid a heavy price. Lt. Edwin H. Gilbert, 23, of Company D informed the brother of Charles W. Phelps that Charles lost his life protecting the flag. "The day your Brother was killed," Gilbert stated, "he was a Corporal of the Color Guard and was killed defending the same and the 4th Michigan could not boast of a braver or better Soldier." Phelps was hit by a gunshot. Harrison Daniels of Company G would write that his friend William H. Plummer, then about 23 and from Washtenaw County, was also a member of the color guard. Plummer was wounded in the leg and remained on the field until Daniels found him after the battle. Sgt. Edwin G. Tripp, 21, of Company H, from the town of Mosherville, may have been a member of the color guard, for he would be remembered later as a man who "fell pierced by five rebel bullets at Gettysburg in defense of the old flag." Tripp died of wounds to his legs and buttocks less than two weeks later. He was one of many men to suffer multiple gunshot wounds.[26]

Corporal Thomas Tarsney, a Company E soldier from the community of Ransom in Hillsdale County, was said to have been carrying the 4th Michigan's flag that day, Henry Seage stated in a letter to a Gettysburg historian years later. "It is reported that just at this juncture our color bearer Thos. Tarsney either surrendered or threw down the colors and ran," he wrote. Tarsney, then 20, escaped while his teenaged brother, John C. Tarsney, was wounded and captured.[27]

One of the attacking Confederates grabbed the flag. "Col. Jeffords seeing our colors (close by) in possession of the Rebs called on my brother [Richard Watson Seage] who was the adjutant of the regiment and 1st Lieutenant M[ichael J.] Vreeland commanding Co. 'I' (since died) to rescue the colors," Henry Seage wrote in 1884. "Those three made a dash for the colors." This description of Vreeland in the fight for the flag is at odds with the account Vreeland shared with his family, in which he described being shot as the Rebel assault struck the regiment's right and rear, as well as his own statement that his company, part of the right wing, was surrounded and wiped out. Vreeland's grandson wrote that the struggle for the flag took place "a few yards away" from where Vreeland had fallen wounded.[28]

It was a bloody and personal fight. Henry Seage claimed in his later account that Jeffords "secured the colors or at least had his left hand on the staff," while Lt. Richard Watson Seage swung his sword, killing the Rebel who was struggling with Jeffords. In his diary entry for July 3, 1863, however, Henry Seage wrote that Jeffords fought Confederates with his sword, cutting down the man who grabbed the flag. The unidentified 4th Michigan officer whose account was published in Detroit agreed, stating the colonel "cut down one or two in a melee around our colors." R. W. Seage was near Jeffords and also "struck them down with his saber, and fell at last severely wounded," the officer wrote. The Reverend John Seage, who wasn't present but soon learned what happened, later reminded Governor Blair of his son's actions. Richard, he wrote, "was terribly wounded in the Battle of Gettysburg defending the Colors by the side of our much love[d] Colonel Jeffords." Richard Watson Seage was hit by two gunshots from two different directions, one striking under his right arm and another in the back below his left shoulder. Both bullets tore through his torso, one damaging his right lung; he was also bayoneted in his left leg, in the inner thigh above the knee.[29]

And the flag? "In the fight the colors were torn in shreds (what little remained)," Henry Seage wrote in his postwar account, "By this time these three were surrounded by Rebs, and in the act of fighting the way out, Col. Jeffords was killed, by bayonet thrust through the body." In fact, various soldiers, Colonel Sweitzer, Lt. Col. George Lumbard, and others would write that Jeffords was not killed in action, but mortally wounded by what an army surgeon noted was a "Bayonet thrust through chest."[30]

John S. Conant, after telling of his regiment breaking and running, also told his family of this. "[O]ur colonel was wounded so he died the next morning," he wrote. "There was a rebel undertook to get our colors[.] the colonel cut him down[,] then they bayoneted him and shot him[.] my Captain fell probably wounded an a prisoner." James Houghton wrote that he was only about 30 feet away from his colonel's deadly fight for the flag when his tent mate, James Johnston, a 19-year-old man who'd been drafted from Shiawassee Township, near the town of Owosso, was shot down. Houghton heard Johnston say, "I am killed." "The rest was groans," Houghton wrote; "there was no help for him."

A bullet hit Lt. Orvey Barrett of Company B in the left leg; he fell to the ground, the action surging around and then beyond him as his comrades retreated, pursued by the Rebels. The Union soldiers had no cover as they stumbled back, and the Confederates kept up their fire. According to Michael Vreeland's grandson, a Rebel stood over the helpless lieutenant, ready to stab him with a bayonet, when an officer stopped that soldier. Though the fighting again raged in the Wheatfield a short time later when other Union forces hit back, Barrett said there was nothing these soldiers could do for those who'd fallen. "They had no time to scoop any of the wounded," Barrett wrote, "as they had all they could attend to in getting out themselves." John Seage would tell the governor of Michigan his son remained on the battlefield until "the next day."[31]

Sweitzer's brigade hurried off the field now littered with dead and wounded men. "[We] were driven back with a heavy loss," Henry Seage wrote in his diary that night. The survivors of the 4th Michigan, the 62nd Pennsylvania, and the 32nd Massachusetts crossed the stone fence at the east end of the Wheatfield. There were friends here, Union soldiers who rose up from behind the wall to fire into the pursuing Confederates, Houghton wrote; their "deadly volley . . . checked the Rebels and sent them back." His brigade comrades weren't the only Union soldiers retreating.

While they'd gone in to support Caldwell's division, two brigades of U.S. Army regulars from the Fifth Corps's Second Division joined the fighting further to the left in the Wheatfield and Rose's Woods. After a short fight, these men were also driven back and retreated to Little Round Top.[32]

Captain James B. McLean of Livingston County, commanding Company K and wounded in the left leg and heel and chin, managed to limp off the field, helped by his men. As they made it to the protection of Union guns, reinforcements and soldiers reforming along lines on Cemetery Ridge, McLean asked if Houghton would get him to one of the hospitals set up by army surgeons. "He put his hand on my Sholder and hobbled along," Houghton wrote. He believed they took a road that wound between the Round Tops, but no such road then existed. Perhaps he referred to a road that lay just north of Little Round Top. While he and others the aided wounded, officers regrouped the remnants of their companies. With an initial estimate of over 171 men from the 4th Michigan killed, wounded, missing, and others scattered, less than 100 soldiers gathered when Lt. Col. George Lumbard tried calling the regiment together after its brigade reached Little Round Top. A letter by a 4th Michigan officer noted there were only 50 men initially, with the number eventually growing to 80.

"With [our] Lt. Col. we rallied by a battery on the hill and met the Penn[sylvania] Reserves just going in to regain the ground as darkness set in," Bancroft wrote in his diary. Those Pennsylvania Reserves, in two brigades, made up the Fifth Corps' Third Division. They charged from the north slope of Little Round Top and drove the Confederates back into the Wheatfield. Other Rebel soldiers were ordered to fall back, since they had no reserves to meet the fresh Union troops. As night fell Confederates occupied the western part of Rose's Woods and the Stony Hill, the ground where some of the 4th Michigan's wounded lay.[33]

The fighting ended as evening gave way to night. Along Cemetery Ridge to the Round Tops stood reformed units, newly arrived Union reinforcements and guns. It was the position that General Meade had wanted in the first place, but that General Sickles, now badly wounded, abandoned by moving his corps out to the Emmitsburg Road. His Third Corps had been effectively destroyed. In front of the hill where the survivors of the 4th Michigan gathered, out in the field, rocks, and the woods lay thousands of dead and wounded men. James Houghton said that while he helped his captain to a hospital, the men of the regiment, their hands and faces smeared with burnt powder, were formed in a defensive line along a path on the western face of Little Round Top that evening.[34]

At some point during the night, these men were moved north with the other outfits from their brigade and division to the edge of Weikert's Woods. Bancroft wrote that he and others worked until after midnight, helping to gather the wounded. Henry Seage bedded down with one of his comrades, who made it off the field slightly wounded. Sgt. John Hewitt of Company E from Hillsdale County sat down and took out his diary. "Having marched 120 miles in 5 days we took a position near Gettysburg," he wrote. "here we met the Rebels & the battle was terrific[.] here the Col. Jeffords was run through with a Rebel bayonet while attempting to retake the colors which are captured." This terrible event—their colonel stabbed trying to rescue the flag—was similarly recorded by Henry Seage in his July 3 diary entry and John S. Conant in a letter home, as well as in the battle report of their division commander, Brig. Gen. James Barnes. And it was reported and published a month later in Detroit in an extract of the letter from that 4th Michigan officer.[35]

HUDSON MUSEUM

Fighting at close quarters at the edge of the woods beyond the Wheatfield, Confederate troops swarm toward the 4th Michigan's line of battle and U.S. flag in a drawing by Lt. Charles Gruner. Note that some soldiers are using clubbed muskets and bayonets; it appears that the artist was rendering the moment before Col. Jeffords was run though and fatally wounded.

At least 25 men had been killed from the 4th Michigan that day, and at least three more would die of their wounds in the days ahead, with others surviving for weeks before succumbing to complications. A modern tabulation would show that 43 from the regiment had been killed or mortally wounded or were missing and presumed killed. Some 66 men were initially reported as wounded, with even more men missing. Men who made it off the field knew that that some of those taken prisoner were also wounded. Lt. Col. George Lumbard soon reported 79 officers and men from the 4th Michigan had been taken prisoner, a number that included Company F's Corporal Irvin Miner. Nineteen of these captured men would die of disease, wounds, or the effects of starvation and Rebel violence over the next two years. But 18-year-old Albert Boies, who'd lost two fingers when he was wounded in the right hand, was only briefly a prisoner. Captured by a lad his age from the 24th Georgia Infantry, Boies was one of the few men who managed that night to escape back to Union lines. He was lucky. His regiment went into battle with 342 men and officers; it came out with 139.[36]

Lt. Orvey Barrett, like scores of other wounded, lay on the battlefield for several hours before he was brought back to one of the Union hospitals. Henry Seage's diary reflects that he wouldn't learn until the next day that his brother Richard Watson Seage was carried back to a hospital after the battle. Not far from these wounded comrades, near the western edge of the field, Lieutenant Vreeland was also alive but severely wounded. He told his son later that his last recollection of the day "was of the blood-red sun sinking in the west through the smoke and haze of battle . . . a sun he never expected to see again."[37]

After nightfall, ambulances and stretcher bearers went out on to the battlefield. So did volunteers like Lieutenant Bancroft. Some veterans later said there was an informal truce in the Wheatfield area, which lay between the pickets, but others said Rebel pickets fired at those who ventured into the field. The Fifth Corps of which the 4th Michigan was part had 81 ambulance crews working until 4:00 A.M. July 3, bringing in 1,300 wounded. Other Union corps also had ambulances and stretcher bearers at work, so the ultimate number of battlefield casualties brought in that night, though not reflected in official reports, was much higher. Some of the 4th Michigan's wounded were closer to Confederate lines than their own and even behind their picket line. Frank Clark, 21, from Morenci, in Company F, had suffered a shattered leg. He was removed by Confederates and taken to one of their hospitals at a farm some three miles west of Gettysburg. Mark W. Taylor, 23, of Company E, was also badly wounded and near Rebel lines; a Confederate picket gave him a drink of water.

But many of the 4th Michigan's wounded were in the Wheatfield area and taken to Union field hospitals that night. Barrett said he, with others, was loaded into an ambulance at about 2:00 A.M., July 3. "Groans and oaths of the wounded were heard on every hand," he wrote. Lieutenant Vreeland, too, was carried back to Union lines. "After the battle was over he was found by his brave comrades still alive, [and] sent to the hospital where he was kindly cared for," stated a Civil War–era newspaper clipping filed with Vreeland's papers. Harrison Jeffords survived his bayonet wound for several hours. "Col. Jeffords died to day at 4:15 am," Sergeant Hewitt noted in his journal on July 3.[38]

Who carried Harrison Jeffords off the battlefield and when remains uncertain. Did his own men carry him off in the retreat from the Wheatfield? Or was he, like Vreeland, Richard W. Seage, and Barrett, removed hours later under the cover of darkness? While a survivor of the battle would state in a stirring speech years later that 4th Michigan men carried Jeffords and the flag off the field, this is not reflected in the available contemporaneous diaries, letters, records, or reports from members of the 4th Michigan.[39] Nor do Jeffords's records answer the question of who removed him. Henry Seage's diary entry for July 3, 1863, showed he was sent that morning to collect Jeffords' body at a Union field hospital, and he wrote about what had happened to the colonel:

> Started with a stretcher with some of the Pioneer Corps & went about a mile to the front to a Hospital to get Col. Jeffords. Soon found him & brot [sic] him down to our Regimental Hosptl. He died yesterday from wounds. One ball through the leg & a bayonet wound through the side. The Col. was killed in trying to save the colors. The colors fell and a Reb got them. The Col. cut

the Reb down with his sword and another Reb run his Bayonet through him. The Pioneers carried him back & will try to send him home.[40]

Henry Seage wrote further in his diary that after he brought the colonel's body back from that unspecified hospital at the front to the regimental hospital, he went on to a division hospital, where he set up a tent and got dinner. Now he learned that his brother Richard had been brought in from the field alive. It appears that Henry's statement that "the pioneers carried [Jeffords] back" referred to the unnamed men who had gone with him that morning to bring the colonel's body from a hospital so arrangements could be made to bury him in Michigan. But could it mean stretcher bearers brought him off the darkened battlefield, dying, in the hours after the fighting ended? Could it mean that they carried him back as the regiment retreated on the evening of July 2?

The report of Capt. James A. Bates, the Fifth Corps chief ambulance officer, stated that stretcher bearers went with the corps when it went into action that day, but his ambulances didn't go onto the battlefield until darkness, after the fighting ended. The letter by the unnamed 4th Michigan officer published in Detroit a month later made reference to the fact that "the point where we fought lay between the pickets all night and next day. The Colonel was helped off by some of our men, every attention being given him by those around." This could mean that he was brought off by men of the 4th Michigan as they left the field, but it could indicate he was carried from that no-man's land between the pickets during the night, as were Barrett, Vreeland, Richard Watson Seage, and hundreds of others.[41]

Whenever he was removed, Jeffords received the attention of a Union doctor, though his life could not be saved. Both Colonel Sweitzer's supplemental report and a reminiscence by Lt. Robert Campbell stated Jeffords, dying, spoke. "He lived till the next day [July 3]," Sweitzer wrote, "was conscious and able to give an account of the occurrence." What Jeffords said and to whom wasn't recorded by Sweitzer and is not reflected in Jeffords's record. Campbell's later account agreed that a doctor looked after the colonel as he lay dying. "He lived in a semi delirious condition for a short time," wrote Campbell in his memoir, "and the surgeon who attended him told me that the last words that he uttered were "Mother! Mother! Mother!"[42]

Though some of the 4th Michigan survivors thought Jeffords had been killed in action or otherwise died on July 2, casualty reports by Lieutenant Colonel Lumbard and General Barnes, like Sergeant Hewitt's diary and John Conant's letter, indicated that he died on July 3. "Thrust through with a bayonet while gallantly attempting to rescue his colors from the grasp of the enemy," Barnes's statement said of Jeffords. A veteran of the 4th Michigan who visited the battlefield in several years later would sum up what had happened in a similar manner: "Just over there on that little rise of ground, is where the gallant Jeffords fell, trying to save our colors."[43]

What became of the 4th Michigan's U.S. flag remains a mystery. Four days after the terrible fight in the Wheatfield, a report appeared in the *New York Herald* by correspondent L. A. Hendricks, giving an account of the fighting by the Fifth Corps on July 2. Within this lengthy report, datelined July 4 from corps headquarters, Hendricks gave a dramatic account of the death of Harrison Jeffords and his fight for his regiment's flag:

> It was from a bayonet thrust that Col. Jefferds [*sic*] fell. It was in the thickest of the fight. A rebel officer had seized the regimental colors. Col. Jefferds shot the rebel dead with his revolver, took the colors in his own hand, reared them aloft and cried out, "Rally round the flag, boys." A rebel bayonet pierced his vitals, and he fell dead, his hand still clutching the flagstaff. The man at whose hands he lost his life was a moment after gasping in death. A bullet from Major Hall's revolver had entered his brain. Conspicuous for gallantry in the hand to hand conflict was Capt. [William F.] Robinson. He killed six rebels with his navy revolver and was then one of the officers to snatch the musket and cartridge box of a dead soldier and kill others.[44]

These few sentences from Hendricks's report, with minor variations in wording and spelling, were quoted in part on July 8 in the *Detroit Free Press*. Other papers in Ann Arbor, Hudson, Monroe, and Jonesville broke this account into individual anecdotes about the three officers. At almost the same time the *Herald*'s report was published, a story by correspondent L. L. Crouse appeared in the *New York Times* stating that Sweitzer's brigade had "won great honors" making a last charge on July 2 with Caldwell's troops. This, too, was recapped in the *Free Press*, which noted that news reports said the 4th Michigan was part of a brigade that "made some splendid charges."[45]

In reality, Sweitzer's brigade had made no splendid charges that day. It had gone into position south of the Wheatfield only to be overwhelmed and battered, with half of its 900 men killed, wounded, or captured. Jeffords was fatally wounded, not killed in action. His officers and men recorded that he fought with his sword, not a revolver. Both New York papers were correct in their overall reporting that the battle of Gettysburg was, after July 3, an important victory for the Union army. But these reports did not reflect the specific, terrible circumstances in which the 4th Michigan and its brigade suffered on July 2 when they were nearly surrounded and driven off the field.

Lt. John Bancroft saw the *Herald*'s report and emphatically dismissed it in a July 21 letter to a friend back in Detroit. "Want of time forbids me to speak of Gettysburg and why and how we were so badly used," he wrote, "or to say anything of the foolish lies printed by the N.Y. Herald and copied by the Mich. Papers." That was all he said on the matter of the press reports, for Bancroft spent most of the letter discussing who would be the regiment's next commander.[46] But fifteen days after Bancroft wrote those words rejecting the news report that described Jeffords's last fight, a lengthy account appeared in the *Detroit Free Press*, headlined "How it Happened the Regiment was so Badly Cut up at Gettysburg." Described as the extract of a private letter written on July 29 by an officer in the 4th Michigan, then camped near Warrenton, Virginia, the account is similar in content, phrasing, and structure to the account in Bancroft's diary and to one he would send to the state adjutant general in 1889.

Regardless of which officer wrote it, the letter published in Detroit gave an accurate description of the regiment's positions and movements and how the 4th Michigan was nearly crushed by the Confederate attack. It described how the regiment's right wing had been shattered and its men taken prisoner, and how the left wing followed the 62nd Pennsylvania in a fast retreat. This officer, who believed that Jeffords had initially been wounded by a bullet, wrote that the colonel was bayoneted in a struggle near the regiment's flag. And he wrote that "Lt. Leage" (*Seage* misspelled by a typesetter or editor) also fought Rebels hand-to-hand until he was wounded. "[T]here was but little chance of re-forming or making any check to a [Confederate] force coming double-quick," this officer explained.

The officer challenged the *New York Herald*'s account about the 4th Michigan, questioning where the information came from and disputing the individual deeds it described. "There was a report printed in the N.Y. *Herald,* written by a reporter who saw no one of us," the officer charged. "Major Hall did well, as he always has, but here he had no personal encounter [close-range or hand-to-hand combat], and was distinctly impressed with the idea we ought to fall back as any." Nor was it true that William F. Robinson shot down several Confederates with his pistol. "Capt. Robinson carries no revolvers," the officer continued, "and was wounded immediately on leaving the [regiment's] first line." Lastly, this officer pointed out that Jeffords died from his wounds (meaning that he had not been killed in action) and that the regiment's U.S. flag had been lost.[47]

Despite this officer's criticism, the *New York Herald*'s brief account, suggesting that Jeffords had saved his regiment's flag, became the basis of the accepted version of the struggle for the colors in the Wheatfield. Adding an even more dramatic dimension to this picture of the fight was a letter written in the fall of 1884 by Henry Seage to Gettysburg historian John Bachelder. In it, Seage wrote of "the recapture of our Regt. Flag" by Jeffords, his brother Richard, and Michael Vreeland, though also noting it was torn to pieces. Historians and authors writing about this struggle have accepted Seage's statement that the 4th Michigan's flag was rescued, though no report, diary, or letter from any soldier or officer from the regiment in the days and week after the battle stated that it was saved.[48]

Sgt. John Hewitt was not the only Gettysburg soldier to record the loss of the regiment's flag. The 4th Michigan officer whose letter extract was published in Detroit put it this way: "With Col. Lombard [*sic*] we had about 50 men that night," he wrote, summing up the aftermath, "and got about one hundred in two or three days. It was found that we had lost the United States colors drawn from the government last winter."[49] Others from their brigade and division noted the loss of the 4th Michigan's flag. Lt. Charles Salter from Detroit, a young officer in the 16th Michigan who survived a harrowing fight on Little Round Top, told friends about this: "The 2nd Brigade, to which the 4th Mich. belongs, did not succeed so well," he wrote 10 days after the battle. "The rebels attacked them with a large force and drove them back about ½ mile. The 4th Mich., 62nd Penn., and 32nd Mass. Regts., all lost their colors. . . . A rebel officer had seized the colors of the 4th and Col. Jeffreys [*sic*] was defending it with his sword. He was bayoneted by the rebels, as also the color bearers, and many others who were trying to recover the colors." Tim Regan of the 9th Massachusetts, which rejoined the battered Second Brigade in the Union line after the battle, recorded the news in his journal. "[T]he Fourth Michigan was nearly annihilated, having lost their Colonel and their colors," he noted.[50]

Another unnamed soldier from the Army of the Potomac who wrote to a Monroe newspaper that month also mentioned the loss of the 4th Michigan's flag in hand-to-hand combat. "Their loss was heavy and they lost their colors, also," he wrote of the regiment, "but the latter circumstance was no disgrace to them, considering the great loss of life they suffered and the desperate character of their engagement."[51]

Lieutenant Campbell of the 4th Michigan, giving an address in 1902, said he had heard the story that the banner had been ripped apart, but he knew it was gone. As regimental quartermaster, he had to replace it. "[O]ur flag was lost, said to have been torn to pieces in the general melee," he said. "I procured another one for the regiment, this time the American eagle, surrounded with stars upon a blue field." He also didn't believe news account that had Jeffords shooting the soldier he'd fought for the flag. "Some have stated that he shot the Rebel with his revolver, but he gave me his revolver the day before," Campbell stated. "I still have it as a relict." Two different members of the 32nd Massachusetts who authored histories of their regiment also wrote that the 4th Michigan's flag was lost. One, Francis Parker, noted that "Colonel Jeffers [*sic*] of the 4th Michigan . . . died in defence of his flag," while the other, Henry B. James, wrote that "Jeffers . . . and a color sergeant of the same regiment were killed, trying to save their flag, but it was captured, and a part of the regiment were taken prisoners."[52]

The U.S. flag was a considered more than just a symbol in the 19th century, but a kind of living incarnation of the country to be revered and protected at all cost. If the 4th Michigan's flag had been rescued, even if only tatters remained, it would have been treated as a sacred object in Michigan and the rest of the pro-Union North. But no memoir or reminiscence or report by a survivor ever addressed what became of the colors Henry Seage claimed 21 years later had been recaptured, yet torn into pieces. To lose a flag to the enemy was something most soldiers didn't care to admit or discuss. Indeed, most letters from the 4th Michigan's officers and men wrote about the battle said nothing about it; they wrote about their friends and neighbors killed or wounded. Of course, other Union regiments also lost flags in this fighting of July 2, and little if anything seems to have been written about them. But Colonel Jeffords had been mortally wounded fighting for his flag, and in doing so evoked a tragic but powerfully heroic image that struck an emotional and patriotic chord with those who believed in the Union cause. Adding to the enormity of Jeffords's sacrifice was that the bayonet was rarely used in Civil War combat; the fact that a Union colonel had been run through was shocking. This news quickly spread to the 4th Michigan's comrades and then far beyond in press reports.

While official reports from Wofford's brigade and Southern newspaper accounts showed that these troops captured three or four Union flags in the Wheatfield on July 2 in hand-to-hand fighting, none was identified as the U.S. flag of the 4th Michigan.[53] According to a history of some of the Georgia soldiers who fought in the Wheatfield, General Wofford wrote a letter that summer in which he passed along information from one of his officers about a Yankee flag that had been grabbed by one of his men that day. "Private Thomas Jolly was bayoneted and killed with a stand of colors in his hand," Wofford wrote (mistakenly, since Jolly, of the Phillips Legion, actually survived his wound). Two of Jolly's comrades, privates named McGovern and Blanton, "avenged" Jolly by each bayoneting a man, Wofford continued, while a third Georgian named Austin grabbed a pistol from the belt of another Yankee, shooting him and two others. What happened to the flag Jolly had in his grasp? Wofford's men weren't sure. The Rebel brigadier wrote that though the Union soldiers lost that stand of colors, it was "supposed to be in the hands of some other regiment."[54]

Was this the 4th Michigan's flag, taken in a hand-to-hand fight in which at least five Union soldiers reportedly were killed or wounded? Capture of a flag was considered a triumph, and

Confederate soldiers who did so were rewarded—the mid-August letter by Wofford shows that in other instances, his men handed over to officers Yankee flags they'd taken in bayonet fights. But Confederate troops had become mixed up by company and regiment during their assault, and they were blasted by Union artillery as they neared Little Round Top. Then the Pennsylvania Reserves attacked, pushing the Rebel advance back.[55] After the battle of Gettysburg was over, soldiers buried the Confederate dead in mass graves on the battlefield. Could it be that Rebel officers never accounted for or reported they had taken the U.S. flag of the 4th Michigan because a Georgian or South Carolinian tucked it into his shirt or haversack, only to be killed minutes later? Did the U.S. banner for which Charles Phelps and Harrison Jeffords fought and died end up buried at Gettysburg? Or was it just that the Rebels who took that U.S. flag didn't know the identity of the regiment from whom they'd captured it?

Whatever became of the 4th Michigan's colors that day, Colonel Jeffords, a brave and respected young officer, became a martyred Union hero, memorialized on the battlefield when a monument was dedicated to his regiment with the image of an officer in bas-relief, clutching the flag. "A better man never lived," wrote Company A's William Gibson about his colonel, who Gibson said was shot and bayoneted after "he cut down a reb in the act of capturing our colors." James Houghton would remember Jeffords as "our Nobel [*sic*] Colonel."[56]

But the immediate response, for the some of the survivors from the 4th Michigan and others from their brigade, division, and corps was anger—anger at the Rebels, for stabbing a respected and well-liked officer, and anger at the Union commanders who had, as Bancroft put it, "so badly used" the regiment and the others in the Second Brigade. Soldiers obviously knew they could be killed or maimed in combat, but they were willing to take this risk as they formed in line of battle, faced the Rebels, and traded volleys with them. They had done so at Gaines' Mill and Malvern Hill a year earlier. But at Gettysburg didn't get that chance, because they'd been badly flanked, taking fire from three directions. Some held their commanders responsible for this vulnerable position. "Gen. Barnes, commanding the division . . . ought to have known what was going on upon his extreme right," complained the 4th Michigan officer whose account was published a month later. "Col. Sweitzer, commanding [the] brigade, also was there [on the right, where the 4th Michigan was hit] a few minutes before the advance was made." In later years, some soldiers continued to blame the high casualties on "the mismanagement of General Barnes," though others who fought that day would live to read the arguments that Gen. Dan Sickles created this deadly situation by moving his Third Corps into an untenable position.

Regardless of the fate of the regiment's flag, the 4th Michigan had lost nearly 200 men and officers, killed, wounded, and missing. "I often wonder," Henry Seage wrote later, "how it was that so many of us crossed that wheatfield and live to tell the story."[57]

CHAPTER 11

We Have Seen a Pretty Hard Campaign

SOME CONFEDERATE SOLDIERS PAID A TERRIBLE PRICE FOR THE BAYONETING OF HARRISON JEFFORDS in the weeks after the fighting at Gettysburg. According to an officer in the division with the 4th Michigan, many Rebels were killed in retribution at Wapping Heights near Manassas Gap on July 23. "We found over 100 bodies of rebels, who had been killed or wounded and afterward bayoneted by our men, who have not forgiven the rebels for their atrocities at Gettysburg and other places," wrote Lt. Charles Salter of the 16th Michigan. "[T]he majority of the 3rd and 5th Corps declare they will bayonet every rebel they can get at, on the battlefield."[1]

But this retaliation was still three weeks off. As darkness fell over the Gettysburg battlefield on July 2, James Houghton, with his wounded captain leaning on him for support, made it to a Third Corps hospital set up in a barn, possibly at the Jacob Snyder farm. Captain McLean was so weak he had to stop frequently. "[A]s we came to the gate we were met by a gard who informed us that they had about 300 wounded in Hospital and could not possibly admit any more," Houghton wrote. "[T]he captain was to[o] weak to go any farther so He layed down on the ground saying He would lye there till they could take Him in." If the violence in the trees near the Wheatfield had been horrific, the scene at the hospital was a nightmare. "The wounded were lying on the ground in rows acrost the yard . . . at the east end of the yard were lying Some of the most hop[e] less cases some were in the agonies of death," Houghton wrote.

The wounded were laid out in rows, with a path between them. He saw "the Surgeons were busily at work probing for bullets and amputating limbs." When he walked back by the barn, "filled . . . with the wounded to its utmost capacity," Houghton couldn't take any more. As he started back to find his regiment, he came across one of his lieutenants. When Houghton told him about McLean's condition and the state of the Third Corps' hospital, the lieutenant decided they had to get their captain out of there. Borrowing a stretcher, they carried McLean to another hospital, where his wounds were quickly dressed. Exhausted, Houghton tried but couldn't find his way back to his regiment. He lay down and fell asleep by a side of a log somewhere on the east side of Little Round Top.[2]

Through the morning of July 3 the ranks of the 4th Michigan slowly grew as men who survived the retreat from the Wheatfield found the regiment in the Union line near the George Weikert farm, north of Little Round Top. So did soldiers who worked through the night bringing in the wounded. While they didn't yet know the score of all their casualties, a soldier from Monroe wrote that the regiment had been "handled more roughly this time than ever before." Yet as bleak and terrible as the previous evening had been, there was some good news. Albert Boies, initially among the scores of men wounded and captured, had escaped from the Confederates during the night. Sgt. Edward Taylor was also wounded and would have been captured, but "managed to escape when they were repulsed by playing wounded and hiding being a large rock," he wrote. About 80 men were missing, and most of them were prisoners. Some survived the experience, some died, and a few escaped. One of the many captured was diarist George W. Millens of Company B, who didn't survive, while one of his comrades from Indiana, Adelbert F. Day, who'd already spent six weeks in Libby Prison after Gaines' Mill, would "hoodwink" the count of his captors and be released in about two months from Belle Isle in a prisoner exchange.[3]

Company D, largely made up of men from the Ann Arbor area, suffered a large number of casualties. Letters and personnel records indicate that two captured men, David Webster, about 27, from Washtenaw County, and Sgt. Oliver Smith, about 25 and from Perry in Shiawassee County, also survived. Webster's family correspondence indicates that both men were taken to Belle Isle prison, but there Smith decided to escape, according to a letter written by Dr. William Clark, the regiment's former surgeon. A prison privy set up over the James River provided Smith, Webster, and an unnamed soldier from the 3rd Michigan Infantry the opportunity. The three prisoners quietly visited the privy in the darkness late that summer, where they lowered themselves into the water and swam for it.

Dr. Clark, serving as a surgeon in a Washington hospital in the fall of 1863, informed Webster's brother that Sergeant Smith and the 3rd Michigan man made it across the river, but Webster, who'd been slightly wounded at Gettysburg, felt he couldn't swim that far. He returned to prison. Smith and his partner kept going, moving along the river by night and hiding in woods by day, eating uncooked corn they grabbed from fields. They stole a canoe and on their fourth morning out landed near a shanty of a black man who fed them a real meal. Trading the canoe for food, they continued down the river and made it to Union forces in the Norfolk area. It had taken them a week. The escapees were returned to Washington from Fortress Monroe.

By September 4, Oliver Smith was back with the Union army. Webster remained in Confederate prison, first in Richmond and then Andersonville in 1864. But he survived illness, was released, and eventually was discharged from the Union army.[4]

Then there were the many wounded of Gettysburg. A bullet had smashed into the right side of the head of Royal W. Hamlin of Company F, about 21, from Lenawee County. The projectile tore through his inner ear and part of his jaw, exiting the back of his neck. He was unconscious for two days and suffered horrible pain in the weeks that followed. He spent months in hospitals before his enlistment ended in the fall of 1864. Quimby H. Crawford of Monroe, about the same age and serving in Company D, had been hit in the temple; the ball grazed the side of his head, tearing away his ear. He, too, was found unconscious after the battle, but improved after a period of delirium and deafness. He eventually was well enough to return to the ranks, but never recovered mentally or emotionally. Capt. William F. Robinson, hit in the leg, assured his parents later that month "it is nothing but a flesh wound and I shall be able to walk with crutches in a little over a week." He insisted that he didn't need his mother to come from Michigan to care for him.[5]

There were scores of other wounded men from their regiment and thousands from other outfits, North and South. As the severity of the 4th Michigan's loss became clearer, men wrote home. "Our loss in killed, wounded and missing is very great," wrote William Tolford of Company F. "We have only ten men left in our company and not much over 100 in the regiment." His comrade Frank Clark, who'd been carried to a Confederate hospital at the John Cunningham farm west of Gettysburg, lost his leg. Clark stayed at the farm for weeks as he recovered. So many of the soldiers of the 4th Michigan had been killed, captured, and wounded that the regiment's 10 companies were soon consolidated, wrote a soldier with the initials "J.W.V." This was Lt. James W. Vesey from Sturgis. "We are temporarily consolidated into five companies," he wrote to a western Michigan newspaper. "Lt. [Charles F.] Gruner [from St. Joseph County] commands the 2nd Co. consisting of companies C and K."

On the morning of July 3 Henry Seage, with other men, helped move and take care of the wounded. They retrieved the body of Colonel Jeffords from a field hospital, the first step in the process of sending his remains back to Dexter, where his funeral "was attended by a large concourse of citizens" from the region. Seage found his badly wounded brother, Lt. Richard W. Seage, at a division hospital, possibly at the Jacob Weikert farm on the Taneytown Road or the nearby Lewis Bushman farm to the west. Henry carried him into the barn for surgery, and here they learned that Lt. Michael Vreeland had also survived and had been brought in. But with so many soldiers killed, wounded, or missing from the 4th Michigan, someone decided that the regiment couldn't afford to have soldiers acting as stretcher bearers and hospital aides. James Quackenbush from Company E appeared with a patrol to take Henry Seage's comrades back to the regiment. Only Seage, for the moment, was allowed to remain behind to take care of his brother and Lieutenant Vreeland.[6]

The survivors of the 4th Michigan were still recovering after the battle, and the main military development of July 3, the famous Confederate attack known as Pickett's Charge, was barely acknowledged by the regiment's diarists. Lieutenant Bancroft of Company H noted that the regiment "lay in position behind a stone wall," remarking on the heavy cannonading, but nothing of the incredible losses the Rebels suffered that afternoon when they attacked across the open fields attempting to break the Union line. Lt. Orvey Barrett, who'd been wounded in the leg, later recalled that "the anxiety was terrible," felt by wounded men who couldn't see the fighting, but who heard the blazing artillery. As more wounded Union troops were brought into the makeshift hospitals, others pressed them. How was the battle going? Were the Confederates gaining? Were the Union troops repelling them? "Finally, the awful noise died away; news was brought by an aide-de-camp 'that the enemy had hauled off,'" Barrett wrote. Even dying men cheered when they heard the news. Lieutenant Bancroft recorded the result: "Rebs fell back from our front during the night," he wrote. In the meantime, Henry Seage stayed with his brother and other 4th Michigan wounded. On July 4 brigade teams arrived, bringing large wall tents as rain fell. Seage helped put up the shelters and move the wounded, and that night shifted Lieutenants Vreeland and Barrett, Samuel Walker, and Sgt. Ezra Brown into a large tent. All of these men survived their Gettysburg wounds.[7]

Lieutenant Bancroft recorded the aftermath of the battle on July 4. "Not very lively," he wrote. Gray clouds hung over the valley in the wake of the fighting. "On the field, sights and smells," he continued. "Bury our dead. Raining." Sgt. John Hewitt of Company E agreed it was quiet, but felt the defeat of Robert E. Lee and the halting of his invasion was reason to celebrate the Fourth of July. James Houghton was one of the men who requested to go back out onto the field to find the body of his tent mate, James Johnston. With a friend from his company named George Tracey, Houghton crossed field where Pickett's Charge occurred. In places, they crossed pools of blood. "It was Rebel Blood so it did not seam so bad," he wrote. Eventually they reached the Wheatfield. "[W]e found men there busily ingaged in burying the dead. They informed me that they had just got my tent mate buried. They showed me his grave." They had buried Johnston near a large rock on the east side of the Wheatfield. One of the soldiers told Houghton that Johnston had seven bullet holes in his body.

Most of the troops that had died in that vicinity were being carried to the trees on the west side of the field, and Houghton said that the Union dead were being carefully put to rest. In some cases, the bloody uniforms were actually being removed and washed and then dried on the branches of the trees, he wrote in his memoir of the battle. Then the bodies were redressed and placed in burial trenches lined with blankets, torn into pieces so that the dead lay on one piece and had a roll for a pillow behind their head. Lastly they were covered over with more blankets, tucked over the bodies. Near the trench lay the body of a large man, a Confederate sergeant whom soldiers claimed had stabbed Colonel Jeffords with his bayonet. This man had been shot through the head, Houghton wrote, his brains spilling out of the wound. Houghton surveyed the scene and went back to his regiment.[8]

Lt. Robert Campbell, the 4th Michigan's quartermaster, also went out to see the carnage, though he didn't record the grisly details as did Houghton. "After the battle I rode for miles over the ghastly field, was at Culp's Hill, Cemetery Ridge, Wheatfield, Little Round Top with its rocky crest from which a fine view is obtained of a large part of the battlefield, and the improvised hospitals. More than 6,000 dead and nearly 30,000 wounded lay upon that field." Harrison Daniels in Company G later wrote that it was on the afternoon of the third day of the battle that he learned his friend William H. Plummer, a member of the color guard, was missing. That night, Daniels said, he volunteered to go with details forming to bring in wounded men from the field, taking with him a canteen of water and a candle. Going back toward the trees at the south edge of the Wheatfield, Daniels found Plummer, alive but wounded. He got help and put Plummer into an ambulance. He survived.

In the meantime the Army of the Potomac again began to march. By July 5, Union advances toward what had been Confederate lines showed that Lee's men already pulled out, starting the long trip back to Virginia. The Union army followed, though the 4th Michigan's William Tolford didn't think it was possible that his outfit could go back into battle. "Our regiment may not be called to go into the fight again, very soon, on account of our numbers, and the loss of our colonel," he wrote. The 4th Michigan waited with its division during the evening on July 5 as thousands of troops tramped out in the rain. At last they marched south toward Emmitsburg, stopping at about 11:00 P.M. to bivouac. The departure of the 4th Michigan from Gettysburg began another separation from the outfit for Henry Seage, who remained behind to take care of his brother and others. Over the course of the next few days, Seage helped take the wounded to Baltimore to a place he called "the Church Home & Infirmary." By the afternoon of July 23, both Vreeland and Barrett were well enough to travel back to Michigan. Though the summer weather tended to make it uncomfortably warm in Richard Seage's room, he recovered to the point that by early September he was able to go home to White Pigeon. Henry Seage wouldn't rejoin the 4th Michigan until September 23 at Culpeper, Virginia.[9]

The 4th Michigan, meanwhile, moved with its brigade, going only about a mile on the morning of July 6, and waiting as other troops marched by. The roads were muddy with the rain and the churning boots of thousands of soldiers and sometimes the columns traveled cross-country as the Union army again stayed between the Confederates and Washington. The rain continued for two days as the regiment moved to near Frederick, Maryland, west to Middletown and over South Mountain and drying ground to Boonsboro. Then they crossed Antietam Creek, north of Sharpsburg, drawing closer to the Army of Northern Virginia. Unable to get their forces across the rain-swollen Potomac in a timely manner, Confederate commanders constructed defensive positions stretching several miles from a point west of Hagerstown southwest to the river. Lieutenant Bancroft heard the firing up ahead as he and his regiment came nearer on July 10. The next day Union soldiers formed in battle lines, and at 6:00 P.M. the 4th Michigan moved forward with thousands of troops, knocking over fences and trampling grain. But there was no attack, only skirmishing. The 4th Michigan went on picket that night.

The regiment again advanced as reserves for the Union skirmish line on July 12 as Lee's army contracted back toward the river. The Fifth Corps moved forward and there was more skirmishing with the Confederates in another line of trenches and breastworks. That afternoon the 4th Michigan was among the outfits that were relieved and moved into some woods to bivouac. "When we saw them [the extensive Rebel works] we thought that another fight was shure to take place," James Houghton remembered. The regiment soon moved back up, constructed works through a cornfield, and appears to have skirmished with Rebels near Williamsport. But it was too late for the Union army to destroy Lee's army now. On July 14, as troops advanced on Williamsport, the soldiers learned what happened. "Rebels all gone acrost the Potomac," Bancroft wrote. John S. Conant of Company H wondered about the decision of their commander, Gen. George Meade, not to throw the Union army against the Confederates while they were cornered. "It was a shame to let Lee get across," he wrote, "if we attacked him probably we would have given him a hard one but they had a strong position but did not want to fight that is pretty certain."[10]

Though the Confederate army crossed the Potomac, Meade continued a pursuit. On July 15 the soldiers of the 4th Michigan and their brigade and division were awakened at 3:00 A.M. and soon were on an exhausting all-day march back over South Mountain to the town of Burkettsville. As troops collapsed from the heat the regiment's number got even smaller. "At one time during the day only 19 all told [were] in the regiment," Lieutenant Bancroft noted. The soldiers got "a good supper" at a farmhouse and it was here, the lieutenant wrote, that the 4th Michigan was reorganized into five companies. The next day began at 2:00 A.M. and the soldiers marched to the town of Berlin near the Potomac, where the men were issued new clothing—they had long since worn out and ripped and torn their uniforms during the Gettysburg campaign. The 4th Michigan camped with the others on the hills above the river that night. Though it was late when the troops went into bivouac, Lieutenant Bancroft stayed up to write a letter to Abraham Purdy of Marathon Township in Lapeer County, father of George Purdy. George, at 18, joined the army in place of his father, who had been drafted in February 1863. The younger Purdy reached the 4th Michigan at Falmouth in late March, and he had been killed in action at Gettysburg.

In the meantime engineers built pontoon bridges over the Potomac at Berlin, and on the afternoon of July 17, the 4th Michigan crossed back into Virginia with its corps. For the next two days the marches south were easier, but Bancroft was getting sick and by the 20th rode in an ambulance with the columns to near Ashby's Gap. The next day, though he was very sick, Bancroft wrote to his friend Theodore H. Hinchman back in Detroit, complaining that the 4th Michigan badly needed new men and that the newspaper reports about the regiment at Gettysburg were inaccurate. "We hope the Governor will send men to fill up our ranks to keep up our good name and to have some one to go home with us," he continued. "We have some good officers as are to be found in the field and enough of them to[o] while we now have only 101 men a captain commands."

Of course, there was the question of what would happen with the command of the 4th Michigan, now that Jeffords was gone. Bancroft said that most of the line officers of the regiment hoped that Major Jairus Hall would "jump" or be promoted past Lt. Col. George Lumbard, just as Jeffords had jumped Lumbard earlier that year at the direction of Governor Blair. Bancroft had heard that "Blair had said he would not commission Lumbard as Colonel and I see no reason why he should reverse his decision." But if Lumbard was made colonel, Bancroft wrote, then Major Hall should be made lieutenant colonel. As a practical matter, that would put Hall in charge of the regiment in terms of day-to-day leadership. Bancroft wrote that he hoped that his friend would raise these views with the governor.[11]

The Union army kept moving over the next few days, to White Plains, toward Manassas Gap, to Salem, and through Warrenton, and there they camped for several days. "Since crossing the river [the Potomac], our line of march has been over the roughest, crookedest, hilliest, dryest roads Virginia has," Lieutenant Vesey complained. "The weather being very hot; the men have suffered much from the heat, several cases of sun stroke occurred." It was here outside of Warrenton that an officer from the 4th Michigan wrote a long letter about what had happened to the 4th Michigan at Gettysburg, and that letter was soon published in a Detroit newspaper. After several days the regiment marched on from the Warrenton area with its comrades on the afternoon of August 3, moving only six or seven miles to Bealton Station, not far from the Rappahannock River. Though the march wasn't far, it was slow and started late, making for a tiresome move. Again on August 8 the soldiers struck their tents and moved their camp to the Rappahannock, near Beverly Ford. Here the regiment would stay with its comrades in the Second Brigade of the First Division of the Fifth Corps for more than a month in the summer heat, tending to regular duties and sometimes greeting comrades who'd been lightly wounded at Gettysburg, now recovered, or who had been placed on hospital details. Several of them arrived on August 9.

Among them was Sgt. John Hewitt of Company E. Hewitt had been assigned temporarily as an attendant in the weeks after the battle, probably at Camp Letterman. This was an army hospital set up in a field south of the York Pike, about a mile or so east of Gettysburg. One of his journal entries mentioned his assignment: "At 2 pm a detail of Cooks Pioneers & nurses was made to stay at the Hos[pital] & I had to stay."[12]

Hewitt recorded visits of the townspeople to the wounded, of their bringing food and his work helping set up the hospital. He had gone out into the country to a dance on July 10, heard preaching by "a celebrated devine [religious leader] from Baltimore" two days later, and seen "an old acquaintance" when a group of women from Adrian came to visit Michigan soldiers in the hospital on July 14. Hewitt's duties ranged from helping to clean the hospital to going to Gettysburg to kill a cow for beef for the men. One night he even managed to attend "singing school" and walk home with the daughter of a local captain.

Slowly but surely Hewitt and his comrades moved wounded soldiers to the railway station for transport to other hospitals and home, and on August 1 "the last of the wounded were taken away," he wrote. Two days later, the attendants themselves boarded a train in Gettysburg and "bid adieu to Penn[sylvania]." They traveled to Washington, D.C., and on August 5 arrived at Camp Convalescence (also given as Convalescent) near Alexandria. Sergeant Hewitt didn't enjoy that place at all: "About come to the conclusion that a convalescent camp is a nuisance," he wrote. "Hope we shall get out of this damned hole soon," he complained again three days later. He got his wish when he and his comrades boarded a train the next day that took them down to their part of the Union army at Bealton Station, where he rejoined his regiment on the Rappahannock.[13]

The soldiers had established their camp on a hill just above the river. The temperature during the day sometimes soared above 100 degrees, but their camp on high ground above the Rappahannock often caught the breeze and they could sometimes take a swim. Tim Regan of the 9th Massachusetts recorded a ghost story he'd heard that reportedly involved a member of the 4th Michigan. According to the tale, an unnamed soldier, while on picket at the river on the night of August 10, got into an increasingly angry argument with a Confederate on the other side over who had the better army. "Both men agreed to fight it out in the middle of the river (considering it neutral territory) accordingly they stripped to the skin and met in the middle of the river[,] each grasping a knife," Regan wrote. The two hotheads fought in the water, until, bleeding from their wounds, he wrote, both "sunk out of sight into the water." The eerie kicker to the story recorded by Regan was that the next night, pickets in the same area were said to have seen the spirits of the two dead combatants rise from the depths of the river and refight their knife fight until both ghostly forms again disappeared into the Rappahannock. It was a fine and macabre story, yet no record, letter, or report from any officer or soldier in the 4th Michigan indicates anything like the deadly fight in the river took place.[14]

During the same evening on which the river duel in Regan's ghostly tale allegedly took place, Edmond R. Bliss of Oakland County, about 23 and serving in Company D, composed a letter about a real battle—the battle of Gettysburg. "[W]e have seen a pretty hard camppaign since I last Rote to you, we was in the battle at gityeesburg," Bliss wrote. "[O]ur company had 31 men when it went in to the fight and when it came out it had six men. I tell you that they fell thick and fast." He explained it was because it had been a season of hard marching and fighting that he had been unable to reply to a letter he received in late May.[15]

Later that month, Lieutenant Vesey noted that those who volunteered back in the spring of 1861 now had nine months left to serve. "We hope to end, or least, help to end this rebellion, and to see Jeff Davis and his gang hung higher than Haman, the volunteers at home and 'in business' before that time," he wrote. But what the regiment needed badly in the meantime was more men. There had been a rumor that the regiment would be sent back to Michigan to recruit more troops, though Vesey admitted there was probably nothing to it. "We are very anxious to have the draft enforced in Michigan immediately, and our regiment filled up," he wrote. "If Gov. Blair will send us 500 men we will be satisfied without going home to recruit."

Still, there was concern about conscription, which could draft any sort of man, no matter what his character might be, into the army. Those who patriotically volunteered at the start wondered about these some of these men. James S. Conant, a Wayne County man himself drafted earlier in the year, commented on them: "Michigan sent . . . a hard lot of boys when the[y] sent the squad that I came with," he wrote. Barely had that group reached Cleveland when the first man deserted. An officer from the 4th Michigan, Capt. Alvan C. Lamson, who'd been serving as a brigade staff officer, expressed doubt about conscripts. Could drafted men really replace volunteers? Though life in the Union army was "almost unbearable," wrote Lamson, "yet to leave it now would only be to rush to 'ills we [k]now not of,' the draft I mean, which according to accounts is not a respecter of persons. I am glad I enlisted when the Regiment was organized, ain't you?" he asked his friend William F. Robinson.[16]

Lamson started out the war as a sergeant major, and now he was serving as the acting assistant inspector general for the Second Brigade. But he still wanted to share gossip about fellow officers. Writing to his friend Captain Robinson, who had been wounded at Gettysburg, he noted that Lt. Benjamin Westfall of Company F, originally a Hudson volunteer who'd also been slightly wounded, had returned to the regiment after a visit home. Lamson had recently seen Lt. George Yates from Detroit, who'd been away from the regiment since late in 1862, now serving on the staff of a Union general. Apparently Yates had proved an entertaining figure while drinking and gambling with his old comrades. "Yates made us a riot a few days ago," Lamson wrote; "we laid him out as usual, sending him home a wiser if not a better man." But the question that really interested Lamson was what was going to happen with the command of the 4th Michigan. "What news do you have about our Regiment, who is to be the Col., Lt Col, and last though not least Major, the latter has many aspirants, myself among the number," he wrote.[17]

Lamson and other officers such as John Bancroft had reason to wonder, after all, since the late Harrison Jeffords had been promoted past Lt. Col. George Lumbard earlier in the year. But in fact Lumbard was eventually promoted to be the colonel of the 4th Michigan this time, while Jairus Hall would soon be commissioned the new lieutenant colonel.

In the days after the regiment's disaster at the Wheatfield, officers wrote to the relatives of those who'd been killed. Lt. Edwin H. Gilbert of Company D wrote to the brother of Cpl. Charles Phelps. "The company—his Corps[,] as well as all that knew him, [knew that] he was a brave man and one that will be missed when the time of action comes, as well as in camp," the lieutenant wrote. "He was buried as well as circumstances would allow us to do and his grave marked with a head board so that his friends could find his remains if they wished to remove him." In another letter to Phelps's brother, Gilbert told Jay Phelps that if his brother had had any personal effects on him when he died, they were lost since "his body was not recovered until the day after the battle." If Jay Phelps wanted to find Charles's grave, he should look on "the left side of the Battlefield," where Charles's name had been "penciled" on a board at the head of the grave. "The 4th Michigan could not boast a braver or better Soldier than Corp. Charles W Phelps," Gilbert wrote.[18]

Lt. John Bancroft had written to the next-of-kin of the men from Company H who died at Gettysburg, and now he heard from some of them. "Yours of the 16th [of July] brings painful tidings to my heart, a great loss to me and family," wrote Abraham Purdy from Lapeer County. "But when I consider the cause in which my son was engaged I forebear to grieve and hope a speedy success to all the brave who are engaged in the defense of our glorious flag." Purdy hoped that Bancroft would soon be able to return home to "enjoy the society of your friends," but he also asked that the lieutenant look into the matter of $20 his son had loaned one of his sergeants. Bancroft had also written to the parents of Charles Wilson, who had signed up for the army in the small town of Litchfield but whose parents lived in Attica, Green County, Wisconsin. "It is hard news but it is the fortune of war," Solomon Wilson wrote. "We have the pleasure of thinking that he died in a good cause, fighting for the flag of his country." Wilson asked Bancroft to send the $20 allotment that Charlie had coming; Mrs. H. Wilson, the young man's mother, hoped Bancroft could tell her more about her son's death. "Now if it would not be asking to[o] much of you I would like to know the surgeon's name that attended Charles in his dying hours," she wrote. "We have not ever had an opportunity of knowing or hearing what kind of soldier he was and we feel anxious to hear something about how he bore the struggle of death, if he had his senses or not. It is painful to think of one dying among strangers and no friend to speak one kind word to them." Whether Bancroft was able to provide those details to Mrs. Wilson is unknown.[19]

Other letters written by officers were to comply with what must have seemed like the endless details of army bureaucracy. Captain Lamson found there was no escaping the government's requirement for accountability regarding its property—in this case, the gear of three soldiers who'd been badly wounded back at Fredericksburg in December. "The Regiment to which my command belongs was directed to advance under the fire of the enemy to take a certain position near Fredericksburg," Lamson explained to government auditors, "in doing so (3) three Privates were severely wounded. The arms carried by these men were left on the field, as we were repulsed, and they could not be recovered." The explanation wasn't good enough, however, and four months later Lamson was asked to give a list of the three lost sets of gear, from .58-caliber Springfield rifles and caps to waist belts and cartridge boxes.[20]

Joel H. Barnes of Company K knew the importance of such paperwork, and he was concerned that his brother Luke, captured by Confederates back on June 26 after falling out on the march toward Gettysburg, would face court-martial and have to pay for losing his rifle. Some months earlier, Joel had sent an army equipment receipt—a kind of "rain check" good for one rifle—back to the western Michigan community of Leonidas. Luke Barnes had been quickly paroled by the Confederates, and his brother thought Luke could use that receipt to try to replace his lost rifle. But Joel had a surefire way to replace Luke's weapon if that didn't work. "[I]f he cannot [get a rifle with the receipt] I will steal one for him," Joel asserted. He also assured family members that the casualties suffered by the U.S. Navy in dramatic sea battles they read about in newspapers were minimal compared to losses of the Army of the Potomac. "[O]ur last battle was the bigest that has been fought or that will be fought for they cannot get two such armies together again very soon," Joel wrote about Gettysburg.[21]

August days continued hot with an occasional rain shower, though by the end of the month there was sometimes cool weather. "Meanwhile we go through the lazy routine of camp life in Virginia in 'dog day,'" wrote Sgt. Edward Taylor, "a little drill—a little parade—much sleep, and 'don't-know-what-to-do-with-oneself.'" A dramatic exception for the soldiers in their division was witnessing the execution of five deserters from the 118th Pennsylvania. Sgt. John Hewitt called it "an impressive scene." James Houghton later recalled that the men were given a postponement of their sentence for three days since three of the men were Catholic and wanted a priest to pardon their sins. The end came for them on August 29. "[W]e were formed in two lines," Houghton wrote, "the deserters were taken from a farm house that was near by and marched down in front of us[.] The Catholic Priest marched with them muttering words of consolation." Then came a band playing the Death March, the drums muffled; the condemned men were walked to their graves, and seated on their coffins made of rough boards "where each one could see His final resting place," Houghton recalled. Two of the men were cousins, and one got up and stepped over to his relative, kissing him and bidding him good-bye. "Each was then asked if they had anything to say, they all shook their heads no," his account continued. Blindfolds were placed on the men and a firing squad of some 60 soldiers marched up. Half of these men had loaded rifles, while the other half had guns that were charged but without bullets. "[T]he order was soon given to ready ame [*sic*] and fire and they were all except one was swept back on to the coffins in an instant," Houghton wrote. The men were marched back to camp. Lt. John Bancroft, who recorded so many experiences in the war, recorded nothing of it.[22]

Private William J. Cunningham, 24, from Company K, mentioned the executions in a letter to his mother, but he stressed that "I have not the room on this page or the time to tell you about it." He promised he would "some other time." Regarding the terrible bloodshed he had witnessed, the soldier from Washtenaw County wrote that it seemed "that God is chastising his children with the fiery rock of correction, but I think [we] will come out of the fire after many trials a purer & wiser nation." Of course, he realized his own enlistment would end in the coming year. "If my life is spared until next spring I will then return[,] but knowing what one day or hour mite [reveal] the hidden future and bring to light which is now hidden from our view." Cunningham wrote. "[B]ut I am resigned to my fate let it be as it may." As he closed his letter, he asked his mother to pray for him.[23]

The 4th Michigan went on picket the day after the executions and came back into camp on September 2, when they received their new stand of colors, Sgt. John Hewitt of Company E noted in his journal. Lt. Robert Campbell, quartermaster, said he also procured this banner for the regiment, later describing its prominent feature as an "American eagle surrounded with stars upon a blue field." Though drill, dress parade, and inspection occupied the soldiers, there was time to construct a race course; after it was completed, "horse racing [was] the order of the day," Hewitt noted. "Major Hall Beat Col. [Gaines?] out of $100."[24]

By now the war in northern Virginia had settled into a kind of stalemate in part because both the Union and Confederate armies in Virginia had grown smaller in the wake of Gettysburg. In the case of the Army of the Potomac, thousands of men were sent to New York because of draft riots. The enlistments of thousands of other soldiers also ended that summer. Yet thousands of new conscripts were arriving and their training began immediately. On the Confederate side, Lee's forces saw Longstreet and his troops leave for Tennessee in September, and soon the Union army knew it. Under pressure from Lincoln and chief general Henry W. Halleck, Meade planned a demonstration or raid.

The day after the soldiers of the 4th Michigan watched the horse racing, Union cavalry moved out on a reconnaissance and clashed with Rebels at Culpeper—the regiment heard firing in the distance on the morning of September 13. The next morning the officers were given their marching orders, though they remained in camp for two more days, continuing to drill, packing on the 15th, and marching the next day. The Fifth Corps tramped in the heat to within a two or three miles of Culpeper. Though the men were tired, they were pleased when the paymaster caught up and began to distribute some of their back pay. In the morning their division marched on through Culpeper and went into camp a short distance beyond it. For about three weeks they remained in this area. But no offensive materialized from the Union army's forward movement, though some of the more advanced elements reached the Rapidan River. The weather started to turn cold, sometimes rainy, and the troops witnessed the execution of yet another deserter, from the 12th New York. After having been absent from the 4th Michigan since Gettysburg, Henry Seage of Company E returned to the regiment, along with his father, the Reverend John Seage. "Boys all glad to see us," the son wrote in his journal that night. Henry Seage had escorted his wounded brother to White Pigeon, arriving on September 10. After several days of socializing with family and friends, Seage and his father, more or less recovered from the wounds he received in May, boarded a train on September 21, arriving at Culpeper about 50 hours later. That same day, Seage later noted, three men from the Second Brigade were hanged for assaulting "an old negro woman."[25]

Major Jairus W. Hall wrote to Gov. Austin Blair that week, asking for an appointment to a new cavalry regiment forming in Michigan. "I am of the opinion that the cavalry service suits my disposition better than Infantry does," Hall wrote hopefully, but ultimately in vain. A Spanish general visited and inspected their division, the 4th Michigan went on picket, and September waned. Sergeant Major Edward "Ned" Taylor thanked his sister Lottie for some tea she'd sent him; he mentioned that he shared some with his cook, an Englishman called "Old Jimmy," who also cooked for Company A. Old Jimmy, he wrote, "declares it is the best he has tasted since leaving England." As September came to a close the next day the regiment returned from uneventful picket duty and on October 1 marched back to Culpeper to witness the punishment of yet another deserter, this time a man from the 32nd Massachusetts whose head was shaved. Then he was branded and "drummed out" of the army. The 4th Michigan went back to its drill and inspections, while Lieutenant Bancroft was appointed to serve on a division court- martial, where he met Col. Joshua L. Chamberlain, the former commander of the 20th Maine Infantry Regiment. Chamberlain, of course, had been hailed as a hero at Gettysburg for charging Rebels at Little Round Top.[26]

In the meantime the effects of that battle continued taking their toll. Corporal David Laird, probably 20, had been in Company A and on the far right of the regiment's ill-fated line in the woods at the southwest corner of the Wheatfield. Like many others, he'd been shot in the back. As he lay in the hospital that summer and on into the fall, he told the Reverend R. J. Parvin of the U.S. Christian Commission that he was concerned about the nature of this wound—that the fact he'd been struck in the back would give people a bad impression of him, Laird said. From Hillsdale County, David's father Robert wrote back to Parvin, saying that David's wound "need give him no uneasiness. None who know him will suppose it to be there on account of cowardice." His parents wrote and prayed, but David's condition deteriorated. A soldier serving at the army hospital telegraphed his father, who arrived in time to be with his son when he died on the morning of September 24. Parvin attempted to comfort Robert Laird, but the father told the pastor that wasn't necessary. "God has given me so much, in seeing the happy death of my boy, that I am perfectly content." But Laird's faith may have been tested days later when he learned that another son, David's brother Sam, had been killed while serving as a sergeant with the 42nd Illinois at the battle of Chickamauga in the western theater of the war.[27]

For just over a week camp life was quiet for the 4th Michigan until word reached the Union army that Confederate forces had crossed the Rapidan River on the Union right flank. Lee heard that two Union army corps had been detached from the Army of the Potomac. To take advantage of this opportunity, he pressed forward. In order to protect Washington, D.C., and his own supply lines, General Meade pulled back in what became several days of marches, dodges, clashes, and general back-and-forth movement nearly 50 miles from the Rapidan northeast toward Washington. Early on October 10, the 4th Michigan came back from picket, collected rations, and broke camp, marching to the southeast with other outfits from their division on what Bancroft described as reconnaissance toward the Rapidan. Soon they were pulled back to the site of their camp near Culpeper. The next day reveille sounded at 5:00 A.M., Sgt. John Hewitt noted, as the Union army marched northeast, back to the Rappahannock. A brass band played "Year of the Jubilee" and other tunes as they went through Culpeper and back across the river.[28]

They were among the troops guarding the Beverly Ford as thousands of wagons and soldiers crossed on October 12, bivouacking that night at the site of their old camp by the ford. The next day, still watching for a Confederate attack, the regiment went into rifle pits near the river and then marched back over on a bridge with other troops from the Fifth and Sixth corps, advancing to Brandy Station, about midway between the Rappahannock and Culpeper, acting as rear guard as Union cavalry skirmished with Confederates. That evening the soldiers of the 4th Michigan and their division set huge campfires on the hills to indicate the presence of a huge Union force, but quietly picked up their gear at 1:00 A.M. on October 13, arriving at the Rappahannock at daylight. All day long the troops trudged to the northeast, covering 25 miles and camping that night at Catlett Station. Henry Seage, detailed to go with the pioneers and musicians who acted as ambulance and medical assistants, complained that his feet were so sore that he could hardly walk.

The long marching continued, the 4th Michigan passing Bristow Station and reaching Manassas Junction. Confederates attacked the Union rear and were repulsed, but commanders decided that the Fifth Corps units needed to hurry back to reinforce those troops. The 4th Michigan ran three or four miles along with others, but the shooting was over when they got there at dark. They turned around at ten o'clock and marched to a point just beyond Bull Run. There they stopped to camp early in the morning of October 15. Lieutenant Bancroft called this "a very tiresome march."[29]

The skies opened up as the Union army moved toward Washington over the next two days. The 4th Michigan marched to Fairfax and then to Centreville and a wet, miserable bivouac. But at last this cat-and-mouse retreat was over. The Union army had prevented the Rebels from threatening the capital, but the ordeal of the weeklong march from Culpeper accomplished little for Lee or Meade. The sun came out on October 17 and dried out men's tents and blankets, and that "put a more cheerful aspect on our conditions and situation," Henry Seage noted. The Confederate army moved back to the southwest and the Union army followed. Early the next morning, the march took the 4th Michigan to Fairfax Court House and then to a place called Fox's Mill. Capt. William H. Loveland of Company B was sent with a group of volunteers to lay an ambush for the infamous Confederate raider Mosby that night, but nothing came of it. On the 19th the 4th Michigan and the 32nd Massachusetts were designated as guards for the wagon train, and they covered about 15 miles that day, crossing over Bull Run and reaching the old battlefield in the evening. The ground was marked with the bones of the dead and entire skeletons that hadn't been buried sufficiently. Bancroft noted that the surviving fence rails on two nearby farms were "full of bullets," another sign of the battles that had been fought here.[30]

The wagon train moved a few miles to Gainesville the next day, where the 4th Michigan camped in the woods. On October 21 the wagons moved on towards Warrenton, and the regiment rejoined its Second Brigade and First Division that evening. Over the next few days the soldiers of the regiment sometimes stayed in bivouac and sometimes marched and camped in rain and mud, finally reaching Warrenton Junction. The location of their camp shifted along the nearby railroad line as the month ended, first to a place called Three Mile Station and again just days later to another point nearby. But there was good news for the soldiers that last week in October—it was now quiet along the lines. They received some soft (fresh) bread and they got paid. And when they were issued hardtack, the men were delighted to find "that it had no worms for the first time in 3 months," Sergeant Hewitt noted.

The regiment was on picket in early November, and Lieutenant Bancroft periodically served on courts-martial. Though he had applied for a 15-day leave after learning that his mother was gravely ill back in Massachusetts, the generals turned him down—the Fifth Corps was under marching orders and no leaves were being granted. The 4th Michigan now numbered 207 soldiers, what with the addition of some drafted men, but it was still a small regiment with an even smaller core of experienced troops. Word began to circulate about the army's new offer to sign up soldiers who had enlisted back in 1861—they were being asked to sign up for another

Having only to observe rather than fight on Nov. 7, 1863, men of the 4th Michigan watch as the artillery fires at Confederate fortifications at Rappahannock Station. Their Union infantry comrades stormed and captured the fort later that same day, but the regiment wasn't in the battle. Drawing by Lt. Charles Gruner.

three-year hitch. "About 100 of our men are willing to reenlist if they can go home to reorganize," Bancroft wrote.[31]

The 4th Michigan returned from picket and the next morning, November 7, was called out at 4:00 A.M. to strike its tents. Three hours later the men were marching with the rest of the Fifth Corps south past Bealton once more toward the Rappahannock River to a place called Rappahannock Station. Here the Confederates had built a fort surrounded by trenches in order to protect a pontoon bridge. The Fifth Corps and the Sixth Corps reached that vicinity in the afternoon and formed in line of battle in woods in front of the Rebel defenses. Corporal Henry Seage wrote that the 4th Michigan halted at the edge of the trees and lay down. Soon two artillery batteries rolled up in front of the regiment and opened fire on the Confederate works, and so did other Union guns up and down the line.

Lieutenant Bancroft had a "fine view" of this battlefield as soldiers from the Sixth Corps, to his right, advanced and traded fire with the Rebels. But the 4th Michigan and its brigade did not have to fight this day. In the evening skirmishers from the Sixth Corps and from the Third Brigade of the Fifth Corps's First Division boldly charged the Confederate works, causing hundreds of Rebels to surrender or flee. Men of the 4th Michigan were on guard duty that night as the soldiers bivouacked near Rappahannock Station, and the next morning marched south on the road to Kelly's Ford with the Fifth Corps. As the men were forming on the west side of the river after crossing on pontoons, General Meade rode by and the proud soldiers "gave him a lusty cheer," Seage wrote. The Second Brigade marched two or three miles from the river and went into bivouac.[32]

The next day many of the men of the First Division of the Fifth Corps found they were short of rations, so they greeted their new temporary division commander, Brig. Gen. Joseph Bartlett, with calls of "hardtack!" as he rode by. Irritated by this lack of respect, Bartlett ordered them out to drill for the rest of the day. Their brigade moved their temporary camps across the river. It was a very cold night as the 4th Michigan went into bivouac, and when the men rose on the morning of November 10 they found everything covered in snow. Rations were issued in the morning and the men marched to a point between Morristown and Bealton Station. Here they stood picket for several days in the rain and cold. It was here that Henry Seage was assigned to the color guard on November 16, just as the man he would identify as having been the flag bearer at Gettysburg, Thomas Tarsney, was demoted to private. New clothing was also issued, and early on the morning of November 18 the 4th Michigan was sent back to Kelly's Ford. They crossed the river and rejoined the Fifth Corps. Using wood and stone from the old Confederate quarters here, the men put up their tents and built fireplaces, believing that now the Union army would be settling into winter camp.

It was not to be. Meade ordered another offensive across the Rapidan River. On November 24, the 4th Michigan moved out with its brigade and division in a rainstorm. "But the progress was slow and difficult," Cyril P. Brown of Company F wrote to his parents. "Artillery wagons sunk in mud to the hubs, and men to the ankles." They'd only moved about a mile when an order came for the troops to head back to camp, which the men cheerfully obeyed.[33]

The Mine Run Campaign

After this false start the men got to stay in camp for a couple of more days. On November 25, the regiment was visited by Michigan adjutant general John Robertson, who made a gift of six new snare drums and a bass drum he had purchased from a sutler. But the next day, Thanksgiving, the offensive began anew, and the 4th Michigan moved out with the Fifth Corps. The troops marched several miles south to the Rapidan, arriving at about 1:00 P.M., crossing that evening at a point Henry Seage described as a mile-and-a-half above Ely's Ford. Two or three miles beyond the river, the column reached the Orange Plank Road and marched about a mile toward Chancellorsville. After that long day's tramp into the night, the soldiers camped on a large hill in the cold.

The march resumed in the morning of November 27 through the rough, forested area called the Wilderness, with the brigade and division trudging along the plank road and then turning off onto a country lane that took them to the Gordonsville Pike. But then came the sound of gunfire from the rear as Confederate cavalry from the brigade of Brig. Gen. Thomas L. Rosser attacked their wagon train. Seage thought that 14 ammunition wagons were captured, but Rosser reported his troopers captured eight ordnance wagons and seven ambulances and destroyed between 35 and 40 wagons. Two 4th Michigan teamsters, Tim Burtch and William Smith, were among the nearly 100 Union wagoners captured by the Rebels; both men ultimately survived the war.

Meade's offensive pressed on. By late morning, the soldiers heard skirmish fire. "We were now hurried forward—the last mile we double-quicked," Cyril Brown wrote. The men moved off the road into the woods, loading their rifles. His company was deployed as skirmishers when the 4th Michigan arrived at the front—the Union army would once again confront the Confederates in strong defensive positions. Shots were exchanged, but that evening the regiment's skirmishers were sent back to their regiment's place in the line. Though Rebel guns opened on them, none of the Michigan troops were injured. The men spent another cold night on their arms, since no fires could be built or food cooked.[34]

This was the opening of Meade's ill-fated Mine Run campaign, named for a high-banked creek that flowed in a northerly direction through the countryside to the Rapidan. The soldiers were roused in the morning, Brown said, a few at a time; they were allowed to walk to the rear to make coffee as rain fell. An expected Confederate attack didn't materialize, and the soldiers of the Fifth Corps were drawn back to the plank road, "where we right-faced and marched to Robertson's Tavern, reaching there about noon," Brown said. The men were again put in line of battle—Sergeant Hewitt said they "layed in the mud all day." It seemed to Lieutenant Bancroft that there would be a fight, but the men ended up encamping in the fields. According to Brown's understanding of the situation, they had moved that day from near the left of the Union line toward its center. The next day, November 29, the soldiers of the 4th Michigan, with the other regiments of their corps, advanced and formed line of battle on the Union right, near Mine Run. But Lee had reacted quickly to this winter offensive, moving his men into strong positions above the steep river banks with trenches for the infantry and strong artillery placement. The orders the Michigan men now received gave many soldiers pause, particularly those who'd seen the results of infantry attacks on strong defensive positions at Fredericksburg and Gettysburg. "[I]n the afternoon we were informed that our corps would storm the Rebel works at sun down," Sergeant Hewitt wrote. The Fifth Corps would be one of four that, according to Meade's plan, would charge across the creek, Lieutenant Bancroft noted. The Third Brigade of the division would go first, as skirmishers, and their Second Brigade would follow.

Orders came for the soldiers to take nothing with them except their weapons and canteens, so the soldiers of the 4th Michigan piled their knapsacks. "Many of the men gave their money and watches to the Chaplain and all felt serious enough," Bancroft wrote. Cyril Brown also noted that men knew many of them wouldn't survive the charge, set for 4:00 P.M. "There naturally were some long faces," he wrote. "None of us knew who would see the morning sun." The men lay down with their rifles at the ready, and darkness fell. But the order to charge didn't come. The men began to feel the tension lift. They were ordered to pull back.[35]

Still, they weren't out of the woods. At 1:00 A.M. on the morning of November 30 the soldiers were told to get to their feet and eat whatever breakfast they could find. Again they were told to prepare to charge and again the soldiers left their packs with a guard. The 4th Michigan marched to the right with its brigade, division, and corps, and began to form into multiple lines of battle in the woods. "Our regiment formed a portion of the 3rd line," Cyril Brown wrote. They waited in the freezing weather. Lieutenant Bancroft wrote that men "tramped around and around until the woods were trodden like a path" as they attempted to keep warm. "It was bitter cold," Brown agreed, "and fires of course could not be allowed. . . . In spite of all exertions, it seemed as though we would freeze." Men who lay down and fell asleep had to be helped off the field. The charge was scheduled for 8:00 A.M., but the hour came and went. They waited.

At 8:30 Union batteries posted on a hill to the left of the 4th Michigan opened fire, and the Confederates responded. This was it, the soldiers thought. "We now fell in and took our guns, every one expecting the hour, and perhaps his last hour[,] had come," Brown wrote. "But the attack is postponed. Slowly the day wears away." "No fires, no coffee, no charge," Lieutenant Bancroft wrote. The soldiers heard that other troops—pickets from the Sixth and Second Corps, who waded the stream and got soaked—froze to death. But more importantly Union commanders looked at the Confederate positions and were surprised by what they saw. Lee's men were in strong, lengthy defenses. The generals made their decision—there would be no assault. Pleased they weren't being sent on a suicidal attack, the Union soldiers tried to keep from freezing throughout the rest of the day. At dark the 4th Michigan pulled back, as did thousands of other soldiers. "Went back to our camping ground of the previous night," Bancroft wrote. "Had a good supper. Felt relieved in not charging."[36]

Brown agreed. The men marched back cold and "sick of the army and everything connected with it. But a good fire and hot cup of coffee soon put me in a better state of mind." Bancroft and others made beds of pine boughs in the shelter of the trees, with huge fires blazing nearby. "Slept soundly, feeling thankful We were not on the hillside between our lines and the rebel works," he wrote. A few days later Brown added a postscript about the Mine Run campaign. "I have since learned that the reason of Meade's abandoning his plan of attack was that he learned by a reconnaissance sent out Sunday night that Mine Run was from three to ten feet deep," he wrote. "For men to charge thro' such a stream, up a craggy hill covered with cannon, supported by thousands of armed men, would be a useless slaughter."

The next day, December 1, the men woke, gathered around their fires, and eventually prepared to move out. "About dark we commenced a retrograde movement," Sergeant Hewitt wrote about the pullout from Mine Run, "arrived at the Rapidan about 12 oc [o'clock] and camped for the night." Henry Seage noted that he and his father took their place in the ordnance train and went along the pike through the nighttime woods and back to the plank road to the Germanna Ford. The 4th Michigan guarded this train, crossing the river at about three in the morning and proceeding on a mile or so to build camp, only to be promptly ordered to take everything down and march another half-mile or so, to be closer to the rest of their division. The men were aggravated as well as exhausted. "About ten minutes after stopping, or five minutes after, everyone was asleep," Lieutenant Bancroft wrote.[37]

The Mine Run campaign was over.

CHAPTER 12

They Say Let the War Go On

THE MARCH BACK FROM THE CANCELLED WINTER OFFENSIVE CONTINUED ON DECEMBER 2. THE men of the 4th Michigan complained that they rose and began moving about seven, without food or coffee, and tramped several hours into the early afternoon to the town of Stevensburg. The next day their corps moved across the Rappahannock, and the Second Brigade of the First Division marched on to Bealton Station, part of the Fifth Corps's deployment along the railroad line. For two days the men were allowed to rest. On December 6, the regiment moved to the other side of the railroad, where the soldiers built their winter camp.

"We then went to work with a will putting up winter quarters," wrote Cyril Brown, the young man from Hudson who joined Company F in the late summer of 1862."We had to bring logs on our backs about a mile, but that's nothing. It only wants time and patience." It took Brown and his bunkmate four days to complete their cabin. "We have as good a fire place and bunk as I could ask for," he wrote with satisfaction. The journals of Henry Seage and John Hewitt, both of Company E, also indicate that the soldiers carried logs and stone to build. They were pleased about its location on the railroad. "I am contented with the place," wrote Brown. "We have no picket duty to do. Guarding supplies at the depot is our duty." Yet within a month's time, Brown became quite ill, and he would soon be discharged for disability.

Lieutenant Bancroft and Capt. William H. Loveland were now the officers for the 5th Company, since the regiment's 10 companies had been consolidated into five, though officers and men continued to identify themselves as members of their old alphabetical company designation. The two officers helped the men put up their cabins, and in doing so, helped themselves. Notes in Bancroft's diary (turned into a scrapbook after the war) contain a copy of a letter he wrote in January, in which he stated there was a lack of horses or mules around the brigade early in December since the vast majority of teamsters were busy bringing food and supplies to the Union soldiers. But by managing to secure the services of a team, Bancroft and Loveland provided their men the use of a wagon for several days to carry logs and rocks. As the men finished their own cabins, the two officers got assistance from grateful troops. They put up a comfortable 9-foot by 11-foot cabin with walls four feet high, topped by two wagon covers for the roof. It had a fireplace, stone chimney, furniture, and door. "We took a great deal of comfort there, called it 'home,'" Bancroft wrote.[1]

The war had come to a close, more or less, for the season, though there was the occasional raid by Confederate cavalry that could result in an alarm or skirmish. "All quiet along the lines," wrote Sgt. John Hewitt. The weather was rainy, but fine days still occasionally appeared. The soldiers drew new clothing and got paid. Capt. William F. Robinson of Company H, the former dentist who had escaped with his life at Gettysburg, still found himself having to explain to the War Department what happened to equipment that had been lost when five of his men had been killed, eight wounded, and four captured: "The arms carried by all these men were left on the field, as we were repulsed, and they could not be recovered," Robinson wrote in a sworn statement about the 17 rifles, belts, cartridge boxes, bayonet scabbards, and various other pieces of gear. He was not alone; Lt. Michael Vreeland, who had barely survived his wounds at the same battle, would also be pressed for an explanation of his company's lost arms and equipment, as were others.

By now word had reached the men of the 4th Michigan of the death of another of their comrades who'd been captured by the Confederates at Gettysburg. This was Sgt. John G. Brownell of Woodstock, who'd been in Company F. Brownell's parents heard that their son had been released in a prisoner exchange in late in October, but died soon after. Was this story true? The parents wanted to know what had really happened, but couldn't get any information. An acquaintance, an officer in the cavalry, investigated and found that it was true; Brownell had been released but died from the effects of starvation suffered at Libby Prison. He was one of several men who died out of a group of 150 prisoners released. After he'd been captured, the Rebels had taken Brownell's shoes, coat, and other clothing, leaving him only his shirt, a pair of pants, and worn-out stockings. He was, the friend wrote, "wasted to a skeleton, and died of sheer starvation and exhaustion." The friend had wanted to send Brownell's body home, but had to have him buried at Annapolis, Maryland.[2]

As the winter camp was established in early December, Lt. Col. George Lumbard penned a politically astute note to Gov. Austin Blair. Lumbard had wanted to become full colonel and commander of the 4th Michigan since the late fall of 1862. Although he now ran the regiment, he still was hoping to get that colonel's commission. But because his regiment was so reduced in number, he needed it filled up in order to justify that promotion, since the War Department seemed to be satisfied with having lieutenant colonels and majors run small regiments. "I have made up my mind to remain the service as long as the war lasts providing I can and [I] shall do all in my power to get this regiment to reenlist," he wrote. "I hope the organization [of the 4th Michigan] will be kept up and that we shall receive in January 5 or 6 hundred men and then by spring we shall have as good a regiment as ever and one that will maintain the reputation of Michigan troops and do its full share in closing up the war, which I hope will be closed ere another year."

This was Lumbard pushing all the right buttons: Linking his request for promotion to colonel to his desire to get hundreds of more men for his regiment in order to help defeat the Confederacy—something that mattered greatly to Blair. Lumbard insisted that "nearly every man in the regiment would reenlist for three years if they could go home soon and remain sixty days." The men of the 4th Michigan were in good spirits, he maintained, but because the regiment was so small, "that spirit of invincibility which they formerly had" was lacking. Still, Lumbard wrote, his men and officers were not discouraged: "They say let the war go on until the Rebels call for quarters and cry enough." Major Jairus Hall and most of the officers would continue to serve, he said.

It would turn out that Lumbard was overconfident when he predicted "nearly every man" would reenlist, but it was the right thing to say to Blair. Lumbard was also careful not to cross the governor on the subject of who should be the next regimental surgeon for the regiment. Initially he had recommended Dr. John Watts, who'd been the 4th Michigan's assistant surgeon for some time. Before he'd been killed, Harrison Jeffords had recommended Watts for the post. But the governor had decided to appoint Dr. Luther French, a physician from Hudson who'd resigned as assistant regimental surgeon because of sickness back in the spring of 1863. That was fine with Lumbard; he just didn't want to make an enemy of Watts. Lumbard needed no reminding of the trouble he had with Blair when the governor appointed then–Captain Jeffords to be colonel early in 1863. Lumbard didn't want a recurrence of this kind of trouble. "I did not wish by refusing to recommend him [Watts] to make myself another enemy, having as I thought[,] incurred the displeasure of the Gov. through the representations of former members of the regiment, under similar circumstances," Lumbard wrote.[3]

While Lumbard lobbied for promotion, the issue facing most of the soldiers of the 4th Michigan was that question of reenlistment. On December 20, Major Jairus Hall read the assembled troops the order that dealt with this. Essentially it was an offer aimed at the men who joined for three years back in the spring of 1861. In six months, their hitch would be up and the spring campaign would be well under way; the government needed these men to reenlist now. In exchange for committing for three more years, they would be formally designated as "Veteran Volunteers." They would also collect a bounty from the state of Michigan of hundreds of dollars, and go home on a 30-day furlough. But it was said that they needed three-quarters of the men present to sign up for that hitch in order to get that leave and those benefits. Sergeant Hewitt noted that "staff officers [are] doing their best to get the men to reenlist."

This "great effort," as Capt. William F. Robinson characterized it, continued over the next several days, and about 20 men reenlisted on Christmas. The next day, the 4th Michigan was formed in a square just outside Lt. Col. George Lumbard's tent; Hewitt said the men heard "some fine speeches but I am not going to enlist." Henry Seage, who joined in September 1861, said he was "taken," apparently swept up by the rhetoric, and he and his cabin mate Amon C. Lake did sign up, though service records shows that Seage mustered out of the army at the expiration of his original three-year hitch, while Lake was fated to die that spring. Neither is listed as a Veteran Volunteer in the state regimental record. How was this possible? Seage's diary shows that within several weeks of his signing up for the extended hitch, he was apparently allowed to change his mind. On February 19, 1864, he went to talk to Captain Monteith about "my term of enlistment." Henry Seage would leave the service in September 1864, the end of his original three-year term. By comparison, Tom Tarsney, who had entered the 4th Michigan when Seage did and who also signed up for the additional hitch, had to serve most of it. Like other 4th Michigan "Veteran Volunteers," Tarsney was not discharged until early in 1866.[4]

Perhaps it was also significant that one of the immediate rewards for men who reenlisted was a party courtesy of Lumbard and Major Hall—a party with plenty of liquor. On the night of December 29, 1863, Seage wrote, probably with sarcasm: "Major & Col. distributed whiskey among the vets and an awful drunk ensued. A fine way to get men to enlist." Hewitt, who'd refused to sign up again, also noted the party in his journal. Another member of the regiment who was refusing to reenlist was Sergeant Major Edward H. C. Taylor. Ever since Ned Taylor had resigned his lieutenant's commission in that feud at the formation of the regiment, he'd longed for a promotion back to an officer's status. But this didn't happen; it had taken him nearly three years to reach the rank of sergeant major. Now that his colonel and major were pressuring him to reenlist, Taylor said no—not unless he was given a commission. "I fear the Colonel and Major don't like it at all," Taylor wrote of his demand. "What do I care?"

Friends in the regiment warned him not to reenlist on the promise of a promotion, and Taylor was taking their advice. "[T]hey can't make me remain in the service longer than the 20th day of June next," he wrote. Another experienced soldier who'd been with the 4th Michigan who'd refused to sign up again was Silas Sadler of Company G. He was sorry that his mother, back in Tecumseh, wrongly believed he was reenlisting, for he heard she had suffered "a crying spell." "But you must not worry any more about it for I won't reinlist now," Sadler wrote his parents. Sadler and other soldiers were hoping their hitch would come to a close while his regiment was doing guard duty along the railroad line near Bealton Station.[5]

Men like Sadler and Hewitt and Taylor had had enough. They had risked their lives and endured hardships for three years. Now they believed it was time for someone else to step up and serve. Nor were they exceptions. More than 150 of the soldiers and officers in the 4th Michigan were unwilling to reenlist, slightly more than half of the men who were eligible to do so. A man who signed his letter to his hometown newspaper "Veteran" gave the example of Company A. Between promotions, casualties, and illness, 35 of the original 106 enlisted men and officers of this company were still present for duty by the spring of 1864. Of those, 13 men, or less than half of those eligible in the company for the reenlistment offer, actually signed up for it. Other companies seem to have had similar situations.[6]

One soldier who had enough of the war was Sgt. Jonas D. Richardson, from Washtenaw County. He was hoping for a discharge or at least a transfer back to Michigan. Richardson, who enlisted at the age of 21 in the spring of 1861, twisted his ankle in the retreat from the Wheatfield at Gettysburg. By the fall of 1863 he'd become sick and lame enough that he was transferred to the

Veteran Reserve Corps, or what had first been called the "Invalid Corps." This was a relatively new branch of the army that allowed men who'd been wounded or sick, but not completely disabled, to do light duty and remain in the service. On Christmas Eve, from Lincoln General Hospital, not far from Washington, Richardson wrote to his brother, convinced that if he could get his hands on $20 to pay a surgeon, he could buy a discharge, just as he said others were doing. Richardson urged his brother to hurry and send this amount. Otherwise, he wrote,

> The chance may slip by. So if you have that amount on hand and can spare it for a short time send it to me by express *without delay*. A Surgeon in the City, whose wife holds the rank of Colonel in the Sanitary Commission has been authorized by the Vice President and ten Senators to make out the discharges of all Soldiers who they think not fit for service, the amount to be paid for *said discharge* is $25. No examination to be *held*[;] the papers are all made out and sent to the Surg. Genl. for his signature[;] *the money* is then forked over and all the accounts settled. I have seen this Surgeon today and paid him $5 to bind the bargain and he says that within 4 or 6 days after I pay him the balance I shal have my discharge.

Once he got his discharge, Richardson wrote, he would get the back pay due him and repay his brother. "If I had the money today, I could get home by New Year's day," he wrote. He wished his brother a merry Christmas and urged him to answer as quickly as he received the letter.[7]

Yet this wasn't the only tactic Richardson tried to get home. He also managed to get Governor Blair to request his transfer to Michigan, and this arrived three days later on December 27 in the form of a letter for Richardson to present to federal authorities. The next day Richardson took that request from Blair to the office of the Provost Marshal General but got a big disappointment when he was "informed that the Secretary of War had forbidden the transferring of any more 'individuals,' only companies." "[I] am bust up on that affair," Richardson wrote. That left open only the possibility of buying a medical discharge. Richardson appealed to his brother again, urging him to "make no delay" in sending the $20 needed to pay the surgeon for signing a discharge. "4 soldiers got there [*sic*] discharges today while I was there," he fretted. But Richardson didn't get the money; he wouldn't get his early discharge, and he remained in the hospital.[8]

December passed slowly by. Lieutenant Colonel Lumbard wrote out the obligatory year-end report to the state adjutant general that summarized the movements, marches, and battles of the regiment through 1863. The regiment had marched over 700 miles that year, he wrote; between November 1, 1862, and the same date in 1863, it had lost 57 killed or mortally wounded; 24 had died of disease, with another 141 discharged for disability; 135 had been wounded, and 57 were missing in action; 105 had been taken prisoner. Another 25 men had deserted the regiment, and 47 had been discharged by order.

There was a train derailment on the line in the vicinity of the 4th Michigan's camp, but no one was injured, and the regiment's clerks were busy preparing muster and pay rolls as the year closed with a gray, rainy day. "Good by 1863," Sergeant Hewitt wrote in his journal; "it has been an eventful year." Henry Seage also bid farewell to the year, "with its toils and hardships." Lt. John Bancroft had been after a furlough for some weeks, and just after the middle of the month December, he was allowed to visit family in Massachusetts. He arrived back in Washington on

New Year's Day and returned to the regiment on January 2. Men were still reenlisting, but the routine of winter camp was monotonous, and Bancroft spent his days studying for an examination before a board of officers from the Ordnance Bureau. He often rode in the countryside with his friend, Captain Loveland. "Life here is now very tedious," he complained as the days dragged on. "Nothing to do."

In the meantime Jairus Hall sent information back to Michigan about the reenlisting of the regiment's veterans. "By a letter from Major Hall, of the 4th Infantry, we learn that 121 men of that regiment were mustered into service on the 8th inst. [of January] as veterans, and would be paid off the next day," a newspaper reported. That number would go up to 124 by later in the month and by another account, tick up to about 140. The paper noted the 4th Michigan's record in battle and mentioned that several of its former officers had gone on to command other regiments—Capt. John Oliver had become the colonel of the 15th Michigan, while Marshall Chapin was now the colonel of the 23rd Michigan. Capt. Charles Doolittle had become colonel of the 18th Michigan, with another 4th Michigan alumnus, George Spalding, serving as Doolittle's lieutenant colonel.[9]

The ties between the 4th Michigan and the communities that sent its men off to war remained strong. Some soldiers from Tecumseh sent $50 back through Lt. Jerome Allen in January 1864 for the building of a new First Methodist Episcopal Church. More importantly, in Hillsdale County and other nearby communities, men were trying to recruit new companies for the 4th Michigan. The first was Cornelius Van Valer, about 47 and a former captain of the 18th Michigan, which formed back in the summer of 1862; now Van Valer was to be a captain of a new company in the 4th Michigan. His lieutenant was 21-year-old William H. Sherman. Another officer with this new company, John V. B. Goodrich, 27, from Lenawee County, would be a familiar face to the regiment's veterans. He had enlisted in the 4th Michigan's Company A in the fall of 1861 but was discharged for disability slightly more than a year later. Now he was given a second lieutenant's commission for helping to recruit the new company. Another supporter of the 4th Michigan, Enos Canniff of Hudson, a former sutler to the regiment, also was attempting to recruit another company, though Canniff himself would not actually serve with it. One man who was signing up, James B. Dickerson of Hudson, essentially rejoined his old regiment. Dickerson was 34 when he originally joined Company F back in the spring of 1861, and he'd been promoted to sergeant that fall. But he'd been discharged for disability after the Seven Days. Now at the age of 37 he enlisted again in the 4th Michigan.

Despite the efforts of Van Valer and Canniff to form two companies, they simply couldn't enlist enough men. They did, however, have enough men between them to make one full company. As a result, within a few weeks, the state adjutant general and the U.S. Army officer in charge of the recruiting office in Detroit would order Van Valer's and Canniff's recruits consolidated into a single company, which was designated "the Independent Company" in the state's published roster of the 4th Michigan after the war. Months would pass, however, before these men finally joined the regiment at the front in Virginia.[10]

Snow and rain kept the 4th Michigan and other soldiers in their division from doing much other than the routines of guard duty and washing. Muddy conditions sometimes helped bring the cancellation of inspections and parades and Henry Seage noted that camp life had indeed become boring. "Hope we will soon have some excitement," he wrote. The only real action came when some Confederate cavalry tried to make a raid on a nearby general's headquarters, but were repulsed. More cerebral and entertaining sorts of conflict came when Dr. John Watts, Capt. James McLean and Lt. Josiah Emerson, among others, organized debate teams that included some privates. The Reverend John Seage, prominent in the debates, was on the team that argued against the proposition "that men in the field are better qualified to elect our National officer than citizens at Home." The chaplain's team lost. Perhaps those who judged the merits of the debate couldn't set aside a belief that they, rather than average civilians, better understood who should be president of the United States. Other pastimes included a dance that was held somewhere in the neighborhood ("but it is [too] muddy to go," Sergeant Hewitt complained), impromptu concerts and speeches, and rabbit hunting in the nearby countryside. One dance, sponsored by some officers, abruptly ended when a brawl broke out. The arrival of four women a couple of days later, seemingly prostitutes who came to the camp from Kelly's Ford, "drew off the looser part of the Regt after them," Henry Seage noted.[11]

Sgt. Maj. Edward Taylor was pleased to take the role of acting regimental adjutant when George Maltz went on leave, and the Reverend John Seage performed a wedding service for Pvt. Daniel W. Langford, a Company B soldier about 28 years old from Lenawee County, when he married a Virginia girl, one Miss Grove. "Bully for him," Henry Seage wrote approvingly. But there was no happy ending for Langford and his wife. Already captured at Gettysburg and afterward exchanged, he was captured again by Confederate troops in less than a few months' time. Langford would die in the notorious Andersonville prison camp before the year was out.

The snow turned to rain, and days of fine weather sometimes appeared in what were otherwise cold times as January gave way to February. Major Hall left for Michigan on recruiting service—as it turned out he wouldn't return to Virginia—and the regiment was called out one night at 11:30 P.M. when what sounded like gunfire came from the direction of the Second Brigade headquarters. "The firing proved to be the falling of the Mule Barn," Henry Seage wrote. A petition circulated among the officers and men asking Gov. Austin Blair to promote George Lumbard to the post of full colonel. Lieutenant Bancroft passed the time reading the novels of Alexander Dumas, while Sergeant Hewitt sometimes was assigned to act as an orderly for Lumbard. As the weather improved late in the month, the men were able to play baseball. But as officers returned from leaves there was also a resumption of favorite officers' activities for the soldiers—inspection, drill, and parade.[12]

At last the time had come for the veterans of the 4th Michigan who had reenlisted to go home on leave, boarding trains for the first leg of the trip back for Michigan on February 25. They arrived in Michigan after three days of travel. The citizens of the town of Adrian had been expecting the soldiers' arrival since late January, "making arrangements to give them a grand reception," one newspaper reported. But this welcome didn't happen. According to the *Detroit Free Press*, the 4th Michigan "did not return as a regiment, with arms and colors." This was because only about half of the regiment's complement of men who'd been with the 4th Michigan since 1861 had reenlisted. Thus the soldiers returned more as a band of weary travelers. "[N]o notice had been given of their arrival, and consequently it was unknown, and no public demonstrations were made," the paper reported. "The men preferred to return quietly."

In Adrian they were issued their furloughs for 35 days and went their various ways. Eight of the officers and 138 of the men took a train to Detroit after getting their leaves. A visit by these returning soldiers was a notable event for small- town newspapers. "We were pleased to receive a call from our old friends Seth Bolles and James Harroun of the 4th Mich. Inft. who are at home on furlough," the editor of the Hillsdale paper reported. "The boys are in good spirits, and say they are bound to see the rebel game played out." The editor of the *Monroe Commercial*, in the town where local volunteers comprised much of Company A, mentioned the names of 13 men and officers as it reported the reenlisting veterans' return home. "These are nearly all left in the service in Co. A who left Monroe in 1861," the paper reported. "Several have been transferred to other Regiments, but the greater portion have departed from life and its scenes and battles, never to return." In fact about half of the original company, or 49 soldiers, remained on the regimental rolls in the spring of 1864, though only a part of this number was fit for duty or otherwise present.[13]

In Indiana, a military ball was thrown in Angola in honor of the return of the men from Steuben County who had joined the 4th Michigan's Company B back in the spring of 1861. The band that provided the music was "Freygang's Quadrille Band," and it is likely that the bandleader was an in-law to the Indiana soldier in the regiment named George E. Young, who had married his sweetheart, Elizabeth Freygang, back in 1861 in Adrian. During his career as a soldier Young had been wounded in battle and captured and held, sick, as a prisoner, before finally being released. But Young was not there at the ball with his wife and family, for he had declined to reenlist. Young wouldn't get back to Indiana until his original enlistment was up in June.[14]

There were honors for Lt. Col. George Lumbard, originally from Hillsdale, fetes he doubtlessly enjoyed. In Detroit, some of the veteran officers and men of the regiment, led by Capt. William H. Loveland, presented him a "beautiful sword, sash and belt, worth at least $150," while the leading citizens from his old hometown sponsored a dinner for him at the Waldon House hotel in Hillsdale. Perhaps just as important if not more so to Lumbard was that he at last was given the commission of colonel of the 4th Michigan Infantry by Governor Blair.[15]

While the reenlisting veterans of the 4th Michigan enjoyed themselves, the weather continued to moderate in Virginia, allowing men like Sgt. John Hewitt to play baseball and to work on their winterized tents. With so many men gone, the officers sometimes cancelled tasks such as inspection and dress parade. "Very pleasant today," Hewitt wrote on March 9, "more Recruits arrived[.] Playing Ball the Chief occupation." A period of relatively good weather was sometimes broken up by rain and even snowfalls, but the soldiers had a comparatively easy time of it. "Some of the 62[nd Pennsylvania] were Drunk tonight," Hewitt wrote about his fellow soldiers on St. Patrick's Day. Henry Seage enjoyed the 9th Massachusetts's celebration of the day with horse racing and jumping, bag races for the men, and a mock parade that poked fun at army discipline and order. Four days later, Hewitt noted that he walked over to the railroad line where one of the Irish regiments from the east was posted. "Had a great time with the Micks," Hewitt wrote, perhaps referring to the men of the 9th Massachusetts.

On other nights men went to dances or attended the regiment's intramural debates on topics like "War is promoter of Civilization," "the U.S. should treat the States in Rebellion as alien enemies," and "women should have the right of Election Franchise in the U.S., the same as men." The team arguing for the proposition won the first debate, while the teams arguing against the latter two propositions won. Henry Seage was proud to have been elected secretary of the regiment's "Lyceum," the organizers of the debates, for the month of March.[16]

There were, however, contests of a physical nature when soldiers had too much to drink. Joseph H. Jagger of Company E, then about 24, from the town of Reading, got into a fight with Lt. James W. Vesey of Sturgis, from Company C. Alcohol seems to have induced Vesey's aggressive behavior, with charges brought against him for instigating the affair. But he apparently paid no serious penalty for it. Other soldiers joined in the brawl, with Francis Waller, 23, of Hillsdale County punching one of his comrades, David Fox, 22, who'd probably been one of his neighbors back home. Each of these men would soon be among the casualties in the coming battles of the spring of 1864. The soldiers of the 4th Michigan lay on their arms in line of battle on the night of March 18 expecting a Confederate raid on their section of the rail line, but nothing came of it.[17] "I took cold owing to the Regiment being obliged one cold damp night to remain up all night under arms in expectation of an attack on the R.R. at this point," Sergeant Major Edward H. C. Taylor complained. "We didn't have an hour's sleep till after daylight and it was so cold and chilly and damp it took me a week to get warm again." Ned Taylor had been acting adjutant and regimental clerk during this period when so many officers and men were on leave, but when Lt. George Maltz returned later in the month, he said: "I sink back to my old rank of Sergt. Major."[18]

A more significant arrival for the Army of the Potomac occurred just two weeks earlier in March, and it portended great and terrible things. Ulysses Grant had come to the front from Washington after being promoted to the rank of lieutenant general, commander of all Union forces. The soldiers knew of Grant's reputation as a leader who would consistently attack—he'd done that in the western theater of the war. But they also knew that fighting in the eastern theater of the war was not at all like combat in the west, where Grant made his name. "Gen. Grant is at Culpepper and superintending the reorganization and remodeling of this Army," Taylor wrote that month. "A large number of troops have been sent out to the front from Washington and things look like a move in less than a month—I think Grant will do well if not hampered by Washington with its dead weight of intrigue and politics." Taylor believed if the new commander was allowed to handle things his way, he would "fight" the Army of the Potomac that summer. "I hope so," Taylor wrote," and have full confidence in his generalship as does most of the army."[19]

New men periodically arrived at the 4th Michigan's camp and those of other regiments, too, and some of them seemed to have to undergo some hazing. "Raised Fits with the recruits," Henry Seage wrote in his diary. "Smoked, burned, etc. This was the initiation." A cold snap brought a sudden snow on March 22, and the some of the men had a snowball fight. Still there were signs that in very short order, the active campaigning of spring would soon resume. "The sick of the Regt were sent off today," Hewitt wrote on March 25. Soldiers understood that when the regimental hospitals were emptied and the sick were sent back to Washington or other towns, it usually meant that a move was coming. But when? As April began, the veteran enlisted men and officers who'd been sent home on furlough arrived back in camp. Some seem to have brought with them the rumor that the 4th Michigan was going to be sent back home within the coming month.

The weather turned rainy and men did household chores or entertained themselves by visiting friends, serenading (holding impromptu musical performances and speeches), attending the "Lyceum" debates, or sometimes going fishing. The men also learned that one of their comrades who'd been captured by the Confederates at Gettysburg, Sgt. William Limbarker of Company F, had been shot down some months earlier while leading a cleanup detail at the Belle Isle prison camp in Richmond. "It seems an officer spoke to him but he did not hear, whereupon a guard drew up and shot him down—C[onfederate] Chivalry!" Ned Taylor wrote with indignation.[20]

Lt. John Bancroft, who had applied for a transfer to another part of the Union army, received orders to report to a board of examiners that would consider his application on April 20. On March 30, he arrived in Washington and took a room, intending to prepare for the exam. During his time in Washington, Bancroft attended a debate in the U.S. Congress and took a day to study philosophy at the Smithsonian; he would meet old friends and attend a festival. The coming spring offensive, however, would derail his plans for a transfer. Back in Virginia the men from the 4th Michigan bided their time, waiting for the new offensive to begin. Reverend Seage, who had survived being shot by Rebel guerillas in the spring of 1863, got leave to travel to New York to perform the marriage ceremony for his own son Richard Watson Seage, who'd survived his Gettysburg wounds. Henry Seage said heavy rains destroyed three railroad bridges over which Union supply trains ran on the night of April 10, but within a couple of days they were rebuilt and the trains were once again bringing men and supplies to the front.

Soldiers who'd been sick or on leave continued to return to the regiment, although one soldier's arrival rankled young Henry Seage. "Tho[ma]s Terwilliger arrived," Seage noted. "This skunk went to Hosp[ital] while at Gains Mill and has been bumming around the convalescent camp until today." In Terwilliger's defense, it should be noted that thousands of other soldiers also hung around the Union's convalescent camps for long periods of time. Some of these long stays were unjustifiable, but a summary of Terwilliger's record shows that he had been transferred to the Invalid Corps in the fall of 1863 until being ordered back to his regiment. It may be that Terwilliger was malingering, but it's also possible the soldier was recovering and moved around at the whim of unknowable reasons for which military bureaucracies are famous.

Jonas D. Richardson, the sergeant with the 4th Michigan who'd been lame for some months and placed in the Veterans Reserve Corps, was now sick and doing what he could to get out of "this worst of all holes[,] Lincoln Hospital." Though unhealthy, Richardson had worked for some weeks in early 1864 delivering messages from one floor to another in the War Department, a job he said would be fatiguing for a person who was well, let alone for a soldier who was sick. His health had deteriorated to the point where he was sent back to the hospital. By early March Richardson was still hoping he could get his medical discharge. "But I have in a measure learned to put up with misfortune and endeavor to console myself with the reflection that I have only 3 months and 17 days to serve Uncle Sam."[21]

Richardson was given the job of doing guard duty at the hospital, and he was hopeful, as were other soldiers in the 4th Michigan who hadn't reenlisted, that he would be discharged on May 16, the date in 1861 that the regiment had come into being with the commission of Dwight Woodbury as its commander. Many of them believed, wrongly, that May 16, 1864, marked the end of their original three-year enlistment, but they would soon find out otherwise. Like other soldiers Richardson was optimistic about the coming of Grant's command. "I think that before the elapse of many weeks that we will hear pleasing news from the Army of the Potomack," he wrote. Still, he was hoping to get home. "I am desirous of seeing some place outside of the military and marshal [martial] law[.] I shall hail my departure from Washington with great joy, feeling and knowing that I am once more free from the clutches of Uncle Sam and his administration," he wrote. But it was death that freed Richardson from the clutches of the Union army. Less than two weeks after he wrote that letter, he died of disease. He was 24.[22]

April days in camp were sometimes rainy and sometimes quiet and uneventful, except for the death of Second Lieutenant James E. Hawks, who was probably 26. A Washtenaw County man who'd joined Company K in the spring of 1861, he died just after returning from Michigan with the reenlisted veterans. Other officers and men continued to arrive, including Dr. Luther C. French from Hudson. French had been assistant surgeon of the 4th Michigan since the late summer of 1862, but had to resign because of illness in the spring of 1863. French regained his health and was given permission to recruit for the regiment in Michigan. Appointed to the post of surgeon by Governor Blair, Dr. French returned on April 16.

About this time the new company for the 4th Michigan under Capt. Cornelius Van Valer, containing between 60 and 70 men and 18 commissioned and noncommissioned officers, left Hudson and arrived in Washington three days later. It would be another three weeks or so before Van Valer's company joined the 4th Michigan, after the new spring offensive had begun. But while some officers returned to the regiment after furlough, others were leaving. Capt. Alvan C. Lamson from Wayne County resigned and was discharged on certificate of disability, and a day later the resignation and discharge of Capt. James McLean from Livingston County, who had been wounded at Gettysburg, was also accepted. Within about two weeks the War Department approved the resignation of Capt. Ebenezer French, 29, from St. Joseph County. French had started as a second lieutenant in Company C and was wounded at both Fredericksburg and Gettysburg.[23]

One of the stranger activities by the men of the regiment in April was a rat hunt, held to rid the camp's dump of vermin. "Killed about 60 rats old and young," Henry Seage wrote. The men played baseball and resumed the typical duties and drill, such as target practice. Col. George Lumbard and one of the senior captains, William H. Loveland, came back from Michigan, while two men from Company E, Charles Hartson and Tom Tarsney, sent a comical letter to a newspaper, hoping they could get "the young lady readers" to correspond with them. "Come, ladies, write to Tom and Charley. We don't care what town you live in, if it isn't Woodbridge. . . . We also certify on our honor that a wife is absolutely necessary, rendered so by the fact that we never had one, and claim that we are entitled to one according to revised army regulations," the soldiers joked.[24]

But the signs pointed to a new offensive. "The sick have been sent away from the army," a soldier from Company A wrote home, "and other preparations made for a move." A man from the Hudson area dashed off a similar note. "Everything betokens a forward movement," the soldier wrote on April 27. "Sutlers and speculators have been sent to the rear, as well as all extra baggage. We have eight days' rations on hand, and under orders to march at a moment's notice." Two days later the men of the 4th Michigan saw the start of the new campaign for themselves. At about ten in the morning, a division of cavalry started to ride by. It was said to be 7,000 strong and took four hours to pass the camp.[25]

The next morning the regiment was ordered to stand for muster at 10:00 A.M., and some men got their washing done before the bugle call known as "The General" sounded, summoning them to assemble, prepared to move out. They marched from Bealton Station with the other regiments of their brigade at about four in the afternoon, covering just a few miles to the place where they bivouacked for the night. "Today began our campaign for the ensuing summer," Henry Seage wrote when the 4th Michigan halted between Rappahannock Station and the headquarters of their division commander, Gen. George Griffin. On the first day of May the regiment formed with its brigade and marched at 9:00 A.M., crossing the Rappahannock an hour later. By early afternoon, the men of the 4th Michigan were camping near Brandy Station as other units from the Fifth Corps, who had been spread out for miles around the countryside, gathered. In the new organization of the Army of the Potomac, Gen. Gouverneur Warren commanded their corps.

They stayed in that bivouac for another day and mustered for pay. Powerful winds picked up, raising clouds of dust and sand before rain set in. On May 3 the 4th Michigan with its division moved a few miles in the afternoon to Culpeper as the Union army continued to assemble. Those soldiers who went to bed early got a couple of hours rest before they were roused about 11:00 P.M. by the call of the buglers. They struck their tents and were under way by midnight for the fords across the Rapidan. At daylight the regiment, numbering about 247 men and around 15 officers, passed with its brigade, division, and corps through the town of Stevensburg and reached the Germanna Ford at 8:00 A.M. Moses Luce of Company E recalled the soldiers stripping down and rolling up their pants and coats around their rifles, which the men carried above their heads as they waded across in water up to their necks. "On the other side we stopped to wring out our socks, put on our shoes again, and marched on," he wrote of May 4. Other accounts say the men were allowed to stop and have some breakfast once they crossed.

The sun was hot and the road was dusty, and Henry Seage, along with many others soldiers, realized the plank road on which they were marching from the ford was taking them back to the vicinity of Chancellorsville—the wooded land called the Wilderness. At the plank road's intersection with the Orange Turnpike the Fifth Corps turned right, heading west. Soon the brigades of Griffin's First Division were filing off the road into battle lines. "Awful tired and foot sore [—] a great many of the boys fell out," Seage wrote that night. Sgt. John Hewitt agreed; he noted that night that they bivouacked "about 3 miles from Robinsons' [Robertsons] Tavern."[26]

This position was several miles west of where they'd skirmished near Chancellorsville, and once again they were in dangerous territory. The last battles in which the men of the original 4th Michigan would fight as a regiment were about to begin, in the Wilderness.

DALE R. NIESEN

Lt. Jerome Allen

STATE ARCHIVES OF MICHIGAN

*Joseph Baker**

ELLA SHARP MUSEUM

John M. Bancroft

ELLA SHARP MUSEUM

Charles Barrett

STATE ARCHIVES OF MICHIGAN

Orvey S. Barrett

HUDSON MUSEUM

Albert Boies

DALE R. NIESEN

Adna Bowen

ELLA SHARP MUSEUM

John Brogan

LENAWEE COUNTY HISTORICAL MUSEUM

William Bradley

MONROE COUNTY HISTORICAL MUSEUM

Ezra Brown

**Reorganized 4th Michigan*

HUDSON MUSEUM

Jay Bush

ELLA SHARP MUSEUM

Marshall Butts

ELLA SHARP MUSEUM

Albert Carpenter

ELLA SHARP MUSEUM

Eastman Carpenter

ELLA SHARP MUSEUM

Henry Case

DALE R. NIESEN

Capt. Marshall W. Chapin

NATIONAL ARCHIVES

Richard Cramer

STATE ARCHIVES OF MICHIGAN

Col. Jonathan Childs

BENTLEY HISTORICAL LIBRARY

John S. Conant

MONROE COUNTY HISTORICAL MUSEUM

Adelbert Day

HUDSON MUSEUM

Capt. Samuel DeGolyer

ELLA SHARP MUSEUM

Lt. Josiah Emerson

STATE ARCHIVES OF MICHIGAN

*Charles Fox**

DEARBORN HISTORICAL MUSEUM

Capt. Ebenezer French

HUDSON MUSEUM

Dr. Luther C. French

ELLA SHARP MUSEUM

Origen Getter

ELLA SHARP MUSEUM

Edwin Gilbert

DALE R. NIESEN

*William Gimbert**

**Reorganized 4th Michigan*

DALE R. NIESEN

*Perrin Goodell**

MONROE COUNTY HISTORICAL MUSEUM

Lt. Henry Grannis

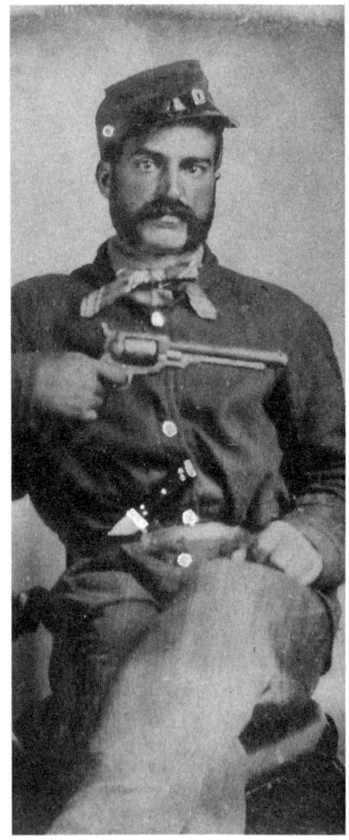

ALLEN MARSHALL

Andrew Guyor

DALE R. NIESEN

Lt. Charles Gruner

ELLA SHARP MUSEUM

Col. Jairus Hall

ELLA SHARP MUSEUM

Edgar Hamlin

ELLA SHARP MUSEUM

Nelson Hazen

STATE ARCHIVES OF MICHIGAN

Lt. Henry Hill

STATE ARCHIVES OF MICHIGAN

Laban Howard*

STATE ARCHIVES OF MICHIGAN

Charles Jenny*

MONROE COUNTY HISTORICAL MUSEUM

Col. Harrison Jeffords

ELLA SHARP MUSEUM

Capt. Alvan Lamson

ELLA SHARP MUSEUM

James Lane

ELLA SHARP MUSEUM

Robert LeBaron

ELLA SHARP MUSEUM

Francis Lumbard

ELLA SHARP MUSEUM

Col. George Lumbard

*Reorganized 4th Michigan

Lt. Horatio Lumbard

ELLA SHARP MUSEUM

Capt. William Loveland

DALE R. NIESEN

John Mackey

ELLA SHARP MUSEUM

Lt. George Maltz

ELLA SHARP MUSEUM

Capt. David D. Marshall

MONROE COUNTY HISTORICAL MUSEUM

Lt. Charles Marvin

ELLA SHARP MUSEUM

Miles Mason

ELLA SHARP MUSEUM

Leroy Mead

WESLEY POWERS

Irvin Miner

STATE ARCHIVES OF MICHIGAN

*Robert Newkirk**

STATE ARCHIVES OF MICHIGAN

Capt. John Oliver

DALE R. NIESEN

Sewell S. Parker

ELLA SHARP MUSEUM

George Patrick

STATE ARCHIVES OF MICHIGAN

Jacob Perine

ELLA SHARP MUSEUM

William H. Plummer

MONROE COUNTY HISTORICAL MUSEUM

Lt. Simon Preston

HUDSON MUSEUM

Jonas Richardson

BENTLEY HISTORICAL LIBRARY

Lt. William F. Robinson

ELLA SHARP MUSEUM

Jason Root

JEREMY IOTT

**Reorganized 4th Michigan*

STEVE ROBERTS

Henry S. Seage

STEVE ROBERTS

Richard Watson Seage

ELLA SHARP MUSEUM

Rev. John Seage

HUDSON MUSEUM

Morris Severance (postwar)

DAVID TAYLOR

Capt. Jeremiah D. Slocum

ELLA SHARP MUSEUM

Marvin Smith

ELLA SHARP MUSEUM

William H. Smith

HUDSON MUSEUM

Lt. Joseph Smith

DALE R. NIESEN

Melvin Stillson

DALE R. NIESEN

Edgar Stoddard

HOBART AND WILLIAM SMITH COLLEGES ARCHIVES

Edward H. C. Taylor (postwar)

STATE ARCHIVES OF MICHIGAN

William Tenbrook

MONROE COUNTY HISTORICAL MUSEUM

Joseph Totten

ELLA SHARP MUSEUM

Sylvester Tripp

DALE R. NIESEN

Lt. Michael Vreeland

ELLA SHARP MUSEUM

Erastus Walters

PRIVATE COLLECTOR

John Walters

ELLA SHARP MUSEUM

Dr. John Watts

MONROE COUNTY HISTORICAL MUSEUM

Lt. Benjamin Westfall

LENAWEE COUNTY HISTORICAL MUSEUM

Col. Dwight Woodbury

BOB COCH

Band of the reorganized 4th Michigan

AUBURN UNIVERSITY LIBRARY

In September of 1861, Lt. Marshall Chapin (1) poses with Sgt. John Bancroft (2), George Multz (3), John F. "Jack" Cooper (4), William G. Robinson of Detroit (5), John Kydd (6), and John Gordon (7). Kydd was killed in action at Gettysburg on July 2, 1863. The picture is from Bancroft's war diary-turned-scrapbook.

AUBURN UNIVERSITY LIBRARY

Sgt. Michael Vreeland (far left) *extends a glass to accept a drink from Sgt. Nolton Stoddard* (far right). *Joining Vreeland in pipe smoking is Lt. Marshall Chapin, while Lt. John Gordon stands, leaning against the tent pole. The child is not identified, but is likely the "young contraband," an escaped slave, mentioned by Dr. Chamberlain. From John Bancroft's diary-scrapbook.*

CHAPTER 13

I Am Well but Don't Know How Long

General George Meade halted two of four Union army corps in the Wilderness on the night of May 4, expecting that Gen. Robert E. Lee would keep his forces in defensive positions nearby. The Fifth Corps, of which the 4th Michigan was part, bivouacked in the woods off of the Orange Turnpike, west of the Wilderness Tavern. But Lee anticipated the advance of the Union army would stop when his forces attacked through the woods, giving his outnumbered men the chance to whittle down the Yankees' numerical advantage. As elements of the Fifth Corps marched south from the turnpike the next morning, they saw Confederate troops from Gen. Richard S. Ewell's corps coming up the road. Reports quickly reached the Union command and, as Lee had hoped, the advance of two other corps stopped, at least for the moment. Soon some of the 4th Michigan's comrades—other soldiers from Gen. Charles Griffin's First Division—were skirmishing with the Rebels. Later that morning, Union commanders were ordered to attack.[1]

The fighting in the woods intensified but the 4th Michigan didn't become exposed to Rebel fire until the afternoon when the brigade was given the order to go in. The diaries of Sgt. John Hewitt and Henry Seage and Seage's later history indicate that the regiment assembled early that morning for the intended march south, but instead was quickly put to work erecting works and digging entrenchments as the fighting began. "Rose at 3 A.M., at daylight advanced down into the woods and formed line," Seage wrote. "Built breastworks of logs and dirt."

As the battle widened south of their location, the 4th Michigan's Second Brigade and others from their division were supposed to attack the Rebels in their front at noon. But their generals were reluctant to send them in without knowing what danger might await them on their flanks on either side of the turnpike, so skirmishing and probing continued into the early afternoon. At last the regiments in the advance, from the First and Third brigades, left the woods, marching west toward a hilly, open piece of ground called Saunders Field (sometimes given as Sanders Field) that stretched along either side of the Orange Turnpike. As their commanders feared, Rebels flanked Griffin's men. Some Union officers later wrote that their line of battle broke up in the thick tangle of brush, trees, and brambles and that different units didn't connect as the generals planned. Scores of Union soldiers were shot down in confused fighting. Although the 4th Michigan and the other regiments of the Second Brigade weren't in the front line of this advance, they too, suffered casualties.

"Our division moved to the front and at 2 [P.M.] engaged the Rebels," Seage wrote in his diary. "Many killed and wounded." Seage had a dangerous job, for he was the color sergeant, a post for which he was probably chosen by officers, months earlier. Lt. Robert H. Campbell in a postwar reminiscence wrote this was the "baptism of fire" for the flag he said he'd gotten to replace the U.S. banner lost in the Wheatfield. "[A] shot smashed the head of one of the color guards and threw his blood and brains upon the flag and into the face of the color-bearer," Campbell wrote. That unfortunate member of the color guard was James Terwilliger. "Terwilligers brains were spattered in my face and coat," Seage wrote in his diary. He would later add in his history that gore also struck the flag. About the same moment Terwilliger was killed, Col. George W. Lumbard was fatally wounded. Another of Seage's comrades, 26-year-old James Tarsney from Hillsdale, of Company E, was killed and at least five other members of his company were wounded. Corporal William Tolford of Company F, who had written home to Hudson to tell of the severe cross fire that hit the regiment at Gettysburg, was among those killed. So was Enoch Davis of Company B, the dark-haired, gray-eyed farmer who had left Ohio to join the Indiana men back in Angola in May 1861; he was about 28. Many more of the 4th Michigan's men were wounded.

The gunfire was even worse for those soldiers in the first two lines of the advance, who fell left and right. Someone gave the order for retreat and Capt. William Loveland took the 4th Michigan's colors from Seage. He ordered the regiment to fall back to the breastworks and then he, too, was wounded. Sergeant Hewitt didn't write the specifics of what he experienced that day, only that "fighting commenced about noon[,] continued all day long, & very heavy loss." Lt. Col. Jairus Hall was in Michigan on a new assignment, so with Lumbard and Loveland wounded, command devolved to the Prussia-born first lieutenant, Charles Gruner of Company C, then the most senior officer and about 27 years old. His comrade Lt. James W. Vesey called Gruner "one of the bravest officers in the army of the Potomac."[2]

The Fifth Corps's advance was beaten back. They retreated to the breastworks built earlier in the day. Another attack was ordered by Grant, but the brigades sent in late that afternoon weren't any more successful. Just as fires had spread through some of the portions of the woods at Chancellorsville, again flames spread in the underbrush that night, killing men who'd been wounded and not removed from the battlefield. Though some soldiers wrote about what a nightmarish time this was, no member of the 4th Michigan seems to have left an account of it. They rested behind the breastworks. Lumbard, in the meantime, was carried to safety, but his wound was fatal. A general from the Fifth Corps later stated that he'd seen stretcher bearers carrying the colonel of the 4th Michigan back for medical attention, but there was nothing the doctors could do. He heard that Lumbard survived for about 20 hours. A correspondent from the *New York World* would write that as Lumbard was borne from the field, the stretcher bearers heard him whisper: "I have fallen for my country."

Lieutenant Campbell wrote that he saw Lumbard "upon that field writhing in the agonies of death. . . . As he groaned and turned, he muttered, 'Must I die and be buried in this hated Virginia soil?'" Abiathar H. Jones from Flat Rock, in Company I, said years later that he and a comrade visited their colonel in the field hospital. "We found him very low and suffering greatly," Jones said. "In trying to relieve him, I found that he rested more comfortably by lying in my arms with his head across my shoulder. I could see he was very near death's door. He spoke once or twice of his intense suffering and said he could not live, and before I was aware he had fallen peacefully asleep and passed away." The colonel's body was wrapped in a blanket and buried by his men at the base of a tree. Jones carved Lumbard's initials in that tree in place of a headstone. Captain Loveland's wound was also fatal, though he lived until the end of May. Both Lumbard and Loveland had been with the regiment since its formation.[3]

Another version of Colonel Lumbard's fatal wounding was given by Moses Luce of Company E, one of the Hillsdale College students who had joined Lumbard's company three years earlier. Luce, an orderly sergeant at the time of the battle, said that as the regiment reached the edge of the woods on the eastern side of one of the clearings in the Wilderness, men knelt and fired at the Rebels on the opposite side. Lumbard, he said, was standing behind a tree but stepped out as the 9th Massachusetts arrived to take the place of the 4th Michigan. As the colonel did so, a bullet struck him in the upper abdomen and he fell to the ground. Luce said he called to several men from his company to carry Lumbard to safety.

"Whom have you there?" asked an officer on horseback, reportedly the colonel of the Massachusetts regiment.

"Colonel Lombard [*sic*] of the 4th Michigan," Luce replied.

"Boys, this is Col. [Lumbard] of the 4th Michigan, and he is dying," the officer shouted to his men. "Give him three cheers."

The soldiers responded with cheers and Lumbard seemed to appreciate the gesture, Luce wrote. After removing him back about a mile, Luce said they propped their colonel against a tree. Lumbard asked Luce about his wound and Luce replied that he thought it was fatal. "He then took from his side pocket a photograph," Luce wrote. "He said, 'This is my wife's photograph, a dear emblem. I want you to be sure to deliver it to her if you ever get back to Hillsdale." Luce wrote that Lumbard died the next day and that he eventually returned the picture to his colonel's wife. Unlike his predecessors—Jeffords, whose body was sent home from Gettysburg, and Woodbury, whose remains were eventually located at Malvern Hill and removed to Michigan—it appears that Lumbard's remains were probably moved into a cemetery, but not identified. In any event, years later his men would not be able to find the spot where they had buried his body in the Wilderness.[4]

After the first day's fighting in the woods and fields, the 4th Michigan probably had fewer than 200 men and officers left present for duty. If they got any rest that night, given the fires and the screams and moans of the wounded and dying that others remembered, it may not have been much. At 3:00 A.M. on May 6, Seage wrote, the men of the 4th Michigan moved up to the front, but it would turn out to be a day of waiting and listening. To the southeast the Second Corps, aided by divisions from other corps, smashed into the Confederate right and drove them back. While it appeared these Union troops would be victorious, the corps of Confederate James Longstreet arrived on the scene, counterattacking. Some of these Rebels were led through an unfinished railroad cut that let them reach the Union left flank and drive the surprised Northern soldiers back to positions along the Brock Road. For hours this area was the scene of intense combat. Later in the day another Confederate attack hit the Union right, a few miles to the northwest and closer to where the Fifth Corps was posted. That assault was halted by their Union army comrades.

But for the 4th Michigan and much of the rest of their division, their sector was comparatively quiet compared to other parts of the long battlefield through the woods. Grant wanted the Fifth Corps to go on the offensive along with thousands of other Union troops in the vicinity of the Orange Turnpike that day, May 6. But with different divisions from their corps detached and sent to other parts of the Union army, and the Confederates well entrenched before them, the commanders of 4th Michigan's brigade, division, and corps didn't order the men to attack. Some accounts say that the Union soldiers were unwilling to charge, knowing that to attack such positions was little better than suicide, but there was skirmishing. Though the 4th Michigan wasn't involved in the fighting, they still came under fire and at some point learned that Colonel Lumbard had died. As the men of the regiment lay in the woods awaiting orders, an exploding shell or fragment hit Sgt. William Cunningham of Company K, killing him instantly. He was about 25 and had been a farmer from Dexter. When the Union's Sixth Corps was attacked just north of their position, the 4th Michigan's brigade went back into the outer line of breastworks, but the regiment was again sent into the woods where it had waited previously, once that Confederate assault was repulsed. At 11:00 P.M. the men were marched to the rear, back to the point where they'd bivouacked on the night of May 4. In the meantime Sgt. John Hewitt, experienced at helping care for wounded men, again was detailed to a field hospital.[5]

Early in the morning of May 7, Henry Seage wrote, the men were awakened by the sound of another Confederate advance, a probing action. The regiment was sent up to the works, and other Union troops and gunners opened fire on the Rebels in heavy skirmishing. This took place at a point out in front of the Union entrenchments, yet apparently far enough away that even though Seage noted there was skirmishing going on, he and his friend Harrison Daniels were able to get water for coffee and to wash. This may have been because Seage, the regiment's color sergeant, didn't have to be out on this line with the flag. Apparently the 4th Michigan's men suffered few if any wounds and casualties during this day behind the breastworks, though a long march was in their immediate future.

The fighting in the Wilderness had cost thousands of Union casualties, and for the 4th Michigan the death toll was at least 12 officers and men killed or mortally wounded. But now Grant decided the Army of the Potomac would leave the Wilderness and march to the southeast, trying to get by Lee and threaten Richmond, forcing the Confederate army to leave its defensive positions. At 10:00 P.M., Seage noted, the 4th Michigan started on the march "to the left," or east and south. The 4th Michigan's Fifth Corps led an exhausting all-night march down the Brock Road toward a crossroads community called Spotsylvania Court House.[6]

Lee anticipated Grant's move, and Confederate forces hurried to get to this important junction first, with Rebel cavalry fighting a delaying action throughout the early morning hours of May 8. As dawn broke the first elements of the Confederate army took positions on a ridge that overlooked the road outside of Spotsylvania Court House, and here they quickly began to dig in. Union soldiers mistakenly called this place Laurel Hill. By 8:30 A.M. the first tired soldiers from the Fifth Corps attacked across a farm field, but were repulsed. As more Confederate troops and guns arrived, they extended their line. And as more of the brigades of the Fifth Corps arrived, they were also sent in to try to drive the Rebels from positions that quickly spread across the Brock Road to the east and along high, tree-covered ground to the west. But these three Union brigades went in piecemeal as they reached the base of the ridge, and each was driven back.

"Laurel Hill"

As Sweitzer's Second Brigade of the First Division of the Fifth Corps arrived on the scene, other Union troops were retreating down the slope, pursued by the Confederates. "About 9 A.M. came on the rebels and formed line," Seage wrote about this fighting. "Drove the rebels at first but they were reinforced and drove us." The Confederates coming down the ridge to the Brock Road, probably South Carolinians, were stopped at a line formed by the 4th Michigan and other regiments and Union gunners. The Confederates fell back to their growing line of defenses.[7]

The 4th Michigan was ordered to reinforce the 22nd Massachusetts as it supported a battery set up on a wooded knoll, which may have been the line described by Henry Seage as "forming at 9 A.M." General Griffin ordered another attack and Union troops moved forward, going south toward the ridge. But the part of their line on the left of the battery was driven back by Confederate musketry and artillery fire. Soon they found Rebels had quietly come through the woods on the left, or to the east, in an attempt to get behind the Union guns and supporting troops on the hill. There was confusion as the battery withdrew and the troops, including the 4th Michigan, came under fire. Some accounts said that as these Union soldiers tried to regroup on the field of the nearby Alsop farm, the Rebel gunners hit them from higher ground, wreaking havoc.[8]

Several members of the 4th Michigan were struck by the artillery fire. Lt. Ben Westfall later recalled he and Lieutenant Vesey took cover behind a cabin as they retreated. But then they heard a cry coming from a short distance away. It was one of their men, wounded in the hip, trying to crawl to safety. The two lieutenants ran out to rescue the man, "the air fairly blue with lead," but they succeeded. The Union soldiers rallied, were ordered forward and threw up breastworks, Seage wrote. This appears to have been on the edge of some woods overlooking a field about several hundred yards north and west of the Spindle farm, and soon the Spindles' house and barn were burning.[9]

As for other descriptions of the action outside Spotsylvania Court House on May 8 from members of the 4th Michigan, there were only brief comments. "The men were all tired and hungry, but they fought well," wrote a soldier who signed his letter to a Monroe newspaper as "Veteran." "The 4th lost eight or ten men killed and wounded." Sergeant Hewitt had rejoined the regiment after the first group of wounded men from the Wilderness was sent off. "Heavy firing," he wrote. "Rebels Repulse [Union attacks] at every point & retreating toward Richmond." While the first part of Hewitt's short account was correct—the Union soldiers had indeed been repulsed—the second part was only a rumor. Lee did not retreat. Instead, the Army of Northern Virginia stayed between Richmond and Grant's forces so as to inflict as many casualties as they could. Union troops couldn't break through the Confederate entrenchments on the ridge.

As night fell, some Union soldiers just east of the 4th Michigan's position were sent in again, and there was confused fighting and many casualties, but the result was the same. The men of the 4th Michigan were fortunate in that their regiment didn't appear to have any role in this night fighting. Their casualties had been relatively low compared to other regiments. George A. Walker of Company E, who had joined the regiment back in the late summer of 1862 from the town of Litchfield and spent nearly six months as a prisoner after Gettysburg, died of his wounds that evening of May 8. A wound ended the war for Lt. Josiah Emerson of Hillsdale, another of the men who enlisted in that company in the spring of 1861. He would muster out at the end of the three-year hitch he'd signed up for as a noncommissioned officer.[10]

Sergeant Major Edward "Ned" Taylor had been struck in the foot. "My wound was received on the 8th, Sunday morning, thro' the right foot from side to side thro' the sole," he wrote to his mother several days later. "[It] is quite painful and prevents walking but am thankful it is not worse." Taylor was placed in a field hospital and then moved to Washington. As with Lieutenant Emerson, the war was over for Taylor. He had declined to reenlist, and his wound meant active service with the 4th Michigan was finished. Experienced officers were among those wounded or whose health gave out in the days after the fighting began near Spotsylvania Court House. On May 21 the War Department authorized the resignation of Capt. William F. Robinson of Company H, discharging him for disability because his earlier wound. Two days later, Lt. Orvey S. Barrett, also wounded at Gettysburg, was issued his discharge for disability. He had commanded Company B for months.[11]

At some point during May 8, the 4th Michigan's most senior surviving officer, Capt. David D. Marshall of Tecumseh, returned to the regiment and took command. Skirmishing continued the following day in the front lines, and Sergeant Hewitt, who helped bury George Walker, noted the large number of Union wounded. By late in the afternoon the 4th Michigan went into the breastworks, while the 9th Massachusetts went out as skirmishers that night to push forward over the open ground. Those men were driven in by Confederates as pioneers attempted to dig a new advanced line of trenches, but members of the 4th Michigan don't appear to have been involved in this fighting.[12]

The next day, May 10, terrible combat began again as Grant ordered his army to attack the bulging Confederate line of works that stretched from the Po River on the Confederate left to beyond Spotsylvania Court House on their right. It was only two miles as the crow flew from the river to the courthouse, but the irregularly shaped Rebel lines twisted and turned twice that far. Thousands of Union soldiers were killed and wounded in the attacks. While Grant wanted massive charges launched, General Warren, the commander of the Fifth Corps, proceeded more cautiously, testing the strength of the Rebel lines.

Moses A. Luce and Asher LaFleur, sergeants, would later write about this, as did veterans of the 22nd Massachusetts. One of Massachusetts men stated that "our regiment with the Fourth Michigan about 11:30 A.M. were ordered in a single deployed line of battle to charge the enemy with fixed bayonets and retake the [Confederate rifle] pits at all hazards. We did so, but at a great sacrifice." Another soldier-historian from the 22nd Massachusetts also told of this bayonet charge. "Our line swept forward at a run and with a wild hurrah, drove them pell-mell," he wrote. They captured the rifle pits with their charge, but then they were directed to keep going toward the edge of the woods before them. As they did, Rebel gunners opened fire. The Massachusetts regiment, more exposed, lost about 80 men to "murderous flank fire" from canister and grapeshot from batteries just inside the woods along the Brock Road at the intersection with the Block House Road. In a report filed later with the Michigan adjutant general, Lt. George Maltz stated that "the regiment with the 22nd Mass. Vol[unteers] on our left, made a charge on the Enemys Rifle Pits, and took them, our loss was 20 killed and wounded."[13]

One of the wounded was Sergeant LaFleur of Company H, who had been at the top of the rifle pits when the Confederate guns opened up. He fell outside of the works, his right leg shattered, as his comrades retreated. In the meantime Sgt. Moses Luce had dropped into a ditch or depression when the volleys of grapeshot ripped from the woods. He waited for the Confederate fire to lessen before he got to his feet and ran back to the relative safety of Union lines, one Rebel bullet slamming into the stock of his rifle and another grazing his face. Luce took his spot in the trenches and joined his comrades when one of them heard a cry for help. "Luce, someone is calling you on the picket line," one of his comrades said. It was his friend LaFleur, out near the rifle pits. "I am bleeding to death, I am bleeding to death," the sergeant cried.

Luce said that he dropped his weapon and scrambled out of the trench. Small arms fire crackled as he ran—"I felt the whiz of the musket balls," he wrote years later. In one account, Luce said that Rebel soldiers stopped shooting at him when they realized he was aiding a wounded man, but LaFleur said Confederate soldiers had quickly resumed positions to fire at the Union troops. He said Luce made his run "amid the greatest peril." But Luce reached LaFleur, whose leg was bleeding badly. He stooped, got his friend up on his back, and carried him to safety to a log cabin behind the Union line. A surgeon first bound up and later amputated LaFleur's leg below the knee. Incredibly, though he would undergo two more surgeries on what was left of his leg, his military career didn't end. LaFleur was one of the men who'd reenlisted for another three-year stint back in December, and he was back on detached service within two months. He ended up serving in the Union army for another year. More than 30 years after this battle, Luce was awarded the Medal of Honor by Congress for dashing out to rescue his friend.[14]

Again the 4th Michigan was relatively fortunate this day that it didn't suffer the terrible casualties that Union regiments suffered further to the east and northeast. It appears that 4th Michigan's specific casualties were three men killed or mortally wounded in the charge near the Brock Road, with others suffering nonfatal wounds. Diarist John Hewitt of the 4th Michigan saw the awful results of the fighting that day as he worked in a nearby field hospital and then helped to transport hundreds of wounded men by wagon to Fredericksburg, where they were sent on to Washington. That night the men of the regiment lay on their arms in line of battle and probably heard the stories passing through the army about the bloody fighting to their left.[15]

Grant allowed the Union army a break from the incessant attacks and planned his next move as rain set in the next day. The men of the 4th Michigan remained at the front and like thousands of other soldiers, dug trenches and cut down trees for breastworks. May 12, however, proved to be another day of fierce fighting and casualties when the Second and Sixth Corps charged, smashed through the Confederate positions and became involved in fierce combat, sometimes hand-to-hand, as rain poured down. Though the violence raged all day the Confederates managed to establish another line of defenses and stop this advance. Further east the Union army's Ninth Corps attacked Lee's line near Spotsylvania Court House, but were also beaten back.

While this battle was unfolding with thousands of casualties, elements of Warren's Fifth Corps again attacked the Rebel defenses at the intersection of the Brock and Block House roads. Three of the regiments in the 4th Michigan's Second Brigade charged "but were repulsed," Henry Seage wrote. That may have been enough for their commanders. After that, the 4th Michigan and one of the Massachusetts regiments were sent out as skirmishers, George Maltz reported. They moved into the advanced rifled pits, "where we laid all night in the mud and the rain," Seage wrote about the close of May 12. They stayed in this area for the next two days. One soldier from the 4th Michigan, Daniel Poyer, a 24-year-old Livingston County man in Company K, was killed. Soldiers in these rifle pits would remember what a terrible time this was in the soaking rain and muddy ground, skirmishing and surrounded by unburied bodies, though Poyer was buried there by his friends.

In the meantime Sergeant Hewitt made the trip to Fredericksburg with loads of wounded men, but "a good many died on acct of such roads," he wrote. He and the other soldiers assigned to hospital duty turned the wounded over to the Christian Sanitary Commission, though he personally saw to it his wounded officer, Lieutenant Emerson, was loaded on a boat. He also saw that help was coming to the 4th Michigan in the form of Capt. Cornelius Van Valer's new company from Michigan, composed of nearly 70 men who just arrived at Fredericksburg on their way to the front.[16]

The hard rain continued through May 13, and the 4th Michigan remained behind the breastworks. The 9th Massachusetts came up and relieved them at about 6:00 P.M., and the soldiers marched back about a mile from the front and began to put up tents for the night, hoping to sleep in shelter. But this was not to be. The Union army was leaving, and all through that night the soldiers made a difficult march. The road was mud a foot deep, and they had to wade the Ny River. Henry Seage called it was "about the hardest march we have made." It ended the next morning around seven. Their Fifth Corps had made a tough trip of several miles around to what had been the eastern portion of the battlefield, about a mile from Spotsylvania Court House. Here they were allowed to rest.

A veteran of one of their fellow regiments, the 22nd Massachusetts, said the 4th Michigan was one of the outfits ordered to support a division artillery battery that evening of May 14. Confederates shelled them as they took their positions but apparently did no damage since the men had protection in several ravines. Sgt. John Hewitt, who was still on hospital detail, noted that the weather was pleasant and wounded troops were continuing to pour in. The Union army was "whipping the Rebels at every point," he wrote proudly. "Gen. Lee asks for an Armistice of two days to bury his dead." The next day he recorded an even grander rumor when he heard that "Richmond is in our possession." These camp stories, some of which made it into newspapers, were among the final entries Hewitt would make in his diary. For the next five days, he continued to help wounded men get enough food to eat.[17]

Of course, Richmond had not been taken. The fighting and skirmishing near Spotsylvania Court House had cost the 4th Michigan at least 10 killed or mortally wounded, with at least two or three times that many suffering nonfatal wounds. Compared to other outfits, their casualties were low. But it was also after this phase of the fighting, sometime in the second week in May, that the 4th Michigan was as small as it had been since the aftermath of Gettysburg. By the estimate of Lt. John W. Vesey of Sturgis, it numbered about 130 at this lowest point.[18]

The men of the 4th Michigan drew three days' rations on May 15 and saw the arrival of Cornelius Van Valer's company, adding some 65 men and about 18 officers to the regiment's depleted ranks. Henry Seage wrote that the addition of these men "makes the regiment about 150 strong," probably meaning that the 4th Michigan had that many riflemen in the ranks. Lieutenant Vesey wrote that the new men now placed the regiment's strength at just under 200. These figures were in general agreement with a soldier from the 4th Michigan who wrote to a Detroit newspaper that although there were about 200 privates and noncommissioned officers in the regiment now, it meant as a practical matter "159 muskets," or men available to go into battle. However they looked at it, the regiment was a shadow of what it once had been.

Lieutenant Bancroft, away from the 4th Michigan since the end of March to take an exam in Washington, made it back to the regiment. Though he had been ordered back as the spring offensive was about to begin, it took to him more than a week to reach the regiment by rail, boat, and wagon train. As evening fell on May 15 another hard rain set it. The men were ordered to pack their gear and form line of battle. They did not move or fight, but lay on their arms all night.[19]

The next day must have been a tense one near Spotsylvania Court House. Many of the men who had joined the 4th Michigan three years earlier, and who hadn't reenlisted for another hitch, were sure that May 16 marked the end of their service since it was on this day three years earlier that their regiment had been created with the commissioning of their first colonel, Dwight Woodbury, by Governor Blair. Had they not fulfilled their duty, then? Hadn't many if not most of these men joined their companies in early May 1861? Henry Seage wrote that the men believed this was the case. The U.S. government, however, did not. The brigade commander arrived in their bivouac to set them straight, letting the Michigan soldiers know that their enlistment dated from their mustering into the federal service on June 20, 1861, and not from the creation of their regiment. Seage's diary indicates that they realized the army had the final word. "Boys all think their time is out today, but will do their duty faithfully until June 20th," he wrote. Lieutenant Bancroft also noted that Sweitzer addressed the men about this, and that the amount of time left in their three-year hitch was a matter of simple math. "Five more weeks to serve," he wrote. But other than this important question, it was a quiet and mild day. The men drew rations and put up their tents as rain again set in that evening.[20]

Their immediate front remained reasonably quiet, given the fighting that had raged around them. The next day the men dug entrenchments, first in the vicinity of their own bivouac and then, once night fell, at the front. Confederate artillery and Union guns in their salient exchanged volleys on May 18, and soldiers continued digging and watching from their place in the second line of trenches with two Massachusetts regiments. On the 19th the soldiers heard heavy firing nearby, probably the battle at the Harris farm a few miles away, but for them the day was uneventful, with pickets happy to live and let live. That evening the Second Brigade was shifted a short distance away to the right when other men from the Fifth Corps became involved in the fighting with troops of Confederate General Richard Ewell. The rain began to fall once more.

The men of the 4th Michigan strengthened their works on May 20. A soldier known as Heman Smith (apparently an alias he sometimes used, for his last name was really Evans) had been on assignment nearby with the Second Brigade staff. But on this day Smith, a Dexter resident, got the chance to write a letter telling a friend back home about the deaths of Dan Poyer and William Cunningham. "I am well at present," he wrote, "but I don't know how long I will remain so." He said that the 4th Michigan had "lost hevy" during the campaign, and he noted that he'd come under Rebel shelling as he scrawled his letter. That same day a Union band and a Confederate band also seem to have held their own musical competition, Bancroft's diary suggested. "Rebel band at the C.H. [Spotsylvania Court House] plays 'Marsellaise Hymn,'" he wrote, misspelling the title of the French national anthem. "Ours plays 'Hail Columbia.'" The music was a pleasant diversion for them men, or perhaps it was an attempt to cover up the sound of what was happening. Thousands of troops on both sides were moving away that night as Grant tried to get around Lee's army. The Fifth Corps was responsible for having to hold their position while the rest of the Union army shifted to the east and south. The soldiers of the 4th Michigan were ordered to quietly strike their tents and pack on the morning of May 21, but they didn't march with their brigade and division until the early afternoon, with both sides still trading artillery shots. The soldiers trudged a few miles to Guinea Station in the heat of the day. Then they followed the railroad line south and bivouacked at about ten o'clock that night.[21]

The Union army pressed south. Some men from the regiment like Sgt. Henry Seage did picket duty that night after they halted. For Seage personally, perhaps the most important development was that, in answer to his own request, he was notified that day he was no longer the carrier of the colors of the regiment. "Went back in the company to my old position," he wrote.[22]

Jericho Mills

There had been Confederate forces just ahead of the Union troops at times throughout the march, but they'd dropped back rather than initiate a confrontation. That changed on May 23. Though the Union commanders didn't yet realize it, the Confederate Army of Northern Virginia was in position on the southern side of the North Anna River, this at a point that was about 20 miles due north of Richmond. The men of the 4th Michigan rose early and began the march with their division that brought them to the river at a place called Jericho Mills, not far from Rebel forces. The Second Brigade forded first, followed by the Third Brigade. Then pontoon bridge builders arrived so that thousands of other troops and supplies could cross more easily. By the afternoon the soldiers of the 4th Michigan and others in their division had walked up a road to the top of the steep banks of the North Anna. Moving southeast, they advanced into the woods.[23]

There, Sgt. Henry Seage wrote, they came on Rebel pickets and drove them back. Lieutenant Bancroft said that one man was killed, and this was George W. Teachout, 24, one of the new soldiers in Van Valer's company. The 4th Michigan men threw up a breastwork. Reports went back to their corps commander, General Warren, that there was a heavy Confederate force nearby, but he didn't believe them. Now he found out the information was accurate. A strong Rebel counterattack smashed into part of a division to the right of Charles Griffin's First Division, and these men broke and retreated. The Rebels charged forward, breaking the Second Brigade's skirmish line and forcing the 4th Michigan back, Bancroft wrote; the 9th Massachusetts retreated, too. Some Michigan soldiers later said that the various companies became separated and that the 4th Michigan fragmented.

Other regiments from their brigade, who had been out as skirmishers, were also driven in but managed to rally at the breastworks they'd built earlier in the day, according to a letter by a soldier of the 22nd Massachusetts. About the same time reinforcements arrived from the Third Brigade, rushing through the woods to join them. Regrouped in squads of various sizes, men from the 4th Michigan followed their regiment's flag or joined in with other outfits. These Union soldiers struck back. "The line is reformed," Bancroft wrote in his diary. Seage agreed. He, too, wrote that the 4th Michigan had fallen back as the Confederates flanked them, but then reformed into line, moved in a counterattack against the Rebels, and "came up to [our] old position and kept up steady fire." The Confederates were driven back, and the 4th Michigan's comrades in the Third Brigade relieved them.

Lee's generals had sprung a trap that could have been far worse for the Fifth Corps, but luck had been with the Union soldiers. The men were issued 50 rounds of cartridges and given four days' rations that evening, in case the battle renewed. But the fight at the North Anna River was over for the 4th Michigan and their comrades in their brigade and division. The soldiers bivouacked in the field. According to a later casualty accounting, the 4th Michigan lost only Teachout that day, though another new soldier, Ambrose Cole, 19, would die of his wounds in a few weeks time. "The 4th was lucky this time," wrote a soldier who signed his letter "Veteran."[24]

The next day was quiet for the soldiers of the Fifth Corps, and the 4th Michigan and other regiments built defensive positions. Grant hoped Lee would attack again, but it was not to be. Union troops tested the strength of the Rebel position and found them strong. The Michigan soldiers were ordered to move out with other troops about five in the afternoon, first marching towards where the front had been previously, and then a mile or so to the west, where again they went to work building breastworks and digging trenches for several hours, using tracks and ties from the nearby railroad in their defenses. The weather turned rainy and it kept on through May 25 as Union troops moved. Grant again would march the Union army to the southeast around the Confederate positions.

The next day Union troops watched and waited in the rain until dark, when they packed quietly, left their entrenchments, and went back to the North Anna River. "Water very high, almost floating our temporary bridge of timbers," Lieutenant Bancroft noted. The soldiers crossed the river and camped, but soon resumed their march. Sergeant Seage described this as an initial march of three muddy, awful miles beyond the mill, where they stopped and drew rations, and then kept moving south through the early morning hours of May 27, stopping for breakfast around eight o'clock in a pine grove. Then they continued on through the muggy heat until 5:00 P.M.[25]

It had been an exhausting march of 20 miles when the 4th Michigan and its brigade finally halted to bivouac by a stream. Sergeant Seage and his comrades went out "sheeping," or foraging livestock for dinner. "[W]e camped for the night, pretty well tired out," wrote "Veteran" to his hometown paper, "but not so tired but that we were able to slaughter some sheep and pigs for supper, and breakfast." Lieutenant Bancroft bathed in the stream, had dinner, and made what he called "a splendid bed" of leaves and went to sleep, only to have Adjutant George Maltz wake him and tell him that he'd been chosen officer of the picket. "Fifty men are awakened after much cursing, etc., and the tired procession follow H. Kingsbury to the picket," Bancroft noted. These unlucky men mistakenly marched another two miles up and down the creek before finding out their post was a just a quarter of a mile from the camp.

The marching continued on May 28, with the regiment crossing the Pamunkey River that afternoon with its corps, reaching Hanovertown. When they halted for the day on the hills above the village, the men went to work as they almost always did now, digging, cutting trees, and building fortifications. They could hear the sound of battle as the cavalry clashed a few miles ahead. The next morning they again moved south with their corps about two miles. Their division crossed the Totopotomy Creek and, stopping short of the Confederate lines, formed line of battle. The soldiers learned that the entire Army of the Potomac was gathered once more. As the 4th Michigan's Second Brigade moved southeast, skirmish fire began to sound. They moved for another mile and a half. As their First Division artillery took a position on a hill and fired into nearby woods to discourage the Confederates, Union skirmishers scrambled up to build more breastworks. Bancroft said the men found corn and potatoes in nearby farm buildings, while one of Henry Seage's comrades brought in a sheep that been out near the skirmish line. Of course, they dined on mutton, just several miles northeast of the town of Mechanicsville, where they had fought in the late June, 1862.

Bethesda Church

The larger picture, however, was that the Confederates had again successfully blocked the Union army. Another clash was taking shape as the Second Brigade moved to the front at 6:00 A.M. the next morning, May 30. Shortly before they marched, Lt. James W. Vesey of Sturgis quickly wrote a letter to his hometown newspaper, since he was sure they were going into battle when his gruff division commander went by, his hat cocked at an angle. "Gen. Griffin just rode by our lines, his hat was at the 'fighting pitch,'" Vesey noted. "We will fight today. It is a sure sign when 'Grif' wears his hat a little on the left." Vesey wasn't wrong. The Michigan troops advanced and the sound of skirmish fire was soon crackling over the countryside.

Accounts by Henry Seage, the soldier who signed his letters "Veteran," and other members of their brigade said that the 22nd Massachusetts was in the advance in their part of this battlefield as brigade skirmishers. They moved west on what some men thought was the Shady Grove Church Road with the 4th Michigan in support. They crossed over fields and through woods, soon firing at Rebel skirmishers and driving them back to breastworks set up at the edge of a clearing. One of the Massachusetts men reported that the Confederates backed up slowly until they reached some farm buildings and fences. Here the 4th Michigan and the Massachusetts men rejoined their brigade's battle line. Then the entire Second Brigade attacked, forcing the Rebels to withdraw to another line of defensive positions. "The rebs were on one side of a clearing and we on the other," wrote "Veteran." "We charged them and drove them back about three miles, to their works." In this last attack the soldiers fixed bayonets, and "we went bounding out of the woods with a yell," a Massachusetts soldier wrote, "and soon drove them out in every direction."

Lieutenant Bancroft wrote that two of the 4th Michigan's men were wounded in the charge across an open field, though some said two men were killed. The regiment and its comrades in the brigade held their position, built works, and established a new skirmish line, working into the night. When they were finally relieved, the hungry Michigan soldiers marched to the rear, received rations, and cooked their dinners early in the morning of May 31. Once again, they had been relatively lucky in terms of low casualties, with other Union regiments suffering higher numbers of killed and wounded. Though they succeeded in pushing back the Rebels who had been directly before them, a Confederate attack hit another part of the Fifth Corps at the nearby Bethesda Church, about a mile away. But for the 4th Michigan, now came two days of rest.[26]

This shifting, moving, clashing, and skirmishing was a matter of the two armies testing each other, probing, jostling for position. Lee's men skillfully extended their trenches and gun emplacements in a line stretching south. The last day of May and the first of June were quiet for the 4th Michigan, though they heard fighting close by. Lieutenant Bancroft saw General Grant ride along the lines—others said the men gave him "tremendous hurrahs." The next day, June 2, the soldiers of the Michigan regiment and other Fifth Corps outfits packed up. The Michigan troops were shifted about a mile to the south southeast and rested in some woods. They were now only a few miles from the village of Cold Harbor. Those who had survived the fighting since the summer of 1862 understood they were back in the neighborhood where they'd lost so many comrades. One of the soldiers, Joel Barnes of Company K, managed to write a letter to a woman back in Michigan. "We are in a thick piece of woods thickly studed with thistle[?]berry, bushes, chinquapin bushes," he wrote. "We build works every half mile[;] it is a good plan. I [had] rather dig than fight[;] it would surprise you to see how quick we throw up a good breast work." At about 3:00 P.M. that hot day the 4th Michigan was pulled out of the woods and built breastworks across a field. Next to them, Gen. Ambrose Burnside's Ninth Corps moved into position, close to Rebel lines. Joel Barnes had just written in his letter that they "expect to have a battle this after noon" and now it happened.

As Confederate commanders realized that Union troops were in motion before them, they sent a force forward, attacking a brigade of the Ninth Corps adjacent to the 4th Michigan and driving them back, Sergeant Seage wrote. "Their pickets [Burnsides's men] leave in the afternoon followed by the rebels," Lieutenant Bancroft agreed, "so we are in a fight. Hurry and confusion." The 4th Michigan fell back, reformed their line, and charged. As they advanced they saw that Burnsides's troops also rallied and were retaking lost ground. Several of the Michigan troops were wounded and at least one was killed. The 4th Michigan was then ordered to support another nearby division of their own corps, since fierce fighting had erupted with other units from the Fifth Corps as well as the Ninth Corps. But for them—for the moment—the battle was over. They returned to their position where they had dug and built breastworks during of the first part of the day, one that had seen 1,500 Union casualties across the entire front. Rain set in that evening and John Bancroft began to get sick, suffering chronic diarrhea that would plague him for days.[27]

Cold Harbor

Now it was June 3, another hot and tragic day for the Union army. Grant had intended to launch an all-out attack on the previous day, but it was postponed for the arrival of more troops. Early in the morning of the third, men from three Union corps charged the Confederate works near Cold Harbor, about two miles south of where the 4th Michigan was dug in with the Fifth Corps near the Bethesda Church battleground. Thousands of Union soldiers died in tragically useless frontal attacks. Though Grant wanted a massive assault all along the line, a soldier who served in the Second Brigade with the 4th Michigan later wrote that their own Fifth Corps' line was too long and too thin for a charge to break through the Rebel defenses before them. All they could do that morning was to engage the Confederates in their front and prevent them from hurrying to the aid of their Rebel comrades just south, where the larger Union attacks took place. At about 6:00 A.M., this officer wrote, the 22nd Massachusetts and 80 men from the 4th Michigan jumped up from their breastworks when ordered out as skirmishers, with the other regiments of their brigade and the other part of the 4th Michigan forming behind them in line of battle. William H. Smith, a 23-year-old Ingham County man who'd been serving in Company K, said this action took place "near Old Church on the Mechanicsville Pike about 8 or 9 miles from Richmond." This referred to the area near Bethesda Church, where the Fifth Corps line was posted.

Other accounts agreed that most of 4th Michigan acted as skirmishers, advancing through the woods into a field and then across it. According to a report filed later with the Michigan adjutant general's office, the Michigan men who went out to the skirmish line were all those present for duty except Captain Van Valer's company. The new men took a position in the battle line on the left of the 9th Massachusetts. The Confederate skirmishers fell back as the Union soldiers pushed forward. "We carried everything before us and halted only when we . . . got within 150 yards of their breastworks," Robert Carter of the 22nd Massachusetts wrote about being on the skirmish line with the 4th Michigan. "We held our own in the edge of the woods, and silenced all their batteries, while the line of battle obliqued [moved at an angle] to the right and drove the enemy." In another letter, Carter described the action as a charge on "the reb line running parallel with the Pole Green Church Road, we approached it from the Bethesda Church."

Yet the Michigan and Massachusetts skirmishers did not silence the Confederate batteries—there were still more than enough Rebel gunners left alive and untouched. Their guns let loose and the skirmishers from the 4th Michigan and 22nd Massachusetts were exposed to an intense cross fire. "The rebs gave our picket or skirmish line a most terrific shelling, the shells rushing through the pines cutting them so they would fall afterwards with the wind," Lieutenant

Bancroft wrote. He felt the advance of the rest of Second Brigade, also forming at the edge of the woods, attracted the attention of the Confederate artillery officers. "Afterward they depressed their pieces and sent them amongst us," he continued. Henry Seage agreed, writing that the Confederates "planted a Battery in the woods in front of our works and shelled us 'right smart.'"

A projectile tore through the body of Lt. James W. Vesey from Sturgis, only 21 but a brave and respected officer, and he died soon after. All told the regiment lost 11 killed and wounded. George Maltz, the regiment's adjutant, was one of the wounded. Lt. John Bancroft took over his job. What was so tragic to the members of the regiment was that a number of the 4th Michigan's casualties were "old men," or those whose hitches were about to elapse in just three weeks. Sergeant Seage wrote in his history that at darkness the Confederates drove the brigade skirmish line back, but then they responded in kind, regaining the ground. After this exhausting back-and-forth movement and a day of fighting and digging in the brutal heat, night came on and the 4th Michigan's skirmishers were allowed to go to their own breastworks, where they made coffee and got rations. Although a subsequent report by George Maltz claimed "the Enemys works were taken" during the fighting this day, the simple fact was that the regiment had help drive the Confederates back to their main line of defense. Yes, the 4th Michigan had tied up Rebel soldiers and gunners before them that day, but the larger, more important picture of the battle of Cold Harbor was that the big Union assault to the south had failed, and at a terrible price.[28]

It rained for two days and it was quiet for the men of the 4th Michigan and most of their brigade, though other regiments sent out on patrols did some skirmishing with Confederates. "The rebs are all gone from our front," noted Bancroft, who was now the regiment's acting adjutant. It had become his responsibility to prepare the paperwork for the "mustering out" of the old 4th Michigan, so he applied (unsuccessfully) for permission to leave the front to finish it. The soldier who used the pseudonym "Veteran" wrote that he went out on June 4 to look at the positions the Confederates had evacuated. "The horses were piled upon each other where they had their batteries, and the trees were cut down by our shells," he wrote of the scene. "It must have been a very warm place for them when our artillery were at work." He guessed by the number of muskets left on the ground that many Rebels had been killed, too.

He and other soldiers of their brigade drew some new clothing, foraged food from area farms and got a chance to bathe. For some men this was the first chance to wash in a month, since the fighting, exhausting marches and hot, humid days had begun. In the meantime, Edward H. C. Taylor, wounded in the foot outside of Spotsylvania Court House, was recovering in Summit Hospital in Philadelphia. He was aware that there had been fierce combat during the month he was separated from his regiment. But the wound through his foot was healing and on June 9 he wrote his mother to say he only had eleven more days to serve. "I will try to get mustered out in Phil[adelphia] when my time is up and so save the trip to Michigan," he wrote. For a Democrat who'd spoken highly of McClellan's cautious tactics earlier in the war, Taylor was supportive of Grant's relentless, costly campaign. "There has been awful fighting since then [May 12], and I suppose the 4th was in also," Taylor said. "Grant means to whip [the Confederates] if fighting will do it, and I hope and believe he will succeed. He certainly has the best of the game now and gets all the reinforcements he wishes."[29]

The 4th Michigan moved a short distance south with its Fifth Corps, covering the Union army as it marched away from Richmond in preparation for Grant's next move. For those men who had been with the regiment since the spring of 1861 and who hadn't reenlisted, their hitch would be over in days—if they could stay alive. But the soldiers also understood now that when the 4th Michigan's three-year term came to a close, the regiment as they had known it would cease to exist, since about half of the men and practically all the officers were going home. What would happen to the regiment's new recruits and the veteran reenlistees? William H. Smith, now the 4th Michigan's sergeant major, wrote that once the "old men" left, "the veterans and normals [i.e., remaining soldiers] whose time is not out will compose 1 or more companies and be transferred to some other Reg't."

Smith had been with the 4th Michigan since the outset and reenlisted back in December. He wasn't happy about the pending transfer of the regiment's "veteran volunteers" and more recent recruits into another outfit, and neither were his comrades. And it turned out Colonel Lumbard's earlier claim that almost all of the officers would stay in the service was not true—they, too, were going to muster out. "Our officers are all going to leave us and it is hard telling what will become of us," he complained. "We are very much disappointed with the way affairs have turned out. But it can't be helped."[30]

CHAPTER 14

The Regiment Is in a Bad Situation at Present

IN THE WAKE OF THE FAILED ATTACK AT COLD HARBOR, GENERAL GRANT DECIDED TO QUIETLY MOVE his army in order to launch a new offensive from south of the James River. Less than two weeks following the terrible losses of June 3, the first of several Union army corps began a march down the York-James Peninsula. Some of the soldiers were sent to board transports to make their way to the region's rivers to reach the James, but most trudged in the dust and heat to points where they could be ferried across or march over a new pontoon bridge built by engineers. Grant intended to surprise the Confederates by coming up from the southeast, striking the town of Petersburg and cutting off Richmond. The Fifth Corps, of which the 4th Michigan was part, acted as a rear guard for the Army of the Potomac. The soldiers of the regiment marched away from the Bethesda Church–Cold Harbor area through the night of June 5 on into the next day, halted, and moved again for a few early morning hours on the seventh, reaching the vicinity of Bottom's Bridge on the Chickahominy River. The Second Brigade dug entrenchments and went on picket, but only once during these few days did Confederate gunners open fire on their division.

The weather was hot. The quartermasters issued clothing before the wagon trains pulled out, so the men replaced those articles worn out over the course of the grinding Overland Campaign. Sgt. Henry Seage remarked on being back in familiar territory. "This is the first time I have been on Picket on the Chickahominy River or have seen it since a year ago," he noted, referring to the summer of 1862. "The mosquitoes I find are so thick and trouble as then." But the Confederate pickets were sociable, so the men of both sides were able to wash, fish, or "lounge listlessly on the banks in the shade," he wrote. In his later history, Seage said they traded coffee for tobacco with the Rebels. Lt. John Bancroft, acting regimental adjutant, continued working on the muster-out papers for those whose enlistments were soon expiring, though he continued to be bothered by diarrhea.

One soldier wrote a short letter to a Detroit newspaper after he read a May 16 news report that said the 4th Michigan had gone into the spring campaign with 270 men, and lost all but 17 men in the fighting in the Wilderness. "There is a mistake in the report," wrote the soldier, who signed his letter "SERGT." "We went into action with 247. We lost seven killed and 27 wounded, including Col. Lombard [*sic*], who subsequently died." Another man had been killed on May 6, he noted. For some reason the soldier said nothing about the casualties the regiment suffered after that. But he explained that with the addition of Captain Van Valer's company, the 4th Michigan now had 205 soldiers and noncommissioned officers and 12 officers. All told, he wrote, this meant an effective regimental strength of 158 rifles.[1]

A soldier from one of the regiments that fought alongside of the 4th Michigan, Robert Carter of the 22nd Massachusetts, wrote in his own history that the men enjoyed rest, washed, and looked over newspaper reports on the battles they'd been in—"much to our amusement, sometimes to our indignation." The accuracy of the correspondents was lacking, he complained. "Were the true history of the War of the Rebellion to be compiled from such as mass of hospital reports, and bird's-eye views of newspaper correspondents and straggling bummers ten miles to the rear, some of our veterans would feel like turning over in their graves."[2]

Now the Fifth Corps's march to the south and east for Grant's new operation began as night fell on June 12, continuing into the next day. Some if not all of the 4th Michigan's men made an important side trip as their comrades withdrew. Sergeant Seage was with a force of soldiers from their division who were sent across the Chickahominy at Long Bridge, moving west on a reconnaissance or patrol, but had no run-ins with the Rebels. Here the 22nd Massachusetts and the 4th Michigan may truly have been the rear guard of the Fifth Corps. They rejoined their brigade as darkness came on. The march for the James River went through the night, covering about 10 miles before they stopped for a brief rest on the morning of June 14. Then they resumed, reaching Wilcox's Landing just south of the town of Charles City Court House. When their columns halted that night to camp in the fields there, the soldiers of the 4th Michigan were about just two miles from the landing.

The next day the Michigan soldiers could see an amazing spectacle when they reached the banks of the river. The James was busy with ships and transports, some ferrying men across to the south side or moving supplies, troops, and munitions up for the new Petersburg offensive. Thousands of other troops were tramping in what must have seemed like endless lines across a newly built bridge. The wagons crossed by the pontoon bridge at about 6:00 A.M. on June 16. Henry Seage received orders to join the division commissary, and that placed him with the wagon train that would carry food supplies for the men. Lieutenant Bancroft, still sick and counting down the days to the muster out, also crossed that morning, probably by transport, as did other regiments of their brigade. But there was a long column of soldiers on the road in front of them with thousands backed up and waiting to march. The 4th Michigan, with others in their brigade and division, had enough time to bathe and eat.

The Second Brigade began to move out at about 1:00 P.M. "Road very dry and dusty," Bancroft noted. "Houses all burned along the road so there is no shelter for stragglers. A very hot dusty and tedious march." It stretched into the evening and then into night, their column halting at 10:00 P.M. at a field to rest. But there was no water in the immediate vicinity, and men had to walk a half-mile to get it. Bancroft, who'd been sharing his horse so that other officers got a turn to ride in the heat and dust, took a nap before they resumed. On the column marched, the men allowed a 10-minute break each hour until they stopped at about two on the morning of June 17. They could hear the sound of heavy fighting up ahead. Later that morning the 4th Michigan arrived with its division outside of Petersburg.[3]

The first Union troops had reached Petersburg and attacked the defenses two days earlier, but their commanders hesitated and lost the chance to take the city. In the days after Cold Harbor, Lee hadn't been sure where Grant's army had gone. Petersburg's defenders were badly outnumbered, but more Confederate troops arrived in the nick of time. Though they were driven from their outer defenses, they managed to hold on in desperate fighting, in part because of the poor leadership and poor communications that plagued Union army generals. Now the men of the Fifth Corps were massed just outside of the scene of this combat at Petersburg's defenses southeast of town. This land on the outskirts of the city was hilly, with open country and woods, but soon it would be cut through with long lines of trenches and forts.

"Very hot," Lieutenant Bancroft wrote in his diary. "Severe fighting going on all the time." The men of the 4th Michigan and the Second Brigade kept low as shells passed over. But to the 150-plus Michigan men and officers whose three-year enlistment was nearly up, the situation must have been truly nerve-wracking. Thousands of Union troops were being sent in to attack the Confederate positions. Every hour these Rebel trenches were being hurriedly strengthened and reinforced. Hundreds of Union soldiers were killed and wounded in the attacks. Would the 4th Michigan, a small regiment with a large number of men about to serve out their term on June 19, be ordered to charge the Confederate defenses?[4]

The morning of June 18 dawned and the Second Brigade moved toward the front and then angled to the south into some woods. Col. Jacob Sweitzer, the brigade commander, promised he would hold the 4th Michigan back and "will call on us only in the case of urgent need," Bancroft noted. Moses Luce later wrote that Gen. Charles Griffin, their division commander, told the soldiers of the 4th Michigan that they should vote on whether they were willing to go into the fighting that day. According to Luce, the men of the regiment voted they would attack, if needed, though apparently some men decided to desert rather than risk being sent into battle. His version of events is supported in part by the memoir of Harrison Daniels from Company G. Daniels, from Lenawee County, who was then 27 years old. He later wrote that their brigade commander—he gave the name "Gen. Barnes," a former division commander, when in fact it was Colonel Sweitzer—called the 4th Michigan into line to address them. Daniels, who admitted in his account that he was writing from memory, gave the date of this talk as the afternoon of June 19, though John Bancroft stated in his diary that it took place on the 18th. Daniels wrote that the brigade commander told them he had no orders to remove them from the front, even though their time in the service was about to end. Still, he "wanted to know if the enemy pushed him if we would stand by him," Daniels wrote in his memoir. "We all said 'Yes.'"[5]

Throughout the afternoon of the 18th, the soldiers of the 4th Michigan heard the battle raging. Wounded troops limped back or were carried from the front, a reminder of the fate that could still befall them. "The ambulances come up near us for their loads," wrote Bancroft. "The limber boys of a battery come back to us and fill from their ammunition boxes and the men tell of the events of the day." The time must have passed slowly, and the tension for the "old men" of the regiment was probably high as the fighting continued. Around 6:00 P.M., the regiments of the Second Brigade were sent in to charge a section of the Confederate line—all of the regiments, that is, but the 4th Michigan. With the three-year hitch of more than 150 officers and men ending in just hours, a commanding officer, likely Gen. Charles Griffin, allowed the Michigan regiment to remain behind. One member of the brigade remembered that the 4th Michigan was excluded from the order to attack when the rest of the troops moved out to assault the Rebel position that evening. The fighting was terrible and scores of men fell dead and wounded, but the Confederate line did not break.[6]

Evening deepened and someone brought mail to the woods where the 4th Michigan waited. This was likely a pleasant distraction, though whether they had light to read their letters is an open question, given their proximity to the fighting. But then the order came that so many must have dreaded: The regiment had to move forward. "Then *fall in* to the front, Col. Sweitzer sends for us and so down we go in the darkness and where the musketry is sounding right lively, too lively for comfort," Bancroft noted. Daniels, in his reminiscence, agreed: "But that night between 8 and 9 while resting in a piece of woods they called us up and into the line in whispers, took us down a hill into a ravine where we relieved another regiment, and only a few rods from the enemies skirmish line." Bancroft wrote in his diary that the 4th Michigan moved out at darkness, shifted positions several times in the hill-and-dale terrain, and then went to work "throwing up earthworks" while Confederates fired at them that night and into the morning of June 19. These accounts show that the Michigan soldiers were not ordered to assault the Rebel works, but to extend the Union line under the cover of darkness. Still, it was dangerous in the hillside trenches. The men of the regiment were digging in just a stone's throw from the Petersburg defenders, with the Confederates continuing to fire. But at last the 4th Michigan's work was over and the men were allowed to rest. Lieutenant Bancroft noted that he "took two [fence] rails and another for a pillow and sleep soundly. No blanket."

In the morning, there was no denying the date: June 19, 1864, the final day of the enlistment term for men who had been mustered into federal service on June 20, 1861. For those who hadn't signed up for another hitch, it meant their service—and their fighting—was over. All they had to do was survive the journey away from their trenches to the rear. But first there was breakfast—"hardtack and sow belly, taken while lying down flat on the ground as it was sure death to stand up," Daniels wrote. "But we kept the other fellows in the same shape."[7]

At 10:00 A.M. the 4th Michigan was relieved by another regiment that had come to take its place. To reach the safety of the woods, beyond the range of the Confederates, the men had to get up and run down the hill, to the trees from where they'd come the previous evening.

Moses Luce said the soldiers scrambled to get away. "We were under fire all the way down the hill, the dirt flew about my feet," he would write later. Harrison Daniels agreed. "[W]hen we rose up and started on the run over the hill, we had one man killed and two wounded whose time of service had expired and who should have been mustered out that day," he wrote later. "Poor fellows, didn't we hate to leave them there after they had been so brave and true." But in fact the man killed was Company F's William H. Palmer, 27, one of the veterans from Lenawee County who had signed on to serve three more years. According to one retelling of the incident decades later, the same bullet that killed Palmer struck Lt. Benjamin Westfall, wounding him in the knee. Lt. Charles Gruner, commanding Company C, was seriously wounded in the thighs and buttocks. Gruner survived, however, and in two months' time he would be discharged. A few other men were also wounded.[8]

But for those who hadn't reenlisted it was now just a matter of traveling back to Michigan and formally mustering out. According to the regiment's figures, 135 men and 22 officers of the 4th Michigan mustered out of the army in Detroit later that month, though Lieutenant Bancroft noted that the returning soldiers numbered 112 men and 12 officers as they left Virginia. During their last hours at the front outside Petersburg, these men said their good-byes to their friends and comrades who had to remain. Then they marched on the road back to City Point, arriving that night. The next day they boarded what Bancroft described as "the mail boat for Washington, homeward bound." One other officer and 32 men who would have also been eligible to go home could not do so because they were prisoners of war. Another 20-some soldiers of the regiment whose terms had expired weren't present, most of them because they were in hospitals. According to the state's tabulation, in their time as soldiers and officers of the original 4th Michigan Infantry, from the regiment's formation to that week outside of Petersburg, 177 of their comrades had been killed or mortally wounded; another 96 died of disease and scores of others had suffered non-fatal wounds. A count of the regiment's combat fatalities by historian William F. Fox put the number of killed and mortally wounded even higher, at 189 men and officers.

Daniels wrote in his memoir that the night of June 20 was the last the departing 4th Michigan soldiers and officers spent with the Army of the Potomac, but other sources indicate it was June 19. Bancroft wrote that they boarded the boat for Washington on the 20th. Their last night in Virginia was at City Point, the great port-depot of the Union army. "Although it was a beautiful night and we were out of danger and where the rebel bullets could not reach us[,] there was no sleep for us," Daniels wrote. "Our minds were filled with thoughts of the dear ones at home and the comrades that were then sleeping in the southland and that could not return with us to the friends that were looking for them." It had been an emotional and ambivalent time, saying good-bye to their comrades who'd reenlisted. "Yes, we were breaking that tie of comradeship that binds the brave and true so firmly together," Daniels wrote. The moment was a bittersweet mix of relief and happiness but also sadness. On one hand, the men who were leaving had been through three years of privation and suffering, illness and wounds, battle and even prison camp with their comrades. Yet the war was still unfinished, and scores of men who had shared the same hardships had chosen to remain. "No man knows the strength of this tie except he who has been in its toils and is then obliged to break it," Daniels wrote.[9]

John Bancroft, who been the regiment's acting adjutant, was now the acting commander of the men who were leaving, since their senior officer, Captain Marshall, was absent when they left Petersburg. "Expect us in Detroit during the week," Bancroft wrote on June 20 in a note to a Detroit newspaper, before their transport sailed from Virginia. The vessel took the men back to Washington, where Moses Luce said he visited the friend he rescued at Laurel Hill, Sgt. Asher LaFleur, in the hospital. The wounded soldier had undergone a second surgery to prevent the spread of gangrene, but was cheery though weak. When those mustering-out soldiers boarded the train for the trip back to Michigan is unclear, but it was typical at that time for a trip between Detroit and Washington to take about two or three days.

In his memoir of his Civil War experiences Harrison Daniels would write that the "old men" of the 4th Michigan were touchingly acknowledged during a Sunday church service in Pittsburgh when they were stopped for a weekend as they made their train trip back to Detroit. Yet it must be noted that the sequence of events in the men's trip home couldn't have placed them at a Sunday sermon in western Pennsylvania. Daniels claimed that their train reached Pittsburgh on a Saturday morning, and that the men couldn't get on a westbound train until Monday morning. "Although we were ragged and dirty and had no money, we were right from the front, an arrangement was made so that all the people might have a chance to see us in a body. We were invited to attend the largest church in the city—it had been a long time since we were in such good hands," Daniels wrote.

The church was packed, according to his account, and these soldiers and officers of the 4th Michigan marched to the seats held for them in front of the altar. The minister arose and led the congregation in the singing of a hymn, Daniels said. "Then he began his prayer for God's blessing on our country, the flag and its defenders," he continued. But the presence in his church of some of those ragged defenders—men like their own brothers and husbands and fathers, back from the battlefields—caused emotion to overcome the pastor, Daniels wrote. His voice broke and tears welled in his eyes, and he had to stop to regain his composure. It was a moving experience, and afterward the people of the church shook hands with the Michigan soldiers, saying, "God bless you." Daniels remembered that many of his comrades' eyes were wet with tears. "Now the ole 4th Michigan will always remember the people of Pittsburgh and their kindness to us on that occasion," he wrote.

While Daniels's description of the event is vivid, his statement that those soldiers from the 4th Michigan were in Pittsburgh on a weekend in late June of 1864 is simply not possible, given the established facts concerning the men's trip home. The officers and men whose enlistments were at an end left Petersburg on Sunday, June 19, and boarded a transport for Washington the next day. Newspaper reports show they arrived in Detroit late on June 25, a Saturday night. In the few days it took for the soldiers to travel to Washington by boat and then to Michigan by rail, they couldn't have been in Pittsburgh on a Sunday. While it is possible that not all of the men who left the 4th Michigan traveled together, it seems that the vast majority of them did so—as many as 140 officers and men, by one contemporaneous account. Daniels's memoir certainly suggests he was part of this large group and mustered out with them. Perhaps the church service he described actually took place during the middle of the week, though no other soldier appears to have mentioned it.[10]

The train carrying the 4th Michigan men home crossed into their home state in the evening of June 25 and soon stopped in Monroe, where about 15 members of Company A were almost certainly the first of the men to get home. It seems their officers had sent a message by telegraph, for the women of the community were expecting them and "had a nice table spread for them" at a local inn called the Humphrey House. Since the soldiers wouldn't be formally mustered out of the service in Detroit for four days, it appears that the men from Monroe were allowed to part with the rest of their comrades on the condition they had to rejoin the others in the city for the official muster out.[11]

The reception the Monroe women prepared for the soldiers of Company A was grand compared to the nongreeting the rest of the men received when they reached Detroit late that night. Moses Luce said the train arrived at about midnight, and the soldiers marched up Woodward Avenue to "some barracks," probably those that had been erected on the old state fair grounds. "There really was but one man to receive us and we recalled to mind how we had been promised many times by leading citizens, when they were needing us in the regiment, that they would make for us a life of glory when we returned," Luce recalled.

The one man there to meet them was Lt. George W. Maltz, the adjutant of the 4th Michigan. He'd come back ahead of the returning soldiers and "procured refreshments for them at his own expense," a Detroit newspaper reported. To thank him, some of the men asked that he be recognized in the press for his thoughtfulness, and he was. In fairness to the residents of Detroit of 1864, it should be noted that this was not the entire regiment returning to Michigan, but only a portion of it, so apparently there had been no official notice or recognition of them or their return by authorities. Still, one Detroit newspaper expressed dissatisfaction with what it called "the shabby treatment" of the returning soldiers from the 4th Michigan.

Moses Luce claimed that their surgeon looked around the barracks and saw they were infested with vermin. No, the doctor ruled, the men were not staying here. The decision was made for the soldiers to sleep out on the sidewalk instead, and Luce's account was confirmed by Henry Seage's later history. Luce wrote that as he bedded down with his knapsack for a pillow, he looked up into the window of a brownstone residence and saw a hand reaching to draw a curtain quickly down. "It was the first thought I had that the soldier now was nobody and I was already a vagrant," he wrote. Luce had made it through his service in the 4th Michigan without getting seriously wounded, but his comrades joked he "finally shed blood for his country" when a rat scrambled over his face and scratched him that morning around dawn.

At least one other editor was appalled at the lack of a greeting for the 4th Michigan soldiers when he heard what had happened in Detroit. The proprietor of the *Lansing State Journal* was particularly peeved that the U.S. government sent these men back without paying them what they were owed, so that the men had "found themselves not only unnoticed and disregarded, but without means to procure even a meal of victuals or a night's lodging." Four days after their arrival, on June 30, these soldiers and officers of the 4th Michigan were formally mustered out of the service. Though these men were free to go home, they almost immediately had a social obligation to fulfill. It had been a group of women in Adrian who donated a customized U.S. flag to the regiment in June 1861, and now, after their arrival back in Detroit, the ex-soldiers were invited by the same women to attend the Fourth of July celebration there.[12]

In the meantime, 23 men from Hillsdale and nearby towns and farming communities left

Detroit. The 4th Michigan's Company E, of course, had been mainly composed of Hillsdale area men. Missing the evening train on the last day of June, the returning survivors arrived in Hillsdale around midnight. Even though they were four hours late, a large crowed of residents came running when the courthouse bell was rung, announcing their return. A bonfire had been lit in the town's Railroad Square and scores of people were waiting to see them when the soldiers, including Moses Luce and John Hewitt, got off the train. The crowd walked with the men to the Western Hotel, where even though it was midnight, a fellow named Loftus Keating, a former classmate of Luce and other soldiers who'd been students at the local college back in 1861, gave a welcoming speech; Luce responded and the men were fed "a sumptuous supper." Though the occasion was supposed to be a happy one, scores of men, the dead, were noticeable by their absence: "[S]ad reflections concerning the brave men who had lost their lives on the battlefield cast a gloom over the enjoyment of the occasion," a correspondent wrote.

Luce was invited to stay with the Keatings. Going back to the home of Keating's mother, Luce found that, after spending the last three years sleeping in tents, on the ground, or on rough platforms of boards and boughs, he couldn't fall asleep in the soft feather bed. "I sunk down in the feathers and nearly smothered to death," he wrote about trying to go to sleep that night. But Keating was an understanding friend. He put the mattress on the floor and covered Luce with a blanket. "[A]t last I went off to sleep and slept the sleep of peace and quietude," Luce wrote.[13]

Four days later, on the Fourth of July in Adrian, about 120 of the soldiers from the 4th Michigan arrived in town. But their train ran late. A large crowd of people from the area had walked to the town's fairgrounds with their marching band and fire companies at 10:30 A.M., but the ex-soldiers hadn't yet arrived. They didn't reach Adrian until noon—after the speeches were already made by Austin Blair and a local judge. Once they arrived, the men from the 4th Michigan were accompanied to the fairgrounds by the town's mayor and council, some of the local fireman, and a hometown militia company, cheered by the crowd. One report said that Harrison Jeffords's father attended the event, riding the "beautiful bright chestnut" horse that had belonged to his son, escorted by eight of the men of the Adrian Guards, a militia company. When the crowd quieted, a local pastor made a welcoming speech that told of their battle record and the deaths of their colonels. One journalist felt it was the best speech given that day, but too long, given the nature of the occasion and the summer heat.

Dr. John S. Watts, the assistant surgeon from Adrian, responded with remarks of thanks. Then it was time for the return of the regiment's banner; again the crowd gave three cheers. The 4th Michigan's former chaplain, the Reverend John Seage, accompanied by Sgt. George Goodsell, a Lenawee County man who'd been in Company F and the original regiment's last color bearer, walked to the platform where the speakers were addressing the crowd. They handed the regiment's flag to Mrs. Josephine Wilcox, the same woman who had presented the 4th Michigan's first regimental colors.

Most of the reports by the assembled correspondents—those printed in the *Hudson Gazette*, *Detroit Free Press*, and *Detroit Advertiser and Tribune*—indicated the returning flag was the original U.S. flag that the women of Adrian had donated back in the spring of 1861. The *Hillsdale Standard*, on the other hand, seemed to indicate that this was the banner carried through the spring campaign of 1864. Its correspondent wrote that the "tattered appearance" of the flag brought back by the men "told a terrible story of war . . . of the old fourth that marched from the Rapidan to the James." Yet Mrs. Wilcox was indirectly quoted as saying that "she knew that the men had kept with unstained honors that [flag] which had been committed to their trust," a reference to the U.S. flag—what has become known as the "Defend It" flag—that she presented three years earlier. She would be the keeper of that original banner for years to come. The flag handed over to her was described as smoke-stained and riddled with bullets, and one article noted that a third of this banner had been shot away. Local businessman Charles Cleveland wrote in his diary that the ceremony marked the return of the 4th Michigan's "tattered colors." This flag truly reflected what the 4th Michigan had been through. "It swayed back and forth in the breeze, a fit emblem of the skeleton regiment that stood below," the Hillsdale paper reported.[14]

The ceremony was over. Perhaps to break the somberness after the talk of the comrades who'd lost their lives, Reverend Seage joked that there were some unmarried men among the ex-regimental officers who might look among the ladies of Adrian "for partners to cheer bachelorhood." Then the fire department and the Adrian Guards marched with the men to the town's Floral Hall, where the women of the Soldiers Aid Society had prepared what a local resident called "a splendid dinner." A concert followed in the afternoon at the hall with singers and musicians, and a grand ball was given that night to raise funds for the soldiers charity and the Agricultural Society of Adrian. How many of the ex-soldiers attended and how many headed back to quiet homes that evening is unknown.[15]

Back in Virginia in the last days of June 1864, there were still 170 or more men on the rolls of the 4th Michigan Infantry Regiment who, because they were 1864 recruits, were drafted men, or had reenlisted for three more years, remained in the service of the United States. The men who were actually present for duty, and not the sick and wounded, represented less than two full companies. Their brigade, Sweitzer's Second Brigade of the First Division of the Fifth Corps, was then in reserve. Capt. Cornelius Van Valer, commander of the company that arrived at the front just a month before, reported that only 127 men were present, and he was the only commissioned officer there. Yet a letter from a member of the regiment put its "strength in the field" at 145.

Because all the other officers were gone, Van Valer was the acting commander of what remained of the 4th Michigan, although the reality was the regiment barely existed. "The regiment is in a bad situation at present," wrote a soldier who initialed his letter to Detroit "W.H.S.," "having no Chaplain, no Surgeon or Steward, no Quartermaster or Quartermaster Sergeant." What happened to these men who were left over after the mustering out of about half the men who remained of the original 4th Michigan? A "special order" that day from Fifth Corps headquarters determined where the remaining soldiers of the regiment were being assigned. "The officers and enlisted men of the Fourth Michigan Volunteers whose term of service has not expired will be transferred to one of the regiments from the same State now serving in the First Division," the order stated.

That turned out to be the 1st Michigan Infantry Regiment, part of the division's Third Brigade. That regiment's number was so reduced that it had temporarily been consolidated with the 16th Michigan for a few weeks previously. Writing back to Detroit from Petersburg in a letter dated July 2, 1864, a member of the 1st Michigan who signed his note "J.H.A." said that the incorporation of the 4th Michigan's remaining men had just been ordered. "The veterans and recruits of the 4th Infantry have been consolidated into our regiment, though they have not yet reported," the soldier wrote.

Even before the "three-year men" mustered out of the 4th Michigan, the veterans who had reenlisted early in 1864 had come to understand that the date of June 19, 1864, marked the end of their regiment as they knew it. Sgt. William H. Smith had complained early in June about how concerned and disappointed the reenlisted men were about this. Some of the remaining men of the 4th Michigan decided they had to try to do something about it, for they soon heard that a new, reorganized 4th Michigan was going to be formed with some of the old regiment's officers. As a result, many of the remaining men signed a petition asking that they be allowed to join this new 4th Michigan organizing back home.[16]

By the third week in July the press in Michigan reported that a reorganized 4th Michigan Infantry Regiment was indeed being formed under Lt. Col. Jairus Hall, who had been away from the old regiment for months, and who was now commissioned colonel of a new incarnation of the regiment. On the 26th, this was confirmed with an order by the state adjutant general of Michigan. Like the original 4th Michigan before it, the men of the reorganized regiment would meet and form at Adrian.

Jairus Hall had been back in Michigan since early in 1864, according a summary of his record, spending the last four months of his initial three-year enlistment at Jackson, running a camp for men drafted into the service. Since not enough of the "old men" of the original 4th Michigan had reenlisted for three more years, Colonel Hall published an appeal in Detroit for enlistees in a new 4th Michigan in mid-August, saying that he was recruiting men from Michigan's First Congressional District. This took in Lenawee, Hillsdale, Monroe, and Wayne counties. Hall noted that while men were being signed up for three years or till the end of the war, he and others didn't really believe the war would go on for another year. Hall also pointed out that men who now joined would receive several hundred dollars in bounties. "We do not ask you to join the 4th Regiment if you can find one of brighter fame, or one that will confer more honor by connection with it," he wrote.

Hall turned to some old comrades to help in this new 4th Michigan Infantry. One was Richard Watson Seage, the officer who'd been shot down at Gettysburg alongside Harrison Jeffords. Hall asked that Seage be commissioned as a first lieutenant and quartermaster. Seage's father, the Reverend John Seage, also joined the reorganized 4th Michigan and was again made chaplain, though he was soon detached on recruiting service for the new regiment. Another former officer of the original regiment, Michael Vreeland, who'd also been wounded at Gettysburg, was authorized to recruit for the reorganized 4th Michigan in the area of his home at Brownstown Township in Wayne County. He was soon commissioned lieutenant colonel.

The remaining men of the original 4th Michigan, absorbed into the 1st Michigan Infantry and serving with the Army of the Potomac at Petersburg, were sure they would soon be joining Hall and their former officers in the new regiment. "Our stay in the 1st [Michigan] bids fair to be temporary one, as the 4th is reorganizing," wrote one of the veterans, whose letter to a Detroit newspaper was initialed "S." "I think the most of the 'old 4th' are pleased with the prospect."[17]

But it was soon established that the new 4th Michigan regiment would, when ready, be sent by the War Department to Tennessee and other points west and south, rather than to Virginia.

As a formality, a Union army staff officer notified George G. Meade, commander of the Army of the Potomac, about this so that he could pass along word to the veterans of the original 4th Michigan: No, they could not be transferred to the reorganized 4th Michigan, at least not yet. "[The reorganized] 4th Regt has gone to the Department of the Cumberland," Assistant Adjutant General Thomas W. Vincent wrote about the new regiment's assignment. "The request therefore cannot be granted."[18]

In fact, most of the surviving veterans of the original 4th Michigan did join the reorganized regiment—in time. "Some [of the original regiment] had veteranized [i.e., reenlisted] and transferred to the 1st [Michigan]," wrote Albert Boies nearly a quarter of a century later. "When the new 4th went to the front, part of the old 4th veterans was sent to them and it was the intention that all the old 4th should be assigned to them." It would take nearly a year for the last soldiers of the original 4th Michigan to join the new regiment.

Throughout the late summer and early fall of 1864, the companies of the reorganized 4th Michigan Infantry Regiment rendezvoused, trained, and received their equipment. The first companies arrived in Adrian, this time on the fairgrounds, in the hottest mid-August weather anyone could remember in more than two decades. Three of the companies were composed of men and officers who initially believed they were going to be a part of a 30th Michigan Infantry Regiment that had been forming in Pontiac, when plans for that outfit were put on hold late in August. Adrian businessman Charles Cleveland noted that there was in excitement in the city as committees from the different wards and from neighboring small towns offered bounties of $300 for enlistees to join the new 4th Michigan regiment. Men continued arriving as September and cooler weather came on and new barracks were erected on the west end of the town.

Just as the presence of the original 4th Michigan had attracted crowds of people to watch drill and parade in the spring of '61, so too did the reorganized 4th Michigan, especially on Sunday afternoons. Cleveland, who again had a contract to provide rations to the regiment, wrote that some 750 men were in camp by mid-October, though other accounts say the number was less than that. "Since its presence here the city has been lively enough," he wrote.

On the morning of October 22 the men of the reorganized 4th Michigan broke camp, marched through Maumee Street to the railroad depot, and boarded a westbound train that pulled out of town at noon. "They presented a fine appearance," wrote Cleveland, who had been busy over the past few days preparing rations for the soldiers to take with them. "A large crowd of our citizens witnessed their departure from the depot," he continued. "Many a moistened eye bade them an affectionate farewell." The train took the 726 men and officers on the first leg of the journey that would take them to Nashville, Tennessee, and then on to Alabama.

Most of the remaining soldiers of the original 4th Michigan Infantry, who had been assigned to the 1st Michigan, would not join the reorganized 4th Michigan until the end of June 1865, at New Orleans. By then the Civil War was over. But in the fall of 1864 as the reorganized 4th Michigan left Adrian, the conflict was still raging.[19]

CHAPTER 15

We Have Broke the Backbone of the Rebellion

SEVERAL DAYS AFTER THE REORGANIZED 4TH MICHIGAN INFANTRY LEFT ADRIAN, ITS MEN ARRIVED at the scene of a major battle in the western theater of the Civil War—the defense of the Union-held town of Decatur, Alabama, in late October and early November 1864. This was the first of two battles for which this regiment was present, though it was not heavily involved.

It was a long trip for the regiment to reach Nashville, and the men were quickly moved on to Decatur, not quite a hundred miles to the south. Gen. William T. Sherman had already taken Atlanta and his devastating "March to the Sea" was under way. The Confederate army of Gen. John Bell Hood, which had tried unsuccessfully to defend Atlanta, pressed north to cut Union supply lines, hoping to halt Sherman's destructive raid and perhaps menace the North. If Hood could overwhelm the Union soldiers at Decatur, an outpost held by elements of the Army of the Cumberland, he could gain a crossing of the Tennessee River and make grief for the Union.

An alumnus of the original 4th Michigan, Col. Charles Doolittle of the 18th Michigan Infantry, was in charge at the defense of Decatur. Regiments from his home state were among the reinforcements hurried to the town, and one was the reorganized 4th Michigan. The defenders of Decatur inflicted serious casualties on the attacking Confederates, and it seemed the worst was over when the new 4th Michigan arrived with other regiments. They were immediately put into defensive positions on the right of the Union line. "We left Nashville yesterday morning and arrived here this morning," wrote Capt. Charles J. Fox about the reorganized regiment in a letter to his father apparently dated October 28. "It looks like war. Hoods Armey is in front of us and they are skirmishing not more than 2 rods from us. We are in the trenches and I don't think there is much danger."

Yet after assuring his father of this, Fox, from Pontiac, went onto say he just saw a soldier who raised his head up above the trenches "fall back down tumble down quicker than he got up." It appears the man's wound was fatal. In another letter two days later, still describing the events of the 28th, Fox wrote that "on[e] man right in front of me was shot in the back and d[ied] this morning." He noted that his regiment "lost 5 men," and a brief summary of the history of the reorganized 4th Michigan by the Michigan adjutant general agreed, stating that one man was killed and four wounded at Decatur.

By the next morning Colonel Doolittle received information that Hood's men were pulling out. That night he put his old comrade Col. Jairus Hall in charge of a force of 950 men, soldiers from several regiments, including a detachment from the reorganized 4th Michigan. They went out at dark on a reconnaissance in force on a route through the country called the Courtland Road. Hall's men clashed with strong Confederate pickets about two miles out, after which Hall ordered them back to camp. Hall was one of the several officers Doolittle acknowledged in this report of the defense of Decatur. William Warner, a soldier with the 18th Michigan, gave the reorganized 3rd and 4th Michigan regiments a backhanded compliment when he wrote home early in November. "The Third and forth Michigon inft. regt are hear, they are new regts and think it hard to go right into a fight the furst thing," Warner wrote; "they dun as well as could be expected of new soldiers."[1]

Within a few days the regiment was moved to Whitesburg, Alabama (given incorrectly as "Whitesboro" in some accounts). "Chaplain," a member of the reorganized 4th Michigan who later sent a letter to the *Detroit Advertiser and Tribune* about their skirmishes and travels, said they were transported on this 35-mile trip by a Union gunboat called the *Stone River.* But after a few days, "Chaplain" wrote, the regiment was moved again, another 45 miles, to the town of Larkinsville. It appears the regiment's companies were spread out and assigned to picket duty to help guard a railway line from Huntsville to a point some 50 miles or more to the east.

Here soldiers of the reorganized 4th Michigan became involved in skirmishes with Confederate raiders. Major D. Williams of the 12th Indiana Cavalry reported that Colonel Hall and 250 of men of the 4th Michigan joined 145 troopers at Brownsboro, about 10 miles east of Huntsville, on November 16. Early the next morning, this force moved out "under command of Colonel Hall, [and] we marched in the direction of New Market [north]." Two or three of miles out, near the town of Maysville, their advance clashed with Confederate cavalry pickets. Hall said his force continued on toward New Market and took a road into the hills to a place called Jones' Cove, where the Confederate raiders had encamped a day earlier. As Hall's force reached a plantation owned by a man whose name was given as "Sandsley," the colonel learned that as many as 500 Rebels under a Colonel Russell were just three miles away. Hall believed this was an appropriate time for his men to breakfast, so they stopped to eat and the troopers fed their horses.

"I then set the column in motion, and after ten minutes' march came upon the enemy in line of battle on the side of the mountain, and advanced upon him with a strong line of skirmishers, from which he retreated," Hall reported. "It then became a running fight. As fast as the infantry could march I drove him around and over the mountains, up Hurricane Branch five miles beyond New Market." Major Williams, one of the Union cavalry officers in the operation, said his troopers and the detachment from the new 4th Michigan broke the Confederate formation, "driving them from their ground in confusion, our men pursuing them. We followed them until night, driving them nine miles, they rallying five times, but were handsomely repulsed and driven back each time." Hall said his men killed nine Rebels and wounded three or four in the running day-long skirmish. They returned to New Market as darkness fell. Major Williams complimented Hall in his report on the fight.

The next day, November 18, was rainy and the roads turned to mud. Hall gave his men a break. They had marched more than 20 miles on the previous day, and even his detachment of cavalry hadn't been able to keep up with Colonel Russell's retreating troopers. Hall's force went back to Brownsboro. But with the Union pressure off, Russell's raiders tore up railroad track of the Memphis & Charleston Railroad between points called Gurney Rock and Point Rock stations. Hall's force went out to find them again on the 19th. "I was informed that the railroad had been torn up five miles north," Hall reported. "A train being at hand I took all the infantry forces then at Brownsborough [*sic*] and proceeded to the place of destruction, leaving orders for Captain Givens to move with the mounted force to that point as soon as possible. The force under him, numbering 124 men, reached there at 11:45 A.M. I then proceeded on Russell's track, coming up with him at dusk at Duckett's plantation, near Paint Rock River."

Hall ordered his soldiers, armed with Enfield rifles, up into the hills to the right of the Confederates. They charged while his cavalry moved on the left of the road that ran along the base of the high ground. "The enemy here made a more stubborn resistance than at any time previous, and I was in hopes that he would stand long enough for us to get within short range," Hall reported, "but I was soon invited to another race, as he showed his heels as usual; it was then dark, and impossible to come up with him again." The Indiana troopers and the 4th Michigan soldiers captured Colonel Russell's camp, food for his troopers and animals alike, bridles, saddles, blankets, about 30 horses, "and canteens which were mostly filled with whisky," Hall wrote. They also seized twenty stands of arms, "including rifles, carbines and shotguns." Most of the captured property was useless to the Union soldiers, so Hall ordered it burned. He used the Confederate camp that night as rains opened up, but the next day, November 20, Russell had moved too far away for pursuit. Hall ordered his men back to Brownsboro. "He has come to grief," a correspondent wrote tersely to the *Cincinnati Gazette* about Colonel Russell.

Hall's men suffered one wounded during this fight. A Union commander in charge of the defense of the railway line, Col. William Lyon of the 13th Wisconsin, expressed his satisfaction with Hall's pursuit and rout of the Confederate raiders, a "rebel force greatly superior in numbers to yours," he wrote to the colonel. His comments were echoed by Maj. General Thomas, commander of the Army of the Cumberland. Thomas acknowledged Lyon's report and noted his appreciation. "Please thank Col. Hall for me for his energetic pursuit and defeat of the rebels on Saturday last," Thomas said in a telegraphed message. The reorganized 4th Michigan remained at Larkinsville for about another week before being sent north on a train on November 27 to Murfreesboro, Tennessee.[2]

The fighting was not yet over in this vicinity. "Chaplain" wrote that the regiment arrived the next afternoon and was sent at first to a Union defensive emplacement called Fort Rousseau, part of the line of fortifications at Murfreesboro. "The day after we arrived a considerable body of the enemy appeared all around us," he wrote. "This produced a panic in the town, and Government and merchant stores were moved with all haste within Fortress Rosencrans." The Union forces and civilians worked on the chain of forts on December 6, "Chaplain" said, and then Confederates attacked "with cannon and musketry." The answering Union guns drove them off. During this fighting, Chaplin said, the new 4th Michigan was placed at one of the defenses called Fort Sheridan. This fort came briefly under attack by a Rebel battery but a shot from a Union gun "took off both legs of the rebel captain," he wrote. "Our regiment went out and drove them pell mell. Having driven the Johnnies and killed quite a number of them, our boys came [back] in good spirits without a scratch, believing they had the best Colonel in the army."

For most of the rest of December, the soldiers of the reorganized 4th Michigan manned fortifications, walked pickets, and guarded supply trains, and it appears they sometimes clashed with Confederate raiders. "Chaplain" wrote that the regiment guarded forage trains every third day. Because the Rebels were able to cut the railroad to Nashville, supplies were tight for several days for Union troops until wagon trains arrived. In the meantime the men were put on half-rations. New soldiers were angry and "grew mutinous" about this, but "Chaplain" wrote that veterans who had served in the Army of the Potomac "took it patiently," and the hard times soon passed.[3]

While accounts and records indicate that most of the regiment was at Murfreesboro during late November, a Tennessee newspaper reported that some men from the reorganized 4th Michigan were in nearby Nashville and that they, too, became involved in a memorable and wild skirmish—not with Rebels, but with regulars of the U.S. Army's 13th Infantry Regiment. In the neighborhood of the Louisville depot—characterized as Nashville's red-light district by one historian—some members of the new 4th Michigan and the 9th Pennsylvania became embroiled in an angry argument with some federal soldiers over who had the better fighting abilities—volunteers, like themselves, or the troops of the 13th U.S. Infantry, who were "regular Army." The disagreement escalated, and given the circumstances and location of this brawl, it is likely strong drink was a factor.

"The controversy moved swiftly from words to pistols and the regulars took refuge in a whorehouse," according to an account of the battle. Surely the combatants' aim must have also been affected by alcohol for it was alleged that over 100 shots were fired. The author who recounted the fight claimed "outsiders were probably most impressed by the amazingly poor display of marksmanship, for the only casualty was one of the women who had part of her shoe cut away by a bullet." The Michigan men, presumably with their allies from Pennsylvania, drove the regulars from the first house to a second house before the provost guard rushed in and put an end to the fracas. No doubt the combatants spent some time in the guardhouse.

Who were these Michigan soldiers and why were they in Nashville while the rest of the regiment was in Murfreesboro? Perhaps they'd been on detached duty of some kind and had time on their hands. In any event, the skirmish with army regulars in the town's red-light district wasn't one that made it into the short histories of the reorganized 4th Michigan published later by the state adjutant general.[4]

The more important battle took place in the Nashville area in mid-December with Major General George Thomas's forces attacking, routing, and effectively neutralizing Hood's army. As 1864 was coming to a close, one of the important figures in the reorganized 4th Michigan, an assistant surgeon named Joseph B. Griswold from Vermontville, proudly wrote home that the soldiers of the corps to which they'd been assigned "have whipped Hood like la diablo" and were pursuing Rebel troops. Griswold, then 22 and just commissioned as a medical officer a month earlier, wasn't initially allowed to be mustered into the regiment because of some sort of red tape. As a result he was ordered to serve with the division's artillery brigade, part of the Fourth Army Corps then posted in the vicinity of Nashville, until the issue could be settled. In the meantime, the reorganized regiment's sick and wounded had been tended in part by the senior assistant surgeon, Dr. Carlos D. Hampton, from Hudson.

Hampton had been commissioned into the new 4th Michigan back in July, though he'd had plenty of experience before then with Rebels and military life. According to a reminiscence by his wife, Dr. Hampton and family left Lenawee County in the fall of 1858 for Texas, where he intended to run a stock farm and practice medicine. But history intervened and the experience was a bad one for the Hamptons. Within a year or so of their arrival in Texas, local Secessionists suspected the doctor of being a "black abolitionist." The family was harassed and threatened until the doctor left, claiming he was joining the Confederate army. In fact, he joined an Illinois cavalry regiment in Arkansas while his wife and sons, still facing abuse by Rebels, eventually escaped and made the long journey back to Michigan.

Joe Griswold, on the other hand, had up until recently been a medical student. Early in the war, he served as a musician in a Michigan cavalry regiment. In his new assignment as an assistant surgeon, he had to deal with the terrible result when men were hit by projectiles. "War is a bloody, terrible, cruel thing," he wrote some several weeks after the battle, "but a necessity." Around Christmas he mentioned to his sister that he'd been busy after the fighting: "I am well," he wrote, "and have had some mighty hard work to do[,] dressing wounded up all one night."[5]

Shortly after the fighting at Nashville, the reorganized 4th Michigan's commander, Jairus Hall, wrote to Michigan Adjutant General John Robertson, hoping for the authority to raise three more companies of men. Hall had left Michigan with just over 700 men, and he was still waiting for Cornelius Van Valer's company to be sent to him from the 1st Michigan Infantry, something that he apparently believed was going to happen sooner rather than later. "As soon as I get his first report I will forward an application which I think will bring the veterans [of the old 4th Michigan] to me," Hall wrote from Tennessee.[6]

Regimental records during this time indicate the presence of some "old men" from the original 4th Michigan in the new regiment, among them Sgt. Irvin Miner. Captured by the Confederates at Gettysburg, he'd been held a month in Richmond's Belle Isle prison camp until his release late in August 1863 and placement in Union convalescent and parole camps in Annapolis, waiting for the processing of his formal exchange as a prisoner of war. Though he wanted to rejoin his regiment, he had continued to be kept as a convalescent in Washington, formally transferred to the Veteran Reserve Corps. In the reorganized 4th Michigan, Miner was the first sergeant of Company B, under Capt. David R. Stroud of Hudson. Before his service was over, he would be commissioned lieutenant. Lt. Michael Vreeland, 26, wounded at Gettysburg, was originally commissioned captain of Company D in the reorganized 4th Michigan but soon became Hall's lieutenant colonel. But his wounds compromised his health, and he wasn't able to march with them just yet. He stayed on detached service in Tennessee when his regiment moved on, and went back to Michigan in the spring of 1865 to get married.

One of the members of the reorganized 4th Michigan was Thomas J. Lowery from Somerset Township in Hillsdale County. Writing from Murfreesboro on New Year's Day, 1865, he told his relatives that he'd learned to appreciate family, home, and peace now that he'd seen comrades taken away by death through battle and disease. "How thankful, how happy every family ought to feel who are surrounded with the blessings of peace," he wrote. "When one comes to witness the Sufferings and privations of poor women and children who are homeless, homeless without food and almost without clothing; then one can realise the blessings of peace and a peaceful home." Lowery implored his relatives to write him, especially since he couldn't get any war news. He insisted he was "as tuff as a bear; I expect to fight, bleed and die for my country and still come home all right and as sound as a bullet."[7]

In mid-January of 1865, the regiment was moved by rail back to Huntsville, where it had been assigned to the Fourth Army Corps's Third Division, Third Brigade. The trip took two days. The soldiers were aggravated when, just as they completed building a camp in a cedar grove, their regiment was ordered back to Nashville by train. Here they camped outside of town for three days, only to move back to Huntsville and find the camp they'd built "more or less demolished," a soldier complained. The back-and-forth movement was actually the result of orders their division had received to be sent to Eastport, Mississippi, but those orders had been canceled after they got to Nashville. Their camp near Huntsville had been torn down in the several days they were gone, and some soldiers blamed that on the local poor folk. But they rebuilt the encampment, which was dry and comfortable and located on the Whitesburg Road about four miles outside of town. "[U]nder the superintendence of our Colonel, who is always up and doing, we have got our huts all up and in first class order," a soldier wrote appreciatively of Hall. Another member of the regiment, Sgt. J. P. Roof of Company D, called their camp's spot "as beautiful piece of ground as ever laid out of doors in the state of Alabama."

Roof estimated that the regiment had lost 20 men (probably from a combination of incapacitating wounds and illness) since it had left Adrian. But the weather was sometimes mild, and a soldier from Hillsdale County named Samuel McLain, about 25, wrote that it was fine for February, as nice as springtime in Michigan could be, though others noted that freezing, rainy weather hit them in early March. But poor McLain didn't survive that month. He soon died in an army hospital in Nashville, where he may have been attended by his regiment's assistant surgeon, Joseph Griswold.

In the meantime Griswold still hadn't been allowed to muster into the service of the reorganized 4th Michigan, but he had met some of its officers. He described Colonel Hall to his sister as a "good looking" man with "a slice of fun in him" who was proud of his position. Griswold was soon attending a Huntsville church and sometimes dining and socializing with local young women, some with pro-Union views and some who were still ardent secessionists, even though the Confederacy was all but crushed.[8]

Michigan officers talked of the possibility that they could still be become involved in major fighting if the Confederacy concentrated what remained of its shrinking forces, and the usual rumors and camp stories circulated as to how or where they might be moved as spring drew near. But what the men of the reorganized 4th Michigan didn't yet know was that the war was now almost over for them—but not their service.

In the second week of March, two divisions of the Fourth Corps were ordered to go into eastern Tennessee, where forces were needed to repair and protect railroad lines the Union army required to move men and supplies. The Third Division of which the reorganized 4th Michigan was part was chosen for this duty. The troops were to move by rail to Knoxville, and Colonel Hall was in charge of escorting or guarding the transportation of the division, with his regiment and the 49th Ohio Infantry. Beginning on March 23, the regiment was ordered to journey to eastern Tennessee with its division, reaching Knoxville on the evening of the 25th, having traveled 112 miles of the distance from Huntsville by rail. Then, by train and over roads, soldiers of their division of the Fourth Corps moved into the countryside to protect the Eastern Tennessee & Virginia Railroad and the crews working on it from guerilla attack.

The day after their arrival at Knoxville the reorganized 4th Michigan went another 15 miles east to the small town of Strawberry Plains and the day after, March 27, another 15 miles or so to the town of New Market. This mission, carried out with other regiments of their brigade, continued on the 29th to a place called Painter's Springs, yet another 15 miles east, and 12 miles more the next morning to the town of Russellville. Specific details of this trek, its conditions, or how the Michigan men were greeted by locals are few, but the country is high and rugged. Even if the roads and weather conditions were good, these may have been laborious patrols and marches, though the soldiers appear to have moved at least some of the time by train. Reports indicate that some Union soldiers often worked on the railroad and clashed with small numbers of guerillas. Continuing on from March 31 to April 7, the regiment camped, worked, and shifted locations, moving more than 50 miles from Bull's Gap, Greenville, and Rheatown to Jonesborough, the easternmost point on this long railroad assignment. It was while they were here that Robert E. Lee surrendered at Appomattox Court House, but there is no account of when and how the reorganized 4th Michigan received this news, or that of the assassination of President Lincoln. They stayed at Jonesborough until April 20, and then began the trip back to Nashville with their division. The regiment arrived on the 27th and camped near the Murfreesboro Pike about six miles from town.[9]

Here they stayed through the month of May, and Colonel Hall was undoubtedly pleased when a brigade inspector declared, "I have never seen a Regiment in a better condition" than the reorganized 4th Michigan, giving much credit to the colonel and his command. The war was over now, and a grand review of the Fourth Corps was held on May 9 for Maj. Gen. George Thomas. Again the reorganized 4th Michigan received kudos, along with the 3rd Michigan, from an observer who noted their "excellent appearance and fine behavior." The men hadn't been paid in nearly half a year, and at last they got their money. This pay due them dated back to the early fall—the time when they'd still been in camp at Adrian.

As the reorganized 4th Michigan camped near Nashville in June, they, like other Union soldiers, were sure that any day now word would come that they were being mustered out and sent home. Instead, orders arrived saying that they were going to be sent down to New Orleans to counter the potential threat of the French invasion of Mexico.

The men weren't happy about this. "[T]here is much dissatisfaction prevailing among the men on account of the understanding which exist among them, and which has been circulated there through the papers, that they are to be sent to New Orleans as a menacing force against Maximillian," a Monroe newspaper reported. "The men say they enlisted to put down the rebellion, and now that the rebellion is put down, they wish to return to their homes." A visitor to the regiment and the reorganized 3rd Michigan reported that the men were willing to wait their turn to be mustered out, but now they were suspicious that the government "intends to hold them for the full three years" of their enlistment. "Many of them declare they will never go to New Orleans, and considerable demoralization is manifesting itself," the paper said.[10]

On the morning June 16 the regiment got on railroad cars for an overnight, 67-mile journey to a town given in a report by an officer as Johnsonville, where, with the rest of the division and corps, the men boarded steamships the next day. The reorganized 4th Michigan got on the *Kate Robison* and embarked down the Tennessee River to the Ohio River, stopping for a short period on the 19th at Cairo, Illinois, the point where the Ohio joins the Mississippi. That same day the journey continued on down the river toward Vicksburg; it took three days to get there. Then the steamboats continued on, arriving in New Orleans on the 24th. According to a later report, the soldiers "camped on the old [1812] battleground of New Orleans." Now a reunion of sorts took place between the reorganized 4th Michigan Infantry and the veterans of the original 4th Michigan, along with those who had enlisted in Captain Van Valer's company early in 1864. Those 172 men who had survived the last year of the war in Virginia were now where they asked to be months earlier, with the reorganized regiment. But the war had been raging then—now the fighting was over. The soldiers wondered why they weren't going home.[11]

Since the summer of 1864, of course, these men from the original 4th Michigan had been part of the 1st Michigan Infantry in the Army of the Potomac. The veterans hadn't wanted this, but there was nothing they could do. "A part of the old 4th Infy was assigned to the 1st Mich. Infty. after the old 4th was discharged," Albert Boies later explained, "but still claimed themselves as [part] of the old 4th." Boies wasn't exaggerating. In the regimental *Record of Service* volume printed by the state of Michigan decades after the war, these men from the old 4th Michigan are listed as having been placed on "detached service" with the 1st Michigan. A soldier's letter from the summer of 1864 states that the remnants of the original 4th Michigan joined their new outfit within about two weeks after the departure from Petersburg of those who hadn't reenlisted.[12]

"On the 5th of July we were turned over to the 1st Michigan, since which time we have been a part of it," wrote a soldier from Capt. Cornelius Van Valer's company, who identified himself only as "S." in a letter to a Detroit paper. "The men of the 4th are scattered throughout the 1st, save my own company." Van Valer's company became Company F in the 1st Michigan. The soldier who initialed his letter "J.H.A." was impressed with his new comrades from the 4th Michigan. "We have got some 'bully' good men by this consolidation, and it seems to give general satisfaction all around," he wrote. Of course, these men from the original 4th Michigan weren't very happy about how this came about. "The boys of the 4th Michigan complain bitterly of the manner in which their [former] officers treated them," J.H.A. continued. "They say they [the officers] gave their word and pledged their honors to stay with them three years more if they would only re-enlist as veterans, and now every one of the old officers skedaddle for home."

Though the men from the original 4th Michigan expected to be with the 1st Michigan temporarily, they soon decided their new officers and comrades were all right. "The officers of the 1st [Michigan] have treated us well," wrote "S" early in August 1864. "We like them generally. The Lieut. Colonel commanding [William A. Throop of Detroit] stands high in the estimation of all." Here they continued to fight Lee's army as part of the Fifth Corp, First Division, Third Brigade at Petersburg and on through the end of the war in Virginia.[13]

The absorbing of the newest recruits and the reenlisted veterans of the original 4th Michigan made for a reunion for George W. Owen, then about 25, from Monroe, and his teenaged brother C. W. Owen, who had joined the 1st Michigan in late March 1864. George and two other Owen brothers in different Union outfits had tried to discourage C.W. from enlisting, but to no avail. Because George and C.W. were in the same division they had periodically seen each other and worried about each other when their brigades were in the terrible battles of 1864. "George . . . lectured me a little because I had not taken his advice and kept out of the army," C.W. wrote about the first visit from his brother after arriving on the front that spring. But both came through the Overland Campaign, and the siblings had become true brothers-in-arms when the remnants of the old 4th Michigan were absorbed into the 1st Michigan at Petersburg. Owen noted that the addition of the 4th Michigan men "doubled our force, and they remained with us until the close of the war." C.W. and George Owen both survived the war.[14]

Another of the 4th Michigan veterans assigned to the 1st Michigan was Jacob Perine, from the community of Tekonsha. He had originally joined the 4th Michigan in the fall of 1862 and was wounded at Gettysburg. Perine had recuperated in New York area military hospitals over the course of many months, but once he was well enough to rejoin the Union army, his old regiment no longer existed. He was also sent to the 1st Michigan outside of Petersburg and was part of the last battles in Virginia.[15]

This was trench warfare at Petersburg, and Joel H. Barnes from Kalamazoo County, now about 30, was another of the veterans of the original 4th Michigan who experienced it. Barnes explained to one of his brothers that the troops learned to quickly dig trenches and "bomb proofs" (bomb shelters, essentially holes in the ground covered by logs) to protect themselves from mortars and artillery whenever they shifted into a new position. Barnes noted that he was writing his letter as he sat in his underwear in his trench, since he'd gotten the chance to boil his clothing—"cold water will not kill lice," he wrote, "but they are all done now. . . . I have burnd pretty bad going out in the sun washing but it had to be done. I had rather have my back burnd then to have the gray backs [lice] charging up and down nights and days." Within about a month's time, Barnes was wounded in action outside Petersburg.[16]

Other letters from veterans of the 4th Michigan sent back to Detroit from the Petersburg trenches showed that they continued to think of themselves as members of their original regiment rather than the 1st Michigan. The headlines over those published letters read: "From the Fourth

Infantry," and "The 4th Michigan Infantry." Nor was this matter of their regimental identity forgotten by their commanders and comrades. When the First Division of the Fifth Corps stormed Confederate fortifications outside Petersburg at a place called Peeble's Farm in late September 1864, an officer from the 83rd Pennsylvanian would write, soldiers of the 4th Michigan acted as skirmishers for their brigade and drove the Confederate pickets back to their breastworks. Just a few days before this battle, their division commander, Brig. Gen. Charles Griffin, in his communications referred to the remnant of the original 4th Michigan as a "battalion" within his Third Brigade. These references show that although these men were assigned to the 1st Michigan, they were proud of their 4th Michigan origins and wanted to be identified as such.[17]

These men would witness the spectacular blowing up of a section of Rebel fortifications at Petersburg by the laying of a huge mine (immediately preceding the infamous and unsuccessful battle of "the Crater"). They took part in the skirmishing and fighting at the Weldon Railroad in August and the capture of Confederate fortifications at the battle of Peeble's Farm (also known as Poplar Grove Church) on September 30, where Joel Barnes was wounded. They were part of the mission to destroy the Weldon railway line far to the south of Petersburg (the so-called "Applejack raid") between December 6 and 12, 1864, when Michigan soldiers and others from their brigade discovered and enjoyed hidden supplies of Rebel brandy.

They were involved in the battle at Dabney's Mill Run on February 6, 1865—a confused fiasco of a fight for the Union army, but one that it could afford. It was here that Van Valer, by then brevetted to the post of major, became acting commander of the 1st Michigan Infantry when the regiment's lieutenant colonel was wounded that day. That spring, the 4th Michigan's veterans and 1864 recruits took part in the push to the west that cut off Petersburg from any further supply from the rest of the shrinking Confederacy in the battles at Hatcher's Run on March 25, on the White Oak Road on March 29 and at Five Forks on April 1. These attacks stretched Lee's remaining forces thin enough that the Union army overwhelmed Petersburg's defenders and made Richmond untenable. Then they participated in the pursuit of Lee's army at Amelia Court House on April 5 and at High Bridge the next day, and the tiring marches that followed. And they were with the First Division and Fifth Corps when they blocked the way of the Army of Northern Virginia at Appomattox Court House, helping to trap and force the surrender of Lee.[18]

Because of this assignment to the 1st Michigan Infantry, some of the original 4th Michigan men who'd been present to witness the Union army's retreat from Bull Run in July 1861 were there at Appomattox Court House when Lee signed his surrender in April 1865. William H. Smith of Ingham County, a 4th Michigan veteran who had become a lieutenant in the 1st Michigan about four months earlier, wrote home that day, "I am so happy I dont know what to say."

> You know I dont drink but I realy think I should like a cup of tea about this time. Well at last we have realy broke the "Back Bone" of the Rebelion. We have had a hard Time of it I assure you, but I feel well repaid. . . . Many are bare foot as the country is rough and stoney. The Soles of my Boots are worn off and for the past Two days I have marched with my feet wound in pieces of cotton tenting. My feet are quite sore but I was bound to see the "Last Ditch" and believe to have found it, for I now consider the Rebelion virtually over.[19]

Lieutenant Smith told of the pursuit of the Confederate army, the parole of their men on the field, and the fact that Grant had allowed Rebel officers to retain their sidearms. "The best of it is the Rebs are as pleased over the affair as we are, and when the surrender was made known to them cheer after cheer went up along their whole line," he wrote. "Their 'Southern Pride' is thoroughly humbled, and I think a majority of them will be better citizens that before."

Smith was pleased and proud of the Army of the Potomac, and he said he "couldn't realize the state of affairs[,] it all seem[s] like a dream." The bands were playing "When Johnny Comes Marking Home," "Hail to the Chief" and "Home, Sweet Home," and the armies cheered in response. "Many, many are the hearts made glad this day, and many more will be by the news," he continued. "I suppose you are all crazy with joy up North." In addendums to the letter the next day, he related that "many of the Rebs are over taking supper with our men. They have a keen relish for a cup of Yankee Coffee. It is [a] jubilee for both armies—A Big Thing."[20]

Another soldier from the old 4th Michigan who had been there for the duration was Alanson R. Piper. A Lenawee County teenager when he joined the regiment along with his older brother Abel in the spring of 1861, Alanson Piper also stood in the ranks of the 1st Michigan as Lee's army surrendered. But he did that without his brother, for Abel had been killed in the 4th Michigan's first major skirmish at New Bridge in 1862. Now 22, Alanson wrote home to his folks that he was all right, but hungry "and feel as if I could eat most anything as I have had no rations for the last five days except fresh beef and corn"—that is, food that the soldiers foraged in the area of Appomattox Court House. But that was fine, he noted. "The men do not complain for we have gained a big victory and they feel quite good over it and think that this war will not last much more and anyway I do not think there will be any more fighting in this department except for bush whacking." As did other Michigan soldiers, Piper cut pieces of surrendered Confederate regimental flags as souvenirs and sent them home. "Enclosed you will find a star from the 34th North Carolina Regt. & after they had surrendered and stacked their arms in front of this regt. with their colors also a piece of silk from the 34th NC and a piece off of the 55th Va regt."[21]

Piper and Smith and their comrades in the 1st Michigan marched back to Washington and participated in the Grand Review of Armies with the Third Brigade, First Division, and Fifth Corps. On June 10 the remaining men of the original 4th Michigan left Washington and, traveling by train and steamboat, joined the reorganized 4th Michigan in New Orleans late that month—"a pleasure ride of about 2400 miles," one soldier joked.

A rumor reached Detroit that angry veterans of the old 4th Michigan mutinied on a steamer on the Mississippi as they made the journey, a story that had the men tying up their officers, seizing control of the ship, and turning it back upstream. The newspaper that printed the story stressed that it was just a rumor. But though the soldiers were indeed angry about being sent on to New Orleans, this hijacking seems to have taken place only in someone's imagination, for there appears to have been no fallout from it. The men did reach New Orleans for the rendezvous with the reorganized regiment, and no further reports about the supposed Mississippi mutiny appeared. The official transfer of those veterans into the reorganized 4th Michigan is dated July 1, 1865.[22]

New Orleans was not, however, the end of the journey for the soldiers of the reorganized 4th Michigan. Now they learned they were going to Texas. To the west there were still the threats of uncertainty and instability in Texas, with Indian attacks on settlers, rumors of Confederate activity in Mexico, and the French incursion. Some Rebel troops, refusing to stay in a reconstituted United States, had gone to Mexico, taking their weapons with them, and there were fears on the part of Union generals that the French were complicit in this. The reorganized regiment, with the corps of which it was part, would go to Texas to help keep the peace and project federal authority.

Of course, the Michigan soldiers were not happy and some vowed they wouldn't stand for it. "The men all think it a shame for the Government to send us off to this hot climate at this time of the year," wrote a member of the original 4th Michigan just before leaving for Texas. "The Government says the war is at an end—that not an armed traitor remains. Therefore why should we be sent here?" He said the men understood that the government might ask them to confront the French in Mexico, but that was not why they had enlisted. "We are now entitled to an honorable discharge," the soldier wrote. "There have been a good many men started for home or some other place, and I think a good many more will go when the Corps takes shipment to Texas." This soldier was not wrong. Before the reorganized 4th Michigan would muster out of the service, scores of men did desert, having decided they had done their duty and had their fill, now that the war was over.[23]

The Michigan soldiers left New Orleans on July 6, boarding steamboats for the Gulf coast village of Indianola, Texas, arriving four days later with the rest of the Second Brigade of the Third Division of the Fourth Corps. They started a grueling march in the summer heat that day, the 10th, and reached Green Lake the next day, a distance of about 20 miles or more. "One of our men died of thirst, and numbers [were] severely injured by heat and fatigue," a soldier from the reorganized 4th Michigan wrote. At Green Lake the regiment spent two terrible months, losing scores of men to disease, many because of bad water and terrible heat.

An officer tried to make a point of the awful conditions to the folks back home. Lt. Samuel Gillespie from Company B wrote late that summer of the soldiers rushing out to do battle with an alligator that had swum up "about twenty rods from shore" near their camp on Green Lake. Someone fired a shot from a three-inch rifled gun at the alligator, and this blast apparently stunned the creature. But when dozens of the soldiers rushed into the water with bayonets to force the beast to shore, the alligator plunged to the bottom of the lake below their feet. That caused the soldiers to beat a hasty retreat. But aside from his tale of the alligator confrontation, Gillespie's subtext was deadly serious. The stagnant Green Lake was the soldiers' only source of water, and it contained parts of animal carcasses, guts, and other refuse and waste. The lake was a watering hole to tens of thousands of cattle, so it was crawling with disease. Yet there was nowhere else for the men to bathe and get water for cooking, coffee, and drinking. "It is gratifying that soldiers can be so pleasantly situated," Gillespie wrote with sarcasm. It was an indeed a bitter situation, for scores of men died because of it. Other members of the regiment agreed.

"Some dissatisfied men say 'that there was no necessity for our going to Texas,'" wrote a man who signed his letter "Veteran." These doubters wondered if a politically connected general had ordered them there for purposes of egotism or career advancement or even for the purposes of land speculation, Veteran wrote. "The mortality among us is fearful," he reported bitterly, with as many as 10 to 20 Union soldiers dying each day. Why, they wondered, were they still there? A member of the reorganized 3rd Michigan Infantry, who was equally angry and disgusted when he described their experiences in a fall letter to a Detroit newspaper, contemptuously referred to the place as "Green Mudhole" and charged the region was only fit for "alligators, [water] moccasins, tarantulas, etc."[24]

On September 10 the brigade was ordered to march inland to San Antonio, a trip of about 170 miles. It took over two weeks. This occurred as their corps established a line that could move in support of other Union army forces on the Rio Grande or to the east. Assistant Surgeon Joseph Griswold of the reorganized 4th Michigan said the soldiers marched out across the open prairie on "one of the hottest" mornings he'd ever known; soon men were dropping of sunstroke in the blazing heat. Miraculously no one died, but more than 60 fell out on the march. Griswold said men collapsed "as though pierced by a bullet," but a heavy rain blew in, lasting for two hours. That, he wrote, saved the lives of half the men who had dropped in the heat. The regiment made about 10 miles and covered about 12 miles the day after, reaching the Guadalupe River and the town of Victoria. Here Griswold was ordered to set up a convalescent camp for those too weak or sick to go on. Soon the men were referring to Griswold as "the little doctor." The others continued the march to San Antonio, where they arrived on the 26th and camped near town with other Union troops by the Salado River.

By mid-October other regiments serving in their brigade received orders to be mustered out, and some of the regiment's senior soldiers, volunteers from the original 4th Michigan, were sent home. But the morale of those who remained was poor. Griswold, who rejoined the reorganized 4th Michigan's camp just outside of San Antonio, estimated that half of the brigade wanted to desert, but men only stayed on duty because they were owed so much back pay. In fact, records for the reorganized 4th Michigan on file with the state of Michigan show that scores of men did desert over the period from the summer of 1865 on into 1866. The records of these men were cleared years later when acts of Congress were passed, granting them honorable discharges.

Late in November their camp was moved into town and the regiment placed on provost (police) duty. Griswold noted that the Texas weather could change dramatically from pleasant temperatures to stifling heat to bitter cold. He visited the Alamo, suffered a bout of diarrhea, and, like other soldiers, wondered when they would go home. "Uncle Sam and his excellency 'Andy' [President Johnson] don't seem inclined to part with us," the young surgeon wrote as the month ended.[25]

The surgeon celebrated part of Christmas with a local family and was impressed with the Tejano-Mexican celebration of the holiday with fireworks, pageantry, the burning of incense, and High Mass. Though he dismissively referred to the locals as "beaners," he had to concede their religious devotion and reverence. He dined and socialized with a onetime Confederate family and walked two "Texas damsels" home before retiring with a good Cuban cigar that night. While Griswold was snubbed by one daughter of a bitter Rebel woman—the young lady had wanted to borrow the surgeon's horse, but refused to go riding with him that January—he noted, perhaps with envy, that Capt. George Rathbun of Adrian became engaged to another Union officer's daughter there in Texas and Lt. Andrew Weir, from Hillsdale, brought his pretty young wife from Michigan.[26]

The duty of the reorganized 4th Michigan dragged on. On January 1, 1866, Colonel Hall was put in charge of what was called the "sub-district of San Antonio" by his superiors at the army's Central District of Texas Headquarters. The area he was responsible for was "east of the Nueces [*sic*] River and north of the Counties of Live Oak, Karnes, DeWitt" and the Colorado, Lavaca, and Navasota rivers. Griswold heard that his regiment would be home by the Fourth of July, 1866, and that may have been a reason that a number of soldiers of the regiment deserted or went absent without leave—they simply had no intention of sticking around that long. A report filed that month by the adjutant of the 4th Michigan showed that 105 men had deserted. Another 99 had died of disease and a whopping 357 men had been discharged for disability, the overwhelming majority of these men because of illness.

Michigan's top military official, State Adjutant General John Robertson, came to see the regiment in San Antonio in February, and the company of the surviving veterans of the original 4th Michigan were soon mustered out, "probably the result of his visit," the young surgeon wrote. Robertson promised that the rest of them would soon follow, perhaps as soon as two months' time. By early March the vast majority of veterans of the 4th Michigan were out of the army—"most of these are probably home by this time," wrote William Bradley, the regiment's adjutant.

Yet many of the Michigan deserters were still in Texas, he noted, angry about the fact they'd been kept in the service so long after the war's end. But when they heard the entire reorganized regiment was going to be mustered out within weeks, many of these men came back, Bradley claimed. It seems some decided that it was better to stay put in the army for the time being, and leave with their last pay and a good record, now that the end of their service was truly in sight. Not all accounts agree with this however. One soldier from the reorganized regiment wrote that "a large number" of men from the 4th and 3rd Michigan regiments were gone and obviously had not come back.[27]

Colonel Hall and detachments of soldiers were sometimes shifted to different towns during this time. At one point during the regiment's Texan sojourn, the *New York Herald Tribune* published a critical report that Hall had "prostituted his [U.S.] flag by ordering it to be 'wrapped up' during the march through the streets of La Grange, a town about halfway between Austin and Galveston. "This was done in deference to the wounded feelings of the reconstructed," the paper charged. But another newspaper quickly denied that report, dismissing the attack on Hall as slander and defending him as an earnest Union man who had served his country gallantly and faithfully. "The above is totally untrue, and the Tribune has been misinformed, probably by some Texan rebel angered against Col. Hall for his straightforward course in that disloyal region," the editor fired back.[28]

The long-awaited orders for the reorganized 4th Michigan's release from duty took longer than Adjutant General Robertson had promised, and trouble continued as men from the regiment and their comrades were kept waiting. "The Third and Fourth Infantry regiments are still here, or perhaps I should say a portion of them, for a large number have furloughed themselves without any official action to speak of and have left," wrote a soldier from the reorganized 4th Michigan. He complained it was harder to get a leave of absence in Texas than it was when the regiment had been facing the Confederates.

"This has given rise to great dissatisfaction and from this cause has arisen a great deal of trouble," the soldier wrote. "The volunteer argues that he enlisted to put down the rebellion. The rebellion has been put down[.] Why then, is he still in the service?" He noted that the soldiers saw only injustice and ingratitude in being kept in the service unnecessarily; the people of Texas were professing loyalty to the Union. On top of that, the men were facing disease and a harsh climate and they were being paid badly. "Cannot something be done to relieve us from this situation?" he asked. "Has the Peninsula State forgotten those who ever proudly maintained the honor of Michigan?"

The days dragged on, but the orders finally came. It was reported in Detroit in mid-May: "We learn from Adjutant General Robertson that the Fourth Michigan Infantry, now in Texas, has been ordered mustered out of the service." On May 26, 1866, the remaining soldiers of the regiment were mustered out at Houston. During the reorganized 4th Michigan's time, only one man had been killed in action and six died of wounds, but 141 men died of disease, and more than twice that number had been discharged for disability, mainly from illness and mainly in Texas. Over 100 men had deserted, and nearly 40 officers and men had resigned or been dismissed by order.

It was a long, slow trip of more than two weeks for the remaining 235 men of the reorganized 4th Michigan to get home, traveling with the reorganized 3rd Michigan Infantry. From Houston, the soldiers were shipped to Galveston, where a steamer took them to New Orleans and then Cairo, Illinois. There the men boarded trains that brought them back to Michigan, arriving in Detroit on at 1:00 P.M. on Sunday, June 10.[29]

Those soldiers of the reorganized 3rd and 4th Michigan regiments who reached Detroit "were immediately marched to the barracks" of the old Fort Wayne. They were, a local paper reported, "the last of those whose record in the great rebellion just closed is now a matter of history" to return home. "The troops brought with them from Texas many curiosities and remembrances of their visit to the Lone Star State, for which they seemed to have a peculiar regard," the paper said.

Local reception committees had been preparing to greet returning Michigan troops in the city, but the notice of the coming of the 3rd and 4th Michigan regiments that Sunday afternoon had been short. The big reception for these men, therefore, came the next day with speeches by Michigan governor Henry H. Crapo, who had succeeded Austin Blair, and William Jennison Jr. of the Soldiers Aid Society. A large banquet was prepared for them that evening at the barracks, with hundreds of soldiers seated at two long rows of tables.

"[T]he veterans did full justice to the handsome spread, and attended as they were by fair hands, they could not but be satisfied as well as gratified with the feeling exhibited towards them," the *Detroit Free Press* said of the feast. A journalist covering the banquet thought Jennison's speech was too political to be appropriate for the returning soldiers—the speech, he said, was better suited for "the stump." But he noted that Crapo, in a short address, asserted that it had been necessary to have the soldiers in Texas, even after so many thousands of others had returned home, "to overawe the spirit of rebellion existing in the hearts of the people." How the soldiers responded to that speech isn't clear, but once it was over, Col. Jairus Hall diplomatically proposed "three cheers for the ladies of the Soldiers Aid Society." On that point, at least, no one could disagree.

The men of the reorganized 3rd and 4th Michigan regiments roared their approval, and the band there for the occasion broke into the popular and sentimental air, "Home, Sweet Home." The next day, June 12, 1866, the men were paid, and these regiments were formally disbanded.

Those who came from the areas around Adrian and the southern tier of Michigan counties boarded westbound trains for home.[30]

It had been five years since Jairus Hall had first joined the companies that would go into the original 4th Michigan back in the spring of 1861, and now his service to his country was finally over.

CHAPTER 16

I Saw Passing a Great Army

IN THE EARLY 1870S THE SURVIVORS OF THE 4TH MICHIGAN, LIKE THOUSANDS OF OTHER VETERANS, began to gather at yearly reunions. The veterans of the regiment timed the event for the anniversary of June 20, the day the first volunteers who comprised the 4th Michigan were sworn into the service of the United States in 1861. For the next half-century these annual reunions were held in the southern Michigan towns (and on occasion, Indiana and Ohio communities) that had seen the men off to the war. The locations of the reunions included Adrian, Hillsdale, Hudson, Jonesville, Sturgis, Eaton Rapids, Lansing, Detroit, Litchfield, Monroe, Reading, Palmyra, North Adams, and Angola, Indiana. These events were put on with fanfare with the support of local merchants and politicians, local chapters of the Grand Army of the Republic, an important postwar veterans association, and their Women's Relief Committee counterparts. Women from these auxiliaries and local churches almost always had charge of the banquets and picnics that were central to the reunions.

News accounts show they were as much civic events as they were get-togethers for the veterans. Local officials, businessmen, and the veterans groups who hosted the gatherings planned entertainment, food, merchant sales, and even fund-raising so that visiting veterans would incur minimal expense, if any, to attend. Invitations were extended to all area men who had been in the Union army. Even a former Confederate soldier from a North Carolina outfit, the Reverend J. M. Barclay, whose name was also given as "Barkley" and "Burkley" and who lived in Hillsdale after the war, was invited to speak at the 1884 reunion. He was made an honorary member of the regiment.[1]

Patriotic and proud, with moments of laughter and remembrance, the gatherings allowed the former comrades-in-arms to enjoy each other's company and honor those who hadn't come home. When an ex-soldier from Hillsdale named Henry W. Magee gave a speech at the 1875 reunion about the regiment's history, "there was hardly a dry eye in the audience while he recounted the trials which they had endured." Surviving programs and reports on the reunions show there was always a speech and moment of silence or prayer for those who had died. More than 200 men from the regiment attended the 1875 reunion, or about half of the membership of the association of the original and reorganized 4th Michigan regiments, according to its 1876 roster.

Committees of GAR members, local officials, and volunteers greeted the veterans as they arrived at the train station of the host community, with the town decked out in flags and bunting. Attending veterans and their wives marched from the depot accompanied by brass bands, reception committees, militia and fire companies, and residents in their carriages. The processions were cheered as they trooped to the local meeting hall, or whatever venue was sufficient to accommodate them. There the veterans conducted a business meeting, electing officers, discussing memorials, and choosing the location of their next gathering. At the 1875 reunion the meeting was adjourned so the veterans could march back to the station to greet the arrival of their "old flag"—the original U.S. banner bearing the words "Defend It"—on the noon train.[2]

Mrs. Josephine Wilcox, the woman who had presented that flag to the 4th Michigan in June 1861, was for years its keeper, and it was routinely brought to the reunions. Newspaper accounts of the reunions don't mention the presence of any other 4th Michigan regimental banners. Often Mrs. Wilcox and the widow of George Lumbard, Mrs. J. D. North of Jackson, made ribbons or badges for the association members.[3]

Then the ex-soldiers convened for dinner or picnic at a local church, hall, or pavilion. Often scores of guests attended with the veterans, and hundreds of members of the public, too. The highlights of these dinners were speeches, prepared by selected veterans and others as responses to preplanned toasts—"To the old Fourth," "The old flag," "To the Ladies," and other topics. Some years, as in the 4th Michigan association's 1884 reunion in Hudson, a "grand regimental ball" capped off the night, held at the local opera house. Concerts and festivities were also scheduled for the reunions. But the years took their toll. At the 1884 reunion in Hudson, 75 veterans of the regiment attended. When the reunion was held in the town of North Adams in 1898, 60 veterans were present. In 1917, the year the United States entered World War I, 33 survivors attended the reunion in Jonesville. And so it went.[4]

Reports about the reunions in the 1870s and 1880s show the members of their association discussed plans to place a memorial to Harrison Jeffords at Gettysburg, a matter that was resolved when the state of Michigan sponsored a monument there and at other locations on the battlefield where regiments from the state had fought. As plans for those monuments took shape in 1889, Thaddeus Huff, a Hillsdale County farmer and veteran who had been wounded at Gettysburg at the age of 22, traveled to the battlefield as a delegate from the 4th Michigan to a national committee dealing with the location of monuments. His job was to help identify the place where Jeffords had fallen. Just a few years earlier, the regiment's artist, Charles Gruner, sold a picture he'd made of the Gettysburg battle "for the nominal sum of ten dollars" to the 4th Michigan association. The association, in turn, intended to sell Gruner's picture for a higher price and put the proceeds toward the proposed marker on the battlefield. Reports about previous reunions state the association also had a painting depicting the 4th Michigan's fight at Malvern Hill—a picture also rendered by Gruner—which was apparently sold by lot as a fund-raiser for a monument to Dwight Woodbury, whose body had been returned to Adrian. What ultimately became of these battle paintings by Gruner is unknown.[5]

Yet by 1888, perhaps as a result of the state's commitment to erect Gettysburg monuments, the 4th Michigan survivors voted to use these funds intended for a Jeffords memorial to instead recover George Lumbard's remains from the Wilderness, return them to Hillsdale, and get an expensive marker for his grave. But the effort by those who tried to locate Lumbard's burial place in Virginia apparently didn't succeed. Details of grave diggers removed the Union dead from the Wilderness shortly after the war for reburial at Fredericksburg, and only a comparatively small number of them could be identified.[6]

The same year the 4th Michigan association took the vote on a monument for Lumbard, Orvey S. Barrett published a brief regimental history titled *The Old Fourth Michigan Infantry* that centered on his old Company B. The members of the 4th Michigan regularly recounted their regiment's experiences and battles and losses in speeches and toasts at reunions, but in 1889 the members discussed the idea of putting their companies' individual histories down on paper, with a "historian" chosen for each company to complete this job. Ultimately only Henry Seage seems to have carried out this assignment, preparing what he titled *History of Co. E, 4th Mich. Infantry, 1861–1864*. It took somewhat longer than a year to complete. The 40-page printed booklet, based largely on Seage's diaries, bears the statement that it was "approved by the old 4th Infantry association at its meeting, June 22, 1897."[7]

The veterans showed their respect for fallen comrades in more than just speeches and moments of silence. When their association met in Adrian in 1889, the old men took the time to march to the sound of fife and drum to Oakwood Cemetery, to the grave of Dwight Woodbury. Those who couldn't make the march were driven out in carriages. The veterans formed around the grave, and the president of their association, Albert V. Cole, a former Lenawee County man who had come from Nebraska to take part in the reunion, read aloud the inscription on the stone. As the veterans filed by his marker before the march back to town, each man removed the flower that had been pinned to his jacket and placed it on the colonel's grave.

John Dean, an English-born Hillsdale County farmer who joined Company H at the age of 28 and saw the finish at Appomattox with the 1st Michigan, also survived the subsequent Texas sojourn with the reorganized 4th Michigan. He suffered wounds and illness in the war and married a volunteer nurse who took care of him in Baltimore. Though his wounds ultimately put him in a wheelchair, he fathered 10 children back in the community of Litchfield and regularly attended regimental reunions. He was, a reporter wrote in 1896, "an interested participant in all the [reunion] exercises," and his comrades made sure he was well cared for.[8]

Irvin Miner, the soldier and diarist from Company F who had been captured at Gettysburg, had spent months in Confederate prison, and ultimately rejoined the reorganized 4th Michigan, hadn't seen Albert Boies since that terrible evening of July 2, 1863. Boies had been captured in or near the Wheatfield, too, but had escaped that night back to Union lines. After the war, Miner eventually moved to the town of Reed City, nearly 200 miles northwest of where he'd lived in 1861, so he didn't see Boies again until the regiment's 1916 reunion. "[B]ut they recognized each other at once as they had not changed like many others," a report said of their meeting. Miner died the next year.[9]

A reunion cleared up a major misunderstanding left over from the war involving Oscar A. Janes, who'd lost an arm when the 4th Michigan was in the trenches outside Petersburg. At the regiment's first reunion in Hillsdale, Janes ran into his old sergeant, James Dickerson. Janes, a student at Hillsdale College before the war, had been wounded as night fell on June 22, 1864, but his comrades thought he had died. In fact ambulance crews had carried him off the field to a hospital. But the next day, Dickerson identified and buried the body of a soldier he thought was Janes, reporting him killed in action. Very much alive, Janes went back to Hillsdale and began practicing law there in 1871. Janes recognized Dickerson at the 4th Michigan's first regimental reunion and greeted him by name. But Janes's former sergeant just couldn't figure out who was talking to him. "Who are you, anyway?" Dickerson finally asked.

"Why, I am Janes, of your company," he replied. "Don't you know me?"

Jim Dickerson was stunned, since standing before him was man he was sure had been killed in action back in 1864.

"My God!" Dickerson exclaimed, staring at Oscar Janes in surprise. "I buried you at Petersburg!"[10]

Regimental reunions weren't the only venues in which the former soldiers gathered. Some were active members of their local GAR posts and in veterans affairs for decades. Some continued to live in or near the southern Michigan communities they had left to serve in the war. For years in the Hillsdale area Company E veterans Tad Huff, Mark Taylor, and William Bird assembled with their wives and families, along with George Kinney of Company B and others on New Year's Day for dinner. Old soldiers from Company F also held annual reunions beginning in the late 1880s. Smaller than a regimental reunion, this company's get-togethers were hosted at the Hudson home of Benjamin E. Westfall, a former officer who was one of six veterans from his area to attend the 50th reunion at Gettysburg in 1913 of the survivors, North and South, who fought there. Surviving to the age of 86, Westfall tragically drowned, apparently while fishing in July 1925 on a lake near the town of White Cloud. His body was brought back to Hudson, where he was buried.[11]

Time marched on, and the small towns and villages that had sent the men off to war no longer used wells to get their water, but now had waterworks and indoor plumbing. There was telephone service, new factories and new technologies and conveniences. Not long after the turn of the century, the old men who came to the reunion weren't given tours of the hosting community in carriages, but in automobiles. "The men of the Old Fourth all falling like leaves," the *Hudson Gazette* opined about the reunion there in 1916. "At the reunion in Hudson twenty years ago the opera house was half filled with members of the regiment; now a half a hundred were gathered."[12]

By 1922 the regimental association became the keeper of what was said to have been Harrison Jeffords's sword when the GAR post at Dexter went out of existence. A news report on that year's reunion said that the 4th Michigan association would keep the sword until its old men were gone, at which time the Michigan State Pioneer and Historical Association in Lansing (predecessor of the state's historical commission) was to receive it. Whether that sword was turned over is not known, but a sword that was said to have been Jeffords's is owned today by a private collector. In the same vein, members of the regiment's association some years earlier became increasingly concerned about their beloved first regimental flag and its safekeeping, what with its possession by a woman who was likely older than most of them. Eventually Mrs. Wilcox and her family relented. By 1898, the colors were being kept in the office of Lester Salsbury, a veteran who'd been badly wounded at Gettysburg but who was then practicing law in Hudson. At the turn of the century, possession of the flag passed to the regiment's old major, James Cole, who had become an evangelist and who kept the colors in a bank vault for a time and also at his home. In 1901 the flag was turned over to the state of Michigan, where it joined other regimental flags carried by her soldiers.[13]

Albert H. Boies believed that, based on government pension records, about 100 members of the 4th Michigan were still alive in 1923, and most of them must have been in their 80s. But now only a handful could attend the reunions. He, Jacob Perine, and two other survivors, Albert W. Veness and Herbert D. Bryan, both of Hillsdale, gathered with their families in Hillsdale in 1928; their dinner at a hotel was sponsored by a local doctor, and the news of their gathering shared space in the local newspaper with a headline about pilot Amelia Earhart in London following her transatlantic flight. "The meeting yesterday was the first that has been held with less than twelve members present," the newspaper said of the reunion. "Time, however, has played havoc with their ranks and the few other men who remained from the old 4th were too feeble to attend."[14]

This gathering, it was reported, was the final reunion of the 4th Michigan.

Not all former soldiers of the 4th Michigan who survived the war attended the reunions, and some continued to suffer its ravages. A shoulder wound Larned B. Partridge of Company B suffered in May 1864 when members of the regiment stormed Rebel rifle pits caused him unrelenting pain, and his suffering was such that friends and family said he was depressed. "[B]efore he was wounded he was cheerful and lively," Orvey Barrett wrote about the ex-soldier. But after leaving the army, Partridge complained there was no relief from pain in his head and shoulder. "[H]e seemed very down hearted and despondent," Barrett wrote; he and others believed that Partridge's inability to work and the pain had driven him mad.[15]

In October 1867 Partridge had asked an old comrade from the 4th Michigan, John Rintz (also given as Rentz), to have a beer with him. Rintz, then in his early 30s, formerly a sergeant, was a shoemaker and store clerk in Blissfield. He recalled Partridge said that "this was the last drink he would take," because he was tired of living and would be "better being dead than alive." About a week letter, Partridge walked into the woods and hanged himself. Rintz lived to be an old man and take part, however briefly, in the new technological age, founding the Blissfield Telephone Company in 1897.

Some survivors of the regiment had distinguished careers in public service and politics.

Oscar Janes served as Hillsdale's city clerk, city attorney, county circuit court administrator, probate judge, and paymaster general on the staff of Michigan governor Russell A. Alger. He also served in the state senate, was a federal pension agent in Detroit, and served on the board of Hillsdale College. And he was an official in the state GAR and an officer of the 4th Michigan association for years.[16]

Moses Luce, who mustered out of the regiment in 1864, also returned to Hillsdale to finish college and went on to law school in Albany. He went back to his home state of Illinois, married, and practiced law, representing banks and railroads. In 1873 he headed west for his health to San Diego, where he went into the practice with an ex-Confederate soldier. He continued to represent big businesses and invested in real estate and mining; he also served as a county court judge for several years and as San Diego's postmaster, appointed by President William McKinley, with whom he went to law school. He helped organize the city's public library and to establish the local Unitarian Church. In modern times, he has been considered by local historians to be one of the most important guiding forces in the shaping of the city of San Diego. Luce, the one member of the regiment to be awarded the Medal of Honor by Congress in 1895 for the rescue of his friend Asher LaFleur, died at the age of 91 on April 29, 1933. He had outlived his comrade LaFleur by some 27 years.[17]

John C. Tarsney, one of three Tarsney brothers to serve in the 4th Michigan's Company E, also went on to a notable career in law and politics. John admitted years later that he was not yet 17 when he enlisted, but lied about his age. His older brother James was killed at the Wilderness, while Tom (whom Henry Seage said had dropped or surrendered the regimental colors at Gettysburg) survived the war. John Tarsney, who was only 18 when he was wounded and captured at the same battle, emerged from the war with what was one of the stranger stories of escape to come out of the regiment.

John Tarsney was taken to Belle Isle and then to Andersonville, and finally to Savannah and Milan, Georgia. In the latter prison camps, Tarsney was a member of the Union prisoners' own police force, self-organized squads of soldiers who suppressed predatory criminal activity among the prisoners. In November 1864, some 17 months after he'd been captured, word spread among the prisoners at Milan that a number of men were to be released. Usually these were the sickest and most disabled prisoners; Tarsney, still reasonably healthy, learned that his name wasn't on the list.

As Tarsney finished his patrol in the camp that night, he talked with a dying man, John Francis of the 54th Pennsylvania. Francis's name *was* on the list; Tarsney made Francis as comfortable as possible and they talked for a while. But when Tarsney returned the next morning to check on him, Francis was dead. Tarsney quickly decided to switch identities with the dead man, pinning a note on Francis's shirt that identified him as John Tarsney of the 4th Michigan. When John Francis's name was called that evening to join the men leaving the prison camp, Tarsney, feigning sickness, took his place. Though he had to convince a Union officer to go along with the ruse, and he was questioned by suspicious Confederates, his identity switch succeeded. John Tarsney was returned to Union lines and rejoined what remained of the old 4th Michigan, by then assigned to the 1st Michigan outside of Petersburg. He would participate in the last battles in Virginia and witness the surrender of Lee.

John Tarsney mustered out of the service in 1865 and went home to Hudson to finish high school. He enrolled in the University of Michigan's law school, graduating in 1869. He married and moved to Kansas City, where he was elected to the post of city attorney and, in 1888, to the U.S. Congress. He was later appointed an associate justice of the Supreme Court of the Oklahoma Territory by President Grover Cleveland, serving in that capacity for three years before returning to Kansas City. Tarsney died a month short of his 75th birthday in September 1920. He outlived his brother Tom, who also became an attorney after the war, by more than 18 years. Tom Tarsney died at the age of 59, probably of heart disease, in Pueblo, Colorado, in the spring of 1902.[18]

William W. Duffield of Detroit, who served for several months as the lieutenant colonel of the 4th Michigan, went on to command the 9th Michigan Infantry and then a brigade in the Army of the Cumberland. He was wounded and captured, but survived. An engineer by training, after the war he worked building railroads and surveying land and served in the Michigan Senate. He also got federal appointments to superintend surveys of the U.S. coast and serve on the board that oversaw the operations of lighthouses.

Scotland-born George Spalding, who'd been a Democrat in the town of Monroe before the war, was a Republican ever after. He became an attorney and served his community as mayor, school board president, congressman, banker, and in other capacities. Having resigned from the 4th Michigan as a captain early in 1864, he'd gone on to be the lieutenant colonel of the 18th Michigan, the provost marshal of Nashville, Tennessee, and the colonel of a Tennessee cavalry regiment that battled Rebel troopers and irregulars, suffering further wounds and earning a brevet rank of brigadier general. When he died in 1915, he was remembered as one of the leading citizens of his community for the past half-century.[19]

George Maltz, a Detroiter who enlisted in the 4th Michigan as corporal and left it as lieutenant and adjutant, worked as a banker and lumberman after the war and also as a cashier for the IRS. He later moved to Alpena, where he founded a bank and served as mayor. He was also elected to serve as a regent for the University of Michigan and later as state treasurer.

Jonathan W. Childs, who had served as major, lieutenant colonel, and colonel of the regiment up to his mysterious resignation in November 1862, rejoined the army about a year later as a captain of Company D of the 2nd U.S. Colored Troops and served beyond the end of the war. He earned his law degree while serving in Florida and was active in Republican politics there during Reconstruction, holding various county and state offices, legislative and judicial, and also federal Interior Department and Internal Revenue collector's posts. He married in Georgia in 1873 and lastly worked as a clerk in the U.S. government's Land Office Surveying Division in Washington, D.C. He died at age 62 on May 24, 1896, of what was characterized as "disease of bladder and kidneys."

Childs was given a pension after the war, having suffered pleurisy during his time in the 4th Michigan because of his exposure to the cold and wet, but his widow Frances tried for decades to show that his kidney disease and death were also linked to his service. Several former officers and men of the 4th Michigan gave affidavits that he'd been ill and in pain before his resignation in November 1862, and a family member said he'd had no urinary problems before his service. A sympathetic U.S. Congress approved an increase in her monthly widow's pension to $30 a month in 1901, but it appears that she never succeeded in convincing the government that Childs died as a result of war-related sickness or condition. Records suggest that as late as 1907 she was still trying to prove her late husband's case.[20]

George Yates, the handsome young man who'd gone from the regiment to serve on the staff of the brigade of which the 4th Michigan was part, survived his wounding at Fredericksburg and went home to Michigan, where he again met George Custer early in 1863. They became good friends. That spring, Custer introduced Yates to a Union cavalry commander, Gen. Alfred Pleasanton. Yates became a staff officer, serving with Pleasanton in the Army of the Potomac and then in Missouri and Kansas, even after many of his comrades had mustered out of the original 4th Michigan in June 1864.

Of course, Custer became a brigadier general and war hero. After a brief postwar marriage in St. Louis and a stint in Washington, D.C., as a government clerk, Yates was back in army in 1866—this time as a lieutenant in the 2nd U.S. Cavalry Regiment and soon after as captain in the 7th U.S. Cavalry, where he took part in Indian battles on the frontier. His friendship with Custer continued to shape the events of Yates's life, his second marriage, and ultimately, his death. Historians believe Yates was probably in command of two companies, one of the wings of the five-company force of the 7th Cavalry, that went into battle at the Little Big Horn on June 25, 1876. Yates's body, scalped and mutilated, was found down the slope from that of his friend, at the place that has since been known as Custer Hill.[21]

William F. Robinson, who'd enlisted as a sergeant in the 4th Michigan and left as a captain, also met with violent death in the west shortly after the war. A brief biography of Robinson noted that the young dentist had been in practice with his father in Ohio before the war and had traveled to New Orleans before returning to Michigan and joining the 4th Michigan. After surviving battles and a wound at Gettysburg, Robinson, who preferred the title "Captain" rather than "Doctor," was reportedly "killed later by Indians at Tucson, Arizona," according to one history. But a news notice of his death filed with family papers stated Robinson was stabbed to death by a group of Mexicans who jumped him on the night of May 11, 1867. Robinson, on his way to California on a business trip, had stopped in the town to visit a friend serving in the U.S. Army's quartermaster department. The Mexicans had lost a bar brawl in a nearby saloon that night, and once thrown out, decided to get even with the next American they came across. That was Robinson, who had nothing to do with their fight. "He was a worthy young man and esteemed by all who knew him," a newspaper said of him.[22]

Albert H. Boies, who had joined the 4th Michigan as a teen from Hudson, lived out most of the rest of his life in his old hometown, working at almost every sort of railroad job and various government inspector positions, too. He enjoyed traveling and for a time appeared with three other veterans in a vaudeville musical act that may have been a kind of reprise of his performance as a cadet who had accompanied the local volunteers to 4th Michigan rendezvous in Adrian back in May 1861. He served as a recruiting officer in both the Spanish-American War and World War I. He also contributed to the historical record of his old regiment by publishing articles, based on his war diaries, in his local newspaper. Boies collected Indian artifacts, outlived his wife, and died at the age of 86 in December 1930. The diary he had in his pocket when a bullet tore into it and knocked him senseless at Malvern Hill remains in the Hudson Museum. "Men are like roosters," Boies reportedly remarked to President Woodrow Wilson about the inevitability of war. "They will fight and there are a lot of things that they will fight about."[23]

Jairus Hall, who'd enlisted in the 4th Michigan in the spring of 1861 and ended up as the colonel of the reorganized regiment, was given the honorary rank of brigadier general for his dedicated service. Hall headed to Colorado in 1866 and became a bank manager, but he was too much an adventurous spirit to stay behind a desk. He also entered the silver-mining business and soon went into it on a full-time basis, developing an operation in a mountain valley that was given his name. He also invested in other mines and served in Colorado's territorial legislature. Hall reportedly won and lost fortunes, risked his life (and nearly lost it) hunting grizzly bears in the Rockies, and became an electrical engineer. He eventually married an old friend's daughter in Jackson, Michigan, where they made their home. Hall outlived her and moved to London, where he died at the age of 63 in November 1903.[24]

James B. Dickerson, the former sergeant who thought he'd buried Oscar Janes at Petersburg, went home to Hudson after mustering out at the rank of lieutenant from the reorganized 4th Michigan at San Antonio early in 1866. An upstate New York native and family man, Dickerson had served with the original 4th Michigan but mustered out after the Seven Days battle in the summer of 1862. He rejoined with Van Valer's company in 1864. Dickerson survived the last year of the Civil War in Virginia and the terrible illness that plagued the Union soldiers in postwar Texas, but he couldn't outlast the infirmities of old age. In December 1909, he was struck by a freight train at the crossing on the east side of his hometown. Had the 80-year-old veteran been stricken at the train track and unable to move out of the way? Did he not hear its approach? Or had he decided to end his life? "We do not know the why or how," the hometown paper said of his death, "but surely this must teach us that the God who rules the universe knows best and in the end will make clear all dark things."[25]

Harrison Daniels, a young farmer living several miles from Tecumseh when he joined what became Company G in the 4th Michigan in the spring of 1861, returned home after mustering out in 1864. He resumed farming, married, raised a family, and was active in the Grand Army of the Republic and his church. As the years went by he eventually had to give up farming and purchased rental property to support himself and his wife. "He availed himself of every opportunity to impress on the younger generation the thought of Country and God and his services were often sought on Memorial Day and other occasions in the county," his local newspaper wrote. At the age of 75 he wrote a memoir of his experiences for his family. He lived for several years as a widower and died at the age of 90. In his reminiscence of the Civil War, Daniels fondly remembered and praised his old regimental chaplain, the Reverend John Seage, as a brave and good man, and also his sons, Henry and Richard Watson Seage. Daniels outlived them, but was sure he'd see them again in the next life. They had, he wrote, "all been mustered out into that Grand Army above, and I expect to meet them at that final reunion."[26]

Jacob Perine, who told the dramatic story of running from the trees at the edge of the Wheatfield with a wounded arm as his regiment was flanked and surrounded, survived the battles of the last year of the war in Virginia with the 1st Michigan Infantry Regiment and witnessed Lee's surrender. He went home to Michigan and rejoined his family, his father having moved from Tekonsha to the town of Albion during the war. Perine spent most of the rest of his long life there, living to see his 100th birthday and beyond, and to become Albion's last Civil War veteran.

His mind stayed sharp into old age. He enjoyed gardening, hated the New Deal, and voted Republican to the end, wrongly predicting in his 90s that the country had enough of FDR and would turn him out of office in 1936. He didn't like depending on others to read him the newspapers after his eyesight gave out, and he didn't mind listening to the radio to stay up on events, though he admitted he sometimes got disgusted with the playing of "too much jazz music." He was 102 when he died.[27]

Edward H. C. Taylor, who had begun the war as a officer, resigned his commission in a feud and spent the rest of his enlistment working his way up to the rank of sergeant major before mustering out in 1864, went home to upstate New York with a wound in his foot. Still a dyed-in-the-wool Democrat, according to an account left by a family member, he got into a controversy at home when he spoke his mind and voted in the election that year—apparently against Lincoln and the conduct of the war.

Taylor moved to California after the war, was involved in railroad building, married, and survived his first wife. Then he went on to Portland, where he worked as an auditor for a steamship company. He married the daughter of a businessman and went into the business of shipping grain overseas until a storm wiped out his investments. He moved his family to St. Paul, Minnesota. There he worked as an accountant and railroad auditor. For 25 years after the war, the wound in his right foot, received near Spotsylvania Court House, did not heal as small pieces of bone worked their way out.

"Doesn't that hurt terrible?" one of his children asked.

"Well, it is not too comfortable," he replied. Taylor told the child that the wound was the reason why he smoked his pipe and two cigars each day—a bad habit, he said, but one that allowed him to tolerate the pain without bothering others. (Of course, when family members later read Taylor's Civil War letters, they realized that he'd been using tobacco before he was wounded.) Taylor led the life of a quiet gentleman and died quietly, sitting in his chair after a Sunday dinner in the summer of 1905. He was 65.[28]

Orvey S. Barrett, who'd been wounded in the leg at Gettysburg and later wrote a short book about the 4th Michigan, went home, married, and worked as a carpenter until his old wound made him dependent on crutches to get around. Finally the disability meant that he could work no more. Less than three years before his death, he sent a letter to Gettysburg historian John Bachelder, praising his research. In an odd statement in which he said nothing about the mauling the 4th Michigan suffered in the Wheatfield and nearby woods, Barrett claimed that he and his regiment fought at Little Round Top on July 2. Of course, Barrett, like many of his comrades, had been wounded when his regiment was driven across the Wheatfield. According to his own book, he was not on Little Round Top. The 4th Michigan had not fought at that place, but had retreated to it and reformed there as the last Union counterattack was launched that evening, with the fighting coming to a close soon after. Barrett also told Bachelder that he witnessed Pickett's Charge on the next day as he lay in an open, unprotected area with other wounded—again, something at direct odds with his book, in which he said he was in a hospital and heard about developments on July 3 from others.

Barrett died in Adrian in February 1892. "I can see you all as you used to appear on the march, in battle, and in the quiet in camp," he wrote in a tribute to his comrades in his book about the 4th Michigan. "Your pranks and repartee are fresh in my memory," he wrote. "You all need to be proud of your record, and the part the glorious old 4th took in suppressing treason. A quarter of a century from now will close the roster for nearly all of us; a much shorter time for myself." Barrett was correct. Within about five years from the time he wrote those words, he was gone.[29]

The Reverend John Seage, the tough chaplain of the 4th Michigan shot by guerillas in the spring of 1863, had joined the reorganized regiment as chaplain, but he was soon put to work recruiting and then acting as chaplain for Union forces at Murfreesboro, Tennessee. He returned to White Pigeon after the war and also lived in Detroit and St. Louis. But he suffered chronically from asthma and hepatitis; the illnesses finally took his life as he visited his son Richard Watson Seage in Jersey City, N.J., in late November 1883. John Seage died just a few days before his 74th birthday.[30]

His son Henry S. Seage was discharged from the Union army in September 1864 outside of Petersburg at the completion of his three-year term. During the final three or four months of his service, he worked as a clerk at the First Division's supply depot. Henry Seage went back to Michigan, married, and raised a family, worked in banking (where he was associated with his old comrade, George Maltz) and went into the insurance business; he was a founding town alderman in Alpena. He was bothered by what he and others described as scurvy for the rest of his years, with doctors writing that it was disease of the liver that eventually took his life. He died in Lansing on April 9, 1899.

As did Orvey Barrett, Henry Seage sent a letter to Gettysburg historian Bachelder that cannot be reconciled with the account he recorded in his 1863 diary or with the facts recorded by others. In the letter, he wrote that his brother helped Colonel Jeffords "recapture" the regiment's flag at Gettysburg, though it was torn to pieces; that Jeffords was killed in the struggle; that he found his brother Richard on the battlefield at daylight the next morning; and that he also found Jeffords's body on the way out of the Wheatfield, where it had been left by stretcher bearers who "probably" discovered he was dead. Of course, this version of events is contradicted by the evidence of his own 1863 diary, by the report of his brigade commander, and memoirs, letters, diaries, and accounts of other officers and men who wrote that the flag was lost and that Jeffords actually died at a hospital on the morning of July 3. Henry's 1863 diary stated he that learned that day his brother was brought to the division hospital, clearly indicating that Richard Watson Seage had been carried off the field by others.

Richard Watson Seage survived his wounds, of course, and married a young woman on Staten Island in a ceremony performed by his father in April 1864. They had three children. Richard's medical and pension records show he lost the use of his right hand. He was part of the reorganized 4th Michigan, resided briefly in Franklin, Tennessee, and then Detroit, where he worked as a clerk. But he eventually went back east where his wife's family lived. There he worked for a time as a typewriter inspector. But the effects of his wounds worsened as the years went by, and Seage was eventually declared an "invalid" by the government pension office. He outlived his younger brother and father and died in New Jersey in November 1908. He was buried with his father on Staten Island.[31]

John Bancroft, the Massachusetts native and architectural draftsman who'd enlisted in Detroit and operated observation balloons for a time during the war, went back east, married, raised a family, and lived out the rest of his life in New Jersey. In 1907, filling out a pension form, Bancroft noted that he was "secretary of the Hammond Typewriter Co." Bancroft died on July 27, 1918; he was 80 years old.[32]

Michael Vreeland, the respected young lieutenant from Wayne County badly wounded at Gettysburg, had been made the lieutenant colonel of the reorganized 4th Michigan. He came back home and got married in the spring of 1865. Within a year, with the support of Jairus Hall and Governor Crapo, Vreeland was awarded the brevet rank of colonel and then brigadier general by the U.S. government for his bravery and faithful service. Vreeland was given a posting with the Internal Revenue office after the war, but he continued to suffer from his injuries, particularly the gunshot that had torn through his lung. It never completely healed. The government gave him a job as the lighthouse keeper at Gibraltar, Michigan, on the western end of Lake Erie. He suffered continued illness from his weakened constitution, yet he survived until January 1876, aged beyond his years.

"They tell me his sufferings in his last hours were dreadful to witness, but he did not cough much or strangle from two or three days previously," wrote his sister Laura; "his mind was perfectly clear." Vreeland was helped from his bed while it was being made up, and rested in a nearby chair. But when he went back into his bed, he turned pale. According to his sister, the old soldier put his finger on his wrist and realized he was dying. "I have no pulse, Mollie, have I?" he quietly asked his wife.

She felt for his pulse—it must have been so weak as to escape her detection. She hesitatingly replied, "No, Michael, you have not."

"I am dying now," he said. "Now all pray for me . . ." Sadly, the old soldier didn't pass away quietly or quickly, but was wracked with pain in his final hour. But he bade his friends good-bye, looked around for his sister and brother-in-law, who had not yet arrived, and expressed his love for his family. Then he closed his eyes and was gone. In addition to his wife, Vreeland left a young son and a baby daughter. But Vreeland had recounted stories of his war experience to family and specifically to his boy, who would pass them on to his own son.

Vreeland's descendants said that there was an ironic postscript to his story, a kind of testament to Army bureaucracy. As a company commander back in 1863 when he'd barely gotten off the Gettysburg battlefield alive, Vreeland was held accountable for the equipment Company I lost when it was wiped out on the regiment's right in the woods at the edge of the Wheatfield. But because he hadn't been able to fill out the required army equipment reports or returns in a timely fashion, he was held responsible for the loss of 22 Springfield rifles and related equipment—bayonets, scabbards, and other items—amounting to a estimated $373 in 1863 prices. Family historians say that the cost of the lost weapons and equipment was deducted from his pay. Vreeland and then his family attempted to get that money back from the army. As late as 1898, his grandson wrote, Vreeland's widow was still trying to recover the pay he'd been docked for the lost arms.[33]

Dr. David Chamberlain, the Hudson physician who served as surgeon and assistant surgeon for the 4th Michigan until his health gave out early in 1863, eventually recovered. He left Hudson after having resided there for 16 years, moving his wife, children, and practice to Toledo, Ohio. As he had in Hudson, Dr. Chamberlain was active in civic improvements and Masonic affairs. He remained a member and participant in the regimental association, sometimes serving as president and in other capacities. He was a popular figure and center of attention at reunions for years. "Dr. Chamberlain was a great favorite among the boys, and all have a kind and genial word to say for their old army physician and surgeon," one newspaper reported. But by the time he was in his late sixties, his health was declining, and he missed reunions for two years. When he made it to the 1895 reunion in Jonesville, the white-haired doctor surprised and delighted his old friends and was the center of attention from the moment he stepped off the train. The next night a large crowd gathered around a campfire in the park to listen him tell of his experiences, "cleaning up the muss" of the soldiers wounded in battle and caring for the sick. The job of an army doctor in war, he said, "was no soft snap."

Chamberlain wasn't able to attend the regiment's reunions in 1899 and 1900 and sent telegrams to the men he'd taken care of nearly 40 years before, expressing his regret. The old soldiers at the 1899 reunion in Jonesville responded by conveying to him "their best wishes for his kindly remembrance of them." Chamberlain died in Toledo two months after the 1900 reunion in Palmyra on August 22, just three months short of his 76th birthday.[34]

Between the reunions of the 4th Michigan association, with all the attending speeches, greetings, remarks, and toasts, the men who served with the regiment must have heard thousands of eloquent words about their battles and losses and their shared experiences. Those who attended the dedication of the Michigan monuments at Gettysburg in 1889 heard even more. Twelve of the men from the regiment who lived in the Hudson area traveled with a handful of younger friends and relatives to the dedication, along with about 30 other 4th Michigan comrades and hundreds of other state veterans. Their hometown newspapers carried accounts of their journey and the dedication of the 4th Michigan's monument, and the speeches and prayer given there were dutifully recorded and published. Lester Salsbury spoke of "the whirlwind of slaughter in the wheatfield," while Richard Watson Seage read a heroic poem he'd written about Gettysburg. Yet very little of their own thoughts and feelings were reflected in the reporting of that time. "The old soldiers were seemingly carried back over a score of years," wrote a man who traveled with the Hudson veterans, "to a time when their visit to Gettysburg was not a holiday, when the great battle was fought. Many had recollections like Comrade A[lbert] H. Boies, who carried Michigan roses to place on the grave of his soldier comrade, who died and was buried on the battlefield." Which of his friends that was Boies didn't say, but he admitted that the ceremony at the Wheatfield was moving. Boies noted that during what he called an impromptu address by Salsbury, "there were few dry eyes among the men who stood upon this same ground 26 years ago and fought for the Union and right." The ceremony closed with the singing of "Nearer My God to Thee."

Former lieutenant and quartermaster Robert Campbell said that about 50 members of the regiment gathered around the monument for a group photograph, and that the experience was indeed strange and moving. This was a place where the dead, dying, and wounded had literally covered the ground. "To the remnant of the regiment who again assembled upon this occasion it seemed like the awakening from a dream, the memories of the past, the thoughts of the present, that the war was over and the victory ours," he wrote. The veterans from Hudson said that they didn't regret attending the dedication, "but of course," an anonymous writer noted upon their return, "the half of said experience will never be told." Nor was that Albert Boies's last visit to Gettysburg. He returned again, 24 years later at the 50th anniversary of the battle with his surviving comrades from that area, Ben Westfall, John A. Dillon, Benjamin F. Bush, and Noah Webster, who had long since moved to California but came back to travel with his old friends to the battlefield. They were among a group of about 20 veterans of the 4th Michigan who attended.[35]

To the veterans of the regiment, these postwar reunions and speeches were fitting remembrance of their service and their sacrifice, since at no point during the war itself, or even at the disbanding of the original 4th Michigan in 1864 had a majority of those survivors ever been honored or feted in their home state. The first group of volunteers had come home from the war in a group of about 150 when their three-year hitch ended in June 1864, and they hadn't been treated as a returning regiment. Others who had joined the regiment later in 1861 returned in the fall of 1864 after having been assigned to the 1st Michigan. Those who had joined later in the war or reenlisted as "Veteran Volunteers" came back from Texas as individuals or in small groups late in 1865 and 1866. And scores of wounded and sick and debilitated soldiers had returned in painful, individual homecomings.

Given this long and varied mustering out of the soldiers of the 4th Michigan, perhaps one of the most memorable salutes came from Moses Luce, the former college student-soldier who had gone on to success as a lawyer and businessman on the West Coast. Luce proudly remembered his service with Company E. Speaking at a Memorial Day service in San Diego's Isle Theater just after the turn of the 20th century, he knew that about half of the men with whom he'd served in the war had died. The survivors, like him, were now old men. "Bright eyes have become dimmed; dark hair had become gray," he said. "Supple limbs and erect bodies have become stiffened and bent by years of toil and the vicissitudes of time."[36]

In his mind, though, Luce still saw a vivid picture of a powerful Union army as he recalled the days of mid-June 1864 when that army was on the move. Though Luce didn't speak of the ambivalence he may have felt with that memory—at that moment in time he had been headed to a last confrontation with Confederates at Petersburg with only a day left to serve in his hitch—he remembered the scene clearly. It was a memory of the 4th Michigan as part of an epic, something larger than life—the Army of the Potomac. They were part of history.

"It was my privilege to stand upon a hillside overlooking the deep waters of the James River," he told his audience about June 15 and 16, 1864, at Wilcox's Landing. "I saw passing a great army with all the material and equipment of war. I heard the continuous marching tread of its armed men and the roll of its cannon wheels as they crossed the bridge which, in a few hours, had been constructed by its engineers. For three days and nights, it moved towards the enemy. More than a thousand flags and banners streamed above them. Far down the river I could see hundreds of flags flying from the masts of the shipping which brought to this army the material and supplies of war."

Now when the old soldiers met, there would be no more pomp and pageantry as in the days when they were young, he knew. And although 40 years had gone by, and though he'd seen war and misery and death, it was a powerful picture Luce painted for his audience—the sight and the sound of endless blue columns marching, and transports and vessels moving on the water. Yes, the occasion for his address was to commemorate the dead. But his eulogy was alive with pride and the energy of that moment in 1864, the stunning view from the hillside in the bright morning light—the ranks of men, the James covered with ships, the flags floating on the breeze—a moment when victory had not yet been achieved, but when confidence was high and the Army of the Potomac was on the march with the clatter of hundreds of horses and wagons, the tread of thousands of feet, and the dust clouds rising in the Virginia sky.

Roster of the 4th Michigan Infantry Regiment

This roster was compiled with information from the Michigan *Record of Service*, vol. 4, service and pension records in the National Archives, and other military records and genealogical sources. All enlistments are for the 4th Michigan and for three-year terms of service, except where noted otherwise. The designation *VV* in parentheses indicates a Veteran Volunteer; for a description, see chapter 12.

A

Abbott, Henry H., Reading, Hillsdale County. Enlisted in Company E, corporal, June 20, 1861, at Adrian, age 22. Farmer living with his parents and seven siblings. Sergeant Sept. 1, 1862. Mustered out at expiration of term at Detroit, June 28, 1864. Resided in Reading after service.

Abbott, James G., Clinton County. Enlisted in Company K, June 20, 1861, at Adrian, age 21. Died of disease in New York City, June 1862. Buried in National Cemetery, Brooklyn, N.Y, Grave No. 29.

Abbott, Oscar B., Reading, Hillsdale County. Enlisted in Company E, age 17, Feb. 1863, for 9 months. Substitute for Griffith Grolaman, drafted Feb. 10, 1863, from Hillsdale. Discharged at Detroit at expiration of term of service Nov. 11, 1863. Resided in Reading and then California after service, a carpenter.

Abbott, Webster H., Hillsdale County. Enlisted in Company E, June 20, 1861, at Adrian, age 19. Brother of Henry Abbott. Discharged for disability at Beverly Ford, Va., Aug. 1, 1863. Resided in Reading after service.

Abrahamski, Paul (*VV*), Lenawee County. Enlisted in Company G, June 20, 1861, at Adrian, age 19. Farmer. Reenlisted Dec. 29, 1863. Died May 21, 1864, of wounds received in action at Wilderness, Va. Born in Germany.

Ackley, John, Hudson. Enlisted in Company F, June 20, 1861, at Adrian, age 23. Cabinet and chair maker. Wounded in action, hit in thigh, at Malvern Hill, July 1, 1862. Died Aug. 6, 1862; buried in National Cemetery, Brooklyn, N.Y., Grave No. 312.

Adair, James H., Williams, Ohio. Enlisted in Company B, June 20, 1861, at Adrian, age 22. Regimental wagoner.

Mustered out at expiration of term of service, June 30, 1864. Resided in Reading, Hillsdale County, after service. Died 1901. Buried West Reading Cemetery.

ADAMS, JAMES F., Monroe. Enlisted in Company A, June 20, 1861, at Adrian, age 24. Farmer; married. Father of a small son. Second lieutenant. Transferred Jan. 29, 1862, to 15th Michigan Infantry. Promoted first lieutenant April 1, 1862. Promoted captain Oct. 1, 1862. Wounded Oct. 3, 1862, Corinth, Miss. Resided in Saginaw after service.

ADAMS, JOHN Q. Enlisted in Company A, June 20, 1861, as corporal at Adrian, age 31. First sergeant. Transferred to 15th Michigan Infantry on Jan. 28, 1862. Promoted captain Oct. 1, 1862. Resigned June 18, 1864, with an honorable discharge.

ADAMS, WILLIAM C., Jackson County. Enlisted in Company D, June 20, 1861, at Adrian, age 23. Farmer. Discharged for disability at Minor's Hill, Dec. 1861 because of hernia. Lived at Grass Lake and Jackson after service.

AESENHUTH, AUGUST, Monroe County. Enlisted in Company G, June 20, 1861, at Adrian, age 20. Wounded May 5, 1863, at Chancellorsville, Va.; left leg amputated by Dr. French. Discharged for disability at Philadelphia, Oct. 6, 1863. Born in Germany.

AINSLEY, GEORGE, Calhoun County. Enlisted in Company C as sergeant June 20, 1861, at Adrian, age 20. Discharged for disability July 30, 1861. Resided in Marshall.

AINSWORTH, RILEY N., Ransom, Hillsdale County. Enlisted in Company E, June 20, 1861, at Adrian, age 21. Taken prisoner at Gettysburg, July 2, 1863. Died while a prisoner in Richmond, Va., Nov. 6, 1863.

AKERS, GEORGE W., Centerville, St. Joseph County. Enlisted in Company C, June 20, 1861, at Adrian, age 21. Laborer working at a hotel. Wounded in arm at Gaines' Mill, Va., June 27, 1862. Discharged for disability at Washington, D.C., March 12, 1863. Buried in Hillside Cemetery, St. Clair.

ALBAN, WILLIAM K., Macomb County. Enlisted in Company I as corporal, age 20. Deserted at Washington, D.C., July 15, 1861.

ALBION, JAMES R., Lenawee County. Enlisted in Company B as corporal, age 25. Father of a young son. Wounded in action July 1, 1862. Transferred to Invalid Corps, Sept. 30, 1863. Resided in Ovid after service.

ALCHIN, FREDERICK, Pittsfield, Washtenaw County. Enlisted in Company D, Sept. 19, 1861, at Hudson, age 25. Transferred to Invalid Corps, Sept. 30, 1863. Resided in Ovid afterward. Died Dec. 21, 1930, and buried Maple Grove Cemetery, Ovid. Born in England.

ALDEN, BUCKLEY A. Enlisted in Independent Company, Feb. 22, 1864, at Scipio, Hillsdale County, age 16. Wounded June 5, 1864. On detached service with Co. F, 1st Michigan Infantry, July 1864 at Petersburg, Va. Transferred to Co. K, reorganized 4th Michigan Infantry, June 6, 1865. Discharged at Detroit, Sept. 8, 1865. Died of lung disease at a Soldiers Home. Buried National Cemetery, Los Angeles.

ALDEN, JOHN A. (*VV*), Scio, Washtenaw County. Enlisted in Company H, as sergeant June 20, 1861, at Adrian, age 21. Student and brother of Samuel and Buckley Alden. Reduced in rank on Feb. 1, 1862, at his own request. Reenlisted Dec. 29, 1863. Detailed as clerk in military office, Detroit, from July 1862 to April 1864. On detached service with Co. H, 1st Michigan Infantry, July 12, 1864, Petersburg, Va. Transferred to Co. C, reorganized 4th Michigan July 1, 1865. Discharged at Detroit, Sept. 11, 1865. Resided in Kalamazoo.

ALDEN, SAMUEL A. Enlisted in Independent Company, Feb. 25, 1864, at Scipio, Hillsdale County, age 19. Died of disease at First Division Hospital, Petersburg, Va., Aug. 10, 1864. Brother of Buckley and John Alden.

ALDRICH, EUGENE, Steuben, Ind. Enlisted in Company B, June 20, 1861, at Adrian, age 19. Farm laborer. Discharged for disability Sept. 6, 1861.

ALDRICH, STEPHEN H., Washtenaw County. Enlisted in Company D, June 20, 1861, at Adrian, age 22. Farmer. Detached temporarily to 18th Rhode Island Lt. Artillery at Minor's Hill, Va. Deserted with John F. Andrews at Aquia Creek, Va., Aug. 22, 1862. On detached service from Co. E, 1st Michigan Infantry, July 2, 1864, at Petersburg. Discharged at expiration of term at Petersburg, Dec. 5, 1864. Buried Oak Hill Cemetery, Grand Rapids.

ALEXANDER, WILLIAM, Fulton County, Ohio. Enlisted in Company H, June 20, 1861, at Adrian, age 26. Farmer. Wounded in right hand during the Peninsula Campaign of 1862. Taken prisoner on the march to Orange Court House, Va., Nov. 27, 1863, during Mine Run Campaign. Discharged at Detroit, Jan. 31, 1865. Admitted to Soldiers Home, Dayton, Jan. 1, 1897. Died March 19, 1913, and buried at the Soldiers Home, Grand Rapids.

ALLEN, CHARLES, Steuben, Ind. Enlisted in Company B, June 20, 1861, at Adrian, age 22. Mustered out at expiration of term, June 30, 1864. Resided in Angola after service.

ALLEN, CHARLES E., Hillsdale. Enlisted in Independent Company, March 23, 1864, at Marshall, age 20. On detached service with 1st Michigan Infantry, Co. F, July 2, 1864, at Petersburg, Va. Transferred to Co. K, reorganized 4th Michigan, June 6, 1865. Discharged at Houston, May 26, 1866.

ALLEN, DELZON C., Hillsdale County. Enlisted in Company E, June 20, 1861, at Adrian, age 19. Missing in action at Malvern Hill, July 1, 1862. Discharged for disability at Detroit, Jan. 24, 1863. Resided in Grand Rapids after service. Buried Greenwood Cemetery, Orange County, Fla.

ALLEN, EDWIN K., Lenawee County. Enlisted in Company B, Sept. 23, 1861, at Hudson. Discharged for disability at Minor's Hill, Nov. 18, 1861.

ALLEN, H. LINDEN, Litchfield, Hillsdale County. Enlisted in Company H, June 20, 1861, at Adrian, age 18. Farmer. Discharged for disability Sept. 27, 1862, at Fortress Monroe, Va. Resided in Ovid after service.

ALLEN, JEROME, Lenawee County. Enlisted in Company G as first sergeant June 20, 1861, at Adrian, age 32. Commissioned second lieutenant May 1, 1862. Commissioned first lieutenant July 1, 1862. Commanding company from July 1863 to May 1864. Mustered out at expiration of term at Detroit, June 30, 1864. Resided in Goshen, Ind., after service.

ALLEN, JESSE I., Lenawee County. Enlisted in Company G, June 20, 1861, at Adrian, age 20. Discharged for disability at Washington, D.C., Aug. 3, 1861.

ALLEN, LEMUEL, Tecumseh. Enlisted in Company G as sergeant June 20, 1861, at Adrian, age 23. Died in Confederate hands, June 28, 1862, of wounds received in action at Gaines' Mill on June 27.

ALLEN, TRISTRAM C. (*VV*), Lenawee County. Enlisted in Company G, June 20, 1861, in Adrian, age 17. Merchant, resided with grandparents and four siblings. Wounded in action Malvern Hill, Va., July 1, 1862. Reenlisted Dec. 29, 1863. Corporal. Wounded in action, shot in hand, Wilderness, Va., May 5, 1864. No further record.

ALLEN, WILLIAM H., Lenawee County. Enlisted in Company I, June 20, 1861, at Adrian, age 21. Farmer. Taken prisoner at Gettysburg, July 2, 1863. Held at Belle Isle, Richmond, Va., and Andersonville, Ga. Released Nov. 20, 1864. Discharged at Detroit Feb. 3, 1865. Resided in Ridgeway Township after service. Sent to Soldiers Home, Grand Rapids, 1892–94. Died June 4, 1927, and buried at Soldiers Home, Grand Rapids.

ALLISON, JOHN M., Saline, Washtenaw County. Enlisted in Company G as sergeant June 20, 1861, at Adrian, age 19. Farmer. Died of disease in Minor's Hill, Va., Dec. 24, 1861. Buried Military Asylum Cemetery, Washington, D.C.

ANDERSON, ALLEN, Litchfield, Hillsdale County. Enlisted in Company H as corporal June 20, 1861, at Adrian, age 22. Farmer. Discharged for disability, lung disease, at Minor's Hill, Va., Jan. 13, 1862. Reenlisted in the 11th Michigan Infantry, March 10, 1865. Mustered out Sept. 12, 1865. Resided in Litchfield. Died Jan. 27, 1892. Buried in Mt. Hope Cemetery, Litchfield.

ANDERSON, FINDLATUR C., St. Joseph County. Enlisted in Company C, June 20, 1861, at Adrian, age 20. Miller. Discharged for disability at Minor's Hill, Va., Nov. 19, 1861.

ANDERSON, JAMES B., Washtenaw County. Enlisted in Company G, June 20, 1861, at Adrian, age 21. Wounded in action at Gaines' Mill, June 27, 1862. Discharged for disability at Newark, N.J., Oct. 29, 1862. Buried Bell Oak Cemetery, Bell Oak.

ANDERSON, JOHN F., Ann Arbor. Enlisted in Company D, June 20, 1861, at Adrian, age 23. Killed in action at Malvern Hill, Va., July 1, 1862.

ANDREWS, CORNELIUS, Jackson County. Enlisted in Company D, June 20, 1861, at Adrian, age 23. Carpenter. Discharged at Sharpsburg, Md., Oct. 25, 1862. Resided in Pennsylvania after service.

ANDREWS, JOHN, Coldwater. Enlisted in Company C, June 20, 1861, at Adrian, age 21. Died Aug. 10, 1862, in hospital at Washington, D.C., of wounds received in action at Malvern Hill on July 1. Buried in National Cemetery, Brooklyn, N.Y., Grave No. 349.

ANDREWS, JOHN F., Washtenaw County. Enlisted in Company D as wagoner June 20, 1861, at Adrian. Farmer. Detached temporarily to 18th Rhode Island Light Artillery at Minor's Hill, Va. Deserted with Stephen H.

Aldrich, at Aquia Creek, Va., Aug. 22, 1862.

Ansel, Henry I., Ida, Monroe County. Enlisted in Company A, June 20, 1861, at Adrian, age 17. Farmer. Wounded in action, scalp injury, during Seven Days battles of 1862. Slightly wounded in action at Gettysburg, July 2, 1863. Detailed as a nurse to the wounded. Mustered out at expiration of term, June 30, 1864. Buried Richardson Cemetery, Monroe County.

Armstrong, George, Montreal. Entered service unassigned to a company. Substitute for William Lewis, drafted Feb. 26, 1863, from Berlin, St. Clair County, for nine months. Deserted. Buried in Pine Tree Cemetery, Shiawassee County.

Ashmore, Obed S., Steuben, Ind. Enlisted in Company H, June 20, 1861, at Adrian, age 19. Farmer. Slightly wounded, shot in left arm, while in action at Fredericksburg, Va., Dec. 13, 1862. Taken prisoner at Gettysburg, July 2, 1863. Held at Andersonville, suffering rheumatism in leg and back while incarcerated. Discharged at expiration of term at Detroit, June 3, 1865. Resided in Corning, N.Y., after service.

Atkinson, Theodore P., Riga, Lenawee County. Enlisted in Company B, June 20, 1861, at Adrian, age 25. Laborer, married. Killed in action at Gaines' Mill, Va., June 27, 1862.

Austin, Albert, Washtenaw County. Enlisted in Company K, June 20, 1861, at Adrian, age 20. Transferred to Battery D, 5th U.S. Artillery, Oct. 9, 1862. Discharged at Sharpsburg, Md., by general order Oct. 25, 1862.

Austin, Charles F., Monroe. Enlisted in Company A, June 20, 1861, at Adrian, age 21. Farmer. Killed in action at Malvern Hill, July 1, 1862. A marker for him is in Woodland Cemetery, Monroe.

Austin, James, Waterloo, Jackson County. Enlisted in Company F, June 20, 1861, at Adrian, age 28. Discharged for disability at Columbia College Hospital, Washington, D.C., Oct. 27, 1861. Resided in Mulliken, Eaton County, after service. Buried Oakwood Cemetery, Grand Ledge.

Austin, Lorenzo D., Monroe County. Enlisted in Company G as musician June 20, 1861, at Adrian, age 43. Discharged for disability at Sharpsburg, Md., Oct. 1862. Buried Burr Oak Cemetery, Burr Oak, Kans.

Avery, Burgess M., Dundee, Monroe County. Enlisted in Company G, June 20, 1861, at Adrian, age 21. Died of disease in Regimental Hospital at Minor's Hill, Va., Dec. 27, 1861. Buried Military Asylum Cemetery, Washington, D.C.

Avery, Elroy M., Monroe. Enlisted in Company G, June 20, 1861, at Adrian, age 17. Student, teacher, and printer's assistant. Enlisted in the 11th Michigan Cavalry Aug. 14, 1863, at Monroe and mustered out as sergeant major. Discharged at Pulaski, Tenn., Aug. 10, 1865. Resided in Ohio and Florida after service, journalist, educator, scientist, and author; also served in the Ohio State Senate and other offices.

Avery, James E., Lenawee County. Entered service in Company B at organization as second lieutenant, June 20, 1861, at Adrian, age 28. Carriage maker. Commissioned first lieutenant Jan. 12, 1862. Admitted to hospital in April 1862 at Yorktown, Va., after washing his face in swamp water and suffering violent inflammation that blinded his right eye and seriously impaired the left. Sent to Fortress Monroe. Resigned and honorably discharged Dec. 4, 1862. Died Dec. 1911, Soldiers Home, Grand Rapids. Buried Saugatuck Cemetery, Saugatuck.

B

Bacon, Reuben C., Washtenaw County. Enlisted in Company D, June 20, 1861, at Adrian, age 23. Corporal. Discharged for disability at Washington, D.C., Jan. 5, 1864. Buried Highland Cemetery, Ypsilanti.

Bacon, William J., Lenawee County. Enlisted in Company F, June 20, 1861, at Adrian, age 17. Shoemaker. Mustered out at expiration of term at Detroit, June 29, 1864. Buried Gleason Cemetery, Reading Township.

Bailey, Albert. Enlisted in Company F. Listed with absentees at special muster, Aug. 18, 1862, with the remark: "Absent with leave." No further record.

Bailey, Isaac, Lenawee County. Enlisted in Company B, Sept. 16, 1861, at Hudson, age 22. Farm laborer. Killed in action at Gaines' Mill, June 27, 1862.

Bailey, Israel, Dexter, Washtenaw County. Enlisted in Company K, sergeant, June 20, 1861, at Adrian, age 45.

Blacksmith, father of six. Discharged for disability at Minor's Hill, Va., Nov. 23, 1861. Born in Canada.

BAILEY, JARED B., Adrian. Enlisted in Company B, June 20, 1861, at Adrian, age 21. Discharged for disability at Minor's Hill, Va., Jan. 6, 1862. Resided in Palmyra, Lenawee County, after service.

BAILEY, THOMAS, Wayne County. Enlisted in Company I, June 20, 1861, at Adrian, age 45. Farmer. Wounded in action and missing at Gaines' Mill, Va., July 27, 1862. Paroled at Dickens's Landing, Va., Aug. 5, 1862. Hospitalized for six months with chronic diarrhea. Transferred to Invalid Corps Sept. 1863. Born in England.

BAILEY, WILLIAM H. (*VV*), Washtenaw County. Enlisted in Company K as musician June 20, 1861, at Adrian, age 21. Laborer. Reenlisted Dec. 29, 1863. On detached service with Co. K, 1st Michigan Infantry, July 2, 1864, Petersburg. Transferred to Co. A, reorganized 4th Michigan, June 6, 1865. Discharged for disability at San Antonio, Jan. 8, 1866. Resided in Wapella, Ill., after service.

BAKER, ALBERT, Hillsdale County. Enlisted in Company H as musician fifer June 20, 1861, at Adrian, age 19. Farmer. Transferred to Co. B, Nov. 31, 1861. Discharged for disability at Minor's Hill, Va., Jan. 5, 1862. Died June 16, 1862.

BAKER, ALVAH, Hudson. Enlisted in Independent Company, March 19, 1864, at Hudson, age 44. On detached service with Co. F, 1st Michigan Infantry, July 2, 1864, Petersburg. Died of disease near Petersburg, Aug. 10, 1864.

BAKER, JOHN F., Monroe County. Enlisted in Company A, Sept. 13, 1861, at Hudson, age 25. Wounded in action at Gettysburg, July 2, 1863, with gunshot wound through right hand. Wounded again, Wilderness, Va., May 5, 1864, gunshot wound to right hip. On detached service with Co. A, 1st Michigan Infantry, July 2, 1864, at Petersburg. Discharged at expiration of term near Petersburg, Oct. 6, 1864. Resided in Carleton after service, working as carpenter. Died April 19, 1921. Buried in Ash Township.

BAKER, MOSES W., Livingston County. Enlisted in Company K, June 20, 1861, at Adrian, age 21. Mustered out at expiration of term June 29, 1864.

BAKER, NEWEL E., Monroe County. Enlisted in Company A, June 20, 1861, at Adrian, age 19. Laborer. Discharged for disability Oct. 22, 1861.

BAKER, PERRY, Monroe. Enlisted in Company A, Sept. 17, 1861, at Hudson, age 22. Died at Belle Isle, Richmond, Va., July 15, 1862, of wounds received in action at Gaines' Mill, Va., June 27, 1862. A GAR post was named for him in Carleton, Monroe County.

BAKER, RANSOM, Hudson. Enlisted in Independent Company, March 29, 1864, at Hudson, age 43. On detached service with Co. F, 1st Michigan Infantry, July 2, 1864, at Petersburg. Died of disease near Petersburg, July 7, 1864. Buried National Cemetery, City Point, Va.

BAKER, WILLIAM F., Steuben, Ind. Enlisted in Company B, June 20, 1861, at Adrian, age 19. Discharged for disability near Falmouth, Va., Jan. 2, 1863.

BALCOM, WILLIAM R., Riley, St. Clair County. Enlisted in Company F, June 20, 1861, at Adrian, age 17. Farmer. Wounded in face and back at Malvern Hill, July 2, 1862. Wounded slightly in action at Fredericksburg, Dec. 13, 1862. Lost thumb on right hand. Discharged for disability at Washington, D.C., Feb. 14, 1863.

BALDINGER, THEODORE. Enlisted in band June 20, 1861, at Adrian, age 23. Shoemaker. Discharged at Harrison's Landing, Va., Aug. 10, 1862. Born in Switzerland.

BALDWIN, EDWARD S. Enlisted as commissary sergeant June 20, 1861, age 19. Commissioned second lieutenant, Co. D, Sept. 1, 1861. Acting regimental quartermaster Jan.–June 1862. Commissioned first lieutenant, Co. K, Sept. 1, 1862. Transferred to Co. F, Nov. 26, 1862. Commanding company from Jan. 29 to June 1863. On leave during battle of Gettysburg. Resigned and honorably discharged July 29, 1863, by special order stating him "to be worthless and incapable." Died Oct. 29, 1890, Marceline, Mo.

BALL, ALLEN, Hudson. Enlisted in Company F as corporal June 20, 1861, at Adrian, age 27. Mechanic. Sergeant. Discharged for disability at Washington, D.C., June 18, 1862. Died of heart disease. Buried in Maple Grove Cemetery, Hudson.

BANCROFT, JOHN M., Wayne County. Enlisted in Company I as sergeant June 20, 1861, at Adrian, age 18. Civil engineering and architectural draftsman. Attended Dartmouth College before the war. Temporarily detached to the Balloon Corps. First sergeant July 1, 1862. Recorded as second lieutenant, July 1862, Co. C. Commissioned first lieutenant, Co. K, to date Sept. 28, 1862. Transferred to Co. H, March 12, 1863. Commanding Co. H from July 2 to Nov. 1863. Commanding Co. B from May 10, 1864. Mustered out at expiration of term of service at Detroit, June 30, 1864. Married in 1865, fathered seven children. Resided in Reading, Mass., and New Jersey after service. Died July 27, 1918.

Bardwell, George W., Washtenaw County. Enlisted in Company D, June 20, 1861, at Adrian, age 24. Deserted at Minor's Hill, Nov. 21, 1861. Had a burial plot, Old Edenville Cemetery, No. 74, Edenville Township, Midland County, yet his grave is reportedly empty.

Barker, Augustus K., Hillsdale. Enlisted in Company E, June 20, 1861, at Adrian, age 18. Corporal. Was tied up for leaving camp with another soldier. Demoted May 13, 1863. Mustered out at expiration of term at Detroit, June 28, 1864. Later resided Soldiers Home, Hot Springs, S.D.

Barlow, Charles H., Livingston County. Enlisted in Company K, June 20, 1861, at Adrian, age 21. Farmhand. Wounded, shot in lung, at Fredericksburg. Discharged at Harper's Ferry, Va., Feb. 19, 1863. Returned to Livingston County, but also resided in Tennessee and elsewhere in the South; then Montcalm and Osceola counties, Mich., farming and working in lumber, before moving to Leroy, Calhoun County; he also wrote poems and prose to newspapers. Buried in Maple Hill Cemetery, Leroy Township.

Barnes, Dexter C., Lenawee County. Enlisted in Company B, June 20, 1861, at Adrian, age 32. Teamster, a husband and father. Discharged for disability at Minor's Hill, Va., March 3, 1862.

Barnes, Henry A. (*VV*), Lenawee County. Enlisted in Company F, June 20, 1861, at Adrian, age 19. Farmer. Promoted to corporal Jan. 1862, and sergeant, Aug. 14, 1862. Wounded in action, shot in arm, May 5, 1864. On detached service with Co. C, 1st Michigan Infantry, July 2, 1864, at Petersburg. Transferred to Co. B, July 1, 1865. Wounded in action at Hatcher's Run, Va., Feb. 6, 1865. Discharged for disability at Philadelphia, Aug. 26, 1865. Buried at Soldiers Home Cemetery, Grand Rapids.

Barnes, Joel H. (*VV*), Kalamazoo County. Enlisted in Company K, June 16, 1861, at Adrian, age 26. Resided with his widowed mother. Cabinetmaker and brother of Luke Barnes. Injured while unloading a barge at West Point, Va., May 1, 1862. Reenlisted Dec. 25, 1863. Wounded at Peeble's Farm, Va., Sept. 30, 1864, hit in right shoulder joint by a bullet. Discharged at Harper Hospital, Detroit, for disability. Resided in Fulton, Gratiot County, after service. Died Sept. 30, 1909, Garrett, Ind. Born in Canada.

Barnes, Lewis, Lenawee County. Enlisted in Company B, June 20, 1861, at Adrian, age 21. Killed in action at Gaines' Mill, June 27, 1862.

Barnes, Luke, St. Joseph County. Enlisted in Company C, June 20, 1861, at Adrian, age 21. Farmer, brother of Joel Barnes. Found guilty by court-martial on April 17, 1863, for sleeping on post and being disrespectful. Taken prisoner at Aldie, Va., June 26, 1863, when he fell out on the march because of sunstroke. Returned to regiment Jan. 1, 1864. Mustered out at expiration of term at Detroit, June 30, 1864. Resided in Adrian and Vicksburg, Mich. Admitted to Soldiers Home, Dayton, Sept. 10, 1889, discharged Feb. 11, 1893. Died in Athens, Calhoun County, Jan. 1922.

Barrett, Charles H. (*VV*), Lenawee County. Enlisted in Company G, June 20, 1861, at Adrian, age 18. Farmer. Reenlisted as sergeant Dec. 29, 1863, at Tecumseh. On detached service with Co. G, 1st Michigan Infantry, July 2, 1864. Commissioned captain of Co. C, reorganized 4th Michigan Infantry, July 1, 1865. Mustered out at San Antonio Feb. 26, 1866. Resided in Bryon Center, Kent County.

Barrett, Orvey S., Lenawee County. Enlisted in Company B as sergeant June 20, 1861, at Adrian, age 26. Engineer. Second lieutenant Sept. 1, 1862. Severely wounded in action at Gettysburg, July 2, 1863, gunshot left leg. Commanding company Feb. 1864. Discharged for disability May 23, 1864, on account of wound. Worked for a time after the war as a carpenter and joiner, until disabled by his wound. Died Feb. 14, 1892. Buried Oakwood Cemetery, Adrian.

Bartlett, John, Ann Arbor. Enlisted in Company D, June 20, 1861, at Adrian, age 47. Farmer. In hospital Georgetown, for chronic kidney inflammation, March 14, 1862. Discharged for disability April 11, 1862. Buried Pray Cemetery, Washtenaw County. Born in England.

Baryan, Lorenzo, Livingston County. Enlisted in Company K, June 20, 1861, at Adrian, age 20. Discharged for disability at Minor's Hill, March 3, 1862.

BASHYETT, JAMES H., Hillsdale County. Enlisted in Company H, June 20, 1861, at Adrian, age 35. Printer. Wounded in ankle at Malvern Hill, July 1, 1862, and captured. Paroled at City Point, Va., July 19, 1862. Sent to U.S. General Hospital, Davids' Island, N.Y. Ordered to return to regiment Nov. 2, 1863, but never reported. Listed as a deserter.

BASSETT, ALMON S., Wright, Ottawa County. Enlisted in Independent Company, March 24, 1864, at Wright, age 17. Carpenter. On detached service with 1st Michigan Infantry, July 2, 1864, Petersburg. Transferred to Co. K, reorganized 4th Michigan, June 6, 1865. Discharged at Houston, May 26, 1866. Resided in Toledo.

BATES, CHARLES. Enlisted in band, June 20, 1861 at Adrian, age 24, as musician. Mustered out at Harrison's Landing, Va., per War Department order, Aug. 10, 1862.

BATES, CHARLES, Williams, Ohio. Enlisted in Company B, June 20, 1861, at Adrian, age 19. Day laborer. Discharged for disability at Fort Woodbury Sept. 6, 1861. Later became a doctor in Florence, Ohio.

BATES, EZRA, Macomb County. Enlisted in Company I, June 20, 1861, at Adrian, age 24. Missing in action at Mechanicsville, Va., June 26, 1862. Cenotaph at Hart Cemetery, Macomb County.

BATES, GORDON, St. Lima Township, Ind. Enlisted in Company C, sergeant, June 20, 1861, at Adrian, age 20. Farm laborer. Discharged for disability, blinded, at Philadelphia, June 4, 1862. Capt. Wood wrote he "is considered the best First Sergeant in the regiment." Resident of Ohio after service.

BATES, HENRY C., Scio, Washtenaw County. Enlisted in Company K, June 20, 1861, at Adrian, age 24. Logger. Transferred to Navy at Erie, Pa., in 1863. Served in Farragut's fleet. Mustered out in Memphis, Tenn. Resided in Augusta, Kans.

BATTEY, WILLIAM F., Lenawee County. Enlisted in Company B as first sergeant June 20, 1861, at Adrian, age 23. Discharged for disability Sept. 2, 1861, at Ft. Woodbury, Va.

BAUER, ANTON, Washtenaw County. Enlisted in Company D, June 20, 1861, at Adrian, age 27. Wounded in action at Gettysburg, July 2, 1863, shot through left arm, also wounded in left side of body. Transferred to Invalid Corps Feb. 15, 1864. Mustered out June 21, 1864. Resided in Adams Township, Hillsdale County.

BAUMIESTER, JOHN. Enlisted in band June 20, 1861, at Adrian, age 43, as musician. Discharged for disability at Minor's Hill, Feb. 14, 1862.

BEACH, EDWARD E., Chelsea, Washtenaw County. Enlisted in Company D as sergeant June 20, 1861, at Adrian, age 23. Discharged for disability June 5, 1862. Buried Pleasant Ridge Cemetery, Lincoln County, Okla.

BEACH, WALLACE F. Enlisted in Company F, Feb. 8, 1864, at Hudson, age 16. Cooper. On detached service with Co. C, 1st Michigan Infantry, July 2, 1864, at Petersburg. Mustered out at Portsmouth Grove, R.I., June 18, 1865. Buried in Maple Grove Cemetery, Hudson.

BEAL, HENRY E., Branch County. Enlisted in Company C, June 20, 1861, at Adrian, age 31. Wounded in action and taken prisoner at Gettysburg, July 2, 1863. Confined in Richmond and paroled at City Point, Va., Aug. 2, 1863; admitted to hospital same day. Returned to regiment Dec. 10, 1863. Mustered out at expiration of term at Detroit, June 30, 1864. Died Nov. 24, 1893. Buried at Manistee.

BEAM, HENRY O., Hillsdale. Enlisted in Independent Company, Feb. 22, 1864, at Hillsdale, age 18. On detached service with Co. F, 1st Michigan Infantry, July 2, 1864, Petersburg. Transferred to Co. K, reorganized 4th Michigan Infantry, June 6, 1865. Died of disease at Green Lake, Tex., Aug. 1, 1865. Buried in National Cemetery, Brownsville, Grave No. 514.

BEAMAN, GEORGE W., Monroe County. Enlisted in Company A, June 20, 1861, at Adrian, age 19. Mustered out at expiration of service, June 30, 1864.

BEASOM, GEORGE. Enlisted in Company F, Feb. 6, 1864, at Hudson, age 28. Wounded in action, shot in right arm, Wilderness, Va., May 5, 1864. On detached service with Co. C, 1st Michigan Infantry, July 2, 1864, Petersburg. Transferred to Co. K, reorganized 4th Michigan, July 1, 1865. Discharged at Houston, May 26, 1866. Resided in South Dakota after service. Buried in Maple Grove Cemetery, Hudson.

BECKER, WILSON, Branch County. Enlisted in Company C, June 20, 1861, at Adrian, age 23. Farmer. Killed in action at Fredericksburg, Va., Dec. 13, 1862.

BECKLEY, GUY, Ann Arbor. Enlisted in Company D as wagoner June 20, 1861, at Adrian, age 31. Painter and constable, husband and father of two. Discharged for disability Sept. 20, 1861, at Ft. Woodbury. Died Nov.

19, 1893, and was buried in Ann Arbor.

Beebe, Corwin, Jackson County. Enlisted in Company H, June 20, 1861, at Adrian, age 19. Blacksmith. Deserted U.S. Hospital, Philadelphia, March 1, 1863. Resided in Warrington, Fla.

Beebe, Darwin C., Litchfield, Hillsdale County. Enlisted in Company H, June 20, 1861, at Adrian, age 21. Cooper. Discharged for disability (wound) at Baltimore, Dec. 7, 1862. Enlisted in 14th Battery, Michigan Light Artillery, Dec. 31, 1863, at Detroit. Corporal, March 1864. Mustered out at Jackson, July 1, 1865. Resided in Litchfield.

Beebe, George E. Enlisted in Company E, Sept. 11, 1861, at Hudson. Discharged for disability at Sharpsburg, Md., Oct. 6, 1862.

Beers, Jeptha W., Tecumseh. Entered service in Company G at organization, as second lieutenant, June 20, 1861, at Adrian, age 40. Blacksmith, husband and father of two. Seriously ill while at Adrian in May 1861, returned to Tecumseh on May 28, to regain his health. Commissioned first lieutenant, Co. K, May 1, 1862. Wounded in action, shot in groin and taken prisoner at battle of Gaines' Mill, Va., June 27, 1862. Died July 6, 1862, at Richmond. Buried in Brookside Cemetery, Tecumseh. GAR post named after him.

Bellows, Alonzo C., Lucas, Ohio. Enlisted in Company B, June 20, 1861, at Adrian, age 24. Corporal. Wounded in action at Gettysburg, July 2, 1863, shot in right leg. Returned to duty Sept. 1863 as clerk and nurse. Mustered out at expiration of term at Detroit, June 30, 1864.

Bender, David, Otsego, Ind. Enlisted in Company B, June 20, 1861, at Adrian, age 23. Cabinetmaker. Corporal July 1, 1863. Reenlisted Dec. 29, 1863. On detached service with Company B, 1st Michigan, July 2, 1864, Petersburg, Va. Transferred to Co C, reorganized 4th Michigan, July 1, 1865. Sergeant Sept. 30, 1864. Mustered out at San Antonio, Feb. 26, 1866. Resided in Hamilton, Ind.

Benderitter, Frank, Monroe County. Enlisted in Company A, June 20, 1861, at Adrian, age 19. Corporal July 1, 1863. Mustered out at expiration of term at Detroit, June 30, 1864. After service was a school custodian in Monroe. Died in 1923 and buried Woodland Cemetery, Monroe.

Bennett, Alexander C., Steuben, Ind. Enlisted in Company H, June 20, 1861, at Adrian, age 25. Thresher. Taken prisoner at Gettysburg, July 2, 1863. Died Oct. 28, 1863.

Bennett, George H., Steuben, Ind. Enlisted in Company H, June 20, 1861, at Adrian, age 19. Killed in action at Malvern Hill, July 1, 1862. Reportedly buried in Genesee County.

Bennett, William, Livingston County. Enlisted in Company K, June 20, 1861, at Adrian, age 20. Farm laborer. Wounded in action at Gaines' Mill, June 27, 1862. Transferred to Battery D, 5th U.S. Artillery. Discharged at Sharpsburg, Md., by order, Oct. 25, 1862. Resided in Fowlerville.

Bensler, Jacob, Washtenaw County. Enlisted in Company D, Sept. 19, 1861, at Hudson. Wounded in action at Gettysburg, July 2, 1863, struck in right shoulder by a shell fragment. On detached service with Co. E, 1st Michigan Infantry, July 1864, at Petersburg. Received flesh wound in the right thigh on March 25, 1865. Transferred to Co. C, reorganized 4th Michigan, July 1, 1865. Discharged at Detroit for disability Aug. 22, 1865. Resided in Manchester, N.J. after war. Admitted to Soldiers Home, Dayton, Sept. 1894, released Aug. 6, 1903. Born in Germany.

Benson, Adelbert, Monroe. Enlisted in Company A, June 20, 1861, at Adrian, age 19. Corporal. Killed in action at Gettysburg, July 2, 1863. Buried near the Rose Barn. Reburied Gettysburg National Cemetery, Michigan Plot, B-16.

Bentley, Jonathan, Lenawee County. Enlisted in Company B, June 20, 1861, at Adrian, age 33. Discharged for disability Oct. 29, 1861.

Berger, Samuel, Homer, Calhoun County. Enlisted in Independent Company, March 26, 1864, at Homer, age 18. On detached service with Co. F, 1st Michigan Infantry July 2, 1864, Petersburg. Transferred to Co. K, reorganized 4th Michigan, June 6, 1865. Admitted to Harper Hospital, Detroit, June 16, 1865. Discharged July 12, 1865. Resided in Homer after service.

Besemer, Charles B. (*VV*), Washtenaw County. Enlisted in Company D, June 20, 1861, at Adrian, age 34. Reenlisted Dec. 29, 1863, at Ann Arbor. On detached service, 1st Michigan Infantry July 2, 1864, Petersburg. Commissary sergeant Dec. 28, 1864. Transferred to Co. C, reorganized 4th Michigan, July 11, 1865. No further record. Resided in Jackson.

BESINGER, ANTONE, Lenawee County. Enlisted in Company G, June 20, 1861, at Adrian, age 27. Cooper. Discharged for disability at New York, Oct. 29, 1862, for wounds received in action at Gaines' Mill, June 27, 1862.

BEST, BENJAMIN, Hillsdale County. Enlisted in Company E, June 20, 1861, at Adrian, age 21. Wounded in action Gettysburg, July 2, 1863, shot in toe. Died May 15, 1864, of wounds received in action at Wilderness, Va., May 5.

BIDWELL, JOHN E., Salem, Washtenaw County. Enlisted in Company D, Aug. 3, 1862, at Minor's Hill, age 25. Farmer, married with young children. Discharged for disability at Yorktown, Va., May 1, 1862.

BIDWELL, JOHN E., Hudson. Enlisted in Company D, Aug. 12, 1862, at Ann Arbor, age 25. Farmer, married with two young children. On detached service with Co. E, 1st Michigan Infantry, July 2, 1864. Discharged May 30, 1865.

BILLINGS, EDGAR M. (*VV*). Enlisted in Company A, June 20, 1861, at Adrian, age 23. Painter. Reenlisted Dec. 29, 1863. Slightly wounded in action May 5, 1864, Wilderness, Va., by shell fragment in hip. On detached service with Co. A, 1st Michigan Infantry, July 2, 1864. Corporal Sept. 1, 1864. Transferred to Co. C, reorganized 4th Michigan, June 6, 1865. Sergeant Nov. 1, 1865. Mustered out at San Antonio, Feb. 26, 1866. Resided in Tuscola after service. Died July 25, 1892. Buried in Flint.

BILLSEN, JOHN W., Ann Arbor. Enlisted in Company K, Aug. 26, 1862, at Ann Arbor, age 20. Laborer. On detached service with Co. K, 1st Michigan Infantry, July 2, 1864. Discharged at Washington, D.C., June 5, 1865.

BILLSON, HENRY, Scio, Washtenaw County. Enlisted in Company K, June 20, 1861, at Adrian, age 24. Died of disease at Falmouth, Va., Dec. 26, 1862. Originally buried at Fitzhugh's Farm, Stafford, Va. Reburied National Cemetery, Fredericksburg, Va.

BING, JOHN, Lenawee County. Enlisted in Company F, June 20, 1861, at Adrian, age 29. Farmer. Discharged for disability at Philadelphia, Oct. 24, 1862. Born in Ireland.

BINGHAM, JAMES H., Homer, Calhoun County. Enlisted in Independent Company, Feb. 22, 1864, at Homer, age 18. On detached service with Co. F, 1st Michigan Infantry, July 2, 1864. Transferred June 6, 1865, to Co. K, reorganized 4th Michigan.

BIRD, JAMES M., Hudson. Enlisted in Company C, May 16, 1861, at Sturgis, age 25. Farmer. Missing in action at Gaines' Mill, June 27, 1862. Wounded and taken prisoner at Gettysburg, July 2, 1863. Died in prison, Dec. 1863. Brother of William Bird. Buried Kirby Cemetery, Mt. Pleasant.

BIRD, WILLIAM, Hillsdale County. Enlisted in Company E, June 20, 1861, at Adrian, age 21. Farmer. Discharged for disability at Warrenton, Va., Nov. 1862, with wounded in right hand. Brother of James Bird. Resided in Adams after service.

BIRDSALL, CHARLES, Hillsdale County. Enlisted in Company H, as second corporal, June 20, 1861, at Adrian, age 39. Mustered out April 25, 1862, for disability, dyspepsia. Buried Grace Lawn Cemetery, Middlebury, Ind.

BIRGE, WILLIAM H., Hillsdale County. Enlisted in Company E, June 20, 1861, at Adrian, age 21. Farm laborer. Hospitalized fall 1862, returned to regiment Nov. 30, 1862. Mustered out at expiration of term at Detroit, June 28, 1864. Resided in Franklin, Pa., after service. Died Oct. 21, 1920. Buried Franklin Cemetery.

BISBEE, CHARLES E., Monroe. Enlisted in Company A, June 20, 1861, at Adrian, age 19. Mason. Discharged for disability at Washington, D.C., Oct. 5, 1862, for wounds received in action at Malvern Hill, July 1, 1862, shot through the left side. Resided in New York after service. Died in April 1880 of erysipelas.

BISONETTE, SAMUEL, Monroe County. Enlisted in Company A, June 20, 1861, at Adrian, age 23. Farmer. Killed in action at Gettysburg, July 2, 1863. Buried Gettysburg National Cemetery, Michigan Plot, 1-C.

BISSELL, HENRY, Tecumseh, Lenawee County. Enlisted in Company G, June 20, 1861, at Adrian, age 21. Photographer. Mustered out at expiration of term at Detroit, June 30, 1864. Died in Tecumseh, March 3, 1930. Buried Brookside Cemetery, Tecumseh.

BISSELL, JOSEPH A., Hillsdale. Enlisted in Independent Company, March 29, 1864, at Hillsdale, age 29. On detached service with 1st Michigan Infantry, July 2, 1864. Admitted to Harper Hospital, Detroit, March 4, 1865. Discharged May 20, 1865.

BIXLER, FRANK M., Steuben, Ind. Enlisted in Company B, June 20, 1864, at Adrian, age 21. Admitted General Hospital, Camp B, Frederick, Md., Nov. 12, 1862, for chronic diarrhea. Transferred to Prince Street Hospital, Alexandria, Va., Dec. 2, 1862. Transferred to Ft. Wood Hospital, N.Y., Dec. 8, 1862. Rejoined regiment Oct. 9, 1863. Discharged for disability at Bealton, Va., March 1, 1864, for chronic hepatitis. Resided in Summit, Ind.

Blanchard, William H., St. Joseph County. Enlisted in Company C, June 20, 1861, at Adrian, age 19. Taken prisoner at Gettysburg, July 2, 1863. Released at Savannah, Ga., Nov. 20, 1864. Discharged at expiration of term at Detroit, March 8, 1865. Resided in Sturgis and South Boardman, Kalkaska County.

Blankman, George, Quebec, Canada. Enlisted in Company K, June 20, 1861, at Adrian, age 20. Missing in action, a straggler on the march and taken prisoner on Nov. 18, 1862. Paroled at City Point, Va., Dec. 14, 1862. Never reported to regiment.

Blatchley, Truman R., Litchfield, Hillsdale County. Enlisted in Company H, corporal, June 20, 1861, at Adrian, age 21. Carpenter. Killed in action at Malvern Hill, July 1, 1862.

Bliss, Edmund, Oakland County. Enlisted in Company D, June 20, 1861, at Adrian, age 21. Farmer. Transferred to Invalid Corps, Sept. 15, 1863. Died March 29, 1897; buried at Oak Ridge Cemetery, Bay County.

Blodgett, Worcester, Dexter. Enlisted in Company K, June 20, 1861, at Adrian, age 27. Farmer. Discharged at Portsmouth, Va., Oct. 11, 1862, on account of gunshot wound chest received at Malvern Hill, July 1, 1862. Portsmouth and Hampton hospitals, discharged Nov. 1, 1862. Married June 1, 1879. Died July 28, 1909, in Dexter. Buried Webster Church Cemetery, Washtenaw County.

Blowers, Martin A., Pittsford, Hillsdale County. Enlisted in Company F, Sept. 10, 1861, at Hudson, age 25. Teacher and farm laborer. Missing in action July 1, 1862. Transferred to Invalid Corps, March 15, 1864. Baptist minister after service. Resided in Minnesota. Died on Aug. 19, 1918, in Fairhaven, Minn.

Boag, Andrew, Lenawee County. Enlisted in Company F, June 20, 1861, at Adrian, age 18. Molder. Wounded at Malvern Hill, July 1, 1862. Assistant division wagon master from Oct. 1862 to April 1864. Mustered out at expiration of term at Detroit, June 29, 1864.

Boies, Albert Hartson, Lenawee. Enlisted in Company F, Sept. 10, 1861, at Hudson, age 17. Farm laborer and musician. Wounded in action July 1, 1862, Malvern Hill, shot in chest by bullet that passed through his diary. Wounded in action at Gettysburg July 2, 1863, in right hand, third and fourth fingers, captured but escaped. Sent to Summit House Hospital, Philadelphia; transferred to Invalid Corps March 15, 1864, as chief musician. Discharged at expiration of term at Elmira, N. Y., Oct. 1, 1864, from Veteran Reserve Corps.

Bolles, George W., Coldwater. Enlisted in Company E, Aug. 21, 1862, at Hudson, age 32. Farm laborer, father of five. Wounded in action, shot in hand, near Spotsylvania Court House, May 10, 1864. Discharged near Washington, D.C., June 5, 1865. Resided in Coldwater after service.

Bolles, Seth (*VV*), Hillsdale County. Enlisted in Company E, June 20, 1861, at Adrian, age 24. Turner in the wood trade. Reenlisted Dec. 31, 1863. Absent from regiment but returned on May 30, 1864. Wounded in action June 3, 1864, near Bethesda Church, Va. On detached service with Co. K, 1st Michigan Infantry July 2, 1864. Transferred to Co. C, reorganized 4th Michigan, July 1, 1865. Discharged at San Antonio, Feb. 10, 1866. Resided in Hudson after service. Died Oct. 10, 1914, buried Oak Hill Cemetery, Grand Rapids.

Bond, Stephen C., Hillsdale. Enlisted in Independent Company, Feb. 12, 1864, at Hillsdale, age 51. Farmer. On detached service with 1st Michigan Infantry, July 2, 1864. Died of disease in Camden Street Hospital, Baltimore, July 1, 1864. Born in England.

Bone, Christian N., Lenawee County. Enlisted in Company F, June 20, 1861, at Adrian, age 27. Blacksmith. Fifth Corps blacksmith. Mustered out at expiration of term at Detroit, June 29, 1864.

Boothby, Henry, Livingston County. Enlisted in Company K, June 20, 1861, at Adrian, age 23. Farm laborer. Discharged for disability at Minor's Hill, Va., Dec. 19, 1861.

Boothe, George W., Wright, Ottawa County. Enlisted in Independent Company, Feb. 26, 1864, at Hudson, age 26. On detached service with Co. F, 1st Michigan Infantry, July 2, 1864. Wounded in action near Petersburg, Aug. 17, 1864; shot in the left arm. Discharged Feb. 28, 1865. Resided in Napoleon, Jackson County, after service. Buried Oak Grove Cemetery, Napoleon Township.

Boothe, Welsley, Lenawee County. Enlisted in Company B, June 26, 1862. Admitted to hospital Aug. 10, 1862. Dropped from rolls by War Department order, Aug. 28, 1863.

Bostwick, Charles, Washtenaw County. Enlisted in Company K, June 20, 1861, at Adrian, age 24. Deserted at Minor's Hill, Va., March 14, 1862.

Boucher, Caleb F., Washtenaw County. Enlisted in Company K, Sept. 15, 1861, at Hudson, age 19. Farmer.

Discharged for disability Dec. 19, 1861. Born in Canada.

BOUCHER, CHARLES W., Sharon, Washtenaw County. Enlisted in Company K, June 20, 1861, at Adrian, age 24. Farm laborer, resided with widowed mother, the oldest of six siblings. Discharged for disability at Minor's Hill, Va., Nov. 14, 1861.

BOVEE, DAVID (*VV*), Dover, Lenawee County. Enlisted in Company K, Sept. 21, 1861, at Hudson, age 22. Farmer. Reenlisted Dec. 25, 1863. Wounded in action, Wilderness, Va., May 5, 1864. On detached service with Co. K, 1st Michigan Infantry, July 2, 1864. Missing in action near Weldon Railroad, Va., Aug. 21, 1864. Resided in Dover after service.

BOWEN, ADNA H., Monroe County. Enlisted in Company A as corporal June 20, 1861, at Adrian, age 19. Commissioned second lieutenant, Co. K, 15th Michigan Infantry, Jan. 31, 1862. Taken prisoner Sept. 1862. Paroled Oct. 1862. Commissioned first lieutenant, Co. I, Oct. 1, 1862. Resigned March 30, 1863. Reentered service as captain, Co. D, 11th Michigan Cavalry at organization. Commissioned Aug. 1, 1863. Promoted major, 6th U.S. Colored Cavalry, Nov. 3, 1864. Resided in Detroit and Hastings, Neb. Died in 1917, Payette, Idaho.

BOWEN, GEORGE W., Monroe. Enlisted as hospital steward, June 20, 1861, at Adrian, age 24. Transferred to 16th Michigan Infantry and commissioned second assistant surgeon Dec. 1, 1862. Discharged May 6, 1863, but again commissioned June 9, 1863. Mustered out Detroit, June 28, 1864. Resided in Groveland Township, Oakland County, after service, a physician.

BOYD, THOMAS, Washtenaw County. Enlisted in Company D, June 20, 1861, at Adrian, age 22. Cooper. Attached to the Balloon Corps in 1861. Wounded in action May 5, 1864, Wilderness, Va., a bullet passing through his left chest and arm. Mustered out at expiration of term, June 30, 1864, at Detroit. Admitted to Soldiers Home, Dayton, Oct. 30, 1886. Buried Riverside Cemetery, Albion.

BOYLE, CHARLES, Monroe County. Enlisted in Company A, Oct. 1, 1861, age 49. Discharged for disability July 6, 1862. Admitted to Soldiers Home, Dayton, where he died Jan. 17, 1880. Buried Sec. B, Row 14, Grave 16, at the Soldiers Home, Dayton. Born in Ireland.

BOYLES, JOHN, Lenawee County. Enlisted in Company H, June 20, 1861, at Adrian, age 21. Farmer residing with his parents. Absent from the regiment Oct. 1862 and never returned. Reported as a deserter March 1, 1863.

BRADDOCK, HARRY B. Enlisted in Company F, Jan. 1, 1864, at Pittsford, Hillsdale County, age 44. On detached service with Co. C, 1st Michigan Infantry, July 2, 1864. Discharged for disability at Bristol, Pa., May 1, 1865. Resided in Trowbridge after the war.

BRADFORD, GEORGE W., LaSalle, Monroe County. Enlisted in Company A, as sergeant, June 20, 1861, at Adrian, age 23. Farmer. Commissioned second lieutenant Sept. 13, 1862. On detached service with ambulance corps from Nov. 1862 to March 1864. Commanding company April 1864. Mustered out at expiration of term at Detroit, June 30, 1864. Resided in Carthage, Mo., after service. Died in 1888.

BRADLEY, WILLIAM F., Adrian. Enlisted in Company G, March 10, 1862, at Adrian, age 17. Clerk. On detached service with Co. G, 1st Michigan Infantry, July 2, 1864. First lieutenant and adjutant, reorganized 4th Michigan, Aug. 31, 1864. Assistant adjutant general of brigade, Oct.–Dec. 1864. Mustered out at Houston, May 26, 1866. Brevet captain and major, U.S. Volunteers, March 13, 1865, for meritorious service. Resided in Grand Rapids.

BRAMAN, WILLIAM C., St. Joseph County. Enlisted in Company C, June 20, 1861, at Adrian, age 24. Farmhand. Mustered out at expiration of term at Detroit, June 30, 1864. Buried Penfield Cemetery, Monroe County, N.Y.

BREEN, WILLIAM P., Wayne County. Enlisted in Company K, June 20, 1861, at Adrian, age 19. Livery keeper. Wounded in action June 27, 1862, Gaines' Mill, shot in left leg; captured June 29, 1862, sent to Richmond, Va. Severe lung infection. Transferred to Veteran Reserve Corps, Jan. 5, 1864.

BRENINGSTOLL, HORACE J., Petersburg, Monroe County. Enlisted in Company A as corporal June 20, 1861, at Adrian, age 17. Laborer. Mustered out at expiration of term at Detroit, June 30, 1864. Resided in Petersburg, postmaster, justice of the peace, and other public offices. Owner of a broom handle company. Died May 30, 1925, age 82; buried in Pleasant View Cemetery, Summerfield Township.

BREWSTER, GEORGE L., Ransom, Hillsdale County. Enlisted in Company E, Sept. 1, 1862, at Hillsdale, age 18. Admitted to hospital early fall of 1862; returned to regiment Oct. 3, 1862. On detached service with Co. K, 1st Michigan Infantry, July 2, 1864. Discharged at Washington, D.C., June 5, 1865.

BRIGGS, DARIUS H., Hillsdale County. Enlisted in Company H, Sept. 30, 1861, at Hudson, age 24. Farmer. On detached service with Co. H, 1st Michigan Infantry, July 2, 1864. Discharged at expiration of term at Detroit, Sept. 6, 1864.

BRIGGS, WILLIAM W., Lenawee County. Enlisted in Company H, Feb. 20, 1862, at Adrian, age 21. Farmer. Discharged at Ft. Hamilton, N.Y., Oct. 28, 1862.

BRIGHAM, LUCIEN, Orangeville, St. Joseph County. Enlisted in Company C, June 20, 1861, at Adrian, age 34. Farmer. Regimental teamster. Mustered out at expiration of term at Detroit, June 29, 1864.

BRINK, JOSEPH, Wayne County. Drafted from Wayne County, Feb. 11, 1863, for nine months, age 20. Farmer. Assigned to Co. H. Killed in action at Gettysburg, July 2, 1863. Buried Gettysburg National Cemetery, Michigan Plot, A-19. Born in Germany

BRISTOL, WILLIAM T., Hillsdale. Enlisted in Company E, as wagoner and teamster, June 20, 1861, at Adrian, age 25. Farmer, husband and father of a young son. Mustered out at expiration of term at Detroit, June 28, 1864. Resided in Toledo.

BRITTON, WILLIAM, Steuben, Ind. Enlisted in Company B, June 20, 1861, at Adrian, age 21. Farmer residing with parents. Discharged for disability at Minor's Hill, Va., Jan. 13, 1862. Resided in Angola after service.

BROCK, DAVID C., Reading, Hillsdale County. Enlisted in Company E as corporal June 20, 1861, at Adrian, age 19. Killed in action at Malvern Hill, July 1, 1862.

BROCKAW, ZACKIUS JACKSON, Everett, Newago County. Enlisted in Company F, June 20, 1861, at Adrian, age 24. Student. In Jarvis Hospital, Baltimore, for chronic bronchitis, he met his future wife, Mary Ann O'Toole, a nurse. Deserted Dec. 5, 1862; later rejoined regiment. Transferred to Second Battalion Invalid Corps, Jan. 15, 1864, because of bronchitis. Resided in Baltimore after service. Died March 17, 1897.

BROCKWAY, GEORGE, Wright, Hillsdale County Enlisted in Company F, June 20, 1861, at Adrian, age 19. Farm laborer. Died of typhoid fever at Union Hotel, Georgetown, Sept. 8, 1861. Born in England.

BROCKWAY, MARTIN, Bela, Lenawee County. Enlisted in Company B, June 20, 1861, at Adrian, age 26. Farmer. Wounded in action, shot in arm, at New Bridge, Va., May 24, 1862. Taken prisoner at Gettysburg, July 2, 1863. Held as a prisoner for 21 months; most of that time at Andersonville, Ga. Discharged at Detroit, July 13, 1865. Brother of Oliver Brockway of 18th Michigan Infantry, also held at Andersonville and dying one day after Martin's arrival; another brother served with 15th Ohio Infantry. Lame and sick after imprisonment, Brockway reported he was unable to work after and resided in Blissfield, Lenawee Township. Died Jan. 29, 1903 Summerfield; buried Pleasant View Cemetery, Ida Township, Monroe County.

BRODOCK, HARRY B., Pittsfield Township, Washtenaw County. Enlisted in Company F, Jan. 31, 1864, at Pittsford, age 44. Farmer, married with four children; father of Henry M. Brodock. Admitted to hospital Aug. 26, 1864, with chronic diarrhea and shell wound to left leg received at Wilderness, Va., May 5, 1864. On detached service with Co. C, 1st Michigan Infantry, July 2, 1864. Corporal Jan. 1, 1865. Transferred to Co. K, reorganized 4th Michigan, July 1, 1865. Mustered out at Detroit, May 26, 1866.

BRODOCK, HENRY M., Pittsfield Township, Washtenaw County. Enlisted in Company F, Jan. 31, 1864, at Pittsford, Hillsdale County, age 15. Farm boy, son of Harry Brodock. Wounded May 5, 1864, Wilderness, Va., leg broken. On detached service with Co. C, 1st Michigan Infantry, July 2, 1864. Corporal Jan. 1, 1865. Transferred to Co. K, reorganized 4th Michigan, July 1, 1865. Mustered out at Detroit, May 26, 1866.

BROGAN, JAMES (VV), Lenawee County. Enlisted in Company K, Sept. 13, 1861, at Hudson. Reenlisted Dec. 19, 1863. On detached service with Co. K, 1st Michigan Infantry, July 2, 1864. Transferred to Co. C, reorganized 4th Michigan, July 1, 1865. Corporal. Mustered out at San Antonio, Feb. 26, 1866.

BRONSON, EDWARD, Milan, Monroe County. Enlisted in Company A, June 20, 1861, at Adrian, age 29. Laborer. Taken prisoner on June 29, 1863, on the march in Gettysburg campaign. Rejoined the regiment Sept. 1863. Discharged for disability at Washington, D.C., March 14, 1864.

BRONSON, WILLIAM H., Brownstown. Enlisted in Company I, June 20, 1861, at Adrian, age 20. Laborer. Killed in action at Malvern Hill, July 1, 1862.

BROWER, EUGENE, Washtenaw County. Enlisted in Company K, June 20, 1861, at Adrian, age 18. Wounded in action Malvern Hill, July 1, 1862. Transferred to Battery D, 5th U.S. Artillery, Oct. 1862. Discharged at Sharpsburg,

Md., Oct. 25, 1862.

Brown, Chauncey A., Hillsdale County. Enlisted in Company E. June 20, 1861, at Adrian, age 21. Discharged for disability at Philadelphia, Oct. 18, 1862.

Brown, Cyril P., Hudson. Enlisted in Company F, Aug. 26, 1862, at Detroit, age 18. Student. Discharged for disability at Bealton, Va., Jan. 9, 1864. Became a doctor and resided at Spring Lake, Ottawa County, after service.

Brown, Ezra, Clinton County. Enlisted in Company K, June 20, 1861, at Adrian, age 40. Farmer and father of six. Corporal Aug. 4, 1861. Sergeant July 1, 1862. Severely wounded in action at Gettysburg, July 2, 1863. Mustered out at expiration of term at Detroit, June 28, 1864. Resided in Harvard, Neb., after war. Admitted to Soldiers Home, Dayton, Nov. 11, 1903, released Dec. 23, 1903.

Brown, George Burt, Hillsdale County. Enlisted in Company E, June 20, 1861, at Adrian, age 19. Shot in foot Sept. 19, 1862. Rejoined regiment Nov. 30, 1862. Later wounded in shoulder and arm. Discharged for disability at Alexandria, Va., April 14, 1863. Resided in Allen Township after war. Died 1925, buried Allen Cemetery.

Brown, John, Amboy, Hillsdale County. Enlisted in Company H, Feb. 11, 1863, for nine months, age 26. Farm laborer. Substitute for Francis P. Sibley. Wounded in action at Gettysburg, July 2, 1863, shot in the back and hand. Died July 19, 1863, at West Philadelphia. Buried in National Cemetery at Philadelphia, Grave No. 285.

Brown, John W., Wheatland, Hillsdale County. Enlisted in Company E, Oct. 8, 1861. Farm laborer, father of two young daughters. Discharged for disability at Minor's Hill, Dec. 18, 1861. Buried Highland View Cemetery, Big Rapids.

Brown, Joseph, Monroe. Enlisted in Company A, Aug. 24, 1862, at Monroe, age 27. Discharged for disability at Bealton, Va., April 1864. Suffered from chronic eye problems. Died in 1911 and buried in Pleasant View Cemetery, Ida.

Brown, William, Jr., Monroe. Enlisted in Company A, Aug. 24, 1862, at Monroe, age 36. Discharged for disability Dec. 31, 1862. Died in 1912; buried in Woodland Cemetery, Monroe.

Brown, William C., Monroe County. Enlisted in Company A as corporal June 20, 1861, at Adrian, age 32. Farmer. Sergeant major Sept. 1, 1862. Commissioned second lieutenant, Co. A, Jan. 1, 1862. Commissioned first lieutenant Sept. 13, 1862. Guilty by court-martial Feb. 1, 1863, for being AWOL for six days, which he said resulted from "railroad problems" and a "marriage contract" with a woman. Fined two months' pay. Wounded in action at Gettysburg, July 2, 1863, shot in the left hip and right side, left lung useless. Commanding company from Oct. 1, 1863, to April 1864. Mustered out at expiration of term at Detroit, June 30, 1864. Stated that he was an invalid after the war, resided in Monroe. Died in 1897 and buried in Woodland Cemetery, Monroe.

Brownell, John G., Rollin/Woodstock, Lenawee County. Enlisted in Company F as corporal June 20, 1861, at Adrian, age 21. Resided with parents. Sergeant. Missing in action (captured) at Gettysburg, July 2, 1863. Died shortly after his release from Richmond, Va., of typhoid fever and diarrhea contracted while prisoner. Buried in Grave 405, Ash Grove Cemetery, Annapolis, Md., Oct. 29, 1863.

Brunner, Charles, Monroe County. Enlisted in Company A, June 20, 1861, at Adrian, age 18. Shoemaker and apple and candy peddler. Corporal. Died May 7, 1864, of wounds received in action at the Wilderness, Va., May 5, 1864.

Bryan, Herbert D., Woodbridge, Hillsdale County. Enlisted in Company E, Sept. 8, 1862, at Hillsdale, age 18. Resided on parents' farm. In hospital fall of 1862; returned to regiment Oct. 3, 1862. On detached service with Co. K, 1st Michigan Infantry, July 2, 1864. Corporal. Discharged at Washington, D.C., June 5, 1865. Resided in Cambria after service. Attended the last reunion of the regiment at Hillsdale in 1928.

Bryant, Martin V. Washtenaw County. Enlisted in Company D, June 20, 1861, at Adrian, age 24. Missing in action at Gaines Mill, June 27, 1862. Corporal. Discharged for disability Nov. 30, 1862.

Bryant, William, Pittsford, Hillsdale County. Enlisted in Independent Company, March 30, 1864, at Hudson, 33. Farm laborer. On detached service with Co. F, 1st Michigan Infantry, July 2, 1864. Transferred to Co. K, reorganized 4th Michigan, June 6, 1865. Discharged Feb. 20, 1865, on account of wounds received in action June 3, 1864. Resided in Kansas after service.

Bryan or Bryon, Joseph (*VV*), Pleasant, Ind. Enlisted in Company B, June 20, 1861, at Adrian, age 24. Miller.

Corporal. Reenlisted Dec. 29, 1863. On detached service with Co. A, 1st Michigan Infantry, July 2, 1865. Mustered out at San Antonio, Feb. 26, 1866. Resided in Deerfield Township, Ohio. Died in 1939.

Buchanan, Charles H., Hillsdale. Enlisted in Independent Company, Feb. 9, 1864, at Hillsdale, age 32. Farmer. On detached service with Co. F, 1st Michigan Infantry, July 2, 1864. Transferred to Co. K, reorganized 4th Michigan, June 6, 1865. Mustered out at Houston, May 26, 1866.

Buck, Luman Dover, Lenawee County. Enlisted in Company F, June 20, 1861, at Adrian, age 21. Laborer on his parents' farm. Listed as missing at Malvern Hill, July 1, 1862. Killed by a shell or fragment near Shepherdstown, Md., Sept. 19, 1862. Buried in National Cemetery, Antietam, Md., Grave No. 2523.

Bullard, George W., Lenawee County. Enlisted in Company F, June 20, 1861, at Adrian, age 39. Discharged for disability, chronic rheumatism, at Washington, D.C., Aug. 3, 1861.

Burce, Joseph, Fairfax, Va. Enlisted in Company B, Sept. 23, 1861. Severely wounded in action at Gettysburg, July 2, 1863. On detached service with Co. B, 1st Michigan Infantry, July 2, 1864. Discharged at expiration of term near Weldon Railroad, Va., Sept. 22, 1864.

Burke, Eli, Hillsdale County. Enlisted in Company E, musician drummer, June 20, 1861, at Adrian, age 61. Discharged for disability Aug. 13, 1861.

Burnett, Chauncey V. "Tip", Hillsdale County. Enlisted in Company E, June 20, 1861, at Adrian, age 21. Resided with his mother and family. Wounded in action at Gettysburg, July 2, 1863, shot in neck slightly. Admitted to a hospital in Philadelphia on July 10, rejoined regiment July 29, 1863. Wounded in action, Wilderness, Va., May 5, 1864, struck in the back of neck/shoulders by a spent bullet. Admitted to a general hospital May 11, 1864; sent to Finley Hospital, Washington, D.C., May 28, 1864. Returned to duty June 3, 1864. Discharged at expiration of term at Petersburg, July 1864. Resided in Jonesville. Died March 25, 1917.

Burns, Edward C., Steuben, Ind. Enlisted in Company B, June 20, 1861, at Adrian, age 22. Farm laborer. Corporal. Taken prisoner at Mine Run, Va., Nov. 10, 1863. Released at Venus Point, Ga., Nov. 20, 1864. Discharged at expiration of term at Detroit, Feb. 7, 1865. Resided in Fremont, Ind. and Dodge County, Neb., where he farmed, raised horses, and served as a county commissioner.

Burr, James D., Mottville, St. Joseph County. Enlisted in Company C, June 20, 1861, at Adrian, age 17. Wounded in action May 5, 1864. Mustered out at expiration of term at Detroit, June 29, 1864. Entered University of Michigan in 1866. Worked in Flint, Pere Marquette Railway, later for the A. T. & S. F. Railroad. Died May 4, 1886, Topeka, Kans.

Burrow, Charles, Calhoun County. Enlisted in Company I, June 20, 1861, at Adrian, age 23. Painter. Wounded in action at New Bridge, May 24, 1862. Transferred to Invalid Corps, July 1, 1863. Died Aug. 8, 1895. Born in Canada West.

Burt, Silas S., Sandstone Township, Jackson County. Enlisted in Company H, Feb. 20, 1862, at Adrian, age 17. Resided on family farm with parents. On detached service with Co. H, 1st Michigan Infantry, July 2, 1864. Died Oct. 20, 1864, at Lincoln Hospital, Washington, D.C., of wounds received in action at Poplar Grove Church, Va., Sept. 30, 1864. Buried Mt. Evergreen Cemetery, Jackson.

Burtch, Timothy B., Cambria, Hillsdale County. Enlisted in Company E, June 20, 1861, at Adrian, age 29. Farm laborer and father of one child. Given extra duty as punishment for AWOL, Nov. 1861–Feb. 1862 at Quartermaster Department. Taken prisoner at Gettysburg, July 2, 1863. Detached to Quartermaster for duration of service. Taken prisoner near Mine Run, Va., Nov. 27, 1863, while a teamster. Confined at Belle Isle, Richmond. Sent to Andersonville, Ga., Jan. 7, 1864. Escaped by hiding on a cart that was used daily to pick up the dead bodies and taken outside of the stockade. Reached safety at Venus Point, Ga., on Nov. 20, 1864. Discharged at expiration of term at Detroit, Feb. 8, 1865. Died in 1931 at the age of 99. Buried in Balcom Cemetery, Ionia.

Burwell, Peter, Jr., Lenawee County. Enlisted in Company I, June 20, 1861, at Adrian, age 17. Farm laborer. Discharged for disability at Washington, D.C., Aug. 7, 1861. Died at Soldiers Home, Grand Rapids, Aug. 8, 1885.

Bush, Benjamin Franklin, Lenawee County. Enlisted in Company F, Sept. 9, 1861, at Hudson, age 18. Farmer. Hospital steward while at Minor's Hill, winter 1861–62, and again in Feb. 1863. On detached service with Co. C, 1st Michigan Infantry, July 2, 1864. Discharged at expiration of term near Weldon Railroad, Va., Sept.

11, 1864. Suffered from sunstroke during service. Resided in Hudson after service. Buried Maple Grove Cemetery, Hudson.

BUSH, JAY S., Pittsford, Hillsdale County. Enlisted in Independent Company, March 16, 1864, at Pittsford, age 18. Corporal April 5, 1864. On detached service with Co. F, 1st Michigan Infantry, July 2, 1864. Transferred to Co. K, reorganized 4th Michigan, June 6, 1865. Sergeant May 1, 1866. Mustered out at Houston, May 26, 1866. Suffered from scurvy, lost all his teeth. Resided in Edmond, Okla. after service. Buried Maple Grove Cemetery, Hudson.

BUSH, RANSOM, Washtenaw County. Enlisted in Company K as sergeant June 20, 1861, at Adrian, age 37. Died of disease, chronic diarrhea, at Philadelphia, Sept. 11, 1862. Buried in National Cemetery at Philadelphia, Grave No. 154.

BUSHEAW, JOHN. Enlisted in Company H, June 20, 1861, at Adrian, age 19. Discharged on account of sickness.

BUSSINS, JOHN (*VV*), Monroe County. Enlisted in Company A, June 20, 1861, at Adrian, age 22. Clerk. Assigned clerk at brigade headquarters, March–June 1863. Reenlisted Dec. 29, 1863. On detached service with Co. A, 1st Michigan Infantry, July 2, 1864. Transferred to Co. C, reorganized 4th Michigan, July 1, 1865. Discharged at San Antonio, Feb. 10, 1866. Born in Germany.

BUTLAND, BENJAMIN P., Litchfield, Hillsdale County. Enlisted in Company H, June 20, 1861, at Adrian, age 19. Farmer. Wounded in action at Gaines' Mill, June 27, 1862. Taken prisoner at Savage's Station, June 30, 1862. Died of wounds.

BUTTS, MARSHALL (*VV*), Lenawee County. Enlisted in Company F, June 20, 1861, at Adrian, age 17. Farmer. Musician bugler. Reenlisted Dec. 29, 1863. On detached service with Co. C, 1st Michigan, July 2, 1864. Transferred to Co. C, reorganized 4th Michigan July 1, 1865. Mustered out at San Antonio, Feb. 26, 1866.

C

CAHOON, CHARLES, Trenton, Wayne County. Enlisted in Company F, June 20, 1861, at Adrian, age 26. Farmer. Captured at Gaines' Mill, Va., June 27, 1862. Paroled Aug. 5, 1862, at Atkins, Va. In hospital at Fortress Monroe, Va., Aug. 1862. Transferred to Invalid Corps, Sept. 30, 1863. Died in Amherstburg, Canada.

CAMPAU, CLAUDE (*VV*). Enlisted in Company I, June 20, 1861, at Adrian, age 19. Reenlisted Dec. 25, 1863. Discharged for disability at Bealton, Va., April 25, 1864. Resided in Wyandotte after service. Buried in Mt. Carmel Cemetery, Wyandotte

CAMPBELL, JOHN E., Ft. Wayne, Ind. Enlisted in Company B, June 20, 1861, at Adrian, age 35. Wounded in action at New Bridge, Va., May 24, 1862. Discharged for disability at Bealton, Va., Jan. 16, 1864. Resided in Sand Lake, Mich., after service. Born in Scotland.

CAMPBELL, ROBERT H., Hillsdale. Entered service as lieutenant, Company E, July 1, 1862, at Falmouth, Va., age 26. Teacher residing with parents and siblings. Commissioned first lieutenant and quartermaster Sept. 1, 1862. Mustered out at expiration of term at Detroit, June 28, 1864. Resided in Ann Arbor after service. Buried Forest Hill Cemetery, Ann Arbor.

CANFIELD, ALBERT, Lenawee County. Enlisted in Company B as corporal June 20, 1861, at Adrian, age 21. Discharged for disability at Minor's Hill, Va., Feb. 21, 1862.

CARL, WILLIAM. Enlisted in band, June 20, 1861, at Adrian, age 33. Discharged on account of disability Aug. 20, 1861, suffering hernia. Born in Germany.

CARNES, CHARLES F., Burr Oaks, St. Joseph County. Enlisted in Company C, June 20, 1861, at Adrian, age 21. Laborer. Discharged for disability at Sharpsburg, Md., Oct. 19, 1862. Resided in Cedar Springs after service. Admitted to Soldiers Home, Dayton, Jan. 1, 1881.

CARNEY, SIMON B., Monroe. Enlisted in Company A, June 20, 1861, at Adrian, age 24. Farmer residing with his parents' family. Sergeant. Taken prisoner at Gettysburg, July 2, 1863. Returned to Annapolis, Md., Nov. 17, 1863. Died of disease contracted while a prisoner in Richmond, at U.S. Hospital, Annapolis, Nov. 18, 1863. Buried Section F, 109, Annapolis Cemetery.

Carpenter, Addison I., St. Joseph County. Enlisted in Company C, June 20, 1861, at Adrian, age 22. 1861. Detailed to brigade hospital, Dec. 3, 1861. Discharged at expiration of term at Detroit, June 1864.

Carpenter, Albert, Hudson. Enlisted in Company F, Sept. 10, 1861, at Hudson, age 21. Carpenter. Slightly wounded in action at Fredericksburg, Va., Dec. 13, 1862. Wounded in action, shot in right shoulder, Wilderness, Va., May 5, 1864. On detached service with Co. C, 1st Michigan Infantry, July 2, 1864. Discharged at expiration of term at Detroit, Sept. 27, 1864. Resided in White Rabbit, Neb., and Long Beach, Calif., where he died on Aug. 31, 1906.

Carpenter, Eastman G. (*VV*). Enlisted in Company K, June 20, 1861, at Adrian, age 21. Harness maker apprentice. Reenlisted Dec. 25, 1863. On detached service with Co. K, 1st Michigan Infantry, July 2, 1864. Transferred to Co. C, reorganized 4th Michigan July 1, 1865. Mustered out at San Antonio, Feb. 26, 1866. Suffered from sunstroke during service. Died Aug. 1921. Buried North Hamburg Cemetery, Livingston County.

Carpenter, Phillip, Wayne County. Enlisted in Company I, June 20, 1861, at Adrian, age 19. Taken prisoner at Gaines' Mill, June 27, 1862. Returned to regiment. Wounded in action near Bethesda Church–Cold Harbor, Va., June 3, 1864, shot in chest. Moved to Douglas Hospital, Washington, D.C., where he died. Buried Arlington National Cemetery, June 22, 1864.

Carpenter, Washington W., Steuben County. Enlisted in Company B, June 20, 1861, at Adrian, age 21. Law student. Clerk at adjutant general's office, Washington, D.C. Deserted Aug. 1863 for 3½ months. Court-martial found him guilty on Dec. 1, 1863, forfeiting all pay due him and deducting $10 per month during the remainder of his enlistment. Wounded in action, Wilderness, Va., May 5, 1864, gunshot in left forearm. Sent to Navy Yard Hospital, Washington. Mustered out at expiration of term, June 30, 1864. After service he resided in Forestville, N.Y., and became a surgeon.

Carrier, William C. Enlisted in Company G, March 18, 1864, at Deerfield, Lenawee County, age 19. On detached service with Co. G, 1st Michigan Infantry, July 2, 1864. Discharged at Detroit, July 1, 1865. Buried at Los Angeles National Cemetery.

Carserrey, John, Hillsdale. Enlisted in Company C, Aug. 26, 1862, at Detroit, age 18. No further record.

Carson, Darius H., Wayne County. Enlisted in Company I, June 20, 1861, at Adrian, age 25. Mustered out at expiration of term, June 30, 1864. Resided in Green Bay, Wis., after service. Admitted to Soldiers & Sailors Home, Milwaukee.

Carter, John, Macon, Lenawee County. Enlisted in Company B, Feb. 22, 1862, at Adrian, age 27. Farm laborer living on his parents' farm. Wounded slightly in action at Fredericksburg, Dec. 13, 1862, shot in right shoulder. Discharged for disability at Washington, D.C., Feb. 26, 1863.

Carver, Orville, Steuben, Ind. Enlisted in Company B, June 20, 1861, at Adrian, age 17. Clerk. Mustered out at expiration of term, June 30, 1864. Reenlisted in Hancock's Veteran Reserve Corps, Ft. Wayne, Ind., April 5, 1865. He was a druggist and postmaster, and served as a state senator, residing in Angola. Died Nov. 20, 1920, in Macomb, Ga.

Case, Charles C., Ovid, Clinton County. Enlisted in Company F as musician drummer June 20, 1861, at Adrian, age 32. Farmer, father of three children. Died of typhoid fever at Harrison's Landing, Va., July 17, 1862.

Case, Henry L. (*VV*), Jonesville. Enlisted in Company H, as musician, June 20, 1861, at Adrian, age 22. Merchant. Reenlisted Dec. 29, 1863. On detached service with Co. H, 1st Michigan Infantry, July 2, 1864. Discharged on disability in the field, June 9, 1865. Died Jan. 23, 1867. Buried in Sunset View Cemetery, Jonesville.

Cassidy, James H., Monroe County. Enlisted in Company G, June 20, 1861, at Adrian, age 20. Deserted soon after. Died in 1901 and buried Maple Grove Cemetery, Dundee.

Caswell, Andrew D., Steuben, Ind. Enlisted in Company B, June 20, 1861, at Adrian, age 24. Discharged for disability, April 15, 1863. Worked as house painter after war. Buried in Old Fremont Cemetery, Fremont, Ind.

Cauchie, William, Monroe County. Enlisted in Company A, June 20, 1861, at Adrian, age 30. Farmer, father of three children. On detached service with ambulance corps from Nov. 1862 to May 1864. Mustered out at expiration of term at Detroit, June 30, 1864. Died in 1899, buried in Maple Grove Cemetery, Dundee. Born in Scotland.

Chamberlain, David P., Hudson. Entered service as Assistant Surgeon at organization, June 20, 1861, at Adrian, age 37. Doctor, husband and father of one child at his commission. Regimental surgeon Aug. 12, 1862. Resigned and discharged for disability March 13, 1863. Resided in Toledo after service. Died on Aug. 22, 1900.

CHAMPION, HENRY B. Enlisted in Company F, Feb. 6, 1864, at Hudson, age 33. Miller. On detached service with Co. C, 1st Michigan Infantry, July 2, 1864. Transferred to Co. K, reorganized 4th Michigan, July 1, 1865. Discharged at Benton Barracks, Mo., Sept. 26, 1865.

CHAMPLIN, WARREN W. Enlisted in Company F, Feb. 2, 1864, at Pittsford, age 40. Mason. On detached service with Co. C, 1st Michigan Infantry, July 2, 1864. Transferred to Co. C, reorganized 4th Michigan, July 1, 1865. Discharged for disability at San Antonio, Jan. 15, 1866. Railroad foreman after service. Buried in Maple Grove Cemetery, Hudson.

CHANDLER, GEORGE A., Sturgis, St. Joseph County. Enlisted in Company C, June 20, 1861, at Adrian, age 43. Carpenter, married and father of four children. Missing in action at Gaines' Mill, June 27, 1862. On detached service with Co. C, 1st Michigan Infantry, July 2, 1864. Discharged at expiration of term, Petersburg, Jan. 18, 1865.

CHAPIN, MARSHALL W., Detroit. Entered service in Company I at organization as first lieutenant, June 20, 1861, age 30. Farmer, married with three children. Commissioned captain, Co. F, Jan. 15, 1862. Commissioned as colonel of the 23rd Michigan Infantry, Aug. 23, 1862. Commanding his brigade in the Twenty-third Corps from July 1863 to Jan. 1864. Resigned and honorably discharged on account of disability April 15, 1864, suffering rheumatism and dysentery. Died in Salt Lake City, Utah, April 13, 1876. Buried in Salt Lake City Cemetery.

CHAPMAN, HENRY A., Pittsford, Hillsdale County. Enlisted in Company F at organization as first lieutenant, June 20, 1861, age 41. Farmer, married with two children. He was rejected but reenlisted in Independent Company, Feb. 25, 1864, at Hudson, age 43. On detached service with Co. F, 1st Michigan Infantry, July 2, 1864. Transferred to Co. K, reorganized 4th Michigan, June 6, 1865. Died of disease in Chestnut Hill Hospital, Philadelphia, June 20, 1865. Buried in National Cemetery, Philadelphia.

CHAPMAN, JONATHAN (*VV*), Monroe County. Enlisted in Company A, May 10, 1861, Reenlisted Dec. 29, 1863. On detached service with Co. A, 1st Michigan Infantry, July 2, 1864. Transferred to Co. C, reorganized 4th Michigan, July 1, 1865. Discharged to date June 25, 1865. Farmer after the war, Corunna, Shiawassee County.

CHARTER, JACKSON, LaSalle. Monroe County. Enlisted in Company A, June 20, 1861, at Adrian, age 22. Resided with his grandmother and siblings. Wounded in action, shot in hand, May 5, 1864. Mustered out at expiration of term at Detroit, June 30, 1864. Resided at Otter Creek, working as a laborer.

CHARTER, WARREN F., LaSalle, Monroe County. Enlisted in Company A, Aug. 19, 1862, at Detroit, age 17. Resided with his parents and siblings. Wounded Nov. 1863, gunshot wound to right hand. On detached service with Co. A, 1st Michigan Infantry, July 2, 1864. Transferred to Co. K, reorganized 4th Michigan, July 1, 1865. Mustered out at Green Lake, Tex., July 31, 1865. Became a lawyer.

CHASE, ISAAC M., Hillsdale County. Enlisted in Company E, May 16, 1861, at Adrian, age 19. Discharged for disability at Minor's Hill, Va., Jan. 20, 1862. Died Feb. 19, 1911. Buried Oakwood Cemetery, Adrian.

CHASE, JAMES F., Dundee, Monroe County. Enlisted in Company A, June 20, 1861, at Adrian, age 20. Gunshot wound to right hand during service. Mustered out at expiration of term at Detroit, June 30, 1864. Resided in South Rockwood. Buried Oak Grove Cemetery, Dundee.

CHASE, WILLIAM H., Branch County. Enlisted in Company C, June 20, 1861, at Adrian, age 24. Received a gunshot wound in the right leg. Discharged for disability at New York, Oct. 20, 1862. Died Jan. 7, 1894.

CHERRY, WILLIAM, St. Joseph County. Enlisted in Company C, June 20, 1861, at Adrian, age 26. Farm laborer. Discharged for disability at Ft. Woodbury, Sept. 16, 1861, suffering from disease of the lung.

CHILDS, JONATHAN W., Augusta, Washtenaw County. Entered service at regiment's organization as major, June 20, 1861, at Adrian, age 28. Teacher and farmer. Commissioned lieutenant colonel Sept. 25, 1861. Commissioned colonel July 1, 1862. Resigned and honorably discharged Nov. 25, 1862. Died 1896, buried in Arlington National Cemetery, Va.

CHOATES, GEORGE, MONROE. Enlisted in Company A as musician June 20, 1861, at Adrian, age 17. Mustered out at expiration of term at Detroit, June 30, 1864. Resided in Detroit after service.

CICOTT, ELVI OR ELROY. Enlisted in Company A, June 20, 1861, at Adrian, age 32. Farmer. Corporal. Discharged for disability at Monroe, Feb. 20, 1863. Resided in Monroe after service, but eventually moved into a Soldiers Home.

Cisco, Lorenzo, Raisinville, Monroe County. Enlisted in Company A, June 20, 1861, at Adrian, age 20. Farmer. Discharged for disability at Washington, D.C., July 22, 1861.

Clago, James E., Grosse Ile. Enlisted in Company I, June 20, 1861, at Adrian, age 23. Farm laborer. Corporal. Killed in action at Mechanicsville, Va., June 26, 1862.

Clark, Frank, Morenci, Lenawee County. Enlisted in Company F, June 20, 1861, at Adrian, age 19. Farmer. Wounded in action July 1, 1862, Malvern Hill, Va., shot in head and leg. Paroled at Annapolis, Md. Corporal. Wounded in action and taken prisoner at Gettysburg, July 2, 1863, shot in thigh, head, and leg; left leg amputated by Confederate surgeons. Sent to Christian Street Hospital, Philadelphia. Mustered out at expiration of term at Philadelphia, June 8, 1864. Worked in an artificial limb factory in Philadelphia, and later served as a justice of the peace. Died July 29, 1894, and buried Greenwood Cemetery, Sedan, Kans.

Clark, James E., Ann Arbor. Enlisted in Company D as corporal June 20, 1861, at Adrian, age 19. Clerk residing with his parents' family. Sergeant. Sergeant major July 1, 1862. Second lieutenant, Co. I, Dec. 4, 1862. Commissioned first lieutenant, Co. B, 1862. Acting adjutant. Killed in action at Fredericksburg, Dec. 13, 1862. Originally buried at Genther's Lot, Fredericksburg. Buried National Cemetery, Fredericksburg. Born in England.

Clark, John, Coldwater. Enlisted in Company K, March 3, 1863, at Auburn, age 21. Substitute for William H. Converse, drafted from Amboy, Hillsdale County. Deserted en route from Detroit to Washington, D.C.

Clark, John, Toronto. Enlisted in Company C, March 3, 1863, for nine months, at Detroit, age 18. Painter, substitute for Henry Hilton, who was a substitute for John H. Lawrence, drafted from Amboy, Hillsdale County. No further record. Born in Ireland.

Clark, William E., Dowagiac. Entered service Aug. 20, 1861, as surgeon, age 42. Doctor. Transferred to 19th Michigan Infantry, Aug. 22, 1862. Resigned and discharged for disability July 18, 1863. Became a surgeon at Carver General Hospital, Washington, D.C. After service resided in Chicago, where he was president of the Medical Society there. Died in 1898 and buried Forest Home Cemetery, Forest Park, Ill.

Clarke, Horace A., Gibraltar, Wayne County. Enlisted in Company I, June 20, 1861, at Adrian, age 20. Killed in action at Mechanicsville, Va., June 26, 1862.

Clarke, Joseph D., Wayne County. Enlisted in Company I, at Adrian, age 18. Wounded in action at Mechanicsville, Va., June 26, 1862, shot in the abdomen. Discharged for disability April 11, 1863. Buried Riverside Cemetery, St. Charles, Saginaw County.

Clay, Samuel, St. Joseph County. Enlisted in Company C, June 20, 1861, at Adrian, age 24. Farmer. Discharged for disability at Detroit, June 4, 1862.

Clegg, John A., Lenawee County. Enlisted in Company G, March 24, 1862, at Adrian, age 31. Laborer. On detached service with Co. G, 1st Michigan Infantry, July 2, 1864. Suffered a broken leg. Discharged at expiration of term at Washington, D.C., March 29, 1865. Buried Maple Grove Cemetery, Hillsdale County. Born in England.

Clegg, Richard, Adrian, Lenawee County. Enlisted in Company G, March 24, 1862, at Adrian, age 43. Butcher, father of daughters. Discharged for disability March 1, 1863. Born in England.

Clements, Arthur, Lenawee County. Enlisted in Company G, June 20, 1861, at Adrian, age 19. Mustered out at expiration of term at Detroit, June 30, 1864.

Cobb, Cyrus P., Litchfield, Hillsdale County. Enlisted in Independent Company, Feb. 26, 1864, at Hillsdale, age 19. Farmer. On detached service with Co. F, 1st Michigan Infantry, July 2, 1864. Transferred to Co. K, reorganized 4th Michigan, June 6, 1865. Died June 1865 of wounds received in action, Columbia Street Hospital, Washington, D.C. Buried Mt. Hope Cemetery, Litchfield.

Cobb, David T., Litchfield. Enlisted in Company H, June 20, 1861, at Adrian, age 21. Farmer. Became ill during the Seven Days Campaign, in hospital at Hampton, Va., till his discharge for disability Jan. 27, 1863. Resided in Litchfield after service. Died 1923, buried Mt. Hope Cemetery, Litchfield.

Coffin, George W., Jefferson, Hillsdale County. Drafted Feb. 11, 1863, for nine months, age 23. Farmer and brother of Seth Coffin. Assigned to Company E. Discharged at expiration of term at Bealton, Va., Nov. 1, 1863. Resided in Pittsford after service. Died Sept. 22, 1913.

COFFIN, SETH, Osseo, Hillsdale County. Drafted Feb. 11, 1863, for nine months, age 21. Farmer residing with widowed mother; brother of George Coffin Assigned to Company E. Died July 6, 1863, of gunshot wound to the head, received in action at Gettysburg, July 2, 1863. Buried at Gettysburg National Cemetery.

COGSWELL, JOHN H., Hudson. Enlisted in Company F, June 20, 1861, at Adrian, age 18. Deserted from camp at Minor's Hill, Va., Dec. 7, 1861. Buried Maple Grove Cemetery, Hudson.

COLE, ALBERT V., Rollin, Lenawee County. Enlisted in Company C, Oct. 13, 1861, Hudson. Corporal. Farm laborer. Sick in brigade hospital, Dec. 1861. Discharged for disability March 2, 1863. Reentered service in Co. G, 6th Michigan Cavalry, Dec. 19, 1863, at Woodstock. Promoted to corporal, March 1, 1864. Wounded in left arm by a pistol shot, Haws Shop, Va., May 28, 1864. Discharged at Washington, D.C., July 6, 1865. Resided in Nebraska, where he eventually became state adjutant general. Died Aug. 13, 1932, Long Beach, Calif.

COLE, AMBROSE. Jefferson, Hillsdale County. Enlisted in Independent Company, Feb. 9, 1864, at Hudson, age 19. Farmer laborer and brother of Marcus Cole. Wounded in action, shot in right hand, May 23, 1864, Jericho Mills, Va. Died of wound July 1, 1864, and was buried Greenwood Cemetery, Pittsford.

COLE, BYRON A. (*VV*), Lenawee County. Enlisted in Company K, Sept. 21, 1861, at Hudson. Reenlisted Dec. 25, 1863. On detached service with Co. K, 1st Michigan Infantry, July 2, 1864. Transferred to Co. C, reorganized 4th Michigan, July 1, 1865. Mustered out at San Antonio, Feb. 26, 1866. Buried Oakwood Cemetery, Grand Ledge.

COLE, JAMES H. Entered service in Company B at organization as captain, June 20, 1861, at Adrian, age 21. Commissioned major Jan. 4, 1862. Resigned and honorably discharged for disability July 18, 1862. Resided in Chicago after service. Died Oct. 30, 1914, buried Oakwood Cemetery, Adrian.

COLE, MARCUS H., Jefferson, Hillsdale County. Enlisted in Independent Company, Feb. 11, 1864, at Jefferson, age 24. Farm laborer. On detached service with Co. F, 1st Michigan Infantry, July 2, 1864. Transferred to Co. K, reorganized 4th Michigan, June 6, 1865. Discharged at Houston, May 26, 1866. Resided in Pittsfield after service. Died March 16, 1907 in Jefferson, buried Greenwood Cemetery, Pittsford.

COLEMAN, ISAAC, Jonesville. Enlisted in Company H, June 20, 1861, at Adrian, age 31. Hostler, brother of John Coleman. Died of disease, typhoid fever, at Harrison's Landing, Va., July 12, 1862.

COLEMAN, JOHN, Hillsdale County. Enlisted in Company H, June 20, 1861, at Adrian, age 35. Teamster, brother of Isaac Coleman. Transferred to Invalid Corps, July 1, 1863. Resided in Jonesville after service. Buried in Sunset View Cemetery, Jonesville.

COLEMAN, LEVI B. (*VV*), Lenawee County. Enlisted in Company G, June 20, 1861, at Adrian, age 28. Reenlisted Dec. 29, 1863, at Tecumseh. Wounded in action at Wilderness, Va., May 5, 1864, gunshot wound to left leg and arm. On detached service with Co. G, 1st Michigan Infantry, July 2, 1864. Transferred to Co. C, reorganized 4th Michigan, July 1, 1865. Mustered out at San Antonio, Feb. 26, 1866. Admitted to Soldiers Home, Dayton, Oct. 30, 1895. Buried Mt. Hope Cemetery, San Diego.

COLLINS, GEORGE, Calhoun County. Enlisted in Company C, June 20, 1861, at Adrian, age 17. Deserted at Adrian, June 25, 1861.

COLLINS, JOHN, Washtenaw County. Enlisted in Company K, June 20, 1861, at Adrian, age 21. Barber. Deserted at Washington, D.C., July 24, 1861. Born in Ireland.

COMFORT, GEORGE W. Hillsdale County. Enlisted in Company E, June 20, 1861, at Adrian, age 22. Discharged for disability at Georgetown, March 3, 1862. Died March 13, 1865.

COMSTOCK, CHESTER W. (*VV*), Washtenaw County. Enlisted in Company D, June 20, 1861, at Adrian, age 23. Farm laborer. Reenlisted Dec. 29, 1863, at Saline. Wounded in action, shot in leg, dated by army records as June 4, 1864, but this was likely June 3, near Bethesda Church, Va. Sergeant. On detached service with Co. E, 1st Michigan Infantry, July 2, 1864. Transferred to Co. C, reorganized 4th Michigan, July 1, 1865. Discharged for disability at Detroit, Sept. 30, 1865.

COMSTOCK, ELLIS B., Salem, Washtenaw County. Enlisted in Company D, Aug. 12, 1862, at Ann Arbor, age 21. Farmer, brother of John W. Comstock. Killed in action at Gettysburg, July 2, 1863. Buried in Gettysburg National Cemetery, Michigan Plot, 11-B.

COMSTOCK, HARRISON, Lenawee County. Enlisted in Company F, May 16, 1861, at Adrian, age 20. Farmer. Mustered out at expiration of term at Detroit, June 29, 1864.

COMSTOCK, JOHN W. (*VV*), Washtenaw County. Enlisted in Company D, June 20, 1861, at Adrian, age 25. Farmer, brother of Ellis Comstock. Reenlisted Dec. 29, 1863, at Saline. Wounded in action May 5, 1864, gunshot, right thigh. On detached service with Co. E, 1st Michigan Infantry, July 2, 1864. Corporal Jan. 25, 1865. Transferred to Co. K, reorganized 4th Michigan, July 1, 1865. Sergeant July 1, 1865. Mustered out at Detroit, Feb. 23, 1866. Buried in Luzerne Cemetery, Luzerne, Oscoda County.

CONANT, JOHN S., Denton, Wayne County. Drafted Feb. 20, 1863, for nine months, from Liberty, Jackson County, age 26. Farm laborer. Assigned to Company H. Discharged at expiration of term at Bealton, Va., Nov. 11, 1863. Died April 11, 1897.

CONKEY, JAMES B. (*VV*), Washtenaw County. Enlisted in Company K, as corporal, June 20, 1861, at Adrian, age 35. Machinist. Sergeant Feb. 10, 1862. Reenlisted Dec. 29, 1863. Wounded in action May 5, 1864, Wilderness, Va., shot in back. Admitted to Campbell Hospital, Washington, D.C. Discharged on disability July 20, 1865.

CONKLIN, WESLEY R., Monroe County. Enlisted in Company G, June 20, 1861, at Adrian, age 25. Shoemaker. Discharged for disability, Sept. 23, 1861. Died of tuberculosis in Eaton County.

CONLON, JOHN, Webster, Washtenaw County. Enlisted in Company A, June 20, 1861, at Adrian, age 19. Farmer. Resided in Saginaw after the war.

CONNOR, JOHN, Lenawee County. Enlisted in Company F, June 20, 1861, at Adrian, age 33. Stone cutter. Deserted at Washington, D.C., Aug. 15, 1861.

CONVERSE, ORRIN M., Jackson County. Enlisted in Company K, Sept. 21, 1861, at Hudson, age 25. Laborer. Wounded July 1, 1862, Malvern Hill, Va., and sent to Ninth St. Hospital, Washington, D.C. Discharged for disability, Feb. 3, 1863, at Detroit for chronic rheumatism. Mustered Co. E, 11th Michigan Cavalry Oct. 7, 1864. Promoted to second lieutenant Jan. 1, 1865. Mustered out Pulaski, Tenn.

COOK, ANDREW J. Enlisted in Company I, Feb. 10, 1864, at Hudson, age 19. Farmer. Wounded in action, shot in arm, Wilderness, Va., May 5, 1864. On detached service with Co. I, 1st Michigan Infantry, July 2, 1864. Transferred to Co. C, reorganized 4th Michigan, July 1, 1865. Transferred to Co. K, Feb. 15, 1866. Mustered out at Houston, May 26, 1866. Resided in Pittsfield, Washtenaw County.

COOK, BYRON H. Enlisted in Company H, Feb. 20, 1862, at Adrian, age 18. Farmer laborer and student. Killed in action at Malvern Hill, Va., July 1, 1862.

COOK, GEORGE, White Pigeon, St. Joseph County. Enlisted in Company C, June 20, 1861, at Adrian, age 21. Regimental blacksmith. Mustered out at expiration of term at Detroit, June 30, 1864. Resided in Wexford after service. Born in England.

COOK, HARRISON P., Lenawee County. Enlisted in Company K, June 20, 1861, at Adrian, age 20. Discharged for disability at Harrison's Landing, Va., July 25, 1862. Buried Leoni Cemetery, Leoni, Jackson County.

COOK, JACOB F., Washtenaw County. Enlisted in Company D, at Hudson, Sept. 19, 1861, age 25. Farm laborer. Taken prisoner at Gettysburg, July 2, 1863. On detached service with 1st Michigan Infantry, July 2, 1864. Dropped from company rolls per order Sept. 9, 1864.

COOLEY, CHARLES, Monroe. Enlisted in Company H as corporal June 20, 1861, at Adrian, age 23. Sailor, resided with parents and family. Transferred on Dec. 1, 1861, to the Navy, serving on gunboats *Carondelet* and *Ajax*. Mustered out Dec. 3, 1864. Reenlisted in the 17th Michigan Infantry. Taken prisoner May 12, 1865, near Spotsylvania, Va. Resided in Rockwood after service.

COOPER, JOHN F., Wayne County. Enlisted in Company I as corporal June 20, 1861, at Adrian, age 27. Mustered out at expiration of term at Detroit, June 30, 1864.

COOPER, WILLIAM B., St. Joseph County. Enlisted in Company C, June 20, 1861, at Adrian, age 18. Blacksmith. Wounded in action at Gettysburg, July 2, 1863, struck on the right side of head above ear with buckshot. Sent to Summit Hospital, Philadelphia. Wounded in action again, Wilderness, Va., May 5, 1864, shot in right knee. Taken to Seminary Hospital, Fairfax, Va. Mustered out at expiration of term at Detroit, June 29, 1864. Described as destitute May 20, 1891, inmate at a "County House" for the poor. Admitted to Soldiers Home, Dayton, Aug. 21, 1891, transferred to General Insane Asylum, July 30, 1892.

COPPINS, CHARLES, Hillsdale County. Enlisted in Company B, Oct. 22, 1861, at Ransom, age 25. Farm laborer, married, no children. Discharged at expiration of term at Detroit, Nov. 7, 1864. Received an injury to his left hand while in the service. Resided in Ransom afterward. Born in England.

CORNELL, DAVID G. Enlisted in Company I, Jan. 29, 1864, at Pittsford, Hillsdale County, age 26. Farmer. On detached service with Co. I, 1st Michigan Infantry, July 2, 1864. Transferred to Co. C, reorganized 4th Michigan Infantry, July 1, 1865. In Harper Hospital April 6, 1865. Discharged at Detroit, May 12, 1865.

CORSER, GEORGE W., Lenawee. Enlisted in Company A, Sept. 17, 1861, at Hudson, age 21. Wounded and missing in action at Gaines' Mill, Va., June 27, 1862, with gunshot wound in right foot. Discharged for disability Dec. 28, 1862. Resided in Hudson after service. Died 1924. Buried Lickly Corners Cemetery, Hillsdale County.

COTRELL, DION H., Lenawee County. Enlisted in Company F, June 20, 1861, at Adrian, age 18. Farmer. Wounded in action at Mechanicsville, June 26, 1862, shot in knee. Discharged for disability at Philadelphia, Sept. 20, 1862.

COURTRIGHT, LEVI J., Reading, Hillsdale County. Enlisted in Company E, as corporal, June 20, 1861, at Adrian, age 37. Farmer and father of six. Died Sept. 3, 1861, of wounds received on picket near Halls House, Arlington Heights, Va. Buried Oak Grove Cemetery, Hillsdale.

COULAN, JOHN, Monroe County. Enlisted in Company A, June 20, 1861, at Adrian, age 23. Mustered out at expiration of term at Detroit, June 30, 1864.

COUSE, EDWARD G., Detroit. Enlisted in Company I, as corporal, June 20, 1861, at Adrian, age 17. Farm laborer. Second lieutenant in 27th Michigan Infantry, Oct. 10, 1862. Resigned May 25, 1863. Resided at Soldier Home, Grand Rapids, Aug. 1894. Died Dec. 27, 1896. Buried at Milwaukee, Wis.

COUTRE, SAMUEL S., Monroe County. Enlisted in Company A, June 20, 1861, at Adrian, age 27. Carpenter. Provost guard at corps headquarters from Nov. 1862 to May 1864. Mustered out at expiration of term at Detroit, June 30, 1864.

COVILLE, ANDREW, Lenawee County. Enlisted in Company F, June 20, 1861, at Adrian, age 24. Farmer living with his mother and two siblings. Sergeant. Missing in action at Gettysburg, July 2, 1863. Presumed to having been killed.

COWGILL, CYRENIUS C., Amboy Township, Hillsdale County. Enlisted in Company C, June 20, 1861, at Adrian, age 23. Sick in General Hospital, Georgetown, Sept.–Oct. 1861. Corporal Jan. 1863. Taken prisoner at Gettysburg, July 2, 1863; arrived in Richmond, July 25, 1863. Admitted Military Prison Hospital No. 21 on Jan. 21, 1864. Died there of pneumonia, Feb. 2, 1864.

CRAIG, ORLANDO, Albion. Enlisted in Company I, June 20, 1861, at Adrian, age 21. Wagon maker. Died at Point Lookout Hospital, Md., Dec. 15, 1862, of severe wounds received in action at Fredericksburg, Va., Dec. 13, 1862.

CRAIN, JOHN F., aka Samuel Crain, Steuben, Ind. Enlisted in Company C, May 16, 1861. Farmer. Wounded slightly in action at Gettysburg, July 2, 1863. Reenlisted Dec. 29, 1863. On detached service with Co. C, 1st Michigan Infantry, July 2, 1864. Deserted at New Orleans, June 25, 1865. Buried at Los Angeles National Cemetery.

CRAMER, RICHARD L., Mt. Clemens. Enlisted in Company I, June 20, 1861, at Adrian, age 18. Shoemaker. Discharged for disability Feb. 16, 1863. Reenlisted in the 1st Michigan Cavalry, Oct. 16, 1863. Taken prisoner at Trevilian Station, Va., June 11, 1864. Mustered out May 29, 1865. Died Nov. 6, 1894. Buried in Oxford.

CRANE, ALEXANDER B., Dexter, Washtenaw County. Enlisted in Company K, June 20, 1861, at Adrian, age 23. Farm laborer, son of Martin L. Crane and brother of George Crane. Discharged for disability at York, Pa., Sept. 5, 1862, on account of wounds received in action at Gaines' Mill, Va., June 27, 1862. Buried Forest Lawn Cemetery, Dexter.

CRANE, ALEXANDER DALLAS, Scio, Washtenaw County. Entered service in Company I at organization as captain, June 20, 1861, at Adrian age 51. Lawyer, general in Michigan's state militia. Resigned and honorably discharged, sprained his ankle when his horse fell. After service served as justice of the peace. Died 1893 and buried in Forest Lawn Cemetery, Dexter.

CRANE, GEORGE, Dexter. Enlisted in Company K, June 20, 1861, at Adrian, age 24. Brother of Alexander B. Crane and son of Martin L. Crane. Carpenter. Discharged for disability at Minor's Hill, Va., Nov. 1, 1861. Reenlisted and was supposed to have died on Sherman's March to the Sea.

CRANE, MARTIN L., Washtenaw County. Enlisted in Company K as wagoner June 20, 1861, at Adrian, age 48. Carpenter, father of seven, including George Crane. Discharged for disability Aug. 2, 1861. Resided in Northville after war. Died July 15, 1896. Buried Novi Cemetery, Novi.

Cranell, William W., Jackson County. Enlisted in Company D, musician, June 20, 1861, at Adrian, age 34. Blacksmith and lawyer. Discharged for disability at Washington, D.C., Aug. 5, 1861, chronic diarrhea and pains in chest.

Cranston, Robert H., Washtenaw County. Enlisted in Company D, June 20, 1861, at Adrian, age 18. Farm laborer. Musician fifer. Dropped from rolls at Bealton, Va., Jan. 3, 1864. Born in Canada.

Cranston, William, Lenawee County. Enlisted in Company K, May 16, 1861, transferred to Co. G. Color bearer. On detached service with Co. G, 1st Michigan Infantry, July 1, 1864. Transferred to Co. C, reorganized 4th Michigan, July 1, 1865. Deserted at New Orleans, June 25, 1865.

Crawford, Quimby H., Monroe County. Enlisted in Company D, June 20, 1861, at Adrian, age 19. Given extra duty Nov. 1861 at U.S. General Hospital, Washington, D.C., for an unknown infraction. Wounded in head while in action at Gettysburg, July 2, 1863, causing unconsciousness, deafness, and derangement. Admitted July 5, 1863, to Satterlee Hospital, Philadelphia. Detailed to Provost Guard, Philadelphia, Jan. 22, 1864. Brought up on charges for helping a prisoner to escape in 1864; sentenced to a period of hard labor and $41 in restitution. Mustered out at expiration of term at Detroit, June 30, 1864. Admitted to Soldiers Home, Dayton, Nov. 11, 1892.

Cressey, Noah, Lenawee County. Enlisted in Company F as musician drummer June 20, 1861, at Adrian, age 53. Farmer. Discharged for disability at Harrison's Landing, Va., July 20, 1862. Buried Main Street Cemetery, Newark, N.Y.

Crisler, Joseph W., Hillsdale County. Enlisted in Company E, June 20, 1861, at Adrian, age 18. Farmer. Wounded in action at Wilderness, Va., May 5, 1864, shot in head and arm. Mustered out at expiration of term at Detroit, June 28, 1864. Resided in Ashton, Osceola County.

Critchfield, Jesse D., Hillsdale County. Enlisted in Company E, June 20, 1861, at Adrian, age 27. Discharged for disability at Georgetown, April 2, 1862.

Crocket, Leroy, Steuben, Ind. Enlisted in Company B, June 20, 1861, at Adrian, age 18. Farmer residing with parents and siblings. Died of disease at Union Hotel, Georgetown, Sept. 14, 1861. Buried in Grave 889, Military Asylum Cemetery, Washington, D.C.

Croghan, George, Washtenaw County. Enlisted in Company K, June 24, 1861, at Adrian, age 19. Miller. In hospital July 15, 1862, for sunstroke. Discharged at Sharpsburg, Md., Oct. 25, 1862. Enlisted with Battery D, 5th U.S. Artillery. Resided in Idaho after service.

Cronenwill, William N., Wayne County. Enlisted in Company D, June 20, 1861, at Adrian, age 24. Wounded twice with gunshots in right thigh in action at Gettysburg, July 2, 1863. Returned to duty Oct. 21, 1863, but transferred to Invalid Corps, Washington, D.C., Nov. 1863.

Cronk, David, Wheatland, Hillsdale County. Enlisted in Company F, May 16, 1861, at Adrian, age 22. Died of disease at Adrian before mustering, June 10, 1861.

Cross, Lorenzo, Wayne County. Enlisted in Company I, June 20, 1861, at Adrian, age 34. Deserted at Adrian, June 23, 1861.

Croxton, Lafayette Jack, Steuben, Ind. Enlisted in Company B, June 20, 1861, at Adrian, age 21. Law student. Wounded in action and taken prisoner at Gaines' Mill, Va., June 27, 1862, shot in left chest. Returned to regiment at Harrison's Landing, Va., Aug. 20, 1862. Discharged for disability on account of wound, Oct. 5, 1862. Resided in Goshen, Ind., after service. Admitted to Soldiers Home, Dayton, Nov. 1871. Died Jan. 25, 1877.

Culver, Adelbert D., Metamora, Ohio. Enlisted in Company B, June 20, 1861, at Adrian, age 19. Wounded in action at Malvern Hill, Va., July 1, 1862. Discharged for disability Sept. 19, 1862. Resided in Fulton County, Ohio, after service.

Cummings, William, Saline, Washtenaw County. Enlisted in Company C, June 20, 1861, at Adrian, age 22. Currier. Sick in camp hospital Dec. 1861. Died of disease at Minor's Hill, Va., Jan. 2, 1862. Buried Jan. 5 in Military Asylum Cemetery, Washington, D.C. Born in Canada.

Cunningham, Henry, Wayne County. Enlisted in Company I, June 20, 1861, at Adrian, age 19. Discharged for disability by order, Nov. 8, 1862.

Cunningham, William J. (*VV*), Dexter. Enlisted in Company K, June 20, 1861, at Adrian, age 22. Farmer, had two brothers, George and James Cunningham, both of whom served in the Union army and died during the war. Wounded and missing in action at Gaines' Mill, Va., June 27, 1862. Reenlisted Dec. 29, 1863. Corporal. Sergeant. Killed at Wilderness, Va., May 6, 1864, by a shell fragment. Buried at Fredericksburg, Va.

CURTIS, AMBROSE, Tecumseh. Enlisted in Company G as corporal June 20, 1861, at Adrian, age 21. First sergeant. Severely wounded in action at Gettysburg, July 2, 1863. Mustered out at expiration of term at Detroit, June 20, 1864. After close of war enlisted in the 8th U.S. Cavalry, served two years fighting Indians. After service was assistant engineer for the Flint & Pere Marquette Railroad. Died in Flint, Feb. 9, 1881. Buried Feb. 17, 1881, Brookside Cemetery, Tecumseh.

CURTIS, BENJAMIN F., Monroe County. Enlisted in Company A, June 20, 1861, at Adrian, age 19. Mustered out at expiration of term at Detroit, June 30, 1864. Resided in Toledo after service.

CURTIS, THOMAS J., Hillsdale. Enlisted in Independent Company, March 25, 1864, age 21. Schoolteacher. On detached service with Co. F, 1st First Michigan Infantry, July 2, 1864. Transferred to Co. K, reorganized 4th Michigan, June 6, 1865. Corporal Oct. 1, 1865. Sergeant May 1, 1866. Discharged at Houston, May 26, 1866. Resumed teaching after the war, married and had a family, residing in Rome, Lenawee County.

D

DALEY, LORENZO, Lenawee County. Enlisted in Company F, June 20, 1861, at Adrian, age 25. Farmer. Assistant division wagon master. Mustered out at expiration of term at Detroit, June 29, 1864.

DALEY, MICHAEL, Blissfield, Lenawee County. Enlisted in Company B, June 20, 1861, at Adrian, age 21. Laborer residing with parents and brother. Wounded at Fredericksburg, Dec. 13, 1862, shot in hip. Discharged Jan. 28, 1863, for disability because of wound. Admitted to Soldiers Home, Dayton, where he died July 28, 1882. Born in Ireland.

DANIELS, HARRISON, Lenawee County. Enlisted in Company G, June 20, 1861, at Adrian, age 24. Mustered out at expiration of term at Detroit, June 30, 1864. Died April 8, 1927, Tecumseh.

DANIELS, MONTROSS, Jackson County. Enlisted in Company H, June 20, 1861, at Adrian, age 21. Farmer. Detached to serve with Arnold's Battery, July 16, 1861. Deserted on March 1, 1862.

DANN, REUBEN, Lenawee County. Enlisted in Company F, June 20, 1861, at Adrian, age 22. Farmer. Deserted at Alexandria, Va., April 21, 1862. Born in Yorkshire, England.

DARKHURST, JAMES A., Lenawee County. In Company F, June 20, 1861, at Adrian. Mustered out June 29, 1864. Suffered from lung disease contracted during war, from which he died Oct. 5, 1876, Devil's Lake, Rollin/ Woodstock townships.

DARROW, JOSEPH, Calhoun County. Enlisted in Company C, June 20, 1861, at Adrian, age 27. Missing in action at Gaines' Mill, June 27, 1862. Discharged for disability at Warrenton, Va., Nov. 21, 1862. Resided in Tecumseh after service. Died March 17, 1893.

DATES, JOHN J., Jackson County. Enlisted in Company D, June 20, 1861, at Adrian, age 40. Farmer, married, with a young son. Discharged for disability at York, Pa., Jan. 19, 1864, for gunshot wound to the left thigh, received in action at Gettysburg, July 2, 1863. Reenlisted 10th Michigan Infantry, March 29, 1864, at Salome. Mustered out April 15, 1865, at Louisville, Ky. Resided in Mankato, Minn. after service.

DAVIDSON, AUGUSTUS, LaSalle, Monroe County. Enlisted in Company A, Aug. 4, 1862, at Monroe, age 25. Farm laborer. Missing in action at Gettysburg, July 2, 1863. On detached service with Company A, 1st Michigan Infantry, July 2, 1864. Taken prisoner at Weldon Railroad, Va., Sept. 8, 1864. No further record.

DAVIDSON, WILLARD, Hudson. Enlisted in Independent Company, Feb. 27, 1864, at Hudson, age 38. On detached service with Co. F, 1st Michigan Infantry, July 2, 1864. Transferred to Co. K, reorganized 4th Michigan, June 6, 1865. Died at Alexandria, Va., May 4, 1866. Buried Old Cemetery, Hudson; a marker for him is at Maple Grove Cemetery, Hudson.

DAVIS, ARTHUR L. Enlisted in Company C. Listed as absent Aug. 18, 1862. No further record.

DAVIS, ENOCH, Defiance County, Ohio. Enlisted in Company B, June 20, 1861, at Adrian, age 25. Farmer. Reenlisted

Dec. 29, 1863. Killed in action at Wilderness, Va., May 5, 1864.

DAVIS, HIRAM H., Washtenaw County. Enlisted in Company D, corporal, June 20, 1861, age 21. Transferred to Invalid Corps, Jan. 6, 1864. Returned April 16, 1864. Wounded in action, shot in neck, Wilderness, Va., May 5, 1864. Mustered out at expiration of term at Detroit, June 30, 1864.

DAVIS, JAMES (*VV*), Shiawassee County. Enlisted in Company I, June 20, 1861, at Adrian, age 19. Taken prisoner at Gettysburg, July 2, 1863. Returned to regiment at Culpeper Va., Oct. 9, 1863. Reenlisted Dec. 29, 1863. Wounded in action, shot in side and arm, May 5, 1864, Wilderness, Va. On detached service with Co. I, 1st Michigan Infantry, July 2, 1864. Transferred to Co. C, reorganized 4th Michigan, July 1, 1865. Mustered out at San Antonio, Feb. 26, 1866.

DAVIS, LAFAYETTE. Enlisted in Company F, Jan. 16, 1864, at Hudson, age 35. Farmer, father of three. Wounded at Wilderness, Va., May 5, 1864, shot in lung and arm. Died of wounds at Fredericksburg, May 13, 1864.

DAVIS or DAVID, ORSON, Calhoun County. Enlisted in Company D, June 20, 1861, at Adrian, age 21. Reportedly killed in action at Gettysburg, July 2, 1863, though he doesn't appear in regiment's list of casualties for that battle. No further record.

DAVIS, WILLIAM, Hillsdale County. Enlisted in Company H, June 20, 1861, at Adrian, age 21. Wounded in action at Fredericksburg, Va., Dec. 13, 1862, loss of index finger right hand. Discharged for disability, April 6, 1863.

DAVIS, WILSON, Tecumseh. Enlisted in Company G, June 20, 1861, at Adrian, age 21. Farm laborer. Died of disease at Georgetown, Sept. 11, 1861. Buried Military Asylum Cemetery, Washington, D.C.

DAY, ADELBERT F. (*VV*), Steuben, Ind. Enlisted in Company B, June 20, 1861, at Adrian, age 16. Wounded in action and taken prisoner at Gaines' Mill, Va., June 27, 1862. Held in Richmond, Va. Paroled at Atkins Landing, Va., Aug. 5, 1862. Taken prisoner at Gettysburg, July 2, 1863; held at Belle Isle, Va., suffering from chronic diarrhea. Paroled at City Point, Va., Aug. 29, 1863. Returned to regiment at Culpeper, Oct. 1863. Reenlisted Dec. 29, 1863. On recruiting duty in Michigan June 1864 to muster out. On detached service with 1st Michigan Infantry, July 2, 1864. Transferred to Co. C, reorganized 4th Michigan, July 1, 1865. Discharged at Detroit, Sept. 11, 1865. Printer after service, served as Angola County recorder. Attended the 50th reunion of the battle of Gettysburg. Died Sept. 26, 1914, Angola.

DAY, LIBERTY, Hillsdale. Enlisted in Independent Company, Feb. 8, 1864, at Cambria, age 23. On detached service with Co. F, 1st Michigan Infantry, July 2, 1864. Mustered out at hospital in Philadelphia, June 9, 1865.

DAY, ROBERT R. Enlisted unassigned to company, Dec. 21, 1863, age 19. No further record.

DEAN, CHARLES B., Washtenaw County. Enlisted in Company D, June 20, 1861, at Adrian, age 23. Corporal. Wounded in action July 1862 during the Seven Days; again wounded in the thigh, Sept. 19, 1862, Shepherdstown Ford. Discharged at Ft. Hamilton, N.Y., Feb. 9, 1863, to enlist in regular army. Discharged at expiration of term near Fredericksburg, Va., May 16, 1864.

DEAN, ELI H., Ann Arbor. Enlisted in Company D, June 20, 1861, at Adrian, age 22. Farmer. Killed in action at Malvern Hill, Va., July 1, 1862.

DEAN, JOHN (*VV*), Hillsdale County. Enlisted in Company H, corporal, June 20, 1861, at Adrian, age 28. Farmer. In hospital from Aug. 15 to Dec. 25, 1861, with typhoid fever. Wounded in action, June 27, 1862, Gaines' Mill, Va., gunshot wounds to face and shoulder. Sent to hospital in Baltimore, where he met a nurse who became his wife. Sergeant Feb. 18, 1862. Reenlisted Dec. 29, 1863. On detached service with Co. H, 1st Michigan Infantry, July 2, 1864. Suffered an injury to his back at Weldon Railroad, Va., summer 1864. Transferred to Co. C, reorganized 4th Michigan, July 1, 1865. Mustered out at San Antonio, Feb. 26, 1866. Resided in Litchfield after service, eventually confined to a wheelchair as a result of spinal injury. Died 1912 and buried Mt. Hope Cemetery, Litchfield. Born in England.

DECKER, CHARLES W., Hillsdale County. Enlisted in Company E, June 20, 1861, at Adrian, age 18. Wounded in action at Gaines' Mill, Va., June 27, 1862. Reenlisted Dec. 29, 1863. Returned to regiment May 15, 1864. On detached service with Co. K, 1st Michigan Infantry, July 2, 1864. Transferred to Co. K, reorganized 4th Michigan, June 6, 1865. Corporal Oct. 1865. Mustered out at San Antonio, Feb. 23, 1866.

DEGOLYER, SAMUEL, Lenawee County. Entered service in Company F at organization as captain, June 20, 1861, at Adrian, age 33. Lawyer and wheel-spoke manufacturer. Married, father of a young daughter. Commissioned major Sept. 25, 1861. Resigned Jan. 13, 1862. Commissioned captain, Battery H, 1st Michigan Light Artillery, March 11, 1862. Died Aug. 8, 1863, of wounds received at Vicksburg, Miss., May 28, 1863. Buried Maple Grove Cemetery, Hudson.

DELAMATER, ADELBERT, Pittsford, Hillsdale County. Enlisted in Independent Company, Feb. 27, 1864, at Hudson, age 18. On detached service with Co. F, 1st Michigan Infantry, July 2, 1864. Transferred to Co. K, reorganized 4th Michigan Infantry, June 6, 1865. Discharged at San Antonio, to date Feb. 14, 1866. Buried Memorial Cemetery, Santa Cruz, Calif.

DELAMATER, SAMUEL A., Jefferson, Hillsdale County. Enlisted in Independent Company, Feb. 11, 1864, age 20. Farmer resided with parents and sister. On detached service with Co. F, 1st Michigan Infantry, July 2, 1864. Transferred to Co. K, reorganized 4th Michigan, June 6, 1865, but was discharged at Washington, D.C., June 10, 1865, on account of wounds received in action Oct. 27, 1864, shot in left ankle. Resided in Pittsford after service.

DELANY, JOHN, Lenawee County. Enlisted in Company F, June 20, 1861, at Adrian, age 21. Farmer. Discharged for disability at Harrison's Landing, Va., July 20, 1862. Died Oct. 1883, buried St Anthony Cemetery, Hillsdale.

DEMMING, BENJAMIN O., Livingston County. Enlisted in Company K, June 20, 1861, at Adrian, age 18. Discharged for disability at Minor's Hill, Jan. 6, 1862. Reentered service in 2nd Michigan Infantry, March 31, 1864, at Centerville. Taken prisoner near Petersburg, Va., July 30, 1864. No further record.

DENMAN, WILLIAM, Washtenaw County. Enlisted in Company D, June 20, 1861, at Adrian, age 22. Mason. Discharged for disability at Washington, D.C., May 13, 1862.

DEPUY, RICHARD G., Ann Arbor. Entered service in Company D at organization as first lieutenant, June 20, 1861, at Adrian, age 30. Lawyer, father of four young children. Commissioned captain, Co. K, Aug. 20, 1861. Killed in action at Gaines' Mill, Va., June 27, 1862.

DEUEL, FREDERICK P., Lenawee County. Enlisted in Company G as orderly sergeant June 20, 1861, at Adrian, age 22. Wounded in right thigh, paralyzing his leg. Discharged for disability at Baltimore, Oct. 29, 1862. Admitted to Soldiers Home, Dayton, Oct. 26, 1906. Died there April 27, 1911, from pneumonia. Buried Grave 25, Sec. Q, Row 11, at the Soldiers Home, Dayton.

DEWEY, GEORGE H., Lenawee County. Enlisted in Company H, Oct. 7, 1861, at Hudson, age 22. Farmer. Discharged for disability June 4, 1862, because of diarrhea and piles. Resided in Hudson after service.

DEXTER, FLAVIUS, J., Washtenaw County. Enlisted in Company D, June 20, 1861, at Adrian, age 21. Taken prisoner at Gettysburg, Pa., July 2, 1863. Returned to regiment at Culpeper, Va., Oct. 9, 1863. Discharged at expiration of term at Detroit, June 1864.

DICKERSON, JAMES B. Enlisted in Company F, June 20, 1861, at Adrian, age 34. Farmer, cooper, and mechanic. Sergeant Sept. 1, 1861. Discharged for disability for deafness at Harrison's Landing, Va., Aug. 14, 1862. Enlisted in Independent Company, March 16, 1864, at Hudson, as sergeant. On detached service with Co. F, 1st Michigan Infantry, July 2, 1864. Transferred to Co. K, reorganized 4th Michigan, June 6, 1865. First sergeant Oct. 1, 1865. Commissioned second lieutenant Oct. 24, 1865. Mustered out at San Antonio, Feb. 23, 1866. Served as a village marshal in Hudson after war. Buried Maple Grove Cemetery, Hudson.

DICKINSON, JOHN E. Enlisted in Company G as corporal June 20, 1861, age 21. Mustered out at expiration of term at Detroit, June 30, 1864. Admitted to Soldiers Home, Dayton, for dropsy, Nov. 28, 1886 where he died on June 24, 1887.

DICKINSON, JOHN R., Monroe County. Enlisted in Company A, June 20, 1861, at Adrian, age 25. Corporal Oct. 18, 1862. Mustered out at expiration of term at Detroit, June 30, 1864. Resided Dundee after service.

DIEHL, AARON J., Wayne County. Enlisted in Company I, June 20, 1861, at Adrian, age 25. Discharged for disability at Warrenton, Va., Nov. 12, 1862, because of gunshot wounds to left arm and left thigh during the Peninsula Campaign. Resided in Knox Township, Ohio, after service.

DILDINE, WILLIAM H., Hillsdale County. Enlisted in Company E, June 20, 1861, at Adrian, age 21. Laborer. Mustered out at expiration of term at Detroit, June 28, 1864. Resided in Sandusky, Ohio, after service.

DILLON, JOHN, Lenawee County. Enlisted in Company F, Sept. 10, 1861, at Hudson, age 16. Farm boy. Was in Georgetown hospital from March to July 1862. On detached service with Co. C, 1st Michigan Infantry, July

2, 1864. Discharged at expiration of term at Weldon Railroad, Va., Sept. 11, 1864. Resided in Hudson. Died in 1927. Buried Maple Grove Cemetery, Hudson.

DILLON, LUMAN H., Hillsdale. Enlisted in Independent Company, March 28, 1864, at Hillsdale, age 16. Farmer. On detached service with Co. F, 1st Michigan Infantry, July 2, 1864. Wounded in action, Oct. 27, 1864, gunshot to left leg at Hatcher's Run, Va. Transferred to Co. K, reorganized 4th Michigan Infantry, June 6, 1865. Corporal May 1, 1866. Mustered out at Houston, May 26, 1866. Resided in Jefferson after service. Died 1926, buried North Lawn Cemetery, North Adams.

DILLON, WILLIAM B., Pittsford, Hillsdale County. Enlisted in Company F, June 20, 1861, at Adrian, age 20. Farmer. Taken prisoner at Gettysburg, July 2, 1863. Died at Belle Isle, Richmond, Va., Dec. 25, 1863. Buried in Locust Cemetery, Pittsford.

DISHER, JOHN (*VV*), Carleton, Monroe County. Enlisted in Company A, June 20, 1861, at Adrian, age 16. Taken prisoner at Gettysburg, July 2, 1863. Held at Richmond. Returned to regiment Oct. 9, 1863, at Culpeper, Va. Reenlisted Dec. 29, 1863. Wounded at Petersburg, Va., June 20, 1864, gunshot wound, right lung. On detached service with Co. A, 1st Michigan Infantry, July 2, 1864. Transferred to Co. C, reorganized 4th Michigan Infantry, June 6, 1865. Discharged at Detroit, July 13, 1865. Resided at Carleton after service, a house builder and butcher. Died Nov. 3, 1916, buried in St. Patrick's Cemetery, Stony Creek. Born in Germany.

DIVELBISS, GEORGE W., Steuben, Ind. Enlisted in Company B, June 20, 1861, at Adrian, age 21. Farmer. Corporal. Wounded in action at Gettysburg, July 2, 1863, shot in both thighs and scrotum. In Fifth Corps Hospital, July 4 to 19; transferred to hospital, York, Pa., until Dec. 18, 1863. Mustered out at expiration of term at Detroit, June 30, 1864. Resided in Allegheny, Pa., and Salina and Ellsworth, Kans., after service, machinist and bridge carpenter.

DODGE, ALVIN, Hillsdale County. Enlisted in Company H, June 20, 1861, at Adrian, age 24. Carpenter and joiner. Discharged for disability March 1, 1864, Bealton, Va., by order. Resided in Chattanooga, Tenn., after service.

DODGE, WILLIAM H., alias Hiram Dodge, Hillsdale County. Enlisted in Company H, June 20, 1861, at Adrian, age 23. Carpenter. Mustered out at expiration of term at Detroit, June 30, 1864. Resided in Manhattan, Kans.

DOLPH, ALFRED, Litchfield, Hillsdale County. Enlisted in Company E, June 20, 1861, at Adrian, age 21. Carpenter apprentice. Killed in action at Malvern Hill, Va., July 1, 1862.

DONLEY, GILES G., Livingston County. Enlisted in Company K, June 20, 1861, at Adrian, age 21. Shoemaker. Wounded in right hand, Malvern Hill, July 2, 1862. Transferred to Invalid Corps, Jan. 15, 1864. Lived in Soldiers Home, Grand Rapids, and was buried there, Row 20, Grave 9.

DONNELLY, ALEXANDER, Wayne County. Enlisted in Company D, June 20, 1861, at Adrian, age 23. Discharged for disability at Ft. Woodbury, Va., Sept. 14, 1861.

DOOLITTLE CHARLES C., Hillsdale. Enlisted in Company E, May 16, 1861, age 29. Banker, married, father of two young sons. First lieutenant. Promoted captain Aug. 20, 1861. Wounded in action at Gaines' Mill, Va., June 27, 1862. Promoted colonel, 18th Michigan Infantry, July 27, 1862; brigadier general of U.S. Volunteers, Jan. 27, 1865; and brevet major general, June 13, 1865, "for meritorious service." Mustered out Nov. 30, 1865. Resided in Toledo after service. Died Feb. 20, 1903. Buried Woodlawn Cemetery, Toledo.

DORN, JOHN J., Howell. Enlisted in Company K, June 20, 1861, at Adrian, age 22. Farmer. Died of disease in New York City, May 1862. Buried in National Cemetery, Brooklyn, N.Y., Grave No. 43.

DOTY, ORASMUS, M., Wheatland, Hillsdale County. Enlisted in Company F, Aug. 23, 1862, at Hudson, age 21. Farmer. Slightly wounded in action at Fredericksburg, Va., Dec. 12, 1863. Wounded slightly and missing in action at Gettysburg, July 2, 1863. Returned to regiment Aug. 12, 1863. On detached service with Co. C, 1st Michigan Infantry, July 2, 1864. Transferred to Co. B, reorganized 4th Michigan Infantry, July 1, 1865. Mustered out at Houston, May 26, 1866. Resided in Albion, Neb., after service.

DOVER, WILLIAM M., Woodland. Enlisted in Company H, June 20, 1861, at Adrian, age 21. Carpenter. Wounded slightly at Fredericksburg, Va., Dec. 13, 1862. Shot in right hand, loss of index finger. Discharged April 6, 1863. Born in Canada.

DOWNER, JACOB R., Washtenaw County. Enlisted in Company K, June 20, 1861, at Adrian, age 23. Blacksmith. Discharged for disability at Minor's Hill, Va., Dec. 19, 1861.

Downing, Christopher F., Monroe County. Enlisted in Company A, June 20, 1861, at Adrian, age 20. Discharged for disability at Washington, D.C., Nov. 19, 1863.

Doyle, Cornelius, Detroit. Enlisted in Company I, June 20, 1861, at Adrian, age 19. Sailor. Sergeant Dec. 4, 1862. Transferred to Invalid Corps, Sept. 15, 1863.

Drake, Charles M., Hillsdale. Enlisted in Company E, June 20, 1861, at Adrian age 21. Joiner. Discharged for disability at Georgetown, March 3, 1862. Resided in St. Elmo, Chattanooga, Tenn. after service.

Drake, Franklin, Adrian. Enlisted in Company B, June 20, 1861, at Adrian, age 18. Died May 24, 1862, of wounds received in action at New Bridge, Va.

Draper, David M., Hillsdale. Enlisted in Independent Company, Feb. 19, 1864, at Hillsdale, age 30. Farmer. Wounded in action June 5, 1864. On detached service with Co. F, 1st Michigan Infantry, July 2, 1864. Transferred to Veteran Reserve Corps, Dec. 2, 1864. Mustered out at Harrisburg, Pa., from Veteran Reserve Corps, Aug. 18, 1865. Resided in Algansee, Branch County, after service. Died Dec. 29, 1889.

Dreher, Antoine. Enlisted in band, June 20, 1861, at Adrian, age 25. Mustered out at Harrison's Landing, Va., Aug. 10, 1862, by order of the War Department.

Drew, William H. (*VV*), Livingston County. Enlisted in Company K, June 20, 1861, at Adrian, age 23. Farmer and laborer, married, no children. Reenlisted Dec. 29, 1863. On detached service with Co. K, 1st Michigan Infantry, July 2, 1864. Wounded in action, gunshot in right thigh at South Side Railroad, Va., April 1, 1865. Transferred to Co. C, reorganized 4th Michigan Infantry, July 1, 1865. Discharged at Detroit, Aug. 5, 1865. Lived in Dexter after service.

Dudley, David T., St. Joseph County. Enlisted in Company C, June 20, 1861, at Adrian, age 22. Farm laborer. Detailed to Camp Hospital, Dec. 1861. Wounded slightly in action at Fredericksburg, Va., Dec. 13, 1862. Taken prisoner at Gettysburg, July 2, 1863. Returned to regiment Oct. 9, 1863. Mustered out at expiration of term at Detroit, June 30, 1864. Resided in Weeping Water, Neb. after service.

Duffenbaugh, Isaac, Tarlton, Ohio. Enlisted in band as drum major and principal musician, June 20, 1861, at Adrian, age 25. Clerk, married with two small daughters. Mustered out Aug. 10, 1862, at Harrison's Landing, Va., per War Department order.

Duffield, Johnson, Monroe County. Enlisted in Company A, June 20, 1861, at Adrian, age 20. Corporal Sept. 25, 1861. Sergeant July 1, 1862. Mustered out at expiration of term at Detroit, June 30, 1864. Resided in Sylvania, Ohio, after service. Buried in Association Cemetery, Sylvania.

Duffield, William, Monroe County. Enlisted in Company A, June 20, 1861, at Adrian, age 22. Discharged for disability at Minor's Hill, Va., Jan. 8, 1862.

Duffield, William Ward, Detroit. Entered service at organization as lieutenant colonel June 20, 1861, at Adrian, age 39. Resigned Sept. 25, 1861. Commissioned colonel, 9th Michigan Infantry at organization, Sept. 25, 1861. Military governor of Kentucky. Wounded and taken prisoner at Murfreesboro, Tenn., July 13, 1862. Exchanged Aug. 27, 1862. Resigned Feb. 6, 1863. Chief engineer of the Kentucky Union Railroad after service. Died 1907, buried in Arlington National Cemetery, Va.

Dugan, John F., Hillsdale County. Enlisted in Company E, June 20, 1861, at Adrian, age 23. Mustered out at expiration of term at Detroit, June 28, 1864.

Duncan, Charles S., Hillsdale County. Enlisted in Company B, June 20, 1861, at Adrian, age 23. Student. Spent most of first year of service in hospital at Baltimore. Listed unfit for duty in 1862; assigned to work as nurse, Baltimore. Discharged near Falmouth, Va., Jan. 2, 1863. Returned to duty, Culpeper, Va., Oct. 6, 1863, per War Department order. Mustered out at expiration of term June 30, 1864. Resided in Iowa after service. Born in Canada.

Dunphey, Addison W., Monroe County. Enlisted in Company G, June 20, 1861, at Adrian, age 20. Mustered out at expiration of term at Detroit, June 30, 1864. Resided in Solon, Kent County, after service.

DuPont, Charles, Dexter. Enlisted in Company K, June 20, 1861, at Adrian, age 19 (later said he was 17). Worked in a drugstore. Wounded in action Gaines' Mill, Va., June 27, 1862, struck in head/face by a bullet, lost his right eye. Admitted to General Hospital, Philadelphia. Discharged for disability July 29, 1862, at Philadelphia. Reenlisted, first lieutenant in 13th Michigan Artillery Battery, Dec. 11, 1863. Promoted captain, June 11, 1864.

Mustered out July 1, 1865. Resided in Detroit, holding various federal and city jobs and posts, and elected register of deeds in the 1870s.

DURYEE, GEORGE W., Jefferson, Hillsdale County. Enlisted in Independent Company, Feb. 9, 1864, at Jefferson, age 42. Farmer; father of James and William Duryee. On leave at times from Feb. 27 to July 26, 1864, with severe inflammation of the lungs and liver, also mumps. On detached service with Co. F, 1st Michigan Infantry, July 1, 1864. Died of disease at Nashville, Tenn., May 3, 1865. Buried Nashville National Cemetery.

DURYEE, JAMES H., Jefferson, Hillsdale County. Enlisted in Company F, Feb. 9, 1864, at Jefferson, age 20. Student and farmer, son of George Duryee and brother of William Duryee. On detached service with Co. C, 1st Michigan Infantry, July 2, 1864. Transferred to Co. C, reorganized 4th Michigan, July 1, 1865. Transferred to Co. K, Feb. 15, 1866. Mustered out at Houston, May 26, 1866. Died July 10, 1910. Buried Los Angeles National Cemetery.

DURYEE, WARREN FRED, Hudson, age 17. Orderly and personal assistant to Dr. David Chamberlain. Never formally enlisted in military service. Resided in Plainville. Died Nov. 22, 1932, buried in Maple Grove Cemetery, Hudson.

DURYEE, WILLIAM BRYON, Jefferson, Hillsdale County. Enlisted in Company F, Feb. 9, 1864, at Jefferson, age 16. Son of George Duryee and brother of James. Wounded in action, shot in side, May 5, 1864, Wilderness, Va. On detached service with Co. C, 1st Michigan Infantry, July 2, 1864. Transferred to Co. K, reorganized 4th Michigan, July 1, 1865. Corporal May 1, 1866. Mustered out at Houston, May 26, 1866. Died Feb. 11, 1886, in a railroad accident.

DUTTON, HENRY, Washtenaw County. Enlisted in Company D, June 20, 1861, at Adrian, age 22. Discharged for disability at Minor's Hill, Va., Jan. 13, 1862.

E

EARLE, FRANCIS S., Grand Rapids. Entered service in Company I at organization as second lieutenant, June 20, 1861, at Adrian, age 24. Commissioned first lieutenant and adjutant to date May 16, 1861. Promoted major and assistant adjutant general of volunteers, July 22, 1862. Resided in Tombstone, Ariz., and died March 14, 1901, in El Paso. Buried Mount Hope Cemetery, San Diego.

EASLICK, WILLIAM, Lenawee County. Enlisted in Company B, June 20, 1861, at Adrian, age 22. Ordnance officer. Discharged for disability at Minor's Hill, Va., Jan. 5, 1862, injured when thrown from a horse. Died May 28, 1899, and buried at Lafayette, Mich.

EASTLICK, NEWMAN A., Macon, Lenawee County. Enlisted in Company G, Feb. 20, 1862, at Adrian, age 25. Farm laborer. Taken prisoner at Gettysburg, July 2, 1863. On detached service with Co. G, 1st Michigan Infantry, July 2, 1864. Lost in explosion of the steamboat *Sultana,* April 28, 1865.

EASTMAN, NORRIS, Jackson County. Enlisted in Company I, June 20, 1861, at Adrian, age 17. Wounded during the Peninsula Campaign and discharged Dec. 27, 1862. Resided in a Soldiers Home in the early 1900s. Buried in Genesee County, Mich.

EASTON, AMBROSE J., Lima, Washtenaw County. Enlisted in Company K as corporal June 20, 1861, at Adrian, age 30. Farmer, listed as head of household, his mother and five siblings residing with him. Sergeant Nov. 14, 1861. Struck by artillery shot at Malvern Hill, Va., June 30, 1862. Buried Lima Center Cemetery.

EATON, WILLIAM H., Monroe. Enlisted in Company A, June 20, 1861, at Adrian, age 20. Farmer residing on parents' farm with younger brother. Sergeant. Killed in action at Malvern Hill, Va., July 1, 1862.

EBERT, JOHN, Adrian. Enlisted in Company A, Sept. 8, 1862, at Adrian, age 38. Died of disease at Frederick, Md., Nov. 30, 1862. Buried in National Cemetery, Antietam, Grave No. 2401.

ELLIS, MARTIN D. Enlisted in Company B, mustered in 1863, age 31. Farmer. Mustered out June 1865. Died Dec. 1870. Buried in village cemetery, Dundee, N.Y.

ELMER, ELIOTT, Wayne County. Enlisted in Company I, June 20, 1861, at Adrian, age 30. Laborer. Sergeant. Captured in action at Gettysburg, July 2, 1863. Held at Belle Isle, Richmond, Va., sick in prison hospital Jan.

1864 to spring of 1864. Paroled March 16, 1864, City Point, Va. Sent to hospital in Baltimore May 20, 1864, unfit for duty because of rheumatism. Discharged at expiration of term at Detroit, June 1864. Resided in Pittsfield, Washtenaw County, later moving west. Died June 4, 1918, and buried in Veterans Circle, Oak Hill Cemetery, Red Bluff, Calif.

Emerson, Josiah D., Hillsdale County. Enlisted in Company E as sergeant June 20, 1861, at Adrian, age 21. Farmer. Wounded in action at Gaines' Mill, Va., June 27, 1862. Commissioned second lieutenant Sept. 3, 1862. Commissioned first lieutenant, Co. B, Dec. 13, 1862. Commanding Co. E, March and April 1864. Wounded in action at Laurel Hill, May 8, 1864, shot in left shoulder and right hip. In a hospital in Philadelphia for three months. Mustered out at expiration of term, June 30, 1864. Resided in Independence, Kans., after service.

English, Amos H. Hillsdale. Enlisted in Independent Company, Feb. 17, 1864, at Hillsdale, age 19. Printer, son of Seth English. On detached service with Co. F, 1st Michigan Infantry, July 2, 1864. Transferred to Co. K, reorganized 4th Michigan, June 6, 1865. Corporal. Mustered out at Houston, May 1, 1866. Resided in Pittsfield, Washtenaw County after service. Died June 21, 1919. Buried Maplewood Cemetery, Reading, Lenawee County.

English, Seth, Jefferson, Hillsdale County. Enlisted in Independent Company, Feb. 13, 1864, at Hillsdale, age 44. Laborer, father of six including Amos English. Died June 21, 1864, of wounds received in action. Buried in National Cemetery, City Point, Va.

Enos, Lewis N. (*VV*), Van Wert County, Ohio. Enlisted in Company I, June 20, 1861, at Adrian, age 20. Wounded in action and taken prisoner at Gaines' Mill, Va. Reenlisted Dec. 25, 1863. On detached service with Co. I, 1st Michigan Infantry, July 2, 1864. Died of wounds at Emory Hospital, Washington, D.C., April 22, 1865.

Enos, Merritt, St. Joseph County. Enlisted in Company C, June 20, 1861, age 18. Taken prisoner at Gettysburg, July 2, 1863. Nurse caring for wounded afterwards; returned to regiment Aug. 1863. Mustered out at expiration of term at Detroit, June 29, 1864.

Eskridge, George, Lenawee County. Enlisted in Company F, Sept. 10, 1861, at Hudson, age 25. Farmer. Discharged for disability at Alexandria, Va., Oct. 31, 1862. Buried Brown Cemetery, Hudson.

Evans, Heman (*VV*), Washtenaw County. Enlisted under the name of Heman Smith in Company K, June 20, 1861, at Adrian, age 19. Reenlisted Dec. 29, 1863. Guard at headquarters, Second Brigade, First Division, Fifth Army Corps, from June 1863 to April 1864. On detached service with Co. K, 1st Michigan Infantry, July 2, 1864, Petersburg. Transferred to Co. C, reorganized 4th Michigan, July 1, 1865. Mustered out at San Antonio, Feb. 26, 1866. Resided at Kawkawlin Bay after service.

Evans, James, Lenawee County. Enlisted in Company B, June 20, 1861, at Adrian, age 17. Farm laborer. Missing in action at Malvern Hill, Va., July 1, 1862. Discharged for disability near Falmouth, Va., Jan. 2, 1863.

Everett, Robert A., Hillsdale. Enlisted May 16, 1861, age 22. While in Adrian, June 1861, was appointed hospital steward. Doctor. Did not muster with regiment into U.S. service and instead was appointed assistant surgeon of the 5th Michigan Infantry, July 31, 1861. Surgeon, 16th Michigan Infantry, April 18, 1863. Mustered out Oct. 11, 1864. Resided in Hillsdale after service, elected mayor there in 1876.

F

Falkner, Andrew J. Rollin, Lenawee County. Enlisted in Independent Company, March 22, 1864, at Hudson, age 18. On detached service with Co. F, 1st Michigan Infantry, July 2, 1864, Petersburg. Transferred to Co. K, reorganized 4th Michigan, June 6, 1865. Discharged for disability at Austin, Tex., April 18, 1866.

Farlaman, Alonzo William (*VV*), Adrian, Lenawee County. Enlisted in Company G, Oct. 3, 1861, at Hudson, age 15. Reenlisted Dec. 29, 1863. On detached service with Co. G, 1st Michigan Infantry, July 2, 1864. Transferred to Co. C, reorganized 4th Michigan, July 1, 1865. Mustered out at San Antonio, Feb. 26, 1866. Resided Coupeville Island, Wash., after service.

Farley, John, Hillsdale County. Enlisted in Company E, June 20, 1861, at Adrian, age 22. Mustered out at expiration of term at Detroit, June 28, 1864. Resided in Plainwell after service before moving west. Buried National Cemetery, Los Angeles.

FARR, ANDREW J., LaGrange, Ind. Enlisted in Company C as corporal June 20, 1861, at Adrian, age 25. Killed in action at Gaines' Mill, Va., June 27, 1862.

FARRAR, DEWITT C., St. Clair. Enlisted in Company B, June 20, 1861, at Adrian, age 22. Corporal. Color guard. Killed in action at Fredericksburg, Va., Dec. 13, 1862. Buried Richmond Cemetery, Richmond, Va.

FAUSETT, FRANCIS, Lenawee County. Enlisted in Company F, June 20, 1861, at Adrian, age 31. Farmer. Discharged for disability at U.S. Hospital, New York, Dec. 15, 1862. Died June 24, 1884.

FENTON, ASAHEL, Washtenaw County. Enlisted in Company G, June 20, 1861, at Adrian, age 23. Corporal. Discharged for disability Oct. 6, 1862.

FENTON, JAMES F., Macomb County. Enlisted in Company I, June 20, 1861, at Adrian, age 42. Sailor, married, father of seven. Wounded in action July 1, 1862. Sergeant. Taken prisoner July 2, 1863. Returned to regiment at Culpeper, Va., Oct. 9, 1863. Died May 13, 1864, of wounds received in action near Spotsylvania Court House, May 10, 1864. Originally buried near Spotsylvania Court House, reburied Fredericksburg National Cemetery. Cenotaph located in Clinton Grove Cemetery, Mt. Clemens. Born in Scotland.

FIDLER, WESLEY D., LaGrange, Ind. Enlisted in Company C, June 20, 1861, at Adrian, age 22. Farmer. Mustered out at expiration of term at Detroit, June 30, 1864.

FIELD, HENRY C., Washtenaw County. Enlisted in Company K, Sept. 21, 1861. On detached service with Co. K, 1st Michigan Infantry, July 1, 1864. Transferred to Co. C, reorganized 4th Michigan, July 1, 1865. Deserted at Washington, D.C., Feb. 17, 1866. Buried Forest Lawn Cemetery, Dexter.

FIELD, NELSON, St. Joseph County. Enlisted in Company C, May 16, 1861, Age 25. Wagon maker, father of a small daughter. Discharged by order of Col. Woodbury, July 1861.

FIELDS, WILLIAM H., Washtenaw County. Enlisted in Company K, June 20, 1861, at Adrian, age 18. Painter. Mustered out at expiration of term June 29, 1864. Resided in Grand Ledge after service. Died Feb. 29, 1904.

FIESTER, WILLIAM T. (*VV*), Hillsdale County. Enlisted in Company E as musician June 20, 1861, at Adrian, age 21. Reenlisted Dec. 29, 1863. On detached service with Co. K, 1st Michigan Infantry, July 2, 1864. Transferred to Co. C, reorganized 4th Michigan, July 1, 1865. Mustered out at San Antonio, Feb. 26, 1866. Resided in Bellevue, Eaton County, after service.

FISH, EZRA M., Wheatland, Hillsdale County. Enlisted in Independent Company, Feb. 17, 1864, at Wheatland, age 18. On detached service with Co. F, 1st Michigan Infantry, July 2, 1864. Transferred to Co. K, reorganized 4th Michigan, June 6, 1865. Discharged at Washington, D.C., June 9, 1865. Lived in Eagle, Clinton County, after service.

FISHBECK, STEPHEN G., Livingston County. Enlisted in Company K as sergeant June 20, 1861, at Adrian, age 21. Day laborer. Deserted Sept. 29, 1862. Worked as a shoemaker after the war, but received a pension after filing a claim that he was "injured in back by a horse." Buried Lakeview Cemetery, Howell.

FISHER, HOMER E., Steuben, Ind. Enlisted in Company B, June 20, 1861, at Adrian, age 21. Clerk, eldest of five siblings. Taken prisoner at Gaines' Mill, Va., June 27, 1862, wounded in right lung and hip. Returned to regiment Aug. 20, 1862. Discharged for disability near Falmouth, Va., Jan. 2, 1863. Resided in Toledo and Orleans, Mich., after war.

FISHER, JOHN, Washtenaw County. Enlisted in Company D, June 20, 1861, at Adrian, age 18. Discharged for disability Feb. 1, 1863, for wound received in action at Fredericksburg, Va., Dec. 13, 1862. Resided in Detroit after service. Buried Forest Hill Cemetery, Ann Arbor.

FISK, CANFIELD, Coldwater. Enlisted in Company C, June 20, 1861, at Adrian, age 21. Mustered out at expiration of term at Detroit, June 30, 1864. Resided in Bethel, Mich., and Topeka, Kans., after service.

FITCH, EDSON J., Steuben, Ind. Enlisted in Company B, June 20, 1861, at Adrian, age 19. Wounded in action Malvern Hill July 1, 1862. Wounded in action again, shot in hand, May 8, 1864. Mustered out at expiration of term, June 30, 1864. Resided in Muskegon.

FITZPATRICK, JOHN, Trenton, Wayne County. Enlisted in Company I, June 20, 1861, at Adrian, age 23. Laborer, supporting his wife and two teenaged relatives. Missing in action at Mechanicsville, June 26, 1862. No further record.

Fitzsimmons, Peter, Hudson. Enlisted in Independent Company, March 28, 1864, at Hudson, age 32. Slightly wounded in the arm June 2, 1864, near Bethesda Church, Va. On detached service with Co. F, 1st Michigan Infantry, July 2, 1864. Discharged at Washington, D.C., June 7, 1865. Resided in Hudson and buried there, Maple Grove Cemetery.

Fleming, John H., Cambria, Hillsdale County. Enlisted in Company E, June 20, 1861, at Adrian, age 18. Farmer residing with his widowed mother and younger siblings. Wounded in action at Gaines' Mill, June 27, 1862, losing index finger. Wounded in action at Gettysburg, July 2, 1863, struck in left thigh by bullet that was never removed. Mustered out at expiration of term at Detroit, June 28, 1864. Resided in Winterfield Township, Clare County, after service. Died March 22, 1922, and buried Greenwood Cemetery, Marion, Osceola County. Born in Canada.

Fletcher, Charles J., Hillsdale County. Enlisted in Company E, as corporal, June 20, 1861, age 23. Dentist. Sergeant. Wounded arm slightly in action at Fredericksburg, Va., Dec. 13, 1862. Found guilty by court-martial of noncommissioned officers Dec. 20, 1862, of cowardice, reduced him to ranks. Wounded in action Wilderness, Va., May 5, 1864, shot in right arm. Sergeant June 1, 1864. Mustered out at expiration of term at Detroit, June 28, 1864. Resided in Enfield, Tompkins County, N.Y., after service.

Flint, Lewis L., Battle Creek. Enlisted in Company C, June 20, 1861, at Adrian, age 21. Apprentice joiner. Discharged for disability at New York, Oct. 3, 1863. Reenlisted in Co. B, 6th Michigan Cavalry. Transferred to 1st Michigan Cavalry, Nov. 17, 1865. Mustered out at Salt Lake City, March 10, 1866. Resided in Flint and Dundee after service.

Flora, James C., Bourbon, Ind. Enlisted in Company C, June 20, 1861, at Adrian, age 29. Farmer, married, father of three young girls. Wounded, a part of a finger taken off by a shell, Gaines' Mill, Va., June 27, 1862. Reduced in rank to private for cowardice at Fredericksburg. Wounded in action at Gettysburg, July 2, 1863, shot in forearm and right thigh, nearly bleeding to death. Amputation of arm. Sent to General Hospital, York, Pa. Mustered out at Detroit, badly disabled at expiration of term of service, June 30, 1864. Died April 27, 1877. Buried in Rickey Cemetery, Mason.

Fogle, George, Saline, Washtenaw County. Enlisted in Company G, June 20, 1861, at Adrian, age 19. Farm laborer, brother of Scott Fogle. Corporal. Color guard, killed in action at Fredericksburg, Va., Dec. 13, 1862.

Fogle, Scott, Washtenaw County. Enlisted in Company G, Feb. 10, 1862, at Adrian, age 18. Farm laborer, brother of George Fogle. On detached service with Co. G, 1st Michigan Infantry, July 2, 1864. Discharged at expiration of term at Petersburg, Feb. 10, 1865.

Folwell, William R., Lenawee County. Enlisted in Company F, June 20, 1861, at Adrian, age 26. Farmer. Discharged for disability at Sharpsburg, Md., Oct. 28, 1862. Resided in Arcadia, Wayne County, N.Y., after service. Died Aug. 15, 1919. Buried East Newark Cemetery, Newark, N.Y.

Fonier, John B., Raisinville, Monroe County. Enlisted in Company A, June 20, 1861, at Adrian, age 28. Farmer, married and father of two small children. Corporal. Killed in action at Malvern Hill, Va., July 1, 1862, shot left side.

Foote, Emery Daniel (*VV*), Lenawee County. Enlisted in Company B, June 20, 1861, at Adrian, age 23. Mechanic. Reenlisted Dec. 25, 1863. On detached service with Co. B, 1st Michigan Infantry, July 2, 1864. Transferred to Co. C, reorganized 4th Michigan, July 1, 1865. Mustered out at San Antonio, Feb. 26, 1866. Resided Buffalo, N.Y., after service.

Forbes, Andrew, Woodstock, Canada West. Enlisted in Company I, May 16, 1861. Discharged June 1862, a minor. Died Dec. 27, 1887.

Force, Alonzo, Madison, Lenawee County, age 17. Entered service in Company K, substitute for William P. Service, drafted for nine months, Feb. 10, 1863. The oldest of four siblings living with their parents. Discharged at expiration of term of service at Bealton, Va., Nov. 11, 1863.

Ford, Oscar. Enlisted in Company F, June 20, 1861, at Adrian, age 23. Discharged for disability at Washington, D.C., Aug. 16, 1861.

Forncook or Forncrook, Frank B., Reading, Hillsdale County. Name also given as Forncock. Enlisted in

Company E, June 20, 1861, at Adrian, age 28. Farm laborer. Killed in action at Malvern Hill, Va., July 1, 1862.

Foster, Martin L. (*VV*), Washtenaw County. Enlisted in Company K, June 20, 1861, at Adrian, age 23. Wounded in action at Malvern Hill, Va., July 1, 1862. Reenlisted Dec. 29, 1863. Wounded in action at Wilderness, Va., May 5, 1864. On detached service with Co. K, 1st Michigan Infantry, July 2, 1864. Transferred to Co. C, reorganized 4th Michigan, July 1, 1865. Discharged at Detroit, Aug. 10, 1865.

Fountain, Hiram B., Hudson, Lenawee County. Enlisted in Company F, June 20, 1861, at Adrian, age 19. Farmer. Corporal. Missing in action at Gaines' Mill, Va., June 27, 1862. Sergeant. Killed in action at Gettysburg, July 2, 1863, buried in the Rose Farm Meadow. Moved to Gettysburg National Cemetery, Michigan Plot, 14-B.

Fournia, Peter (*VV*), Monroe County. Enlisted in Company E, June 20, 1861, at Adrian, age 32. Lumberman, married, with two small children. Transferred to Company A, Sept. 1, 1861. Reenlisted Dec. 29, 1863. On detached service with Co. A, 1st Michigan Infantry, July 2, 1864. Transferred to Co. C, reorganized 4th Michigan, July 1, 1865. Discharged to date June 11, 1865. Resided in Slaytown, Eaton County, after service. Buried at Charlotte Cemetery, Charlotte. Born in Canada.

Fournia, Samuel D. (*VV*), Monroe. Enlisted in Company A, Oct. 1, 1861, at Monroe. Reenlisted Dec. 29, 1863. Stated he was held at Andersonville, Ga., for 11 months. On detached service with Co. A, 1st Michigan Infantry, July 2, 1864. Transferred to Co. A, reorganized 4th Michigan, June 6, 1865. Discharged at Detroit, Aug. 21, 1865. Resided in Toledo after service. Died in 1901, buried St. Joseph Cemetery, Erie, Mich.

Fowler, Hudson K., Lenawee County. Enlisted in Company F, June 20, 1861, at Adrian, age 21. Carpenter. Discharged for disability at Washington, D.C., June 15, 1862. Reentered service in 9th Michigan Cavalry as sergeant, Nov. 18, 1862, at Hillsdale. Transferred to Battery L, 1st Michigan Light Artillery, May 1, 1863. Mustered out at Jackson, Aug. 22, 1865.

Fowler, John W., Hillsdale. Enlisted in Independent Company, March 21, 1864, at Hillsdale, age 21. Farmer. On detached service with Co. F, 1st Michigan Infantry, July 1864. Discharged at New York City, May 30, 1865.

Fox, David, Hillsdale County. Enlisted in Company E, June 20, 1861, at Adrian, age 17. Farmer, oldest of four siblings. Wounded in action, Chancellorsville, Va., May 4, 1863. Wounded in action May 23, 1864, Jericho Mills, Va., gunshot wound to left thigh. Treated at Finley Hospital, Washington, D.C., May 10, remained for months. Mustered out at expiration of term, June 28, 1864. Enlisted in Co. G, 30th Michigan Infantry, at Allen, for one year as sergeant, Jan. 9. 1865. Mustered out at Jackson, June 17, 1865. Resided in Kinderhook, Branch County, where he died in 1932. Buried Kinderhook Cemetery.

Fox, John W. Enlisted in Company C as corporal, June 20, 1861, age 21. Laborer. Died of disease at Yorktown, Va., April 17, 1862. buried in Yorktown National Cemetery, Grave 361.

Freeman, Allen (*VV*), Lenawee County. Enlisted in Company F, June 20, 1861, at Adrian, age 21. In regimental hospital Jan. and Feb. 1863. Reenlisted Jan. 31, 1864. Wounded in the hand at Old Church near Cold Harbor, Va., Overland Campaign (probably June 2 or 3), 1864 while on the skirmish line. On detached service with Co. C, 1st Michigan Infantry, July 2, 1864. Transferred to Co. C, reorganized 4th Michigan, July 1, 1865. Discharged to date June 5, 1865. Died in 1896 and buried East Plains Cemetery, Matherton, Clinton County.

Freeman, Edmund, Oakland. Died at Fairfax, Va., Dec. 16, 1862. No further record.

French, Ebenezer, St. Joseph County. Entered service in Company C at organization as second lieutenant, June 20, 1861, at Adrian, age 26. Printer. Commissioned first lieutenant Sept. 1, 1861. Commissioned captain, Company A, Sept. 1, 1862. Wounded in action, hit in left chest, face, and lower leg, Fredericksburg, Va., Dec. 13, 1862. Sent to Douglas Hospital, Washington, Dec. 19, 1862. Returned to regiment March 1, 1863. Slightly wounded in action at Gettysburg, July 2, 1863, right arm. Discharged on account of disability May 9, 1864. Tried to reenlist in the Invalid Corps but was pronounced unfit. Reentered service in Co. E, 11th Michigan Infantry as captain, March 1, 1865. Commanding garrison at Charlestown, Tenn., June 1865. Mustered out at Nashville, Sept. 16, 1865. Buried in Oak Hill Cemetery, Section B., San Jose, Calif.

French, Luther Calvin, Hudson. Entered service as Assistant Surgeon, age 42, commissioned Aug. 23, 1862. Druggist, married, no children. Commissioned surgeon March 13, 1863. Resigned on account of disability, a hernia, May 18, 1863, at Stoneman's Switch, Va. Died April 12, 1895, buried in Maple Grove Cemetery, Hudson.

Fry, Mahlon, St. Joseph County. Enlisted in Company C, June 20, 1861, at Adrian, age 18. Dropped from rolls at Culpeper, Va., Oct. 4, 1863.

FUCHS, MICHAEL. Enlisted in Band, June 20, 1861, at Adrian, age 40. Mustered out at Harrison's Landing, Va., per order, Aug. 10, 1862. Lived in Allegheny, Pa., after service.

FULLER, JOHN P., Pittsford, Hillsdale County. Enlisted in Company F, Jan. 25, 1864, at Pittsford, age 35. Cooper, married father of three children. Wounded in action, May 12, 1864, left leg; leg amputated June 21, 1864. Died at Washington, D.C., June 20, 1864, of wounds. Buried Wolf Cemetery, Pittsford.

FULLER, ORSON, Steuben, Ind. Enlisted in Company B, June 20, 1861, at Adrian, age 17. Day laborer, oldest of three siblings. Discharged for disability at Ft. Woodbury, Sept. 6, 1861.

FULLER, SAMUEL, Lenawee County. Enlisted in Company C, May 16, 1861, at Sturgis, age 22. Farm laborer, oldest of four siblings. Died of disease at Washington, D.C., Jan. 28, 1864.

FULLER, WATSON W., North Adams, Hillsdale County. Enlisted in Company H, June 20, 1861, at Adrian, age 26. Shoemaker. Corporal. Taken prisoner, wounded, at Malvern Hill, Va., July 2, 1862. Died of wounds. Buried North Lawn Cemetery, North Adams.

FULLER, WILLIAM R., Hillsdale County. Enlisted in Company E, June 20, 1861, at Adrian, age 21. Corporal. Taken prisoner at Gettysburg, July 2, 1863. Confined at Richmond, Va. Mustered out at expiration of term at Detroit, May 29, 1865. Resided in Addison after service. Died in 1924 and buried North Lawn Cemetery, North Adams.

FULLERTON, JOHN, Washtenaw County. Enlisted in Company G, June 20, 1861, at Adrian, age 16. Farm laborer. Discharged for disability at Minor's Hill, Va., Dec. 29, 1861, because of heart and kidney trouble. Reenlisted in the 4th Michigan Cavalry. Discharged for disability. Reenlisted the 6th Michigan Cavalry, headquarters staff. Discharged for disability. Resided in Augusta Township after service.

FUNK, MOSES A., Jonesville. Entered service in Company H at organization as captain, June 20, 1861, at Adrian, age 47. Millinery store owner and carpenter. Resigned and honorably discharged Sept. 7, 1861. Died Feb. 12, 1865. Buried Oak Grove Cemetery, Hillsdale.

FURMAN, EDWARD, White Lake. Enlisted in Company H, June 20, 1861, at Adrian, age 25. Laborer. Taken prisoner at Mechanicsville, Va., June 26, 1862, and confined at Richmond. Died of disease at Fairfax Hospital, typhoid fever, on Dec. 16, 1862, contracted while a prisoner.

G

GAHAGAN, PETER, Hudson. Enlisted in Company K, Sept. 13, 1861, at Hudson, age 20. Farm laborer, unmarried. Died Sept. 7, 1863, of wounds received in action at Gettysburg, July 2, 1863. His body was returned to Michigan for burial.

GALE, FRANK B., Monroe. Enlisted in Company A, as corporal, June 20, 1861, at Adrian, age 19. Middle child of five siblings. Killed in action at Malvern Hill, Va., July 1, 1862, shot in heart. Stone marker at Woodland Cemetery, Monroe.

GARNSEY, ALBERT L. (*VV*), Metamora, Ohio. Enlisted in Company B, June 20, 1861, at Adrian, age 22. Farmer, brother of Roswell Garnsey. In brigade hospital at Minor's Hill, Va., with typhoid fever. Rejoined regiment March 1, 1862. Relapsed and hospitalized; rejoined regiment at Yorktown, Va., April 1862. Wounded in action Gaines' Mill, Va., June 27, 1862, losing forefinger of right hand and middle finger of left hand, again hospitalized. Unable to keep up on march to Gettysburg, he was charged with desertion in the face of the enemy. Fined $25.64 for lost property (this was restored under a general order) and had to forfeit pay to Feb. 11, 1864. Reenlisted Feb. 18, 1864. Wounded in shoulder Old Church (Bethesda Church), Va., June 3, 1864. Sent to hospital at White House Landing. On detached service with Co. B, 1st Michigan Infantry, July 2, 1864. Corporal Sept. 1, 1865. Transferred to Co. C, reorganized 4th Michigan, July 1, 1865. On duty as guard at prison in San Antonio, Dec. 1865. Mustered out and honorably discharged Feb. 26, 1866. Died Dec. 15, 1899, in Toledo and buried Amboy Township Cemetery, Fulton County, Ohio.

GARNSEY, ROSWELL L., Fulton County, Ohio. Enlisted in Company B, June 20, 1861, at Adrian, age 21. Brother of Albert Garnsey. Killed in action at Gaines' Mill, Va., June 27, 1862.

GARRISON, SAMUEL J., Washtenaw County. Enlisted in Company K, June 20, 1861, at Adrian, age 32. Discharged for disability Aug. 2, 1861.

GARVIN, EUGENE, St. Joseph County. Enlisted in Company C, as musician drummer, June 20, 1861, at Adrian, age 22. Mustered out at expiration of term at Detroit, June 30, 1864. Resided in Mendon after service.

GATES, GEORGE E., Hillsdale County. Enlisted in Company E, June 20, 1861, at Adrian, age 17. Farmer, oldest of three siblings. Discharged for disability, chronic diarrhea, at Washington, D.C., July 16, 1861. Reenlisted in 2nd Michigan Cavalry, Nov. 11, 1862. Mustered out on Sept. 1, 1865. Resided in Reading after service.

GATES, JOHN A., Washtenaw County. Enlisted in Company D, as corporal, June 20, 1861, at Adrian, age 21. Carpenter. In Seminary General Hospital, Georgetown, Aug. 20, 1861, fever. Discharged at Sharpsburg, Md., to enlist 2nd U.S. Cavalry. Died June 19, 1914, Ann Arbor.

GATES, JONATHAN P., Cambria, Hillsdale County. Enlisted in Company H, Feb. 11, 1863, at Moscow, for nine months, age 18. Farmer, substitute for John Kesslering, farmer from Moscow Township. Died of disease, typhoid fever at Lovell Hospital, Portsmouth Grove, R.I., July 25, 1863. Buried in National Cemetery, Brooklyn, N.Y., Grave No. 3383.

GAUNTLETT, JOSEPH. Enlisted in Company G, June 20, 1861, at Adrian, age 18. Blacksmith, oldest of five siblings. Wounded in action, Gaines' Mill, Va., June 27, 1862. Mustered out at expiration of term at Detroit, June 30, 1864. Resided in Detroit after service. Born in England.

GAVETT, EDWARD, Hillsdale County. Enlisted in Company D, 1st Michigan Infantry, April 24, 1861, at Coldwater, for three months, age 25. Laborer, married, father of a baby daughter. Enlisted in Company E, 4th Michigan, March 26, 1862, at Adrian as musician. Taken prisoner at Gaines' Mill, Va., June 27, 1862. Held at Belle Isle, Richmond. Suffered sunstroke. Returned to regiment Oct. 3, 1862, at Harper's Ferry, Va. Was unable to keep up with the march, June 30, 1863, Gettysburg Campaign, and was sent to Camp Distribution. Transferred to Invalid Corps, Aug. 1, 1863. Died April 15, 1881, and buried Wyllys-Sebring Cemetery, Cambria Township.

GAY, WILLIAM I., Hillsdale County. Enlisted in Company H, Sept. 27, 1861, at Hudson, age 30. Farmer. Corporal. Discharged for disability at York, Pa., Jan. 12, 1863, because of illness. Resided in Hudson and then Girard, Ill., after service.

GEE, ORRIN, Dundee, Monroe County. Enlisted in Company G, June 20, 1861, at Adrian, age 26. Farmer. Transferred to Invalid Corps, Jan. 1, 1864, because of back and hip injuries from a wagon turning over on him. Resided in Dundee after service. Buried Oak Grove Cemetery, Dundee.

GETTER, ORIGEN H., Manistee. Enlisted in Company H, June 20, 1861, at Adrian, age 26. Painter. Reenlisted Dec. 29, 1863. On detached service with Co. H, 1st Michigan Infantry, July 2, 1864. Transferred to Co. C, reorganized 4th Michigan, July 1, 1865. Mustered out at San Antonio, Feb. 26, 1866. Resided in San Antonio after service.

GIBBS, JOHN H., Rollin, Lenawee County. Enlisted in Company F, Aug. 26, 1862, at Hudson, age 23. Shoemaker, brother of Robert R. Gibbs. Wounded in action at Fredericksburg, Va., Dec. 13, 1862, shot through right leg. On detached service with Co. C, 1st Michigan Infantry, July 2, 1864. Discharged for disability, deafness, at Detroit, Sept. 8, 1864. Died in 1928, buried Smith Hill, Otisville Cemetery, Genesee County.

GIBBS, ROBERT, Cairo, Illinois, age 23, sailor. Enlisted in Company H, March 6, 1863, at Riley, substitute for Robert Clary. Deserted March 13, 1863, en route from Detroit to Washington. Born in London, England.

GIBBS, ROBERT R., Rollin, Lenawee County. Enlisted in Company F, Aug. 26, 1862, at Detroit, age 17. Brother of John H. Gibbs. Discharged for disability, March 2, 1863. Resided in Wheatland, Hillsdale County, after service. Buried Norvell Cemetery, Jackson County.

GIBSON, WILLIAM H., Monroe. Enlisted in Company A, June 20, 1861, at Adrian, age 25. Mason. Wounded, shot in side, and missing in action Gaines' Mill, Va., June 27, 1862. Returned to regiment Oct. 1862. Wounded in action at Fredericksburg, Va., Dec. 13, 1862. Mustered out at expiration of term at Detroit, June 30, 1864. Resided in Hamlin, Eaton County, after service. Died in 1915 and buried Woodland Cemetery, Monroe.

GILBERT, EDWIN H., Ann Arbor. Enlisted in Company D as first sergeant June 20, 1861, at Adrian, age 22. Saddle and harness maker. Commissioned second lieutenant July 1, 1862; first lieutenant Nov. 26, 1862. Commanding company from Dec. 14, 1862, to March 1863, and from June 1863 to Nov. 1863. Acting regimental quartermaster Nov. 1863. Commanding company from Jan. to May 1864. Mustered out at expiration of term at Detroit, June 30, 1864.

GILBERT, OLIVER, Litchfield, Hillsdale County. Enlisted in Company H, June 20, 1861, at Adrian, age 24. Carpenter. Died of disease, typhoid fever, at Union Hill, Va., Oct. 27, 1861. Buried Mount Hope Cemetery, Litchfield.

GILCHRIST, ARCHIBALD, Hillsdale County. Enlisted in Company E, June 20, 1861, at Adrian, age 23. Cabinetmaker. Discharged for disability at Alexandria, Va., Jan. 29, 1863. Resided in Virginia and Bradford, Pa., after service. Born in Canada.

GILL, WILLIAM EDGAR, Hillsdale. Enlisted in Independent Company, Feb. 11, 1864, at Hillsdale, age 27. Farmer, married, father of one child. Corporal. Slightly wounded in action, in the face, at Bethesda Church, Va., June 3, 1864. On detached service with Co. F, 1st Michigan Infantry, July 2, 1864. Transferred to Veteran Reserve Corps, May 4, 1865. Discharged at Detroit, July 21, 1865. Resided in Baltimore after service. Died Jan. 22, 1890. Buried at Clayton, Lenawee County.

GILLELAND, JAMES G., Lenawee County. Enlisted in Company B, June 20, 1861, at Adrian, age 21. Mustered out at expiration of term June 30, 1864. Suffered from epilepsy after service. Resided in Adrian.

GILLELLAND, WILLIAM W., Pittsford, Hillsdale County. Enlisted in Independent Company, March 21, 1864, at Hudson, age 19. On detached service with Co. F. 1st Michigan Infantry, July 2, 1864. Transferred to Co. K, reorganized 4th Michigan Infantry. Transferred to Veteran Reserve Corps, by order, Jan. 6, 1865. Discharged at Brattleboro, Vt., Oct. 3, 1865, from Veteran Reserve Corps.

GILMORE, FRANKLIN JAMES, Lenawee County. Enlisted in Company G, Feb. 20, 1862, at Adrian, age 27. Farmer. Discharged for disability at Washington, D.C., Oct. 24, 1862, because of sunstroke. Died July 3, 1925. Buried Ridgeway Township Cemetery.

GLEASON, ALVARO F., Reading, Hillsdale County. Enlisted in Company E, June 20, 1861, at Adrian, age 17. Farmer, one of seven siblings. Discharged for disability at Washington, D.C., July 16, 1861.

GODFROY, FREDERICK. Enlisted in Company A, June 20, 1861, at Adrian, age 19. Discharged for disability June 1861.

GONIER, XAVIER, Monroe County. Enlisted in Company A, June 20, 1861, at Adrian, age 29. Mustered out at expiration of term at Detroit, June 30, 1864. Resided in Monroe after service.

GOODELL, THOMAS (*VV*), Wayne County. Enlisted in Company I, June 20, 1861, at Adrian, age 16. Farm boy, one of 10 siblings. Wounded in action July 1, 1862. Reenlisted Dec. 29, 1863. Wounded in action May 5, 1864, Wilderness, Va., a flesh wound in the arm from gunshot. On detached service with Co. I, 1st Infantry, July 2, 1864, Petersburg. Transferred to Co. C, reorganized 4th Michigan, July 1, 1865. Discharged to date Feb. 15, 1866. Resided in Ecorse after service. Admitted to Soldiers Home, Dayton, March 19, 1888. Born in Canada.

GOODELL, TITUS (*VV*), Wayne County. Enlisted in Company I as corporal June 20, 1861, at Adrian, age 19. Reenlisted Dec. 29, 1863. First sergeant Feb. 29, 1864. Wounded in action May 5, 1864. Admitted Campbell Hospital, Washington, D.C., wound from gunshot, right leg above the knee. Transferred to Veteran Reserve Corps, Jan. 10, 1865, at Washington, D.C. On detached service with Co. I, 1st Michigan Infantry, July 2, 1864, Petersburg. Discharged from Veteran Reserve Corps, Aug. 2, 1865. Resided in Ecorse after service, also at Soldiers and Sailors Home, Erie County, Ohio.

GOODENBERGER, JOHN, Somerset, Hillsdale County. Enlisted in Company F, Aug. 26, 1862, at Hudson, age 44. Farmer. Died May 13, 1864, at Armory Hospital, Washington, D.C., of wounds received in action at Wilderness, Va., May 5, 1864, shot in shoulder and chest. Buried Arlington National Cemetery, May 22, 1864.

GOODHUE, ELMER, Ann Arbor. Enlisted in Company D as corporal June 20, 1861, at Adrian, age 24. Killed in action at Malvern Hill, Va., July 1, 1862.

GOODRICH, GEORGE W., Branch County. Enlisted in Company C, June 20, 1861, at Adrian, age 18. Corporal. Discharged for disability April 14, 1863, varicose veins. Reenlisted in 14th Michigan Artillery Battery for one year, Sept. 5, 1864. Mustered out at Jackson, July 1, 1865.

GOODRICH, JOHN V. B., Hudson. Enlisted in Company A, Sept. 17, 1861, at Hudson, age 25. Teacher. Discharged for disability at Falmouth, Va., Dec. 10, 1862, gunshot wound to left thigh. Enlisted in Independent Company, Feb. 6, 1864, at Hudson. Commissioned second lieutenant Feb. 24, 1864. On detached service with Co. F, 1st Michigan Infantry, July 2, 1864, Petersburg. Transferred to Co. K, reorganized 4th Michigan, June 6,

1865. Resigned and honorably discharged for disability July 21, 1865. Became an attorney and lived in Ottawa County, serving as probate judge and later in the House of Representatives 1887–90; moved to California and died in 1914.

Goodrich, Morrell, Washtenaw County. Enlisted in Company D, June 20, 1861, at Adrian, age 49. Farmer, father of five. Discharged for disability July 14, 1862, for chronic diarrhea and rheumatism. Enlisted in Co. H, 27th Michigan Infantry on Dec. 9, 1862. Hospitalized at Davids' Island, N.Y., for wound and other disabilities July 1864. Transferred to Veteran Reserve Corps, Jan. 28, 1865. Discharged for disability on July 25, 1865. Resided in Dexter and died Aug. 14, 1898.

Goodsell, George A., Lenawee County. Enlisted in Company F as corporal June 20, 1861, at Adrian, age 25. Farmer. Wounded at Chancellorsville, Va., May 1863, and hospitalized with wounds from gunshot and shell to his right arm and head, disfiguring his face. First sergeant. Wounded in action at Gettysburg, July 2, 1863. Mustered out at expiration of term at Detroit, June 29, 1864.

Goodwin, Charles W., Saline. Enlisted in Company G, June 20, 1861, at Adrian, age 22. Died of disease at Washington, D.C., March 23, 1862. Buried Military Asylum Cemetery, Washington.

Gordon, John A., Detroit. Enlisted in Company I as corporal, age 24. Commissioned second lieutenant Sept. 1, 1861. Commissioned first lieutenant Jan. 15, 1862. Wounded in action at Malvern Hill, Va., July 1, 1862, musket ball penetrating his right shoulder. Sent to Judiciary Square Hospital, Washington, D.C. Commissioned captain Sept. 3, 1862. Wounded in action at Shepherdstown Ford, Va., Sept. 19, 1862, ball striking upper left lung. Sent to Washington, D.C., returning to duty Feb. 27, 1863. Acting assistant provost marshal in Detroit from May 1863 to May 1864. Mustered out at expiration of term in California under War Department order, June 30, 1864. Worked as a hotel proprietor in San Diego. Died 1891 and buried San Francisco National Cemetery.

Gould, William H., Livingston County. Enlisted in Company K, June 20, 1861, at Adrian, age 21. Corporal March 10, 1864. Mustered out at expiration of term June 29, 1864. Resided in Mason after war. Buried Maple Grove Cemetery, Mason.

Graham, Robert. Enlisted, unassigned to company, June 21, 1864, at Jackson, age 30. Deserted.

Granger, David A., Trenton. Entered service in Company I at organization as captain, June 20, 1861, at Adrian, age 33. Civil engineer, married, no children. Resigned June 1861. Enlisted in Co. C, 11th Massachusetts Infantry, Sept. 20, 1861. Second lieutenant. First lieutenant Aug. 11, 1862. Captain Sept. 5, 1863. Wounded in action Nov. 27, 1863; died of wound Oct. 27, 1864.

Grannis, Henry A., Adrian. Entered service in Company C at organization as first lieutenant June 20, 1861, at Adrian, age 32. Express agent, married, no children. Quartermaster, acting division quartermaster from Jan. to Oct. 1862. Commissioned captain of Co. F, Sept. 1, 1862. Resigned and honorably discharged Nov. 26, 1862. Resided in St. Thomas, Canada, after service.

Grannison, George, Monroe County. Entered service in Company A, June 20, 1861, at Adrian, age 22. Discharged Dec. 28, 1862, by order; transferred to 2nd U.S. Calvary, Nov. 1, 1862, by order of War Department.

Graviot, Hiram, Monroe County. Enlisted in Company A, June 20, 1861, at Adrian, age 20. Discharged for disability at Washington, D.C., July 1861. Died on Sept. 22, 1861, and buried Port Creek Cemetery, Ash Township.

Green, James S., Burr Oak, St. Joseph County. Enlisted in Company C, June 20, 1861, at Adrian, age 20. Wounded in head at Gaines' Mill, Va., June 27, 1862. Wounded in action, Wilderness, Va., May 5, 1864. Mustered out at expiration of term at Detroit, June 30, 1864.

Green, Newton, Hillsdale County. Enlisted in Company E, June 20, 1861, at Adrian, age 22. Discharged for disability at Washington, D.C., Sept. 6, 1861. Resided in Osseo after service.

Green, Philip, Washtenaw County. Enlisted in Company C, June 20, 1861, at Adrian, age 24. Discharged for disability at Washington, D.C., Aug. 6, 1861.

Gregery, Charles W., Jonesville (name is spelled Gregory in regimental casualty list). Enlisted in Company H, June 20, 1861, at Adrian, age 18. Post office clerk, had two brothers. Killed in action at Gettysburg, July 2, 1863, and buried Rose Farm. Reburied Gettysburg National Cemetery, Michigan Plot, 16-A.

Gregory, Thomas, Monroe County. Enlisted in Company E, June 20, 1861, at Adrian, age 23. Miller. Discharged for disability at Minor's Hill, Nov. 25, 1861.

Grinnage John, Bedford, Monroe County. Enlisted in Company A, June 20, 1861, at Adrian, age 26. Laborer. Transferred to U.S. Cavalry in 1862.

Grisson, Charles E., Hamburg, Livingston County. Enlisted in Company D, June 20, 1861, at Adrian, age 19. Student, resided on farm with parents and siblings. Discharged for disability June 17, 1862. Enlisted in Co. D, 26th Michigan Infantry. Second lieutenant. Wounded near Spotsylvania Court House, May 1864. Appointed to the staff of Gen. Nelson Miles. Mustered out in 1866 as first lieutenant.

Griswold, George, Monroe County. Enlisted in Company A, Sept. 24, 1861, at Hudson. Corporal. Wounded in action Aug. 1863. On detached service with Co. A, 1st Michigan Infantry, July 2, 1864, Petersburg. Discharged at expiration of term, Sept. 10, 1864.

Griswold, Lewis, Rome, Lenawee County. Enlisted in Company A, June 20, 1861, at Adrian, age 17. Transferred and discharged, fall of 1862.

Gruner, Charles F., St. Joseph County. Enlisted in Company C as first sergeant June 20, 1861, at Adrian, age 24. Painter and chair maker. Commissioned second lieutenant Sept. 1, 1861. Commissioned first lieutenant Sept. 1, 1862. Found guilty by court-martial, March 1, 1863, for conduct prejudicial to good order for unauthorized three-day absence at Falmouth, Va.; forfeited one month's pay. Commanding company from June to Nov. 1863 and from Jan. to June 1864. Commanded regiment May 5–8, 1864, after Col. Lumbard was fatally wounded. Wounded in action again, Petersburg, June 20, 1864, gunshot striking left hand, passing through both thighs, injuring rectum. Admitted to Carver General Hospital, Washington, D.C., June 21 until Aug. 18, 1864. Honorably discharged. Resided in Monroe after service. Died in 1912 and buried in Woodland Cemetery, Monroe. Born in Prussia.

Gue, Leonard L., Highland. Enlisted in Company F, June 20, 1861, at Adrian, age 26. Blacksmith. Wounded in action June 27, 1862, Gaines' Mill, shot in right thigh and captured. Exchanged and returned to duty Sept. 1862. Corporal in color guard Jan. 1863. Severely wounded in action at Gettysburg, July 2, 1863, in left arm. Sent to hospital at Chester and Germantown, Pa. Declared unfit for further field service. Transferred to Invalid Corps at Washington, D.C., March 15, 1864. Discharged from Veteran Reserve Corps; enlisted in Battery G, 1st Michigan Light Artillery, Sept. 5, 1864, at Pontiac for one year. Appointed artificer Jan. 28, 1865. Mustered out at Jackson, Aug. 6, 1865. Resided Burdell (Tustin), Osceola County after service. Died Nov. 23, 1896. Buried Burdell Township Cemetery.

Guyor, Andrew Kibbie, Monroe County. Enlisted in Company A, May 16, 1861, age 25. Discharged for disability July 10, 1862. Buried in St. Joseph Cemetery, Monroe.

Guyor, Lewis, Erie, Monroe County. Enlisted in Company H, age 17. Farmer residing with his mother, a widow. Substitute for Joseph Ream, drafted for nine months. Discharged at expiration of term at Frederick, Md., Nov. 11, 1863.

H

Haberfelder, Theodore, Monroe. Enlisted in Company A, June 20, 1861, at Adrian, age 19. Clerk. Corporal. Slightly wounded in action at Fredericksburg, Va., Dec. 13, 1862. Killed in action at Chancellorsville, Va., May 3, 1863. Born in Germany.

Hackett, Andrew, Steuben, Ind. Enlisted in Company B, June 20, 1861, at Adrian, age 21. Mustered out at expiration of term June 30, 1864. Resided in Beatrice, Neb., after service.

Hadley, Cornelius, Litchfield, Hillsdale County. Enlisted as corporal in Company H, June 20, 1861, at Adrian, age 23. Farmer, resided on parents' farm with six siblings. Brother of Jesse and Simon Hadley. Discharged for disability Oct. 23, 1862, at Philadelphia. Reenlisted in Co. M, 9th Michigan Cavalry, May 9, 1863, as sergeant. Awarded the Medal of Honor April 5, 1898, for having voluntarily carried a dispatch from Gen. Grant through enemy lines at Knoxville, Tenn., to Gen. Burnside. Promoted to lieutenant in Co. F, 1st U.S. Cavalry, June 17, 1864. Mustered out April 3, 1866. Resided in Litchfield after service. Died March 22, 1902, and buried in Mount Hope Cemetery, Litchfield.

Hadley, Jesse L., Litchfield. Enlisted in Company H, June 20, 1861, at Adrian, age 21. Farmer, brother of Simon and Cornelius Hadley. Discharged for disability at Minor's Hill, Dec. 18, 1861, weakness and typhoid fever. Reenlisted in Co. I, 4th Michigan Cavalry, July 10, 1862. Mustered out July 2, 1865. Resided in Litchfield after service.

Hadley, Simon B., Litchfield. Entered service in Company H at organization as first lieutenant, June 20, 1861, at Adrian, age 35. Schoolteacher, brother of Jesse and Cornelius Hadley. Resigned Aug. 10, 1861. Reenlisted Aug. 13, 1862, Co. D, 4th Michigan Cavalry. First sergeant. Discharged due to onset of mental illness Aug. 25, 1864. Considered insane, he resided in Litchfield after service, hospitalized in the state asylum in Kalamazoo for a period. Died Aug. 6, 1906.

Haight, Benjamin, Wyandotte. Enlisted in Company F, June 20, 1861, at Adrian, age 32. Farmer. Died from the effects of an ulcer of the right leg at U.S. Hospital, Philadelphia, May 15, 1862.

Haight, Daniel M., Wayne County. Enlisted in Company I, June 20, 1861, at Adrian, age 24. Wounded slightly in action at Gettysburg, July 2, 1863. Mustered out at expiration of term at Detroit, June 30, 1864. Resided in Taylor after service.

Hall, Jairus W., Adrian. Entered service in Company D at organization as second lieutenant, June 20, 1861, at Adrian, age 21. Commissioned first lieutenant, Sept. 1, 1861. Commissioned captain, Co. A, July 1, 1862. Transferred to Co. D, Sept. 1, 1862. Commissioned major May 22, 1863. Commissioned lieutenant colonel July 3, 1863. Commissioned colonel of reorganized 4th Michigan to date July 26, 1864. Commanded brigade in Tennessee during Hood's invasion, winter 1864. Post commander, San Antonio; mustered out and honorably discharged at Houston, May 1, 1866. Appointed brevet brigadier general, U.S. Volunteers, March 1, 1865, for gallant and meritorious service during the war. Lived in Colorado, working in banking and mining, and served in the Territorial Legislature; married and resided in Jackson, Mich. Also became an electrical engineer. Died St. Thomas Hospital, London, England, Nov. 5, 1903.

Hall, Jeremiah M., Hillsdale County. Enlisted in Company E, June 20, 1861, at Adrian, age 27. Day laborer. Deserted March 11, 1862.

Hall, John L. (*VV*), Hudson. Enlisted in Company G as bugler June 20, 1861, at Adrian, age 18. Blacksmith, three siblings. Reenlisted Dec. 29, 1863. Assigned to work as nurse at Fifth Corps Hospital, City Point, Va., Jan. 1864. On detached service with Co. G, 1st Michigan Infantry, July 2, 1864, Petersburg. Transferred to Co. C, reorganized 4th Michigan, July 1, 1865. Mustered out at San Antonio, Feb. 26, 1866. Died in Syracuse, N.Y., March 29, 1932. Buried Brookside Cemetery, Tecumseh.

Hall, Joseph, Morenci, Lenawee County. Enlisted in Company G, Oct. 1, 1862, at Tecumseh, age 23. Printer. Wounded twice, Wilderness, Va., May 5, 1864, and again days later, in the left leg, Laurel Hill, Va. Leg amputated. Died July 2, 1864, in Douglas Hospital, Philadelphia. Buried Arlington National Cemetery, Va., July 6, 1864. Born in England.

Hall, Lorenzo James, Lenawee County. Enlisted in Company G, June 20, 1861, at Adrian, age 22. Corporal. Wounded and missing in action at Gaines' Mill, June 27, 1862, wounded in right thigh. Discharged for disability at New York, Oct. 29, 1862. Admitted to Soldiers Home, Dayton, Jan. 15, 1871, died there Jan. 26, 1881.

Hall, Mifflin, Monroe County. Enlisted in Company A, June 20, 1861, at Adrian, age 35. Hospital steward Feb. 1, 1862. Mustered out at expiration of term at Detroit, June 28, 1864.

Hamilton, Joseph H., Lenawee County. Enlisted in Company F, June 20, 1861, at Adrian, age 25. Farmer. Wounded in action at Fredericksburg, Va., Dec. 13, 1862. Died at Kalorama Hospital, Washington, D.C., April 28, 1863, of smallpox. Buried at Harmony Burial Ground, Washington.

Hamlin, Edgar V., Hudson. Enlisted in Company F, Sept. 8, 1862, at Hudson, age 17. Farmer. Slightly wounded in action at Fredericksburg, Va., Dec. 12, 1862, scalp wound. Missing in action and taken prisoner at Gettysburg, July 2, 1863. Exchanged March 1864. Sent to hospital, Annapolis, Md., April 30, 1864. Discharged near Washington, D.C., June 5, 1865. Resided Omaha, Neb. Died in Hudson, March 14, 1926. Buried in Oak Grove Cemetery, Morenci.

Hamlin, Harrison, Lenawee County. Enlisted in Company F, Sept. 10, 1861, age 21. Farmer. On detached service with Co. C, 1st Michigan Infantry, July 2, 1864, at Petersburg. Discharged at expiration of term at Weldon Railroad, Va., Sept. 11, 1864. Resided in Massachusetts after service.

HAMLIN, JAMES B., Williamston, Ingham County. Enlisted in Company H, March 6, 1863, age 33. Machinist. Substitute for William R. House, drafted from Williamston for nine months. Deserted en route from Detroit to Washington, March 13, 1863. Resided in Fayette, Ohio.

HAMLIN, ROYAL W., Lenawee County. Enlisted in Company F, Sept. 10, 1861, at Hudson, age 20. Farmer. Wounded slightly at Fredericksburg, Dec. 13, 1862. Wounded in action, struck in the head, Gettysburg, July 2, 1863. Sent to hospital in York, Pa., and released Aug. 22, 1863. Admitted to Fairfax Seminary Hospital May 31, 1864; admitted June 7, 1864, to Haddington Hospital, Philadelphia; admitted June 11, 1864, to Satterlee Hospital, Philadelphia, and then Aug. 5, 1864, to St. Mary Hospital, Detroit. Discharged at expiration of term at Detroit, Sept. 12, 1864.

HAMM, RICHARD P., Lenawee County. Entered service in Company B as first lieutenant, May 16, 1861. Resigned at Meridian Hill, Va., Aug. 5, 1861, on a surgeon's certificate of disability.

HAMMOND, LUCIUS G., Lenawee County. Enlisted in Company F, June 20, 1861, at Adrian, age 45. Farmer. Corporal. Sergeant. Transferred to Invalid Corps at Beverly Ford, Va., Sept. 15, 1863.

HAMP, CLARK G., Fulton County, Ohio. Enlisted in Company H, June 20, 1861, at Adrian, age 18. Farmer. Slightly wounded in action at Gettysburg, July 2, 1863. Sick and wounded in hospital at York, Pa.; rejoined company June 26, 1864. Mustered out at expiration of term at Detroit, June 20, 1864. Resided in Ohio after service.

HAMP, FREDERICK, Swanton, Lucas County, Ohio. Enlisted in Company F, June 20, 1861, at Adrian, age 47. Farmer, father of six children, including William Hamp. Discharged for disability May 21, 1863, General Hospital, Washington, D.C. Born in Germany.

HAMP, WILLIAM, Swanton, Lucas County, Ohio. Enlisted in Company F, June 20, 1861, at Adrian, age 18. Farmer, son of Frederick Hamp. Brigade commissary baker. Returned to regiment April 28, 1863. Deserted while on the march, June 30, 1863.

HAMPTON, CHARLES E., Franklin, Lenawee County. Enlisted in Company G, June 20, 1861, at Adrian, age 19. Farm laborer. Mustered out at expiration of term at Detroit, June 30, 1864. Died Oct. 16, 1917, Fowler, Ind.

HARDY, JOHN D. (*VV*), Adams, Hillsdale County. Enlisted in Company H, June 20, 1861, at Adrian, age 24. Sawyer and lumberjack. Wounded at Gettysburg, July 2, 1863, shot in leg. Admitted to hospital, York, Pa. Reenlisted Dec. 29, 1863. Captured at Long Bridge, Va., June 14, 1864, while on the march to the James River. Sent to Andersonville, Ga., June 21, 1864. Admitted to camp hospital for diarrhea July 8, 1864, and died same day. Buried in Grave No. 3015, Andersonville.

HARLEY, JONATHAN P., Washtenaw County. Enlisted in Company D, June 20, 1861, at Adrian, age 25. Captured at Warrenton Junction, Va., Aug. 29, 1862. Confined at Richmond, Aug. 31, 1862. Paroled at Annapolis, Md., Nov. 18, 1862. Deserted from hospital Aug. 31, 1863. Dropped from rolls at Beverly Ford, Va., per War Department. Died in 1936.

HARMON, FREDERICK, Monroe County. Enlisted in Company A, June 20, 1861, at Adrian, age 20. Died of disease in hospital at Georgetown, Sept. 1, 1861. Buried Military Asylum Cemetery, Washington, Sept. 13. Born in Germany.

HARRINGTON, ERASTUS, Adrian. Enlisted in Company I, Aug. 2, 1861, age 18. Taken prisoner at Gettysburg, Pa., July 2, 1863. No further record.

HARRINGTON, JEROME F. or T. Enlisted as hospital steward May 16, 1861, at Ann Arbor, age 26. Transferred to 1st Michigan Infantry, Sept. 1, 1861. Discharged for disability, May 28, 1862. Resided in Jackson after service.

HARRIS, CHARLES W., Hillsdale County. Enlisted in Company H, June 20, 1861, at Adrian, age 17. Clerk. Wounded in left hand, July 1, 1862, Malvern Hill, Va. Admitted to General Hospital, Annapolis, Md., July 29, 1862. Accidentally wounded by discharge of his own gun while on patrol, suffering the loss of a finger and injury to his head. Admitted to General Hospital, Washington, D.C., Sept. 21, 1862. Discharged for disability at Convalescent Camp, Alexandria, Va., Feb. 28, 1863. Enlisted in Co. K, 27th Michigan Infantry, Dec. 23, 1863, at Hillsdale. Mustered out and honorably discharged July 26, 1865. Worked as a guard at the state prison in Jackson and later owned a grocery store in St. Cloud, Fla. Died 1911 in St. Cloud.

Harris, Henry H., Washtenaw County. Enlisted in Company K, June 20, 1861, at Adrian, age 22. Slightly wounded in action, May 5, 1864, Wilderness, Va., flesh wound (gunshot) right thigh. Admitted Campbell Hospital, Washington, D.C. Mustered out at expiration of term June 29, 1864. Buried Mt. Rest Cemetery, St. Johns, Mich.

Harris, William, St. Joseph County. Enlisted in Company C, May 16, 1861. Farmer, father of three young children. Discharged by order of Col. Woodbury at Adrian, June 20, 1861. Born in England.

Harrison, William H., Palmyra, Lenawee County. Enlisted in Company B, June 20, 1861, at Adrian, age 31. Wounded in action May 1864, Wilderness, Va., shot in leg. Amputation. Died May 23, 1864, at Carver Hospital, Washington, D.C., and buried Arlington National Cemetery.

Harroun, James H. (*VV*), Hillsdale County. Enlisted in Company E, June 20, 1861, at Adrian, age 22. Wounded slightly in action at Fredericksburg, Va., Dec. 12, 1862. Reenlisted Feb. 13, 1864. Returned to regiment May 30, 1864. On detached service with Co. K, 1st Michigan Infantry, July 2, 1864, at Petersburg. Transferred to Co. C, reorganized 4th Michigan, July 1, 1865. Mustered out at San Antonio, Feb. 26, 1866.

Hart, Lewis. Enlisted in Company C, May 16, 1861, at Sturgis, age 20. Discharged for disability Oct. 1, 1862.

Hartson, Charles T. (*VV*), Hudson. Enlisted in Company E, Oct. 5, 1861, at Hudson. Reenlisted Dec. 29, 1863. Wounded in action, shot in hand, May 8, 1864. Returned to regiment June 5, 1864. On detached service with Co. K, 1st Michigan Infantry, July 2, 1864, at Petersburg. Transferred to Co. C, reorganized 4th Michigan Infantry, July 1, 1865. Mustered out at San Antonio, Feb. 26, 1866. Resided in Eaton Rapids after service.

Hartson, Hiram L., Ransom Township, Hillsdale County. Enlisted in Company E, June 20, 1861, at Adrian, age 21. Wounded in action near Spotsylvania Court House, Va., in the left arm, May 8, 1864. Mustered out at expiration of term at Detroit, June 28, 1864. Resided in Ransom after service. Died April 3, 1903. Buried Evergreen Cemetery, Ransom.

Haven, William W., Trenton. Enlisted in Company I, June 20, 1861, at Adrian age 19. Died at Annapolis, Md., July 24, 1862, of wounds received in action at Malvern Hill, Va., on July 1, 1862.

Havens, Truman, Centerville. Enlisted in Company C, June 20, 1861, at Adrian, age 39. Severely wounded in leg at Gaines' Mill, Va., June 27, 1862. Corporal. Dropped from the rolls at Culpeper, Va. Resided in Hillsdale after service, then moved west. Buried Oak Hill Memorial Cemetery, San Jose, Calif.

Haviland, Delos M., Iosco, Livingston County. Enlisted in Company K, June 20, 1861, at Adrian, age 20. Farmer and brother of Lewis Haviland. Killed in action at Gaines' Mill, Va., June 27, 1862.

Haviland, Lewis Alonzo, Livingston County. Enlisted in Company K, June 20, 1861, at Adrian, age 24. Farmer, brother of Delos Haviland. Discharged for disability at Washington, D.C., Jan. 15, 1863, for gunshot wound in right arm received in action at Gaines' Mill, Va., June 27, 1862.

Hawk, Fayette, St. Joseph County. Enlisted in Company C as corporal June 20, 1861, at Adrian, age 28. Discharged for disability April 28, 1863. Reenlisted as a landsman, U.S. Navy, on Sept. 3, 1863. Mustered out Aug. 6, 1865. Resided in Michigan after service.

Hawks, James E., Washtenaw County. Enlisted in Company K as corporal June 20, 1861, at Adrian, age 23. Student. Commissioned second lieutenant Sept. 28, 1862. Died of disease at Bealton, Va., April 9, 1864.

Hazen, Nelson T., Milan, Monroe County. Enlisted in Company G, Sept. 9, 1862, at Monroe, age 17. On detached service with Co. G, 1st Michigan Infantry, July 2, 1864, Petersburg. Discharged June 5, 1865. Resided in Azalia, Monroe County, after the service. Buried Azalia Cemetery.

Heald, James, Monroe County. Enlisted in Company A, June 20, 1861, at Adrian, age 32. Mustered out at expiration of term at Detroit, June 30, 1864. Resided in Monroe after service.

Heath, Charles, Medina, Lenawee County. Enlisted in Company F, June 20, 1861, at Adrian, age 16. Farm boy, brother of Chauncy Heath. Wounded in action, shot in face, July 1, 1862, at Malvern Hill, Va. Wounded severely in action at Fredericksburg, Va., Dec. 13, 1862. Died of smallpox in New York City, March 1863. Buried in National Cemetery at Brooklyn, N.Y., Grave No. 3356.

Heath, Chauncy, Hillsdale. Enlisted in Company F, June 20, 1861, at Adrian, age 20. Farmer, brother of Charles Heath. Corporal. Wounded slightly in action at Fredericksburg, Va., Dec. 13, 1862. Taken prisoner at Gettysburg, July 2, 1863. Mustered out at expiration of term at Detroit, June 29, 1864. Resided in Owosso after service. Drowned in 1913.

HEEMAN, THOMAS. Enlisted in Independent Company, March 25, 1864, at Hudson, age 18. On detached service with Co. F, 1st Michigan Infantry, July 2, 1864, at Petersburg. Admitted to Harper Hospital, Detroit, Aug. 5, 1864. Discharged at Detroit on May 10, 1865.

HEINE, PAUL, Cleveland, Ohio. Enlisted in band, June 20, 1861, at Adrian, age 33. Painter, father of four young children. Listed as deserted on Feb. 21, 1862. Mustered out Aug. 10, 1862, by War Department order. Born in Baden, Germany.

HEINTZEN, J. GEORGE, JR., Wayne County. Enlisted in Company I as first sergeant June 20, 1861, at Adrian, age 30. Reduced in rank to corporal June 25, 1861. Wounded in action, Malvern Hill, Va., July 1, 1862, shot in left foot and ankle. Captured and held for six weeks in Richmond. Sick and wounded in general hospital, Philadelphia. Discharged as unfit for service Dec. 3, 1862. Resided in California after service. Died Jan. 29, 1906, Brown Valley, Calif. Born in Germany.

HENDERSHOT, WILLIAM, Macon, Lenawee County. Enlisted in Company G, June 20, 1861, at Adrian, age 22. Farm laborer, oldest of seven siblings. Suffered from hearing loss, Dec. 13, 1862, at Fredericksburg. Taken prisoner at Gettysburg, July 2, 1863. Paroled at City Point, Va., Dec. 28, 1863. Mustered out at expiration of term at Detroit, June 30, 1864. Resided in Emerson after service. Died Feb. 5, 1895.

HENDERSHOTT, PATTERSON, Tecumseh. Enlisted unassigned to a company, Oct. 3, 1862, at Tecumseh, age 34. Married and father of two children. Resided in Tecumseh after service.

HENDERSON, DAVID, Monroe County. Enlisted in Company A, June 20, 1861, at Adrian, age 24. Transferred to Co. E, Aug. 12, 1861. Detailed to gunboat service July 1862 to Nov. 1863. Discharged at Washington, D.C., Nov. 16, 1863.

HENFREY, RICHARD. Drafted for nine months early in 1863, age 32. Farmer. Joined regiment at Falmouth, Va., March 23, 1863. Assigned to Co. H. Listed sick June 17, 1863; captured and paroled Oct. 1, 1863. Discharged at expiration of term at Bealton, Va., Nov. 11, 1863. Buried in Bryon, Genesee County. Born in England.

HENRY, JAMES, Jonesville. Enlisted in Company H, June 20, 1861, at Adrian, age 25. Farmer. Discharged at Washington, D.C., Jan. 15, 1863, for gunshot wound to the right arm while in action at the Second Battle of Bull Run, the only man in the 4th Michigan to have taken part in the battle after he fell in on the march with the 11th Massachusetts Infantry, which was engaged. Sent to a general hospital, Washington, D.C., Sept. 1, 1862, until his discharge Jan. 15, 1863. Resided in Chico, Calif., after service.

HEWITT, JOHN W., Hillsdale County. Enlisted in Company E as sergeant June 20, 1861, at Adrian, age 19. Mustered out at expiration of term at Detroit, June 28, 1864. Resided in Capac, St. Clair County, after service.

HIBNER, DANIEL, Washtenaw County. Enlisted in Company G, June 20, 1861, at Adrian, age 22. Farmer, oldest of two brothers on farm with their mother. Mustered out at expiration of term at Detroit, June 30, 1864. Resided in Alpena area after war. Buried Long Rapids Cemetery, Alpena.

HIGBY, LEVI, H., Ransom, Hillsdale County. Enlisted in Company H, Oct. 8, 1861, at Hudson, age 18. Farm laborer, oldest of five siblings. Wounded severely in action at Fredericksburg, Va., Dec. 13, 1862. Died Dec. 22, 1862, in Division Hospital, Ninth Army Corps, of wounds.

HILFE, NICHOLAS, Cuyahoga, Ohio. Enlisted in band as musician, June 20, 1861, at Adrian, age 28. Mustered out at Harrison's Landing, Va., per order, Aug. 10, 1862.

HILL, FRANCIS E., Hillsdale. Enlisted in Independent Company, March 9, 1864, at Hillsdale, age 18. On detached service with Co. F, 1st Michigan Infantry, July 2, 1864, at Petersburg, Va. Wounded in action Sept. 30, 1864, at Peeble's Farm, Va., gunshot in right foot. Transferred to Co. K, reorganized 4th Michigan, June 6, 1865. Discharged at Harper Hospital, Detroit, Aug. 29, 1865. Resided in Quincy, Branch County, after service.

HILL, HENRY G., Ann Arbor. Enlisted in Company D as sergeant June 20, 1861, at Adrian, age 23. Stonemason. First sergeant. Commissioned second lieutenant Nov. 26, 1861. Commanding Co. F, July 1863. Commanding Co. D, Nov. 1863. Provost guard at brigade headquarters from Dec. 1863 to March 1864. Mustered out at expiration of term at Detroit, June 30, 1864. Had a brother in the 1st Michigan Infantry killed in the war. Died Feb. 26, 1899, and buried at Valley City Cemetery, Grand Rapids. Born in Canada.

HILL, LEANDER F. Enlisted unassigned to company, Feb. 11, 1864, at Hudson, age 24. No further record.

HILLIARD, ALFRED J., Lenawee County. Enlisted in Company F, June 20, 1861, at Adrian, age 19. Farmer. Served on detached duty as division teamster. Mustered out at expiration of term at Detroit, June 29, 1864. Resided in Muskegon after service.

HILLS, JOHN, Wayne County. Enlisted in Company I as sergeant June 20, 1861, at Adrian, age 23. Laborer. In hospital Harrison's Landing, Va., July 1862, chronic diarrhea. Admitted to field hospital Gettysburg, July 6, 1863. Mustered out at expiration of term at Detroit, June 30, 1864. Resided in Wyandotte after service. Died Dec. 20, 1906. Buried Oakwood Cemetery, Wyandotte. Born in England.

HINSDALE, JAMES W. (*VV*), Dundee. Enlisted in Company A, June 20, 1861, at Adrian, age 19. Laborer. Wounded slightly in the neck in the Peninsula Campaign, 1862. Reenlisted Dec. 29, 1863. On detached service with Co. A, 1st Michigan Infantry, July 2, 1864. Wounded in action at Hatcher's Run, Va., March 25, 1865. Transferred to Co. C, reorganized 4th Michigan, July 1, 1865. Discharged at San Antonio, Feb. 10, 1866.

HOAG, ISAAC R., Fairfield, Lenawee County. Enlisted in Company H, April 8, 1862, at Adrian, age 18. Farmer, one of six siblings. Wounded June 27, 1862, at Gaines' Mill, Va., gunshot wound in chest, right lung. Discharged for disability at Philadelphia, Sept. 8, 1862. Died before the end of the war, date unknown. Buried in Jasper, Lenawee County.

HOAGLAND, FRANKLIN B., LaGrange, Ind. Enlisted in Company C, June 20, 1861, at Adrian, age 22. Farm laborer, oldest of five siblings. Wounded slightly in action at Fredericksburg, Va., Dec. 13, 1862. Taken prisoner and wounded at Gettysburg, July 2, 1863. Died on Belle Isle, Richmond, Oct. 24, 1863, of wounds received in action.

HOAGLAND, THOMAS V., Lenawee County. Enlisted in Company G, June 20, 1861, at Adrian, age 22. Taken prisoner at Gettysburg, July 2, 1863. Mustered out at expiration of term at Detroit, June 30, 1864. Resided in Ridgeway Township after service.

HODGE, RILEY, Washtenaw County. Enlisted in Company K, June 20, 1861, at Adrian, age 22. Corporal. Transferred to Battery D, 5th U.S. Artillery, Oct. 9, 1862. Discharged at Sharpsburg, Md., Oct. 25, 1862.

HODGES, THEODORE, Fowlerville. Enlisted in Company K, June 20, 1861, at Adrian, age 18. Died of disease at regimental hospital, Minor's Hill, Va., Dec. 1, 1861. Buried Military Asylum Cemetery, Washington, D.C., Dec. 7, 1861.

HOFFMAN, FELIX, Washtenaw County. Enlisted in Company K, June 24, 1861, at Adrian. Discharged March 1, 1863, on account of wounds received in action at Gaines' Mill, Va., June 27, 1862.

HOFFMAN, FREDERICK, Monroe. Enlisted in Company A, June 20, 1861, at Adrian, age 24. Tailor. Killed in action at Chancellorsville, Va., May 1863. Born in Germany.

HOGAN, THOMAS, Jackson. Enlisted in Company I, June 20, 1861, at Adrian, age 32. Brought up on charges Feb. 1, 1862, for being drunk and absent without leave; found guilty. Killed in action at Mechanicsville, Va., June 26, 1862.

HOISINGTON, ADDISON J., Hudson. Enlisted in Company F, June 20, 1861, at Adrian, age 19. Farmer. Wounded in action at Malvern Hill, Va., July 1, 1862, shot in leg. Killed in action at Gettysburg, July 2, 1863, first buried on the Rose Farm. Reburied Gettysburg National Cemetery, Michigan Plot, B-12.

HOLCOMB, WILLIAM H., Branch County. Enlisted in Company C, June 20, 1861, at Adrian, age 25. Wounded severely in action at the battle of Fredericksburg, Va., Dec. 13, 1862, shot in head. Sent to hospital at Washington, D.C., where he died Dec. 21, 1862.

HOLISTER, ALVIN F., Lenawee County. Enlisted in Company F, June 20, 1861, at Adrian, age 22. Farmer. Deserted at Washington, D.C., July 29, 1861

HOLLINGER, JAMES H., Hillsdale County. Enlisted in Company E, June 20, 1861, at Adrian, age 22. College student. Wounded slightly in action at Fredericksburg, Va., Dec. 13, 1862. Mustered out at expiration of term at Detroit, June 28, 1864.

HOLLINGSHEAD, JAMES B., Napoleon, Ohio. Enlisted in Company I, June 20, 1861, at Adrian, age 22. Corporal. Killed in action at Malvern Hill, Va., July 1, 1862.

HOLMES, ALEXANDER, Lenawee County. Enlisted in Company B, Sept. 16, 1861. Discharged for disability near Falmouth, Va., Jan. 2, 1863. Resided Hudson after service. Buried Maple Grove Cemetery, Hudson.

Holt, Ira E., Livingston County. Enlisted in Company K, June 20, 1861, at Adrian, age 18. Resided with his parents on farm. Corporal. Discharged at Washington, D.C., March 7, 1863, on account of wounds; shot in right arm, at Fredericksburg, Va., Dec. 13, 1862. Resided in Howell after war. Buried Lakeview Cemetery, Howell.

Hooker, W. H. Enlisted in Company C. Died Dec. 21, 1862. Buried in Military Asylum Cemetery, Washington, D.C.

Hopes, William, Hudson. Enlisted in Independent Company, Feb. 27, 1864, at Hudson, age 21. Deserted at Hudson, April 5, 1864.

Hopkins, Daniel, Corunna. Enlisted in Company E, Dec. 31, 1863, at Grand Rapids, age 24. Mustered out July 11, 1865. No further record.

Horner, John A., Branch County. Enlisted in Company C, June 20, 1861, at Adrian, age 18. Corporal. Sergeant. Discharged for disability Feb. 28, 1863.

Horton, Robert P., Lenawee County. Enlisted in Company I, Oct. 1, 1861, at Hudson, age 21. Wounded in action, shot in right leg, May 4, 1863. Transferred to Veteran Reserve Corps Feb. 15, 1864. Discharged at expiration of term at Washington, D.C., Oct. 1, 1864. Resided in Woodstock after service. Buried Chapman Cemetery, Lenawee County.

Hough, Judson B., Lenawee County. Enlisted in Company G, June 20, 1861, at Adrian, age 27. Farmer, married and father of three young children. Missing in action at Gaines' Mill, Va., June 27, 1862. Returned. Again missing in action at Chancellorsville, May 1863. No further record.

Houghton, James. Drafted Feb. 10, 1863, for nine months, from Cohoctah, Livingston County, age 21. Assigned to Company K. Joined regiment April 19, 1863. Discharged at expiration of term at Bealton, Va., Nov. 11, 1863. Resided in Cohoctah.

House, Eri, Scio, Washtenaw County. Enlisted in Company K, June 20, 1861, at Adrian, age 31. Painter, married, no children. Discharged at Sharpsburg, Md., Aug. 18, 1862, on account of gunshot wound received in action at battle of Malvern Hill, Va., July 1, 1862. Resided near St. Louis, Mo., after service.

Howe, Marion F., Hillsdale County. Enlisted in Company H, June 20, 1861, at Adrian, age 21. Farm laborer. Discharged for disability, chronic diarrhea and rheumatism, Minor's Hill, Va., Dec. 10, 1861. Reentered service in Co. G, 18th Michigan Infantry as corporal, Aug. 2, 1862, at Jonesville. Taken prisoner at Snow's Pond, Ky. Sept. 23, 1862. Paroled Nov. 1862. Sergeant May 15, 1865. Discharged at Detroit, June 21, 1865. Resided Moscow Township, Hillsdale County, after service.

Hoy, Hugh (*VV*), Monroe County. Enlisted in Company I, June 20, 1861, at Adrian, age 19. Reenlisted Dec. 29, 1863. On detached service with Co. I, 1st Michigan Infantry, July 2, 1864. Wounded in action at Gravelly Run, Va., March 31, 1865. Transferred to Co. C, reorganized 4th Michigan, July 1, 1865. Mustered out at San Antonio, Feb. 26, 1866. Resided in Ecorse and then Hennepin, Minn., after service. Born in Ireland.

Hubbard, Erastus C., Tecumseh. Enlisted in Company G, Aug. 25, 1862, age 42. Discharged for disability March 13, 1863. Resided in Battle Creek.

Hubble, Jerome, Monroe County. Enlisted in Company I, June 20, 1861, at Adrian, age 23. Clerk. Left foot amputated at Jarvis General Hospital, Baltimore; discharged for disability Oct. 13, 1862.

Hudler, James M., Waterloo, Jackson County. Enlisted in Company D, June 20, 1861, at Adrian, age 29. Miller. Discharged on disability at Baltimore, Md., May 27, 1864, on account of wound received in action at Gettysburg, July 2, 1863, shot in left ankle, followed by amputation of the leg, Aug. 5, 1863. Sent to Davis General Hospital, Baltimore. Fitted with artificial leg, Haddington General Hospital, Philadelphia. Died July 1, 1898. Buried in Oak Grove Cemetery, Chelsea.

Huff, Thaddeus, Hillsdale County. Enlisted in Company E, June 20, 1861, at Adrian, age 20. Farmer, lived with his father. Wounded slightly in action at Fredericksburg, Va., Dec. 13, 1862. Corporal. Severely wounded in leg in action at Gettysburg, July 3, 1863. Mustered out at expiration of term at Detroit, June 28, 1864. Resided in Hillsdale after service. Died 1928. Buried Oak Grove Cemetery, Hillsdale.

Huffman, Samuel, Steuben, Ind. Enlisted in Company G, June 20, 1861, at Adrian, age 27. Farmer. Missing in action at Chancellorsville, May 1, 1863. Discharged for disability at Detroit, July 30, 1863.

Hughes, George L. C., Washtenaw County. Enlisted in Company D, Sept. 9, 1861, at Hudson, age 21. Gunsmith. Wounded in action at Gettysburg, July 2, 1863, shot in left ankle. Sent to hospitals in Philadelphia. Discharged for disability at Detroit, Dec. 24, 1863, on account of wound. Died March 31, 1874 at Adrian and buried there at Oakwood Cemetery.

HUGHES, GEORGE W., Hillsdale County. Enlisted in Company E, May 16, 1861, at Adrian, age 26. Printer, married. Transferred to Veteran Reserve Corps March 31, 1864. Discharged at expiration of term at Washington, D.C., June 20, 1864.

HULSTED, FRANK G., St. Joseph County. Enlisted in Company C, June 20, 1861, at Adrian, age 22. Collection agent. Corporal. Sergeant. Taken prisoner at Gettysburg, July 2, 1863. Released at Venus Point, Ga., Nov. 18, 1864. First sergeant. Discharged at expiration of term at Detroit, March 11, 1865.

HUNT, F. MARION, Hillsdale County. Enlisted in Company E, June 20, 1861, at Adrian, age 21. Gone from regiment, rejoining May 30, 1864. Mustered out at expiration of term at Detroit, June 28, 1864. Resided in Osseo after service. Died May 9, 1928, Ada, Ohio.

HURD, LEWIS G., Ann Arbor. Enlisted in Company D, June 20, 1861, at Adrian, age 21. Resided with father and mother. Died at Minor's Hill, Va., March 11, 1862. Body brought back to Michigan for burial on March 25, 1862.

HURLBURT, THOMAS J. (*VV*), Branch County. Enlisted in Company C, June 20, 1861, at Adrian, age 18. Corporal April 1863. Reenlisted Dec. 29, 1863. On detached service with Co. E, 1st Michigan Infantry, July 2, 1864. Transferred to Co. C, reorganized 4th Michigan, July 1, 1865. Discharged to date June 18, 1865. Buried Boyne Valley Cemetery, Boyne Falls.

HUTCHINS, GEORGE, Detroit. Enlisted in Company I, Sept. 20, 1861, at Detroit, age 21. Killed in action at Gettysburg, July 2, 1863.

HUTT, MYRON D., St. Joseph County. Enlisted in Company C, June 20, 1861, at Adrian, age 21. Mustered out at expiration of term at Detroit, June 30, 1864. Died Dec. 25, 1891. Buried Center Riverton Cemetery, Mason County.

HUXFORD, WILLIAM P., Washtenaw County. Enlisted in Company D, June 20, 1861, at Adrian, age 17. Clerk, resided on a farm with father and mother. Shot in right side of face and head, Malvern Hill, Va., July 1, 1862. Suffered loss of sight in right eye, loss of hearing, and paralysis. Hospitalized in Philadelphia until Aug. 11, 1862. Discharged for disability at Sharpsburg, Md., Sept. 15, 1862, because of wounds. Reenlisted in 162nd New York Infantry. Promoted captain of the 42nd U.S. Infantry. Brevet major for gallant and meritorious service in the assault on Port Hudson, La. Mustered out Sept. 10, 1868, because of epileptic fits resulting from his wound. Died in 1910 from hemorrhage of the brain relating to the wound.

HYATT, JAMES E., Washtenaw County. Enlisted in Company K, June 20, 1861, at Adrian, age 27. Corporal Aug. 28, 1862. Sergeant. Wounded in action at Gettysburg, by a gunshot July 2, 1863. Mustered out at expiration of term June 29, 1864. Resided in Littlefield, Emmet County, after service. Died Jan. 17, 1907.

HYNDELL, JOHN, Calhoun County. Enlisted in Company I, June 20, 1861, at Adrian, age 20. Discharged for disability at camp April 15, 1863.

I

IDE, BRAINARD T., Howell. Enlisted in Company K, June 20, 1861, at Adrian, age 21. Farm laborer. Died of disease at Georgetown, Aug. 23, 1861. Buried Military Asylum Cemetery, Washington, D.C.

IHRIG, WILLIAM G., Dexter. Enlisted in Company K as first sergeant June 20, 1861, at Adrian. Killed in action at Gaines' Mill, Va., June 27, 1862. Born in Russia and was said to have served in the Russian army.

ILIFF, ELIAS D., Camden, Hillsdale County. Enlisted in Company E, June 20, 1861, at Adrian, age 17. Farm laborer. Died July 6, 1862, of wounds received in action at Malvern Hill, Va., July 1, 1862.

INGALL, HENRY E., Medina, Lenawee County. Enlisted in Company F, June 20, 1861, at Adrian, age 16, also given as 19. Resided with his uncle, having come to the U.S. from England a year before. Discharged near Gaines' Mill, June 15, 1862, by order of the secretary of war because he was considered a British citizen; he left on return to England Aug. 10, 1864.

IRISH, ALFRED A., Hillsdale. Enlisted in Independent Company, Feb. 15, 1864, at Hillsdale, age 20. Farmer and brother of John Newton Irish, he resided on farm with his parents and four younger siblings. In regimental hospital for diarrhea, May 1864, and continued to be in and out of hospital for next year. On detached service with Co. F, 1st Michigan Infantry, July 2, 1864. Wounded in action, Peeble's Farm, Va., Sept. 30, 1864. Absent on furlough Jan. and Feb. 1865. Transferred to Co. K, reorganized 4th Michigan Infantry, June 6, 1865. Discharged to date Feb. 16, 1866. Died in 1871.

IRISH, JOHN NEWTON, Moscow, Hillsdale County. Enlisted in Independent Company, Feb. 13, 1864, at Hillsdale, age 17. Farm boy, brother of Alfred Irish. On detached service with Co. F, 1st Michigan Infantry, July 2, 1864. Wounded Sept. 30, 1864, losing vision in one eye at Peeble's Farm, Va. Transferred to Co. K, reorganized 4th Michigan, June 6, 1865. Discharged to date Feb. 16, 1866. Died in Elkhart, Ind., in 1940. Buried Grace Lawn Cemetery, Elkhart.

IRWIN, JAMES, Brownstown, Wayne County. Enlisted in Company G, June 20, 1861, at Adrian, age 22. Laborer. Wounded while on picket Sept. 1861. Discharged for disability at Philadelphia, Dec. 12, 1862.

ITZKINS, GEORGE, DeKalb, Ind. Enlisted in Company C, June 20, 1861, at Adrian, age 17. Resided on farm with parents. Wounded. Transferred to Co. G, 4th U.S. Artillery. Discharged at Alexandria, Va., Dec. 24, 1862.

J

JACKSON, JOHN W. (*VV*). Enlisted in Company G, Sept. 26, 1861, age 24. Farmer. Missing in action at Chancellorsville, Va., May 1863. Returned to company at Warrenton, Va., July 28, 1863. Reenlisted Dec. 29, 1863. On detached service with Co. G, 1st Michigan Infantry, July 2, 1864. Died of disease in hospital at Washington, D.C., May 26, 1865. Buried at Arlington National Cemetery. Born in Germany.

JACKSON, JOSEPH. Died of disease at Union Hotel, Georgetown, Aug. 20, 1861. Buried Military Asylum Cemetery, Washington, D.C., Aug. 29, 1861.

JACKSON, WILLIAM H., Detroit. Enlisted in Company I, June 20, 1861, at Adrian, age 20. Promoted corporal Dec. 3, 1862. Sergeant. Killed in action at Gettysburg, July 2, 1863. Buried Gettysburg National Cemetery, Michigan Plot, I-17.

JAGGER, JOSEPH H., Reading, Hillsdale County. Enlisted in Company E, Aug. 22, 1862, at Hillsdale, age 21. Absent in early fall, joining regiment Oct. 3, 1862. Wounded in action, shot in shoulder, May 10, 1864, near Spotsylvania Court House, Va. Returned May 30, 1864. On detached service with Co. K, 1st Michigan Infantry, July 2, 1864. Discharged at Washington, D.C., June 5, 1865. Resided in Coldwater after service. Died May 28, 1930.

JANES, OSCAR A., Hillsdale. Enlisted in Independent Company, Feb. 15, 1863, at Hillsdale, age 21. On detached service with Co. F, 1st Michigan Infantry, July 2, 1864. Discharged for disability Nov. 5, 1864, on account of wounds received in action before Petersburg, Va., at Weldon Railroad, June 22, 1864, which resulted in the loss of his left arm. In Haddington Hospital, Philadelphia, from July 1 to Nov. 15, 1864. Resided in Hillsdale and Detroit after service, attorney, serving in Hillsdale as city clerk, attorney, circuit court commissioner and probate judge; also served as paymaster general for Michigan, staff of Gov. R. A. Alger, and Hillsdale College trustee. Died in 1933 and buried Oak Grove Cemetery, Hillsdale.

JEFFERS, CHARLES T., Hillsdale County. Enlisted in Company H as sergeant June 20, 1861, at Adrian, age 24. Painter and boatman on the Mississippi and Great Lakes. Discharged for disability at Minor's Hill, Va., Dec. 13, 1861, on account of wounds received while on picket, shot in right hand. Enlisted in Co. K, 27th Michigan Infantry at organization, sergeant, Dec. 16, 1863, at Hillsdale. Wounded in action at Spotsylvania, Va., May 12, 1864. Discharged Jan. 22, 1865, to accept promotion as first lieutenant in 8th U.S. Colored Heavy Artillery. Resided in Sioux Falls, N.D. after service, worked as a deputy warden in state penitentiary.

JEFFERS, GEORGE W., Coldwater. Enlisted in Company H, June 20, 1861, at Adrian, age 22. Shoemaker. Discharged for disability, rheumatism, at Ft. Woodbury, Sept. 6, 1861. Resided in Coldwater after service.

JEFFORDS, HARRISON HERBERT, Dexter. Entered service in Company K at organization as first lieutenant, June 20, 1861, at Adrian, age 24. Attorney, oldest of four siblings. Commissioned captain, Co. C, May 1, 1862. Commissioned colonel to date from Nov. 26, 1862, taking command March 1863. Died July 3, 1863, at

Gettysburg, of bayonet wound received in action July 2. Buried Dexter Cemetery.

JEHU, DAVID, Wayne County. Enlisted in Company I, June 20, 1861, at Adrian, age 41. Had resided in Wheeling, Va., before coming to Michigan for employment. Left his son in the care of his parents. After being hospitalized at Gettysburg, he died at Baltimore, Aug. 3, 1863, reportedly after he fell from a train car on from Baltimore to Washington, D.C. Born in Wales.

JENNISON, SEWELL A., Hillsdale. Enlisted in Company E, June 20, 1861, at Adrian, age 23. College student. Corporal. Complained of dropsy and was admitted to division hospital at Stoneman's Switch, Va., March 10, 1863. Died Stafford, Va., March 30, 1863. Originally buried at Fitzhugh's Farm, Stafford; reburied National Cemetery, Fredericksburg.

JEWETT, GEORGE, Caledonia, Kent County. Enlisted in Company K, June 20, 1861, at Adrian, age 16. Student, had four siblings. Deserted while at Adrian on June 22, 1861.

JOHNSON, FREEMAN, Lenawee County. Enlisted in Company F as corporal June 20, 1861, at Adrian, age 26. Farmer. Wounded June 27, 1862, at Gaines' Mill, Va. Transferred to Invalid Corps Aug. 1, 1863.

JOHNSON, JAMES H., Hudson. Enlisted in Company H, Oct. 7, 1861, at Hudson, age 20. Carpenter. Died of typhoid fever at DeCamp General Hospital, Davids' Island, N.Y., June 1, 1862, buried New Rochelle Beachwood Cemetery, Grave No. 8.

JOHNSON, ORRIN, Wheatland, Hillsdale County. Enlisted in Company I, Sept. 4, 1862, at Hudson, age 22. Farmer. Transferred to Co. F Nov. 1, 1861. Died of typhoid fever, July 15, 1862.

JOHNSON, THOMAS A., Lenawee County. Enlisted in Company F, June 20, 1861, at Adrian, age 41. Farmer, African-American. Discharged for disability Aug. 17, 1861.

JOHNSTON, JAMES, Shiawassee Township. Drafted Feb. 10, 1863, for nine months, age 19. Laborer, had four siblings. Assigned to Company K. Killed in action at Gettysburg, July 2, 1863, shot through body and reportedly buried on the field.

JONES, ABIATHAR H., Flat Rock. Enlisted in Company I as wagoner June 20, 1861, at Adrian, age 30. Company drummer July 1861. Wounded at Mine Run, Nov. 29, 1863. Mustered out at expiration of term at Detroit, June 20, 1864. Reenlisted as fireman in the Navy on *Black Hawk*. Mustered out in Feb. 1867. Resided in Flat Rock after service. Died Jan. 1, 1898, buried Brookside Cemetery, West Branch.

JONES, EDWARD, Cleveland, Ohio. Substitute for Francis W. Pratt, drafted March 2, 1863, for nine months, from Ottawa, Cass County. Reportedly deserted.

JONES, GEORGE. Enlisted unassigned to a company, Feb. 5, 1864, at Corunna, Shiawassee County, age 21. Not listed on returns of muster-out roll.

JONES, JONATHAN B. Enlisted in Independent Company, Feb. 12, 1864, at Hillsdale, age 25. Corporal April 5, 1864. On detached service with Co. F, 1st Michigan Infantry, July 2, 1864, Petersburg, Va. Missing in action Dec. 9, 1864, near Petersburg. Returned to regiment May 20, 1865. Discharged at Washington, D.C., per general order June 8, 1865. Resided in Michigan after service. Died June 23, 1886, Vassar, Tuscola County.

JONES, MILES L., Litchfield, Hillsdale County. Enlisted in Company H, June 20, 1861, at Adrian, age 18. Farmer, resided with parents. Missing in action at Mechanicsville, Va., June 26, 1862, captured at Meadow Bridge. Spent months in general hospitals and discharged for disability, enlarged heart, at Fortress Monroe, Va., March 13, 1863. Died May 5, 1898. Buried in Allen Cemetery, Hillsdale.

JONES, THOMAS D. (*VV*), Coldwater. Enlisted in Company B as sergeant June 20, 1861, at Adrian, age 23. Saloon hand. Discharged for disability Aug. 24, 1861. Reenlisted Sept. 24, 1861, as first sergeant. Commissioned second lieutenant, Co. F, Jan. 13, 1862. Transferred to Co. B, Jan. 13, 1862. Wounded in action at Gaines' Mill, Va., June 27, 1862, and died July 23, 1862, in New York Harbor.

JONES, TIMOTHY T., Steuben, Ind. Enlisted in Company B as corporal June 20, 1861, at Adrian, age 21. Teamster. Reenlisted Dec. 29, 1863. On detached service with Co. B, 1st Michigan Infantry, July 2, 1864, Petersburg. Transferred to Co. C, reorganized 4th Michigan, July 1, 1865. Resided in Crystal, Mich. after war. Admitted to Soldiers Home, Dayton, for rheumatism Nov. 2, 1901.

JUDSON, THOMAS H. Enlisted in Company F, June 20, 1861, at Adrian, age 22. Molder. Promoted to corporal June

1862. Slightly wounded in the left shoulder, Chancellorsville, Va., May 1863. Killed in action at Wilderness, Va., May 5, 1864. Born in England.

K

KAISER, ANDREW JACKSON, St. Joseph County. Enlisted in Company C, June 20, 1861, at Adrian, age 20. Brick mason. In hospital with pneumonia, Aug. 11, 1861, at Georgetown. Wounded, shot in foot and thigh, at Malvern Hill, Va., July 1, 1862. In Emory General Hospital, Washington, Nov. 4, 1863, for chronic diarrhea. Returned to duty May 1, 1864. Mustered out at expiration of term at Detroit, June 30, 1864. Resided in Hillsdale and Sturgis after service. Died 1902.

KANE, MORRIS, Toledo, Ohio. Enlisted in Company K, June 20, 1861, at Adrian, age 35. Wounded in the right leg in Virginia. Transferred to Invalid Corps, Washington, D.C., Sept. 30, 1863. Admitted to Soldiers Home, Dayton, Aug. 19, 1868. Released Sept. 25, 1868. Buried Lakeview Cemetery, Howell. Born in Ireland.

KEEDLE, JAMES (*VV*), Washtenaw County. Enlisted in Company D, June 20, 1861, at Adrian, age 23. Reenlisted Dec. 29, 1863, at Ann Arbor. On detached service with Co. E, 1st Michigan Infantry, July 2, 1864, Petersburg. Dropped from company rolls per order near Petersburg, Sept. 9, 1864.

KEELER, LEWIS W. (*VV*), Washtenaw County. Enlisted in Company D, June 20, 1861, at Adrian, age 26. Reenlisted Dec. 25, 1863, at Ann Arbor. On detached service with Co. E, 1st Michigan Infantry, July 2, 1864, Petersburg. Transferred to Co. K, reorganized 4th Michigan, July 1, 1865. Mustered out at San Antonio, Feb. 23, 1866.

KELCH or KELSH, HENRY, Washtenaw County. Enlisted in Company K, June 20, 1861, at Adrian, age 43. Farm laborer. Discharged for disability at Washington, D.C., Sept. 11, 1861, for wounds. Born in Germany.

KELEN, JOHN, Metamora, Lapeer County. Enlisted in April 3, 1863, at Ft. Wayne, Detroit, age 40. Machinist. Substitute for John French. Discharged for disability at Convalescent Camp, Va., July 16, 1863, for chronic rheumatism and thickening of the tissues in feet. Reported as unfit for duty in Invalid Corps and that his actual age was 50. Born in Germany

KELLEY, EMERY B. Enlisted in Company I, Feb. 11, 1864, at Jefferson, Hillsdale County, age 17. Killed in action at Wilderness, Va., May 5, 1864. Buried Leonardson Cemetery, Pittsford.

KELLEY, ROBERT W., Washtenaw County. Enlisted in Company K, June 20, 1861, at Adrian, age 18. Discharged for disability at Philadelphia, Dec. 15, 1862, for wounds. Buried Mt. Hope Cemetery, Lansing.

KELLOGG, E. LYMAN, Washtenaw County. Enlisted in Company K, June 20, 1861, at Adrian, age 19. Blacksmith, had one sibling. Taken prisoner at Gettysburg, July 2, 1863. Mustered out at expiration of term, June 29, 1864.

KELLY, EDWIN C., Lenawee County. Enlisted in Company G, March 6, 1862, at Adrian, age 21. Spent two months in a hospital in Maryland and discharged to date April 9, 1863. Resided in Kansas after service.

KELLY, WILLIAM H., Lenawee County. Enlisted in Company G, June 20, 1861, at Adrian, age 39. Harness maker and sailor. Mustered out at expiration of term at Detroit, June 30, 1864. Enlisted Co. K, 67th Ohio Infantry, Nov. 14, 1865. Resided in Nebraska after service. Buried Gibbon-Riverside Cemetery, Gibbon, Neb. Born on Isle of Man.

KELSER, GEORGE J., Rollin, Lenawee County. Enlisted in Independent Company, March 18, 1864, at Hudson, age 25. On detached service with Co. F, 1st Michigan Infantry, July 2, 1864, Petersburg. Corporal. Transferred to Co. K, reorganized 4th Michigan Infantry, June 6, 1865. Wounded in action, shot in left thigh, at Five Forks, Va., April 1, 1865. Discharged at Satterlee Hospital, Philadelphia, July 7, 1865. Resided in Clayton after service.

KEMERY or KEMORY, ABSALOM, Steuben County, Ind. Enlisted in Company B, June 20, 1861, at Adrian, age 28. Discharged for disability Dec. 10, 1861. Resided in Angola after service.

KEMPT, GODFREY, Monroe County. Enlisted in Company A, June 20, 1861, at Adrian, age 23. Taken prisoner on June 29, 1863, on the march to Gettysburg, while guarding a house along the route. Rejoined the regiment Sept. 1863. Discharged at Washington, D.C., June 12, 1865. Buried Oak Grove Cemetery, Chelsea.

KENDALL, HARRY, Monroe. Enlisted in Company A as corporal June 20, 1861, at Adrian, age 19. Died of disease at Minor's Hill, Va., Oct. 27, 1861. Buried Woodland Cemetery, Monroe.

KENNEDY, JOHN, St. Joseph County. Enlisted in Company C as corporal June 20, 1861, at Adrian, age 27. Farmer, resided with nine siblings. Sergeant. Discharged for disability Feb. 8, 1863. Born in Ireland.

KENYON, LEWIS L., Hudson, Lenawee County. Enlisted in Company F, June 20, 1861, at Adrian, age 19. Farmer. Killed in action at Malvern Hill, Va., July 1, 1862.

KESSELRING, JACOB, Macomb County. Enlisted in Company I, June 20, 1861, at Adrian, age 22. Taken prisoner in action at Gaines' Mill, Va., June 27, 1862. Discharged for disability at Alexandria, Va., Nov. 15, 1862.

KETCHUM, ALVAH, Calhoun County. Enlisted in Company C, June 20, 1861, at Adrian, age 19. Mustered out at Detroit, June 30, 1864. Resided in Olivet, Mich., and Meagher County, Mont. after service.

KEYES, WILLIAM, Wayne County. Enlisted in Company I, June 20, 1861, at Adrian, age 38. Corporal. Discharged on disability Dec. 17, 1861.

KIDDER, SAMUEL C., London Township, Monroe County. Enlisted in Company A, June 20, 1861, at Adrian, age 20. Detached to Lowe's Balloon Corps from Oct. to Dec. 1861 at Washington; back with regiment Feb. 28, 1862. Wounded and missing in action at Malvern Hill, Va., July 1, 1862. In regimental hospital July 1862 for fever. Taken prisoner at Chancellorsville, May 4, 1863. Returned to regiment at Auburn, Va., Oct. 26, 1863. In regimental hospital, May 6, 1864, with gunshot wound in a finger of right hand received at Wilderness, Va. Mustered out at expiration of term at Detroit, June 30, 1864. Reenlisted Sept. 6, 1864, in 18th Michigan Infantry for one year. Nashville General Hospital, Jan. 10, 1865, with syphilis. Resided in Hawkins, Mich., after service, working as a clerk and preacher. Died July 27, 1907.

KIDNEY, JOHN P., Branch County. Enlisted in Company C, June 20, 1861, at Adrian, age 23. Farm laborer by trade. Wounded in action, gunshot to the left shoulder, at Gaines' Mill, Va., June 27, 1862. Missing in action at Chancellorsville, May 1, 1863. Taken prisoner at Gettysburg, July 2, 1863. Returned to regiment Dec. 10, 1863. Mustered out at expiration of term at Detroit, June 30, 1864. Resided in Union City after service.

KILMER, ALONZO, White Pigeon, St. Joseph County. Enlisted in Company C as wagoner June 20, 1861, at Adrian, age 28. Papermaker and local marshal. Married, father of a small daughter. Ambulance driver. Mustered out at expiration of term at Detroit, June 29, 1864. Served as deputy sheriff of St. Joseph County after service; moved to Kansas and became a judge. Died July 8, 1908, in Sedan, Kansas. Buried in Greenwood Cemetery, Sedan.

KIMBALL, DUANE C., Adrian. Enlisted in Company B as corporal June 20, 1861, at Adrian, age 17. Oldest of three siblings. Sergeant. Died July 6, 1863, of wounds received in action at Gettysburg, July 2, 1863, shot in body, leg amputated. Buried Gettysburg National Cemetery, Michigan Plot, E-13.

KING, LAWRENCE, Hudson. Enlisted in Independent Company, March 25, 1864, at Hudson, age 19. Wounded in action June 18, 1864. On detached service with Co. F, 1st Michigan Infantry, July 2, 1864, Petersburg. Transferred to Co. K, reorganized 4th Michigan Infantry, June 6, 1865. Discharged by order at St. Louis, Mo. Sept. 25, 1865. Born in Ireland.

KING, MARTIN, Hudson. Enlisted in Independent Company, March 30, 1864, at Hudson, age 24. On detached service with Co. F, 1st Michigan Infantry, July 2, 1864, at Petersburg. Sergeant. Missing in action Aug. 21, 1864, at Weldon Railroad, Va.

KING, NORMAN, Ann Arbor. Enlisted in Company D, June 20, 1861, at Adrian, age 22. Corporal. Killed in action at Gettysburg, July 2, 1863. Buried in Gettysburg National Cemetery, Michigan Plot, B-10.

KING, THOMAS JR., Hudson. Enlisted in Independent Company, March 28, 1864, at Hudson, age 22. Wounded during the Overland Campaign in Virginia, May 1864; underwent left leg amputation surgeries May 31 and June 11, 1864. Died of wounds at Hudson, Oct. 24, 1864. Buried Maple Grove Cemetery, Hudson.

KING, WALLACE A., Tecumseh. Enlisted in Company G as first lieutenant, age 24. Landscape artist, student at Norwich University, Vermont. Not mustered because a case of bilious fever and was hospitalized for four weeks. Enlisted in Co. B, 7th Rhode Island Cavalry. Mustered out Sept. 26, 1864.

KINGSLEY, ANDREW J., Steuben County. Enlisted in Company B, June 20, 1861, at Adrian, age 31. Discharged for disability at Minor's Hill, Va., March 3, 1862.

KINNEY, GEORGE H., Hillsdale County. Enlisted in Company H, June 20, 1861, at Adrian, age 21. Schoolteacher. Missing at Gaines' Mill, Va., June 27, 1862, wounded by a gunshot through his body. Discharged Dec. 1,

1862, for disability at Davids' Island, N.Y. Employed as forage master in the Quartermaster Department, Western Theater, 1864. Resided in North Adams after the war, postmaster. Died in June 1904 and buried North Lawn Cemetery, North Adams.

KITTLE, JESSE, Monroe. Enlisted in Company A, June 20, 1861, at Adrian, age 22. Resided on his father's farm, the eldest of two siblings; his brother, John serving in the 5th Michigan Cavalry. Killed in action at Malvern Hill, Va., July 1, 1862

KNAGGS, JOHN WESLEY, Raisinville, Monroe County. Enlisted in Company A, June 20, 1861, at Adrian, age 22. Farmer. Badly wounded and captured in action, Malvern Hill, Va., July 1, 1862; left arm amputated. Held at Libby Prison and exchanged one month later. Discharged for disability at Washington, D.C., Nov. 11, 1862. Resided in Bay City after service.

KNAPE, AUGUST, Monroe. Enlisted in Company A, June 20, 1861, at Adrian, age 25. Killed in action at Malvern Hill, Va., July 1, 1862.

KNOWING, EDWARD. Died of disease, typhoid fever, at Seminary Hospital, Georgetown, Oct. 5, 1861. Buried in Military Asylum Cemetery, Washington, D.C.

KREIGER, CHRISTIAN B., Wayne County. Enlisted in Company I, June 20, 1861, at Adrian, age 22. Severely wounded in action at Gettysburg, July 2, 1863, right arm, with forearm amputated July 30, 1863. Discharged Jan. 1, 1864.

KRONBACH, ADAM, Monroe County. Enlisted in Company A, May 15, 1861, Mustered out at expiration of term at Detroit, June 30, 1864. Lost an eye in the service. Resided in Monroe and buried Trinity Lutheran Cemetery, Monroe.

KULMAN, AUGUST. Enlisted in Band as Musician, June 20, 1861, at Adrian, age 34. Mustered out at Harrison's Landing, Va., Aug. 10, 1862, by War Department order.

KYDD, JOHN H., Detroit. Enlisted in Company I, June 20, 1861, at Adrian, age 19. Carpenter residing with parents and two siblings. Corporal. Promoted first sergeant April 4, 1863. Killed in action at Gettysburg, July 2, 1863. Initially buried in the Wheatfield, but moved to Gettysburg National Cemetery, Michigan Plot, H-5. Born in Scotland.

L

LADD, CHARLES H., Monroe County. Enlisted in Company A, June 20, 1861, at Adrian, age 23. Promoted corporal, May 1862. Sick in hospital Aug. 1862. Detached to brigade Provost Guard, March and April 1863. Killed in action at Gettysburg, July 2, 1863. Buried near Rose Barn, reburied in Gettysburg National Cemetery, Michigan Plot, B-13.

LAFLEUR, ASHER B. (*VV*), Litchfield, Hillsdale County. Enlisted in Company H, June 20, 1861, at Adrian, age 21. Farmer. Corporal Jan. 1, 1863. Wounded and missing in action at Gettysburg, July 2, 1863, shot through the body. Returned to regiment Aug. 1, 1863. Reenlisted Dec. 19, 1863. Sergeant. Wounded in action May 10, 1864, near Spotsylvania Court House, Va., leg smashed by grapeshot and amputated. Discharged at Detroit, June 5, 1865. Later served as township treasurer in Litchfield and treasurer of Hillsdale County. Died in 1906 and buried Mt. Hope Cemetery, Litchfield.

LAFOUNTAIN, PAUL, LaSalle, Monroe County. Enlisted in Company I, June 20, 1861, at Adrian, age 20. Farm laborer. Died of disease, typhoid fever, at Georgetown, Oct. 20, 1861. Buried Military Asylum Cemetery, Washington, D.C., Oct. 27, 1861.

LAIRD, DAVID C., Pittsford, Hillsdale County. Enlisted in Company A, June 20, 1861, age 19. Farmer laborer, resided on parents' farm with two siblings. Died Sept. 24, 1863, of wounds received in action at Gettysburg, July 2, 1863, shot in back. Buried Camp Letterman Hospital, Gettysburg. Moved to Gettysburg National Cemetery, Michigan Plot, B-22.

LAKE, AMON C., Hillsdale. Enlisted in Company E, June 20, 1861, at Adrian, age 21. Wounded in action at Gaines' Mill, June 27, 1862. Corporal. Wounded slightly in thigh in action at Gettysburg, July 2, 1863. Died May 14, 1864, of wounds received in action at Wilderness, Va., May 5, 1864. Originally buried at Woolen Factory Lot,

Fredericksburg, Va.; reburied Fredericksburg National Cemetery, Row W, 2430.

LAMPMAN, AMASA. Enlisted in Company K, June 20, 1861, at Adrian, age 24. Farm laborer. Discharged for disability at Minor's Hill, Va., Dec. 14, 1861. Enlisted in Co. H, 22nd Michigan Infantry, Aug. 11, 1862, at Howell. Transferred to Invalid Corps March 22, 1864, on account of wounds received in action at Chickamauga, Ga., Sept. 20, 1863. Buried Lakeview Cemetery, Howell.

LAMPMAN, LAWSON W., Livingston. Enlisted in Company K, June 20, 1861, at Adrian, age 18. Wounded in action at Gaines' Mill, Va., June 27, 1862. Killed in action at Gettysburg, July 2, 1863. Buried Gettysburg National Cemetery, Michigan Plot, I-2.

LAMSON, ALVAN C., Wayne County. Enlisted as sergeant major, June 20, 1861, at Adrian, age 22. Commissioned second lieutenant, Co. K, Sept. 1, 1861. Commissioned first lieutenant, Co. H, Dec. 11, 1861. Commissioned captain July 18, 1862. On detached service as acting assistant inspector general on Col. McQuade's brigade staff, March 26, 1863. Transferred to Co. C, April 11, 1863. On brigade staff of Col. J. Sweitzer, May 22, 1863, detailed as acting assistant inspector general to March 1864. Resigned and honorably discharged for disability April 20, 1864. Buried Elmwood Cemetery, Detroit.

LANE, JAMES T. (*VV*), Macon Township, Lenawee County. Enlisted in Company G, March 5, 1862, at Adrian. Carpenter. Reenlisted March 6, 1864. On detached service with Co. G, 1st Michigan Infantry, July 2, 1864, at Petersburg. Transferred to Co. C, reorganized 4th Michigan, July 1, 1865. Corporal Sept. 1, 1865. Mustered out at San Antonio, Feb. 26, 1866. Resided in Holloway after service. Buried Raisin Presbyterian Cemetery, Lenawee County.

LANGFORD, DANIEL W. (*VV*), Lenawee County. Enlisted in Company B, June 20, 1861, at Adrian, age 25. Farm laborer. Reenlisted Dec. 29, 1863. Taken prisoner at Gettysburg, July 2, 1863. Returned to company Aug. 12, 1863. Married Sarah Grove on Feb. 6, 1864, at Bealton Station, Va. Langford was recorded as a straggler while on the march and taken prisoner June 14, 1864. Died of yellow fever at Savannah, Ga., Oct. 14, 1864; his wife gave birth to a daughter a month later in Fairfield, Lenawee County.

LAPHAM, GEORGE, Detroit. Enlisted in Company I, June 20, 1861, at Adrian, age 19. Farmer. Killed in action at Gettysburg, July 2, 1863.

LAPHAM, WILLIAM B., Wayne County. Enlisted in Company I, June 20, 1861, at Adrian, age 22. Day laborer. Discharged for disability by order, Feb. 19, 1863. Resided in Albion, Neb., after service.

LARZELERE, WILLIAM F., Tecumseh. Enlisted in Company G, June 20, 1861, at Adrian, age 25. Clerk. Discharged for disability at Ft. Woodbury, Va., Sept. 5, 1861. Resided in Saline, Washtenaw County, after service. Died July 16, 1923.

LARZILIER, GEORGE, Detroit. Enlisted in Company H, Feb. 9, 1863, for nine months, age 21. Farmer, substitute for John Robert Lowry, drafted from Jackson County. Wounded in the right leg, Gettysburg, July 2, 1863. Taken to hospital in York until Dec. 1863; sent to Detroit. Discharged at expiration of term at Detroit, Dec. 25, 1863. Died Oct. 2, 1885, and buried Reynolds's Corner Cemetery, Manchester.

LASSEY, JOHN G., Raisinville, Monroe County. Enlisted in Company A, July 26, 1862, at Monroe, age 28. Farmer, married, brother of Richard and William Lassey. Wounded in action, in the side, Wilderness, Va., May 5, 1864. On detached service with Co. A, 1st Michigan Infantry, July 2, 1864, at Petersburg. Discharged near Washington, D.C., by order, June 9, 1865. Resided in Monroe after service. Buried King (Old Sackett) Cemetery, Raisinville.

LASSEY, RICHARD R., Raisinville. Enlisted in Company A as corporal June 20, 1861, at Adrian, age 28. Farmer, married with two young daughters; brother to John and William Lassey. Sergeant. Wounded slightly in left arm at Malvern Hill, Va., July 1, 1862. Taken prisoner at Gettysburg, July 2, 1863. Died at Richmond, Va., Dec. 26, 1863. Buried at National Cemetery, Richmond, Section 8A, Site 1572. Born in England

LASSEY, WILLIAM, Monroe County. Enlisted in Company A, June 20, 1861, at Adrian, age 19. Brother to John and Richard Lassey. Corporal Sept. 25, 1861. Wounded by a spent ball at Malvern Hill, Va., July 1, 1862. Sergeant Aug. 8, 1862. Mustered out at expiration of term at Detroit, June 30, 1864. Resided in Monroe after service, then moved to Independence, Kans., in 1878. Died Oct. 28, 1915, and buried in Mount Hope Cemetery, Independence.

LATTA, MARTIN M., LaGrange, Ind. Enlisted in Company C, June 20, 1861, at Adrian, age 21. Farm laborer, had five siblings. Died of disease in camp near Falmouth, Va., Dec. 30, 1862.

LAUGHLIN, PATRICK. Enlisted in Company K, June 20, 1861, at Adrian, age 19. Farm laborer. Transferred to Battery D, 5th U.S. Artillery, Oct. 9, 1862. Discharged at Sharpsburg, Md., per general order, Oct. 25, 1862. Born in Ireland.

LAVERTY, ELIJAH, Lansing. Enlisted in Company H, Feb. 11, 1863, at Leroy, age 21. Farmer residing on parent's farm. Substitute for Gilbert Putney, drafted from Leroy, for nine months. Died of illness in Douglas Hospital, Washington, D.C., July 19, 1863. Buried Military Asylum Cemetery, Washington. Born in Canada.

LAW, CHARLES E., LaGrange, Ind. Enlisted in Company C, May 16, 1861, at Sturgis. Discharged for disability July 30, 1862.

LAWRENCE, HENRY L., Hudson. Enlisted in Company F, June 20, 1861, at Adrian, age 21. Farmer, married. Shot in chest, died May 6, 1863, of wounds received in action at Chancellorsville, Va. Buried near camp at Falmouth, Va.

LAWSON, GEORGE C., Hudson, Lenawee County. Enlisted in Company F as sergeant June 20, 1861, at Adrian, age 35. Shoemaker. Killed accidentally by a comrade, Corporal Lucius Hammond Aug. 31, 1861, at Hall's Hill, Va. Buried in Plot 66, Block D, Maple Grove Cemetery, Hudson.

LEBARON, ROBERT. Entered service as second assistant surgeon, May 5, 1863, at Aldie, Va., age 26. Mustered out at Detroit, June 28, 1864. Died 1925 and buried Oak Hill Cemetery, Pontiac.

LEE, ANDREW J., Lenawee County. Enlisted in Company G, June 20, 1861, at Adrian, age 22. Corporal. Mustered out at expiration of term at Detroit, June 30, 1864. Resided in Manchester after service. Died Oct. 28, 1889, and buried Oak Grove Cemetery, Manchester.

LEE, EDWIN, Cambridge, Lenawee County. Enlisted in Company G, June 20, 1861, at Adrian, age 18. Farmer, resided with mother and three siblings. Corporal Co. E. Aug. 25, 1861. Resided in Tipton after war service. Buried Cambridge Junction Cemetery.

LEE, GEORGE H., St. Joseph County. Enlisted in Company C, June 20, 1861, at Adrian, age 23. Discharged for disability at Philadelphia, Dec. 30, 1862.

LEIGHTON, PHILLIP, Trenton, Wayne County. Enlisted in Company I, June 20, 1861, at Adrian, age 23. Killed in action at Fredericksburg, Va., Dec. 13, 1862.

LEMING, HENRY, Wayne County. Enlisted in Company I as musician, age 14. Discharged for disability at camp, March 16, 1863. Reenlisted in Co. B, 24th Michigan Infantry, March 23, 1865. Discharged June 30, 1865, at Detroit. Resided in New Buffalo after service. Admitted to Soldiers Home, Dayton, for rheumatism, June 14, 1892. Released Sept. 19, 1892. Died June 1, 1901, Soldiers Home, Grand Rapids. Buried there June 6, 1901.

LEONARD, FREEMAN, LaSalle. Monroe County. Enlisted in Company A, June 20, 1861, at Adrian, age 22. Blacksmith, relative of John D. Leonard. Died of typhoid fever in hospital at Harrison's Landing, Va., July 8, 1862, and buried on the bank of James River; reburied at National Cemetery, Glendale, Va.

LEONARD, JOHN D., LaSalle, Monroe County. Enlisted in Company A, June 20, 1861, at Adrian, age 17. Resided on parents farm with three siblings; related to Freeman Leonard. Died of disease in hospital at Mound Hill, Va., Feb. 11, 1863. Originally buried at Stafford, Va., but reburied National Cemetery, Fredericksburg, Va.

LEWIS, ALONZO, Lenawee County. Enlisted in Company B, Feb. 25, 1862, at Adrian, age 23. Laborer. Wounded at Gettysburg, July 2, 1863, shot right leg. On detached service with Co. B, 1st Michigan Infantry, July 2, 1864, at Petersburg. Transferred to Co. C, reorganized 4th Michigan, July 1, 1865. Admitted to Harper Hospital, Detroit, Dec. 1865. Transferred to Co. K, Feb. 5, 1866. Transferred to Veteran Reserve Corps. Resided in Hamilton, Neb., after service, operating a farm implement dealership. Died at 80 in York, Neb., Feb. 28, 1917.

LEWIS, EDWARD, Macon, Lenawee County. Enlisted in Company D, 3rd Michigan Cavalry, Sept. 27, 1861. Enlisted in Co. B, 4th Michigan Infantry, Feb. 27, 1862, at Adrian, age 20. Killed in action at Gettysburg, July 2, 1863. Buried in Macon Cemetery, Macon.

LEWIS, GEORGE W., Adrian. Enlisted in Company F, June 20, 1861, at Adrian, age 29. Barber and farmer, married, household of nine. Wounded in action at Gettysburg, July 2, 1862, shot through right arm. Transferred to Invalid Corps at Washington, D.C., Feb. 15, 1864. Resided in Franklin Township after service. Buried

Springville Cemetery, Lenawee County.

LEWIS, HARVEY (*VV*), Lenawee County. Enlisted in Company F, June 20, 1861, at Adrian, age 21. Miller. Reenlisted Feb. 16, 1864. Wounded in action, shot in hand, at Malvern Hill, Va., July 1, 1862. Wounded in action, shot in neck, May 8, 1864, Laurel Hill, Va. In a hospital in Washington, D.C. On detached service with Co. C, 1st Michigan Infantry, July 2, 1864, at Petersburg. Transferred to Co. C, reorganized 4th Michigan, July 1, 1865. Discharged to date June 25, 1865. Buried at Etheridge Cemetery, Lawrence County, Tenn.

LEWIS, JOHN, Kalamazoo. Enlisted Feb. 22, 1864, at Kalamazoo, age 44. Veterinary surgeon.

LIBBEY, GEORGE W., Monroe County. Enlisted in Company G, Sept. 28, 1861, at Hudson. Discharged for disability, hernia, at Minor's Hill, Va., Feb. 13, 1862. Resided in Duplain, Clinton County, after service. Buried Mt. Rest Cemetery, St. Johns, Michigan.

LIMBARKER, WILLIAM E. (spelling also interpreted as Lembocker, Limbocker, Lenbocker and Limbocker), Lenawee County. Enlisted in Company F as sergeant June 20, 1861, at Adrian, age 26. Printer. Wounded in action, in hand, Gaines' Mill, Va., June 27, 1862. Taken prisoner at Gettysburg, July 2, 1863. Shot and killed Oct. 25, 1863, at Belle Isle, Va., by Confederate prison guard. Buried Section 4A, Grave 335, National Cemetery, Richmond.

LINDENBOWER, WHEELER, Hudson. Enlisted in Company C, Sept. 30, 1861, age 21. Farmer. Col. Woodbury's aide and hostler. Injured Feb. 1862 when kicked in the head by the colonel's horse, injuring his left eye. Missing in action at Malvern Hill, Va., July 1, 1862. Allowed leave from July 5 to Aug. 5, 1862, to take Woodbury's horses home. Hostler for Col. Jeffords. Discharged for disability at Bealton, Va., March 29, 1864. Was a teamster after war. Died in Medina, Lenawee County, in 1926 and buried Evergreen Cemetery, Ransom Township.

LINDSLEY, WILLIAM, Saline, Washtenaw County. Enlisted in Company H as sergeant June 20, 1861, at Adrian, age 21. Farmer. Mustered out May 5, 1862, Washington, D.C., on account of disability. Reenlisted in 1st Michigan Sharpshooters Oct. 3, 1864. Mustered out July 28, 1865. Died June 2, 1900, and buried at Saline.

LIVINGSTON, JAMES, St. Joseph County. Enlisted in Company C, June 20, 1861, at Adrian, age 15. Resided on family farm, one of several children. Taken prisoner Aug. 29, 1861. Discharged for disability at Washington, D.C., Feb. 12, 1863.

LOCKWOOD, ELIAS, Lenawee County. Enlisted in Company B, June 20, 1861, at Adrian, age 25. On gunboat service in western theater flotilla from July 1862 to May 1863. Discharged at Washington, D.C., Nov. 16, 1863, for formal transfer to gunboat service. Resided in Romeo after service. Died March 4, 1911, and buried Romeo Cemetery.

LONG, WILLIAM, Hudson. Enlisted in Independent Company, March 31, 1864, at Hudson, age 38. On detached service with Co. F, 1st Michigan Infantry, July 2, 1864, at Petersburg. Transferred to Co. K, reorganized 4th Michigan Infantry, June 6, 1865. Discharged at Louisville, Ky., July 3, 1865.

LOURIN, JOHN, Alexandria, Va. Enlisted in Company I, at Union Hill, Va., age 19, Nov. 1, 1861. Listed as sick and wounded in hospital. Deserted camp Jan. 3, 1863.

LOSS, CHARLES P., Brownstown. Enlisted in Company I, June 20, 1861, at Adrian, age 17. Resided with family on their farm, oldest of seven siblings. Taken prisoner at Gettysburg, July 2, 1863. Mustered out at expiration of term June 30, 1864.

LOSSING, JEHIAL B., Adrian. Enlisted in Company F, June 20, 1861, at Adrian, age 18. Wagon maker. Discharged for disability at New York City, Jan. 5, 1863. Died 1864. Buried Section B-5, Plot 5, Oakwood Cemetery, Adrian.

LOVELAND, WILLIAM H. Enlisted in Company D, as sergeant, June 20, 1861, at Adrian, age 21. Sergeant major Jan. 10, 1862. Commissioned first lieutenant, Co. D, Sept. 10, 1862. Commissioned captain, Co. B, Sept. 10, 1862. Wounded in action, Wilderness, Va., May 5, 1864, shot in the middle left femur with wound not dressed for three days; leg amputated. Died May 31, 1864. Buried in Carroll Hill Cemetery, Fairfax, Vt.

LOVETT, GEORGE E., Calhoun County. Enlisted in Company I, June 20, 1861, at Adrian, age 21. Detached to brigade bakery Jan. 3, 1863. Wounded in left leg, May 5, 1864, at Wilderness, Va. Mustered out at expiration of term at Detroit, June 30, 1864. Resided in Albion after war. Died at Soldiers Home, Grand Rapids, Feb. 14, 1916.

LOW, HENRY, Mendon, St. Joseph County. Enlisted in Company C, June 20, 1861, at Adrian, age 21. Died at Epiphany Hospital, Washington, D.C., July 17, 1862, of severe wounds in side and shoulder received in action at Malvern Hill, Va., July 1, 1862. Buried Military Asylum Cemetery, Washington, D.C., July 18, 1863.

LOW, DAVID (*VV*), Washtenaw County. Enlisted in Company D, June 20, 1861, at Adrian, age 31. Farmer, married, with a small daughter. Reenlisted Dec. 25, 1863. Mustered Jan. 1, 1864. Killed in action near Laurel Hill, Va., May 10, 1864. Born in England

LOWE, ROBERT, Ann Arbor. Enlisted in Company K, Feb. 20, 1863, at Waterloo, Jackson County, age 25. Substitute for John Segrist, drafted for nine months, from Jackson County. Deserted en route from Detroit to Washington, D.C.

LUCE, CONSTANT, Monroe. Entered service as captain, Company A, at organization, June 20, 1861, at Adrian, age 40. Married, with a son. Resigned on account of disability, Nov. 23, 1861. Reentered service in 17th Michigan Infantry as lieutenant colonel at organization, Aug. 8, 1862. Commanding regiment from Oct. 16 to Oct. 26, 1862. Wounded by explosion of a shell at South Mountain, Md., Sept. 1862. In hospital for five days at Alexandria, Va. Commissioned colonel March 21, 1863. Honorably discharged Dec. 4, 1864. In March 1865 Luce was court-martialed for mismanagement of funds during 1861 while he was in the 4th Michigan. Resided in Monroe after service, real estate dealer and register of deeds. Died Feb. 28, 1904. Buried Woodland Cemetery, Monroe.

LUCE, MOSES AUGUSTINE, McDonough, Ill. Enlisted in Company E, June 20, 1861, at Adrian, age 18. College student. Sergeant Jan. 1, 1863. Mustered out at expiration of term at Detroit, June 28, 1864. Awarded the Medal of Honor by Congress in 1895 for his rescue of a wounded comrade near Spotsylvania Court House. Lawyer; vice president of the California Southern Railroad Company; county judge, San Diego. Died April 25, 1933, and buried Greenwood Cemetery, Hawthorne section, San Diego.

LULL, LEONARD, Hudson. Enlisted in Independent Company, March 16, 1864, at Hudson, age 58. Farmer, married, and father of Leonard D. Lull. On detached service with Co. F, 1st Michigan Infantry, July 2, 1864, at Petersburg. Returned to duty from McClellan Hospital, Philadelphia, Sept. 23, 1864. Transferred to Co. K, reorganized 4th Michigan, June 6, 1865. No discharge furnished.

LULL, LEONARD D., Lenawee County. Enlisted in Company K, Sept. 15, 1861, at Hudson, Farmer. His father was Leonard Lull. Killed in action at Malvern Hill, Va., July 1, 1862.

LUMBARD, FRANCIS M., Jackson. Drafted in Company I, March 31, 1864, at Jackson, age 28. Railroad conductor. On detached service with Co. E, 1st Michigan Infantry, July 2, 1864, at Petersburg. Transferred to Co. I, reorganized 4th Michigan Infantry, June 6, 1865. Sergeant. Commissioned second lieutenant June 6, 1865. Mustered out at Detroit, Oct. 17, 1865. Buried Lakeview Cemetery, Whitmore Lake.

LUMBARD, GEORGE W., Hillsdale County. Entered service in Company E at organization as captain, June 20, 1861, at Adrian, age 31. Lawyer, married, father of a young son. Commissioned lieutenant colonel July 1, 1862. Commanding regiment from Nov. 25, 1862, to spring 1863. Commissioned colonel July 3, 1863. Died May 6, 1864, of wounds received in action at Wilderness, Va., May 5, 1864. Buried by his men in the Wilderness, but his remains were likely moved, unidentified, into the national cemetery at Fredericksburg after the war.

LUMBARD, HORATIO G., Hillsdale. Entered service in Company K as first lieutenant, Nov. 14, 1862, age 38. Master bookbinder, married and father of a teenage daughter. Acting regimental adjutant from Jan. to July 1863. Wounded and taken prisoner at Gettysburg, July 2, 1863, loss of a thumb. Held at Libby Prison, Richmond. Mustered out and honorably discharged Dec. 19, 1864, by War Department order. Resided in Philadelphia after service.

LYNCH, WILLIAM, Washtenaw County. Enlisted in Company D, June 20, 1861, at Adrian, age 24. Missing in action at Gettysburg, July 2, 1863. No further record, but it was believed he was killed and buried on the Rose Farm property.

LYON, LYMAN J., Hudson. Enlisted in Independent Company, Feb. 29, 1864, at Hudson, as musician drummer. Age 46. Mason, married, father of three. On detached service with Co. F, 1st Michigan Infantry, July 2, 1864, Petersburg. Transferred to Co. K, reorganized 4th Michigan, June 6, 1865. Mustered out at Houston, May 26, 1866. Resided in Hudson after service. Buried Plot 11, Block J, Maple Grove Cemetery, Hudson.

M

Mackey, John H. (*VV*). Enlisted in Company G, June 20, 1861, at Adrian, age 25. Reenlisted Dec. 29, 1863. Wounded in action at Gettysburg, July 2, 1863, shot in right foot. On detached service with Co. G, 1st Michigan Infantry, July 2, 1864, Petersburg. Transferred to Co. C, reorganized 4th Michigan, July 1, 1865. Corporal July 1, 1865. Mustered out at San Antonio, Feb. 26, 1866. Suffered from lung disease after war. Resided in Sand Creek, S.D., after service.

Macoy, Justus, Hudson. Enlisted in Independent Company, March 19, 1864, at Hudson, age 43. On detached service with Co. F, 1st Michigan Infantry, July 2, 1864, Petersburg. Died at White Hall Hospital, Philadelphia, Oct. 6, 1864.

Magee, Henry W., Hillsdale County. Enlisted in Company E, June 20, 1861, at Adrian, age 20. Mustered out at expiration of term at Detroit, June 28, 1864. Resided in Chicago after service and practiced law

Mallory, Stephen H., Hillsdale County. Enlisted in Company E, June 20, 1861, at Adrian, age 22. Farmer, resided with his parent and two siblings. Mustered out at expiration of term at Detroit, June 28, 1864. Resided in Roxand, Eaton County, after service. Died Sept. 25, 1917.

Maltz, George L., Detroit. Enlisted in Company I as corporal June 20, 1861, at Adrian, age 19. Sergeant Sept. 1, 1861. Wounded in action at Mechanicsville, Va., June 26, 1862. Taken prisoner in the field hospital at Savage's Station; prisoner at Libby Prison for two months until exchanged. First sergeant Nov. 1, 1862. Sergeant major Dec. 4, 1862. Commissioned second lieutenant, Co. E, Dec. 13, 1862. Commanding company March and April 1863. Acting adjutant from July 5, 1863, to Dec. 1863, and from Feb. 1864 to May 1864. Wounded in action near Bethesda Church, June 3, 1864. Commissioned first lieutenant March 21, 1864. Mustered out and honorably discharged June 28, 1864. Resided in Alpena after service, bank president; mayor 1874–76, also served as state treasurer and regent, University of Michigan. Buried Elmwood Cemetery, Detroit.

Mangus, James, Tecumseh. Enlisted in Company G as corporal June 20, 1861, at Adrian, age 25. Farm laborer, resided on farm with six relatives. Sergeant. Died of disease at Philadelphia, Dec. 25, 1862.

Mann, Chauncey L., LaGrange, Ind. Enlisted in Company C, May 16, 1861, at Sturgis, age 22. Never mustered into the U.S. service.

Mann, Harlow S., Livingston County. Enlisted in Company K, June 20, 1861, at Adrian, age 20. Merchant clerk, resided with parents and sister. Discharged for disability, June 18, 1862. Resided in Saginaw after service.

Maples, Andrew (*VV*), Tecumseh. Enlisted in Company B, June 20, 1861, at Adrian, age 21. Corporal Jan. 1, 1862. Sergeant July 1, 1862. Reenlisted Dec. 29, 1863. Wounded in action, Wilderness, Va., May 5, 1864, gunshot to right arm. On detached service with Co. B, 1st Michigan Infantry, July 2, 1864, Petersburg. Transferred to Co. C, reorganized 4th Michigan, July 1, 1865. Commissioned first lieutenant July 1, 1865. Mustered out and honorably discharged at San Antonio, Feb. 26, 1866. Resided in Shelby and Harbor Springs after service.

Marcey, Lyman (*VV*), Lenawee County. Enlisted in Company G, June 20, 1861, at Adrian, age 25. Wounded slightly in action at Fredericksburg, Va., Dec. 13, 1862. Reenlisted Dec. 29, 1863. Wounded in left arm, Wilderness, Va., May 5, 1864. On detached service with Co. G, 1st Michigan Infantry, July 2, 1864, Petersburg. Discharged at Washington, D.C., Sept. 21, 1864. Buried Oak Hill Cemetery, Grand Rapids.

Marks, William H. (*VV*), Moscow, Hillsdale County. Enlisted in Company H, June 20, 1861, at Adrian, age 21. Farmer, resided with parents and nine siblings. Reenlisted Dec. 29, 1863. On detached service with Co. H, 1st Michigan Infantry, July 2, 1864, Petersburg. Transferred to Co. C, reorganized 4th Michigan, July 1, 1865. Mustered out at San Antonio, Feb. 26, 1866. Resided in Kansas after service.

Marsh, William H., Hillsdale County. Enlisted in Company H, June 20, 1861, at Adrian, age 29. Blacksmith apprentice and railroad employee, resided with parents and two siblings. Deserted with fellow soldiers, C. Harris and Jarvis Smith, while passing though Washington, D.C., Sept. 12, 1862. Returned to regiment Jan. 13, 1864. Restored to duty March 1, 1864, but ordered to forfeit pay for the period he was absent and to make up that time. On detached service with Co. H, 1st Michigan Infantry, July 2, 1864, Petersburg. Transferred to Co. C, reorganized 4th Michigan Infantry, July 1, 1865. Admitted to Harper Hospital, Detroit, Sept. 11,

1865. Discharged at Detroit, Sept. 26, 1865. Buried Hillside Cemetery, St. Clair.

MARSHALL, DAVID D., Lenawee County. Entered service in Company G at organization, as captain, June 20, 1861, at Adrian, age 34. Constable, married, father of a young daughter. In regimental hospital, Falls Church, Va., typhoid fever. Sent to hospital at Georgetown from Oct. 10 to Nov. 13, 1861. Hospitalized again July 19 to Aug. 1862. Commanding regiment from Feb. 25 to April 1864. Mustered out at expiration of term at Detroit, June 30, 1864. Reenlisted captain, Co. D, 30th Michigan Infantry, Nov. 28, 1864. Mustered out at Detroit, June 30, 1865. Died Oct. 14, 1886, Bay City. Buried Brookside Cemetery, Tecumseh.

MARSHALL, GEORGE E., Washtenaw County. Enlisted in Company D, Sept. 19, 1861, at Hudson. Sick and wounded in general hospital and convalescent camp at Alexandria, Va., from Nov. 1862 to May 1863. Taken prisoner at Gettysburg, July 2, 1863. After his capture was admitted to hospital in Richmond, Va., Oct. 21, 1863, and under treatment Nov. 1, 1863. Buried Oak Lawn Cemetery, Stockbridge.

MARTIN, CULWELL, Clinton County. Enlisted in Company K, June 24, 1861, age 32. Laborer. Married, father of young children. Discharged for disability at Sharpsburg, Md., Sept. 1, 1862. Reenlisted in Co. M, 1st Michigan Engineers and Mechanics, Aug. 31, 1863. Corporal July 1864. Mustered out at Nashville, Tenn. Sept. 22, 1865. Buried Maple Hill Cemetery, Elmira, Otsego County.

MARTIN, JAMES (*VV*), Wayne County. Enlisted in Company I as corporal June 20, 1861, at Adrian, age 26. Transferred to 1st Michigan Cavalry, Dec. 10, 1861. Reenlisted at Minor's Hill, Va., Feb. 25, 1862. Discharged, Washington, D.C., Nov. 10, 1862, by reason of his enlistment in 2nd U.S. Cavalry.

MARTIN, RICHARD, Montreal, Canada West. Enlisted in Company I, June 20, 1861, at Adrian, age 18. Discharged for disability at Minor's Hill, Va., Jan. 27, 1862. Resided in San Francisco after service.

MARVIN, CHARLES N., Hillsdale County. Enlisted in Company E as ordnance first sergeant June 20, 1861, at Adrian, age 22. Merchant, resided with parents and five siblings. Commissioned second lieutenant Sept. 1, 1861. Commissioned first lieutenant, Co. F, June 27, 1862. Commissioned captain, Nov. 26, 1862. Resigned and honorably discharged, Jan. 29, 1863. Resided in Buffalo, N.Y., after service.

MASON, MILES T., Wayne County. Enlisted in Company D, June 20, 1861, at Adrian, age 22. Mustered out at expiration of term at Detroit, June 30, 1864. Resided in Newport, Ky., after service.

MATHEWS, WILLIAM, Franklin, Lenawee County. Enlisted in Company G, June 20, 1861, at Adrian, age 18. Resided on his father's farm with three siblings. Died at Georgetown Hospital, Aug. 16, 1861.

MCAFEE, JOHN, St. Joseph County. Enlisted in Company C as corporal June 20, 1861, at Adrian, age 19. Sergeant. Mustered out at expiration of term at Detroit, June 30, 1864. Resided in Windsor, Canada, after service.

MCBRIDE, QUINTUS J., Blissfield, Lenawee County. Enlisted in Company B, June 20, 1861, at Adrian, age 17. Resided on parent's farm with four siblings. Died of disease at Union Hotel, Georgetown, Aug. 20, 1861. Buried Military Asylum Cemetery, Washington.

MCCANN, JAMES, Trenton. Enlisted in Company I, June 20, 1861, at Adrian, age 23. Corporal. Reduced in rank, March 1862, by court-martial. Attached to provost guard at brigade headquarters until mustered out at expiration of term at Detroit, June 30, 1864. Resided in Wyandotte after service.

MCCARTHY, ALEXANDER A., Lenawee County. Enlisted in Company I, Oct. 5, 1861, at Hudson, Discharged for disability, Jan. 1, 1863.

MCCARTY, WILLIAM F. D., Hillsdale County. Enlisted in Company E as corporal June 20, 1861, at Adrian, age 22. Listed as sick and in the hospital, York, Pa., May and June 1862. Reduced in rank after battle of Malvern Hill, Va., July 1, 1862, to private. Discharged by War Department order at Washington, D.C., Nov. 3, 1862.

MCCAUSSEY, CHARLES A., Lenawee County. Enlisted in Company K, June 20, 1861, at Adrian, age 21. Discharged at Baltimore, April 24, 1863, on account of wound received in action at Fredericksburg, Va., Dec. 13, 1862. Resided in Scotts, Kalamazoo County.

MCCLURG, WILLIAM, Macomb County. Enlisted in Company I, June 20, 1861, at Adrian, age 24. Discharged for disability at Washington, D.C., Aug. 5, 1861.

MCCOLLISTER, CHARLES E., St. Joseph County. Enlisted in Company E as sergeant June 20, 1861, at Adrian, age 24. Quartermaster sergeant Sept. 1, 1861. Transferred back to company Nov. 1, 1861. Discharged on disability at Minor's Hill, Va., Dec. 18, 1861.

McConnell, Martin, Hillsdale County. Enlisted in Company H, June 20, 1861, at Adrian, age 21. Farmer. Discharged at Harrison's Landing, Va., July 19, 1862, disability. Died of disease Aug. 3, 1862. Buried Military Asylum Cemetery, Washington, D.C.

McConnell, William H., Hillsdale County. Entered service in Company H as second lieutenant at organization, June 20, 1861, at Adrian, age 23. Sick Sept. 20, 1861, sent to Seminary Hospital, Georgetown; did not rejoin regiment. Resigned Jan. 2, 1862. Resided in Monroe after service. Died March 18, 1872.

McCormick, Charles, Superior, Washtenaw County. Enlisted in Company D, June 20, 1861, at Adrian, age 21. Farmer, resided on his father's farm with five siblings. Discharged for disability at Philadelphia, Feb. 24, 1863.

McDermott, James, Lenawee County. Enlisted in Company G, March 8, 1862, at Adrian. On detached service with Co. G, 1st Michigan Infantry, July 2, 1864, Petersburg. Discharged at expiration of term at Washington, D.C., March 8, 1865. Resided in Clinton after service. Buried Riverside Cemetery, Clinton.

McDonald, Charles, Wayne County. Enlisted in Company I, as corporal, June 20, 1861, at Adrian, age 31. Discharged for disability at camp, March 13, 1863.

McDonald, Robert S., Brownstown. Enlisted in Company I, June 20, 1861, at Adrian, age 22. Police officer. Wounded in action, Mechanicsville, Va., June 26, 1862. Sick and wounded in General Hospital, Baltimore. Discharged at Baltimore, Oct. 4, 1862. Resided in Detroit after service. Born in Scotland.

McDonough, Michael, Saugatuck, St. Joseph County. Enlisted in Company C, June 20, 1861, at Adrian, age 21. Slightly wounded in action at Fredericksburg, Va., Dec. 13, 1862. Corporal. Transferred to Invalid Corps at Washington, D.C., Oct. 1, 1863. Later resided at Soldiers Home, Grand Rapids.

McDougall, James, Adrian. Enlisted in Company B, May 16, 1861, at Adrian, age 38. Died of disease at Minor's Hill, Va., Jan. 1, 1862.

McDougall, John A., Lenawee County. Enlisted in Company I, Oct. 10, 1861, at Union Hill. Discharged for disability at Minor's Hill, Va., Jan. 20, 1862.

McDougall, William M., Rollin, Lenawee County. Enlisted in Company B, Oct. 1, 1861, at Hudson. Died of disease at Minor's Hill, Va., Jan. 8, 1862. Buried Military Asylum Cemetery, Washington, D.C.

McEvoy, John, Wayne County. Enlisted in Company I, June 20, 1861, at Adrian, age 21. Sick and wounded in Hospital Alexandria, Va., Dec. 1862. Wounded in action, shot in the arm, Wilderness, Va., May 5, 1864. Mustered out at expiration of term at Detroit, June 30, 1864.

McFadden, Michael (*VV*), Washtenaw County. Enlisted in Company D, June 20, 1861, at Adrian, age 23. Carpenter. Reenlisted Dec. 29, 1863, at Ann Arbor. Wounded in action, shot in leg, Wilderness, Va., May 5, 1864. On detached service with Co. E, 1st Michigan Infantry, July 2, 1864, Petersburg. Discharged for disability Feb. 12, 1865.

McFarland, John, Wayne County. Enlisted in Company I, June 20, 1861, at Adrian, age 19. Check clerk in railroad freight office. Absent without leave July Nov. 1862. Mustered out at expiration of term at Detroit, June 30, 1864. Born in Scotland.

McKenzie, William, Wayne County. Enlisted in Company D, June 20, 1861, at Adrian, age 27. Sergeant. Wounded in action, Wilderness, Va., May 5, 1864, gunshot wound in right eye. Admitted to Stanton Hospital, Washington, D.C., May 11, 1864. Transferred to Satterlee Hospital, Philadelphia, May 18, 1864. Mustered out at expiration of term Aug. 3, 1864, Adrian. Resided in Leroy, Osceola County, after service.

McKeown, James, Tecumseh. Enlisted in Company G as corporal June 20, 1861, at Adrian, age 19. Cabinetmaker, oldest of two siblings. Died of disease in hospital at Baltimore, Nov. 1, 1861.

McKinsty Walter, Lapeer. Enlisted in Company H, Feb. 11, 1863, at Ft. Wayne, Detroit, for nine months, age 24. Farmer. Deserted en route to join regiment on March 13, 1863. No further record.

McKiver, Robert, Monroe County. Enlisted in Company H, June 20, 1861, at Adrian, age 17. Laborer, resided with his widowed mother. Discharged for disability at Washington, D.C., May 29, 1862. Died in 1916. Born in Canada.

McKnight, George, Watertown, Canada West. Enlisted in Company I, June 20, 1861, at Adrian, age 27. Reported to have committed suicide at Ft. Woodbury, Va., Sept. 3, 1861.

McLean, James B., Livingston County. Enlisted in Company K as sergeant June 20, 1861, at Adrian, age 28.

Commissioned second lieutenant Jan. 29, 1862. Promoted first lieutenant June 27, 1862. Commissioned captain Sept. 28, 1862. Contracted disease of the lungs at Falmouth, Va., during winter of 1862–63. Wounded, shot in shin and left heel while in action at Gettysburg, July 2, 1863. Resigned and honorably discharged on account of disability April 21, 1864.

Mead, LeRoy, Lenawee County. Enlisted in Company G as corporal June 20, 1861, at Adrian, age 30. Butcher and farmer. Sergeant Jan. 1, 1862. Commissioned second lieutenant Feb. 12, 1863. Commanding Co. K, May 1, 1864, and wounded in action, shot in shoulder, Wilderness, Va., May 5, 1864. Rejoined the regiment June 21, 1864, at City Point, Va., and mustered out at expiration of term at Detroit, June 30, 1864. Resided in Macon Township after war. Died March 23, 1883.

Meech, Frederick W., Steuben, Ind. Enlisted in Company B, June 20, 1861, at Adrian, age 24. Sergeant Nov. 1, 1861. Killed in action at Gaines' Mill, Va., June 27, 1862.

Meek, David (*VV*), Northwest Ohio. Enlisted in Company B, June 20, 1861, at Adrian, age 24. Farm laborer. Wounded and in general hospital Dec. 1862. Reenlisted Dec. 29, 1863. On detached service with Co. B, 1st Michigan Infantry, July 2, 1864, Petersburg. Transferred to Co. C, reorganized 4th Michigan, July 1, 1865. Mustered out at Detroit to date Feb. 26, 1866.

Mellions, John, Jonesville, Hillsdale County. Enlisted in Company H, June 20, 1861, at Adrian, age 22. Farmer. Killed in action at Gaines' Mill, Va., shot in forehead, July 27, 1862.

Melville, William Harry, St. Joseph County. Enlisted in Company C, June 20, 1861, at Adrian, age 19. Resided on parents' farm with eight siblings. Corporal. Sergeant. Transferred to Veteran Reserve Corps, March 17, 1864. Resided in Mendon after service, but buried Melville-Brown Cemetery, Winfield, Kans.

Merrifield, Marc A., Tekonsha, Calhoun County. Enlisted in Company E, June 20, 1861, at Adrian, age 21. Discharged for disability at Warrenton, Va., Nov. 18, 1862. Resided Union City after service. Buried Riverside Cemetery, Union City.

Merritt, Billings B., Hillsdale County. Enlisted in Company E, as sergeant, June 20, 1861, at Adrian, age 23. Discharged for disability at Sharpsburg, Md., Oct. 27, 1862.

Metty, Eli, Frenchtown, Monroe County. Enlisted in Company E, June 24, 1861, at Ft. Wayne, Detroit, age 26. Farmer and father of four. Discharged for disability March 8, 1862.

Miliken, John, Raisin, Lenawee County. Enlisted in Company F, June 20, 1861, at Adrian, age 18. Farmer. Deserted at Philadelphia, Nov. 15, 1862. Reenlisted in U.S. Cavalry.

Millard, Melancthon, Adrian. Enlisted in Company G, Feb. 24, 1862, age 17. Law student, resided with parents and three siblings. Promoted second lieutenant, Co. B. Resigned citing "Dissatisfaction among officers of Regt." Oct. 23, 1862. Enlisted in Co. D, reorganized 4th Michigan, Sept. 3, 1864, at Adrian, age 20. Sergeant Oct. 13, 1864, and transferred to Co. E. Commissioned second lieutenant, Co. D, Nov. 21, 1864. Commissioned first lieutenant, Co. I, Oct. 24, 1865. Mustered out and honorably discharged Feb. 11, 1866. Resided in Cleveland, Ohio, an attorney.

Millens, Cyrus, Medina, Lenawee County. Enlisted in Company B, June 20, 1861, at Adrian, age 25. Farmer, resided on parents' farm with four siblings; brother of George Millens. Corporal July 1, 1862. Discharged for disability April 11, 1863. Resided in Ogden after service. Buried Palmyra Cemetery, Palmyra.

Millens, George W., Medina, Lenawee County. Enlisted in Company B, June 20, 1861, at Adrian, age 22. Farmer, brother of Cyrus Millens. Corporal. Taken prisoner at Gettysburg, July 2, 1863. Confined at Richmond, Va., July 21, 1863. Sent to Andersonville, Ga., but while en route, admitted to hospital in Augusta. Died Feb. 28, 1864. Buried Marietta National Cemetery.

Miller, Brazilla S., Hillsdale. Enlisted in Independent Company, Feb. 10, 1864, at Hillsdale, age 16. On detached service with Co. F, 1st Michigan Infantry, July 2, 1864, Petersburg. Transferred to Co. K, reorganized 4th Michigan, June 6, 1865. Discharged at Harper Hospital, Detroit, Aug. 29, 1865.

Miller, Frank, Reading, Hillsdale County. Enlisted in Company E, June 20, 1861, at Adrian, age 22. Farm laborer. Musician. Mustered out at expiration of term at Detroit, June 28, 1864. Born in Switzerland.

Miller, Ira G., Hillsdale. Enlisted in Independent Company, Feb. 10, 1864, at Hillsdale, age 21. Farm laborer. Corporal April 5, 1864. On detached service with Co. F, 1st Michigan Infantry, July 2, 1864, Petersburg.

Discharged at Wilmington, Del., from Tilton General Hospital, Feb. 6, 1865, on account of wounds received in action. Resided in Fulton after service.

MILLER, JOHN, Montreal, Canada. Enlisted in Company K, March 3, 1863, at Warren, age 30. Farmer, married with four young children. Substitute for Christopher Rothy, drafted from Warren. Deserted en route from Detroit to Washington, D.C. Born in England.

MILLER, JOHN MORTON, Gibraltar, Wayne County. Enlisted in Company I, June 20, 1861, at Adrian, age 23. Wounded at Gaines' Mill, Va., June 27, 1862, shot in right leg. Amputations of the lower third of limb, Fortress Monroe, Va., on July 7, 1862. Died July 19, 1862, at Satterlee Hospital, Philadelphia. Buried Woodland Cemetery, Grave 14, Philadelphia. Body removed and buried Gibraltar Cemetery, Gibraltar.

MILLER, MICHAEL, Litchfield, Hillsdale County. Enlisted in Company H, June 20, 1861, at Adrian, age 19. Farmer, resided on parents' farm with nine siblings. Discharged for disability, described as disease of the lungs, at Minor's Hill, Va., Nov. 23, 1861. Resided in Litchfield after service.

MILLER, RILEY, Macon, Lenawee County. Enlisted in Company B, Feb. 27, 1862, at Adrian, age 23. Farm laborer, married. Transferred to Invalid Corps, March 1864. Corporal, Veteran Reserve Corps. Discharged for disability at Washington, D.C., Feb. 27, 1865. Resided in Tecumseh after service and buried Ridgeway Township Cemetery.

MILLS, ALMYRON, Greenfield, LaGrange, Ind. Enlisted in Company C, June 20, 1861, at Adrian, age 19. Farm laborer, brother of Charles Mills. Detailed to take care of his brother at Georgetown Hospital, Dec. 1861. Sergeant. Taken prisoner at Gettysburg, July 2, 1863. Mustered out at expiration of term, July 29, 1864.

MILLS, CHARLES, Johnson Township, LaGrange, Ind. Enlisted in Company C, June 20, 1861, at Adrian, age 15. Resided on parents' farm, brother of Almyron Mills. Sick in hospital, Georgetown, Dec. 1861. Corporal. Taken prisoner at Gettysburg, July 2, 1863. Returned to regiment Oct. 30, 1863. Mustered out at expiration of term at Detroit, June 29, 1864.

MINER, AUSTIN D., Hudson. Enlisted in Company F, June 20, 1861, at Adrian, age 20. Farmer, half-brother of Irvin Miner. Wounded in action at Malvern Hill, Va., July 1, 1862, shot in side. Corporal. Killed in action at Chancellorsville, Va., May 1863. Buried Greenwood Cemetery, Pittsford.

MINER, IRVIN S., Locust Corners, Pittsford Township, Hillsdale County. Enlisted in Company F as corporal June 20, 1861, at Adrian, age 22. Farmer, half-brother of Austin Miner and Orlando Miner, who served in the reorganized 4th Michigan. Captured on June 27, 1862, at Gaines' Mill, Va., and exchanged on Aug. 6, 1862. Sergeant. Wounded and taken prisoner at Gettysburg, July 2, 1863. Held at Belle Isle and Libby prisons, Richmond, Va. Returned to Annapolis, Md., Dec. 10, 1863. Transferred to Invalid Corps, Dec. 23, 1863. Reenlisted and mustered in Co. B of the reorganized 4th Michigan as first sergeant on Aug. 29, 1864, at Hudson, age 26. Commissioned second lieutenant Feb. 9, 1865; first lieutenant Aug. 8, 1865. Mustered out and honorably discharged at Houston, May 26, 1866. Resided in Reed City, Osceola County, farmer, also served as township clerk and librarian. Died in Reed City, Jan. 30, 1917, and buried in Maple Grove Cemetery, Hudson, Maple Plot 5, Block U.

MINER, JOHN, Attica, Lapeer County. Enlisted in Company K, April 3, 1863, at Attica, substitute for Genius Spencer, drafted from Metamora. Discharged for disability at Washington, D.C., Aug. 17, 1863.

MINER, JOHN C., Manchester. Enlisted in Company G, June 20, 1861, at Adrian, age 25. Wounded and missing in action at Malvern Hill, Va., July 1, 1862. Later died in Ascension Hospital, Washington, D.C., of wound. Buried Military Asylum Cemetery, Washington, D.C., July 23, 1862.

MITCHELL, LUTHER E. Enlisted unassigned to company, Feb. 27, 1864, at Medina, Lenawee County, age 21. Not on regimental returns or muster-out roll.

MOCHMER, ADAM. Enlisted in Company F, Feb. 13, 1864, age 55. On detached service with Co. C, 1st Michigan Infantry, July 2, 1864, Petersburg. Hospitalized and deserted. Returned to duty Nov. 3, 1864. Transferred to Co. C, reorganized 4th Michigan, July 1, 1865. Transferred to Co. K, Feb. 15, 1866. Absent in hospital at Washington, D.C. No discharge furnished.

MOHORTER, CHARLES, Lenawee County. Enlisted in Company C, June 20, 1861, at Adrian, age 21. Wounded in action and taken prisoner at Gettysburg, July 2, 1863, shot in hand. Transferred to Invalid Corps at Washington,

D.C., Jan. 15, 1864. Mustered out at expiration of term, June 30, 1864.

Monroe, Calvin, Saline, Washtenaw County. Enlisted in Company G, June 20, 1861, at Adrian, age 21. Killed in action at Malvern Hill, Va., July 1, 1862.

Monteith, George, Adrian. Entered service with Company G as first lieutenant at organization, June 20, 1861, at Adrian, age 21. Schoolteacher. Appointed Sept. 28, 1862, aide-de-camp on staff of Gen. F. J. Porter. Commissioned captain, Co. E, Feb. 1, 1863. Acting assistant adjutant general, Second Brigade, from June 7, 1863, to May 1864. Commissioned captain and assistant adjutant general, U.S. Volunteers, April 20, 1864. Resigned and honorably discharged Jan. 1, 1865. Resided in Cincinnati after service.

Montonye, Sidney B. (*VV*), Lenawee County. Enlisted in Company G, June 20, 1861, at Adrian, age 22. Reenlisted Dec. 29, 1863. On duty in hospital from July 1862 to April 1863. On detached service with Co. G, 1st Michigan Infantry, July 2, 1864, Petersburg. Transferred to Co. C, reorganized 4th Michigan, July 1, 1865. Mustered out at San Antonio, Feb. 26, 1866. Buried Rice Cemetery, Milan, Monroe County.

Moody, Robert, Wyandotte. Enlisted in Company K, June 20, 1861, at Adrian, age 22. Died July 15, 1863, of wounds, gunshot in back, received in action at Gettysburg, July 2, 1863. Buried Gettysburg National Cemetery, Michigan Plot, E-16.

Moon, George E., Hillsdale County. Enlisted in Company E, June 20, 1861, at Adrian, age 22. Wounded, shot in right leg, Gaines' Mill, Va., June 27, 1862. Discharged for disability at Philadelphia, Oct. 23, 1862. Reentered service in Co. I, 9th Michigan Cavalry, as sergeant on Dec. 15, 1862. Killed in action at Fayetteville, N.C., March 12, 1865.

Mooney, John, Canada West. Enlisted in Company I, June 20, 1861, at Adrian, age 22. Deserted at Fairfax Court House, Va., July 21, 1861.

Moore, John R., Hudson. Enlisted in Company I, Aug. 26, 1862, at Detroit, age 35. Shoemaker, married with four young children. Listed as killed in action at Gettysburg, July 2, 1863, shot in the chest; however, listed in some records as missing, no further information.

Morehouse, Henry L., Litchfield, Hillsdale County. Enlisted in Company H, June 20, 1861, at Adrian, age 19. Farmer. Killed in action at Malvern Hill, Va., July 1, 1862.

Morehouse, William M., Pittsford, Hillsdale County. Enlisted in Company H, June 20, 1861, at Adrian, age 19. Discharged for disability Jan. 31, 1863, at Fortress Monroe, Va. Resided in Concord and Pittsford after service. Died 1916 and buried Greenwood Cemetery, Pittsford.

Morgan, Moses (*VV*), Monroe County. Enlisted in Company G, May 16, 1861, at Adrian, age 47. Farmer, father of eight children. Corporal Dec. 29, 1863. Wounded in action at Gettysburg, July 2, 1863, gunshot wound to right leg. On detached service with Co. G, 1st Michigan Infantry, July 2, 1864, Petersburg. Wounded in action near Petersburg, Aug. 1864. Transferred to Co. C, reorganized 4th Michigan, July 1, 1865. Discharged for disability at Detroit, Feb. 9, 1866. Resided in Newaygo after service. Buried Azalia Cemetery, Azalia, Monroe County.

Morhut, Michael, Coldwater. Enlisted in Company D, Sept. 19, 1861, at Hudson. Discharged for disability Feb. 20, 1863, and died of disease March 5, 1863. Buried Military Asylum Cemetery, Washington, D.C.

Morse, Birdsey H., Jackson County. Enlisted in Company D, June 20, 1861, at Adrian, age 23. Farm laborer, resided on parents' farm with six siblings. Discharged at Sharpsburg, Md., by order, Oct. 25, 1862.

Morse, Sanford, Pleasant, Ind. Enlisted in Company B, June 20, 1861, at Adrian, age 22. Farmer, resided with parents and five siblings. Reenlisted Dec. 29, 1863. Wounded in action and taken prisoner at Malvern Hill, Va., June 27, 1862. Returned to regiment Aug. 20, 1862. On detached service with Co. B, 1st Michigan Infantry, July 2, 1864, Petersburg. Transferred to Co. C, reorganized 4th Michigan, July 1, 1865. Mustered out at San Antonio, Feb. 26, 1866.

Morsman, Albert, Lenawee County. Enlisted in Company G, Sept. 19, 1861, at Hudson, age 17. Resided on his parent's farm with seven siblings. On duty in hospital from July 1862 to April 1864. On detached service with Co. G, 1st Michigan Infantry, July 2, 1864, Petersburg. Discharged at expiration of term at Weldon Railroad, Va., Sept. 1, 1864. Resided in Tipton after service. Buried Brookside Cemetery, Tecumseh.

Moses, Norris, St. Joseph. Enlisted in Company C, June 20, 1861, at Adrian, age 27. Railroad conductor, married, with a young daughter. Guilty by court-martial for desertion in the face of the enemy, Oct. 1, 1863. Sent to prison for the rest of his enlistment. Born in Canada.

Mosher, Abraham, White Lake. Oakland County. Enlisted in Company H, June 20, 1861, at Adrian, age 27. Farm laborer, resided on parents' farm with 10 siblings. Brother of Nathaniel Mosher. Captured at Malvern Hill, Va., July 1, 1862. Discharged for disability at Detroit July 1862 by order of Lt. Col. Smith, U.S. Army. Resided in Gladwin and Montrose after service. Died 1916 and buried in Oakwood Cemetery, Fenton, Genesee County.

Mosher, Nathaniel (*VV*), Highland, Oakland County. Enlisted in Company H, June 20, 1861, at Adrian, age 21. Farm laborer, resided on parents' farm with family. Brother of Abraham Mosher. Wounded in action Fredericksburg, Va., Dec. 13, 1862. Reenlisted Dec. 29, 1863. On detached service with Co. H, 1st Michigan Infantry, July 2, 1864, Petersburg. Transferred to Co. C, reorganized 4th Michigan, July 1, 1865. Mustered out at San Antonio, Feb. 26, 1866. Died in 1900 at New Lothrop, Shiawassee County.

Mosier, Isaac, Monroe County. Enlisted in Company A, June 20, 1861, at Adrian, age 42. Discharged for disability Dec. 18, 1861. Died in 1887; buried in National Cemetery, Brooklyn, N.Y., Grave No. 302.

Mosier, Aaron, Raisinville. Enlisted in Company A, June 20, 1861, at Adrian, age 19. Killed in action at Malvern Hill, Va., July 1, 1862, shot in the chest.

Mott, Charles. Enlisted in Company F, June 20, 1861, at Adrian, age 20. Farmer, resided on parents' farm with three siblings. Wounded in action at Malvern Hill, July 1, 1862, shot in shoulder. Died July 17, 1862, in hospital at Washington, D.C., and buried Military Asylum Cemetery, Washington.

Mott, Sylvanus, Jr., Gibraltar, Wayne County. Enlisted in Company I, June 20, 1861, at Adrian, age 19. Died of disease on a steamer traveling from Harrison's Landing, Va., to New York, July 1862. Buried in National Cemetery at Brooklyn, N.Y., Grave No. 186.

Mowry, Granville G., Washtenaw County. Enlisted in Company D as corporal June 20, 1861, at Adrian, age 23. Clerk, resided with his parents and younger siblings. Sergeant July 1, 1862. Quartermaster sergeant July 22, 1862. Mustered out at expiration of term at Detroit, June 28, 1864. Resided in Detroit after service.

Mulloy, James, Livingston County. Entered service in Company K as second lieutenant at organization, June 20, 1861, at Adrian, age 40. House painter; married, father of five. Resigned and honorably discharged at Meridian Hill, Va., July 29, 1861. Born in Ireland.

Munger, Thomas J., Coldwater. Enlisted in Company B, June 20, 1861, at Adrian, age 21. Killed in action at Gaines' Mill, Va., June 27, 1862.

Murdock, Ira, Hillsdale County. Enlisted in Company H, June 20, 1861, at Adrian, age 24. Hunter and trapper, resided on parents' farm with four siblings. Discharged for disability, chronic diarrhea and lame back, at Washington, D.C., July 29, 1861. Resided in Eaton Rapids after service.

Murphy, Edward H., Washtenaw County. Enlisted in Company K, June 20, 1861, at Adrian, age 21. Died of disease, inflammation of the lungs, at Adrian, July 1, 1861. Buried at Oakwood Cemetery, Adrian.

Murphy, James H. (*VV*), Washtenaw County. Enlisted in Company D, June 20, 1861, at Adrian, age 22. Laborer. Reenlisted Dec. 29, 1863, at Ann Arbor. On detached service with Co. E, 1st Michigan Infantry, July 2, 1864, Petersburg. Transferred to Co. K, reorganized 4th Michigan, June 6, 1865. Mustered out at San Antonio, Feb. 23, 1866. Resided in the Soldiers Home, Grand Rapids, 1887.

Murphy, William H., Wyandotte. Enlisted in Company F, June 20, 1861, at Adrian, age 19. Farmer. Killed in action at Malvern Hill, Va., July 1, 1862. Born in Canada.

Murry, Charles, Lenawee County. Enlisted in Company G, June 20, 1861, at Adrian, age 19. Not mustered. No further record.

Myer, George, Lenawee County. Enlisted in Company B, June 20, 1861, at Adrian, age 25. Discharged for disability at Alexandria, Va., Feb. 6, 1863, for wounds received in action at Fredericksburg, Va., Dec. 13, 1862.

N

Nash, Orlando, Hillsdale County. Enlisted in Company F, June 20, 1861, at Adrian, age 19. Farm laborer. Discharged for disability, gunshot wound at camp, Jan. 2, 1863. Resided in Hillsdale after service. Died in

1927 and buried Plot 850, Oak Grove Cemetery, Hillsdale.

NAVARRE, ALEXANDER Frenchtown, Monroe County. Enlisted in Company E, June 20, 1861,, at Adrian, age 24. Resided on parents' farm with seven siblings. Wounded slightly in action at Fredericksburg, Va., Dec. 13, 1862. Transferred to Invalid Corps, Nov. 15, 1863. Enlisted in 7th Michigan Infantry as quartermaster sergeant, Jan. 22, 1864, at Exeter. Commissioned first lieutenant and adjutant Nov. 4, 1864. Mustered out at Jeffersonville, Ind., July 5, 1865. Died in 1916 and buried in St Joseph Cemetery, Monroe.

NAVARRE, ISAAC, Monroe. Enlisted in Company A, June 20, 1861, at Adrian, age 20. Killed in action at Malvern Hill, Va., July 1, 1862; also reported to have been fatally wounded in the battle, dying in a hospital on July 5, 1862.

NEAL, JOHN D., Scipio, Hillsdale County. Enlisted in Company E, June 20, 1861, at Adrian, age 17. Farm laborer. Discharged for disability at Georgetown, April 22, 1862.

NELSON, FRANK B., Monroe County. Enlisted in Company A, June 20, 1861, at Adrian, age 22. Carpenter. Wounded severely in the neck at Fredericksburg, Va., Dec. 13, 1862. Mustered out at expiration of term at Detroit, June 30, 1864. Resided in Monroe after service. Died in 1920 and buried in Woodland Cemetery, Monroe.

NEWELL, WILLIAM E., Jefferson, Hillsdale County. Enlisted in Independent Company, Feb. 8, 1864, at Jefferson, age 25. Farm laborer, resided on parents' farm with seven siblings. On detached service with Co. F, 1st Michigan, July 2, 1864, Petersburg. Transferred to Co. K, reorganized 4th Michigan, June 6, 1865. Sergeant. Mustered out at Houston, May 26, 1866. Resided in Lansing after service.

NEWMAN, CHARLES, Jefferson, Hillsdale County. Enlisted in Independent Company, Feb. 15, 1864, at Jefferson, age 34. On detached service with Co. F, 1st Michigan Infantry, July 2, 1864, Petersburg. Wounded in action Sept. 30, 1864, shot in right leg. Admitted to Harper Hospital, Detroit, March 13, 1865. Discharged at Detroit, May 25, 1865. Resided in Adams Township after service.

NEWTON, HENRY W., Washtenaw County. Enlisted in Company D, June 20, 1861, at Adrian, age 18. Son of Thomas Newton. Killed in action at Chancellorsville, Va., May 3, 1863. Originally buried at Bullock's Farm, Spotsylvania; reburied Row U, 2231, Fredericksburg National Cemetery.

NEWTON, THOMAS W. (*VV*), Washtenaw County. Enlisted in Company D, June 20, 1861, at Adrian, age 43. Father of Henry Newton. Reenlisted Dec. 29, 1863, at Ann Arbor. On detached service with Co. E, 1st Michigan Infantry, July 2, 1864, Petersburg, Va. Transferred to Co. K, reorganized 4th Michigan, July 1, 1865. Mustered out at San Antonio, Feb. 23, 1866.

NICHOLS, CHARLES E., Jefferson, Hillsdale County. Enlisted in Company I, Feb. 11, 1864, at Jefferson, age 18. Farmer, resided with parents and two siblings. On detached service with Co. I, 1st Michigan Infantry, by order, July 2, 1864, Petersburg, Va. Hospitalized with measles, Jan. 31, 1865. Wounded April 1, 1865, by shell outside of Petersburg, Southside Railroad. Discharged at Washington, D.C., June 15, 1865. Resided in Hillsdale after service. Died at Soldiers Home, Grand Rapids, Feb. 14, 1916. Buried Lot 15, North Lawn Cemetery, North Adams.

NICHOLS, HENRY A., Winfield Lake, Ind. Enlisted in Company B as musician drummer June 20, 1861, at Adrian, age 36. Farmer, married, father of two children. Reenlisted Dec. 29, 1863. On detached service with Co. A, 1st Michigan Infantry, July 2, 1864, Petersburg. Transferred to Co. I, reorganized 4th Michigan, July 1, 1865. Mustered out at San Antonio, Feb. 23, 1866. Resided in Angola, Ind., after service.

NICHOLS, JAMES, Wayne County. Enlisted in Company I, June 20, 1861, at Adrian, age 23. Mustered out at expiration of term at Detroit, June 30, 1864. Died Oct. 4, 1894.

NOBLE, EDGAR (*VV*), Flint. Enlisted in Company K as corporal June 20, 1861, at Adrian, age 22. Farmer. Sergeant July 1, 1862. Wounded in action Aug. 1863. Reenlisted Dec. 29, 1863. Wounded in action Wilderness, Va., May 5, 1864. On detached service, Co. K, 1st Michigan Infantry, July 2, 1864, Petersburg. Transferred to Co. I, reorganized 4th Michigan, July 1, 1865. Discharged on disability at Washington, D.C., Aug. 20, 1865. Resided in Howell, Livingston County, after service. Died 1924 and buried section B1–2, Plot 48A, Lakeview Cemetery, Howell.

NOBLES, ENOS S. (*VV*). Enlisted in Company H, June 20, 1861, at Adrian, age 21. Farmer. Reenlisted Dec. 29, 1863. Corporal Feb. 1, 1863. On detached service with Co. H, 1st Michigan Infantry, July 2, 1864, Petersburg. Transferred to Co. C, reorganized 4th Michigan, July 1, 1865. Sergeant. Mustered out at San Antonio, Feb.

26, 1866. Resided in North Adams, Hillsdale County.

NOLAN, THOMAS (*VV*), Monroe County. Enlisted in Company A, June 20, 1861, at Adrian, age 19. Sailor. Transferred to gunboat service, Feb. 27, 1862. Reenlisted Dec. 29, 1863. Failed to report from veteran furlough.

NORTH, JOHN W., Washtenaw County. Enlisted in Company G, June 20, 1861, at Adrian, age 23. Mustered out at expiration of term at Detroit, June 30, 1864.

NORTH, WILLIAM P., Washtenaw County. Enlisted in Company G, June 20, 1861, at Adrian, age 21. Missing in action at Malvern Hill, Va., July 1, 1862. Died in Washington, D.C., of wounds received in action at Malvern Hill.

NORTHRUP, CLARENCE L., Hillsdale County. Enlisted in Company E, March 18, 1862, at Adrian. In hospital fall of 1862, returned to regiment Oct. 3, 1862. Wounded in action, shot in leg, May 10, 1864, near Spotsylvania Court House. On detached service with Co. K, 1st Michigan Infantry, July 2, 1864, Petersburg. Discharged at expiration of term in the field, March 18, 1865. Resided in Osseo after service.

NULL, HENRY, Washtenaw County. Enlisted in Company D, June 20, 1861, at Adrian, age 24. Discharged for disability at New York, Nov. 24, 1862.

NUTTON, BYRON F., Moscow, Hillsdale County. Enlisted in Company H, June 20, 1861, at Adrian, age 21. Farmer, lived with parents and four siblings. Discharged for disability, rheumatism, at Union Hill, Va., Nov. 21, 1861. Resided in Jefferson City, Mont., after service. Buried Soldiers Home Cemetery, Hot Springs, S.D.

NYE, SIMONS S., Lenawee County. Enlisted in Company F, Sept. 10, 1861, at Hudson, age 18. Photographer. Discharged for disability at Fortress Monroe, Nov. 23, 1862. Buried in Goodrich (Lane) Cemetery, Pittsford Township.

O

O'BRIEN, MICHAEL, Lenawee County. Enlisted in Company G, June 20, 1861, at Adrian, age 21. Mustered out at expiration of term at Detroit, June 30, 1864.

OLIVER, JOHN M., Monroe. Enlisted in Company A, June 20, 1861. Druggist, married, father of four young children. First lieutenant. Captain Sept. 25, 1861. Promoted colonel, 15th Michigan Infantry, Jan. 15, 1862. Commendation for conspicuous bravery and efficient service, Shiloh, Tenn., April 6 and 7, 1862. Brevet brigadier general, U.S. Volunteers, Jan. 12, 1865; brevet major general March 13, 1865. Mustered out Aug. 24, 1865, and honorably discharged. Practiced law in Little Rock, Ark.; also appointed assessor of Internal Revenue and to postal service superintendent. Died March 30, 1872, in Washington, D.C.

OLMSTEAD, EDWIN (*VV*), Washtenaw County. Enlisted in Company G, May 16, 1861. Sergeant. Wounded slightly at Fredericksburg, Va., Dec. 13, 1862. Reenlisted Dec. 29, 1863. On detached service with Co. G, 1st Michigan Infantry, July 2, 1864, Petersburg. Transferred to Co. C, reorganized 4th Michigan, July 1, 1865. Discharged on account of disability at San Antonio, Jan. 15, 1866. Resided in Wellsville, Lenawee County.

OLMSTEAD, LEWIS E., Tecumseh. Enlisted in Company G, June 20, 1861, at Adrian, age 24. Molder. Corporal. Sergeant. Wounded in action at Fredericksburg, Va., Dec. 12, 1862. Mustered out at expiration of term at Detroit, June 30, 1864. Buried Forest Lawn Cemetery, Dexter.

OLNEY, GEORGE W., Monroe County. Enlisted in Company A, June 20, 1861, at Adrian, age 19. Carpenter apprentice. Taken prisoner at Gettysburg, July 2, 1863. Died of illness at Andersonville, Ga., June 20, 1864, and buried in Grave No. 2267.

OLSON, MARTIN, Monroe County. Enlisted in Company A, June 20, 1861, at Adrian, age 26. Corporal. Taken prisoner at Gettysburg, July 2, 1863. Died in Richmond, Va., Oct. 27, 1863. Buried National Cemetery, Belle Isle, Richmond.

O'NEILL, JOHN, Washtenaw County. Enlisted in Company K, June 20, 1861, at Adrian, age 30. Wounded in action at Malvern Hill, Va., July 1, 1862. Mustered out at expiration of service June 29, 1864.

OSBORNE, HORACE, Hudson. Enlisted in Company B, Sept. 16, 1861, at Hudson, age 16. Died of typhoid fever at Minor's Hill, Va., Dec. 1861. Buried Military Asylum Cemetery, Washington, D.C., Dec. 31, 1861.

OSBURN, LYMAN. Drafted for nine months, Company H, Feb. 11, 1863, at Allen, age 28. Blacksmith. Transferred to

Veteran Reserve Corps. Discharged at expiration of term, Dec. 12, 1863. Resided in Ross, Ind., after service. Died Dec. 3, 1916.

Ostrander, James H., Hillsdale County. Enlisted in Company H, June 20, 1861, at Adrian, age 19. Farmer. Discharged for disability, tuberculosis, at Ft. Woodbury, Va., Sept. 6, 1861.

Owen, Andrew, Steuben, Ind. Enlisted in Company G, June 20, 1861, at Adrian, age 22. Missing in action at Gettysburg, July 2, 1863. Mustered out at expiration of term at Detroit, June 30, 1864. Buried Oak Hill Cemetery, Shiawassee County.

Owen, George (*VV*), Monroe County. Enlisted in Company A, June 20, 1861, at Adrian, age 21. Painter. Slightly wounded in action, left thigh, during Seven Days Battles of 1862. Reenlisted Dec. 29, 1863. Received gunshot wounds to the head and groin in the Overland Campaign, 1864. On detached service with Co. A, 1st Michigan Infantry, July 2, 1864, Petersburg. Transferred to Co. C, reorganized 4th Michigan, July 1, 1865. Mustered out at San Antonio, Feb. 26, 1866. Worked for years at *Detroit Tribune*, a foreman; started a daily newspaper in Owosso and later operated a printing business in Norfolk, Va. Died in Feb. 1915.

Owen, Martin Wesly (*VV*), Lenawee County. Enlisted in Company F, June 20, 1861, at Adrian, age 24. Farmer and day laborer at a harness shop. Reenlisted Dec. 29, 1863. Wounded and in hospital June 1863. On detached service with Co. C, 1st Michigan Infantry, July 2, 1864, Petersburg. Transferred to Co. C, reorganized 4th Michigan, July 1, 1865. Mustered out at San Antonio, Feb. 26, 1866. Resided in Hudson after service. Buried in Rollin Center Cemetery in Rollin Township.

P

Page, Charles W., Jefferson, Hillsdale County. Enlisted in Company F, Feb. 9, 1864, at Jefferson, age 18. Farmer residing on with parents and brother. On detached service with Co. C, 1st Michigan Infantry, July 2, 1864, Petersburg, Va. Missing in action at Hatcher's Run, Va., Feb. 6, 1865. No further record.

Page, Erastus W., Hillsdale County. Enlisted in Company H, June 20, 1861, at Adrian, age 18. Farmer. Discharged for disability, chronic bronchitis, at Minor's Hill, Va., Jan. 16, 1862.

Palmer, William H. (*VV*), Ridgeway, Lenawee County. Enlisted in Company F, June 20, 1861, at Adrian, age 24. Farmer, resided on parents' farm with four younger siblings. Reenlisted Dec. 29, 1863. Killed in action at Petersburg, Va., June 19, 1864.

Parker, George, Frankford, Canada. Enlisted in Company K, March 3, 1863, at Richfield, age 22. Resided on his parents' farm with younger sister. Substitute for William Clemens, age 18, of Richfield, drafted for nine months. Deserted en route from Detroit to Washington, D.C.

Parker, Horatio B., Litchfield, Hillsdale County. Enlisted in Company H, June 20, 1861, at Adrian, age 21. Farm laborer, resided with parents and three siblings. Died of disease, typhoid fever, at Harrison's Landing, Va., Aug. 4, 1862.

Parker, Philo C., Burr Oak, St. Joseph County. Enlisted in Company C, June 20, 1861, at Adrian, age 20. Killed in action at Malvern Hill, Va., June 27, 1862.

Parker, Samuel S., Monroe County. Enlisted in Company H, June 20, 1861, at Adrian, age 41. Merchant and lawyer, married, father of Senter and Sewell Parker. Discharged for disability, dyspepsia and symptoms of a broken constitution, Minor's Hill, Va., Jan. 6, 1862.

Parker, Senter S. (*VV*), Monroe. Enlisted in Company H as sergeant June 20, 1861, at Adrian, age 22. Clerk in family's store; served with his father Samuel Parker and brother Sewell Parker. Regimental commissary sergeant Sept. 1, 1861. Reenlisted Dec. 29, 1863. On detached service with Co. H, 1st Michigan Infantry, July 2, 1864, Petersburg. Commissioned second lieutenant, Co. B, reorganized 4th Michigan, July 26, 1864. Resigned Jan. 31, 1865.

Parker, Sewell S., Monroe. Enlisted in Company A, June 20, 1861, at Adrian, age 20. Clerk working in family's store, his father Samuel S. Parker, and brother Senter S. Parker. Commissioned second lieutenant, Co. A, 26th Michigan Infantry, Sept. 1, 1862. Commissioned first lieutenant March 13, 1863. Commissioned captain

Oct. 12, 1863. Major of the reorganized 4th Michigan, Oct. 3, 1864. Commanding regiment Sept. and Dec. 1865. Mustered out at Houston, May 26, 1866. Resided in Toledo after service

PARKHURST, ABEL, Washtenaw County. Enlisted in Company D, June 20, 1861, at Adrian, age 34. Discharged for disability at Sharpsburg, Md., Sept. 30, 1862.

PARKHURST, JAMES A., Tecumseh. Enlisted in Company F as wagoner June 20, 1861, at Adrian, age 32. Farmer. Detached to corps headquarter as wagoner. Mustered out at expiration of term at Detroit, June 29, 1864.

PARKS, ORSON L., Adams, Hillsdale County. Enlisted in Company H, June 20, 1861, at Adrian, age 28. Carpenter. Shot in arm June 26, 1862, at Mechanicville, Va. Discharged for disability at Ft. McHenry, Va., Nov. 12, 1862.

PARMALEE, NOBEL S., Lenawee County. Enlisted in Company F, June 20, 1861, at Adrian, age 20. Farmer. Mustered out at expiration of term at Detroit, June 29, 1864. Resided in Osseo and Duplain, Clinton County.

PARMELEE, EZERIAH, Coldwater. Enlisted in Independent Company, March 27, 1864, at Hudson, age 35. Sergeant April 5, 1864. On detached service with Co. F, 1st Michigan Infantry, July 2, 1864, at Petersburg. Transferred to Co. K, reorganized 4th Michigan Infantry, June 6, 1865. Listed sick, paralyzed on his right side, Oct. 10, 1864. Resided in Morenci, Lenawee County. Died Jan. 29, 1897, and buried in Hudson.

PARSONS, ALEXUS B., St. Joseph County. Enlisted in Company C, June 20, 1861, at Adrian, age 43. Died of disease at the General Hospital, Georgetown, July 7, 1861.

PARSONS, CHARLES B. Entered service in Company E at organization as second lieutenant, June 20, 1861, at Adrian, age 26. Commissioned first lieutenant Sept. 1, 1861. Commissioned captain July 1, 1862. Resigned and honorably discharged for disability, March 4, 1863. Resided in Bonne Terre, Mo., after service.

PARSONS, OLIVER S., Ann Arbor. Enlisted in Company D, Aug. 12, 1862, at Ann Arbor, age 23. Farm laborer. Wounded in action, shot in hand, Wilderness, Va., May 5, 1864. On detached service with Co. E, 1st Michigan Infantry, July 2, 1864, Petersburg. Transferred to Veteran Reserve Corps, Nov. 16, 1864, near Petersburg. Discharged from Veteran Reserve Corps, Washington, D.C., June 27, 1865.

PATRICK, ALEXANDER L., Detroit. Enlisted in Company B, June 20, 1861, at Adrian, age 24. Regimental mail carrier. Mustered out at expiration of term at Detroit, June 30, 1864. Died March 26, 1900. Buried Elmwood Cemetery, Detroit.

PATRICK, GEORGE, Washtenaw County. Enlisted in Company D, June 20, 1861, at Adrian, age 21. Discharged for disability at Ft. Woodbury, Sept. 10, 1861. Died Dec. 29, 1899, and buried White Oak Cemetery, Ingham County.

PARTRIDGE, LARNED (*VV*), Lenawee County. Enlisted in Company B, June 20, 1861, at Adrian, age 21. Farmer; eldest of six siblings. Wounded in action at Gettysburg, July 2, 1863, shot in leg. Reenlisted Feb. 13, 1864. Wounded in shoulder near Spotsylvania Court House, May 1864, shot in right shoulder. On detached service with Co. B, 1st Michigan Infantry, July 2, 1864, Petersburg. Transferred to Co. C, reorganized 4th Michigan, July 1, 1865. Mustered out at San Antonio, Feb. 26, 1866. Committed suicide in 1867.

PAUL, GEORGE D., Frenchtown, Monroe County. Enlisted in Company A, June 20, 1861, at Adrian, age 30. Cooper. Corporal Sept. 25, 1861. Wounded at Malvern Hill, Va., July 1, 1862, shot through the body. Sergeant Sept. 13, 1862. Wounded and taken prisoner at Gettysburg, July 2, 1863, gunshot wound to the right side. Held at Libby, Belle Isle, Andersonville, Savannah, and Milan prisons for about 18 months and released on parole Nov. 20, 1864. Discharged at expiration of term at Detroit, Jan. 16, 1865. Resided in Monroe after service, served as city clerk 1882–83. Died Sept. 21, 1916. Buried Woodland Cemetery, Monroe. Born in Scotland.

PAULDING, CORNELIUS, Monroe County. Enlisted in Company A, June 20, 1861, age 20. Clerk in father's store, resided with his family; brother of William Paulding. Color sergeant. Died of typhoid fever at Washington, D.C., Aug. 12, 1861. Buried Woodland Cemetery, Monroe.

PAULDING, WILLIAM G., Monroe County. Enlisted in Company A as corporal June 20, 1861, at Adrian, age 22. Clerk in father's store, resided with parents and brothers. Brother of Cornelius Paulding. Discharged for disability at Union Hill, Feb. 27, 1862. Died May 27, 1864 and buried at Woodland Cemetery, Monroe.

PEASE, CONSTANTINE, Burr Oak, St. Joseph County. Enlisted in Company C, as corporal, June 20, 1861, at Adrian, age 20. Farmer, resided with parents and six siblings. Wounded and taken prisoner in the Seven Days battle, late June 1862. Paroled at Turkey Island, Va., July 13, 1862. Sent to the hospital, Ft. Hamilton, N.Y., then to

Annapolis, Md. Wounded in action at Gettysburg, July 2, 1863, shot in left hip. Taken to field hospital on July 7; transferred to Camp Letterman hospital, July 24, 1863. Died Aug. 7, 1863, from wounds received in action at Gettysburg, July 2, 1863. Buried in National Cemetery, Michigan Plot, B-23.

PEASE, WASHINGTON, Jefferson, Hillsdale County. Enlisted in Independent Company, Feb. 15, 1864, at Hillsdale, age 19. Farm laborer. On detached service with Co. F, 1st Michigan Infantry, July 2, 1864, at Petersburg. Died of typhoid fever, hospital of the First Division, Fifth Corps, May 25, 1865.

PENCE, WILLIAM H. (*VV*), Monroe County. Enlisted in Company A, June 20, 1861, at Adrian, age 30. Reenlisted Dec. 29, 1863. On detached service with Co. A, 1st Michigan Infantry, July 2, 1864, Petersburg. Transferred to Co. C, reorganized 4th Michigan, June 6, 1865. Discharged for disability at San Antonio, Jan. 15, 1866. Buried London Cemetery, Milan.

PENDELTON, JAMES H., Litchfield, Hillsdale County. Enlisted in Company H, June 20, 1861, at Adrian, age 18. Carpenter. Wounded slightly in action at Fredericksburg, Va., Dec. 13, 1862. Killed in action at Gettysburg, July 2, 1863. Buried Gettysburg National Cemetery, Michigan Plot, A-17.

PENNOCK, ALONZO, Tecumseh. Enlisted in Company G, Feb. 11, 1862, at Adrian, age 18. Day laborer, brother of Martin Pennock. Wounded in action, shot in head, May 8, 1864. On detached service with Co. G, 1st Michigan Infantry, July 2, 1864, at Petersburg. Discharged at expiration of term at Detroit, Feb. 13, 1865. Resided in Tecumseh after service. Died July 14, 1908, of cancer and buried Brookside Cemetery, Tecumseh,

PENNOCK, MARTIN V., Lenawee County. Enlisted in Company G, June 20, 1861, at Adrian, age 19. Brother of Alonzo Pennock. Corporal. Taken prisoner at Gettysburg, July 2, 1863, and confined at Richmond, Va. Died of disease at Tecumseh, Jan. 6, 1864. Buried Brookside Cemetery, Tecumseh.

PERCY, PERRIN E., Washtenaw County. Enlisted in Company K, May 16, 1861. No further record.

PERINE, JACOB H., Tekonsha, Calhoun County. Enlisted in Company E, Aug. 5, 1862, at Tekonsha, age 22. Farmer, resided on parents' farm with five siblings. Wounded in action, shot or grazed by bullets in upper thigh and elbow at Gettysburg, July 2, 1863. Admitted to hospital at Ft. Schuyler, N.Y.; transferred to hospital at Davids' Island, N.Y. On detached service with Co. K, 1st Michigan Infantry, July 2, 1864, at Petersburg. Discharged at Washington, D.C., June 5, 1865. Died in 1942, age 102. Buried Riverside Cemetery, Albion.

PERKINS, GUY C., Washtenaw County. Enlisted in Company K, June 20, 1861, at Adrian, age 18. Brother of Leonard Perkins. Discharged for disability at Washington, D.C., Jan. 30, 1863. Reenlisted Nov. 1, 1864, as a substitute for George N. Clark of Birch Run, in Co. H, 17th Michigan Infantry. Transferred to Co. I, 12th Michigan Infantry, May 31, 1865, Washington, D.C. Mustered out July 28, 1865. Resided in Cokato, Minn., after service.

PERKINS, LEONARD W., Sylvan, Washtenaw County. Enlisted in Company K, June 20, 1861, at Adrian, age 44. Constable and farmer, married, no children. Brother of Guy Perkins. Detailed as an army postmaster June 30 to Oct. 21, 1862. Charged with cowardice and desertion, intentionally allowing himself to be taken prisoner. Found guilty; head shaved and drummed out of camp on Feb. 9, 1863. Reenlisted as a substitute for a man drafted into the 17th Michigan Infantry, Oct. 1, 1864. Transferred to Co. I, 12th Michigan, May 31, 1865, at Washington, D.C. Mustered out July 28, 1865.

PERKINS, MARION D., Lenawee County. Enlisted in Company B, June 20, 1861, at Adrian, age 18. Found guilty by court-martial of a charge of desertion and cowardice after the Second Battle of Bull Run. Missing in action at Chancellorsville, Va., May 1863.

PERRY, EDWIN S. (*VV*), Washtenaw County. Enlisted in Company D, June 20, 1861, at Adrian, age 27. Farm laborer, resided on parents' farm. Reenlisted Dec. 29, 1863. On detached service with Co. E, 1st Michigan Infantry, July 2, 1864, Petersburg. Transferred to Co. K, reorganized 4th Michigan, July 1, 1865. Corporal. Mustered out at San Antonio, Feb. 23, 1866. Died in 1914 and buried in Oak Grove Cemetery, Morenci, Lenawee County.

PERRY, ORRIN E., Clinton County. Enlisted in Company K, June 20, 1861, at Adrian, age 31. Wounded, shot in right leg below knee, while in the skirmish line, and captured at Wilderness, Va., May 5, 1864. Held at Andersonville, Ga., suffering with rheumatism. Released at Venus Point, Ga., Dec. 6, 1864. Discharged at expiration of term at Detroit, Feb. 23, 1865. Resided in Canton, Mo., after service, running an express mail service. Entered a Soldiers and Sailors Home in 1889; died Jan. 2, 1902, Quincy, Ill.

PETERS, CHARLES W., Adrian. Enlisted in Company F, June 20, 1861, at Adrian, age 18. Stone cutter, resided with parents and four siblings. Killed in action at Malvern Hill, Va., July 1, 1862.

Peters, George W., Medina, Lenawee County. Enlisted in Company F, Sept. 10, 1861, at Hudson, age 34. Farmer, married, father of a young son. Discharged for disability at Minor's Hill, Va., Nov. 20, 1861.

Peterson, John. Enlisted in Company G, May 16, 1861, at Adrian. Discharged Dec. 27, 1861.

Petre, Henry, Steuben, Ind. Enlisted in Company K, June 20, 1861, at Adrian, age 16, ward of a local court, living with an attorney's family. Wounded in action at Gaines' Mill, Va., June 27, 1862, gunshot through right shoulder and lung, lodging in his spine, also wounded in left foot. Mustered out at expiration of term at Detroit, June 29, 1864. Resided in Arlington, Ore., after service, becoming a doctor. Died in 1896 in Tillamook, Ore.

Petrie, Henry C., Cambria, Hillsdale County. Enlisted in Independent Company, March 25, 1864, at Hillsdale, age 18. Farmer, resided with parents and five siblings. Wounded in action near Bethesda Church, June 3, 1864. Discharged for disability at Philadelphia, Nov. 26, 1864. Resided in Hillsdale after service. Died in 1924.

Phelps, Burton L., Lenawee County. Enlisted in Company I, Sept. 14, 1861, at Hudson, age 18. Corporal. Wounded slightly in action at Fredericksburg, Va., Dec. 13, 1862. Severely wounded in action at Gettysburg, July 2, 1863, upper extremities. Discharged for disability at Philadelphia, Dec. 14, 1863. Resided in Jackson after service. Buried Plot 15, Block Q, Maple Grove Cemetery, Hudson.

Phelps, Charles W., Washtenaw County. Enlisted in Company D, June 20, 1861, at Ann Arbor, age 21. Laborer. Corporal in color guard, killed in action at Gettysburg, July 2, 1863. Buried in the National Cemetery, Michigan Plot, A-11.

Philips, Elias. Enlisted in Company C, May 16, 1861, at Ann Arbor. Compiled military record states that he served, but was never mustered into the service.

Pier, Henry, Ann Arbor. Enlisted in Company I, Aug. 15, 1862, at Detroit, age 28. Killed in action at Wilderness, Va., May 5, 1864.

Pier, William D., Lenawee County. Enlisted in Company B, June 20, 1861, at Adrian, age 25. Discharged for disability near Falmouth, Va., Jan. 2, 1863. Buried Forest Hill Cemetery, Evart.

Pierce, Norman O., Detroit. Enlisted in Company I, July 25, 1862, at Detroit, age 27. Discharged for disability, syphilis, at Sharpsburg, Md., Oct. 22, 1862.

Pierce, William J., Manchester, Ohio. Enlisted in Company B, June 20, 1861, at Adrian, age 22. Died of disease at Minor's Hill, Va., Dec. 6, 1861.

Pierson, Henry, Adrian. Enlisted in Company F, June 20, 1861, at Adrian, age 23. Painter. Deserted Nov. 28, 1861, Minor's Hill, Va., along with Henry Ryerson, of Co. F.

Pierson, William C., Tecumseh. Enlisted in Company G, June 20, 1861, at Adrian, age 19. Farmer, part of an eight-member family residing together. Killed in action at Gaines' Mill, Va., June 27, 1862. Born in Canada.

Piersons, James, St. Joseph County. Enlisted in Company C as corporal June 20, 1861, at Adrian, age 22. Discharged for disability at Sharpsburg, Md., Oct. 22, 1862. Buried Oak Lawn Cemetery, Sturgis.

Piper, Abel M. D., Lenawee County. Enlisted in Company B, June 20, 1861, at Adrian, age 24. Brother of Alanson Piper. Killed in action at New Bridge, May 24, 1862.

Piper, Alanson R. (*VV*), Lenawee County. Enlisted in Company B, June 20, 1861, at Adrian, age 18. Farm laborer, brother of Abel Piper. Corporal July 1, 1863. Reenlisted Dec. 29, 1863. Wounded in action, shot in arm, near Spotsylvania Court House, May 10, 1864. On detached service with Co. B, 1st Michigan Infantry, July 2, 1864, Petersburg. Transferred to Co. D, reorganized 4th Michigan Infantry, July 1, 1865. Sergeant. Mustered out at San Antonio, March 13, 1866. Resided in Kalamazoo after service.

Piquet, Peter, Washtenaw County. Enlisted in Company D, June 20, 1861, at Adrian, age 25. Discharged by order at Washington, D.C., Nov. 25, 1862. Enlisted in 1st U.S. Cavalry. Died July 10, 1897, and buried Oakwood Cemetery, Saline.

Pitwood, John, Hillsdale County. Enlisted in Company H, June 20, 1861, at Adrian, age 18. Farmer, resided with parents and three siblings. Discharged for disability at Washington, D.C., July 29, 1861. Wounded during Bull Run Campaign, his thumb shot off. Reenlisted 1st Michigan Engineers and Mechanics as a bugler, Oct. 2, 1861. Mustered out Oct. 31, 1864. Resided in Newaygo after service. Born in England.

PLODECH, PAUL. Enlisted in band, June 20, 1861, at Adrian, age 27. Mustered out at Harrison's Landing, Va., Aug. 10, 1862, by War Department order. Resided in Cleveland after service.

PLUM, CHARLES W. Enlisted in Company G, May 16, 1861, at Adrian, age 21. Killed in action during the Overland Campaign, Virginia, May 1864.

PLUMLEY, THOMAS J., Hillsdale. Enlisted in Company E, Aug. 29, 1862, at Adrian, age 25. Wagon maker by trade. Deserted on the march June 25, 1863. No further record.

PLUMMER, CHESTER W., Bridgewater, Washtenaw County. Enlisted in Company G, June 20, 1861, at Adrian, age 18. Farmed with his family, brother of William Plummer. Killed in action at Chancellorsville, Va., May 5, 1863.

PLUMMER, JAMES (*VV*), Detroit. Enlisted in Company I as corporal June 20, 1861, at Adrian, age 31. Sergeant. Wounded in action, Mechanicsville, Va., June 26, 1862. Discharged. Reentered service in Co. G, 27th Michigan Infantry as first lieutenant, April 4, 1863. Acting assistant quartermaster from Nov. 1863 to April 1864. Killed in action at Wilderness, Va., May 8, 1864.

PLUMMER, WILLIAM H., Washtenaw County. Enlisted in Company G, June 20, 1861, at Adrian, age 21. Brother of Chester Plummer. Wounded in action, gunshot in right thigh at Gettysburg, July 2, 1863, causing him spinal problems. Corporal. Mustered out at expiration of term at Detroit, June 30, 1864. Resided in Lansing after service. Died March 8, 1866. Buried Oakwood Cemetery, Adrian.

PLUSE or PLUES, SHERMAN D., Raisinville, Monroe County. Enlisted in Company A, June 20, 1861, at Adrian, age 21. Wounded and missing in action at Malvern Hill, Va., July 1, 1862, shot through both jaws. Corporal. Discharged for disability at Washington, D.C., Nov. 15, 1862. Resided in Monroe and then Saginaw after service.

POMEROY, CHARLES, Woodstock. Lenawee County. Enlisted in Company D, June 20, 1861, at Adrian, age 29. Blacksmith, resided with parents and six siblings. Discharged for disability, Dec. 9, 1862.

PORDON, JOHN (*VV*), Monroe County. Enlisted in Company A, June 20, 1861, at Adrian, age 23. Reenlisted Dec. 29, 1863. Wounded in action, in leg, Wilderness, Va., May 5, 1864. On detached service with Co. A, 1st Michigan Infantry, July 2, 1864, Petersburg. Sergeant July 2, 1865. Transferred to Co. C, reorganized 4th Michigan, July 1, 1865. Mustered out at San Antonio, Feb. 26, 1866. Resided in Grafton, Monroe County, after service.

POSKETT, GEORGE, Lenawee County. Enlisted in Company F, June 20, 1861, at Adrian, age 22. Sawyer, lumberman. Corporal June 1862. Discharged for disability, Oct. 26, 1862, Philadelphia. Born in England.

POST, JOHN, Liberty, Jackson County. Enlisted in Company F, Feb. 28, 1863, at Liberty, Butcher, father of three small children. On detached service with Co. C, 1st Michigan Infantry, July 2, 1864, Petersburg, Va. Transferred to Co. K, Feb. 15, 1866. Discharged at expiration of term at San Antonio, Feb. 28, 1866. Resided in Empire after service.

POTTER, ALVINZI, Washtenaw County. Enlisted in Company K as corporal June 20, 1861, at Adrian, age 25. Cabinetmaker. Transferred to Invalid Corps, Sept. 15, 1863. Discharged June 21, 1864. Resided in Dexter after service. Died Jan. 14, 1891.

POTTERFIELD, SAMUEL D., Lenawee County. Enlisted in Company I, June 20, 1861, at Adrian, age 22. Professional actor and dancer. Married, father of infant son born in 1862. Transferred to Co. D, at Washington, D.C., Aug. 9, 1861. Temporarily assigned to Balloon Corps. Wounded in action at Gaines' Mill, Va., June 27, 1862. Died of lockjaw on July 18, 1862, at Annapolis, Md., as a result of wound. Buried at National Cemetery, Annapolis.

POWELL, BENJAMIN W., LaGrange, Ind. Enlisted in Company C, June 20, 1861, at Adrian, age 20. Laborer. Taken prisoner at Gettysburg, July 2, 1863. Died of disease while prisoner of war at Richmond, Va., Sept. 15, 1863.

POYER, DANIEL F., Livingston County. Enlisted in Company K, June 20, 1861, at Adrian, age 21. Resided with parents and sister. Killed in action on skirmish line near Spotsylvania Court House, Va., May 12, 1864.

PRESTLE, THOMAS, Reading, Hillsdale County. Enlisted in Company E, June 20, 1861, at Adrian, age 24. Died at Fortress Monroe, July 15, 1862, of wounds received in action at Malvern Hill, Va., July 1, 1862.

PRESTON, SIMON B., Hudson. Entered service in Company F at organization as first lieutenant, June 20, 1861, at Adrian, age 35. Lawyer, married, with two sons. Brother-in-law of William Henry Terpening. Taken prisoner at Bull Run, Va., on July 21, 1861. Held in Richmond for two months, transferred Tuscaloosa, Ala. for six months. Returned to regiment Feb. 1862. Died June 30, 1862, of wounds received in action at Gaines' Mill, Va., June 27, 1862. Buried in unmarked grave; Cenotaph Plot 23, Block M, in Maple Grove Cemetery, Hudson.

PRICE, GEORGE P., Lenawee County. Enlisted in Company F as corporal June 20, 1861, at Adrian, age 23. Printer. Discharged at Philadelphia, Dec. 12, 1862. Resided in Lyons, N.Y., after service and buried there.

PRICE, JOSEPH, Coldwater. Enlisted in Company C, June 20, 1861, at Adrian, age 32. Farmer, married and father of five. Wounded in action, gunshot wound to left shoulder, Malvern Hill, Va., July 1, 1862. Died at Washington, D.C., July 21, 1862. Buried Military Asylum Cemetery, Washington, D.C.

PRIEST, GEORGE SCOTT, Steuben, Ind. Enlisted in Company B, June 20, 1861, at Adrian, age 21. Farm laborer, resided on parents' farm with eight siblings. Brother of Mathias Priest. Discharged for disability at camp, March 30, 1863.

PRIEST, MATHIAS, Steuben, Ind. Enlisted in Company B, June 20, 1861, at Adrian, age 22. Farm laborer, brother of George Priest. Discharged for disability near Falmouth, Va., Jan. 2, 1863, for amputation of leg. Not having discharge papers, he tried for two years to get a pension. Resided in Orangeville, Barry County, and was buried Mountain Home Cemetery, Allegan County.

PRYOR, WILLIAM A., Ann Arbor. Enlisted in Company D, June 20, 1861, at Adrian, age 26. Corporal. Killed in action at Gettysburg, July 2, 1863. Buried Gettysburg National Cemetery, Michigan Plot, A-13.

PURDY, COLUMBUS L., Wheatland, Hillsdale County. Enlisted in Company H, Sept. 3, 1861, at Hudson, age 23. Farmer. Died of typhoid fever on hospital boat en route to New York, Aug. 7, 1862. Buried Row 5, Somerset Cemetery, Somerset Township.

PURDY, GEORGE, Lapeer County. Enlisted in Company H, Feb. 11, 1863, at Lapeer, for nine months, age 18. Resided on his parents' farm with them and his younger brother. Substitute for Abram Purdy, his father, age 42, who was drafted at Marathon, Lapeer County, Feb. 10, 1863. Killed in action at Gettysburg, July 2, 1863. Buried Gettysburg National Cemetery, Michigan Plot, A-18.

Q

QUACKENBUSH, JAMES A. (*VV*), HILLSDALE COUNTY. ENLISTED IN COMPANY E, JUNE 20, 1861, AT Adrian, age 19. Painter, resided with his mother and four siblings. Reenlisted as sergeant Dec. 29, 1863. Wounded in action, shot in arm, May 28, 1864. On detached service with Co. K, 1st Michigan Infantry, July 2, 1864, Petersburg. Deserted for five days at Weldon Railroad, Va. Missing in action near Petersburg, Dec. 13, 1864. Returned to regiment at Alexandria, Va., May 19, 1865. No further record. Resided in Canada after service and buried in Fairfield Cemetery, Spencerport, N.Y. Born in Canada West.

QUICK, WILLIAM E., Lenawee County. Enlisted in Company B, Feb. 20, 1862, at Adrian, age 23. Farm labor residing with parents and sister. Discharged for disability in general hospital July 15, 1862.

QUINN, JAMES. Assigned to ambulance corps. Discharged for disability at Washington, D.C., April 13, 1863. Buried in Carleton Cemetery, Monroe County.

R

RAMSEY, REUBEN W., Huron. Enlisted in Company I, June 20, 1861, at Adrian, age 23. Farmer, residing with his mother and three younger siblings. Died of disease at Georgetown, Aug. 27, 1861.

RANDALL, ALBERT L., Tecumseh. Enlisted in Company G, June 20, 1861, at Adrian, age 19. Resided with parents and younger sibling Discharged for disability June 1862.

RANDALL, AVERY, Cambria, Hillsdale County. Enlisted in Company E, June 20, 1861, at Adrian, age 18. Died of disease at Minor's Hill, Va., Dec. 19, 1861, of typhoid fever after a short illness. Body shipped home and buried in Hillsdale.

RANDALL, EDMUND, Ann Arbor. Enlisted in Company D, Aug. 20, 1862, at Adrian, age 20.

RANDOLPH, JOHN M., Ann Arbor. Entered service in Company D at organization as captain, June 20, 1861, at Adrian, age 34. Mason, married, with a young son. Commissioned major July 18, 1862. Discharged for physical disability, May 22, 1863, by War Department order. Buried in Fairview Cemetery, Ann Arbor.

Rankin, Erastus, Monroe County. Enlisted in Company G, June 20, 1861, at Adrian, age 22. Resided with parents and five siblings on family farm. Taken prisoner in action at Chancellorsville, Va., May 1863. Returned to regiment July 28, 1863, at Warrenton, Va. Wounded, shot in chest, at Laurel Hill, Va., May 8, 1864. Mustered out at expiration of term at Detroit, June 30, 1864.

Rankin, Simon, Monroe County. Enlisted in Company G, June 20, 1861, at Adrian, age 19. Mustered June 20, 1861. Wounded in action at Fredericksburg, Va., Dec. 13, 1862. Missing in action at Chancellorsville, May 1, 1863. No further record.

Rapson, John (*VV*), York, Washtenaw County. Enlisted in Company G, June 20, 1861, at Adrian, age 22. Reenlisted Dec. 29, 1863. On duty in a hospital from July 1862 to Jan. 1864. On detached service with Co. G, 1st Michigan Infantry, July 2, 1864, Petersburg, Va. On duty at brigade headquarters from Oct. 1864 to May 1865. Transferred to Co. C, reorganized 4th Michigan, July 1, 1865. Mustered out at San Antonio, Feb. 26, 1866. Buried Romulus Cemetery, Romulus.

Rauch, Peter, LaSalle, Monroe County. Enlisted in Company H, June 20, 1861, at Adrian, age 39. Married, father of three young children. Discharged for disability, a wound, from a convalescent camp, Jan. 17, 1863. Died in 1916 and buried in LaSalle Protestant Cemetery.

Rayner, Charles B., Allen, Hillsdale County. Enlisted in Independent Company, Feb. 11, 1864, at Hillsdale, age 28. Carpenter and joiner. First corporal May 5, 1864. Seriously wounded in action, shoulder, June 3, 1864, at Bethesda Church, Va. Died in U.S. Hospital, Alexandria, Va., July 2, 1864.

Reagan, Timothy, Hudson. Enlisted in Company F as private June 20, 1861, at Adrian, age 44. Shoemaker, married, father of three children. Promoted to corporal July 1861; sergeant Jan. 1862. Suffered rupture of groin Aug. 28, 1862. At Convalescent Camp, Alexandria, Va., until discharged. Jan. 3, 1863. Resided in Hudson after service and died Sept. 21, 1876. Buried in Plot 41, Block E, Maple Grove Cemetery, Hudson. Born in Ireland.

Redfield, James. Enlisted in Company A as sergeant June 20, 1861, at Adrian, age 21. College student. Commissioned second lieutenant Nov. 1, 1861. Commissioned first lieutenant Jan. 1, 1862. In regimental hospital July 11–17, 1862, typhoid fever, chronic diarrhea, and rheumatism. Transferred to hospital at Fortress Monroe, Va., July 17–22, 1862. Admitted Chesapeake Hospital, Hampton Roads, Va., July 22 to Sept. 6, 1862. Transferred to Episcopal Church Hospital, Washington, D.C., from Sept. 6 to Sept. 13, 1862. Resigned and honorably discharged for disability Sept. 13, 1862. Lived in Charlottesville, Va., and Bolivia, N.Y., a farmer, after service. Died at Canandaigua, N.Y., on Feb. 8, 1904 of acute alcoholic insanity. Buried in Batavia Pioneer Cemetery, Batavia, N.Y.

Reed, David J., Hillsdale. Enlisted in Company E, Aug. 30, 1861, at Hillsdale, age 16. Resided with his parents and two siblings. In the hospital Sept. 1862, returning to regiment Oct. 3, 1862. Severely wounded in action, right side, Fredericksburg, Va., Dec. 13, 1862. Transferred to Carver General Hospital, Washington, D.C., Dec. 20, 1862. Died Jan. 29, 1863, Camp Distribution, Alexandria, Va.

Reeve, Selah V., Detroit. Enlisted as regimental quartermaster sergeant, June 20, 1861, at Adrian, age 27. Transferred to 2nd Michigan Infantry, second lieutenant, Sept. 1, 1861.

Reeves, Charles, Monroe County. Enlisted in Company D, June 20, 1861, at Adrian, age 28. Killed in action at Gaines' Mill, Va., June 27, 1862.

Regal, Isaiah, Monroe. Enlisted in Company A, Aug. 24, 1862, at Monroe, age 21. Wounded in action at Gettysburg, July 2, 1863, gunshot to left forearm; in Summit Hospital, Philadelphia, July 11, 1863. Transferred to Invalid Corps, Washington, D.C., Jan. 1, 1864. Discharged at Washington, June 27, 1865, from Veteran Reserve Corps.

Regets, John, Wayne County. Enlisted in Company I, June 20, 1861, at Adrian, age 24. Taken prisoner at Chancellorsville, May 2, 1863. Returned to regiment at Culpeper, Va., Oct. 8, 1863. Wounded in action at Wilderness, Va., May 5, 1864. Mustered out at expiration of term at Detroit, June 30, 1864.

Reneau, Peter, Wayne County. Enlisted in Company I, June 20, 1861, at Adrian, age 21. Wounded in action Malvern Hill, July 1, 1862. Discharged for disability at Washington, D.C., Jan. 3, 1863.

Reynolds, Ely H., Hillsdale. Enlisted in Independent Company, Feb. 10, 1864, at Hillsdale, age 25. Sergeant April 5, 1864. On detached service with Co. F, 1st Michigan Infantry, July 2, 1864, Petersburg. First sergeant

March 16, 1865. Transferred to Co. K, reorganized 4th Michigan, June 6, 1865. Discharged at Detroit, Feb. 23, 1866. Resided in Nebraska after service. Died in 1913 and buried in Sunset View Cemetery, Jonesville.

Rheyport, Charles H., Hillsdale County. Enlisted in Company E, June 20, 1861, at Adrian, age 25. Carpenter. Mustered out at expiration of term at Detroit, June 28, 1864. Died Oct. 8, 1881, in Grundy County, Mo.

Rhodes, Edward, Hillsdale. Enlisted in Independent Company, March 25, 1864, at Hillsdale, age 17. Resided with parents and four siblings, a brother of Martin Rhodes. On detached service with Co. F, 1st Michigan Infantry, July 2, 1864, Petersburg. Missing while on picket Aug. 21, 1864, at Weldon Railroad, Va., captured; in Libby Prison and Belle Isle; in hospital 40 days from exposure while prisoner, after his release. Returned Dec. 28, 1864. Discharged at Alexandria, Va., June 20, 1865. Resided in Pittsfield, Washtenaw County, after the service.

Rhodes, Martin V. B., Jefferson, Hillsdale County. Enlisted in Company E, Feb. 24, 1863, at Hillsdale, for nine months, age 22. Substitute for Daniel A. Wisner, drafted from Moscow Township. Farmer, brother of Edward Rhodes. Transferred to Co. H. Discharged at expiration of term at Detroit, Dec. 22, 1863. Resided in Fairfield, Lenawee County, after service.

Richards, Albert D., Grand Rapids. Enlisted under the alias of Joseph Spingstead. Enlisted in Company B as wagoner June 20, 1861, at Adrian, reportedly age 12. Resided with parents and five siblings. Discharged for disability, the loss of three fingers on right hand, April 19, 1862. Reenlisted in the Michigan Provost Guard, Dec. 18, 1862. Mustered out May 9, 1865. In Soldiers Home, Grand Rapids, Nov. 3, 1889 to April 22, 1893.

Richardson John, Steuben, Ind. Enlisted in Company B, June 20, 1861, at Adrian, age 24. Blacksmith, resided on farm with parents and five siblings. Discharged Aug. 23, 1862, for wound received in action during the Seven Days, severe, to left arm and hand, June 1862. Resided in Angola after service.

Richardson, Jonas D., Washtenaw County. Enlisted in Company D as corporal June 20, 1861, at Adrian, age 21. Resided with his parents and brother. Sergeant. Injured ankle at Gettysburg July 2, 1863. Transferred to Invalid Corps, Washington, D.C., Sept. 30, 1863. Died of disease, spring 1864.

Richmond, James, Lenawee County. Enlisted in Company G, June 20, 1861, at Adrian, age 21. Discharged for disability at camp, March 1, 1863.

Rickett, Don A., Mendon, St. Joseph County. Enlisted in Company C, June 20, 1861, at Adrian, age 23. Farm laborer, resided on parents' farm with three younger siblings. Wounded in thigh at Shepherdstown Ford, Md., Sept. 19, 1862. In a hospital, Washington, D.C. Sergeant. Wounded in action at Gettysburg, July 2, 1863, shot in back of shoulder. Admitted to Summit House Hospital, Philadelphia. Reported absent wounded April 1864. Mustered out at expiration of term at Detroit, June 29, 1864. Resided in Mendon and Grand Traverse County after service.

Riley, Luke, Chelsea, Washtenaw County. Enlisted in Company K, June 20, 1861, at Adrian, age 21. Transferred to Battery D, 5th U.S. Artillery, Oct. 9, 1862. Discharged at Sharpsburg, Md., per order, Oct. 25, 1862. Resided in Chelsea after service.

Riley, Phillip (*VV*), Jackson. Enlisted in Company B, June 20, 1861, at Adrian, age 23. Reenlisted Dec. 29, 1863. On detached service with Co. B, 1st Michigan Infantry, July 2, 1864, Petersburg. Transferred to Co. C, reorganized 4th Michigan, July 1, 1865. Mustered out at San Antonio, Feb. 26, 1866. Served a short sentence in the state prison after the war for horse theft.

Rintz, John (*VV*). Also given as Rentz. Enlisted in Company B as sergeant June 20, 1861, at Adrian, age 24. Shoemaker and clerk. First sergeant Oct. 23, 1862. Reenlisted Dec. 29, 1863. On detached service with Co. B, 1st Michigan Infantry, July 2, 1864, Petersburg. Transferred to Co. H, reorganized 4th Michigan, July 1, 1865. Honorably discharged May 26, 1866. Resided in Blissfield, Lenawee County, after service, founding the Blissfield Telephone Company in 1897.

Ritter, Lewis Fredrick, Washtenaw County. Enlisted in Company D, June 20, 1861, at Adrian, age 23. Accidentally wounded, struck in hip with "buck and ball" shot by James D. Murphy, who was drunk, on Nov. 24, 1861. Discharged for disability at Minor's Hill, Va., 1862. Reenlisted in Co. H, 1st Michigan Engineers and Mechanics, Dec. 22, 1862. Mustered out Sept. 22, 1864. Resided in Concord, Mich. after service. Died on May 25, 1909, from an accidental injury to his foot and buried in Concord. Born in Germany

Roberts, John B. (*VV*). Enlisted in Company A, June 20, 1861, at Adrian, age 21. Reenlisted Dec. 29, 1863.

Wounded in action, Wilderness, Va., May 5, 1864; left arm amputated by Surgeon Kerr of 62nd Pennsylvania. Discharged at Harper Hospital, Detroit, March 1, 1865, on account of wound. Resided in Monroe; died in 1929 and buried in Woodland Cemetery, Monroe.

ROBERTS, RUSSELL, Lenawee County. Enlisted in Company F, June 20, 1861, at Adrian, age 22. Farmer. Discharged for disability at Washington, D.C., Aug. 9, 1861, because of imperfect vision.

ROBINSON, CHARLES W., Marshall. Enlisted in Independent Company, Feb. 13, 1864, at Hillsdale, age 19. Farm laborer. Corporal. On detached service with Co. F, 1st Michigan Infantry, July 2, 1864, Petersburg. Sergeant March 16, 1865. Transferred to Co. K, reorganized 4th Michigan, June 6, 1865. Commissioned second lieutenant Feb. 28, 1866. Mustered out at Houston, May 26, 1866. Resided in Marshall after service.

ROBINSON, HENRY, Monroe County. Enlisted in Company A, June 20, 1861, at Adrian, age 21. Corporal July 1, 1862. Wounded in action a Gettysburg, July 2, 1863, by a shell fragment striking the left side of his back. Sergeant May 1, 1864. Mustered out at expiration of term at Detroit, June 30, 1864. Resided in Bridgewater, N.Y., after service.

ROBINSON, WESLEY, Waterloo, Jackson County. Enlisted in Company D, June 20, 1861, at Adrian, age 28. Suffered from rheumatism in right hip and back, caused by shell explosion injury during the Peninsula Campaign, June 1862. Reentered service in Co. F, 20th Michigan Infantry at organization as second lieutenant, July 29, 1862. Discharged for promotion at Sharpsburg, Va., Sept. 14, 1862. Resigned because of disability and honorably discharged May 23, 1863. Physician after service, residing at Blue Creek, Adams County, Ohio.

ROBINSON, WILLIAM F., Hillsdale County (also said he lived in Jackson). Enlisted in Company H as first sergeant June 20, 1861, at Adrian, age 24. Dentist. Commissioned second lieutenant Dec. 2, 1861. Commissioned first lieutenant July 18, 1862. Commanding Co. F from Oct. 30, 1862, to Feb. 4, 1863. Commissioned captain Jan. 27, 1863. Wounded in leg in action at Gettysburg, July 2, 1863. Resigned and honorably discharged for disability May 21, 1864. Reported murdered May 11, 1867, Tucson, Ariz..

ROBINSON, WILLIAM G., Detroit. Enlisted in Company I, June 20, 1861, at Adrian, age 21. Sailor, resided with parents and younger brother. Wounded in action Malvern Hill, Va., July 1, 1862. Discharged for disability at Detroit, Sept. 2, 1862. Resided in Detroit after service. Born in Ireland.

ROBINSON, WILLIAM W. (*VV*), Hillsdale County. Enlisted in Company H, June 20, 1861, at Adrian, age 21. Carpenter. Reenlisted Dec. 29, 1863. On detached service with Co. H, 1st Michigan Infantry, July 2, 1864, Petersburg. Transferred to Co. C, reorganized 4th Michigan, July 1, 1865. Transferred to Veteran Reserve Corps. Discharged at Washington, D.C., July 31, 1865.

ROCKFELLOW, ANDREW H., Wayne County. Enlisted in Company G, June 20, 1861, at Adrian, age 28. Corporal. Sergeant. Killed in action near Bethesda Church, Va., July 3, 1864.

ROCKWELL, JAMES K., Mendon, St. Joseph County. Enlisted in Company C, June 20, 1861, at Adrian, age 21. Wounded in head Malvern Hill, Va., July 1, 1862. Transferred to Invalid Corps, July 1, 1863. Resided in Mendon after service.

RODGERS, JOHN L., Brownstown, Wayne County. Enlisted in Company G as sergeant June 20, 1861, at Adrian, age 31. Blacksmith, married. Commissioned second lieutenant July 1, 1862. Listed sick with consumption, Dec. 1862, treated by Dr. Chamberlain. Resigned and honorably discharged Feb. 11, 1863. Died in 1869 and buried in Oak Forest Cemetery, Flat Rock.

RUDOLPH, JACOB (*VV*), Exeter. Enlisted in Company E, June 20, 1861, at Adrian, age 22. Laborer in a brick works. Reenlisted Dec. 25, 1863. Wounded in action in the Overland Campaign in Virginia, May 9 and June 3, 1864, shot in left leg, which was amputated. Died Sept. 16, 1864, in U.S. Hospital at Washington, D.C. Born in Germany.

ROLFE, JARVIN D., Hillsdale County. Enlisted in Company E, June 20, 1861, at Adrian, age 30. Discharged for disability from regiment's camp, Jan. 1, 1863.

ROLLINS, CHARLES, Lenawee County. Enlisted in Company B as corporal June 20, 1861, at Adrian, age 26. Discharged for disability Sept. 6, 1861.

ROMEYN, JAMES W., Detroit. Commissioned first lieutenant, Company I, age 22. Attorney, graduate of Columbia College, N.Y., 1858. Became senior aide-de-camp on Gen. Orlando Wilcox's staff. Resigned Oct. 17, 1862.

Later served as U.S. consul to Chile, congressman, and senator.

RONEY, BARNEY, Howell. Enlisted in Company K, June 20, 1861, at Adrian, age 22. Farmer, married and father of small son. Killed in action at Malvern Hill, Va., July 1, 1862.

ROOT, JASON, Monroe County. Enlisted in Company A, June 20, 1861, at Adrian, age 19. Resided with his parents and five siblings. Mustered out at expiration of term at Detroit, June 30, 1864. Resided in Monroe after service. Died on March 23, 1917, and buried Woodland Cemetery, Monroe.

ROOT, MANLY, Hillsdale County. Enlisted in Company H, Sept. 27, 1861, at Hudson, age 34. Farmer. Wounded in action at July 1, 1862, Malvern Hill, Va., gunshot wound in left shoulder. Discharged for disability at Fortress Monroe, Feb. 29, 1863. Died Oct. 2, 1888.

ROSA, HIRAM, Hudson. Enlisted in Independent Company, March 31, 1864, at Hudson, age 24. Farmer, resided on parents' farm with two siblings; brother of Moses Rosa. On detached service with Co. F, 1st Michigan Infantry, July 2, 1864, Petersburg. Died at Staunton General Hospital, Washington, D.C., of typhoid fever, July 9, 1864.

ROSA, MOSES, Hudson. Enlisted in Independent Company, March 19, 1864, at Hudson, age 23. Farmer, brother of Hiram Rosa. Died of disease near Fredericksburg, Va., May 14, 1864.

ROSE, A. MORELL, Monroe. Entered service in Company A at organization as second lieutenant, June 20, 1861, at Adrian, age 29. Principal of the Union Academy School, Monroe. Commissioned first lieutenant Sept. 25, 1861. Commissioned captain Jan. 1, 1862. Killed in action at Malvern Hill, Va., July 1, 1862.

ROSE, MYRON, Detroit. Enlisted in Company I, July 22, 1862, at Detroit, age 44. Farmer. Slightly wounded in action at Fredericksburg, Va., Dec. 13, 1862. Wounded in action at Gettysburg, July 2, 1863. Transferred to Veteran Reserve Corps April 13, 1864. Mustered out at Washington, D.C., June 26, 1865. Buried Highland Cemetery, Ypsilanti.

ROSS, WILLIAM H., Fayette Township, Hillsdale County. Enlisted in Company E, June 20, 1861, at Adrian, age 21. Farmer, resided with parents and three siblings. Wounded in action June 26, 1862, Mechanicsville, Va. Discharged for disability at Sharpsburg, Md., Oct. 6, 1862.

ROSS, WILLIAM H., Hillsdale. Enlisted in Independent Company, Feb. 9, 1864, at Hillsdale, age 23. Corporal April 5, 1864. On detached service with Co. F, 1st Michigan Infantry, July 2, 1864, Petersburg. Transferred to Co. K, reorganized 4th Michigan, June 6, 1865. Twice wounded in action near Petersburg, June 18, 1864, and Feb. 6, 1865. Mustered out at San Antonio, Feb. 23, 1866.

ROUPP, JACOB, Branch County. Enlisted in Company C, June 20, 1861, at Adrian, age 32. Transferred to Invalid Corps at Beverly Ford, Va., Sept. 15, 1863. Transferred back to regiment from Washington, D.C., Feb. 10, 1864. Mustered out at expiration of term June 30, 1864.

ROUSE, CHARLES A., Ann Arbor. Enlisted in Company D, June 20, 1861, at Adrian, age 19. Carpenter apprentice. Killed in action at Gettysburg, July 2, 1863. Buried in Gettysburg National Cemetery, Michigan Plot, A-14.

ROUSE, JOHN, Washtenaw County. Enlisted in Company K, June 20, 1861, at Adrian, age 18. Tanner. Injured falling from rail car while in route from Michigan near Harrisburg, Pa., June 27, 1861, fracturing his skull. Returned to regiment in camp on Aug. 3, 1861, but was deemed unfit for duty, showing signs of imbecility, and discharged for disability by Dr. Chamberlain on Aug. 17, 1861.

ROZELL, DANIEL R., Jackson County. Enlisted in Company D, June 20, 1861, at Adrian, age 20. Farmer, resided with parents and eight siblings. Discharged for disability at Baltimore, Nov. 3, 1862, on account of wounds received in battle at Gaines' Mill, Va., June 27, 1862.

RUSSELL, JEREMIAH, Lenawee County. Enlisted in Company F, June 20, 1861, at Adrian, age 18. Farmer. Wounded in neck and shoulder while in action, Malvern Hill, July 1, 1862, his left side paralyzed. Discharged for disability at Philadelphia, Dec. 12, 1862.

RUSSELL, JUSTIN, Hillsdale County. Enlisted in Company E, June 20, 1861, at Adrian, age 16. Discharged for disability June 24, 1862.

RYERSON, HENRY, Lenawee County. Enlisted in Company F, May 16, 1861, at Adrian, age 24. Farmer. Deserted Nov. 28, 1861, at Munson Hill, Va., with Henry Pierson of Co. F.

S

SADLER, SILAS W., Tecumseh. Enlisted in Company G, June 20, 1861, at Adrian, age 18. Resided with parents. Mustered out at expiration of term at Detroit, June 30, 1864. Reenlisted Co. D, 30th Michigan Infantry, Nov. 30, 1864, as sergeant. Mustered out June 30, 1865. Resided in Owosso after service. Died in 1930, buried in Oak Hill Cemetery, Owosso.

SALIOTTE, GILBERT, Ecorse. Enlisted in Company I, June 20, 1861, at Adrian, age 19. Clerk, resided with father and three siblings. Taken prisoner in action at Gettysburg, July 2, 1863. Returned to regiment at Annapolis, Md., Dec. 10, 1863. Wounded in action May 5, 1864, shot in jaw, Wilderness, Va. Admitted Campbell Hospital, Washington, D.C. Mustered out at expiration of term at Detroit, June 30, 1864.

SALSBURY, LESTER H., Dover. Enlisted in Company B as corporal June 20, 1861, at Adrian, age 21. Farmer residing on his parents' farm. Sergeant. Wounded in action at Gettysburg, July 2, 1863, shot through hand and lung, with bullet also lodging in left thigh. In a field hospital at Gettysburg for three weeks, then moved to hospital at Harrisburg, Pa., for three months. Discharged for disability at Bealton, Va., Jan. 23, 1864. Became a lawyer after service and resided in Hudson.

SANDBAR, JOSEPH (*VV*), Monroe County. Enlisted in Company H, June 20, 1861, age 35. Laborer. Reenlisted Dec. 29, 1863. On duty at brigade headquarters from April 1863 to April 1864. On detached service with Co. G, 1st Michigan Infantry, July 2, 1864, Petersburg. On duty at division headquarters from Sept. 1864 to April 1865. Mustered out at San Antonio, Feb. 26, 1866. Buried LaSalle Protestant Cemetery. Born in Paris, France.

SANDERS, JOHN, Washtenaw County. Enlisted in Company D, June 20, 1861, at Adrian, age 35. Farm laborer. Wounded and captured at Gaines' Mill, June 27, 1862, but reportedly released. Wounded in action again, struck in chest with "buck and ball" gunshot, Gettysburg July 2, 1863; sent to Westminster, Md. Wounded again in the thigh in Virginia in the Overland Campaign, May 1864. Mustered out at expiration of term, June 30, 1864. Reenlisted in Co. K, 182nd Ohio Infantry. After the war he enlisted again in 1866 in the 27th U.S. Infantry Regiment for two years; enlisted Dec. 29, 1869, in Co. I, 18th U.S. Infantry for five years; enlisted March 8, 1876, Co. F, 19th U.S. Infantry for five years. Discharged for disability Feb. 18, 1878. Resided in Soldiers Home, Dayton. Born in Scotland.

SARGENT, JOHN PARKER, St. Joseph County. Enlisted in Company C, June 20, 1861, at Adrian, age 18. Taken prisoner at Gettysburg, July 2, 1863. Escaped from Andersonville, Ga., Aug. 21, 1864, reporting to provost marshal at Atlanta on Sept. 16, 1864, from thence was transferred to Camp Distribution, Va. Discharged at expiration of term at Detroit, Oct. 20, 1864. Resided in St. Croix Falls, Wis., after war. Died Middleport, N.Y.

SAVERY, STEPHEN P., Washtenaw County. Enlisted in Company K, June 20, 1861, as musician at Adrian, age 20. Resided on his parents' farm with four younger siblings. Discharged for disability July 28, 1861.

SAWYER, CHARLES E., Washtenaw County. Enlisted in Company K, June 20, 1861, at Adrian, age 19. Corporal July 29, 1862. Mustered out at expiration of term at Detroit, June 29, 1864. Buried Maple Grove Cemetery, Mason.

SAXTON, CHARLES, Tecumseh. Enlisted in Company G, June 20, 1861, at Adrian, age 20. Brother of James Saxton. Killed in action, shot in the head, at Malvern Hill, Va., July 1, 1862.

SAXTON, JAMES, Lenawee County. Enlisted in Company G, June 20, 1861, at Adrian, age 18. Brother of Charles Saxton. Wounded in action at Gaines' Mill, Va., June 27, 1862, from gunshot to right thigh and shell wound to right knee. Wounded in action, North Anna River, Va., May 25, 1864, from gunshot. Mustered out at expiration of term of service at Detroit, June 30, 1864. Enlisted in Co. D, 30th Michigan Infantry, Nov. 30, 1864, at Jackson, for one year. Sergeant Jan. 4, 1865. Mustered out and honorably discharged at Detroit, June 30, 1865. Resided in Farwell after service. Died May 16, 1894.

SAYERS, FRANK, Washtenaw County. Enlisted in Company D, June 20, 1861, at Adrian, age 21. Discharged for disability at Warrenton, Va., Nov. 7, 1862. Reenlisted, Co. C, 1st Michigan Cavalry. Dec. 16, 1863. at Mt. Clemens. Transferred to Co. M, Nov. 17, 1865. Discharged at Ft. Bridger, Utah, March 25, 1866. Resided in Mason after service, bartender. Died Oct. 9, 1881. Buried Maple Grove Cemetery, Mason.

SCHAFFER, ALBERT, St. Joseph County. Enlisted in Company C, June 20, 1861, at Adrian, age 21. Farmer. Sick in

Brigade Hospital, Dec. 1861. Discharged for disability, chronic rheumatism, at Philadelphia, June 4, 1862. Buried Westminster Cemetery, Bala Cynwyd, Pa.

SCHAFFER, LEWIS, St. Joseph County. Enlisted in Company C, June 20, 1861, at Adrian, age 31. Died of disease at brigade hospital, Nov. 20, 1861. Buried Military Asylum Cemetery, Washington, D.C., Nov. 23, 1861.

SCHNAITTER, CORNELIUS. Enlisted in band, June 20, 1861, at Adrian, age 30. Mustered out at Harrison's Landing, Va., Aug. 10, 1862, per War Department.

SCHNICKENBURGER, JOHN, Lenawee County. Enlisted in Company F as sergeant June 20, 1861, at Adrian, age 26. Shoemaker. On detached duty in U.S. Hospital, Baltimore. Reportedly resigned Nov. 1861, though state records reflect him missing in action near Spotsylvania Court House, May 10, 1864. Born in Germany.

SCHOLFIELD, LEISTER T., Steuben, Ind. Enlisted in Company H, June 20, 1861, at Adrian, age 22. Farmer. Discharged for disability at Warrenton, Va., Nov. 17, 1862, because of wound suffered earlier. Resided in Barnes, Kans., after service. Died in 1922.

SCHOTT, ISAAC WILLIAM. Enlisted in Company H, Sept. 19, 1861, age 18. Millwright. Discharged for disability, chronic diarrhea, Jan. 2, 1863. Resided in Grand Ledge.

SCHULTZE, CHARLES L., Sandwich, Canada West. Enlisted in Company I, June 20, 1861, at Adrian, age 25. Killed in action at Malvern Hill, Va., July 1, 1862.

SCOTT, EZRA S., Adrian. Enlisted in Company H, Oct. 8, 1861, at Adrian, age 19. Shoemaker. Discharged for disability at Detroit, June 26, 1862.

SCOTT, JOHN D., LaGrange, Ind. Enlisted in Company C, June 20, 1861, at Adrian, age 21. Mustered out at expiration of term at Detroit, June 29, 1864. Resided in Ontario, Ind.

SCRANTON, ALPHONSO, Monroe. Enlisted in Company A, Aug. 28, 1862, at Detroit, age 21. Missing in action at Gettysburg, July 2, 1863. On detached service with Co. A, 1st Michigan Infantry, July 2, 1864. Taken prisoner Sept. 8, 1864, at Weldon Railroad, Va. Returned to regiment after being listed as missing in action at Hatcher's Run, Va., Feb. 22, 1865. Discharged at Washington, D.C., June 9, 1865. Buried Boughton Cemetery, Kalamazoo County.

SCRIVER, WILLIAM, Lenawee County. Enlisted in Company B. Sept. 16, 1861, at Hudson. No further record.

SCULLY, ANDREW, Detroit. Enlisted in Company I as musician June 20, 1861, at Adrian, age 16. Resided with his parents and siblings. Discharged for disability at camp, Jan. 10, 1863, unable to do the duty of a soldier because of his youth and lack of endurance. Resided in Brooklyn, N.Y., after service. Born in Ireland.

SEAGE, HENRY S. Enlisted in Company E, Sept. 27, 1861, at Hudson, age 17. Resided on farm with parents and three siblings, the son of the Reverend John Seage, then living in White Pigeon, and brother of Richard Seage. Corporal Dec. 18, 1862; sick with scurvy Dec. 1862. Color sergeant, wounded slightly, May 5, 1864, Wilderness, Va. On detached duty, clerk at division commissary depot, May–Sept. 1864. On detached service with Co. K, 1st Michigan Infantry, July 2, 1864, Petersburg. Discharged at expiration of term near Petersburg, Sept. 10, 1864. Insurance agent after service. Died April 9, 1899, in Lansing and buried at Mount Hope Cemetery.

SEAGE, JOHN, White Pigeon, St. Joseph County. Entered service as regimental chaplain, summer of 1862, joining the regiment in Sept. at Falmouth, Va., age 52. Baptist minister, married and father of four, including Henry and Richard Seage. Seriously wounded June 8, 1863, near Deep Run, Va., by guerillas, multiple gunshots, as he carried money to be mailed and deposited. Mustered out at expiration of term at Detroit, June 29, 1864. Enlisted in Co. F, reorganized 4th Michigan, Aug. 28, 1864, at Adrian. Chaplain. Mustered out at Detroit, May 26, 1866. Resided in St. Louis, Mo. after service. Buried Fountain Cemetery, N.Y. Born in England.

SEAGE, RICHARD WATSON (*VV*), White Pigeon. Enlisted in Company E as corporal June 20, 1861, at Adrian, age 23. Clerk, brother of Henry Seage and son of John Seage. Sergeant. Wounded in action and captured at Malvern Hill, Va., July 1, 1862, his skull dented by a bullet; prisoner for 19 days. Admitted to hospital at Ft. Hamilton, N.Y. Rejoined the regiment Oct. 9, 1862, at Sharpsburg, Md. Sergeant major Dec. 13, 1862. Commissioned second lieutenant, Company I, April 1, 1863. Severely wounded in action at Gettysburg, July 2, 1863. Honorably discharged Dec. 31, 1863, for disability because of his wounds. Commissioned first lieutenant and quartermaster, reorganized 4th Michigan, July 26, 1864, but resigned March 6, 1865. Commissioned captain, U.S. Volunteers, March 13, 1865, for gallant and meritorious service during the war.

Died Nov. 1908, Jersey City, N.J. Buried Fountain Cemetery, N.Y.

SEBRING, NORMAN B., Fulton, Ohio. Enlisted in Company B, Feb. 27, 1862, at Adrian, age 21. Resided on parents' farm with five siblings. Discharged for disability at Detroit, July 24, 1863, for lung disease. Reenlisted in Co. H, 11th Michigan Cavalry, Aug. 28, 1863. Mustered out on Sept. 15, 1865. Resided in Odgen, Lenawee County, after service.

SENTER, WILLARD, Hillsdale. Enlisted in Independent Company, Feb. 26, 1864, at Hillsdale, age 18. On detached service with Co. F, 1st Michigan Infantry, July 2, 1864, Petersburg, Va. Transferred to Co. K, reorganized 4th Michigan, June 6, 1865. Dishonorably discharged with loss of pay, bounty, and allowances to date Aug. 12, 1865, date of his desertion. Resided in Olivet after service.

SEVERANCE, MORRIS P., Lenawee County. Enlisted in Company F, June 20, 1861, at Adrian, age 21. Farmer residing with parents and two siblings. Wounded in action at Mechanicsville, Va., June 26, 1862, gunshot left side of lung, leaving him disabled. Sent to hospital in Philadelphia, Oct. 16, 1862. Resided in Pittsford after service. Died on March 2, 1915. Buried Plot 12, Block Y, Maple Grove Cemetery, Hudson.

SEWARD, WILLIAM H., Lenawee County. Enlisted in Company G, June 20, 1861, at Adrian, age 18. Discharged for disability at Philadelphia, Dec. 12, 1862.

SHADBOLT, FRANK (*VV*). Rollin, Lenawee County. Enlisted in Company E, Sept. 16, 1861, at Hudson, age 18. Farmer, resided with parents and younger sister. In hospital fall of 1862, returned to regiment Nov. 8, 1862. Reenlisted Jan. 20, 1864. On detached service with Co. K, 1st Michigan Infantry, July 2, 1864, Petersburg. Transferred to Co. C, reorganized 4th Michigan, July 1, 1865. Discharged at Detroit, Sept. 11, 1865, Resided in Hudson after service. Buried Plot 17, Block M, Maple Grove Cemetery, Hudson.

SHAFER, ALEXANDER (*VV*), Lenawee County. Enlisted in Company B, June 20, 1861, at Adrian, age 19. Reenlisted Dec. 29, 1863. Wounded in action June 3, 1864, Cold Harbor Va., bullet entered back of right hand. In hospital, Alexandria, Va. Transferred to Summit House Hospital, Philadelphia. On detached service with Co. B, 1st Michigan Infantry, July 2, 1864, Petersburg. Transferred to Co. C, reorganized 4th Michigan, July 1, 1865. Mustered out at San Antonio, Feb. 10, 1866. Resided in Reading, Hillsdale County, after service. Died May 21, 1897, at Fawn River, St. Joseph County.

SHAFER, ALPHONZO, Pleasant, Ind. Enlisted in Company B as corporal June 20, 1861, age 21. Painter. Reenlisted Dec. 29, 1863. On detached service with Co. B, 1st Michigan Infantry, July 2, 1864, Petersburg, Va. Transferred to Co. K, 4th reorganized 4th Michigan Infantry, July 1, 1865. Discharged at Detroit, Feb. 3, 1866. Resided in Hillsdale after service. Died in 1917. Buried in section G, plot 20, Maplewood Cemetery, Reading Township.

SHARP, JONATHAN S. (*VV*), Livingston County. Enlisted in Company K as sergeant June 20, 1861, at Adrian, age 27. Blacksmith and teamster, married father of a small daughter. Reenlisted Dec. 29, 1863. Wounded in action, Wilderness, Va., May 5, 1864. No further record.

SHAW, GEORGE, Monroe County. Enlisted in Company G as corporal June 20, 1861, at Adrian, age 26. In Seminary Hospital. No further record.

SHAW, GILMORE M., Washtenaw County. Enlisted in Company D, June 20, 1861, at Adrian, age 21. Listed sick and wounded in general hospital. No further record.

SHEETS, FREDRICK A., Ann Arbor, Washtenaw County. Enlisted in Company D, sergeant, June 20, 1861, age 42. Wounded in action, shot in right arm and left leg, at Gettysburg, July 2, 1863. Died July 25, 1863, of wounds. Buried in Gettysburg National Cemetery, Michigan Plot, E-17.

SHERMAN, WILLIAM H., Hillsdale. Entered service in Independent Company at organization as first lieutenant, Feb. 8, 1864, at Hillsdale, age 21. Resided with his parents and two siblings. On detached service with Co. F, 1st Michigan Infantry, July 2, 1864, Petersburg. Resigned on account of disability Sept. 13, 1864. Died in 1937.

SHERRY, THOMAS, Muir, Ionia County. Enlisted in Company K, June 20, 1861, at Adrian, age 18. Wounded in action at Malvern Hill, Va., July 1, 1862, gunshot wound. Corporal March 7, 1863. Mustered out at expiration of term at Detroit, June 29, 1864. Resided in Ionia.

SHICK, CHARLES, Steuben, Ind. Enlisted in Company B, June 20, 1861, at Adrian, age 21. Discharged for disability April 19, 1862. Resided in Jackson, Mich., after service. Buried Mt. Evergreen Cemetery, Jackson.

SHOTT, WILBER M., Lenawee County. Enlisted in Company H, Sept. 16, 1861, at Hudson, Discharged for disability at camp, Jan. 2, 1863. Died June 11, 1896. Buried in St. Catherines, Canada.

Showers, Andrew J., Jackson County. Enlisted in Company D, June 20, 1861, at Adrian, age 22. Discharged by order at Washington, D.C., Nov. 25, 1862, to enlist in the 5th U.S. Artillery.

Silsbee, John O., Lenawee County. Enlisted in Company F, June 20, 1861, at Adrian, age 31. Farmer. Discharged for disability at Baltimore, Aug. 21, 1862, for insanity. In the Soldiers and Sailors Home at Western Insane Asylum, July 15, 1875.

Silsby, Frederick R., Washtenaw County. Enlisted in Company D, June 20, 1861, at Adrian, age 24. Dropped from the rolls at Beverly Ford, Va., per War Department order, Aug. 20, 1863.

Silsby, James P., Wayne County. Enlisted in Company D, June 20, 1861, at Adrian, age 24. Married, father of a baby. Wounded in the left shoulder at Mechanicsville, Va., by a shell fragment. Wounded at Malvern Hill, July 1, 1862, in same shoulder. Admitted to hospital for five weeks. Taken prisoner at Gettysburg, July 2, 1863. Held at Belle Isle, Richmond. Sent to Andersonville, Ga., Feb. 21, 1864; sent to Savannah, Ga., Sept. 3, 1864. Exchanged Nov. 9, 1864. Discharged at Detroit, Jan. 5, 1865. Became a doctor, resided in Kansas.

Simmons, Watson C., Hillsdale County. Enlisted in Company E, June 20, 1861, at Adrian, age 22. Discharged for disability at Georgetown, April 22, 1862.

Skirvin, Charles M., Sherman Township, St. Joseph County. Enlisted in Company C, Jan. 12, 1863, at Sherman, age 18. Wounded slightly at Gettysburg, July 2, 1863. On detached service with Co. C, 1st Michigan Infantry, July 2, 1864, Petersburg. Hospital steward, Jan. 6, 1865. Transferred to Co. C, reorganized 4th Michigan, July 1, 1865. Admitted to Harper Hospital, Detroit, July 2, 1865. Mustered out at Detroit, Oct. 31, 1865.

Skirvin, Francis M. Enlisted in Company C, June 20, 1861, at Adrian, age 18. Lost an index finger by gunshot. Mustered out at expiration of term at Detroit, June 30, 1864. Resided in Sturgis after service. Died Aug. 18, 1896.

Slater, John M., Franklin, Lenawee County. Enlisted in Company G as corporal June 20, 1861, at Adrian, age 32. Farm laborer, married, father of three children. Sergeant. Discharged for disability at Alexandria, Va., Nov. 20, 1862. Resided in New Haven after service. Buried Franklin Township Cemetery, Lenawee County.

Sloan, William H., Amboy, Hillsdale County. Enlisted in Company H, June 20, 1861, at Adrian, age 22. Died of typhoid at regimental hospital at Minor's Hill, Va., Dec. 3, 1861. Buried Military Asylum Cemetery, Washington, D.C.

Slocum, Jeremiah D., Adrian. Entered service in Company B as first lieutenant, at organization, June 20, 1861, at Adrian, age 24. Bookseller. Commissioned captain, Co. I, June 20, 1861. Absent with leave July to Sept. 1862. Resigned and honorably discharged Sept. 28, 1862, because of disability, rheumatism. Resided in Jersey City, N.J., after service.

Smith, Ames, Cambridge, Lenawee County. Enlisted in Company F, Feb. 1864, at Detroit, age 28. No further record.

Smith, Albert, Hudson. Enlisted in Company F, June 20, 1861, at Adrian, age 15. Resided with his older brother and sister-in-law. Promoted to corporal Aug. 1862. Wounded and missing in action at Gettysburg, July 2, 1863, wounded and left on field. No further record.

Smith, Austin T., Iosco, Livingston County. Enlisted in Company K, June 20, 1861, at Adrian, age 21. Farmer, resided with parents and two younger siblings. Corporal. Died of disease in camp near Falmouth, Va., March 8, 1863.

Smith, Charles, Girard, Branch County. Enlisted in Company E, as corporal. June 20, 1861, at Adrian, age 18. Farm laborer. On recruiting service in Michigan, Aug. 12, 1862. Appointed second lieutenant, 9th Michigan Cavalry, March 27, 1863. First lieutenant Jan. 17, 1864; captain Aug. 19, 1865. Mustered out as first lieutenant July 21, 1865, and honorably discharged. Resided in Missouri.

Smith, George, Wayne County. Enlisted in Company I, June 20, 1861, at Adrian, age 21. Student. Discharged for disability at Washington, D.C., July 20, 1861.

Smith, George W., Ingham County. Enlisted in Company K, June 20, 1861, age 18. Resided on parents' farm with siblings. Discharged for disability at Washington, D.C., Aug. 20, 1861. Buried Pleasant View Cemetery, Blissfield, Lenawee County.

Smith, Heman. *See* Evans, Heman.

SMITH, HUBERT D., Litchfield, Hillsdale County. Enlisted in Company H, June 20, 1861, at Adrian, age 23. Farmer, resided on parents' farm with two younger siblings. Wagoner. Appointed sergeant Aug. 1, 1861. In hospital June 1862 by accidental overdose. Discharged at expiration of term at Detroit, June 13, 1864. Resided in Litchfield after service. Died 1905 and buried Mt. Hope Cemetery, Litchfield, row 2, plot 5,

SMITH, JACKSON H., Washtenaw County. Enlisted in Company K, Sept. 20, 1861, at Hudson, age 16. Mustered Sept. 20, 1861. Missing on the march to Frederick, Md., June 27, 1863. Transferred to the Navy, July 20, 1863. Resided in Evart after service.

SMITH, JAMES P., Detroit. Enlisted in Company I, Nov. 3, 1862, at Detroit, age 17. Wounded slightly in action at Gettysburg, July 2, 1863. Transferred to Invalid Corps at Washington, D.C., per order, Jan. 15, 1864. Buried Deerfield Cemetery, Deerfield, Mich.

SMITH, JARVIS B., Hillsdale County. Enlisted in Company H, June 20, 1861, at Adrian, age 24. Farmer residing on his parents farm with three siblings. Deserted on the march through Washington, D.C., Sept. 12, 1862. Mustered out in 1864, suffering impaired hearing and rheumatism. Resided in Presque Isle after war.

SMITH, JOHN, Hudson, Lenawee County. Enlisted in Company F, June 20, 1861, at Adrian, age 17. Lived with his parents on their farm with two siblings. Mustered out at expiration of term at Detroit, June 29, 1864. Buried Woodland Cemetery, Monroe.

SMITH, JOHN, Blissfield, Lenawee County. Enlisted in Company I, Aug. 25, 1862, age 18. Cooper. Discharged for disability while in camp, Jan. 1, 1863.

SMITH, JOSEPH L., Hudson. Entered service in Company F as second lieutenant, June 20, 1861, at Adrian, age 31. Married, father of two small children. Wounded in action and captured at Gaines' Mill, Va., June 27, 1862, resulting in amputation of left leg. Resigned and honorably discharged March 7, 1863. Reenlisted in the Veteran Reserve Corps as a lieutenant on Sept. 30, 1863. Mustered out Aug. 16, 1865. Resided in Dover, Lenawee County, after service. Admitted to Solders Home, Dayton, June 20, 1867. Died May 30, 1882.

SMITH, JULIUS D., Livingston County. Enlisted in Company K as corporal June 20, 1861, at Adrian, age 21. Printer. Discharged for disability, July 27, 1861. Died 1897. Buried Lakeview Cemetery, Howell.

SMITH, LORENZO C., Franklin, Lenawee County. Enlisted in Company G, June 20, 1861, at Adrian, age 23. Carpenter and joiner, residing on parents' farm with six siblings. Corporal. Sergeant. Died May 28, 1864, in Emory Hospital, Washington, D.C., of wounds received in action at Laurel Hill, Va., his leg having been amputated because of gunshot wound. Buried National Cemetery, Arlington, Va.

SMITH, MARVIN (*VV*), Rollin, Lenawee County. Enlisted in Company F, as musician fifer, June 20, 1861, at Adrian, age 29. Reenlisted Dec. 29, 1863. On detached service with Co. C, 1st Michigan Infantry, July 2, 1864, Petersburg, Va. Transferred to Co. I, reorganized 4th Michigan, July 1, 1865. Discharged at San Antonio, Feb. 23, 1866. Resided in Addison, Lenawee County, and Oceana County after service. Died Nov. 15, 1892.

SMITH, NATHANIEL M. (*VV*), Lenawee County. Enlisted in Company F, June 20, 1861, at Adrian, age 21. Farmer. Reenlisted Dec. 29, 1863. Mustered out at expiration of term at Detroit, June 2, 1864. Resided in Lawton, Van Buren County.

SMITH, OLIVER S. (*VV*), Washtenaw County. Enlisted in Company D, June 20, 1861, at Adrian, age 22. Farm laborer. Reenlisted Dec. 29, 1863, at Perry. Sergeant. Missing in action at Gettysburg, July 2, 1863. Prisoner of war at Belle Isle, Richmond; returned Sept. 4, 1863. Wounded in action, shot in leg, May 5, 1864. On detached service with Co. E, 1st Michigan Infantry, July 2, 1864, Petersburg. Discharged to accept commission as captain, 123rd U.S. Colored Infantry, June 20, 1865. Died Nov. 10, 1889. Buried Oak Hill Cemetery, Owosso.

SMITH, OLNEY J. (*VV*), Litchfield, Hillsdale County. Enlisted in Company H, June 20, 1861, at Adrian, age 19. Farmer residing with parents and two siblings. Discharged for disability because of wounds, Warrenton, Va., Nov. 17, 1862. Reentered service in Co. C, 6th Michigan Infantry, enlisted Feb. 24, 1864, age 22. Mustered out at New Orleans, Aug. 20, 1865. Resided in Schuyler, Neb., after service.

SMITH, WASHINGTON I., Washtenaw County. Enlisted in Company D, June 20, 1861, at Adrian, age 26. Died of wounds received in action at Gettysburg, July 2, 1863.

SMITH, WILLIAM, Hillsdale. Enlisted in Company H, June 20, 1861, at Adrian, age 19. Blacksmith, resided with his parents and five siblings. Discharged for disability at Fairfax Seminary, Va., by order Jan. 20, 1863.

Smith, William E., Hudson. Enlisted in Company I, Sept. 14, 1861, at Hudson, age 17. Painter. Died of disease at camp near Falmouth, Va., Jan. 1, 1863.

Smith, William H. (*VV*), Stockbridge. Enlisted in Company K, June 20, 1861, at Adrian, age 20. Post Office clerk. resided with parents and siblings. Reenlisted Dec. 29, 1863. Recommended for promotion by officers June 14, 1864, for meritorious conduct in battle. On detached service with 1st Michigan Infantry, July 2, 1864, Petersburg. Sergeant major. Commissioned first lieutenant, Co. H, Nov. 1, 1864. Commanding company from Jan. 1, 1865, to June 1, 1865. Mustered out near Jeffersonville, Ind. July 9, 1865. Resided in Michigan after service, working in real estate. Died Dec. 19, 1917, in Cheboygan. Buried in Gaylord.

Smith, William H., Hillsdale County. Enlisted in Company E, June 20, 1861, at Adrian, age 21. Taken prisoner at battle of Mine Run, Va., Nov. 27, 1863. Discharged at expiration of term at Detroit, March 25, 1865. Resided in Youngstown, Ohio, after service. Buried Perryville Cemetery, Fenner, N.Y.

Snyder, Andrew C., Lenawee County. Enlisted in Company G, June 20, 1861, at Adrian, age 18. Discharged for disability at Minor's Hill, Va., Jan. 13, 1862.

Spade, Abraham, Allen, Hillsdale County. Enlisted in Company H, June 20, 1861, at Adrian, age 21. Farm laborer residing with his widowed mother and four younger siblings. Detailed to the Balloon Corps, Columbia Armory, Washington, D.C. Rejoined regiment Nov. 2, 1861. Brought up charges March 1, 1862, for sleeping on post; found guilty. Killed in action at Malvern Hill, Va., July 1, 1862.

Spafford, Charles R., Tecumseh. Enlisted in Company G, June 20, 1861, at Adrian, age 26. Printer, married, father of a small son. Discharged for disability at Washington, D.C., Aug. 3, 1861. Resided in Rollin Township after service.

Spalding, George W. (*VV*), Monroe. Enlisted in Company A as first sergeant June 20, 1861, at Adrian, age 24. Clerk and schoolteacher. First lieutenant, Co. B, Aug. 5, 1861. Commissioned captain Jan. 13, 1862. Wounded in action July 1, 1862. Resigned July 18, 1862. Reentered service as lieutenant colonel, 18th Michigan Infantry, at organization, July 18, 1862. Provost marshal from June 14, 1863, to Jan. 1864. Colonel, 12th Tennessee Cavalry, Feb. 21, 1864. Brevet brigadier general, U.S. Volunteers, March 21, 1865, for valuable service in battle of Nashville. Honorably discharged Oct. 24, 1865. Served as Monroe postmaster, federal treasury agent, Monroe mayor, school board and worked as an attorney and bank director. Died Sept. 13, 1915, and buried in Woodland Cemetery, Monroe. Born in Perthshire, Scotland.

Spath, Frederick, Monroe. Enlisted in Company A, June 20, 1861, at Adrian, age 20. Laborer. Wounded in thigh May 5, 1863, at Chancellorsville, Va. Stayed behind at Gettysburg to care for wounded. Transferred to Invalid Corps Sept. 1, 1863, by War Department order. Resided in Monroe after service. Died 1887 and buried in Trinity Lutheran Cemetery, Monroe. Born in Bavaria, Germany.

Spellman, Frank, LaGrange, Ind. Enlisted in Company C as corporal June 20, 1861, at Adrian, age 19. Killed in action at Malvern Hill, Va., July 1, 1862.

Spence, James K., Hillsdale County. Enlisted in Company E, June 20, 1861, at Adrian, age 28. Mustered out at expiration of term at Detroit, June 28, 1864.

Spencer, Le Roy Milton, Fowlerville, Livingston County. Enlisted in Company K, Sept. 18, 1862, at Handy, age 16. Farm boy residing with parents and siblings. Musician drummer. Discharged by general order of the War Department at Washington, D.C., June 5, 1865. Resided in Marquette after the war, died July 23, 1930. Buried Park Cemetery, Marquette.

Spencer, Samuel H., Hillsdale. Enlisted in Company E, age 15. Missing in action at Malvern Hill, Va., July 1, 1862. On detached service with Co. K, 1st Michigan Infantry, July 2, 1864. Discharged at Washington, D.C., June 5, 1865. Died in 1930. Buried in Oak Hill Cemetery, Owosso.

Spencer, Tenant R., Washtenaw County. Enlisted in Company D, June 20, 1861, at Adrian, age 29. In hospital at Harrison's Landing, Va., Aug. 10, 1862, for chronic diarrhea. Died of the disease at a Philadelphia hospital, Nov. 25, 1862. Buried in Mt. Mariah Cemetery, Philadelphia.

Sperry, Alford E., Adrian. Enlisted in Company B, June 20, 1861, at Adrian, age 21. Resided with his parents and four siblings. Wounded and taken prisoner at Malvern Hill, Va., July 1, 1862. Returned to regiment at Harrison's Landing, Aug. 20, 1862. Died of disease at Falmouth, Va., April 20, 1863. Originally buried at

Fitzhugh's Farm, Stafford, Va.; moved to Row T, Plot 2102, Fredericksburg National Cemetery.

Spies, Joseph, Cleveland. Enlisted in band, June 20, 1861, at Adrian, age 36. Painter and musician. Mustered out at Harrison's Landing, Va., Aug. 10, 1862. Born in Germany.

Spoors, Robert, Washtenaw County. Enlisted in Company D, Sept. 19, 1861, at Hudson. Discharged for disability April 19, 1862, because of amputation of a leg in Virginia. Admitted to Soldiers Home, Dayton, for chest ulcers Nov. 3, 1867. Died on May 14, 1884. Buried Scadin Cemetery, Washtenaw County.

Springer, Arnold D., Oakland County. Enlisted in Company I, June 20, 1861, at Adrian, age 15. Resided on his parents' farm. Missing in action at Fredericksburg, Va., Dec. 13, 1862. Transferred to Invalid Corps, Aug. 1, 1863, by War Department order.

Springer, Jerome, Lenawee County. Enlisted in Company B, Feb. 24, 1862, at Adrian. Discharged for disability at Bealton, Va., March 8, 1864.

Stacey, George H., Hillsdale County. Enlisted in Company E, June 20, 1861, at Adrian, age 22. Wounded and missing in action at Gettysburg, July 2, 1863. Returned Aug. 1, 1863. Discharged at Detroit, Aug. 7, 1866, to date June 28, 1864. Resided in Brooklyn, Jackson County. Buried Highland Cemetery, Brooklyn.

Staley, John M., Jonesville. Enlisted in Company H, as June 20, 1861, at Adrian, age 22. Blacksmith and drug store clerk, married. Sergeant. Wounded in action, shot in hip at Wilderness, Va., May 5, 1864. Mustered out at expiration of service.

Stanback, Philip, Hillsdale County. Enlisted in Company E, June 20, 1861, at Adrian, age 19. Farm laborer. Wounded in action at Gettysburg, July 2, 1863, in left leg. In hospitals, York and Germantown, Pa. Transferred to Veteran Reserve Corps, Jan. 31, 1864. Reenlisted as sergeant, April 16, 1864. Mustered out Nov. 18, 1865. Resided in Hillsdale after service. Admitted to Soldiers Home, Dayton, April 23, 1902.

Stark, Jacob H., Allen, Hillsdale County. Enlisted in Independent Company, 4th Michigan, Feb. 23, 1864, at Allen, age 27. First sergeant April 5, 1864. On detached service with Co. F, 1st Michigan Infantry, July 2, 1864, Petersburg. Commissioned first lieutenant Sept. 13, 1864. Transferred to Co. K, reorganized 4th Michigan, June 6, 1865. Mustered out at Houston, May 26, 1866. Resided in Ann Arbor after service. Died April 18, 1892, and buried Riverside Cemetery, Clinton, Lenawee County.

Starr, Eli L., Centreville, St. Joseph County. Enlisted in Company C as sergeant June 20, 1861, at Adrian, age 21. Killed in action at Malvern Hill, Va., July 1, 1862.

Statson, Joseph F., Hudson, Lenawee County. Last name also given as Stutson. Enlisted in Company F, June 20, 1861, at Adrian, age 31. Farmer, resided with his elderly mother. Died of congestion of the lungs at camp near Falmouth, Va., March 1, 1863.

Stedman, Edwin A., Washtenaw County. Enlisted in Company D, June 20, 1861, at Adrian, age 27. Marble engraver. Transferred to band, Sept. 1, 1861. Discharged at Harrison's Landing, Va., Aug. 10, 1862. Enlisted in band, 2nd U.S. Cavalry, Aug. 11, 1862. Discharged at Monrovia Station, Md., Aug. 11, 1865. Died 1906. Buried in Oak Hill Cemetery, Owosso.

Stephens, William H., St. Joseph County. Enlisted in Company C, June 20, 1861, at Adrian, age 18. Farmer resided with parents and younger siblings. Discharged for disability at Ft. Woodbury, Va., Sept. 13, 1861.

Stevens, John W., Hillsdale County. Enlisted in Company E, June 20, 1861, at Adrian, age 37. Tailor, married and father of two small children. Wounded in action at Gaines' Mill, June 27, 1862. Sick and wounded in general hospital and in convalescent camp, Alexandria, Va. No further military record. Died in 1907.

Stevens, Joseph W., Hillsdale County. Enlisted in Company E, June 20, 1861, at Adrian, age 19. Taken prisoner June 29, 1862. Discharged for disability at Philadelphia, Dec. 3, 1862. Enlisted in 1st Michigan Sharpshooters, Kalamazoo. Sergeant and drill master. Captured at Petersburg, Va., June 17, 1864; held at Andersonville, Ga.; and survived the *Sultana* disaster. Resided in Buffalo, N.Y., after service. Born in England.

Stevens or Stephens, Nelson, Washtenaw County. Enlisted in Company D, June 20, 1861, at Adrian, age 21. Discharged for disability Dec. 11, 1861, at Minor's Hill.

Stevenson, Isaiah, Wayne County. Enlisted in Company I, June 20, 1861, at Adrian, Musician bugler, age 27. Plasterer. Detached as Gen. Morell's bugler. Transferred to Invalid Corps at Washington, D.C., Aug. 1, 1863. Discharged from Veteran Reserve Corps at Washington, D.C., June 21, 1864. Resided in Detroit after service.

Born in Ireland.

Stewart, William S., Monroe. Enlisted in Company A, June 20, 1861, at Adrian, age 23. Discharged for disability at Detroit, July 1862. Resided in Exeter Township after service. Died in 1909 and buried in McIntire Cemetery. Born in Canada.

Stiles, George. Enlisted, unassigned to company, Feb. 11, 1864, at Adrian, age 22. Deserted at Detroit, Feb. 25, 1864.

Stillson, Melvin, Tecumseh. Enlisted in Company G, June 20, 1861, at Adrian, age 30. Shoemaker. Discharged for disability, chronic rheumatism, at Ft. Woodbury, Va., Sept. 12, 1861. Reenlisted 3rd Michigan Cavalry as first sergeant, promoted second lieutenant, Nov. 1, 1862. Resigned Jan. 23, 1864. Resided in Otsego after service and admitted to Soldiers Home, Grand Rapids.

Stilwell, James I., Litchfield, Hillsdale County. Enlisted in Company H, June 20, 1861, at Adrian, age 19. Farmer. Corporal. Taken prisoner at Gettysburg, July 2, 1863. Discharged at expiration of term at Detroit, Jan. 13, 1865. Resided in Litchfield after service.

Stoddard, Edgar C., Monroe County. Enlisted in Company A, June 20, 1861, at Adrian, age 19. Merchant in father's store, residing with parents and siblings. brother of Herbert Stoddard. Discharged Sept. 1, 1861. Resided in Toledo.

Stoddard, Herbert Lee, Monroe County. Enlisted in Company A, as corporal, June 20, 1861, at Adrian, age 21. Merchant in father's store, resided with his parents and siblings; brother of Edgar Stoddard. Discharged Sept. 1, 1861. Resided in Chicago.

Stoddard, Nolton F., Brownstown. Enlisted in Company I, June 20, 1861, at Adrian, age 29. Carpenter. Brother of William Stoddard. Sergeant Sept. 1, 1861. First sergeant. Second lieutenant Jan. 15, 1862. Resigned and honorably discharged Nov. 4, 1862, because of asthma. Resided in Detroit after service, became a founder of Detroit Edison Company and was president of an engineering company. Died Dec. 6, 1895.

Stoddard, William H., Gibraltar. Enlisted in Company I, June 20, 1861, at Adrian, age 22. Laborer residing with parents and siblings, brother of Nolton Stoddard. Discharged for disability. July 20, 1861. Reenlisted in Co. I, Oct. 24, 1862. Discharged for disability at Washington, D.C., Aug. 1863. Resided in Gibraltar.

Stone, Henry C., Hudson. Enlisted in Company B, Sept. 16, 1861, age 21. Farm laborer, resided with parents and two sisters. Severely wounded in action at Fredericksburg, Va., Dec. 13, 1862. Discharged for disability at Detroit, March 10, 1863. Buried at National Cemetery, Los Angeles.

Stone, Oliver P., Hudson. Enlisted in Company E, June 20, 1861, at Adrian, age 18. Corporal. Discharged at Washington, D.C., by general order. Nov. 1862. Reenlisted in the 5th U.S. Artillery same date. Resided in Swanton, Ohio. Died May 12, 1899 and buried at Blissfield, Lenawee County.

Storms, Abram W., Lima, Washtenaw County. Enlisted in Company K, June 24, 1861, at Adrian. Farm laborer, resided on parents' farm with siblings. Missing in action at Gettysburg, July 2, 1863. Discharged at expiration of term at Detroit, Aug. 22, 1865. Buried Porter Cemetery, Washtenaw County.

Storms, James H., LaGrange, Ind. Enlisted in Company C, June 1861, at Adrian, age 26. Discharged for disability Oct. 15, 1861.

Stott, Mark. Enlisted in Company I, June 20, 1861, at Adrian, age 30. Corporal. Wounded in action May 5, 1864. Mustered out at expiration of term at Detroit, June 30, 1864. Died June 11, 1896, and buried in St. Catherine's Cemetery, Ontario, Canada.

Stout, Amos, Adrian. Enlisted in Company G, June 20, 1861, at Adrian, age 20. Laborer. Never mustered. Enlisted in 6th Michigan Infantry, March 20, 1864, at Palmyra. Discharged on disability at New Orleans, Aug. 1, 1865.

Stout, William, Wayne County. Enlisted in Company I, June 20, 1861, at Adrian, age 20. Taken prisoner at Chancellorsville, Va., May 1863. Buried Mt. Evergreen Cemetery, Jackson.

Strong, Amos (*VV*), Hillsdale County. Enlisted in Company E, June 20, 1861, at Adrian, age 21. Reenlisted Dec. 31, 1863. Wounded in action; shot in arm May 5, 1864. On detached service with Co K, 1st Michigan Infantry, July 2, 1864, Petersburg. Transferred to Co. C, reorganized 4th Michigan, July 1, 1865. Discharged at Detroit, Aug. 5, 1865. Buried North Lawn Cemetery, North Adams.

Strong, Edward. Enlisted in band as musician, June 20, 1861, at Adrian, age 34. Gunsmith. Mustered out at

Harrison's Landing, Va., Aug. 10, 1862, by War Department order. Resided in Cleveland after service. Born in Germany.

STRONG, HENRY N. Entered service as chaplain at organization, June 20, 1861, at Adrian, for age 35. Episcopal clergyman. Resigned and honorably discharged July 20, 1862. Resided in Milwaukee after war. Died Aug. 6, 1886, at St. Mark's Home & Hospital, Grand Rapids.

STUART or STEWART, EDWIN, Lenawee County. Enlisted in Company G, Feb. 23, 1862. Discharged for disability at Philadelphia, Dec. 12, 1862.

SULLINGER, ASA, Lenawee County. Enlisted in Company F, June 20, 1861, at Adrian, age 31. Farmer. Discharged for disability at Washington, D.C., Aug. 3, 1861, suffering kidney and liver disease. Resided in Bethany after service.

SUMNER, EDWARD, Sylvan, Washtenaw County. Enlisted in Company A, Sept. 13, 1861, age 21. Farm laborer residing with six siblings. Corporal July 1, 1862. Wounded in hand while advancing May 4, 1863, at Chancellorsville, Va. Transferred to Invalid Corps, Washington, D.C., Sept. 1, 1863. Resided in Traverse City.

SUTHERLAND, HENRY WILLIAM. Drafted from Jefferson, Hillsdale County, for 9 months, age 30. Farmer. Assigned to Company E. Transferred to Co. H. Discharged at expiration of term at Bealton, Va., Nov. 11, 1863. Resided in Adams after war. Died Sept. 19, 1886. Buried in Plot 24, East Hill Cemetery, Osseo.

SUZOR, JOSEPH, Monroe County. Enlisted in Company A, June 20, 1861, at Adrian, age 20. Discharged for disability, rheumatism, April 12, 1863. Resided in Wyandotte and also the town of Texas, Wis.

SWARTOUT, THOMAS, Monroe. Enlisted in Company A, Sept. 24, 1861, at Adrian, age 26. Killed in action at Malvern Hill, Va., July 1, 1862.

SWEET, WILLIAM, Salem, Washtenaw County. Enlisted in Company D, June 20, 1861, at Adrian, age 34. Discharged for disability for illness at Warrenton, Va., Nov. 17, 1862. Joined 9th Michigan Cavalry, May 9, 1863. Mustered out June 12, 1865. Resided in Salem.

T

TARSNEY, JAMES, Hillsdale County. Enlisted in Company E, corporal, June 20, 1861, at Adrian, age 23. Blacksmith and brother of John and Thomas Tarsney. First sergeant. Killed in action at the Wilderness, Va., May 5, 1864.

TARSNEY, JOHN, Ransom, Hillsdale County. Enlisted in Company E, Aug. 26, 1862, at Hillsdale, age 16, though he claimed to be 18. Farm laborer and brother of Thomas and James Tarsney. Hospitalized early fall of 1862, returned to regiment Oct. 3, 1862. Wounded slightly at Fredericksburg, Va., Dec. 13, 1862. Taken prisoner at Gettysburg, July 2, 1863. Captured again at Wilderness, Va., May 5, 1864. Held at Belle Isle, Andersonville, and Milan prisons. Returned to 1st Michigan Infantry at Petersburg, Jan. 10, 1865. Discharged at Washington, D.C., June 5, 1865. Graduated from the University of Michigan in 1867. Resided in Kansas City, Mo., and served as city attorney, Kansas City, Kans. Elected to Congress and appointed by President Cleveland to Supreme Court of Oklahoma. Died in Kansas City, Sept. 4, 1920.

TARSNEY, THOMAS (*VV*), Ransom. Said he was a locomotive fireman, age 18, and enlisted in three-month 9th Indiana Infantry at Ft. Wayne, Ind., April 1861. Enlisted in Company E, 4th Michigan, Oct. 8, 1861, age 19, at Hudson. Brother of John and James Tarsney. Promoted to corporal May 16, 1863. Reenlisted Dec. 29, 1863. Wounded in action, shot in hand, May 5, 1864. On detached service with Co. K, 1st Michigan Infantry, July 2, 1864. Transferred to Co. C, reorganized 4th Michigan, July 1, 1865. First sergeant July 1, 1865. Discharged to date Feb. 15, 1866. Resided in Grand Rapids and Denver, Colo., an attorney. Died April 19, 1902, age 59, Pueblo, Colo.

TASKER, RICHARD (*VV*), Steuben, Ind. Enlisted in Company B, June 20, 1861, at Adrian, age 22. Farmer, residing with parents and siblings. Taken prisoner at Gettysburg, July 2, 1863. Returned to regiment Oct. 6, 1863. Reenlisted Dec. 29, 1863. Corporal. Wounded at Wilderness, Va., May 5, 1864. Underwent surgeries May 5 and May 25, amputation of right arm. Died at Finley Hospital, Washington, D.C., June 7, 1864. Buried in Arlington National Cemetery, Va. Born in England.

Taylor, Adison A., LaSalle, Monroe County. Enlisted in Company A, June 20, 1861, at Adrian, age 19. Mustered out at expiration of term at Detroit, June 30, 1864.

Taylor, David Wayne, New York. Enlisted in Company B, June 20, 1861, at Adrian, age 21. Discharged at Alexandria, Va., Nov. 1, 1862. Transferred to 2nd U.S. Cavalry, Oct. 1, 1862. Resided in Harrison, Mich., after service.

Taylor, Edward Henry Courtney, Trenton. Enlisted in Company A, June 20, 1861, at Adrian. Tutor. Sergeant major June 1, 1863. Wounded in action near Spotsyslvania Court House, May 8, 1864, shot in foot. Mustered out at expiration of term at Detroit, June 28, 1864. Died Aug. 13, 1905, St. Paul, Minn.

Taylor, Edward M., Allen, Hillsdale County. Enlisted in Company E, June 20, 1861, at Adrian, age 18. Farmer. Severely wounded in action at Gettysburg, July 2, 1863, in leg and foot, a ball entering middle of thigh, traveling down leg to ankle. In hospital at Philadelphia, transferred to Harrisburg. Ball extracted from his ankle on Oct. 13, 1863. Discharged on disability at Rochester, N.Y., Feb. 24, 1864. Buried at National Cemetery, Milwaukee.

Taylor, Levi S., Lenawee County. Enlisted in Company G, June 20, 1861, at Adrian, age 23. Farmer. Resided with parents and siblings. Mustered out at expiration of term at Detroit, June 30, 1864. Resided in Jackson after service. Buried Woodland Cemetery, Jackson.

Taylor, Mark W., Hillsdale County. Enlisted in Company E, May 16, 1861, at Adrian, age 21. Wounded severely and missing in action at Gettysburg, July 2, 1863. Discharged on disability General Hospital, Davids' Island, N.Y., June 7, 1864. Resided in Hillsdale after service. Died May 11, 1907. Buried in Oak Grove Cemetery, Hillsdale, Row 6, Plot 736.

Taylor, Samuel. *See* Tyler, Samuel.

Taylor, William J., Washtenaw County. Enlisted in Company D, June 20, 1861, at Adrian, age 23. Discharged for disability at Fairfax, Va., Nov. 28, 1862. Buried Rice Cemetery, Milan, Monroe County.

Teachout, Charles, Dundee, Monroe County. Enlisted in Company A, June 20, 1861, at Adrian, age 19. Wounded twice and taken prisoner at Malvern Hill, Va., July 1, 1862. Died while a prisoner.

Teachout, George W., Hillsdale. Enlisted in Independent Company, Feb. 20, 1864, at Hillsdale, age 24. Killed in action near North Anna River, May 23, 1864.

Tenbrook, William L. (*VV*), Adrian. Enlisted in Company B as musician June 20, 1861, at Adrian, age 22. Resided on parents' farm with four siblings. Discharged for disability Sept. 3, 1861. Again entered service Dec. 5, 1861. Corporal July 1, 1862. Sergeant July 1862. Reenlisted Dec. 29, 1863. Wounded in action at Wilderness, Va., May 5, 1864, gunshot wound to an ankle. Admitted to Campbell Hospital, Washington, D.C. On detached service with Co. B, 1st Michigan Infantry, July 2, 1864, Petersburg. Commissioned first lieutenant, Company A, reorganized 4th Michigan, July 26, 1864. Commissioned captain Feb. 9, 1865. Mustered out and honorably discharged to date Feb. 13, 1866. Buried Austin Cemetery, Austin, Mo.

Teneyck, Moseley, Litchfield, Hillsdale County. Enlisted in Company H, June 20, 1861, at Adrian, age 17. Farmer. Discharged for disability because of feebleness of constitution at Ft. Woodbury, Sept. 24, 1861.

Terpening, Henry, Lenawee County. Enlisted in Company F as sergeant June 20, 1861, at Adrian, age 21. Farmer. Brother-in-law of Simon Preston and brother of William Terpening. Wounded in action Malvern Hill, Va., July 1, 1862, fractured right thigh by a gunshot. Discharged for disability at Baltimore, Oct. 16, 1862. Resided in Wisconsin.

Terpening, William, Reading, Hillsdale County. Enlisted in Company F, June 20, 1861, at Adrian, age 26. Carpenter, married and father of two children. Brother-in-law of Simon Preston and brother of Henry Terpening. Discharged for disability at Washington, D.C., Aug. 14, 1861. Reenlisted Co. F, Jan. 26, 1864. Wounded, shot in right hip, Wilderness, Va., May 5, 1864. Sent to hospital at Alexandria, Va. Mustered out from the reorganized 4th Michigan, Jan. 20, 1866, San Antonio. Resided in Ellsworth, Wis., after the war. Died 1913. Buried Section B-6, Plot 13, Oakwood Cemetery, Adrian.

Terwilliger, James, Hillsdale County. Enlisted in Company E, Oct. 5, 1861, at Hillsdale. Killed in action at Wilderness, Va., May 5, 1864, shot in the head.

Terwilliger, Thomas D., Hillsdale County. Enlisted in Company E, Sept. 16, 1861, at Hudson, Transferred to Invalid Corps, Nov. 15, 1863; transferred from Invalid Corps back to the regiment, March 14, 1864. On detached service with Co. K, 1st Michigan Infantry, July 2, 1864, Petersburg. Discharged at expiration of term of service at Weldon Railroad, Sept. 12, 1864. Resided in Pentwater after service. Died in Hudson in July 1917 and was buried at Addison, Lenawee County.

THEWING, EDWARD. Enlisted in Company I as private June 20, 1861, at Adrian, age 19. Died of typhoid fever Seminary Hospital, Georgetown, Oct. 5, 1861.

THEWING, HERMAN S., Hillsdale. Enlisted in Independent Company, March 26, 1864, at Hillsdale, age 18. Wounded in action near Bethesda Church, June 2, 1864, both legs, one amputated. Died June 19, 1864, at Mt. Pleasant Hospital, Washington, D.C. Buried National Cemetery, Arlington.

THIELL, WILLIAM H., Hillsdale County. Enlisted in Company E as sergeant June 20, 1861, at Adrian, age 19. Appointed second lieutenant July 1, 1862. Commissioned first lieutenant Sept. 1, 1862. Dismissed by sentence of court-martial March 4, 1863, for overstaying his leave, which he said occurred because he was arrested and detained for not knowing the "counter-sign" or password when he returned to camp. Resided in Bloomington, Ill., and Chicago after service. Died 1890. Buried Forest Home Cemetery, Forest Park, Ill.

THOMAS, ASAHAEL, Rollin, Lenawee County. Enlisted in Independent Company, Feb. 23, 1864, at Rollin, age 44. Laborer. On detached service with Co. F, 1st Michigan Infantry, July 2, 1864, Petersburg, Va. Transferred to Co. K, reorganized 4th Infantry, June 6, 1865. Absent, sick. No further record.

THOMAS, JOHN J., St. Joseph County. Enlisted in Company C, June 20, 1861, at Adrian, age 17. Farm laborer. Discharged for disability at Washington, D.C., April 20, 1862. Admitted to the Soldiers Home, Dayton, June 23, 1893.

THOMPKINS or TOMPKINS, WESLEY JOSEPH, Sturgis. (Also given in one contemporaneous record as Thomskins.) Enlisted in Company C, May 16, 1861, at Sturgis, age 18. Carpenter. Wounded by a shell in head, neck, and lower back on April 5, 1862, near Yorktown Va. Admitted to hospital at Fortress Monroe, Va. Transferred to Judiciary Square Hospital, Washington, D.C. Discharged July 1862. Reenlisted in 2nd Michigan Infantry, March 31, 1864. Wounded in shoulder and captured on June 17, Petersburg, Va. Sent to Andersonville, Ga. Discharged at expiration of term at Detroit, June 3, 1865. Survived the *Sultana* disaster on the Mississippi River, admitted Overton Hospital, Memphis, Tenn. Resided in Ft. Wayne, Ind. Admitted to the Soldiers Home, Dayton, on June 12, 1877 and released Jan. 11, 1881. Died Jan. 12, 1907, and reportedly buried in Genesee County, Mich.

THOMPSON, HUGH. Enlisted in Company G, June 20, 1861, at Adrian, age 19. No further military record. Died 1921 and buried Mt. Hope Cemetery, Litchfield, Hillsdale County.

THOMPSON, JAMES, Hudson. Enlisted in Company E, Sept. 17, 1861, at Hudson. Severely wounded in action at Fredericksburg, Va., Dec. 13, 1862; died from wounds. Buried Old Protestant Cemetery, Hudson.

THURLACK, CHARLES, Monroe County. Enlisted in Company A, June 20, 1861, at Adrian, age 22. Killed in action at Gettysburg, July 2, 1863, buried near the Rose Barn. Reburied in the Gettysburg National Cemetery, Michigan Plot, A-15.

THURSTON, EPAMINONDAS, Colon, St. Joseph County. Enlisted in Company C, June 20, 1861, at Adrian, age 21. Farmhand. Sent to hospital, Aug. 12, 1862, for two months. Wounded in action at Gettysburg, July 2, 1863; sent to Summit House Hospital, Philadelphia. Wounded in action, Wilderness, Va., May 5, 1864, shot through the neck. On detached service with Co. C, 1st Michigan Infantry, July 2, 1864. Transferred to Co. C, reorganized 4th Michigan, July 1, 1865. Mustered out at expiration of term at New York City, July 17, 1865. Stated he was a prisoner of war at Andersonville, Ga. Resided in Burr Oak and Pullman, Wash., after service.

TICE, PETER, Washtenaw County. Enlisted in Company D, June 20, 1861, at Adrian, age 19. Deserted at Gaines' Mill, Va., June 24, 1862. Found guilty by court-martial and ordered to pay a $10 fine and serve additional year. On detached service with Co. E, 1st Michigan Infantry, July 2, 1864. Transferred to Co. B, reorganized 4th Michigan, July 1, 1865. Discharged at expiration of term at Detroit, Aug. 4, 1865.

TICHNOR, HENRY (*VV*). Enlisted in Company B, June 20, 1861, age 19. Reenlisted Dec. 29, 1863. On detached service with Co. B, 1st Michigan Infantry, July 2, 1864. Transferred to Co. C, reorganized 4th Michigan, July 1, 1865. Discharged at Detroit, Sept. 5, 1865. Resided in Fairfield, Lenawee County, after service.

TILLOTSON, GEORGE, Steuben, Ind. Enlisted in Company B, June 20, 1861, at Adrian, age 25. Mechanic. Corporal July 1, 1862. Reenlisted Dec. 19, 1863. On detached service with Co. B, 1st Michigan Infantry, July 2, 1864.

Sergeant. Killed in action at Hatcher's Run, Va., Feb. 6, 1865.

TODD, ARTEMUS C., Girard, Branch County. Enlisted in Company E, Aug. 29, 1862, at Girard, age 16. Died of disease at Falmouth, Va., Dec. 12, 1862.

TODD, ELLIOT, Litchfield, Hillsdale County. Enlisted in Company H, June 20, 1861, at Adrian, age 18. Farmer, residing with parents and siblings. Died of disease, typhoid fever, at Fortress Monroe, Va., Sept. 18, 1862.

TOLFORD, WILLIAM HENRY (*VV*). Enlisted in Company F, Sept. 10, 1861, at Hudson, age 31. Farmer. Reenlisted as corporal Jan. 1, 1864. Killed in action at Wilderness, Va., May 5, 1864. Buried Maple Grove Cemetery, Hudson, Plot 17, Block J.

TOMLINSON, CHARLES (*VV*), Clinton, Lenawee County. Enlisted in Company G, June 20, 1861, at Adrian, age 18. Resided with mother and sister. Reenlisted Dec. 29, 1863. Killed in action near Cold Harbor, Va., June 3, 1864.

TOMPSON, JAMES H. Enlisted in Company C, June 20, 1861, at Adrian, age 19. Absent without leave. No further record.

TORPY, SILVANUS E., Washtenaw County. Enlisted in Company K, June 20, 1861, at Adrian, age 27. Discharged for disability Sept. 28, 1862, because of rheumatism. Resided in the State Veterans Home, Waupaca, Wis., after service.

TOTTEN, JOSEPH H., Monroe County. Enlisted in Company G, June 20, 1861, at Adrian, age 18. Farmer. Absent and sick in a hospital, Philadelphia, May through Aug. 1863. Mustered out at expiration of term at Detroit, June 30, 1864. Enlisted as a sergeant in 30th Michigan Infantry on Nov. 28, 1864, for one year's service, discharged on June 17, 1865. Resided in Dundee.

TOUPANCE, CHESTER (*VV*), Kalamazoo. Enlisted in Company C, June 20, 1861, at Adrian, age 18. Reenlisted Dec. 29, 1863. Wounded in action May 5, 1864. On detached service with Co. C, 1st Michigan Infantry, July 2, 1864, Petersburg. Transferred to Co. C, reorganized 4th Michigan, July 1, 1865. Mustered out at San Antonio, Feb. 26, 1866. Resided in Kalamazoo and Indiana after service.

TRACEY, GEORGE, Lenawee County. Enlisted in Company K, Sept. 16, 1861, at Hudson. On detached service with Co. K, 1st Michigan Infantry, July 2, 1864, Petersburg. Discharged at expiration of term of service at Weldon Railroad, Sept. 12, 1864. Resided in Matherton after service.

TRAIN, HENRY, Detroit. Enlisted in Company H, March 6, 1863, at Richfield, age 21. Farmer. Substitute for John W. Moon, drafted at Richfield, Genesee County, Feb. 10, 1863. Deserted on the march to Frederick, Md., June 28, 1863.

TRIPP, EDWIN G., Mosherville, Hillsdale County. Enlisted in Company H, June 20, 1861, at Adrian, age 19. Farm laborer. Sergeant Jan. 1, 1863. Died in First Division (Fifth Corps) Hospital, Gettysburg, July 15, 1863, of wounds, shot in both legs, received in action July 2, 1863. Buried Gettysburg National Cemetery, Michigan Plot, E-9.

TRIPP, SYLVESTER SIDNEY (*VV*), Washtenaw County. Enlisted in Company G, June 20, 1861, at Adrian, age 25. Reenlisted Dec. 29, 1863. On detached service with Co. G, 1st Michigan Infantry, July 2, 1864, Petersburg. Transferred to Co. C, reorganized 4th Michigan, July 1, 1865. Failed to return from furlough in Michigan, Nov. 1, 1865. Resided in Saline after war. Buried Oakwood Cemetery, Saline.

TROMBLY, RICHARD, Lenawee County. Enlisted in Company I, June 20, 1861, at Adrian, age 23. Clerk in father's store, lived with parents and family. Discharged for disability, June 22, 1861.

TRUAIR, FRANK B., Washtenaw County. Enlisted in Company D as corporal June 20, 1861, at Adrian, age 27. Carpenter. Injured by a horse, July 3, 1862, and transferred to Invalid Corps at Meridian Hill, Va., Aug. 19, 1863. Died April 11, 1897. Buried Riverside Cemetery, St. Charles, Saginaw County.

TUCKER, JOHN M., Livingston County. Enlisted in Company K, June 20, 1861, at Adrian, age 21. Farmer. Corporal. Discharged for disability at New York City, Aug. 28, 1862, for wounds received in action at battle of Gaines' Mill, June 27, 1862. Resided in Grass Lake. Died 1904, buried Berg Cemetery.

TUFFS, JOHN, Webster, Washtenaw County. Enlisted in Company K, June 20, 1861, at Adrian, age 18. Farmer, residing on parents' farm with their family. Brother of Richard Tuffs. Transferred to Battery D, 5th U.S. Artillery, Oct. 9, 1862. Discharged at Sharpsburg, Md., per general order, Oct. 25, 1862. Suffered from sunstroke at Gettysburg, Pa., on July 1, 1863. Mustered out on May 16, 1864, at expiration of term. Resided in Scio and died May 31, 1913. Buried Forest Lawn Cemetery, Dexter. Born in England.

TUFFS, RICHARD M., Webster, Washtenaw County. Enlisted in Company K, June 20, 1861, at Adrian, age 21. Teamster, residing on parents' farm. Brother of John Tuffs. Transferred to Battery D, 5th U.S. Artillery, Oct. 9, 1862. Discharged at Sharpsburg, Md., general order, Oct. 25, 1862. Died in Dexter on March 22, 1917. Born in England.

TUNNICLIFF, JOSEPH W., JR., Jackson. Entered service in as surgeon June 20, 1861, at Adrian, age 42. Doctor. Transferred to 1st Michigan Infantry as surgeon, Aug. 20, 1861. Discharged on account of disability Dec. 10, 1862. Appointed in 1863 by Gov. Blair to be assistant state military agent of Michigan in Washington, D.C., serving to the end of the war. Appointed U.S. examining surgeon for pensions in 1867 and served until 1873. Died March 20, 1881. Buried Mount Evergreen Cemetery, Jackson.

TURNER, JAMES H., Monroe County. Enlisted in Company A, June 20, 1861, at Adrian, age 20. On detached service with ambulance corps, from Nov. 1862 to May 1864. Mustered out at expiration of term at Detroit, June 30, 1864. Resided in Toledo.

TURPING, WILLIAM H. Enlisted in Company F, Jan. 26, 1864, at Hudson, age 36. Slightly wounded in action, shot in thigh, May 5, 1864, Wilderness, Va. Wounded again in action May 9, 1864, Laurel Hill, Va. On detached service with Co. C, 1st Michigan Infantry, July 2, 1864, Petersburg. Transferred to Co. K, reorganized 4th Michigan, June 6, 1865. Discharged for disability at San Antonio, Jan. 20, 1866.

TUTTLE, JAMES G., Wayne County. Enlisted in Company F, June 20, 1861, at Adrian, age 21. Sailor. Taken prisoner at Falls Church, Va., Aug. 10, 1861, with Stiles H. Wirts while on picket. Held at Richmond, transferred to Castle Pinckney, Charleston, S.C. Transferred to Columbia, S.C., Jan. 1, 1862. Escaped and recaptured 31 days later, Winnsboro, Tenn. Sent to Libby Prison, Richmond. Paroled May 20, 1862. Discharged for disability June 30, 1862. Enlisted in Co. A, 17th Michigan Infantry, Dec. 30, 1863, at Brownstown; transferred to 2nd Michigan Infantry, June 3, 1865. Mustered out and discharged, July 28, 1865. Resided in Clay, Mich., after service.

TUTTLE, MOSES S., Tecumseh. Enlisted in Company K, June 25, 1861, at Adrian, age 25. Carpenter. Discharged for disability, chronic diarrhea, July 11, 1862. Resided in Ypsilanti after service.

TUTTLE, SMITH, Washtenaw County. Enlisted in Company K, June 20, 1861, at Adrian, age 25. Listed as sick and wounded in general hospital. No further record.

TWING, EDWIN, Geauga County, Ohio. Enlisted in Company I, June 20, 1861, at Adrian, age 31. Died of disease at Georgetown, Oct. 5, 1861.

TYLER, SAMUEL JACKSON. Enlisted in Company H, June 20, 1861, at Adrian, age 24. Day laborer, married. Died at Washington, D.C., April 25, 1862, at the Patent Office, of accidental wounds received at Fairfax, Va., shot through both legs by a Union cavalry trooper, March 12, 1862. Buried at Military Asylum Cemetery, Washington, D.C.

U

UNDERWOOD, DEXTER, Tecumseh. Enlisted in Company G, June 20, 1861, at Adrian, age 18. Killed in action at Malvern Hill, Va., July 1, 1862.

UPTHEGROVE, HENRY, Jonesville. Enlisted in Company H, June 20, 1861, at Adrian, age 18. Farmer. Discharged for disability, rheumatism, at Minor's Hill, Va., Jan. 2, 1862. Reenlisted in Co. F, 15th Michigan Infantry as color sergeant, Jan. 29, 1862. Reenlisted Jan. 25, 1864, Scottsboro, Ala. Mustered out Sept. 9, 1865. Resided in Jackson County after service. Admitted to the Soldiers Home, Dayton, for rheumatism, Aug. 13, 1896; released March 12, 1905.

V

Van Allen, Darwin G., Jonesville. Enlisted in Company H, sergeant, June 20, 1861, at Adrian, age 23. Farmer. Shot himself in the foot with a revolver on Nov. 5, 1861, and was sent to brigade hospital. Reduced to rank at his own request. Wounded at Gaines' Mill, June 27, 1862, struck in the hip by a cannon ball. Discharged for disability at Davids' Island, N.Y., Dec. 1862. Enlisted in Co. K, 27th Michigan Infantry, Dec. 21, 1863, at Hillsdale. Sergeant. Captured at Wilderness, Va., May 6, 1864; imprisoned at Andersonville, Ga., but exchanged. His father brought him home, but he lived only about a year. His brother, also in the 27th Michigan and captured at the same time, died in prison.

Van Dawarca, George, Hudson. Enlisted in Company F, Feb. 8, 1864, at Detroit, age 18. Cooper. Wounded in action, shot in hand, May 5, 1864. On detached service with Co. C, 1st Michigan Infantry, July 2, 1864, Petersburg. Discharged for disability, Dec. 5, 1864. Resided in Reynolds, Mich., after service. Died Nov. 1908.

Van Etten, Peter, Hudson. Enlisted in Independent Company, Feb. 27, 1864, at Hudson, age 32. On detached service with Co. F, 1st Michigan Infantry, July 2, 1864, Petersburg. Deserted May 4, 1865.

Van Horn, Columbus, Washtenaw County. Enlisted in Company D, June 20, 1861, at Adrian, age 27. Farm laborer. Discharged for disability Dec. 20, 1862. Resided in Northfield after service.

Van Lieu, James J., Lenawee County. Enlisted in Company G, June 20, 1861, at Adrian, age 43. Discharged for disability at Sharpsburg, Md., Oct. 27, 1862.

Van Olker, John, Cleveland. Enlisted in band as lieutenant and leader, June 20, 1861, at Adrian, age 35. Musician, married and father of five young children. Discharged at Harrison's Landing, Va., Aug. 10, 1862, per War Department order. Resided in Cleveland after service. Born in Germany.

Van Scoter, Alonzo B., Hillsdale County. Enlisted in Company H, June 20, 1861, at Adrian, age 30. Carpenter and joiner, resided with parents and two younger siblings. Sergeant Feb. 1, 1862. Discharged for disability at York, Pa., Dec. 22, 1862, on account of gunshot wound in the shoulder received at Malvern Hill, Va., July 1, 1862. Resided in Concord, Jackson County, after service.

Van Valer, Cornelius B. (*VV*), Hillsdale County. Entered service in Company D, 18th Michigan Infantry, at organization as captain, July 27, 1862, age 46. Master carriage and wagon maker. Single parent of three children. Resigned at Nashville, Tenn., Aug. 1, 1863. Entered service in Independent Company of the 4th Michigan Infantry as captain at organization, Feb. 8, 1864, at Hillsdale. On detached service with Co. F, 1st Michigan Infantry, July 2, 1864, Petersburg. Brevet major U.S. Volunteers Sept. 30, 1864, for gallant service at battle of Peeble's Farm, Va. Commanding regiment Feb. 1865. Transferred to Co. C, reorganized 4th Michigan, June 6, 1865. Resigned and discharged Oct. 2, 1865. Resided in Hillsdale after service. Died Oct. 26, 1889, Hillsdale.

Van Volkenburgh, Thomas, Hillsdale County. Enlisted in Company F, June 20, 1861, at Adrian, age 23. Discharged for disability at Washington, D.C., Feb. 4, 1863, because of wound in left lung. Resided in Muskegon after service.

Van Wagnen, Rynear, Allen, Hillsdale County. Enlisted in Independent Company, Feb. 26, 1864, at Allen, age 36. Carpenter and farm overseer. Corporal April 5, 1864. On detached service with Co. F, 1st Michigan Infantry, July 2, 1864, Petersburg. Died in Third Division Hospital, Alexandria, Va., of dysentery July 6, 1864. Buried National Cemetery, Alexandria.

Vanakin, Adison, Wayne. Enlisted in Company F, Feb. 1864, at Detroit, age 29. Resided with parents and siblings. Listed as sick and hospitalized soon after joining company.

Vance, Joseph, Hudson. Enlisted in Company F, Sept. 10, 1861, at Hudson, age 19. Farmer. Killed in action at Malvern Hill, July 1, 1862.

Vandemark, Abram, Washtenaw County. Enlisted in Company K, June 20, 1861, at Adrian, age 18. Laborer. Discharged for disability Nov. 15, 1862, because of wound in the groin. Reenlisted in Co. E, 5th U.S. Artillery, Feb. 2, 1864. Discharged Feb. 3, 1866. Resided in Liberty, Jackson County, after service.

Vanderpool, Oliver C., Jonesville. Enlisted in Company H, June 20, 1861, at Adrian, age 17. An only child, he resided with his parents. Killed in action at Malvern Hill, July 1, 1862.

Vandeventer, William, Lenawee County. Enlisted in Company F, June 20, 1861, at Adrian, age 26. Farmer. Discharged for disability at Philadelphia, Nov. 28, 1862, because of wound from Seven Days battles of 1862, also suffering from diarrhea and neuralgia. Resided in Isabella after service.

Vaneps, Cornelius, Pittsfield, Washtenaw County. Enlisted in Company F, Feb. 6, 1864, at Hudson. Farmer, father of four children. Wounded in face, shot through the jaw, May 5, 1864, at Wilderness, Va. Admitted to a General Hospital, Alexandria, Va., May 14, 1864. On detached service with Co. C, 1st Michigan Infantry, July 2, 1864, Petersburg. Discharged June 22, 1865, on account of wounds. Died 1893, buried in Glenwood Cemetery, Flint.

Vanguilder, Orrin, Branch County. Enlisted in Company C, June 20, 1861, at Adrian, age 21. Farm laborer. Discharged at Alexandria, Va., Dec. 24, 1862. Transferred to U.S. Cavalry. Resided in Orleans, Mich., after service.

Vanhouton, Thaddeus, Lenawee County. Enlisted in Company F, June 20, 1861, at Adrian, age 26. Farmer. Discharged for disability at Minor's Hill, Va., Jan. 6, 1862.

Vanmeeter, Madison J., Litchfield, Hillsdale County. Enlisted in Company H, June 20, 1861, at Adrian, age 21. Farmer residing with parents and siblings. Died of disease, typhoid fever, at Seminary Hospital, Georgetown, Aug. 23, 1861.

Vanzant, Oliver, Calhoun County. Enlisted in Company C, June 20, 1861, at Adrian, age 21. Wounded in action May 5, 1864. Mustered out at expiration of term at Detroit, June 30, 1864.

Vanzile, Riley E., Livingston County. Enlisted in Company K, June 20, 1861, at Adrian, age 21. Farm laborer. Missing on march to Frederick, Md., June 27, 1863.

Vanzile, Wells, Livingston County. Enlisted in Company K, June 20, 1861, at Adrian, age 22. Transferred to Invalid Corps, July 16, 1863.

Vaughn, Eugene, LaGrange, Ind. Enlisted in Company C as corporal June 20, 1861, at Adrian, age 24. Sergeant. Wounded slightly in action at battle of Fredericksburg, Dec. 1862. Missing in action at Chancellorsville, May 1, 1863. Returned to regiment at Culpeper, Va., Oct. 9, 1863. Mustered out at expiration of term June 29, 1864.

Veness, Albert W., Fulton, Ohio. Enlisted in Independent Company, Feb. 6, 1864, at Hillsdale, age 26. Blacksmith, married, father of a small child. On detached service with Co. F, 1st Michigan Infantry, July 2, 1864, Petersburg. Transferred to Co. K, reorganized 4th Infantry, June 6, 1865. Corporal May 1, 1866. Mustered out at Houston, May 26, 1866. Resided in Prattville, Hillsdale County, after service. Died in 1938; buried in Jefferson Township.

Veness, John W., Hillsdale. Enlisted in Independent Company, Feb. 24, 1864, at Hillsdale, age 18. On detached service with Co. F, 1st Michigan Infantry, July 2, 1864, Petersburg. Missing in action Aug. 21, 1864, at Weldon Railroad, Va., Taken prisoner; died of disease at Andersonville, Ga., Nov. 7, 1864.

Vessey or Vesey, James W., Sturgis. Enlisted in Company C as sergeant June 20, 1861, at Adrian, age 18. Printer apprentice by trade. Commissioned second lieutenant Nov. 18, 1862. Commanding Co. I, from July to Dec. 1863, and Feb. and March 1864. Died June 3, 1864, of massive wounds received hours earlier when hit by artillery at Bethesda Church, Va.

Villett, Charles, LaSalle, Monroe County. Enlisted in Company A, May 16, 1861, age 57. Postmaster and town clerk. Hospital nurse in Washington. Discharged for disability, March 21, 1863. Born in France.

Vreeland, Michael J. (*VV*), Brownstown. Enlisted in Company I as sergeant June 20, 1861, at Adrian, age 22. Farmer and cousin to William Vreeland and Marshall Chapin. First sergeant Jan. 13, 1862. Commissioned second lieutenant, Co. D, Sept. 1, 1862. Transferred to Co. I, Sept. 21, 1861. Commissioned first lieutenant Oct. 16, 1862. Commanding Co. I from Sept. 19, 1862, to April 1863. Wounded, shot in breast and hand while in action at Gettysburg, July 2, 1863. Mustered out at expiration of term at Detroit, June 30, 1864. Reentered service as captain, Co. D, reorganized 4th Michigan, Sept. 1864. Commissioned lieutenant colonel to date July 26, 1864. Mustered out and honorably discharged at Houston, May 26, 1866. Brevet colonel and brigadier general U.S. Volunteers March 13, 1865, for gallant and meritorious service during the war. Died in 1876 from the effects of his wounds and buried in Woodmere Cemetery, Detroit.

VREELAND, WILLIAM J., Brownstown. Enlisted in Company I, June 20, 1861, at Adrian, age 17. Farm boy, residing with his parents' family. Cousin of Michael Vreeland and Marshall Chapman. Discharged on disability, July 30, 1861, because of dislocated elbow. Reenlisted in reorganized 4th Michigan, Sept. 12, 1864. Mustered out July 2, 1865. Resided in Flat Rock after service. Died March 15, 1902, Detroit.

W

WADEMAN, CHARLES H., Branch County. Enlisted in Company C, June 20, 1861, at Adrian, age 18. Farm laborer. Mustered out at expiration of term at Detroit, June 30, 1864. Buried Fair Plains Cemetery, Grand Rapids.

WAGNER, LEVI, Monroe County. Enlisted in Company A, June 20, 1861, at Adrian, age 19. Discharged on account of disability Oct. 22, 1861, Minor's Hill, because of rheumatism. Reenlisted in Co. K, 18th Michigan Infantry, Aug. 11, 1862, at Monroe. Received a gunshot wound to right shoulder at Athens, Ga. Mustered out at Nashville, Tenn., June 26, 1865. Resided in Monroe after service.

WAIT, ALONZO, Oxford, Oakland County. Enlisted in Company I, June 20, 1861, at Adrian, age 19. Laborer. Wounded in action at Malvern Hill, July 1, 1862. Discharged at Washington, D.C., Jan. 12, 1863, for wounds.

WALKER, GEORGE A., Litchfield, Hillsdale County. Enlisted in Company E, Aug. 25, 1862, at Hillsdale, age 25. In hospital fall of 1862, returned to regiment Oct. 3, 1862. Missing in action at Gettysburg, July 2, 1863. Prisoner. Returned to Annapolis, Md., Dec. 10, 1863. Died of wounds received at Spotsylvania Court House, Va., May 1864. Originally buried at Hart's Farm, Spotsylvania; reburied Row E, Plot 491, National Cemetery, Fredericksburg.

WALKER, HINCKLEY, Lenawee County. Enlisted in Company F June 20, 1861, at Adrian, age 19. Discharged for disability, chronic rheumatism, at Washington, D.C., Aug. 19, 1861.

WALKER, SAMUEL G., Litchfield, Hillsdale County. Enlisted in Company H, as corporal, June 20, 1861, at Adrian, age 19. Farmer. Sergeant Jan. 1, 1862. Commissioned second lieutenant July 18, 1862. Wounded in action and captured at Gettysburg, July 2, 1863, shot through the arm and back; escaped. Transferred to Invalid Corps, Sept. 5, 1863. Mustered out at expiration of term at Detroit, June 30, 1864. Resided in Buffalo, N. Y. after service. Died Nov. 5, 1912 and buried Forest Lawn Cemetery, Buffalo.

WALKER, WARREN E., Ann Arbor. Enlisted in Company D, Aug. 12, 1862, age 20. Clerk in his father's hotel. Discharged for disability at Washington, D.C., Oct. 31, 1863. Became a wheelwright in the U.S. Army Quartermaster Department in 1864. Resided in Ann Arbor and graduated from the University of Michigan, became an attorney.

WALLACE, JOHN, Lyndon, Washtenaw County. Enlisted in Company I, Feb. 1, 1864, at Pittsford, Hillsdale County, age 19. Lived on parents' farm with family. On detached service with Co. I, 1st Michigan Infantry, July 2, 1864, Petersburg. Discharged at U.S. Hospital, York, Pa., May 19, 1865, gunshot wounds to the left forearm and right shoulder. Resided in Pittsford after service. Died in 1920 in Hillsdale.

WALLER, FRANCIS, Hillsdale County. Enlisted in Company E, June 20, 1861, at Adrian, age 20. Blacksmith. Wounded in action at Wilderness, Va., May 5, 1864, shot in the right shoulder. Mustered out at expiration of term at Detroit, June 28, 1864. Resided in Bay City.

WALSER, CHARLES, Washtenaw County. Enlisted in Company D, June 20, 1861, at Adrian, age 24. Musician. Discharged for disability Aug. 15, 1862. Enlisted as musician in Co. D, 1st Michigan Sharpshooters June 18, 1863, at Springport. Taken prisoner at Petersburg, Va., Oct. 27, 1864. Returned May 10, 1865. Discharged at Washington, D.C., June 29, 1865.

WALSH, JAMES, Cincinnati. Enlisted in Company H, March 6, 1863, at West China, age 20. Shoemaker. Substitute for Peter Robel, drafted from West China, St. Clair County. Deserted en route from Detroit to Washington, D.C. Born in Canada.

WALTER, EDWARD LORRAINE, Litchfield, Hillsdale County. Enlisted in Company H, June 20, 1861, at Adrian, age 16. Wheelwright apprentice living with his parents and siblings. Assigned to be a telegrapher during the war. Discharged for disability, chronic diarrhea, Feb. 20, 1863. Resided in Ann Arbor and entered the

University of Michigan as a student of the classics in 1864. Became assistant professor of Greek and Latin, and professor of modern languages and literature. Died on July 4, 1898, while aboard the ship *La Bourgogne* off the coast of Sable Island, Canada.

Walterhouse, Daniel Lewis, Livingston County. Enlisted in Company K, June 20, 1861, at Adrian, age 32. Farm laborer. Dropped from rolls July 21, 1863. No further record.

Walters, Abram, Hudson. Enlisted in Independent Company, Feb. 25, 1864, at Hudson, age 16. Resided with his parents and sibling. On detached service with Co. F, 1st Infantry, July 2, 1864, Petersburg. Transferred to Co. D, 12th Veteran Reserve Corps, Dec. 31, 1864. Discharged at Washington, D.C., Sept. 1, 1865.

Walters, Erastus (*VV*), Washtenaw County. Enlisted in Company G, June 20, 1861, at Adrian, age 19. Student. Reenlisted Dec. 29, 1863, as corporal. Severely wounded in action at Gettysburg, July 2, 1863. On detached service with Co. G, 1st Michigan Infantry, July 2, 1864, Petersburg. Discharged to date June 25, 1865. Resided in Rush Township, Shiawassee County, after service.

Walters, John, LaSalle, Monroe County. Enlisted in Company A, June 20, 1861, at Adrian, age 17. Lived with his widowed mother and siblings. Killed in action at Malvern Hill, July 1, 1862.

Ward, George T., Hillsdale County. Enlisted in Company E, June 20, 1861, at Adrian, age 18. Laborer. Wounded in action at Gettysburg, July 2, 1863. Again wounded in action at Wilderness, Va., May 5, 1864, shot in right thigh. Mustered out at expiration of term at Detroit, June 28, 1864. Buried at National Cemetery, Los Angeles.

Ward, Gilbert D., Camden, Hillsdale County. Enlisted in Company E, Aug. 30, 1862, at Hillsdale, age 41. Hospitalized sick early fall of 1862; returned to regiment Oct. 3, 1862. Severely wounded in action at Gettysburg, July 2, 1863, shot in thigh. Discharged for disability at York, Pa., Oct. 14, 1863. Resided in Camden Center after war. Admitted to the Soldiers Home, Dayton, July 1, 1890. Buried at Boyne City, Mich.

Ward, Joseph L., Ann Arbor. Enlisted in Company D, as corporal, June 20, 1861, at Adrian, age 35. Painter. Killed in action at Malvern Hill, July 1, 1862.

Waring, Joshua, Tecumseh. Enlisted in Company G, June 20, 1861, at Adrian, age 19. Died of disease at Fortress Monroe, Va., April 16, 1862.

Warne, Harvey, Lenawee County. Enlisted in Company B, Sept. 16, 1861. Taken prisoner at Gettysburg, July 2, 1863. Died of diarrhea, July 31, 1864, at Andersonville, Ga., Grave No. 4419.

Warner, George P., Wyandotte. Enlisted in Company F, June 20, 1861, at Adrian, age 20. Farmer residing with parents' family. Deserted at Washington, D.C., Aug. 3, 1861.

Warner, Harvey L. (*VV*), Franklin, Lenawee County. Enlisted in Company B, June 20, 1861, at Adrian, age 27. Farmer residing with parents and siblings. Taken prisoner Gaines' Mill, June 27, 1862. Returned to company Aug. 20, 1862. Corporal. Taken prisoner at Gettysburg, July 2, 1863. Rejoined regiment. Court-martial Oct. 1, 1863, for conduct prejudicial to good order, accused of straggling and thus being captured on the march near Kelly's Ford. Va.; he pleaded guilty, saying he was sick and unable to keep up. Sentenced to forfeit pay for the five months he was absent and to make up the time lost. Reenlisted Dec. 29, 1863. On detached service with Co. B, 1st Michigan Infantry, July 2, 1864, Petersburg. Wounded in action July 28, 1864, at Petersburg and died of wounds Aug. 22, 1864, Davids' Island, N.Y.

Warren, John, Hillsdale County. Enlisted in Company H as wagoner June 20, 1861, at Adrian, age 49. Carpenter, married and father of five. Discharged July 29, 1861, for disability after hurting his ankle and back while loading the train on which his regiment departed Adrian, June 24, 1861, for Washington, D.C.

Washburn, William, Camden, Hillsdale County. Enlisted in Company E, Aug. 30, 1862, at Hillsdale, age 39. Farmer, married. Had two brothers and two brothers-in-law serving in the Union army. Listed as sick July 7, 1863, and in a hospital, Philadelphia, for four weeks with ague and fever. Returned to regiment Oct. 3, 1862. On detached service with Co. K, 1st Michigan Infantry, July 2, 1864, Petersburg. Discharged near Washington, D.C., June 5, 1864. Resided in Hillsdale and died April 17, 1898. Buried Row 2, Plot 36, Bankers Cemetery, Hillsdale Township.

Waterman, Willis E. Enlisted in Company K, Oct. 22, 1863, at Putnam, Livingston County, age 16. Farm boy residing with grandparents. Killed in action at Wilderness, Va., May 5, 1864.

Watkins, William H., Bedford, Monroe County. Enlisted in Company A, June 20, 1861, at Adrian, age 20. Farm laborer. Killed in action at Fredericksburg, Va., Dec. 13, 1862.

WATSON, CLARKE, Ash, Monroe County. Enlisted in Company A, June 20, 1861, at Adrian, age 25. Laborer. Killed in action at Malvern Hill, July 1, 1862.

WATSON, GEORGE. Enlisted in Company H, substitute for David L. Godfrey, age 32, drafted from Elba, Lapeer County, Feb. 21, 1863. Age 21. Farmer. Deserted March 13, 1863, en route from Detroit to Washington, D.C.

WATSON, WILLIAM C., Carleton, Monroe County. Enlisted in Company A, June 20, 1861, at Adrian, age 25. Wounded and captured in action at Malvern Hill, July 1, 1862, with a gunshot in left hip joint that disabled him. Admitted Episcopal Hospital, Philadelphia, July 30, 1862. Transferred March 18, 1862, to Master Street Hospital, and again May 11, 1862, to South Street Hospital. Mustered out of service May 5, 1864, his left leg deformed. Resided in Ash Township after service. Died Jan. 8, 1914, and buried Grafton Cemetery, Carleton.

WATTS, JOHN S., Adrian. Entered service as second assistant surgeon of the regiment, July 25, 1862, age 44. Doctor, married and father of six. Commissioned assistant surgeon March 13, 1863. Mustered out at Detroit June 28, 1864. Died Jan. 15, 1889, Richmond, Ind.

WEATHERWAX, CHARLES H., Macomb County. Enlisted in Company I, June 20, 1861, at Adrian, age 21. Discharged at Sharpsburg, Md., Oct. 22, 1862. Transferred to 2nd U.S Infantry. Resided in Roulette, Pa., after service.

WEAVER, ORLANDO FORREST. Cambria, Hillsdale County. Enlisted in Company E, June 20, 1861, at Adrian, age 21. Farmer. Absent and sick, July and Aug. 1863. Discharged for disability, chronic nephritis, "kidney inflammation," at Convalescent Camp. Washington, D.C., Oct. 13, 1863. After service, went into wet plate photographic business with his brother in Chicago. Died in 1910 and buried in Oakwood Cemetery, Beaver Dam, Wis.

WEBSTER, ANDREW J., Pittsford, Hillsdale County. Enlisted in Independent Company, Feb. 6, 1864, at Hudson, age 48. Farmer, husband, and father of seven, including Edgar J. and Noah Webster. Became ill June 26, 1864, mustered out Aug. 4, 1864, on general discharge. Webster was reportedly killed in Dakota Territory while in mail service. Buried in plot 18, block A, Maple Grove Cemetery, Hudson.

WEBSTER, CHARLES H. Enlisted in Company I, July 22, 1862. Discharged at disability camp, March 1, 1863. Resided in Detroit after service. Died Oct. 10, 1900, at the Soldiers Home, Dayton.

WEBSTER, DAVID, Washtenaw County. Enlisted in Company D, Sept. 23, 1861, at Ann Arbor, age 25. Married, father of a young son. Taken prisoner at Gettysburg, July 2, 1863, where he was slightly wounded. On detached service with Co. E, 1st Michigan Infantry, July 2, 1864, Petersburg. Discharged at expiration of term at Detroit, Jan. 5, 1865. Resided in Detroit.

WEBSTER, EDGAR, Pittsford, Hillsdale County. Enlisted in Independent Company, March 2, 1864, at Hudson, age 16. Farm laborer. Son of Andrew J. Webster. Wounded in action June 3, 1864, at Old Church, Va., flesh wounds in both legs. On detached service with Co. F, 1st Michigan Infantry, July 2, 1864, Petersburg. Wounded in action a second time and in a hospital at Washington, D.C., but no further record. Became a lawyer after service and resided in Spokane, Wash.

WEBSTER, EDWIN (*VV*), Monroe County. Enlisted in Company G, Sept. 19, 1861, at Hudson. Wounded and missing in action at Gaines' Mill, Va., June 27, 1862. Reenlisted Dec. 29, 1863. On detached service with Co. G, 1st Michigan Infantry, July 2, 1864, Petersburg. Transferred to Co. C, reorganized 4th Michigan, July 1, 1865. Corporal Nov. 1, 1865. Mustered out at San Antonio, Feb. 26, 1866. Died in 1869 and buried Azalia Cemetery, Azalia, Monroe County.

WEBSTER, LOREN, Milan, Monroe County. Enlisted in Company G, June 20, 1861, at Adrian, age 22. Sawmill employee. Killed in action near Spotsylvania Court House, Va., May 11, 1864.

WEBSTER, NOAH, Pittsford, Hillsdale County. Enlisted in Company F, Sept. 10, 1861, at Hudson, age 19. Farmer, son of Andrew Webster and brother of Edgar Webster. On detached service with Co. C, 1st Michigan Infantry, July 2, 1864, Petersburg. Discharged at expiration of term near Weldon Railroad, Va., Sept. 11, 1864. Resided in Berkeley, Calif., after service. Died July 1, 1931, in Oakland, Calif.

WEEKS, ROBERT, Wayne County. Enlisted in Company I, June 20, 1861, at Adrian, age 27. On detached duty gunboat service, Jan. 1862, on the *Carondelet*. Transferred Nov. 21, 1863. Saw action at Forts Henry and Donelson Feb. 6, 1862, and Island 10, April 1862. Mustered out at Detroit, June 30, 1864.

WEIR, ARCHIBALD, Hillsdale County. Enlisted in Company E, June 20, 1861, at Adrian, age 23. Shoemaker, brother of Thomas and Andrew Weir of the reorganized 4th Michigan. Detached to ambulance corps for term of service. Mustered out at expiration of term at Detroit, June 28, 1864. Resided in Jackson County, Ind., and Moscow, Hillsdale County. Died in 1921 and buried in Blackmark Cemetery, Moscow Township. Born in Scotland.

WEISS, VALENTINE, Monroe. Enlisted in Company A, Aug. 28, 1862, at Monroe, age 38. On detached service with Co. A, 1st Michigan Infantry, July 2, 1864, Petersburg. Discharged near Washington, D.C., June 9, 1865. Died on Nov. 24, 1884, and buried in St. Joseph Cemetery, Monroe.

WELLS, CHARLES, Wayne County. Enlisted in Company A, June 20, 1861, at Adrian, age 21. Died in New York, Aug. 27, 1862, of wounds received in action at Malvern Hill, July 1, 1862. Buried July 13, 1862, Military Asylum Cemetery, Washington, D.C.

WELLS, HENRY SPENCER, Wheatland, Hillsdale County. Enlisted in Company K, 17th New York Infantry, July 1, 1861, age 16. Store and post office clerk in Knowlesville, N.Y. Captured at Bull Run, Va., July 21, 1861. Held at Richmond, New Orleans, and Salisbury, N.C. from Sept. 21, 1861, to May 1862. Mustered out in Elmira, N.Y., on May 31, 1863. Enlisted in Independent Company, 4th Michigan Infantry, Feb. 3, 1864, at Hillsdale, age 18. Sergeant April 5, 1864. Wounded in action late May 1864. On detached service with Co. F, 1st Michigan Infantry, July 2, 1864, Petersburg. Transferred to Co. K, reorganized 4th Michigan, June 6, 1865. Wounded in action Sept. 30, 1864, at Peeble's Farm, Va., shot in left hip. Discharged at Washington, D.C., June 8, 1865. Enrolled in Hillsdale College, Feb. 13, 1864, and later resided in Bushnell, Ill. Died Dec. 10, 1916, and buried in Quincy, Ill.

WELLS, JAMES H. (*VV*), Lenawee County. Enlisted in Company B, June 20, 1861, at Adrian, age 19. Reenlisted Feb. 15, 1864. On detached service with Co. B, 1st Michigan Infantry, July 2, 1864, Petersburg. Transferred to Co. C, reorganized 4th Michigan, July 1, 1865. Corporal Nov. 1, 1865. Mustered out at San Antonio, Feb. 26, 1866. Resided in Petoskey after service. Buried Greenwood Cemetery, Petoskey.

WELCH, JAMES. Enlisted in Company H, March 6, 1863, at Ft. Wayne, Detroit, age 20. Sailor. Deserted March 13, 1863, en route from Detroit to Washington, D.C. Born in Ireland.

WEST, REUBEN H. (*VV*), Lenawee County. Enlisted in Company B, Sept. 6, 1861, at Hudson, age 20. Farmer. Reenlisted Dec. 29, 1863. On detached service with Co. B, 1st Michigan Infantry, July 2, 1864, Petersburg. Transferred to Co. C, reorganized 4th Michigan, July 1, 1865. Received two gunshot wounds, one in left hand. Discharged at Detroit, Aug. 8, 1865. Died June 20, 1901, and buried in Kalkaska.

WESTFALL, BENJAMIN, Hudson. Enlisted in Company F as corporal June 20, 1861, at Adrian, age 22. Butcher, brother of Charles Westfall. First sergeant Aug. 1861. Commissioned second lieutenant March 7, 1863. Wounded in action at Gettysburg, July 2, 1863, shot in right hand. Commanding company from Aug. 1863 to April 1864. Wounded in action again at Petersburg, shot in knee, June 19, 1864. Mustered out at expiration of term of service at Detroit, June 29, 1864. Reenlisted in Co. G, 30th Michigan Infantry, Jan. 9, 1865; mustered out June 30, 1865. Resided in Hudson, a carpenter and justice of the peace. Drowned July 20, 1925. Buried Plot 44, Block G, Maple Grove Cemetery, Hudson.

WESTFALL, CHARLES J., Hudson. Enlisted in Company F, Aug. 16, 1862, at Hudson, age 21. Farmer and brother of Benjamin Westfall. Wounded in action at Gettysburg, July 2, 1863, shot in right arm and elbow. In hospital, Germantown, Pa. On detached service with Co. C, 1st Michigan Infantry, July 2, 1864, Petersburg. Discharged near Washington, D.C., June 6, 1865.

WESTGATE, ALBERT, Adrian. Enlisted in Company G, June 20, 1861, at Adrian, age 21. Farm laborer. Killed in action at Malvern Hill, Va., July 1, 1862.

WHEATON, ANDREW SCOTT, Steuben, Ind. Enlisted in Company B, June 20, 1861, at Adrian, age 22. Mason. In hospital at Harrison's Landing with typhoid fever and diarrhea; admitted to a hospital in Maryland. Wounded in action at Gettysburg, July 2, 1863, shot in leg below the knee. Mustered out at expiration of term June 30, 1864. Resided in Angola, then Wayne, Neb., after service.

WHEELER, CHARLES D., Medina. Lenawee County. Enlisted in Company F, Feb. 28, 1862, at Hudson. Farmer. Wounded in leg near Spotsylvania Court House, Va., May 1864.

Wheeler, Chester G., Lenawee County. Enlisted in Company F, June 20, 1861, at Adrian, age 28. Discharged Aug. 3, 1861. Died of disease at Georgetown, Sept. 3, 1861. Buried in Old Protestant Cemetery, Hudson, but his headstone is at Maple Grove Cemetery, Hudson.

Wheeler, Edmond H., Hudson. Enlisted in Company F, June 20, 1861, at Adrian, age 20. Farmer. Died of disease, typhoid fever, at Georgetown, Sept. 3, 1861, and buried in the Military Asylum Cemetery, Washington, D.C.

Wheeler, Frank (*VV*), Tecumseh. Enlisted in Company G, June 20, 1861, at Adrian, age 21. Farmer. Reenlisted Dec. 29, 1863. On detached service with Co. G, 1st Michigan Infantry, July 2, 1864, Petersburg. Transferred to Co. C, reorganized 4th Michigan, July 1, 1865. Sergeant. Commissioned second lieutenant July 1, 1865. Mustered out at San Antonio, Feb. 26, 1866.

Wheeler, John, Macomb County. Enlisted in Company I, June 20, 1861, at Adrian, age 21. Wounded and missing at Gaines' Mill, June 27, 1862, shot in the left hand. Discharged at Alexandria, Va., Oct. 11, 1862, on account of wound. Died 1910. Buried in Flushing, Genesee County.

Wheelock, John F., Dexter. Enlisted in Company K, June 20, 1861, at Adrian, age 30. Blacksmith, married father of three small children. Wounded and missing at Gaines' Mill, June 27, 1862. Mustered out at expiration of term at Detroit, June 28, 1864. Resided in Chelsea after service. Buried in Lima Center Cemetery, Washtenaw County.

Whelan, Edwin M., Lenawee County. Enlisted in Company G, June 20, 1861, at Adrian, age 21. Taken prisoner at battle of Gettysburg, July 2, 1863. Mustered out at expiration of term, June 30, 1864.

Whipple, George, Monroe. Enlisted in Company A, May 15, 1861. Clerk, residing with parents and brothers. Corporal May 4, 1863. Taken prisoner at Gettysburg, July 2, 1863. Died at Andersonville, Ga., April 25, 1864.

Whipple, George M., Flat Rock. Enlisted in Company A, Sept. 17, 1861, at Hudson, age 23. Farmer. Corporal. Taken prisoner at Gettysburg, July 2, 1863. Returned to regiment. Died of disease at Alexandria, Va., April 15, 1864.

Whipple, John C., Monroe. Enlisted in Company A, May 20, 1861, as a wagoner, age 22. Sergeant. Wounded by gunshot, left temple, at Gaines' Mill, Va., June 27, 1862. Promoted Aug. 1862 to second lieutenant in 18th Michigan Infantry. Employed as a store clerk after service and resided in Alpena. Died from the effects of his war wound in Sept. 1893.

White, Charles P., Litchfield, Hillsdale County. Enlisted in Company H, June 20, 1861, at Adrian, age 22. Cooper. Discharged for disability at Minor's Hill, Va., Nov. 21, 1862. Reentered service in Co. F, 7th Michigan Cavalry, enlisted as corporal Dec. 22, 1862. Taken prisoner at Funkstown, Md., July 6, 1863. Held at Belle Isle, Andersonville, Savannah, and Milan prisons for 505 days. Sergeant April 30, 1865. Honorably discharged at Ft. Leavenworth, Kans., Nov. 21, 1865. Resided in Litchfield. Died in 1911 and buried Sand Creek Cemetery, Litchfield.

White, John Baldridge, Monroe County. Enlisted in band as principal musician, June 20, 1861, at Adrian, age 48. Farmer, father of eight, including Johnson White. Suffered from sunstroke near Meridian Hill on July 1, 1861. Mustered out at Harrison's Landing, Va., Aug. 10, 1862. Died on Nov. 15, 1892, at University Park, Ore.

White, Johnson, Lenawee County. Enlisted in Company B, June 20, 1861, at Adrian, age 19. Farmer, son of John White. Hospitalized with illness from Sept. 1862 until June 1864 at Meridian Hill and Camp Distribution near Alexandria, Va. His father claimed his sickness was from a poisoned pie he'd bought from a woman in July 1861. Transferred to Veteran Reserve Corps, March 16, 1864. Resided in Oakville, Ore., after service. Died on Dec. 14, 1914, in Wasco County, Ore. Buried in Multnomah County, Ore.

White, Newell, Lenawee County. Enlisted in Company B, June 20, 1861, at Adrian, age 21. Sickened after the crossing at Shepherdstown Ford, Md., on Sept. 19, 1862, and sent to regimental field hospital, then to a hospital in Philadelphia; to Convalescent Camp in Alexandria, Va., on April 10, 1863. Discharged at Washington, D.C., for disability, April 24, 1863. Resided in Oakville, Oregon, and Macon counties, Missouri, after service. Died on June 19, 1885, in Macon County, killed by lightning after reportedly having survived a previous lightning strike.

White, Walter C., Hudson. Enlisted in Company A, Sept. 17, 1861, at Hudson, age 26. Carpenter residing with his parents. Killed in action at Fredericksburg, Va., Dec. 13, 1862, shot in the head.

Whitmore, Fontelle D. Enlisted in Independent Company, Feb. 27, 1864, at Rollin, Lenawee County, age

40. Wounded in action June 3, 1864. On detached service with Co. F, 1st Michigan Infantry, July 2, 1864, Petersburg. No further record.

WHITMORE, JOHN M., Allen, Hillsdale County. Enlisted in Company E, June 20, 1861, at Adrian, age 24. Day laborer, married, father of a young child. Deserted June 20, 1862.

WHITMORE, LEWIS F., Washtenaw County. Enlisted in Company D, June 20, 1861, at Adrian, age 24. Corporal. Killed in action at Gettysburg, July 2, 1863.

WHITMORE, PETER D., Rollin, Lenawee County. Enlisted in Independent Company, Feb. 22, 1864, at Hillsdale, age 21. Farm laborer. On detached service with Co. F, 1st Michigan Infantry, July 2, 1864, Petersburg. Transferred to Co. K, reorganized 4th Michigan, June 6, 1865. Mustered out at U.S. Hospital at Chester, Pa., June 14, 1865. Resided in Allen after service. Died May 1885. Buried in Allen Cemetery, Hillsdale.

WHITNEY, CHAUNCEY B., Onondaga, Ingham County. Enlisted in Independent Company, Feb. 29, 1864, at Rollin, age 54. Miller, grandfather of Jason Whitney. On detached service with Co. F, 1st Michigan Infantry, July 2, 1864, Petersburg. Transferred to Co. K, reorganized 4th Michigan, June 6, 1865. Resided in Sumner, Gratiot County.

WHITNEY, JASON B., Onondaga, Ingham County. Enlisted in Independent Company, Feb. 27, 1864, at Rollin, Lenawee County, age 22. Grandson of Chauncey Whitney. On detached service with Co. F, 1st Michigan July 2, 1864, Petersburg. Transferred to Co. K, reorganized 4th Michigan June 6, 1865. Corporal May 1, 1865. Discharged at Houston, May 26, 1866.

WHITTEN, SETH, Hillsdale. Enlisted in Independent Company, Feb. 25, 1864, at Hudson, age 17. Farm boy living with parents. On detached service with Company F, 1st Michigan Infantry, July 2, 1864, Petersburg. Transferred to Co. K, reorganized 4th Michigan, June 6, 1865. Discharged to date July 3, 1865.

WHITTLESY, THOMAS B., St. Joseph County. Enlisted in Company C, as musician bugler, June 20, 1861, at Adrian, age 20. Wounded in the hip. Mustered out at expiration of term at Detroit, June 29, 1864. Resided in Omaha, Neb., after service. Died in 1904.

WILBER, ALBERT M., Hillsdale County. Enlisted in Company E, June 20, 1861, at Adrian, age 24. Wounded in leg at Shepherdstown Ford, Sept. 19, 1862. Discharged for disability at Frederick, Md., Dec. 2, 1862. Resided in Brady, Ohio, after service.

WILCOX, CALVIN, Livingston County. Enlisted in Company K as corporal June 20, 1861, at Adrian, age 21. Farmer residing with parents. Discharged for disability at Washington, D.C., Sept. 20, 1861, for chronic diarrhea and rheumatism. Resided in Howell after service. Buried Lakeview Cemetery, Howell.

WILCOX, CHARLES W., Wheatland, Hillsdale County. Enlisted in Company F, June 20, 1861, at Adrian, age 21. Deserted at Ft. Woodbury while on picket duty, Sept. 8, 1861. Buried Maple Grove Cemetery, Hudson.

WILCOX, HARRISON, Lenawee County. Enlisted in Company F, as first sergeant, June 20, 1861, age 21. Deserted at Ft. Woodbury while on picket duty, Sept. 8, 1861. Died on Dec. 13, 1915 at Milan, Monroe County.

WILDER, WILLIAM, Hillsdale County. Enlisted in Company H, June 20, 1861, at Adrian, age 22. Dougherty man (stagecoach driver). Discharged for disability chronic diarrhea at Washington, D.C., July 29, 1861.

WILDT, FRED R., Ann Arbor. Enlisted in Company D, June 20, 1861, at Adrian, age 19. Resided on parents' farm. Killed in action at Fredericksburg, Va., Dec. 13, 1862. Originally buried at Genther's Lot, Fredericksburg; reburied Row AA, Plot 2863, Fredericksburg National Cemetery.

WILEY, JAMES W., Lenawee County. Enlisted in Company B, June 20, 1861, at Adrian, age 24. Died of disease at Union Hotel, Georgetown, Sept. 6, 1861. Buried Military Asylum Cemetery, Washington, D.C.

WILKINSON, JOHN, Taylor, Wayne County. Enlisted in Company I, June 20, 1861, at Adrian, age 43. Laborer. Discharged for disability, April 15, 1863. Born in England.

WILLIAMS, EDWIN K., Washtenaw County. Enlisted in Company D, June 20, 1861, at Adrian, age 19. Resided with parents on family farm. Killed in action at Gaines' Mill, June 27, 1862. Buried Lima Center Cemetery, Washtenaw County.

WILLIAMS, EDWIN W. (*VV*), Woodstock, Lenawee County. Enlisted in Company F, June 20, 1861, at Adrian, age 17. Shoemaker residing with parents. On detached duty with ambulance corps. Reenlisted Feb. 21, 1864. Wounded in action at Wilderness, Va., May 5, 1864. On detached service with Co. C, 1st Michigan Infantry,

July 2, 1864, Petersburg. Transferred to Co. C, reorganized 4th Michigan, July 1, 1865. Discharged at San Antonio, Feb. 5, 1866. Resided in Big Rapids.

WILLIAMS, GEORGE, Branch County. Enlisted in Company C, June 20, 1861, at Adrian, age 18. Died of disease at Philadelphia, Aug. 10, 1862. Buried in National Cemetery at Philadelphia, Grave No. 82.

WILLIAMS, GEORGE (*VV*), Lenawee County. Enlisted in Company B, June 20, 1861, at Adrian, age 22. Taken prisoner at Gettysburg, July 2, 1863. Returned to regiment at Culpeper, Va., Oct. 6, 1863. Reenlisted Feb. 18, 1864. Wounded in action May 5, 1864, gunshot through right arm and shoulder. On detached service with Co. B, 1st Michigan, July 2, 1864. Transferred to Co. C, reorganized 4th Michigan, July 1, 1865. Mustered out at San Antonio, Feb. 26, 1866. Died May 5, 1923, at Attica, Lapeer County.

WILLIAMS, HARMON HARRISON G., Lenawee County. Enlisted in Company B as sergeant June 20, 1861, at Adrian, age 24. Laborer, married with a young daughter. Deserted at Minor's Hill, Va., Dec. 1, 1861.

WILLIAMS, IRA (*VV*), Hillsdale County. Enlisted in Company E, as corporal, June 20, 1861, at Adrian, age 21. Discharged for disability at Washington, D.C., Dec. 26, 1862. Reentered service in Co. K, 6th Michigan Infantry, Dec. 16, 1863, at Hudson. Died at Ft. Morgan, Ala., Oct. 17, 1864.

WILLIAMS, JULES L., Hillsdale County. Enlisted in Company H, June 20, 1861, at Adrian, age 20. Student. Discharged for disability at Minor's Hill, Va., Jan. 2, 1862. Born in Wales.

WILLIS, A. Sidney, Hillsdale County. Enlisted in Company H, as corporal, June 20, 1861, at Adrian, age 18. Resided with parents on family farm. Sergeant. Missing in action, captured, Gettysburg, July 2, 1863, but escaped during the night. Transferred to Invalid Corps at Beverly Ford, Va., Sept. 15, 1863.

WILSAY, SOLOMON, Webster, Washtenaw County. Enlisted in Company K, June 20, 1861, at Adrian, age 32. Machinist, married and father two young children. Discharged for disability at Philadelphia, July 15, 1862.

WILSEY, HENRY, Lenawee County. Enlisted in Company I, Sept. 6, 1861. Farmer. Brother of Jeremiah Wilsey. Taken prisoner at Gettysburg, July 2, 1863. Died Jan. 29, 1864, while a prisoner in Richmond.

WILSEY, JEREMIAH, Lenawee County. Enlisted in Company I, Sept. 16, 1861. Farmer, brother of Henry Wilsey. Wounded in the Peninsula Campaign, summer 1862. Taken prisoner at Gettysburg, July 2, 1863. Held at Belle Isle, Richmond, Va., and Andersonville, Ga., until March 31, 1865. Sent to Vicksburg, Miss., after his release and then to Jefferson Barracks, Mo., and Benton Barracks. Furloughed for 30 days, reporting to Camp Chase, Ohio, June 2, 1865. Discharged at expiration of term at Detroit, June 1865. Resided in Addison village, Lenawee County, after service. Died on May 31, 1928, in Jackson.

WILSON, CHARLES, Litchfield, Hillsdale County. Enlisted in Company H, June 20, 1861, at Adrian, age 19. Lived on family farm with parents. Died at First Division Hospital (Fifth Corps), July 5, 1863, of wounds received in action at Gettysburg on July 2. Buried Gettysburg National Cemetery, Michigan Plot, E-15.

WILSON, DAVID A., Washtenaw County. Enlisted in Company D, June 20, 1861, at Adrian, age 20. Discharged for disability at Ft. Woodbury, Sept. 7, 1861.

WILSON, HENRY H., Washtenaw County. Enlisted in Company D, June 20, 1861, at Adrian, age 29. Farmer and mason. Discharged for disability, heart disease, at Minor's Hill, Va., Jan. 13, 1862. Resided in Webster Township after service.

WINN, JAMES, Lenawee County. Enlisted in Company G, Oct. 3, 1861, at Hudson, age 16. Resided with parents. Wounded slightly in action at battle of Fredericksburg, Dec. 13, 1862. On detached service with ambulance corps, Fifth Corps, from Nov. 1863 to April 1864. On detached service with Company G, 1st Michigan Infantry, July 2, 1864, Petersburg. Discharged at expiration of term at Petersburg Oct. 6, 1864.

WINTERS, CHRISTOPHER D., Enlisted in Company E, June 20, 1861, at Adrian, age 24. Discharged on account of sickness. No further record.

WIRTS, STILES H., Lenawee County. Enlisted in Company F, June 20, 1861, at Adrian, age 18. Taken prisoner at Falls Church, Va., Aug. 10, 1861. Captured while on picket with James Tuttle. Held at Richmond, Va., and at Castle Pinckney, Charleston, S.C.; transferred to Columbia, S.C., Jan. 1, 1862, with others. Escaped and recaptured at Winnsboro, Tenn. Sent to Libby Prison, Richmond, until paroled on May 20, 1862. Discharged at Washington, D.C., May 21, 1862.

WISDOM, ALBERT S., Brownstown. Enlisted in Company I, June 20, 1861, at Adrian, age 19. Farmer residing on parents' farm. Reported to have been taken prisoner at Chancellorsville, May 2, 1863.

WISHART, WILLIAM M. (*VV*), Tecumseh. Enlisted in Company G, Sept. 16, 1861, at Hudson, age 15. Farm boy, resided with parents. Wounded slightly in action at Fredericksburg, Va., 1862, shot in right leg. Reenlisted Feb. 21, 1864. On detached service with Co. G, 1st Michigan Infantry, July 2, 1864, Petersburg. Sergeant Sept. 10, 1864. Resided in New Windsor, Md.

WISNER, JEHIEL, Lenawee County. Enlisted in Company B, Sept. 16, 1861, age 41. Farmer, married, father of six. Discharged for disability May 25, 1862.

WOOD, ABRAM R., Sturgis. Entered service in Company C at organization, as captain, June 20, 1861, age 34. Carpenter, married, father of one child. Mistakenly shot and killed by one of his own men, Luke Barnes, while on picket at Yorktown, Va., April 18, 1862.

WOOD, DAN A., Richmond. Enlisted in Independent Company, March 31, 1864, at Hudson, age 49. Stonemason. On detached service with Co. F, 1st Michigan Infantry, July 1, 1864, Petersburg, Va. Discharged at Alexandria, May 4, 1865. Resided in Hudson after service.

WOOD, JAMES T., Lenawee County. Enlisted in Company H, June 20, 1861, at Adrian, age 25. Farmer on parents' farm. Admitted to the hospital from Harrison's Landing, Va., Aug. 10, 1862, for diarrhea. Died of disease, chronic diarrhea, at Philadelphia, Aug. 25, 1862. Buried in National Cemetery, Philadelphia, Grave No. 340.

WOOD, OSCAR, Bruce, Macomb County. Enlisted, unassigned to company, Feb. 19, 1864, at Hudson, age 23. Farm laborer residing with parents. No further record.

WOODBURY, DWIGHT A., Adrian. Commissioned colonel of the regiment May 16, 1861, at Adrian, age 36. Hotel keeper, colonel of local militia battalion, married, father of a seven-year-old daughter. Killed in action at Malvern Hill, July 1, 1862, shot in the head. Buried on the battlefield initially, his body was retrieved after war. Buried section B-9, Plot 44, Oakwood Cemetery, Adrian.

WOODFIELD, NATHANIEL. Enlisted in Company B, June 20, 1861, at Adrian, age 35. Laborer. Admitted to hospital Oct. 13, 1861, at Ft. Woodbury, Va. Discharged because of tuberculosis on Oct. 29, 1861. Reenlisted in Battery H, 1st Michigan Light Artillery, "DeGolyer's Battery," Dec. 12, 1861, at Tecumseh. Reenlisted Jan. 1, 1864, at Big Black, Miss. Mustered out at Jackson, Mich., July 22, 1865. Born in England.

WOODS, WILLIAM, Trenton. Enlisted in Company I, June 20, 1861, at Adrian, age 57. Farmer, married father of four. Corporal. Discharged for disability at Georgetown, April 24, 1862.

WOODWARD, EDWARD (*VV*), Monroe. Enlisted in Company A, June 20, 1861, at Adrian, age 20. Molder, married. Wounded in action, left wrist, during Seven Days battles 1862. Taken prisoner at Chancellorsville, Va., May 4, 1863, and held at Libby Prison, Richmond. Returned to duty Oct. 26, 1863. Reenlisted Jan. 20, 1864. On detached service with Co. A, 1st Michigan Infantry, July 2, 1864, Petersburg, Va. Transferred to Co. C, reorganized 4th Michigan, July 1, 1865. Resided in Monroe.

WOODWARD, HARLOW W. Enlisted in Company F, June 20, 1861, at Adrian, age 18, but quickly discharged by order of mustering officer at Adrian for disability.

WORDEN, DAVID, Reading, Hillsdale County. Enlisted in Company E, June 20, 1861, at Adrian, age 30. Brother of Freeman Worden. Died of disease at Yorktown, Va., April 21, 1862.

WORDEN, FREEMAN P., St. Joseph County. Enlisted in Company C, June 20, 1861, at Adrian, age 29. Farm laborer, brother of David Worden. Corporal. Killed in action at Gettysburg, July 2, 1863, and buried near the Rose Barn. Reburied Gettysburg National Cemetery, Michigan Plot, A-12.

WORDEN, HERMAN B., Lenawee County. Enlisted in Company C, May 16, 1861, age 19. Farm laborer at parents' home and farm. Wounded in action May 5, 1864. Mustered out at expiration of term at Detroit, June 30, 1864.

WORDEN, WILLIAM M., Cambria, Hillsdale County. Enlisted in Company E, June 20, 1861, at Adrian, age 45. Farmer, husband and father of three children. Died of disease at Camp Convalescent, Alexandria, Va., March 2, 1863.

WORDIN, IRA (*VV*), Somerset, Hillsdale County. Enlisted in Company H, Sept. 16, 1861, at Hudson, age 17. Farmer residing with parents. Reenlisted Dec. 29, 1863. Killed in action near Bethesda Church, Va., June 3, 1864. Buried National Cemetery, Section B, No. 51, Seven Pines, Va.

WRIGHT, JAMES H. (*VV*), Calhoun County. Enlisted in Company D, June 20, 1861, at Adrian, age 22. Reenlisted Dec. 29, 1863. On detached service with Co. E, 1st Michigan Infantry, July 2, 1864, Petersburg, Va. Transferred to Co. K, reorganized 4th Michigan, June 6, 1865. Mustered out at San Antonio, Feb. 23, 1866. Resided in Hudson after service.

WRIGHT, LAWRENCE C., Hillsdale County. Enlisted in Company E, June 20, 1861, at Adrian, age 18. Discharged Nov. 3, 1862. Reenlisted in 2nd Maryland Cavalry for six months. Reenlisted 3rd Maryland Cavalry. Mustered out July 1865. Resided in Quincy, Branch County.

WRIGHT, SAMUEL F., Lenawee County. Enlisted in Company G, June 20, 1861, at Adrian, age 26. Discharged for disability at Washington, D.C., Aug. 5, 1861.

WRIGHT, WALTER W., Hillsdale County. Enlisted in Company E, June 20, 1861, at Adrian, age 19. Wounded in action at Malvern Hill, July 1, 1862, shot in right thigh, and captured. Returned to regiment Nov. 8, 1862. Discharged for disability at Warrenton, Va., Nov. 18, 1862. Resided in Hudson, a bricklayer and mason. Buried Maple Grove Cemetery, Hudson.

WRIGHT, WILLIAM D., Blissfield, Lenawee County. Enlisted in Company B, June 20, 1861, at Adrian, age 25. Killed in action at the Wilderness, Va., May 5, 1864.

WYANT, JOHN W., Burr Oak, St. Joseph County. Enlisted in Company C, June 20, 1861, at Adrian, age 18. Killed in action at Chancellorsville, May 4, 1863.

Y

YATES, GEORGE W. M., Detroit. Enlisted in Company A, June 20, 1861, at Adrian, age 18. Clerk residing with his widowed mother. Regimental quartermaster sergeant Feb. 29, 1862. Commissioned first lieutenant and adjutant Sept. 26, 1862. Detailed on staff of Col. Sweitzer, commanding brigade, from Nov. 10, 1862, to March 1863, as acting assistant adjutant general. Wounded Dec. 13, 1862, Fredericksburg, Va., when a shell struck and exploded in his horse. On staff of Col. McQuade from March to June 1863. On staff of Gen. Pleasanton from June 1863 to April 1864. Mustered out at expiration of term at Detroit, June 29, 1864. Appointed captain 13th Missouri Cavalry. Remained on Pleasanton's staff, mustering out Jan. 11, 1866. Second lieutenant in 2nd U.S. Cavalry, May 5, 1866. Transferred and promoted captain 7th U.S. Cavalry, Aug. 19, 1867. Died June 25, 1876, at the Little Big Horn. Initially buried on the battlefield, reburied at Ft. Leavenworth, Kans.

YATES, JOHN C., Hillsdale. Enlisted in Independent Company, Feb. 20, 1864, at Hillsdale, age 32. Farmer, resided with his mother. On detached service with Co. F, 1st Michigan Infantry, July 2, 1864, Petersburg. Transferred to Co. K, reorganized 4th Michigan, June 6, 1865. Discharged to date Feb. 16, 1866.

YAWGER, CHESTER S., North Adams, Hillsdale County. Enlisted in Company H, June 20, 1861, at Adrian, age 19. Farmer. Recruiting officer in Michigan, Nov. 1861. Rejoined regiment at Yorktown, Va., April 1862. Taken prisoner at Gettysburg, July 2, 1863. Held a prisoner for 17 months, 15 days, at Belle Isle, Va., Andersonville, Ga., Savannah, Ga., and others. Discharged at Detroit, Jan. 4, 1865. Brother of Francis Yawger; another brother in the 11th Michigan Cavalry died in the war. A businessman after service, resided in Jerome, Hillsdale County. Died Dec. 20, 1890. Buried in plot 254M, North Lawn Cemetery, North Adams.

YAWGER, FRANCIS, North Adams. Enlisted in Company H, June 20, 1861, at Adrian, age 20. Farmer residing with his parents. Brother of Chester Yawger. Died of typhoid fever at Minor's Hill, Va., Nov. 16, 1862. Buried plot 224N, North Lawn Cemetery, North Adams, Hillsdale County.

YEARNCE, William H., Scio, Washtenaw County. Enlisted in Company K, June 20, 1861, at Adrian, age 21. Harness maker. No further record.

YOUNG, GEORGE A. (*VV*), Lenawee County. Enlisted in Company I, June 20, 1861, at Adrian, age 27. Farmer. Reenlisted Dec. 29, 1863. Accidentally drowned in Michigan, April 25, 1864, while on furlough. Born in England.

YOUNG, GEORGE E., Steuben, Ind. Enlisted in Company B, at Adrian, age 21. Farmer. Wounded in action at New Bridge, Va., May 24, 1862, shot in right arm and shoulder. Corporal. Taken prisoner at Gettysburg, July 2, 1863. Held Belle Isle, Va.; in hospital in Aug. 1863 with camp diarrhea. Formally exchanged Oct. 26, 1863. Commissioned as assistant provost marshal till end of service. Mustered out at expiration of term at Detroit, June 30, 1864. Reenlisted as adjutant of the 152nd Indiana Infantry. Died Nov. 19, 1905, at Angola.

YOUNG, LAFAYETTE, Litchfield, Hillsdale County. Enlisted in Company H, June 20, 1861, at Adrian, age 17. Lived with parents on their farm. Corporal Jan. 1, 1862. Discharged for disability at Washington, D.C., Sept. 18, 1862, for a wound received in action previously. Enlisted as first sergeant in Second Company Sharpshooters, 27th Michigan Infantry, Feb. 15, 1864, at Hillsdale. Died Aug. 14, 1864, at Litchfield of wounds received in action at Wilderness, Va., May 6, 1864. Buried Mt. Hope Cemetery, Litchfield.

YOUNG, WILLIAM, Ann Arbor. Enlisted in Company D, Sept. 12, 1862, at Ann Arbor, age 40. On detached service with Co. E, 1st Michigan, July 2, 1864, Petersburg, Va. Discharged July 8, 1865. Became photographer in Dexter and Plymouth after service.

YOUNGHAUSE, CHARLES. Enlisted in band, June 20, 1861, at Adrian, age 38. Professional musician, married, father of two small children. Mustered out Aug. 10, 1862, per War Department. Born in Saxony, Germany.

YOUNGS, HENRY L. Enlisted in Company I, June 20, 1861, at Adrian, age 18. Discharged for disability July 22, 1861.

YOUNGS, JEROME B., Branch County. Enlisted in Company C, June 20, 1861, at Adrian, age 22. Transferred to Invalid Corps, Jan. 15, 1864.

Z

ZIMMERMAN, DIONIS, Ann Arbor. Enlisted in Company D, June 20, 1861, at Adrian, age 24. Listed as killed in action Gettysburg, July 2, 1863, shot in head. However, other records indicate he was critically wounded in action and died in the First Division hospital, July 9, 1863. Buried Gettysburg National Cemetery, Michigan Plot, E-7.

Notes

After a full first reference in the endnotes, abbreviations are used for the names of the following references and sources.

MOLLUS	Michigan Military Order of the Loyal Legion of the United States, a collection of post–Civil War articles written by veterans who belonged to this organization. The papers are at the University of Michigan's Bentley Historical Library.
OR	United States War Department, *The War of the Rebellion: A Compilation of the Official Records of the Union and Confederate Armies.* 70 volumes in 128 parts. Washington, D.C.: Government Printing Office, 1880–1901.
USAMHI	United States Army Military History Institute, an archive at Carlisle Barracks, Pennsylvania, where papers of Michael Vreeland and Jairus Hall are filed.

Chapter 1. We Will Strive to Do Our Duty as American Soldiers

1. Woodbury to Blair, January 10, 1861, Austin Blair Papers, Burton Historical Collection, Detroit Public Library.
2. *Adrian Watchtower,* July 5, 1860; *Adrian Expositor,* February 6, 1866, and June 20, 1901.
3. *Adrian Watchtower,* July 5, 1860; *Adrian Expositor,* February 6, 1866.
4. Woodbury to Blair, April 16, 1861, Blair Papers.
5. Charles Monroe Cleveland diary, April 16 and 17, 1861, Bentley Historical Library, University of Michigan. Cleveland was an Adrian merchant.
6. C. Luce to Gen. Robertson, April 25, 1861, 4th Michigan records, Box 59-14, Military Establishment, State Archives of Michigan, Lansing; Yates and Custer: Annie Gibson Roberts Yates, "Colonel George W. Yates," *Research & Review* (Little Big Horn Association), vol. 15, 1989, p. 16; and Brian Pohanka, "George Yates, Captain of the Band Box Troop," *Greasy Grass* (Custer Battlefield, Historical & Museum Association), vol. 8,

May 1992, pp. 11–12.

7. *Steuben (County, Angola, Ind.) Republican,* April 27, 1861; *Adrian Expositor,* May 11, 1861. Arguments about Meech's offense and his rescue from the sheriff appeared in the *Republican,* June 1, 1861. The editor wrote in Meech's defense that he was "a good steady young man," the charge against him a misdemeanor.
8. D. Knipple to E. Starr, May 10, 1861; Starr to Bro. Hank, no date (May?) 1861; Starr to Brother Hank, May 16, 1861, Bentley Library. Knipple was killed by an accidental gunshot wound later that summer.
9. Barry resignation, Randolph election: *Michigan (Ann Arbor) Argus,* May 15, 1861, *Detroit Free Press,* May 17, 1861; Barry Guard training: *Michigan State (Ann Arbor) News,* May 9, 1861.
10. Phelps to his brother, May 23, 1861 (transcript), courtesy of Jeff Phelps. On June 28, Charles Phelps wrote his brother, "I enlisted in the 4th Reg. a week ago."
11. Lumbard to Robertson, April 29, 1861, 4th Michigan records, State Archives; *Jonesville Independent,* May 2, 1861; *Detroit Free Press,* May 11, 1861.
12. Moses Luce autobiographical sketch, provided by his grandson, Edgar A. Luce Jr.
13. *Hudson Gazette,* April 20 and April 23, 1861; DeGolyer to J. Robertson, April 29, 1861, Blair Papers.
14. *Adrian Expositor,* May 21, 1861; Harrison Daniels reminiscence, provided by Craig and Ann Emery and Hal Flynn. Daniels noted in his text that he was nearly 76 when he composed it, mainly from memory.
15. *Detroit Free Press,* May 8, 1861; William Vreeland statement, Vreeland pension record, National Archives and Records Administration, Washington, D.C.
16. Taylor to dear Mother, May 7, 1861 and Taylor to dear Sister, May 8, 1861, Edward H. C. Taylor Civil War letters, G. Taylor Collection, Warren Hunting Smith Library, Hobart and William Smith Colleges, Geneva, N.Y. Taylor's background is from letters written in 1860 on into the spring of 1861.
17. Crane to Robertson, April 25, 1861, and Crane to Robertson, April 28, 1861, 4th Michigan records, State Archives; *Detroit Free Press,* May 23, 1861; *Adrian Expositor,* May 24, 1861; Franklin Ellis, *History of Livingston County, Michigan* (Philadelphia: Everts & Abbot, 1880), p. 62; *Michigan State (Ann Arbor) News,* photocopy of undated clipping in the authors' possession (June 1861), a resolution of thanks to the ladies of Dexter from Company K, dated June 14, 1861.
18. Will and Testament of Harrison H. Jeffords, May 22, 1861, Jeffords pension file, National Archives. A history of Lenawee County containing biographies of Jeffords's family gives for him a birth date of Aug. 21, 1834, in Monroe County, N.Y., but this year was apparently a typographical error. The Michigan 1850 and 1860 censuses show his ages for those years as 14 and 23 respectively, which makes the year of his birth 1836 or 1837. This is confirmed by mustering papers in his service record showing him to be 24 in 1861, 25 in 1862, and 26 in 1863.
19. DeGolyer to Robinson [Robertson], April 20, 1861, photocopy in Hudson Museum, Hudson.
20. *Tecumseh Herald,* May 11, 1861.
21. E. Starr to Bro. Hank, May 16, 1861, Bentley Library.
22. Ibid.; Starr to unknown, undated (May 17 or 18, 1861); Starr to Bro. Hank, May 19, 1861, Bentley Library.
23. *Adrian Expositor,* May 1, 6, 9, 11, 17, 1861; *Jonesville Independent,* May 1, 1861; *Detroit Free Press,* May 4, 9, 1861; John Robertson, *Michigan in the War* (Lansing: W. S. George, 1882), p. 220.
24. *Cleveland Plain Dealer,* June 6, 1861; Jonathan Childs's background: William A. Ellis, *Norwich University, 1819–1911: Her History, Her Graduates, Her Roll of Honor,* vol. 2 (Montpelier: Capital City Press, 1911), p. 615; *Hudson Gazette,* June 19, 1896 (a reminiscence by Dr. Chamberlain).
25. J. Fountain to Woodbury, May 20, 1861, Dwight Woodbury Papers, Bentley Library; *Adrian Expositor,* May 23, 24, 28, 1861.
26. Bancroft diary-scrapbook, May 29, 1861, RG 95, Special Collections & Archives, Auburn University Library, Auburn, Alabama. Bancroft turned his Civil War diaries into a scrapbook of his time in the Union army, adding to it various orders, letters, pictures, and newspaper clippings about his regiment's postwar reunions. A typed transcript of the diary is also on file at the Bentley Library, University of Michigan. Bancroft sometimes wrote to Detroit newspapers and to his friend Theodore Hinchman of Detroit; the letters to Hinchman are in the Detroit Public Library's Burton Collection.

27. *Adrian Expositor,* May 28, 29, 1861; *Monroe Commercial,* June 6, 1861.
28. *Hillsdale Standard,* May 28, 1861. One of the young men who decided on the spot to go with the company that day, a James Smith, was never mustered into service. He may have just wanted to go along with them to Adrian.
29. *Tecumseh Herald,* May 30, 1861; *Hudson Gazette,* June 1, 1861.
30. *Jonesville Independent,* May 30 and Aug. 22, 1861.
31. Miranda Goheen diary (Tecumseh area), May 28, 1861, Bob Coch Collection; Albert H. Boies, "War Memories," one of a series of articles based on Boies's diary published in the *Adrian Daily Times,* the first of which ran on March 20, 1886.
32. Boies, "War Memories," *Adrian Daily Times,* March 20, 1886. The performance of Boies, Carleton, and the cadets was also remembered in the *Hudson Gazette,* Aug. 13, 1897.
33. Barlow to Friend Charley, June 4, 1861, Charles Bates Papers, Bentley Library; *Michigan (Ann Arbor) Argus,* May 29, 1861.
34. Bancroft diary, May 30, 1861; DePuy letter, June 6, 1861, in the *Ann Arbor Journal,* May 29, 1861; Richardson to parents, May 31, 1861, Bentley Library; *Hillsdale Standard,* June 4, 1861.
35. Starr to Brother Hank, June 4, 1861, Bentley Library.
36. Richardson to parents, May 31, 1861, Bentley Library; Bancroft diary, June 5, 1861; James Gilmore Tuttle memoir (described as having been written by Tuttle in 1900 and early 1901), Bentley Library.
37. Taylor to sister, June 31, 1861, Taylor Collection; Robertson, *Michigan in the War,* p. 837.
38. *Jonesville Independent,* May 30, 1861; *Hillsdale Standard,* June 4, 1861; *Adrian Expositor,* June 7, 17 1861; *Hudson Gazette,* June 8, 1861; Brawl over food: *Adrian Expositor,* June 12, 1861; *Detroit Free Press,* June 15, 1861; Examination of enlistees: Barlow to Friend Charley, June 4, 1861, Bates Papers; William Vreeland statement, Vreeland pension file, National Archives; Wirts to friend Bill (transcript), June 9, 1861, William Carleton Papers, Hillsdale College Archives.
39. Richardson to parents, May 31, 1861; and Cleveland diary, June 5, 1861; Bancroft diary, June 1–3, 5, 7, 1861.
40. Monteith to parents, June 19, 1861, Bentley Library.
41. *Detroit Free Press,* June 15, 1861; Richardson to his brother, June 16, 1861, Bentley Library.
42. Woodbury to friends at home, June 16, 1861, Burton Collection; *Detroit Daily Tribune,* June 13 and 19, 1861.
43. *Cleveland Herald,* June 5, 1861; *Adrian Expositor,* June 7, 1861; *Hillsdale Standard,* June 11, 1861; *Detroit Tribune,* June 19, 1861.
44. Fountain to Woodbury, June 13, 1861, Woodbury Papers; *Peninsular (Ann Arbor) Courier,* June 25, 1861. Minié muskets were old-model smooth-bore weapons fitted with rifled barrels for better accuracy.
45. *Detroit Daily Tribune,* June 22, 1861; *Steuben Republican,* June 22 and June 30, 1861; Monteith to parents, June 19, 1861, Bentley Library.
46. Cameron to Blair, June 20, 1861 (telegram), Woodbury Papers; Robertson, *Michigan in the War,* p. 223; *Adrian Expositor,* June 20, 1861.
47. *Adrian Expositor,* June 22, 1861; *Detroit Free Press,* June 23, 1861.
48. *Adrian Expositor,* June 22, 1861; *Detroit Free Press,* June 18 and 23, 1861; *Hudson Gazette,* June 15, 1861; Bancroft diary, June 21, 1861.
49. *Adrian Expositor,* June 22, 1861. While some have questioned whether the regiment also had a flag bearing the state seal on a blue field—a typical regimental banner—John Bancroft's diary and news accounts of this ceremony refer only to this customized "stars and stripes" presented by Mrs. Wilcox. A historical sketch of the first several months of the regiment, undated but written by Chaplain Henry Strong, in the regiment's records in the State Archives of Michigan, also described the presentation of "a regimental flag"—that is, a single banner—by the Adrian women. This U.S. flag, known as the "Defend It" flag, is in the possession of the State of Michigan, in a secure, climate-controlled room with other state battle flags in the building housing the state library, museum, and archives.
50. *Detroit Free Press,* June 23, 1861; Bancroft diary, June 22, 1861. Bar fight: *Adrian Expositor,* June 22, 1861. Woodbury's stated policy about minors: *Jonesville Independent,* May 30, 1861; *Adrian Expositor,* June 27, 1861;

William Vreeland statement, Vreeland pension file, National Archives. Bill Vreeland eventually joined the second incarnation of the 4th Michigan, the "reorganized" regiment in 1864.

51. Michigan Military Dept. to Woodbury, June 22, 1861 (telegram), Woodbury Papers; Bancroft diary, June 22, 24, 1861; *Adrian Expositor,* June 23, 1861.
52. *Hudson Gazette,* June 29, 1861; Bancroft diary, June 25, 1861.
53. *Hudson Gazette,* June 29, 1861; Whitney to John Robertson, Nov. 28, 1881, 4th Michigan records, State Archives. Whitney said kept his promise to Woodbury, returning his body from Virginia to Michigan in 1866, with the people of Adrian covering the expense.
54. *Hudson Gazette,* June 29, 1861; *Adrian Expositor,* June 25, 1861.
55. Bancroft diary, June 25, 1861.

Chapter 2. The Loss Is Great, the Confusion Greater

1. *Toledo Blade,* June 25, 1861; *Hudson Gazette,* June 29, 1861; *Hillsdale Standard,* July 9, 1861; Eli Starr to his father, June 27, 1861, Bentley Historical Library; and Bancroft diary, June 25 (26), 1861, RG 95, Special Collections & Archives, Auburn University Library; *Cleveland Plain Dealer,* June 25, 1861.
2. Orvey S. Barrett, *The Old Fourth Michigan Infantry* (Detroit: W. S. Ostler, 1888), p. 4. *Hardtack* was often spelled by soldiers as two words, "hard tack." *Cleveland Herald,* June 26, 1861; *Detroit Free Press,* June 28, 1861; *Steuben Journal,* July 6, 1861.
3. Bancroft diary, June 25 (26), 1861; *Detroit Free Press,* June 28, 1861; Warren's injury: *Adrian Expositor,* June 27, 1861, and *Jonesville Independent,* July 4, 1861. The *Dunkirk Union* story about the injured soldier appeared in the *Detroit Free Press;* this article about the woman who aided the soldier didn't give his name, but the account matches reports on Warren's accident in the Adrian and Jonesville newspapers.
4. *Hudson Gazette,* July 6, 1861; *Detroit Free Press,* June 28, 1861; *Hillsdale Standard,* June 29, 1861; Barrett, *Old Fourth Michigan Infantry,* p. 4; *Detroit Advertiser,* July 2, 1861. In a speech at a regimental reunion decades later, Cole indicated the men made the racket in cattle cars at a point after they left Cleveland but before they reached Harrisburg (*Adrian Daily Times & Expositor,* June 20, 1901) and appears to have occurred as they left Elmira. The injured Rouse was discharged later that summer.
5. Starr to his father, June 27, 1861, Bentley Historical Library, University of Michigan; Bancroft diary, June 26 (27), 1861.
6. Bancroft diary, June 26 (27), 1861; Richardson to parents, June 28, 1861, Bentley Library; *Hudson Gazette,* June 26, 1861.
7. Barrett, *Old Fourth Michigan Infantry,* p. 4; James Gilmore Tuttle memoir, pp. 1, 2, Bentley Library; *Detroit Free Press,* July 2, 3, 6, 1861; *Detroit Tribune,* July 5, 1861; *Detroit Advertiser,* June 3, 1861; Bancroft diary, July 1, 1861. "Buck and ball" muskets fired a lead ball or bullet and buckshot.
8. Tom Jones to friend Pete, June 28, 1861, in the *Steuben Journal,* July 6, 1861; Barrett, *Old Fourth Michigan Infantry,* pp. 4, 5; *Detroit Free Press,* July 6 and 9, 1861; Starr to his mother, July 4–5, 1861, Bentley Library.
9. *Detroit Free Press,* July 6, 9, 1861; Tuttle memoir, pp. 2, 3; Barrett, *Old Fourth Michigan Infantry,* p. 5.
10. *Detroit Free Press,* July 9, 1861; DePuy's letter appeared in the *Michigan (Ann Arbor) Argus,* July 7, 1861; Starr to mother, July 4–5, 1861, and Spence to J. P. Cook, July 10, 1861, Bentley Library.
11. Bancroft diary, July 4, 1861; Allen to brother and sister (transcript) July 5, 1861, courtesy of Nancy Findley; Harrison Daniels reminiscence, Craig and Ann Emery and Hal Flynn; Barlow to Friend Charley, July 6, 1861, Charles Bates Papers, Bentley Library.
12. Spence to Cook, July 10, 1861, Bentley Library; *Hudson Gazette,* July 13, 1861.
13. *Steuben Republican,* July 13, 1861; *Hudson Gazette,* July 20, 1861.
14. United States War Department, *The War of Rebellion: A Compilation of the Official Records of the Union and Confederate Armies,* 70 vols. in 128 parts (Washington, D.C.: Government Printing Office, 1880–1901), series 1, vol. 2, p. 315.

15. *Jonesville Independent,* July 25, 1861; Starr to mother, July 20, 1861, Bentley Library; *Steuben Republican,* July 27, 1861; *Hudson Gazette,* July 27, 1861, and Feb. 14, 1863.
16. Robert Garth Scott, *Forgotten Valor: The Memoirs, Journals, & Civil War Letters of Orlando B. Willcox* (Kent, Ohio: Kent State University Press, 1999), p. 188; Richardson to his mother, July 20, 1861, Bentley Library; Monteith to dear parents, July 18, 1861, Bentley Library; Barrett, *Old Fourth Michigan Infantry,* pp. 5–6; *Steuben Republican,* July 27, 1861.
17. Tuttle memoir, pp. 3, 4.
18. Bancroft diary, July 16, 21, 1861; Barlow to Bates, Aug. 3, 1861, Bates Papers; William Limbarker diary, July 21, 1861, Clarke Historical Library, Central Michigan University. This soldier's name has also been variously spelled and interpreted as "Lembocker" and other variations, but the authors believe that Limbarker is correct.
19. *Hudson Gazette,* Aug. 3, 1861; extracts of McConnell's letters to his parents, *Jonesville Independent,* Aug. 8, 1861; Bush to wife, July 20 (21, 23), 1861, Bentley Library.
20. *Hudson Gazette,* Aug. 3 and 10, 1861; Robinson to Father & Mother, July 25, 1861, Bentley Library. Accounts show that the 1st South Carolina Infantry wasn't at the battle of Bull Run, but other troops from the state were there that day.
21. *Hudson Gazette,* Aug. 3 and 10, 1861; Barrett, *Old Fourth Michigan Infantry,* p. 7.
22. Taylor to Marie, Sept. 3, 1861, G. Taylor Collection, Warren Hunting Smith Library, Hobart and William Smith Colleges.
23. Bush to wife, July 23, 1861 (transcript), Bentley Library; Barlow to Bates, Aug. 3, 1861, Bates Papers; *Hudson Gazette,* Aug. 3, 1861; *Steuben Republican,* Aug. 3, 1861; *Michigan (Ann Arbor) Argus,* July 25, 1861; Limbarker diary, July 21 (22), 1861.
24. Robinson to parents, July 25, 1861, and Monteith to parents, July 26, 1861, Bentley Library; Bancroft diary, July 22, 1861; *Steuben Republican,* Aug. 3, 1861.
25. *Hudson Gazette,* Aug. 10, 1861.
26. Tuttle memoir, p. 4; Monteith to parents, July 31, 1861, Bentley Library; Taylor to mother, brother, and sisters, Aug. 2, 1861, Taylor Collection.
27. *Hudson Gazette,* Aug. 3, 1861.
28. *Hudson Gazette,* Aug. 10, 1861, and June 19, 1896.
29. *Hudson Gazette,* Aug. 10, 1861; Scott, *Forgotten Valor,* p. 188; Woodbury to Robertson (telegram), Aug. 1, 1861, 4th Michigan regimental records, State Archives of Michigan.
30. Michael Vreeland's Aug. 7, 1861, letter to a friend, quoted in an article by Carl Vreeland, his grandson, in the *Oregon (Portland) Journal,* June 24, 1964, p. 8J. This was first of a three-part series titled "Letter from Civil War Battlefields" that ran on successive days on the paper's features page. Wirts to friend William, Aug. 5, 1861, Carleton Papers, Hillsdale College Archives; Limbarker diary, July 30, 1861; Bancroft diary, Aug. 11, 16, 29–31, 1861; *Detroit Advertiser,* Aug. 24, 1861; *Steuben Republican,* Aug. 24, 1861.
31. Monteith to parents, Aug. 10, 1861, Bentley Library; *Jonesville Independent,* Aug. 22, 1861.
32. *Steuben Republican,* Aug. 31, 1861; Redfield's Aug. 13 letter in the Batavia, N.Y. *Republican Advocate,* Aug. 24, 1861; *Detroit Advertiser,* Aug. 24, 1861 (signed J.M.B., the letter was probably written by Bancroft; on Oct. 5, 1861, Bancroft noted in his diary, "I occasionally write my friend, Col. Scripps of the Detroit Advertiser").
33. Barrett, *Old Fourth Michigan Infantry,* pp. 7–8.
34. Richardson to parents, Aug. 17, 1861, Bentley Library; *Jonesville Independent,* Aug. 22, 1861; Childs to Uncle, Aug. 15, 1861 (transcript), Hudson Museum.
35. Childs to Uncle, Aug. 15, 1861, Hudson Museum; *Hudson Gazette,* Aug. 10, 1861, and June 19, 1896; Monteith to parents (transcript), Aug. 20, 1861, Bentley Library.
36. Childs to Dear Uncle, Aug. 15, 1861, Hudson Museum; Taylor to Maria, Aug. 27, 1861, Taylor Collection.
37. Childs to Dear Uncle, Aug. 15, 1861, Hudson Museum; Taylor to Maria, Aug. 27, 1861, Taylor Collection; and Richardson to parents, Aug. 17, 1861, Bentley Library.
38. Tuttle memoir, pp. 9–10.

Chapter 3. McClellan Moves Slow but Sure

1. *Jonesville Independent,* Aug. 22, 1861.
2. This passage, taken from a Civil War–era newspaper, was quoted in a history of DeGolyer's community by Verdie Yager, *Reflections on the Bean: History of the Hudson Area in Prose and Picture* (Brooklyn, Mich.: Exponent Press, 1983), pp. 21–22.
3. An account of the escape appeared in *Washington Star,* Aug. 24, 1861, and was published in the *Hudson Gazette* on Aug. 31, 1861; Yager, *Reflections on the Bean,* pp. 21–22.
4. *Hudson Gazette,* Aug. 31, 1861; Yager, *Reflections on the Bean,* pp. 21–22.
5. *Hudson Gazette,* Aug. 31 and Sept. 7, 1861; Yager, *Reflections on the Bean,* pp. 21–22.
6. *Hudson Gazette,* Aug. 31 and Sept. 7, 1861; Yager, *Reflections on the Bean,* pp. 21–22; United States Naval War Records Office, *Official Records of the Union and Confederate Navies in the War of the Rebellion,* 30 vols. (Washington, D.C.: Government Printing Office, 1894–1922), series 1, vol. 4, p. 768.
7. Yager, *Reflections on the Bean,* p. 22.
8. Tuttle memoir, pp. 6–7, Bentley Historical Library, University of Michigan. Scott, *Forgotten Valor,* pp. 307, 309, *n.*, 314, *n.* Various histories that discuss the issue of the status of prisoners held as criminals center on Union and Confederate officers, not enlisted men. The names of Union officers who faced retaliatory execution were published, but Tuttle, who was not an officer, is not listed among them.
9. Tuttle memoir, pp. 13–15. The Withington diary was cited in a Michigan newspaper article, "Diary Tells the Story of Confederate Jail," by Philip Mason, historian and Wayne State University professor, dated January 29, 1961. This article was part of a Civil War centennial series written for the Associated Press.
10. Tuttle memoir, pp. 16–18; Scott, *Forgotten Valor,* p. 313.
11. Tuttle memoir, pp. 21–23.
12. Ibid., pp. 24–27.
13. Ibid., pp. 28–29.
14. Ibid., pp. 30–34.
15. Chamberlain's opinion on Dr. Clark: *Hudson Gazette,* June 19, 1896; Lumbard's illness: *Jonesville Independent,* Sept. 19, 1861.
16. Woodbury to Blair, Aug. 29, 1861, Austin Blair Papers, Burton Historical Collection, Detroit Public Library; *Michigan (Ann Arbor) Argus,* Sept. 27, 1861; Vreeland to Dear Sister, Sept. 19, 1861, quoted in Carl Vreeland, "Letters from Civil War Battlefields," pt. 1, in the *Oregon (Portland) Journal,* June 24, 1964.
17. *Hudson Gazette,* Sept. 7, 14, 21, 1861; *Jonesville Independent,* Sept. 19, 1861; *Sturgis Journal,* Sept. 12, 1861; Michigan Adjutant General, *Records of Service of Michigan Volunteers in the Civil War,* vol. 4 (Kalamazoo: Ihling Bros & Everard, 1905), p. 10; *Hudson Gazette,* Sept. 21, 1861; Richardson to parents and brother, Sept. 13, 1861, Bentley Library. Levi Courtright's name is given as Cortright in news accounts and some records.
18. Richardson to parents and brother, Sept. 13, 1861; and Monteith to parents, Sept. 12, 1861, both in the Bentley Library.
19. Taylor to mother, Sept. 22, 1861, G. Taylor Collection, Warren Hunting Smith Library, Hobart and William Smith Colleges.
20. Jeffords to friends, Sept. 20, 1861, Jeffords pension file, National Archives.
21. Richardson to parents and brother, Sept. 21, 1861, Bentley Library; Jeffords to Dear Friends, Sept. 20, 1861, Jeffords pension file, National Archives; *Michigan (Ann Arbor) Argus,* Sept. 27, 1861.
22. Richardson to ——, Sept. 30, 1861, Bentley Library.
23. Blair to Robertson, Sept. 25, 1861, 4th Michigan regimental records, State Archives of Michigan; Albert H. Boies, "War Memories No. 2," *Adrian Daily Times,* March 27, 1886; *Hudson Gazette,* Sept. 7, 14, Oct. 18, 1861.
24. Woodbury to Blair, Oct. 10, 1861, Blair Papers.
25. Woodbury to Blair, Oct. 10, 1861, Blair Papers. A resident of Hudson wrote to the *Detroit Free Press* saying that DeGolyer had been a Democrat who favored Stephen Douglas in the 1860 presidential election, but

that his experience as a prisoner of the Confederates made him into an "out and out abolitionist." DeGolyer gave a speech about this conversion when he got back to Michigan in the fall of 1861, and Governor Blair approved of his change of heart. "This speech won for him the promotion to Major," claimed the writer, who signed his letter "Junius." *Detroit Free Press,* April 2, 1862.

26. Jeffords to friends, Oct. 12 [1861], Jeffords pension file, National Archives; Taylor to Dear Maria, Aug. 16, 1861, Taylor Collection; Taylor to (Michigan) Adjutant General, Sept. 24, 1861, 4th Michigan records, State Archives of Michigan; Allen to sisters, Oct. 2, 1861 (transcript), continuation of a letter begun on Sept. 28, 1862, courtesy of Nancy Findley.
27. *OR,* series 1, vol. 5, p. 219.
28. Phelps to brother (transcript), Oct. 5, 1861, Jeff Phelps.
29. *Hudson Gazette* (excerpt of Woodbury's correction to the *New York Times*), Oct. 19, 1861
30. *Hudson Gazette,* Oct. 19, 1861; Moses Luce memoir, Edgar A Luce Jr.; *OR,* series 1, vol. 5, p. 217.
31. Bancroft diary, Sept. 30, Oct. 1, 1861, RG 95 Special Collections & Archives, Auburn University; and Richardson to ——, Oct. 5, 1861, Bentley Library.
32. *Hillsdale Standard,* Oct. 22, 1861; *Hudson Gazette,* Oct. 26, 1861; *Jonesville Independent,* Oct. 30, 1861.
33. Robinson to father & mother, Oct. 27, 1861, Bentley Library; *Hudson Gazette,* Nov. 2, 1861; *New York World* dispatch printed in *Detroit Free Press,* Oct. 26, 1861.
34. *Hudson Gazette,* Nov. 2, 9, 16, and Dec. 7, 1861; Seage diary, Oct. 18, 1861, Steve Roberts. Captain DePuy explained James Murphy's sentence in a Feb. 19, 1862, letter published in the *Michigan (Ann Arbor) Argus,* Feb. 28, 1862. Limbarker's court-martial record, Feb. 20, 1862, National Archives.
35. Jeffords to friends, (date illegible, but probably Nov. 24, 1861), Jeffords pension file, National Archives; Richardson to Dear Parents & Brother, Nov. 23, 1861, and Robinsòn to Dear Father, Nov. 24, 1861, Bentley Library. The dateline of Jeffords's letter from Minor's Hill and the description of the review indicate it occurred on Nov. 20, 1861.
36. *Hillsdale Standard,* Oct. 29, 1861; Richardson to parents & brother, Oct. 5, 13, and 27, 1861, Bentley Library; J. Barnes to Dear Ma & Father, Oct. 27, 1861, Roger Walcott Collection, Archives and Regional History Collections, Western Michigan University, Kalamazoo.
37. Westgate to Dear Brother, Nov. 2, 1861 (copy and transcript), provided by Kenneth D. Andrews. The "town where Uncle Silas was from" may be Westgate's reference to Tecumseh, where Company G was formed. Harrison Daniels, who served in the company and wrote a brief memoir of his Civil War experience for his family, made no mention of women in the company or regiment.
38. Limbarker diary, Aug. 29, 1861; Bancroft diary, Oct. 31, 1861; *Hudson Gazette,* Dec. 7, 1861.
39. Taylor to Lottie, Nov. 25, 1861, Taylor Collection.
40. *Hudson Gazette,* Dec. 7, 1861.
41. Richardson to Dear Parents & Brother, Dec. 14, 1861, Bentley Library.
42. McCarty to friend William, Dec. 7, 1861, Will Carleton Papers, Hillsdale College Archives; Seage diary Nov. 2, 10, 12, 1861; *Monroe Monitor,* probably December, n.d., 1861; *Ann Arbor Journal,* Jan. 1, 1862; *Hillsdale Standard,* n.d., probably Feb. 1862; *Hudson Gazette,* Dec. 21, 1861.
43. Barrett, *Old Fourth Michigan Infantry,* pp. 30–33; Richardson to Parents and Brother, Dec. 22, 1861, Bentley Library; *Hudson Gazette,* Dec. 21, 1861.

Chapter 4. We Shall Go into the Storm of Battle with Brave Hearts

1. Sadler to Father and Mother, Jan. 4, 1862, from a private collector (copies of Sadler's letters are in the Bentley Historical Library, University of Michigan); Richardson to Dear Parents & Brother, Dec. 22 and 29, 1861, Bentley Library; Henry Seage diary, Dec. 25, 1861, Steve Roberts; McCarty to Friend Will (transcript), Jan. 2, 1862, Will Carleton Papers, Hillsdale College Archive; *Hudson Gazette,* Jan. 18 and Feb. 22, 1862; Limbarker's second diary, Dec. 25, 1861, Clarke Historical Library, Central Michigan University; *Hillsdale*

Standard, February 4, 1862; Monteith to My dear mother, Jan. 2, 1862, Bentley Library.

2. Limbarker diary, Dec. 23, 1861. A letter in the *Detroit Free Press,* April 3, 1862 by "Junius" stated DeGolyer was given a new commission by Blair after he got in this trouble and resigned from the 4th Michigan. He was made captain of the 1st Michigan Light Artillery, Battery H. DeGolyer was fatally wounded near Vicksburg, Mississippi, on May 28, 1863.
3. Limbarker diary, Dec. 15 and 23, 1861, and Jan. 22, 1862; Blair to Robertson (for Cole's commission to major), Jan. 4, 1862, 4th Michigan records, State Archives of Michigan, Lansing; the story about Preston's return in Feb. 1862 was reprinted 75 years later in the *Hudson Post Gazette,* Feb. 11, 1937; Lumbard to Col. Backus, Feb. 5, 1862, regimental records, State Archives; Charles Doolittle diary, Jan. 11 and 14, 1862, private collector; Enoch Davis diary, Jan. 6–31, 1862, Fulton County Historical Museum, Wauseon, Ohio.
4. Starr to Dear Father, Jan. 9, 1862, Bentley Library. Akers, Starr's friend, joined the regiment after having a scrape with the law—an incident in which Akers stole 50 cents from a man. Starr wrote this was Akers's first offense and that it was better for him to be allowed to join the army than be prosecuted.
5. Starr to Dear Father, Jan. 9, 1862; Richardson to Dear Parents & Brother, Jan. 12, 1862, and Clark to Em, Jan. 19, 1862, all from Bentley Library; Irvin Miner diary, Jan. 13 and 17, 1862, Robert Walkowiak; Silas Sadler diary, Jan. 23, 1862, private collector.
6. Limbarker diary, Jan. 17, 1862. A two-page document from the records of the Adjutant General in the National Archives, dated Feb. 20, 1862, at Hall's Hill, Va., and marked "Special Orders No. 80," shows the charges and specifications against Limbarker, as well as the record of his acquittal. Boies, "War Memories No. 2"; Barrett, *Old Fourth Michigan Infantry,* pp. 33–34.
7. For example, Regan noted on February 27, while skirmishing with Confederates over possession of a barn, that some of his comrades built their own "cannon" using a stovepipe, wagon wheels, and a pole, causing Rebel cavalrymen second thoughts about attacking. When pickets from the 4th Michigan came to relieve Regan's comrades, they turned this field piece over to the Michigan soldiers. Timothy J. Regan, *The Lost Civil War Diaries* (Victoria, B.C.: Trafford Publishing, 2003), p. 38.
8. Blowers letter, March 3, 1862 in *Hudson Gazette,* March 15, 1862.
9. *Hillsdale Standard,* March 25, 1862; Jeffry D. Wert, *The Sword of Lincoln: The Army of the Potomac* (New York: Simon & Schuster, 2005), pp. 62–63; Albert H. Boies, "War Memories No. 3," *Adrian Daily Times,* April 3, 1886; *Hudson Gazette,* March 29, 1862; George Millens diary, March 9, 10, 11, 1862, Glen McQueen.
10. Taylor to dear Mother, April 2, 1862, G. Taylor Collection, Warren Hunting Smith Library, Hobart and William Smith Colleges; Robinson to Dear Father & Mother, April 28, 1862, Bentley Library; Millens diary, March 12, 1862; *Hillsdale Standard,* March 25, 1862.
11. Millens diary, March 15, 16, 22, 23, 1862; Cressey to Dear Brother, March 17, 1862, Lynn Bryant; Seage diary, March 18, 1862; Sadler diary, March 20, 1862; Doolittle diary, March 21, 1862; Phelps to Dear Brother, March 31, 1862, Jeff Phelps; Monteith to dear Mother (transcript) March 24, 1862, Bentley Library.
12. Seage diary, March 22 and 23, 1862; Monteith to dear Mother, March 24, 1862, Bentley Library; Phelps to Dear Brother, March 31, 1862, Jeff Phelps; Webster to Dear Mother (transcript), March 25, 1862, Steve Bucher and Rose Miller; *Hudson Gazette,* May 10, 1862; Richardson's letter published in the *Ann Arbor Journal,* April 9, 1862.
13. Millens diary, March 23–28, 1862; Davis diary, March 23–28, 1862; Daniels reminiscence, Craig and Ann Emery, Hal Flynn; Henry Seage, *History of Co. E, 4th Mich. Infantry, 1861–1864* (Lansing: Thompson & Van Buren, 1897), p.10.
14. Taylor to Dear Mother, April 2, 1862, Taylor Collection; *OR,* vol. 11, pt. 1, pp. 298–99.
15. Boies's story: "War Memories No. 4," *Adrian Daily Times,* April 10, 1886. Boies wrote that the incident occurred on April 3 near Big Bethel, but other accounts place it on April 4 near Cocklestown: Seage diary, April 4, 1862.
16. *Hudson Gazette,* April 13, 1862; Taylor to dear Sister Lottie, April 14, 1862, Taylor Collection; *Detroit Free Press,* April 12, 1862; *Hillsdale Standard,* April 23, 1862.
17. Millens diary, April 5 and 6, 1862; Doolittle diary, April 5, 1862; Thomskins (probably Thompkins) pension

record, National Archives; *Hudson Gazette,* April 13, 1862; *Monroe Commercial,* May 1, 1862.

18. *OR,* vol. 11, pt. 1, pp. 299–300; Wert, *The Sword of Lincoln,* p. 72; Miner diary, April 6–9, 1862.
19. Miner diary, April 7, 1862; Davis diary, April 8, 1862; Doolittle diary, April 8, 1862; Millens diary, April 9, 1862; Seage, *History of Co. E,* pp. 11–12; *Hudson Gazette,* May 10, 1862; Heintzelman's compliment: *Supplement to the Official Records of the Union and Confederate Armies* (Wilmington, N.C.: Broadfoot Publishing, 1996), vol. 2, p. 31.
20. *Sturgis Journal,* April 17, 1862; Miner diary, April 8–18, 1862; *Michigan (Ann Arbor) Argus,* April 23, 1862; Millens diary, April 10–18, 1862. Chamberlain's story about Carver in an 1884 publication called *The Veteran,* printed semimonthly and then weekly between 1883 and 1885, first in Lansing and then in Detroit. A copy of this clipping in the authors' possession quotes Chamberlain's tale. Carver survived the war, became a druggist in Angola, and served in various public positions, including postmaster and state senator; Jesse H. Carpenter, *The War for the Union, 1861–1865: A Record of its Defenders Living and Dead from Steuben County, Indiana* (Angola, Ind.: R. H. Carpenter, 1888–89), p. 8.
21. Davis diary, April 17, 1862; Alfred Davenport, *Camp and Field Life of the Fifth New York Volunteer Infantry* (New York: Dick & Fitzgerald, 1879), p. 160; Doolittle diary, April 18, 1862; *Hudson Gazette,* May 16, 1862; *Monroe Commercial,* May 1, 1862; Earle (4th Michigan adjutant) to John Robertson, April 26, 1862, Bentley Library; death of the Reverend Strong's children: April 7, 1862, telegram to Woodbury; and Strong to Woodbury, April 11, 1862 (application for leave), both in military pension records of Strong, National Archives.
22. William Clark to Blair, April 22 and June 30, 1862, and Joseph Clark to Blair, June 21, 1862, all in Austin Blair Papers, Burton Historical Collection, Detroit Public Library; Boies, "War Memories No. 2" and "War Memories No. 3."
23. Millens diary, April 29, 1862; Taylor to Sister Lottie, April 14 (15), 1862, Taylor Collection; Sadler to Father and Mother, April 22, 1862, private collector.
24. Woodbury to Blair, May 2, 1862, Blair Papers.
25. Miner diary, May 2–4, 1862; Seage diary, May 2–4; Richardson to Dear Parents & Brother, May 4 (5), 1862, Bentley Library; *Hudson Gazette,* May 24 and 31, 1862; Phelps to Dear Brother, May 17, 1862, Jeff Phelps.
26. Davis diary, May 12, 1862; *Hudson Gazette,* May 24 and May 31, 1862; *Monroe Commercial,* May 29, 1862; *Ann Arbor Journal,* May 12, 1862; Seage diary, May 13, 1862; Millens diary, May 13, 1862; Doolittle diary, May 13, 1862.
27. Bancroft, Miner, Millen, and Seage diaries, May 14–19, 1862; *Monroe Commercial,* May 29, 1862.
28. Davis diary, May 20–23, 1862; Seage diary, May 20–23, 1862; Millens diary, May 21–23, 1862; Miner diary, May 20–23, 1862; Sadler diary, May 22, 23, 1862; Edward Taylor to sister Lottie, May 21, 1862, Taylor Collection; *Monroe Commercial,* May 29, 1862.
29. Fisher court-martial: Davis diary, May 23, 1862; Carpenter, *War for the Union,* p. 7; Letter by "Volunteer," a pen name attributed to Woodbury, in *Williams County (Bryan, Ohio) Leader,* June 5, 1862. While printers dated the letter May 25, it was probably written on May 23, given that it says nothing of the New Bridge skirmish that took place on May 24 and gained national attention for Woodbury's regiment. Biographical materials about Woodbury state he lived in Ohio before making Adrian his home. This is one of three letters to the Bryan paper attributed by archivists to Woodbury in the Bowling Green State University's Center for Archival Collections, Newspaper Collection, Bowling Green, Ohio.
30. *OR,* vol. 11, pt. 1, pp. 652–54; a story about this day from the *New York Herald,* datelined Cold Harbor, March 24, 1862, was printed in the *Hillsdale Standard* of June 3, 1862; *Detroit Free Press,* May 29, 1862.
31. *OR,* vol. 11, pt. 1, p. 665; *Monroe Commercial,* June 12, 1861; James (Jay) Monaghan, *Custer: The Life of General George Armstrong Custer* (Lincoln: University of Nebraska Press, 1971), p. 81; Richardson's May 25 letter in the *Ann Arbor Journal,* June 4, 1862.
32. *OR,* vol. 11, pt. 1, p. 665; *Ann Arbor Journal,* June 4, 1862; *Steuben Republican,* June 7, 1862. Robinson to Dear Father & Mother, May 5 (June 5), 1862, Bentley Library. Robinson clearly described the May 24 skirmish at New Bridge in this letter, which he wrongly dated May rather than June; Orvey S. Barrett would write in his book, *The Old Fourth Michigan Infantry,* that he saw Custer cross the river four times that day, p. 13.

33. Millens diary, May 24 and 25, 1862; *Ann Arbor Journal,* June 4, 1862; Barrett, *Old Fourth Michigan Infantry,* p. 13; *Sturgis Journal,* June 8, 1862; Miner diary, May 24, 1862; Phelps to Dear Brother, May 30, 1862, Jeff Phelps; *OR,* vol. 11, pt. 1, pp. 654, 665.
34. Spalding story: his obituary, *Monroe News Courier,* September, 1915; Fisher: Carpenter, *War for the Union,* p. 7. As noted previously, Fisher's court-martial on May 23 was recorded by diarist Enoch Davis, also in Company B.
35. *OR,* vol. 11, pt. 1, pp. 652, 654; *Steuben Republican,* June 7, 1862; Phelps to Dear Brother, May 30, 1862, Jeff Phelps; Monaghan, *Custer,* p. 82; *OR,* vol. 11, pt. 1, pp. 652, 654.
36. *OR,* vol. 11, pt. 1, pp. 652, 654; Robertson, *Michigan in the War,* p. 224; *New York Herald,* June 3, 1862; *Hudson Gazette,* June 7, 1862; *Steuben Republican,* June 19, 1862; "Volunteer" (Woodbury) to Editor Leader, May 26, 1862, in the *Williams County Leader,* June 12, 1862, Bowling Green University Newspaper Collection.
37. Joseph B. Clark to Blair, June 21, 1862, Blair Papers; Robinson to parents, May (June) 5, 1862, Bentley Library.
38. *OR,* vol. 11, pt. 1, pp. 651, 654; Seage diary, May 24, 1862.

Chapter 5. A Whirlwind of Bullets, Yells, and Shrieks

1. George Millens diary, May 25 and 26, 1862, Glen McQueen; Henry Seage diary, May 25, 1862, Steve Roberts; Charles Doolittle diary, Mary 25 and 26, 1862, private collector; *Sturgis Journal,* June 8, 1862; Irvin Miner diary, May 26, 1862, Robert Walkowiak.
2. Millens diary, May 27, 1862; *OR,* vol. 11, pt. 1, pp. 33, 717.
3. *OR,* vol. 11, pt. 1, p. 34; Millens diary, May 27, 1862.
4. Millens diary, May 27, 1862; *Michigan (Ann Arbor) Argus,* June 6, 1862; *OR,* vol. 11, pt. 1, p. 718; Robinson to Dear Father, May 28, 1862, Bentley Historical Library, University of Michigan; Miner diary, May 27, 1862.
5. Millens diary, May 28, 1862; Phelps to Dear Brother, May 30, 1862, Jeff Phelps; Miner diary, May 28, 1862; *Ann Arbor Journal,* June 11, 1862; Robinson to Dear Father, May 28, 1862, Bentley Library; *Hudson Gazette,* Aug. 26, 1862.
6. Barrett, *Old Fourth Michigan Infantry,* pp. 16, 17; Albert H. Boies, "War Memories No. 6," *Adrian Daily Times,* April 24, 1886. Boies later thought that this incident happened on the regiment's march back with its brigade after the fighting at Mechanicsville on June 26, but Barrett placed the incident on the return from Hanover Court House, a month earlier on the same road.
7. Millens diary, May 30, 31, 1862; Silas Sadler diary, May 30, 1862, private collector; Wert, *The Sword of Lincoln,* pp. 84–89; *Ann Arbor Journal,* June 11, 1862; Barrett, *Old Fourth Michigan Infantry,* p. 14; *Hudson Gazette,* Aug. 26, 1862; Miner diary, June 1, 1862.
8. *Michigan (Ann Arbor) Argus,* July 4 and 11, 1862; Richardson to parents, June 8, 1862, Bentley Library.
9. Richardson to parents, June 8, 1862, Bentley Library; Phelps to Dear Brother, June 14, 1862, Jeff Phelps.
10. Boies, "War Memories No. 5," *Adrian Daily Times,* April 17, 1886.
11. Taylor to Dear Sister, July 14, 1862, G. Taylor Collection, Warren Hunting Smith Library, Hobart and William Smith Colleges. In this letter, Taylor estimated that Cole had gone crazy from sunstroke "some six weeks" earlier; Doolittle diary, June 3, 1862; Cole to Blair, June 24, 1862, Austin Blair Papers, Burton Historical Collection, Detroit Public Library; McCarty to Friend Will, June 22, 1862 (transcript), Will Carleton Papers, Hillsdale College Archives.
12. Clark to Blair, June 12, 1862, Blair Papers.
13. Taylor to dear Mother, Bro. & Sisters, May 28, 1862; Taylor to dear friends at home, June 9, 1862; and Taylor to Sister Lottie, June 18, 1862; and Taylor to dear Sister Anna, June 21, 1862, all from Taylor Collection.
14. Bancroft diary, June 7, 8, 1862, RG 95, Special Collections & Archives, Auburn University Library; Davenport, *Camp and Field Life,* fn. p. 203; Miner diary, June 18, 1862; Enoch Davis diary, June 14, 1862, Fulton County (Ohio) Historical Museum; Seage diary, June 12, 1862; Millens diary, June 8, 15, 1862.
15. Starr note to ——, June 8, 1862, Bentley Library; Bancroft diary, June 15, 1862.

16. Millens diary, June 20, 22, 23, 1862; Miner diary, June 25, 1862; Bancroft diary, June 25, 26, 1862.
17. *Hudson Gazette,* Aug. 16, 1862.
18. Chapin to Dear Thad, July 4, 1862, Marshall W. Chapin Papers, Burton Collection; *Hudson Gazette,* Aug. 16, 1862; *OR,* vol. 11, pt. 2, pp. 227, 271, 272, 312, 384, 386, 399.
19. Chapin to Dear Thad, July 4, 1862, Chapin Papers; Davis diary, June 26, 1862; Doolittle diary, June 26, 1862; *Hudson Gazette,* Aug. 16, 1862; *OR,* vol. 11, pt. 2, pp. 313, 399.
20. Wert, *The Sword of Lincoln,* pp. 102–3.
21. *Hudson Gazette,* Aug. 16, 1862; Chapin to Thad, July 4, 1862, Chapin Papers; Randolph to Robertson, July 5, 1862, 4th Michigan records, State Archives of Michigan; Doolittle diary, June 27, 1862; Bancroft diary, June 27, 1862.
22. *OR,* vol. 11, pt. 2, pp 272, 273, 313; Barrett, *Old Fourth Michigan Infantry,* pp. 16–17; Chapin to Thad, July 4, 1862, Chapin Papers; A. H. Boies, "Brave Old Woodbury," *National Tribune,* March 19, 1896; Randolph to Robertson, July 5, 1862, 4th Michigan records, State Archives.
23. *OR,* vol. 11, pt. 2, pp. 273, 313, 420; Millens diary, June 27, 1862; Chapin to Thad, July 4, 1862, Chapin Papers.
24. Shelby Foote, *The Civil War: A Narrative* (New York: Random House, 1958), pp. 485–89; *OR,* vol. 11, pt. 2, p. 273; Chapin to Thad, July 4, 1862, Chapin Papers.
25. Robertson, *Michigan in the War,* p. 226; *OR,* vol. 11, pt. 2, p. 313; Randolph to Robertson, July 5, 1862, regimental records, Archives of Michigan; Chapin to Thad, July 4, 1862, Chapin Papers. Randolph's report stated that Childs was wounded, as do casualty sheets filed in Childs's pension papers, National Archives. Yet some subsequent newspaper reports in the summer of 1862 list him as sick and removed from the front to recover. Years afterward his wife would say a bullet had struck a tobacco box in his pocket.
26. Chapin to Thad, July 4, 1862, Chapin Papers.
27. Chapin to Thad, July 4, 1862, Chapin Papers; Converse's description of DePuy's death: Barry to E. B. Pond, July 13, 1862, in the *Michigan (Ann Arbor) Argus.*
28. Millens's diary, June 27, 1862; Barlow's account: transcript of a letter, Barlow to DuPont, March 1, 1885, Archive and Regional History Collection, Western Michigan University. A copy of this letter is also in the Bentley Historical Library. Boies, "War Memories, No. 6" and "Brave Old Woodbury"; Chapin to Thad, July 4, 1862, Chapin Papers; Seage diary, June 27, 1862.
29. Chapin to Thad, July 4, 1862, Chapin Papers; Seage diary, June 27, 1862; Millens diary, June 27, 1862.
30. Millens diary, June 27, 1862; Barlow to DuPont, March 1, 1885, Western Michigan University.
31. Bancroft diary, June 27, 1862; Chapin to Thad, July 4, 1862, Chapin Papers; *Hudson Gazette,* Aug. 30, 1862; William F. Fox, *Regimental Losses in the American Civil War* (Albany: Albany Publishing, 1889), p. 383; Michigan Adjutant General, *Records of Service,* pp. 8, 23, 31, 49; Loveland report, July 28, 1862, 4th Michigan records, State Archives; Miner diary, June 27, 1862.
32. The story is in *War Anecdotes and Incidents of Army Life: Reminiscences from Both Sides of the Conflict between North and South* by Albert Lawson (Cincinnati: E. H. Beasley, 1888), pp. 23–24. Some regimental records give Sanders's name as Saunders. Magruder was brevetted lieutenant colonel for his actions during the Mexican War.

Chapter 6. At It We Went Tooth and Nail

1. Henry Seage diary, June 28, 1862, Steve Roberts; *Hudson Gazette,* Aug. 30, 1862; Michigan Adjutant General, *Records of Service,* p. 66.
2. *Hudson Gazette,* Aug. 30, 1862; Chapin to Dear Thad, July 4, 1862, Marshall W. Chapin Papers, Burton Historical Collection, Detroit Public Library; George Millens diary, June 29, 30, 1862, Glen McQueen; John Bancroft diary, June 29, 1862, RG 95, Special Collections and Archives, Auburn University Library.
3. *Hudson Gazette,* Aug. 30, 1862; Millens diary, June 30, 1862; *OR,* vol. 11, pt. 2, p. 274.

4. *Hudson Gazette,* Aug. 30, 1862; *Hillsdale Standard,* July 22, 1862; Millens diary, June 30, 1862; Jeffords to Friend Tip, July 7, 1862, Bentley Historical Library, University of Michigan.
5. Joseph Clark to Blair, June 21, 1862, and Dr. Clark to Blair, June 30, 1862, Austin Blair Papers, Burton Collection. Clark's controversial service with the 19th Michigan is in William M. Anderson's *They Died to Make Men Free: A History of the 19th Michigan Infantry in the Civil War* (Dayton: Morningside Books, 1994). Years later Chamberlain claimed Governor Blair made Clark the 4th Michigan's surgeon, rather than promoting him from assistant surgeon, as a slap. Chamberlain said he considered resigning over this insult, but officers and men of the regiment asked him to stay. After this affair created hard feelings among some voters back home, Chamberlain wrote, Governor Blair did make him the regiment's surgeon after moving Clark to another regiment. *Hudson Gazette,* June 19, 1896.
6. Bancroft diary, July 1, 1862; Millens diary, July 1, 1862; Chapin to Dear Thad, July 4, 1862, Chapin Papers; Lumbard's account, *Hillsdale Standard,* July 22, 1862; Phelps to Dear Brother (transcript), July 4, 1862, Jeff Phelps; *Hudson Gazette,* Sept. 20, 1862; *OR,* vol. 11, pt. 2, pp. 274, 275, 279, 314.
7. *Hillsdale Standard,* July 22, 1862; Bancroft diary, July 1, 1862; Millens diary, July 1, 1862; *OR,* vol. 11, pt. 2, pp. 275, 276; Randolph to Robertson, July 5, 1862, regimental records, State Archives of Michigan. Sgt. James Vesey, in a letter to a local newspaper in Michigan after the battle, wrote that Childs was "very sick" but said nothing about him being wounded; other news reports listed him as sick, though Randolph reported him as wounded.
8. Millens diary, July 1, 1862; Chapin to Dear Thad, July 4, 1862, Chapin Papers.
9. Phelps to Dear Brother (transcript), July 4, 1862, Jeff Phelps; Chapin to Dear Thad, July 4, 1862, Chapin Papers; Millens diary, July 1, 1862; Barrett, *Old Fourth Michigan Infantry,* p. 17; Boies, "Malvern Hill," *National Tribune,* Feb. 13, 1896; *Hillsdale Standard,* July 22, 1862; Regan, *Lost Civil War Diaries,* p. 63; J. F. Gilmore, "With the 4th Mich.," *National Tribune,* July 7, 1910.
10. Chapin to Dear Thad, July 4, 1862, Chapin Papers; *Hillsdale Standard,* July 17 (including information from the Adams letter, dated July 7) and July 22, 1862; *Jackson Eagle,* Aug. 2, 1862, quoting Chamberlain in the *Adrian Watchtower;* Randolph to Robertson, July 5, 1862, Bentley Library; *Monroe Monitor,* July 9, 1862.
11. Randolph to Robertson, July 5, 1862, regimental records, State Archives; *Hillsdale Standard,* July 22, 1862
12. *Hillsdale Standard,* July 22, 1862; *Hudson Gazette,* Feb. 22, 1924; Boies told in three different postwar accounts of the bullet tearing through his diary: "War Memories No. 4," "War Memories No. 6," and "Malvern Hill." Forncrook: Moses Luce, "A Brave Cook," *National Tribune,* March 23, 1915; McCarty pension file, National Archives. McCarty lost rank as a result of his actions that day.
13. *OR,* vol. 11, pt. 2, p. 314; Taylor to Dear Mother, July 4, 1862, G. Taylor Collection, Warren Hunting Smith Library, Hobart and William Smith Colleges; *Hillsdale Standard,* July 17 and 22, 1862.
14. *OR,* vol. 11, pt. 2, p. 279; Chapin to Dear Thad, July 4, 1862, Chapin Papers; Woodbury's body: *Hudson Gazette,* July 26, 1862; Randolph to Robertson, July 5, 1862, State Archives.
15. Fox, *Regimental Losses,* p. 383; *OR,* vol. 11, pt. 2, p. 314; *Hillsdale Standard,* July 22, 1862.
16. Bancroft diary, July 1, 1862; Vesey's July 12 letter published in *Sturgis Journal,* undated clipping in the files of the authors, late July or Aug. 1862; Charles Doolittle diary, July 1, 1862, private collector; Enoch Davis diary, July 1, 1862, Fulton County Historical Museum.
17. Boies, "Malvern Hill," and *Hudson Post Gazette,* Feb. 22, 1924; Doolittle diary, July 2, 1862; Seage diary, July 14–15, 1862; *Monroe Commercial,* July 31, 1862; Webster to Dear Mother, July 5, 1862, Steve Bucher and Rose Miller; *Hudson Gazette,* July 26 and Sept. 20, 1862. Woodbury's body was recovered in 1866 and taken back to Adrian for burial.
18. Millens diary, July 3, 6, 7, and 8, 1862; Phelps to Dear Brother, Aug. 9, 1862, Jeff Phelps; Moses Luce memoir, p. 9, Edgar A. Luce Jr.; Bancroft diary, July 3–7, 1862; *Cleveland Plain Dealer,* July 11, 1862.
19. Jeffords to Friend Tip, July 7, 1862, Bentley Library. The promotions within the regiment are from Griffin to Locke, July 12, 1862, 4th Michigan regimental records, State Archives of Michigan; Fifth Corps' Special Order No. 75, July 14, 1862, reported in the *Hillsdale Standard;* and a letter, J. Webster Childs to Blair, July 15, 1862, Blair Papers. In this letter, Colonel Child's father wrote that his son wanted Lumbard commissioned

lieutenant colonel. The July 15, 1862, diary entry of Capt. Charles Doolittle also noted the promotions of Childs, Lumbard, and Randolph by Porter. Strong's resignation: Special Order No. 84, July 20, 1862, Fifth Army Corps, National Archives; Harrison Daniels reminiscence, Craig and Ann Emery and Hal Flynn.

20. Taylor to dear Sister, July 14, 1862, Taylor Collection; Seage diary, July 14 and Aug. 2, 1862; Millens diary, July 18, 20, 23, Aug. 1, 2, 1862; *Hudson Gazette,* July 26, 1862; *Monroe Commercial,* July 3 and Aug. 7, 1862; Bancroft diary, Aug. 1 and 2, 1862.
21. Vesey's July 12, 1862, letter to the *Sturgis Journal;* Bancroft diary, Aug. 5, 1862.
22. Davenport, *Camp and Field Life,* pp. 121–22.
23. The recording of the muster-out of the 4th Michigan's band on Aug. 10, 1864: *Supplement to Official Records,* pt. 2, vol. 30, p. 606. The order for the mustering out of regimental bands: *OR,* series 3, vol. 2, p. 336.
24. The summation of Miner's experiences as a prisoner to his release: Various entries in his diary, June 28–Aug. 6, 1862. Tim Regan of the 9th Massachusetts was among the prisoners released with Miner. Regan said that on Aug. 5, when the marching column of prisoners was halted in the town of Manchester, a drunken Rebel soldier challenged "some Yankee to fight him," and that "a man from the 4th Michigan accommodated him," giving the Reb "a good whipping" before any Confederate officers could stop it; Regan, *Lost Civil War Diaries,* p. 76.
25. Bancroft diary, Millens diary, Miner diary, and Seage diary, Aug. 10–16, 1862.
26. Diaries of Bancroft, Millens, Miner, and Seage, Aug. 17–27, 1862.
27. Diaries of Bancroft, Millens, Miner, and Seage, Aug. 28–29, 1862. The background regarding Pope and Porter is from Otto Eisenschiml, *The Celebrated Case of Fitz John Porter* (New York: Bobbs-Merrill, 1950). Dr. William F. Breakey of the 16th Michigan also witnessed soldiers foraging from the old woman's cabin and property: "Recollections and Incidents of Medical Military Service," Michigan Military Order of the Loyal Legion, *War Papers,* vol. 2 (Detroit: James H. Stone, 1898), pp. 126–27.
28. Bancroft diary, Aug. 29, 30, 1862; Seage diary, Aug. 29, 30, 1862; Millens diary, Aug. 30, 1862.
29. Bancroft diary, Aug 31, 1862; Taylor to My dear Sister Lottie, Sept. 20, 1862, Taylor Collection; Phelps to Dear Brother, September (n.d.), 1862, Jeff Phelps. The saga of Porter's court-martial and quest for justice is in Eisenschiml, *Celebrated Case.*
30. James Henry's wound while marching with the 11th Massachusetts: Henry pension record, National Archives; Chamberlain told the story of the controversies involving Blair, Clark, and himself in the *Hudson Gazette,* Jan. 19, 1896. A letter supporting Chamberlain for regimental surgeon was sent to Blair by a member of the Boies family in Hudson, July 30, 1862, Blair Papers.
31. Bancroft and Seage diaries, Sept. 1–3, 1862; *Hudson Gazette,* Sept. 20, 1862, and April 19, 1895.

Chapter 7. The Sight Was Horrible and One I Hope I Never See Again

1. John Bancroft, Henry Seage, George Millens, Charles Doolittle, Silas Sadler, and Irvin Miner diaries, various dates Sept. 3–12, 1862, respectively from the Special Collections and Archives, Auburn University; Steve Roberts; Glen McQueen, a private collector (Doolittle and Sadler), and Robert Walkowiak; Doolittle resignation, Sept. 4, 1862, 4th Michigan records, State Archives of Michigan.
2. Bancroft, Seage, Millens, Sadler, and Miner diaries, Sept. 13–16; Phelps to Dear Brother, September (no date), 1862, courtesy of Jeff Phelps; Seage, *History of Co. E,* p. 17.
3. Bancroft, Seage, and Miner diaries, Sept. 17, 1862; Phelps to Dear Brother, September (no date), 1862, Jeff Phelps; Chamberlain to Hinchman, Oct. 13, 1862, Theodore Hinchman Papers, Burton Historical Collection, Detroit Public Library; *Hudson Gazette,* Oct. 11, 1862.
4. *OR,* vol. 19, pt. 1, p. 349; *OR,* vol. 19, pt. 1, p. 345; Seage diary, Sept. 18, 1862; Miner diary, Sept. 18, 1862; Millens diary, Sept. 18, 1862.
5. Seage and Bancroft diaries, Sept. 19, 1862; *Sturgis Journal,* Oct. 9, 1862; Phelps to Dear Brother, Sept.

1862, Jeff Phelps; *Hudson Gazette,* Oct. 11, 1862. Campbell, "Service with the Old 4th Michigan Infantry," a handwritten paper for the Michigan Military Order of the Loyal Legion of the United States (MOLLUS), Bentley Historical Library, University of Michigan.

6. *Sturgis Journal,* Oct. 9, 1862; Taylor to dear Sister Lottie, Sept. 20, 1862, and Taylor to dear Sister Marie, Oct. 11, 1862, G. Taylor Collection, Warren Hunting Smith Library, Hobart and William Smith Colleges; *Hudson Gazette,* Oct. 11, 1862.
7. *Sturgis Journal,* Oct. 9, 1862; Bancroft and Miner diaries, Sept. 19, 1862; William H. Powell, *The Fifth Corps, Army of the Potomac* (New York: G. P. Putnam, 1896), p. 301; Sadler to Dear Father and Mother (transcript), Sept. 26, 1862, a private collector; *Hillsdale Standard,* Nov. 15, 1862.
8. The account of General Porter urging a medal of honor be given to Colonel Childs is from an unidentified fragment, possibly from the *Monroe Commercial,* in group of post–Civil War newspaper clippings dating from the late 19th century to the 1960s. These are in the Heckert Papers, Monroe County Historical Museum, Monroe, Michigan.
9. Bancroft diary, Sept. 19, 1862; Miner diary, Sept. 19, 1862; Taylor to dear Sister Lottie, Sept. 20, 1862, Taylor Collection; Sadler to Dear Father and Mother, Sept. 26, 1862, a private collector; Phelps to brother, Sept. 1862, Jeff Phelps.
10. *Hudson Gazette,* Oct. 11, 1862; Bancroft diary, Sept. 28; Seage diary, Sept. 25 and 27, 1862; "Descendants of John Seage," a genealogy by John DeVinney; Harrison Daniels reminiscence, Craig and Ann Emery and Hal Flynn.
11. Miner diary, Oct. 3; Millens diary, Oct. 3, 12, 1862; Moses Luce memoir, pp. 11–12, Edgar A. Luce Jr.; Taylor to Sister Marie, Oct. 11, 1862, Taylor Collection; Jeffords to Dear Friends, Oct. 19, 1862, Jeffords pension file, National Archives.
12. Diaries of Millens, Bancroft, Seage, and Miner, Oct. 16, 1862; Sadler diary, Oct. 17, 1862; Jeffords to Dear Friends, Oct. 19, 1862, Jeffords pension file, National Archives.
13. Phelps to dear Brother, Oct. 26, 1862, Jeff Phelps; Childs to Blair, Oct. 22, 1862, 4th Michigan records, State Archives. The list of recommended promotions is not attached to Child's letter.
14. Diaries of Millens, Bancroft, Seage, and Miner, Oct. 30–Nov. 9, 1862.
15. Millens diary, Nov. 10, 13, 1862; Bancroft diary, Nov. 11, 1862; Miner diary, Nov. 10, 11,12; Taylor to My dear Sister (undated, but written Nov. 10, 1862), Taylor Collection.
16. Robinson to Dear Father, Nov. 14, 1862, Bentley Library.
17. Childs's resignation, Nov. 2, 1862, Childs's service and pension records, National Archives; Childs to Blair, Nov. 10, 1862, Austin Blair Papers, Burton Collection; Jerome Allen's notes are part of a form in Childs's pension record.
18. Seage diary, Nov. 14, 15, 1862; Bancroft diary, Nov. 16, 17, 1862; Miner diary, Nov. 12, 18, 1862; *Hudson Gazette,* Dec. 13, 1862.
19. Seage, Bancroft, Miner, and Millens diaries, Nov. 19–23, 1862.
20. Bancroft, Miner, and Millens diaries, Nov. 24–29, 1862; Sadler diary, Nov. 28, 1862; Robinson to Dear Father, Nov. 14, 1862, Bentley Library; Taylor to My dear Mother, Feb. 20, 1863, Taylor Collection.
21. Watts's statement and the findings of Assistant Secretary Webster Davis in the matter of Childs's pension are part of his pension file, National Archives. Several other statements about his poor health and apparent kidney and bladder problems are in this file. Millens diary, Nov. 29, 1862.
22. *Hudson Gazette,* Dec. 13, 1862.
23. Miner, Phelps, Bancroft, and Millens diaries, Dec. 1–10, 1862.
24. Wert, *The Sword of Lincoln,* p. 190.
25. *Adrian Watchtower,* Jan. 5, 1863; *OR,* vol. 21, pp. 404, 410.
26. *OR,* vol. 21, p. 410; Millens diary, Dec. 12, 1862; Seage diary, Dec. 12, 1862; Bancroft diary, Dec. 12, 1862; Miner diary, Dec. 12, 1862.
27. Bancroft, Millens, Seage, and Miner diaries, Dec. 13, 1862; *Adrian Watchtower,* Jan. 5, 1863.
28. *Adrian Watchtower,* Jan. 5, 1863; Taylor to dear Mother, Dec. 13, 1862, Taylor Collection.

29. Henry S. Seage, "War Reminiscences of the Battle of Fredericksburg" (typescript), papers of Michigan Military Order of the Loyal Legion Commander, Bentley Library; *Hudson Gazette,* Jan. 3, 1863; Seage, *History of Co. E,* p. 20 (entry for Dec. 13, 1862).
30. Seage diary, Dec. 13, 1862; Seage, *History of Co. E,* p. 20.
31. Seage; "War Reminiscences"; *Adrian Watchtower,* Jan. 5, 1863; *OR,* vol. 21, p. 405; *Hudson Gazette,* Jan. 3, 1863.
32. *Adrian Watchtower,* Jan. 5, 1863; *OR,* vol. 21, p. 405; *Hudson Gazette,* Jan. 3, 1863.
33. Seage; "War Reminiscences"; Robinson to Dear Father, Dec. 18, 1862, Bentley Library.
34. *Adrian Watchtower,* Jan. 5, 1863; Seage, *History of Co. E,* p. 20 (Dec. 13, 1862).
35. Seage, *History of Co. E,* p. 20 (Dec. 13, 1862); Seage; "War Reminiscences"; *Adrian Watchtower,* Jan. 5, 1863; Lumbard to (Michigan) Adjutant General (photocopy), Dec. 17, 1862, report of casualties, Heckert Papers.
36. *Adrian Watchtower,* Dec. 26, 1862. The paper carried a letter from Taylor to White's father, dated Dec. 17, 1862, informing him of the death of his son; Phelps to Dear Brother, Dec. 20, 1862, Jeff Phelps; Yates wounded: House of Representatives' Committee on Pensions, April 13, 1888, Report on H.R. 7708, pension of Annie Gibson Yates, from a private collector; Carl Vreeland, "Letters from Civil War Battlefields," pt. 1, *Oregon (Portland) Journal,* June 24, 1964.
37. Lumbard to (Michigan) Adjutant General (photocopy), Dec. 17, 1862, report of casualties, Heckert Papers; Seage, "War Reminiscences"; Fox, *Regimental Losses,* p. 383; Bancroft diary, Dec. 13, 1862; Wert, *The Sword of Lincoln,* p. 202; Millens diary, Dec. 14, 1862.
38. Robinson to Dear Father, Dec. 18, 1862, Bentley Library; Phelps to Dear Brother, Dec. 20, 1862, Jeff Phelps; Seage diary, Dec. 13, 1862; Bancroft diary, Dec. 14, 1862.
39. *Adrian Watchtower,* Jan. 5, 1863; Bancroft, Seage, and Millens diaries, Dec. 14, 1862.

Chapter 8. Three Cheers for Colonel Jeffords

1. Phelps to dear Brother, Dec. 20, 1862, Jeff Phelps; Taylor to Sister Lottie, Jan. 15, 1863, G. Taylor Collection, Warren Hunting Smith Library, Hobart and William Smith Colleges.
2. John Bancroft diary, Dec. 15 and 16, 1862, RG 95, Special Collections & Archives, Auburn University; Irvin Miner diary, Dec. 15 and 16, 1862, Robert Walkowiak; Henry Seage diary, Dec. 15 and 16, 1862, Steve Roberts; George Millens diary, Dec. 15 and 16, 1862, Glen McQueen; Seage, *History of Co. E,* p. 21.
3. Bancroft, Miner, and Millens diaries, Dec. 17–25, 1862; Seage diary, Dec. 20, 1862; Michigan Adjutant General, *Records of Service,* p. 27; *Hudson Gazette,* Jan. 3, 1863.
4. Miner diary, Dec. 30 and 31, 1862; Seage diary, Dec. 30 and 31; Bancroft diary, Dec. 30 and 31; Millens diary, Dec. 30 and 31, 1862; and *OR,* vol. 21, p. 743.
5. Miner diary, Jan 1, 1863; Seage diary, Jan. 1, 1863; Taylor to Sister Lottie, Jan. 15, 1863, Taylor Collection; Wert, *The Sword of Lincoln,* pp. 211–12; Barnes to Affectionate Brother, Jan. 11, 1863, Roger Walcott Collection, Archives and Regional History Collections, Western Michigan University.
6. Barnes to Affectionate Brother, Jan. 11, 1863, Walcott Collection.
7. Fund-raising for new colors: *Adrian Watchtower,* Jan. 21, 27, 29, 1863. New flag: Robert H. Campbell, "Pioneer Memories of the War Days 1861–65," in *Michigan Pioneer and Historical Collections,* vol. 30 (Lansing: Van Koop, Hallenbeck Crawford, 1906), p. 567, and "Service with the Old 4th Mich. Infantry," MOLLUS; also Seage diary, March 24, 1863; and Seage, *History of Co. E,* p. 22. In his paper written after the war and in a 1902 speech to the Washtenaw County Pioneer Society, Campbell specified that he requisitioned a U.S. flag in Washington and that it was hailed and saluted by passersby as he carried it to his regiment. Henry Seage noted in his diary for March 24, 1863, that the quartermaster brought "a new flag" for the regiment, but in his later *History of Co. E* he wrote that this was a blue flag with a gold eagle.
8. Millens diary, Jan. 8, 1863; Taylor to Sister Lottie, Jan. 15, 1863, and Taylor to dear Mother, Feb. 20, 1863, Taylor Collection; Barnes to Affectionate Brother, Jan. 11, 1863, Walcott Collection.

9. Millens diary, Jan. 15, 1863; Miner diary, Jan. 16, 1863; Bancroft diary, Jan. 20, 1863.
10. Millens, Seage, and Miner diaries, Jan. 21–22, 1863; John W. Hewitt diary, Jan. 21, 1863, Clarke Historical Library, Central Michigan University; Bancroft diary, Jan. 22, 1863; Taylor to Dear "Bill," Jan. 25, 1863, Taylor Collection; Vreeland to Dear Mother, Jan. 25, 1863, Michael Vreeland Papers (photocopy), U.S. Army Military History Institute, Carlisle Barracks, Pa. (USAMHI).
11. Bancroft diary, Jan. 22, 1863; Miner diary, Jan. 23–26, 1863; Millens diary, Jan. 24–26, 1863; Vreeland to Dear Mother, Jan. 25, 1863, Vreeland Papers.
12. Childs biography: Ellis, *Norwich University*, p. 616; Charles Doolittle diary (transcript), Dec. 9, 1862, and Jeffords to the assistant adjutant general, Center Grand Division, Feb. 1, 1863, from a private collector; Lumbard to Blair, Feb. 7, 1863, 4th Michigan records, State Archives. As an example of soldiers assuming that a senior officer would typically be promoted as vacancies occurred, Charles W. Phelps wrote his brother on Dec. 2, 1862, that "Col. Childs of our reg't has resigned and gone home, Lt. Col. Lombard [*sic*] will be Colonel I think" (Jeff Phelps).
13. Miner diary, March 10, 1863; Bancroft to Hinchman, Feb. 8, 1863, and March 16, 1863, Hinchman Papers, Burton Historical Collection, Detroit Public Library; Blair to Robertson, Feb. 12, 1863, 4th Michigan regimental files, State Archives; *Detroit Free Press*, Feb. 14, 1863.
14. Miner diary, Feb. 16–17 1863; L. Barnes to Dear Mother, March 7, 1863, Walcott Collection; Bancroft to Hinchman, Feb. 8, 1863, Hinchman Papers; Phelps to Dear Brother, March 16, 1863, Jeff Phelps.
15. Miner, Seage, and Hewitt diaries, from Feb. 1 to March 16, 1863; Campbell, "Service with the Old 4th Michigan Infantry," pp. 12–13, MOLLUS, and "Pioneer Memories," p. 567; Taylor to sister Lottie, May 21, 1863, Taylor Collection.
16. Miner diary, March 17, 1863; *Hudson Gazette*, April 4, 1863.
17. Taylor to Sister Lottie, April 1, 1863, Taylor Collection.
18. The charges against Jeffords, dated March 20, 1863, appear on p. 5 of General Orders No. 13, "proceedings of a general Court Martial . . . 1st Division, 5th Army Corps, February 28, 1863," National Archives.
19. Jeffords to Smith, March 18, 1863, Jeffords service record, National Archives.
20. Jeffords Court-Martial, National Archives.
21. Ibid.
22. Ibid.
23. Ibid.
24. Ibid.
25. Ibid.; Griffin's General Orders No. 20, April 18, 1863, is part of this record in the National Archives.
26. Maltz to Hinchman, April 5, 1863, and Bancroft to Hinchman, April 10, 1863, both Hinchman Papers.
27. Jeffords's letter in the *Michigan State (Ann Arbor) News*, May 5, 1863; Jeffords to Dear Friends, April 17, 1863, private collector.
28. Miner diary, March 22, April 5, 1863; Chamberlain's Jan. 1863 leave: *Hudson Gazette*, Jan. 31, 1863; Bancroft to Hinchman, April 10, 1863, Hinchman Papers; French: Jeffords to Blair, March 13, 1863, 4th Michigan records, State Archives.
29. Taylor to sister Lottie, April 1, 1863, Taylor Collection.
30. Miner's letter in the *Hudson Gazette*, April 4, 1863.
31. Richardson letter in the *Ann Arbor Journal*, May 7, 1863.
32. Seage diary, March 23, 24, 26, April 6, 7, 8, 1863. New flag: Campbell, "Service with the Old 4th Michigan Infantry," p. 13, MOLLUS; Bancroft to Hinchman, April 10, 1863, Hinchman Papers; Vreeland to Dear Brother Alpheus, April 1, 1863, Vreeland Papers.
33. Miner diary, April 10 and 12, 1863; Seage diary, April 12, 14, 1863; Phelps to Dear Brother, April 14, 1863, Jeff Phelps; Richardson letter, *Peninsular (Ann Arbor) Courier*, May 7, 1863.

Chapter 9. Christ How the Canister Flew

1. Henry Seage diary, April 19, Steve Roberts. A typed transcription called "the Houghton Journal," a short, partial daily record of some his experiences with an incomplete narrative written after the war, is in the Bentley Historical Library, University of Michigan.
2. John W. Hewitt diary, April 23, 26, 27, 1863, Clarke Historical Library, Central Michigan University; Seage diary, April 26, 27, 1863; Irvin Miner diary, April 25–27, 1863, Robert Walkowiak; John Bancroft diary, April 27, 1863, RG 95, Special Collections and Archives, Auburn University Library; Edgar Noble diary, April 27, 1863, Thomas Spain. For a detailed history and examination of this campaign, see *Chancellorsville* by Stephen W. Sears (New York: Houghton Mifflin, 1996).
3. Bancroft diary, April 28–29, 1863; Hewitt diary, April 28–29, 1863; Miner diary, April 28–29, 1863; Noble diary, April 29, 1863.
4. Bancroft, Hewitt, Miner, and Noble diaries, April 30, 1863; *OR*, vol. 25, pt. 1, p. 517.
5. Seage diary, May 1, 1863; *OR*, vol. 25, pt. 1, p. 517; Jeffords to Dear Friends (transcript), May 7, 1863, used by permission of a private collector; Seage, *History of Co. E*, p. 23; Bancroft diary, May 1, 1863.
6. Seage diary, May 1, 1863; Houghton journal; Miner diary, May 1, 1863; Hewitt diary, May 1, 1863; Maltz to Hinchman, May 12, 1863, Hinchman Papers, Burton Collection, Detroit Public Library; Phelps to Dear Brother, May 5, 1863, Jeff Phelps; Jeffords to Dear Friends, May 11, 1863, private collector; Seage, *History of Co. E*, p. 23; Noble diary, May 1, 1863.
7. Houghton journal; Miner diary, May 2, 1863; Bancroft diary, May 2, 1863; Maltz to Hinchman, May 12, 1863, Hinchman Papers; Taylor to Sister Lottie, May 7, 1863, G. Taylor Collection, Warren Hunting Smith Library, Hobart and William Smith Colleges.
8. Seage, *History of Co. E*, p. 24; Seage diary, May 3, 1863.
9. *Adrian Watchtower*, May 13, 1863; Phelps to Dear Brother, May 5, 1863, Jeff Phelps; Campbell, "Service with the Old 4th Mich. Infantry," MOLLUS.
10. *OR*, vol. 25, pt. 1, p. 517; Salter's May 4 letter in *Detroit Advertiser and Tribune*, May 14, 1863. When the story was retold over the years by Michigan men, Gen. George Meade replaced Gen. Joseph Hooker
11. Bancroft diary, May 3, 1863; Houghton journal; Salter letter, *Detroit Advertiser and Tribune*, May 14, 1863; Seage, *History of Co. E*, p. 24; Seage diary, May 3, 1863.
12. *Monroe Monitor*, May 14, 1863; Houghton journal; Bancroft diary, May 3, 1863.
13. *OR*, vol. 25, pt. 1, p. 518; Sears, *Chancellorsville*, p. 406; Maltz to Hinchman, May 12, 1863, Hinchman Papers; Bancroft diary, May 4, 1863; Houghton journal and John S. Conant to Dear Parents Brothers and Sisters, May 4–5, 1863, Bentley Library; Barrett, *Old Fourth Michigan Infantry*, p. 20; Miner diary, May 4, 1863; Phelps to Dear Brother, May 5, 1863, Jeff Phelps.
14. Barrett, *Old Fourth Michigan Infantry*, p. 20; Phelps to Dear Brother, May 5, 1863, Jeff Phelps; Miner diary, May 4, 1863; Seage diary, May 4, 1863; *Hudson Gazette*, May 23, 1863; Maltz to Hinchman, May 12, 1863, Hinchman Papers; *OR*, vol. 25, pt. 1, p. 518.
15. Harrison Daniels reminiscence, Hal Flynn and Craig and Ann Emery.
16. Hewitt diary, May 5–6, 1863; Seage diary, May 5–6, 1863; Jeffords to Dear Friends, May 7, 1863, private collector; Bancroft diary, May 5–6, 1863; Houghton journal; Phelps to Dear Brother, May 23, 1863, Jeff Phelps.
17. Fox, *Regimental Losses*, p. 383, stated eight men from the 4th Michigan were killed or mortally wounded at Chancellorsville, but it is not clear whether this includes Austin Miner or the other man missing. Miner was later determined to have been killed. A contemporaneous army tabulation for the regiment—*OR*, vol. 25, pt. 1, p. 180—indicated six men killed and 12 wounded, but infection and complications usually caused the deaths of a number of wounded men weeks and months after a battle.
18. Taylor to Sister Lottie, May 7, 1863, and May 12, 1863, Taylor Collection; Jeffords to Dear Friends, May 7, 1863, private collector.
19. Maltz to Hinchman, May 12, 1863, Hinchman Papers; Vreeland to Dear Mother, May 18, 1863, Vreeland

Papers, USAMHI.

20. Jeffords to Dear Friends, May 7, 1863, and May 13, 1863, private collector; Henry Seage and Irvin Miner both used the term "splendid horse" in describing the animal, and John Hewitt also commented that it was a "beautiful war horse"; Bancroft diary, May 13 and 16, 1863. Lt. George Maltz wrote, specifically, that it was "the enlisted men" who gave Jeffords this gift: Maltz to Hinchman, May 12, 1863, Hinchman Papers; McQuade to Blair, May 10, 1863, Abraham Lincoln Presidential Library, Springfield, Ill.
21. Maltz to Hinchman, May 12, 1863, Hinchman Papers.
22. Hewitt diary, May 25–26, 1863; Houghton journal, May 25–26, 1863; Bancroft to Hinchman, May 28–29, 1863, Hinchman Papers; Jeffords to Blair, May 28, 1863, 4th Michigan regimental records, State Archives of Michigan; Phelps to Dear Brother, May 23, 1863, Jeff Phelps. Phelps's reference to the date, May 16, reflected the incorrect belief by many men that their enlistments in the spring of 1861 dated from the appointment of Dwight Woodbury to raise and lead the 4th Michigan. In fact, their enlistments dated from their muster into federal service in June 1861.
23. Bancroft to Hinchman, May 28–29, 1863, Hinchman Papers; Miner diary, May 27, 1863.
24. Bancroft to Hinchman, May 28–29, 1863, Hinchman Papers; Bancroft diary, June 1–2, 1863; Daniels reminiscence; *Monroe Monitor,* June 10, 1863; Hewitt diary, June 4, 1863; Houghton journal, June 4, 1863; Miner diary, June 5, 1863; Phelps to Dear Brother, June 10, 1863, Jeff Phelps.
25. John Seage wrote two different letters recounting this incident: J. Seage to Gov. Blair, Dec. 23, 1863, and J. Seage to Robertson, June 1, 1866, 4th Michigan regimental records, State Archives; Campbell, "Service with the Old 4th Michigan, p. 18, MOLLUS; Jeffords to Dear Friends, May 13, 1863, private collector.
26. J. Seage to Robertson, June 1, 1866, and Seage to Blair, Dec. 23, 1863, regimental records, State Archives; Seage diary, June 8, 9, 15–24, 1863.
27. Taylor to Sister Lottie, June 12, 1863, Taylor Collection; Barrett, *Old Fourth Michigan Infantry,* pp. 37–39.
28. Miner diary, June 9–10, 1863; Houghton journal, June 11–12, 1863; Barrett, *Old Fourth Michigan Infantry,* p. 21. Barrett claimed that the regimental "smart aleck" who asked the question was later shot and killed while on picket, but the regiment's contemporaneous records, letters to hometown newspapers, and diary keepers don't mention a fatality along the river at that time.
29. Taylor to dear Sister Lottie, June 12, 1863, Taylor Collection; Bancroft, Miner, Hewitt, and Seage diaries, June 12–20, 1863; Houghton journal; Bancroft to Hinchman, June 23, 1863, Hinchman Papers.
30. Miner, Bancroft, Seage, and Hewitt diaries, June 21–26, 1863; Houghton journal; *Hillsdale Standard,* June 30, 1863. The fact Luke Barnes fell out and was captured is in a subsequent letter by his brother, Joel Barnes to Dear Brother Judge, Aug. 21, 1863, Roger Walcott Collection, Archives and Regional Historical Collections, Western Michigan University, and also in his service record, National Archives.
31. Miner diary, June 26–30, 1863; Hewitt diary, June 26–30, 1863; Seage diary, June 26–30; and Bancroft diary, June 26–30, 1863; Houghton journal.

Chapter 10. They Were Soon on All Sides of Us

1. Campbell, "Service with the Old 4th Michigan Infantry," MOLLUS.
2. James Houghton journal, Bentley Historical Library, University of Michigan; John Bancroft diary, July 1, 1863, Special Collections and Archives, Auburn University; Bancroft Gettysburg narrative and letter to the state adjutant general, June 17, 1889, Record Group 59-14, 4th Michigan Infantry records, Box 97, State Archives of Michigan, Lansing; John W. Hewitt diary, July 1, 1863, Clarke Historical Library, Central Michigan University; Irvin Miner diary, July 1, 1863, Robert Walkowiak; Barrett, *Old Fourth Michigan Infantry,* pp. 21–22.
3. Henry Seage diary, July 2, 1863, Steve Roberts; Bancroft Gettysburg narrative; *OR,* vol. 27, pt. 1, p. 610.
4. Houghton journal; Bancroft diary, July 2, 1863; Bancroft Gettysburg narrative.
5. Houghton journal. For accounts of the Fifth Corps's movement onto the battlefield at Gettysburg, see Harry P. Pfanz, *Gettysburg: The Second Day* (Chapel Hill: University of North Carolina Press, 1987), p. 208, and

Edwin P. Coddington, *The Gettysburg Campaign* (Dayton: Morningside Books, 1979), p. 389. Oliver Norton, bugler for the commander of the Third Brigade of the First Division, recalled they marched on what must have been the School House Road, turned south on Taneytown Road, and then went across country.

6. Coddington, *The Gettysburg Campaign*, p. 389.
7. *OR*, vol. 27, pt. 1, p. 610; Coddington, *The Gettysburg Campaign*, p. 400; Bancroft to Adjutant General of Michigan, June 17, 1889, 4th Michigan records, State Archives; Houghton journal; Pfanz, *Gettysburg*, pp. 242–45.
8. Houghton journal; *OR*, vol. 27, pt. 1, p. 611; *Detroit Free Press*, Aug. 4, 1863, "an extract of a private letter from an officer of the Fourth Infantry, dated Warrenton, July 29th, giving an account of how it happened the regiment suffered so at Gettysburg." The description of the changes in the 4th Michigan's position also in Bancroft diary, July 2, 1863, and the Bancroft Gettysburg narrative.
9. Pfanz, *Gettysburg*, pp. 252–53, 256–59; Jay Jorgensen, *Gettysburg's Bloody Wheatfield* (Shippensburg, Pa.: White Mane Books, 2001), pp. 79–82; *Detroit Free Press*, Aug. 4, 1863; *Supplement to Official Records*, vol. 5, p. 192; *OR*, vol. 27, pt. 1, p. 611.
10. For accounts of Caldwell's attack, see Pfanz, *Gettysburg*, pp. 267–87, and Stephen W. Sears, *Gettysburg* (New York: Houghton Mifflin, 2003), pp. 301–4.
11. *OR*, vol. 27, pt. 1, p. 611; Sweitzer wrote another version of his report that appears in the *Supplement to Official Records*, vol. 5, pp. 189–95; his meeting with Caldwell and subsequent brigade march is on pp. 192–93, as is his description of the low ground where the 4th Michigan moved; Bancroft Gettysburg narrative; Houghton journal.
12. Houghton journal; Sears, *Gettysburg*, pp. 302–3; Bancroft Gettysburg narrative.
13. Pfanz, *Gettysburg*, p. 287.
14. *OR*, vol. 27, pt. 1, p. 611; *Supplement to Official Records*, vol. 5, p. 193; *Detroit Free Press*, Aug. 4, 1863; Bancroft diary, July 2, 1863; Bancroft Gettysburg narrative; Houghton journal.
15. Hillyer's account, "The Battle of Gettysburg: Address Before the Walton County, Georgia, Confederate Veterans," Aug. 2, 1904, *Walton Tribune*, is quoted in Pfanz, *Gettysburg*, p. 295. The 4th Michigan's U.S. flag, selected in late March, had been in camp except for the march to Chancellorsville, where the regiment was involved in skirmishing. Since regimental flags weren't usually carried on skirmish lines, this flag was still in good shape.
16. Houghton journal; Perine account: *Battle Creek Enquirer & News*, n.d. (late January), 1935, provided by Sharon Mershon; *Supplement to Official Records*, vol. 5, p. 193; Francis J. Parker, *The Story of the Thirty-second Regiment, Massachusetts Volunteer Infantry* (Boston: C. W. Calkins, 1880), p. 169.
17. *Detroit Free Press*, Aug. 4, 1863; Carl Vreeland, "Letters from Civil War Battlefields," *Oregon (Portland) Journal*, June 25, 1964; Bancroft to the Michigan Adjutant General, June 17, 1889, 4th Michigan records, State Archives, and enclosed Bancroft Gettysburg narrative. In the letter, Bancroft cited his comrade, State Treasurer (former Lieutenant) George Maltz, about burying Kydd and Jackson after the battle; also *Detroit Free Press*, July 13, 1863.
18. Vreeland statement on Company I's lost arms and accoutrements, copy provided by Cecile Vreeland; Laird's wounding: Gregory A. Coco, *Killed in Action: Eyewitness Accounts of the Last Moments of 100 Union Soldiers Who Died at Gettysburg* (Gettysburg: Thomas Publications, 1996), pp. 46–47; Bancroft diary, July 2, 1863.
19. Sweitzer's reports: *OR*, vol. 27, pt. 1, pp. 611–12 (in which Sweitzer quotes Martin); and *Supplement to Official Records*, vol. 5, pp. 193–95; John Coxe, "The Battle of Gettysburg," *Confederate Veteran*, vol. 21, no. 9, September 1913, p. 435.
20. Houghton journal; Perine account: *Battle Creek Enquirer & News*, n.d. (late Jan.), 1935; Bancroft diary, July 2, 1863; and Bancroft Gettysburg narrative.
21. *OR*, vol. 27, pt. 1, p. 612; *Supplement to Official Records*, vol. 5, p. 193; Pfanz, *Gettysburg*, p. 293; Houghton journal.
22. Bancroft diary, July 2, 1863; Bancroft Gettysburg narrative. Bancroft wrote that his account was "taken from notes I made at that time and a letter written a few days after the battle." Bancroft to Adjutant General, June

17, 1889, 4th Michigan file, State Archives.

Seage to Bachelder, Sept. 23, 1884, in Dale A. Ladd and Audrey J. Ladd, eds., *The Bachelder Papers: Gettysburg in their Own Words*, 3 vols. (Dayton: Morningside, 1994–95), vol. 2, pp. 1070–72; *Detroit Free Press*, Aug. 4, 1863.

23. Conant to Dear Parents Brothers and sisters, July 5, 1863, Bentley Library; Coxe, "The Battle of Gettysburg," p. 435; Parker, *Thirty-second Regiment*, p. 170.
24. Tolford's letter, *Hudson Gazette*, July 11, 1863; Houghton journal; Pfanz, *Gettysburg*, p. 295; *OR*, vol. 27. pt. 2, pp. 399–400
25. *OR*, vol. 27, pt. 1, p. 612; *Supplement to Official Records*, vol. 5, p. 193; *Detroit Free Press*, Aug. 4, 1863.
26. Gilbert to J. E. Phelps, Aug. 16, 1863, Jeff Phelps; Harrison Daniels reminiscence, Hal Flynn and Craig and Ann Emery; Tripp remembered at a regimental reunion, the *Coffee Cooler* (monthly veterans newspaper, published at Sturgis, Michigan), Aug. 1892.
27. Seage to Bachelder, Sept. 23, 1884, in Ladd and Ladd, *The Bachelder Papers*, vol. 2, pp. 1070–72. Tom Tarsney, one of three Tarsney brothers in the regiment, was reduced in rank to private four months later, according to Henry Seage's diary, Nov. 16, 1863. John Tarsney: Michigan Adjutant General, *Records of Service*, p. 107. John Tarsney's military record shows he was captured, but other biographical materials say he was also wounded.
28. Seage to Bachelder, Sept. 23, 1884, Ladd and Ladd, *Bachelder Papers*, vol. 2, p. 1071; Carl Vreeland, "Letters from Civil War Battlefields," *Oregon (Portland) Journal*, June 25, 1964. There is no statement or reference in Vreeland's voluminous pension file that he was involved in the struggle for the flag. His own statement to the army about the loss of his company's rifles was that they were "surrounded" on the regiment's right. Henry Seage's statement that Vreeland was part of the fight for the flag was made nearly nine years after Vreeland died.
29. Seage to Bachelder, Sept. 23, 1884, Ladd and Ladd, *Bachelder Papers*, vol. 2, p. 1071; Seage diary, July 3, 1863; *Detroit Free Press*, Aug. 4, 1863; John Seage to Blair, Dec. 23, 1863, 4th Michigan records, State Archives; R. W. Seage medical examinations in his pension file, National Archives.
30. H. Seage to Bachelder, Sept. 23, 1884, Ladd and Ladd, *Bachelder Papers*, vol. 2, p. 1071. Henry Seage recorded in his diary on July 3 that Jeffords died from his wounds, but he thought this took place on July 2. Col. Lumbard stated the circumstances of Jeffords's wounding in battle and subsequent death the next day in his year-end report, Lumbard to Robertson, Dec. 1863, 4th Michigan records, State Archives; Sweitzer's supplemental report, *Supplement to Official Records*, vol. 5, p. 194; *Medical and Surgical History of the War of the Rebellion, prepared under the direction of Surgeon General Joseph K. Barnes, United States Army*, 3 vols. in 6 parts (Washington, D.C.: Government Printing Office, 1870–88), pt. 1, vol. 2, p. 468.

    The diaries of John Bancroft and John Hewitt, the letter by William Tolford, and the reminiscence of Robert Campbell state that Jeffords survived for a time after he was bayoneted; so do official reports, such as the casualty statement on Jeffords authorized by Gen. James Barnes; that statement is part of Jeffords's service record, National Archives.
31. Conant to Dear Parents Brothers and sisters, July 5, 1863, Bentley Library; Houghton journal; Carl Vreeland, "Letters from Civil War Battlefields," *Oregon (Portland) Journal*, June 25, 1964; Barrett, *Old Fourth Michigan Infantry*, pp. 22–23; John Seage to Blair, Dec. 23, 1863, regimental records, State Archives. Richard W. Seage was likely removed from the field in the early morning hours of July 3.
32. Seage diary, July 2, 1863; Houghton journal; Sears, *Gettysburg*, p. 304.
33. Houghton journal; *Detroit Free Press*, Aug. 4, 1983; Bancroft diary, July 2, 1863; Sears, *Gettysburg*, pp. 321–22; Pfanz, *Gettysburg*, p. 428.
34. Bancroft diary, July 2, 1863; Houghton journal.
35. Bancroft diary, July 2, 1863; Seage diary, July 2 and 3, 1863; Hewitt diary, July 2, 1863; Conant to Dear Parents Brothers and sisters, July 5, 1863, Bentley Library; *OR*, vol. 27, pt. 1, p. 604; *Detroit Free Press*, Aug. 4, 1863.
36. List of 4th Michigan casualties at Gettysburg, July 2, 1863, G. Lumbard, 4th Michigan records, State Archives. The regiment's killed, mortally wounded, and missing and presumed dead: John W. Busey, *These Honored Dead: The Union Casualties at Gettysburg* (Hightstown, N.J.: Longstreet House, 1996), pp. 70–72; Boies,

"The Spirit of Comradeship," *Confederate Veteran,* vol. 23, September 1915, p. 424; *OR,* vol. 27, pt. 1, p. 613. A tabulation of the regiment's prisoners who died in Rebel prisons by the late William Heckert is in the Heckert Papers, Monroe County Historical Museum.

37. Barrett, *Old Fourth Michigan Infantry,* p. 23; Seage diary, July 3, 1863; Carl Vreeland, "Letters from Civil War Battlefields," *Oregon (Portland) Journal,* June 25, 1964; unidentified newspaper clipping about Vreeland, marked "Adrian Paper, June 8, 1865," Vreeland file, USAMHI.
38. Pfanz, *Gettysburg,* pp. 428, 432; Coddington, *The Gettysburg Campaign,* p. 442; Wert, *The Sword of Lincoln,* p. 295; Frank Clark is in Gregory A. Coco, *A Vast Sea of Misery* (Gettysburg: Thomas Publications, 1988), pp. 151–52; Mark Taylor: *Michigan (Sturgis) Democrat,* June 26, 1890; Barrett, *Old Fourth Michigan Infantry,* p. 23; Vreeland removed from battlefield: clipping identified as "Adrian paper, June 8, 1865," Vreeland Papers, USAMHI; Hewitt diary, July 3, 1863.
39. In a patriotic reunion speech, Lester H. Salsbury said that members of the regiment were victorious in a hand-to-hand fight for the colors and were able to "bring off the flag and the body of our lion-hearted colonel." *Hudson Post,* June 29, 1876. Salsbury was seriously wounded at Gettysburg with bullets striking him in the thigh, hand, and lung and was almost certainly carried off the field himself.
40. Seage diary, July 3, 1863.
41. Seage diary, July 3, 1863; Bates report, *OR,* vol. 27, pt. 1, p. 597; *Detroit Free Press,* Aug. 4, 1863. The authors were not able to find any Civil War account, letter, report, or diary of the 4th Michigan that unequivocally stated the men of the regiment carried their wounded colonel off the battlefield during the retreat.
42. Sweitzer report, *Supplement to Official Records,* vol. 5, p. 194; *Detroit Free Press,* Aug. 4, 1863; Campbell, "Service with the Old 4th Michigan Infantry," MOLLUS. This was Campbell's handwritten reminiscence; a shorter version of Campbell's paper, a speech given after 1900 called "Pioneer Memories of the War Days of 1861–65," edited and with punctuation and quotation marks added, was published in the *Michigan Pioneer and Historical Collection,* vol. 30; the anecdote about Jeffords's death appears on p. 570. The surgeon who attended Jeffords was not named.
43. Casualty sheet authorized by General Barnes, Jeffords service record, National Archives; Lumbard to Robertson, Dec. 1863, 4th Michigan records, State Archives. A transcription of this letter is in Robertson, *Michigan in the War,* pp. 229–30. Several casualty statements are in Jeffords's records, some that are correct and some wrongly stating that he was killed in action. Letter of "Lieutenant," a former member of the 4th Michigan, in the *Hudson Gazette,* July 21, 1871.
44. *New York Herald,* July 6, 1863.
45. *Detroit Free Press,* July 8 and 22, 1863; *Monroe Commercial,* July 16, 1863. Another version of this brief report appeared in the *Hudson Gazette,* July 18, 1863, in which the spelling of Jeffords's name was corrected; his name was also corrected when the report was reprinted in the *Michigan (Ann Arbor) Argus.* The anecdote about William F. Robinson was reprinted in the *Jonesville Independent,* July 23, 1863. The Hudson paper didn't include the statement that Jeffords shot a Confederate, possibly because it had learned from someone in the regiment that this wasn't correct. Crounses's report of the charge of the brigades of Caldwell and Sweitzer: *New York Times,* July 4, 1863.
46. Bancroft to Hinchman, July 21, 1863, Theodore Hinchman Papers, Burton Historical Collection, Detroit Public Library. Bancroft wasn't the only soldier who was critical of the news reports about battles and skirmishes. In September 1861, Luke Barnes warned his brother at home, "you must not believe the papers for they do not tell the truth." After the Seven Days battle in 1862, Lt. Charles Salter of the 16th Michigan wrote a friend in Detroit: "I can assure you no matter how grand it may be for people up North to read accounts of splendid victories, it is not very pleasant for those engaged in it." Less than a year after Gettysburg, Robert Carter of the 22nd Massachusetts wrote about reporting on the Fifth Corps near Spotsylvania Court House: "I observe that the newspapers report very erroneously, and the reports are deficient as a general thing, in the true facts of this campaign; they are full of the most exaggerated blunders, and many absurd stories are circulated. . . . Even Hendricks, our Fifth Corps correspondent, as been strangely misled . . . they dare not come to the front for *reliable information,* but derive their knowledge from those at the rear." See L. Barnes to

Dear Brother, Sept. 10, 1861, Roger Walcott Collection, Archives and Regional History Collections, Western Michigan University; Salter to I. Duffield, July 12, 1862, Duffield Papers, Burton Collection; Robert G. Carter, *Four Brothers in Blue* (Norman: University of Oklahoma Press,1999), p. 403.

47. *Detroit Free Press,* Aug. 4, 1863. Bancroft and Lt. George Maltz both wrote to Hinchman, and their letters are in the Detroit Public Library's Burton Collection. Of course, there is no letter dated July 29, 1863, in Hinchman's papers. We think it likely that Bancroft wrote this letter, following up his brief but harsh criticism of the *Herald's* account in his July 21 letter with specifics on July 29, when he was in camp; and that Hinchman took this letter to the *Free Press* for publication.

    Hinchman was a businessman active in Detroit civic affairs, and during the war was a supporter of the "Union" party (a coalition of Republicans and "War Democrats"). At times, Bancroft had asked Hinchman to pass word of officers' opinions on matters such as promotions to Governor Blair. George Maltz and Dr. Chamberlain also wrote to him. Why was there no name attached to this July 29 letter when it was printed? Because it was common practice; Detroit's Civil War newspapers regularly published information contained in private letters sent by soldiers to friends and family who shared the contents with editors. Even when soldiers sent letters directly to the editors, their full names were usually not given. *A Guide to the Material in the Detroit Newspapers 1861–1866* by Helen Ellis (Lansing: Michigan Civil War Centennial Observance Commission, 1965) shows that it was routine for as many as 400 or more officers and soldiers writing hundreds of letters directly to Detroit newspapers not to be identified by name, but by initials and pseudonyms. Small weekly papers also often used initials and pen names for correspondents serving in the army.

48. Seage to Bachelder, Sept. 23, 1884, Ladd and Ladd, *Bachelder Papers,* vol. 2, p. 1071; Pfanz, *Gettysburg,* p. 294; Sears, *Gettysburg,* p. 304. Pfanz specifically cited Seage's letter to Bachelder as the source for the recapture of the 4th Michigan flag. Sears cited Colonel Sweitzer's reports, which state Jeffords was wounded fighting for his colors but make no claim that he saved the flag; and Houghton's narrative, which stated Jeffords "regained the flag" before he was bayoneted.

49. Hewitt diary, July 2, 1863; *Detroit Free Press,* Aug. 4, 1863.

50. Salter to My Dear Friend, July 12, 1863, Duffield Papers, Burton Collection; David L. Poremba, ed., *If I Am Found Dead* (Ann Arbor: Ann Arbor Media Group, 2006), p. 126; Regan, *Lost Civil War Diaries,* p. 144. A fatal bayonet stab wound was rare and undoubtedly shocking news. George W. Adams's study of Union army medicine notes that less than 0.4 percent of all reported Civil War wounds were inflicted with sword or bayonet, and that chest wounds "made by cutting weapons had a mortality rate of 9 percent, but were few in number." *Doctors in Blue* (Dayton: Morningside Books, 1985), pp. 113, 136.

51. *Monroe Monitor,* July 22, 1863. A number of men from Monroe served in the 7th Infantry Regiment, also in the Army of the Potomac. The soldier who wrote to the paper may have been from this outfit, since he was not a member of the 4th Michigan.

52. Campbell, "Pioneer Memories," pp. 567, 571. Campbell claimed this blue post-Gettysburg flag went through the spring campaign of 1864 and that it was returned to Michigan, where it was on display in a military museum after the turn of the century. Yet the curator in charge of Michigan's Civil War flags, Kerry Chartkoff, in an interview with the authors in 2008, said evidence indicates the remaining part of a blue regimental flag (with the state seal painted on one side, a federal coat of arms on the other) was an expensive presentation flag given to the reorganized 4th Michigan regiment, formed in the late summer of 1864. This couldn't have been the flag Campbell "procured" in the summer of 1863. Parker, *Thirty-second Regiment,* p. 172; Henry B. James, *Memories of the Civil War* (New Bedford, Mass.: F. E. James, 1898), p. 39.

53. Email discussions between the authors and Kurt D. Graham, coauthor with Richard M. Coffman of *To Honor These Men: A History of the Phillips Georgia Legion Infantry Battalion* (Macon, Ga.: Mercer University Press, 2008), and Gregory C. White, *This Most Bloody & Cruel Drama—A History of the 31st Georgia Volunteer Infantry* (Baltimore: Butternut & Blue, 1997); *Richmond Enquirer,* Aug. 5, 1863.

54. Coffman and Graham, *To Honor These Men,* pp. 168–69. Some interpret the words about the colors "supposed to be in the hands of some other regiment" to mean that a Union regiment must have rescued that flag. But because of the contemporaneous accounts that the 4th Michigan's flag was lost, and the fact that the Union

soldiers were driven off the field, we believe Wofford was saying that the flag was taken by Confederates who were not part of his brigade. Rebel units were mixed up in their advance across the Wheatfield.

Three of the soldiers mentioned in Wofford's description of this fight for a Yankee flag—privates Thomas B. Jolly, who was thought killed, Michael McGovern, and J. A. Blanton—were named in a Confederate "Roll of Honor" issued later that summer. See *OR*, ser. 1, vol. 27, pt. 2, p. 775.

55. Coffman and Graham, *To Honor These Men*, pp. 168, 171; Houghton journal.
56. *Monroe Commercial*, July 16, 1863; Houghton journal.
57. "Mismanagement" by Barnes, letter by a "former Hudson boy" who served in the 4th Michigan in *Hudson Gazette*, July 21, 1871; Seage to Bachelder, Sept. 23, 1884, Ladd and Ladd, *Bachelder Papers*, vol. 2, p. 1072. The debate about who was ultimately responsible for sending Barnes's division into that dangerous position in the woods south and west of the Wheatfield raged on for decades in newspapers. Orvey Barrett gave his opinion, holding George Meade responsible, in a letter to the *National Tribune*, Sept. 23, 1886.

Chapter 11. We Have Seen a Pretty Hard Campaign

1. Salter to My Dear Friend, July 29, 1863, Duffield Papers, Burton Historical Collection, Detroit Public Library. The letter is also in Poremba, *If I Am Found Dead*, p. 129.
2. James Houghton journal, Bentley Historical Library, University of Michigan.
3. The George Weikert farm, east of Trostle's Woods and just north of the Wheatfield Road, should not be confused with the Jacob Weikert farm on the Taneytown Road and site of a temporary hospital set up by surgeons of the Third and Fifth corps. *Monroe Commercial*, July 16, 1863 (July 5 letter of William Gibson); *Hudson Gazette*, July 11, 1863 (July 5 letter of William B. Tolford); Taylor to Dear Mother, July 4, 1863, G. Taylor Collection, Warren Hunting Smith Library, Hobart and William Smith Colleges; John Bancroft diary, July 2–3, 1863, RG 95, Special Collections & Archives, Auburn University Library. Death of Millens: summary of his service record with his diary transcription, Glen McQueen, and service record documents, National Archives. A War Department filing in Millens's record states he died at Augusta, Georgia, on February 28, 1864. Exchange of A. Day: Carpenter, *War for the Union*, p. 8.
4. The experiences of Sgt. Oliver Smith and David Webster are from Webster family letters and letter transcriptions, Steve Bucher and Rose Miller: Clark to S. M. Webster, Oct. 19, 1863; D. Webster to Dear Father, Jan. 15 (1864), from Pemberton Castle Crew Prison, Webster to Dear Mother, Jan. 27, 1864; and Webster to Dear Mother, May 11, 1864, from Andersonville. Also Michigan Adjutant General, *Records of Service*, pp. 66, 77.
5. Service and pension records for Hamlin and Crawford, National Archives; Robinson to his parents, July 22, 1863, Bentley Library.
6. *Hudson Gazette*, July 11, 1863; Coco, *Vast Sea of Misery*, p. 152; Houghton journal. Vesey's Aug. 20 letter appeared in the *Sturgis Journal*, Sept. 10, 1863; Henry Seage diary, July 3, 1863, Steve Roberts; Jeffords's funeral: *Detroit Free Press*, July 12, 1863.

   An Aug. 20, 1863 letter sent to the Army by H. B. Wescott of Dexter on behalf of Jeffords's family, part of Jeffords's record in the National Archives, states that a man named "E.R. Snyder of Littleton" (Littlestown, Pennsylvania), took Jeffords's body to Hanover where a Union Army doctor embalmed it for $50. The body was taken to Baltimore and sent to Michigan by rail at a cost of $50. Other correspondence by officers and doctors shows the man who embalmed the body, Dr. P. Gardner of the 1st Virginia (Union) Cavalry, was investigated to see if his embalming business was improper. Authorities ruled the doctor, though showing "indiscretion and imprudence," violated no regulation.
7. Bancroft diary, July 3, 1863; Barrett, *Old Fourth Michigan Infantry*, pp. 23–24.
8. Bancroft diary, July 4, 1863; John W. Hewitt diary, July 4, 1863, Clarke Historical Library, Central Michigan University; Houghton journal. Houghton, apparently writing his reminiscence years later, included the story of Major Hall shooting the Confederate sergeant who had stabbed Jeffords—something the *New York Herald* reported, but which the unnamed officer from the regiment wrote did not happen in a letter extract in the

Detroit Free Press, Aug. 4, 1863.

9. Campbell, "Pioneer Memories," p. 571; Bancroft diary, July 5, 1863; Harrison Daniels reminiscence, Hal Flynn and Craig Emery and Ann Emery. Other accounts say men of the regiment went out to pick up wounded on the night of July 2, yet Daniels placed his retrieval of Plummer on the night of July 3; *Hillsdale Independent,* July 14, 1863; *Hudson Gazette,* July 11, 1863; Seage diary, July 5–Sept. 23, 1863.
10. Bancroft diary, July 6–14, 1863; Houghton journal; Conant to Dear Parents Brothers and sisters, July 17, 1863, Bentley Library.
11. Bancroft diary, July 15–21, 1863; Bancroft to Hinchman, July 21, 1863, Hinchman Papers, Burton Collection.
12. *Sturgis Journal,* Sept. 10, 1863; Bancroft diary, July 22–Aug. 9, 1863; Hewitt diary, July 28, 1863.
13. Hewitt diary, July 5–Aug. 9, 1863.
14. Regan, *Lost Civil War Diaries* (Aug. 29, 1863), p. 158.
15. Bliss to Mrs. Hacker, Aug. 10,1863, Hacker Brothers Papers, Schoff Civil War Collection, William L. Clements Library, University of Michigan.
16. *Sturgis Journal,* Sept. 10, 1863; Conant to Dear Parents Brothers and Sisters, March 13, 1863, and Lamson to Robinson, Aug. 20, 1863, Bentley Library.
17. Lamson to Robinson, Aug. 20, 1863, Bentley Library.
18. Gilbert to J. E. Phelps, Aug. 1 and 16, 1863, Jeff Phelps.
19. A. Purdy to Bancroft, July 27, 1863, and S. Wilson to Bancroft, Aug. 25, 1863 (transcriptions), enclosed with the Bancroft diary transcript by Peter Bancroft, Bentley Library. The original letters are part of the Bancroft diary-scrapbook at Auburn University.
20. Handwritten copy of Lamson's statement regarding lost gear, Aug. 28, 1863, with addendum dated Dec. 13, 1863, Bentley Library.
21. J. Barnes to Judge William Barnes, Aug. 21, 1863, Roger Walcott Collections, Archives and Regional Historical Collections, Western Michigan University. It may be that Luke Barnes just wasn't cut out to be a soldier. Letters show that after he accidentally shot Captain Wood in 1861, he was caught asleep while on duty and was disrespectful to an officer; he had other run-ins with soldiers. Joel Barnes wrote that Luke was "kind of strange" and "inclind to be fieble minded." Lieutenant Col. Lumbard invented a word on Aug. 21, 1863, when he reported Luke was "indiscipline-able." Records show Luke later applied for an invalid pension, but the government rejected it.
22. Taylor to My dear sister, Aug. 20, 1863, Taylor Collection; Hewitt diary, Aug. 29, 1863; Houghton journal.
23. Cunningham to Dear Mother, Aug. 30 or 31, 1863, Cunningham pension file, National Archives.
24. Hewitt diary, Aug. 30, Sept. 2–12, 1863; Campbell, "Pioneer Memories," p. 571. Campbell wrote around the turn of the century that this blue flag was eventually placed in Michigan's "military museum" in Lansing, but no 4th Michigan flag of that description is in the state's possession. What does survive is part of a blue, two-sided "presentation" flag, identified as a banner of the reorganized 4th Michigan Infantry Regiment, which formed in the late summer and fall of 1864.
25. Bancroft diary, Sept. 13–30, 1863; Hewitt diary, Sept. 13–30, 1863; Seage diary, Sept. 23, 1863; Seage, *History of Co. E,* p. 27.
26. Hall to Blair, Sept. 22, 1863, Blair Papers, Burton Collection; Taylor to My dear Lottie, Sept. 29, 1863, Taylor Collection; Bancroft diary, Oct. 1, 1863; Hewitt diary, Sept. 28, 30, Oct. 1, 1863.
27. Coco, *Killed in Action,* pp. 46–47; *Hudson Gazette,* Oct. 5, 19, 1863. Coco and the state's *Record of Service* volume for the 4th Michigan give a hometown of Adrian for Ladd, but contemporaneous news articles and records show he had lived with his parents in Pittsford Township, Hillsdale County.
28. Bancroft diary, Oct. 5, 10, 11, 1863; Hewitt diary, Oct. 10, 11, 1863; Seage diary, Oct. 10, 11, 1863.
29. Seage, Bancroft, and Hewitt diaries, Oct. 12–14, 1863; Bancroft to Hinchman, Nov. 5, 1863, Hinchman Papers.
30. Seage, Bancroft and Hewitt diaries, Oct. 15–19, 1863.
31. Seage, Bancroft, and Hewitt diaries, Oct. 20–Nov. 2, 1863; Bancroft to Lt. Col. Fred Locke, Oct. 22, 1863, in the Bancroft diary, with responses on back; Bancroft to Hinchman, Nov. 5, 1863, Hinchman Papers.
32. Bancroft diary, Nov. 7–8 1863; Seage diary, Nov. 7–8, 1863.

33. Bancroft, Seage, and Hewitt diaries, Nov. 9–24, 1863; *Hudson Gazette,* Dec. 19, 1863.
34. Bancroft, Seage, and Hewitt diaries, Nov. 25–27, 1863; Seage, *History of Co. E,* p. 31; *OR,* series 1, vol. 29, pt. 1, pp. 689–90, 904.
35. Seage, *History of Co. E,* p. 32; Bancroft diary, Nov. 29, 1863; Hewitt diary, Nov. 9, 1863; *Hudson Gazette,* Dec. 19, 1863.
36. *Hudson Gazette,* Dec. 19, 1863; Bancroft and Seage diaries, Nov. 30, 1863.
37. Bancroft, Seage, and Hewitt diaries, Dec. 1, 1863.

Chapter 12. They Say Let the War Go On

1. *Hudson Gazette,* Dec. 19, 1863; John W. Hewitt diary, Dec. 2–9, 1863, Clarke Historical Library, Central Michigan University; Henry Seage diary, Dec. 2–14, 1863, Steve Roberts; John Bancroft diary, Dec. 2, 1863, and a letter dated January 27, 1864, describing the building of winter camp, RG 95, Special Collections and Archives, Auburn University Library.
2. Robinson statement regarding lost stores, Dec. 22, 1863, Bentley Historical Library, University of Michigan; Brownell: *Hudson Gazette,* Nov. 28, 1863.
3. Lumbard to Blair, Dec. 8, 1863, Austin Blair Papers, Burton Historical Collection, Detroit Public Library.
4. Hewitt diary, Dec. 11–17, 20, 26, 1863; Seage diary, Dec. 20, 24, 26, 1863; Robinson to Lt. Col. J. R. Smith, Dec. 26, 1863, Bentley Library.
5. Hewitt and Seage diaries, Dec. 29, 1863; Taylor to Dear Will, Jan. 11, 1864, G. Taylor Collection, Warren Hunting Smith Library, Hobart and William Smith Colleges; Sadler to Dear Father and Mother (no date, but at a point after Feb. 28, 1864, most likely March 1864), from a private collector. Sadler did, however, enlist in the 30th Michigan Infantry late in 1864.
6. *Monroe Commercial,* April 28, 1864. Figures about the reenlistment are from John Robertson, *Michigan in the War,* p. 231.
7. Richardson to Dear Brother, Dec. 24, 1863, Bentley Library.
8. Richardson to Dear Brother, Dec. 28, 1863, Bentley Library.
9. Lumbard to Robertson, December (no date) 1863, Bentley Library; Hewitt and Seage diaries, Dec. 31, 1863; Bancroft diary, Jan. 1, 2, 23, 1864; *Detroit Advertiser and Tribune,* Jan. 16, 1864; Taylor to Dear Lottie, Jan. 31, 1864, Taylor Collection; *Hillsdale Standard,* Jan. 26, 1864.
10. Church donation: *Tecumseh Herald,* Jan. 21, 1864; Recruitment of new soldiers: *Hudson Gazette,* Jan. 9 and March 20, 1864; *Hillsdale Standard,* Feb. 15, 1864; Blair to Michigan Adjutant General (commissioning Goodrich), Feb. 24, 1864, Blair Papers; Order No. 48, Office of the Superintendent of Volunteer Recruiting Service, Lt. Col. B. H. Hill, March 30, 1864, 4th Michigan records, State Archives of Michigan.
11. Seage diary, Jan. 14, 17, 21, 23, 29, 31, 1864; Hewitt diary, Jan. 6, 13, 14, 16, 25, 28, 29, 1864.
12. Taylor to Dear Lottie, Jan. 31, 1864, Taylor Collection; Seage diary, Feb. 6, 10, 1864; Michigan Adjutant General, *Records of Service,* p. 43; Watts et al. (15 officers and 166 men), to Blair, Feb. 15, 1864, Blair Papers; Hewitt diary, Feb. 4, 14, 19, 20.
13. *Detroit Free Press,* March 1, 1864; *Hillsdale Standard,* Jan. 26 and March 8, 1864; *Hudson Gazette,* March 12, 1864; *Monroe Commercial,* March 2 and April 28, 1864.
14. *Steuben County Republican,* March 11, 1864.
15. *Hudson Gazette,* March 21, 1864; *Hillsdale Standard,* March 21, 1864; Blair to Robertson, March 21, 1864, Blair Papers.
16. Seage diary, Feb. 25, March 4, 8, 17, 1864; Hewitt diary, March 3, 9, 17, 21, 1864.
17. Seage diary, March 12, 18, 1864.
18. Taylor to Dear Will, March 27, 1864, Taylor Collection.
19. Ibid.
20. Seage diary, March 11, 22, 31, April 1, 2, 5, 1864; Hewitt diary, April 1–4, 1864; Blair to Robertson (Lumbard

commission), March 21, 1864, Blair Papers.

21. Bancroft diary, March 28, 30, April 12, 15, 25, 29, 30, 1864; Seage diary, April 7, 12, 13, 1864; Richardson to Dear Brother, March 3, 1864, and Richardson to Dear Brother, April 3, 1864, Bentley Library.
22. Richardson to Dear Brother, April 3, 1864, Bentley Library. Notes from a family genealogy filed with Richardson's letters state that he died on April 15, 1864.
23. Hawk's death: McLean to Robertson, April 10, 1864, and Special Orders (discharges) for Lamson, McLean, and E. French, 4th Michigan records, State Archives; Seage diary, April 16, 1864; *Hudson Gazette,* April 23 and May 7, 1864.
24. Seage diary, April 13 and 15, 1864; Henry Seage's third diary, April 20, 1864, John DeVinney collection; Hewitt diary, April 14, 15, 20, 1864; the Hartson-Tarsney letter to the *Hillsdale Standard* was reprinted in the *Hudson Gazette,* May 7, 1864.
25. *Monroe Commercial,* April 28, 1864; *Hudson Gazette,* May 7, 1864; Seage, *History of Co. E* (April 29, 1864), p. 33; Hewitt diary, April 27, 29, 1864.
26. Moses Luce memoir, p. 20, Edgar Luce Jr.; Hewitt diary, April 30–May 4, 1864; Seage diary, April 30–May 4, 1864, John DeVinney; Seage, *History of Co. E,* p. 33. Other accounts indicate the 4th Michigan had significantly less manpower than this 260 soldiers and officers. This may reflect only the number of men present and not those detached to serve in other duties at the direction of their brigade, division, and corps commanders. An unsigned account of regimental casualties dated May 27, 1864, seemingly by an officer, stated the 4th Michigan went into the Wilderness campaign with "190 guns." *Detroit Advertiser and Tribune,* May 27, 1864.

Chapter 13. I Am Well but Don't Know How Long

1. Wert, *The Sword of Lincoln,* pp. 334, 335.
2. John W. Hewitt diary, May 5, 1864, Clarke Historical Library, Central Michigan University; Henry Seage diary, May 5, 1864, John DeVinney; Seage, *History of Co. E,* p. 34; Robert H. Campbell, "Service with the Old 4th Michigan," pp. 32–33, MOLLUS; *Hudson Gazette,* May 28, 1864; *Sturgis Journal,* June 16, 1864; *Detroit Advertiser and Tribune,* May 27, 1864. Letters indicate that Jairus Hall was in Jackson at a camp for the rendezvous of men drafted into the Union army in the spring of 1864.
3. *Detroit Advertiser,* May 16, 1864; Campbell, "Service with the Old 4th Michigan," pp. 32–33, MOLLUS; Hewitt diary, May, 5, 1864; Jones's account of Lumbard's death: *Hillsdale Standard,* June 27, 1893, a report on a postwar 4th Michigan reunion.
4. Moses Luce memoir, pp. 23, 24, Edgar A. Luce Jr. The effort to find Lumbard's grave and remove his remains for reburial in Michigan is related in chapter 16.
5. Seage, *History of Co. E* (May 6, 1864), p. 34; Hewitt diary, May 6, 1864.
6. Seage, *History of Co. E* (May 7, 1864), p. 34; Seage diary, May 7, 1864; *Monroe Commercial,* June 23, 1864; Fox, *Regimental Losses,* p. 383.
7. Historians and men who were there pointed out that "Laurel Hill" was actually the name of a farm located a mile north of the high ground where the battle took place. The battlefield actually spanned the Spindle Farm and the Perry Farm properties. This ridge where the fighting occurred was about two miles northwest of Spotsylvania Court House. Seage, *History of Co. E* (May 8, 1864), pp. 34–35; Gregory A. Mertz, "General Gouverneur K. Warren and the Fighting at Laurel Hill," *Blue & Gray* magazine, vol. 21, issue 4, summer 2004, p. 20.
8. Seage diary, May 7, 1864; Seage, *History of Co. E* (May 8, 1864), p. 35; Mertz, "Gen. Warren," p. 21.
9. Powell, *Fifth Corps,* pp. 634–35; *Hudson Post,* March (n.d.), 1915, Hudson Museum.
10. *Monroe Commercial,* June 23, 1864; Hewitt diary, May 8, 1864. 4th Michigan strength: Vesey letter in the *Sturgis Journal,* June 16, 1864; and Seage, *History of Co. E* (May 8, 1864), pp. 34–35.
11. Taylor to Dear Mother, May 16, 1864, G. Taylor Collection, Warren Hunting Smith Library, Hobart and William Smith Colleges; discharges of Robinson and Barrett, War Department orders regarding officers

from the regiment, 4th Michigan regimental records, Box 59-14, State Archives of Michigan, Lansing.

12. *Monroe Commercial,* June 23. 1864; Seage diary, May 9, 1864; *Strugis Journal,* June 16, 1864; Hewitt diary, May 9, 1864.
13. Carter, *Four Brothers in Blue,* pp. 395, 398, 404; John L. Parker, *History of the 22nd Massachusetts Infantry* (1887; Baltimore: Butternut and Blue, 1997), p. 435; Powell, *Fifth Corps,* p. 664; Maltz to Robertson, June 30, 1864, regimental records, State Archives.
14. Luce memoir, p. 26; Walter F. Beyer and Oscar F. Keydel, *Deeds of Valor: How America's Heroes Won the Medal of Honor,* vol. 1 (Detroit: Perrien-Keydel, 1907), pp. 327–28; LaFleur deposition quoted in Minnie Dubbs Millbrook, *A Study in Valor—Michigan Medal of Honor Winners in the Civil War* (Lansing: Michigan Civil War Centennial Observance Commission, 1966), p. 98.
15. Seage diary, May 10, 1864; Hewitt diary May 10, 1864.
16. Hewitt diary, May 11, 12, 1864; Seage, *History of Co. E,* p. 35; Seage diary, May 12, 1864, p. 35; Poyer's death was mentioned in a letter by Heman Smith (whose real name according to census records was Heman Evans), in Smith to Dear Friend, May 20, 1864, miscellaneous file, Charles Bates Papers, Bentley Historical Library, University of Michigan. Poyer's burial in the entrenchment was related in a statement by a comrade, William Gould, part of a pension application by Poyer's family, Poyer pension file, National Archives. Accounts of the skirmishes and attacks by regiments in the same division as the 4th Michigan during this time are in Carter, *Four Brothers in Blue,* pp. 404–5; and Parker, *22nd Massachusetts Infantry,* p. 439.
17. Seage, *History of Co. E* (May 13, 14, 1864), p. 35; Hewitt diary, May 13–20, 1864; Fox, *Regimental Losses,* p. 383; Carter, *Four Brothers in Blue,* p. 400.
18. 4th Michigan strength: Vesey letter in the *Sturgis Journal,* June 16, 1864.
19. *Sturgis Journal,* June 16, 1864; *Detroit Advertiser and Tribune,* May 27, 1864; *Detroit Free Press,* June 27, 1864; Seage, *History of Co. E* (May 15, 1864), p. 35; John Bancroft diary, May 15, 1864, Special Collections and Archives, Auburn University Library. Van Valer's company is referred to in the state's regimental records for the 4th Michigan as "the Independent Company."
20. Bancroft diary, May 16, 1864; Seage diary, May 16, 1864.
21. Bancroft and Seage diaries, May 17–21, 1864; Parker, *22nd Massachusetts Infantry,* p. 444; H. Smith (Evans) to Dear Friend, May 20, 1864, Bates Papers.
22. Seage diary, May 22, 1864.
23. Bancroft diary, May 22–23, 1864; Seage, *History of Co. E* (May 23, 1864), p. 36.
24. Bancroft diary, May 23, 1864; Seage diary, May 23, 1864; *Michigan Record of Service* vol. 4, p. 70; Fox, *Regimental Losses,* p. 383; Parker, *22nd Massachusetts Infantry,* p. 448; Carter, *Four Brothers in Blue,* p. 429; *Monroe Commercial,* June 23, 1864

    A letter critical of Lt. William H. Sherman of the new company, written by soldier Henry S. Wells and printed in Hillsdale, set off angry charges and countercharges involving personnel of the 4th Michigan. The controversy raged for months in papers of the towns from where the men hailed. Before it ended, Sherman, accused of cowardice by Wells, resigned and ran for the state legislature as a Democrat that fall. He lost. One veteran sergeant called the dispute "foolish" and noted that many soldiers had been separated from the regiment during this fighting. Wells, he said, shouldn't have been so critical.
25. Bancroft diary, May 24–27, 1864; Seage diary, May 24–27, 1864; Seage, *History of Co. E,* p. 37.
26. *Sturgis Journal,* June 16, 1864; Bancroft diary, May 28–30, 1864; Seage diary, May 28–29, 1864; *Monroe Commercial,* June 23, 1864; Seage, *History of Co. E* (May 30, 1864), pp. 37–38; *Four Brothers in Blue,* p. 417; Powell, *Fifth Corps,* p. 666.
27. Bancroft diary, May 31–June 2, 1864; Seage diary, May 31–June 2, 1964; J. Barnes to Friend Harriet, June 2, 1864, Archive and Regional History Collection, Western Michigan University; Carter, *Four Brothers in Blue,* p. 417; Seage, *History of Co. E,* p. 38.
28. Bancroft and Seage diaries, June 3, 1864; William H. Smith to Dear Sister (transcription), June 12, 1864, copy provided by William P. Watson; Parker, *22nd Massachusetts,* p. 460; Carter, *Four Brothers in Blue,* pp. 424–25, 437; Maltz to Robertson, June 30, 1864, regimental records, State Archives.

29. Seage diary, June 4–5, 1863; Bancroft diary, June 4, 1864; *Monroe Commercial,* June 23, 1864; Taylor to Dear Mother, June 8, 1864, Taylor Collection.
30. Bancroft diary, June 5, 1864; *Monroe Commercial,* June 23, 1864; Taylor to Dear Mother, June 8, 1864, Taylor Collection; William Smith to sister (transcription), June 12, 1864, William P. Watson.

Chapter 14. The Regiment Is in a Bad Situation at Present

1. Henry Seage diary, June 5–12, 1864, John DeVinney; Seage, *History of Co. E,* pp. 38–39; John Bancroft diary, June 4–11, 1864, Special Collections and Archives, Auburn University Library; *Detroit Free Press,* June 23, 1864.
2. Carter, *Four Brothers in Blue,* p. 420.
3. Bancroft and Seage diaries, June 12–16; *OR,* vol. 40, pt. 1, p. 455; Carter, *Four Brothers in Blue,* p. 437.
4. Bancroft diary, June 17, 1864.
5. Bancroft diary, June 18, 1864; Moses Luce memoir, Edgar A. Luce Jr.; Harrison Daniels reminiscence, Craig and Ann Emery and Hal Flynn.
6. Bancroft diary, June 18, 1864; Carter, *Four Brothers in Blue,* p. 440.
7. Bancroft diary, June 18 and 19, 1864; Luce memoir; Daniels reminiscence.
8. Daniels reminiscence; Luce memoir; Michigan Adjutant General, *Records of Service,* pp. 32 and 54; *Hudson Gazette,* March 7, 1915; Bancroft diary; Seage, *History of Co. E,* (June 19, 1864), p. 40.
9. Daniels reminiscence; Maltz to Robertson, June 30, 1864, regimental records, State Archives of Michigan; *Detroit Advertiser and Tribune,* June 24, 1864 (evening edition, June 20 letter of Bancroft); Roberstson, *Michigan in the War,* p. 232; Fox, *Regimental Losses,* p. 383; Seage, *History of Co. E,* p. 40. While Seage didn't muster out with the "old men," his company history accurately described the major events of these days.
10. Daniels reminiscence; *Detroit Free Press,* June 28, 1864; *Hillsdale Standard,* June 28, 1864. Henry Seage's *History of Co. E,* p. 40, states that the men of the 4th Michigan arrived in Detroit on June 26, and it appears to have been early in the morning.
11. *Monroe Monitor,* June 29, 1864.
12. Luce memoir; *Hillsdale Standard,* June 28 and July 5, 1864, quoting the *Detroit Advertiser and Tribune; Hudson Gazette,* July 2, 1864, also quoting the *Detroit Advertiser; Monroe Monitor,* July 4, 1864, quoting the *Lansing State Journal.*
13. *Hillsdale Standard,* July 6, 1864; Luce memoir.
14. Reports on the ceremony of the returning flag at Adrian: *Hudson Gazette,* July 2 and 9, 1864; *Detroit Advertiser and Tribune,* July 9, 1864; *Detroit Free Press,* July 2, 1864; *Hillsdale Standard,* July 12, 1864; Charles Cleveland diary, July 4, 1864, Bentley Historical Library, University of Michigan.

    Was the flag presented to Mrs. Wilcox that day the original flag? Ned Taylor had written to his sister on May 21, 1863 that the original flag was sent home; Quartermaster Lt. Robert Campbell, speaking years later, agreed. By the time Taylor wrote his letter, the original colors had already been replaced with a new flag, brought by Campbell from Washington, as indicated in Henry Seage's diary entry for March 24, 1863, and as Campbell would maintain in his later accounts. Campbell wrote that this second banner was a U.S. flag, though Seage later wrote in his company history that it was a blue flag with a gold eagle. Of course, the historical evidence indicates it was a U.S. flag that was lost at Gettysburg, just as Campbell maintained.

    Harrison Jeffords had described the poor condition of the regiment's original "Defend It" U.S. flag in a late April letter to the *Michigan (Ann Arbor) Argus,* published on May 4, 1863. Letters printed in the *Adrian Watchtower* early in 1863 made clear that the officers of the 4th Michigan intended for Mrs. Wilcox to have this flag. Perhaps the "Defend It" flag was already back in Michigan when these men returned, and they simply brought it with them for the July 4th ceremony.

    Writing and speaking about regimental flags decades later, Robert Campbell said that the flag he got to replace the one captured at Gettysburg (the regiment's second U.S. flag) was blue with an American eagle and white stars. He said this was the regiment's third flag, and claimed in 1902 that both "our first and third flag may be seen at the military museum in the State capitol in Lansing." For years, Civil War banners carried by Michigan regiments were on display in the state capitol.

Yet the surviving evidence, in the form of the flags themselves, doesn't support Campbell about the blue flag. According to Kerry Chartkoff, head of Michigan's Civil War flags preservation effort, the State of Michigan has five flags associated with the 4th Michigan: First, a small "Dexter Union Guard" militia flag, which didn't go to war; second, the original U.S. "Defend It" flag presented by the women of Adrian in June 1861; and two other "fragmentary" U.S. flags—one that is truly a ragged fraction of its original size, about which nothing is known—and a second Stars and Stripes flag, parts of which were apparently cut away for souvenirs and which was turned over to the state in a large ceremony in Detroit on July 4, 1866.

The fifth flag associated with the 4th Michigan in the state's possession is a portion of a blue regimental banner with a finely painted Michigan coat-of-arms on one side and a federal eagle on the other. Mrs. Chartkoff describes this as "an expensive presentation flag" that has on its staff the inscription "New Organization," referring to the reorganized 4th Michigan. This flag also bears a motto, "Be As Brave." This blue, partial flag was also turned over to the state with numerous other Civil War flags in the 1866 ceremony and was recorded as having belonged to the reorganized 4th Michigan. Given that it is an expensive presentation flag for the reorganized 4th Michigan, it couldn't have been "procured" by Lieutenant Campbell to replace the U.S. flag lost at Gettysburg.

15. *Hudson Gazette*, July 9, 1864; *Hillsdale Standard*, July 9, 1864; *Detroit Advertiser and Tribune*, July 9, 1864; Cleveland diary, July 2, 1864.
16. Van Valer to Austin Blair, June 29, 1864, Austin Blair Papers, Burton Historical Collection, Detroit Public Library; William H. Smith letter, June 12, 1864 (transcription), William P. Watson; *Detroit Advertiser and Tribune*, July 4, 1864; Fifth Corps "special orders No. 146," *OR*, vol. 40, pt. 2, p. 217; *Detroit Free Press*, July 8, 1864.
17. *Detroit Advertiser and Tribune*, Aug. 14 and 16, 1864; Hall to Robertson, Aug. 1, 1864, 4th Michigan regimental records, State Archives of Michigan, Lansing; R. W. Seage pension application, National Archives; Hall to Capt. Knight (of the reorganized 4th Michigan at Adrian) authorizing Vreeland to recruit, Aug. 1, 1864, National Archives.

    Hall's spending March–June 1864 in Michigan is mentioned in a summary of his military record in a letter sent "To the President of the U. States," dated Aug. 1866, signed by Col. Michael Shoemaker of the 13th Michigan and six other individuals. Though Andrew Johnson was then president, the letter is from the files of the Abraham Lincoln Presidential Library. A letter by Hall, dated May 23, 1864, and written on stationery labeled "Headquarters Draft Rendezvous, Jackson, Mich.," also shows him assigned to duty away from the regiment. Hall signed this letter as major of the 4th Michigan, though records reflect his commission as lieutenant colonel dated from July 13, 1863. Heckert Papers, Monroe County Historical Museum.
18. Fifth Corps "special orders No. 146," *OR*, vol. 40, pt. 2, p. 217. The fact that men of the old 4th Michigan signed a petition to be attached to the reorganized 4th Michigan is reflected in War Department letter, Thomas Vincent, Adjt. General's Office, to George G. Meade, July 1864, Heckert Papers.
19. Boies to the Adjutant General, State of Michigan, May 25, 1888, Hudson Museum, Hudson, Michigan; Robertson, *Michigan in the War*, p. 234; Cleveland diary, Aug. 14, 16, 27, Sept. 25, Oct. 14, 18, 22, 1864; Charles Lanman, *The Red Book of Michigan; a Civil, Military and Biographical History* (Detroit: E. B. Smith, 1871), containing John Robertson's *History of Michigan During the Rebellion*, p. 180.

Chapter 15. We Have Broke the Backbone of the Rebellion

1. *OR*, vol. 39, pt. 1, pp. 453, 702, 703; Robertson, *Michigan in the War*, p. 234; Fox to Dear Father, Oct. 28 and 30, 1864, private collector; W. Warner to Dear Sister and also Dear Brother, Nov. 6, 1864, Bentley Historical Library, University of Michigan. A man who signed his letter "Chaplain," published Jan. 9, 1865, in the

Detroit Advertiser and Tribune, said the reorganized 4th Michigan arrived in Nashville on Oct. 29 and reached Decatur on Nov. 2, but this doesn't correspond with the earlier date given by Captain Fox and official reports. If "Chaplain" really was the regiment's chaplain—at this time, the Reverend John Seage—it seems he was traveling separately from the rest of the regiment, perhaps helping to care for the sick or carrying out other duties.

2. *OR*, vol. 45, pt. 1, pp. 612, 636–37; an unidentified newspaper clipping, probably from a Michigan paper in Nov. 1864, quoting the *Cincinnati Gazette*, Nov. 23, 1864; clippings (photocopied pages), Heckert Papers, Monroe County Historical Museum, marked as coming from the "Jarius W. Hall, 4th Michigan Papers, Civil War Miscellaneous Collection, U.S. Army Military History Institute, Carlisle Barracks, Carlisle, Pa."; telegraph message (copy), Gen. Thomas to Col. Snow, Nov. 21, 1864, 4th Michigan records, State Archives of Michigan; Lyon to Hall, Nov. 22, 1864, Abraham Lincoln Presidential Library, Springfield, Ill.; *Detroit Advertiser and Tribune*, Jan. 9, 1865.
3. *Detroit Advertiser and Tribune*, Jan. 9, 1865.
4. The story of the fight between men of the 4th Michigan and the regulars appears in *The Life of Billy Yank: The Common Soldier of the Union* by Bell I. Wiley (Indianapolis: Bobbs-Merrill, 1951), pp. 324–25. That account, in turn, is largely based on the *Nashville Dispatch*, Nov. 27, 1864.
5. Griswold to My Dear Sister, Feb. 22, 1865, and Dec. 20, 1864, Bentley Library; Hampton: "A Saga of Secession Days in the Southern States, Personal recollection of Mrs. C. C. Hampton, wife of Dr. Carlos D. Hampton, and mother of Will E. Hampton as told to him and taken down in short hand, and later printed in his paper, the Charlevoix Courier," Bentley Library.
6. Hall to Robertson, Dec. 29, 1864, 4th Michigan files, State Archives.
7. Miner was listed in a roster of Company B, reorganized 4th Michigan, in the *Hudson Gazette*, Jan. 28, 1865; Vreeland, "Letters from Civil War Battlefields," pt. 3, by Carl Vreeland, *Oregon (Portland) Journal*, June 28, 1964, and *Adrian Watchtower*, June 8, 1865; Lowery to Dear Mother, Jan. 1, 1865, Mrs. Glen (Lucy) Rutan Collection, Samuel McLain Letters, Archives and Regional History Collections, Western Michigan University, Kalamazoo.
8. Lowery to Dear Mother Jan. 1, 1865; and McLain to Dear Mother, Feb. 12, 1865, both in the Archives and Regional History Collections, Western Michigan University; *Detroit Free Press*, March 3, 1865; the Jan. 29 letter from Sgt. Roof is on a clipping that appears to be from the *Adrian Watchtower*, Feb. 9, 1865, in Heckert Papers, marked as coming from the "Jarius W. Hall, 4th Michigan Papers, Civil War Miscellaneous Collection, U.S. Army Military History Institute, Carlisle Barracks, Pa."; *OR*, vol. 49, pt. 1, pp. 19–20; Griswold to My Dear Hattie, Jan. 22, 1865.
9. *OR*, vol. 49, pt. 1, pp. 21–23, 917; report to Michigan Adjutant General from Maj. S.S. Parker, Jan. 21, 1866 (regarding the movement of the reorganized 4th Michigan throughout 1865), 4th Michigan files, State Archives.
10. *Detroit Free Press*, March 3, and May 16, 1865; Griswold to Hattie, Jan. 22, 1865; Jan. 28, 1865; Feb. 6, 1865; March 1, 1865, and March 9, 1865, all Bentley Library; Army of the Cumberland, May 11, 1865, extract of letter by Capt. R. S. Walker, inspector, Third Brigade, Third Division, Fourth Corps, 4th Michigan files, State Archives; *Monroe Commercial*, June 15, 1865.
11. June report to Michigan Adjutant General from Maj. S. S. Parker, Jan. 21, 1866 (regarding the movement of the reorganized 4th Michigan throughout 1865), 4th Michigan files, State Archives.
12. Boies to the Adjt. General, State of Michigan, May 25, 1888, Hudson Museum, Hudson, Michigan.
13. *Detroit Free Press*, July 13, 1863; *Detroit Advertiser and Tribune*, Aug. 14, 1864.
14. C. W. Owen, *The First Michigan Infantry—Three Months and Three Years* (Quincy, Mich.: Quincy Herald Print, no date), pp. 23. 38, 52.
15. Perine biographical clippings and statement, Sharon Mershon.
16. J. Barnes to Dear Brother Judge, July 20, 1864, Roger Walcott Collection, Archives and Regional History Collections, Western Michigan University.
17. *Detroit Free Press*, July 27, 1864; *Detroit Advertiser and Tribune*, Aug. 14, 1864; Amos Judson, *History of the*

83rd Regiment Pennsylvania Volunteers (Erie, Pa.: B.F.H. Lynn, 1865), p. 232; *OR*, vol. 42, pt. 2, p. 999.

18. Robertson, *Michigan in the War*, p. 234.
19. Smith to Dear Friends, April 9, 1865, University of Washington Digital Collection, http://content.lib.washington.edu/. The library's collection is searchable. A transcription of the letter is also in the Schoff Civil War Collection, Clements Library, University of Michigan.
20. Ibid.
21. Piper to Dear Parents, April 14, 1865, Lewis Leigh collection, USAMHI.
22. *Detroit Advertiser and Tribune*, July 7, 1865; *Monroe Commercial*, July 13, 1865.
23. William L. Richter, *The Army in Texas during Reconstruction, 1865–1870* (College Station: Texas A&M University Press, 1987), pp. 17–18; *Monroe Commercial*, July 13, 1865.
24. *Detroit Free Press*, Aug. 17 and Oct. 22, 1865; *Hudson Gazette*, Sept. 2, 1865.
25. Richter, *Army in Texas*, p. 18; Griswold to Hattie, Sept. 11, Oct. 17, Oct. 19, Nov. 19, Nov. 30, Dec. 11, 1865; Bentley Library; Major S. Parker to Robertson (report), Jan. 21, 1866, Heckert Papers.
26. Griswold to Hattie, Dec. 26 and 31, 1865, and Jan. 15 and 24 and Feb. 26, 1866, Bentley Library.
27. General Orders No. 1, regarding Hall as commander of the San Antonio subdistrict, Lincoln Presidential Library; Bradley to Robertson, report of Jan. 21, 1866, and March 11, 1866, 4th Michigan files, State Archives; *Detroit Free Press*, April 4, 1866.
28. The New York paper's accusatory report is in an unidentified newspaper clipping from 1865 or 1866, originally from the Jairus Hall file, Civil War Miscellaneous Collection, USAMHI. A photocopy of this and other newspaper clippings is in Heckert Papers.
29. *OR*, vol. 48, pt. 2, p. 1223; Robertson, *Michigan in the War*, pp. 234–35; *Detroit Free Press*, April 22 and May 16, 1866.
30. *Detroit Free Press*, June 12, 1866.

Chapter 16. I Saw Passing a Great Army

1. The *Hillsdale Standard*, June 22, 1875, suggests yearly reunions began for the 4th Michigan in 1873, but other reports on reunions indicate the first was held in 1872. Community planning for the reunions: *Hudson Post*, May 19, 25 and June 15, 1876, and June 16 and 23, 1916; *Hudson Gazette*, May 20, 1876, May 15, 1896, and May 18, 1916.

   Women's role in the reunions: The *Hudson Gazette* credited the 1875 reunion dinner to 'the ladies of Hillsdale," while an undated clipping from the *Hillsdale Standard* in 1878 said "the ladies of Tecumseh" handled that year's reunion dinner. The local Women's Relief Committee preparing dinner is in the *Adrian Weekly Times and Expositor* of June 28, 1889. The WRC is also credited in reports on 4th Michigan reunions in the *Coffee Cooler*, Aug. 1892 (the *Cooler* was a monthly newspaper for veterans published in Sturgis); also *Hillsdale Standard*, June 27, 1893; *Adrian Times*, June 20, 1911; and *Hudson Gazette*, June 15, 1916, to cite just a few examples. Women from the local Methodist Church making dinner, *Hudson Post*, June 23, 1916. Participation of ex-rebel "Burkley"or Barkley: *Hudson Post*, June 27, 1884; *Hudson Gazette*, June 27, 1884; *Adrian Times*, June 19, 1911.
2. Magee's emotional speech: unidentified Hudson newspaper clipping about the reunion in Hillsdale, June 1875, Hudson Museum; host communities decorated in patriotic fashion: *Hudson Post*, June 22, 1876; *Hudson Gazette*, June 26, 1896; *Jackson Citizen Press*, June 18, 1913; *Hudson Gazette*, June 23, 1916.

   Coverage in the Hudson paper of the 1875 reunion in Hillsdale reflects the veterans marching to greet the flag at the railroad depot, and citizens marching with them; this is also in the *Hudson Post*, June 25, 1876, and June 27, 1884, and many others. Clippings about the regimental reunions routinely showed the presence of the regiment's first flag at the events year after year.
3. For example, at the 1890 reunion, Lumbard's widow made badges featuring a picture of Little Round Top, the Gettysburg landmark, *Michigan (Sturgis) Democrat*, June 26, 1890. She also made badges for the 1893

reunion in Hillsdale, according to an unidentified clipping in the Hudson Museum; the *Steuben County Republican,* June 25, 1902, reported she sent 75 "beautiful button-hole bouquets" for that year's reunion. Mrs. Wilcox made silk badges for the survivors' 1889 reunion in Adrian, from an unidentified clipping from a Jackson newspaper; the *Adrian Weekly Times and Expositor,* June 28, 1889, reported the men received flowers that were pinned to their lapels when they arrived in town for the reunion.

4. Dinner speeches and toasts are reflected in most accounts of the reunions, sometimes in detail. A sampling of articles that mentioned or covered them are *Hudson Post,* June 29, 1876 and June 27, 1884; *Hudson Gazette,* June 25, 1876; *Adrian Times & Expositor,* June 28, 1889; *Monroe Commercial,* July 2, 1897. Declining numbers: unidentified news clipping on the North Adams reunion in 1898, Hudson Museum, and *Jonesville Independent,* June 28, 1917.
5. Memorandum by Henry Seage, then president of the 4th Michigan association about the plan to memorialize Jeffords at Gettysburg, dated Jan. 5, 1886, is in the Hudson Museum. Gruner's paintings for fund-raising: Malvern Hill picture, in *Hillsdale Standard,* June 22, 1875, and *Hudson Post,* June 22, 1876. Gettysburg painting: a clipping about a reunion in Eaton Rapids, likely the *Eaton Rapids Journal* of late June 1886, in John Bancroft's diary-scrapbook, Special Collections and Archives, Auburn University Library. Huff traveling to Gettysburg to identify his regiment's place: a copy of an unidentified clipping in the authors' possession, apparently from a Hillsdale newspaper on which the date "Sept. 29 84" was written. Huff was from the Hillsdale area and lived there after the war.
6. Members of the 4th Michigan association voting to locate Lumbard's remains and pay for a monument, *Hillsdale Standard,* July 3, 1888, Bancroft diary; men unable to locate Lumbard's grave: *Adrian Weekly Times & Expositor,* June 28, 1889; authors' discussion by email with Donald Pfanz, staff historian, Fredericksburg and Spotsylvania National Military Park.
7. Seage's *History of Co. E* adopted by the members of the regiment: *Monroe Commercial,* July 2, 1897.
8. Dean's participation is in the *Michigan (Sturgis) Democrat,* June 26, 1890, and *Hudson Gazette,* June 23, 1896.
9. Miner and Boies meet, *Hudson Gazette,* June 22 and 29, 1916.
10. Paul Leake, *History of Detroit—a Chronicle of its Progress, its Industries, its Institutions, and the People of the Fair City of the Straits* (Chicago: Lewis Publication Co., 1912), pp. 966–67. The story about Dickerson and Janes was repeated in other various published biographical sketches of the men.
11. Many clippings about Company F's reunions survive in Hudson's local museum, including *Hudson Gazette,* Feb. and 23, 1910, and March 18, 1915, and *Hudson Post,* May 19 and 26, 1916. The report of Westfall's death in the *Hudson Post-Gazette* is datelined July 20, 1925. Westfall had been wounded in the right hand at Gettysburg.
12. The visiting veterans took rides in automobiles in Jackson: *Jackson Citizen Press,* June 21, 1913; "falling like leaves": *Hudson Post,* June 23, 1916.
13. Jeffords's sword: *Hillsdale Daily News,* June 20, 1922. Concern about the keeping of the regiment's first flag was expressed in a vote by the veterans at their 1898 reunion in North Adams; they planned to place it in "the war office in Lansing": unidentified (June) 1898 clipping in the files of the Hudson Museum.

    An article in the *Reading (Mich.) Telephone,* June 28, 1899, noted the flag was then being kept in "Comrade Salsbury's back office." An unidentified clipping, dated June 28, 1900, in the Hudson Museum about the regiment's 1900 reunion in Palmyra, and *Adrian Times & Expositor,* n.d., June 1901, also mentioned the original regimental flag and that it was to be turned over to the state of Michigan. It was.
14. "One hundred now living": *Hudson Post-Gazette,* May 8, 1923; the last reunion: *Hillsdale Daily News,* June 21, 1928, and *Hudson Post-Gazette,* July 3, 1929.
15. Partridge's state of mind, wounds, and suicide: Affidavits in his pension record, National Archives.
16. Leake, *History of Detroit,* pp. 965–67.
17. James M. Guinn, *Historical and Biographical Record of Southern California* (Chicago: Chapman Publishing Co., 1902), pp. 483–84; "Alumni Spotlight—Luce . . . Among 25 Who Shaped 'America's Finest City,'" *Hillsdale (College) Magazine,* Winter 1987, pp. 8–9; Moses Luce biographical materials and information provided by

Edgar Luce Jr.

18. The story of John Tarsney's escape by switching identities with the dead man is from *Kansas City: Its Resources and their Development . . . A Souvenir of the Kansas City Times* (Kansas City, 1890); *Hudson Post-Gazette*, Sept. 14, 1920. Tom Tarsney's death certificate is part of his pension record, National Archives.
19. Duffield biographical information: S. D. Bingham, *Michigan Biography* (Lansing: Thorp & Godfrey, 1888), pp. 238–39; Spalding biography: *Monroe Courier News*, Sept. (n.d.), 1915.
20. Childs's biography in Ellis, *Norwich University*, p. 616; letters regarding Childs's pension and disability applications are in his pension file, National Archives.
21. Pohanka, "George Yates," 13–19.
22. Death of Robinson: Henry Lovejoy Amber, *History of Dentistry in Cleveland* (Cleveland, 1911), pp. 85–86; unidentified news clipping, marked "1867," on his death, Robinson Family Papers, Bentley Historical Library, University of Michigan.
23. *Hudson Post Gazette*, Feb. 22, 1924, and Dec. 23, 1930.
24. *Colorado (Georgetown) Weekly Miner*, Feb. 22, 1872; "Col. Hall's Big Bear Fight," *Chicago Sunday Times-Herald*, Dec. 22, 1895; photocopy of Hall's 1903 death certificate, General Register Office, Lambeth District, County of London; *Omaha (Neb.) World-Herald*, Dec. 16, 1903.
25. *Hudson Gazette*, December, n.d., 1909, Hudson Museum.
26. Harrison Daniels reminiscence and newspaper obituary clipping, Craig and Ann Emery and Hal Flynn.
27. Perine clippings, Jan. (n.d.), 1934, 1935, 1936, 1940, *Battle Creek Enquirer & News*, and biographical statement, all provided by Sharon Mershon.
28. Taylor biographical data, introduction to Taylor letters, G. Taylor Collection, Warren Hunting Smith Library, Hobart and William Smith College Archives.
29. Barrett to Bachelder, July, 8, 1889, in Ladd and Ladd, *Bachelder Papers*, vol. 2, p. 1606.
30. John Seage pension file, National Archives; "Descendants of John Seage," a genealogy by John DeVinney.
31. Henry Seage pension file and Richard W. Seage pension file, National Archives; Ladd and Ladd, *Bachelder Papers*, vol. 2, pp. 1071–72; "Descendants of John Seage," by John DeVinney.
32. Bancroft pension file, National Archives.
33. Vreeland pension file, National Archives; Carl Vreeland, "Letters from Civil War Battlefields," pt. 3, *Oregon Journal*, June 26, 1964; copies of letters about commissions for Vreeland for brevet colonel and brigadier general are in Vreeland Papers, USAMHI, and in the National Archives, Records of the Adjutant General's Office, Letters Received by the Commission Branch, file V173CB1866.
34. *Hudson Gazette*, July 5, 1895; *Reading Telephone*, June 28, 1899; clippings about the 1900 reunion in Palmyra, Hudson Museum; Chamberlain obituaries (clippings from unidentified 1900 newspapers), the Toledo Public Library and Hudson Museum.
35. *Hudson Post*, June 14 and June 21, 1889; Campbell, "Pioneer Memories," p. 572.
36. Luce's Memorial Day speech was printed in the *Evening (San Diego) Tribune* in 1903. The clipping is undated, from materials from his family's history files courtesy of Edgar Luce Jr. and the San Diego Library.

Bibliography

Archives and Libraries

Archives and Regional History Collections, Western Michigan University, Kalamazoo. Charles Barlow letter transcript; Joel and Luke Barnes letters, Roger Walcott Collection; Samuel McLain and Thomas J. Lowery letters, Mrs. Glen Rutan Collection.

Auburn University Library, Special Collections and Archives, Auburn, Alabama. John Bancroft diary-scrapbook.

Bentley Historical Library, University of Michigan, Ann Arbor. Charles Bates Papers; Ransom Bush letter; Robert H. Campbell, "Service with the Old 4th Michigan Infantry," Michigan Military Order of the Loyal Legion of the U.S. (MOLLUS); Henry S. Seage, "War Reminiscences of the Battle of Fredericksburg," read in Detroit, March 2, 1899 (MOLLUS); Charles Cleveland diary; James Houghton journal; George Monteith letters; Jonas Richardson letters; William F. Robinson letters; copies of Silas Sadler letters; Eli Starr letters; James K. Spence letter; James G. Tuttle memoir; William Limbarker 1862 diary; John S. Conant letters; Harrison Jeffords July 7, 1862, letter.

Burton Historical Collection, Detroit Public Library. Austin Blair Papers; John M. Bancroft letters; George Maltz letters; Theodore Hinchman Papers; Marshall W. Chapin letter.

Center for Archival Collections, Bowling Green State University Library, Bowling Green, Ohio. Dwight Woodbury 1862 letters in the *Williams County (Bryan, Ohio) Leader.*

Clarke Historical Library, Central Michigan University, Mt. Pleasant. William Limbarker 1861 diary; John W. Hewitt diary.

William L. Clements Library, University of Michigan. Schoff Civil War Collection; Hacker Brothers Papers; letters of Edmond Bliss.

Fulton County Historical Museum, Wauseon, Ohio. Enoch Davis diary.

Hillsdale College Archives, Hillsdale, Michigan. Will Carleton Papers.

Hudson Museum, Hudson, Michigan. Various 4th Michigan and biographical newspaper clippings, letters, photocopies, and transcriptions.

Monroe County Historical Museum, Monroe, Michigan. Heckert Papers.

National Archives and Records Administration, Washington, D.C. Harrison Jeffords service and pension records and court-martial; Joseph Thompkins pension; Michael J. Vreeland pension record; William Vreeland pension; records of the adjutant general (courts-martial); Jonathon Childs pension; and the service and pension records of other soldiers and officers.

State Archives of Michigan, Lansing. 4th Michigan Infantry regimental correspondence and records.

U.S. Army Military History Institute, Carlisle Barracks, Carlisle, Pennsylvania. Michael Vreeland papers (photocopies); Jairus Hall file (newspaper clippings).

Warren Hunting Smith Library, Hobart and William Smith Colleges, Geneva, N.Y. Edward H. C. Taylor Civil War letters, G. Taylor Collection. http://academic.hws.edu/library/archives/taylor.asp.

Unpublished Items and Privately Held Manuscripts

Moses Luce autobiographical statement [memoir], Edgar A. Luce Jr.; Harrison Daniels reminiscence, Craig and Ann Emery and Hal Flynn; "Descendants of John Seage," a genealogy by John DeVinney; Miranda Goheen diary, Bob Coch; Lemuel Allen letters (transcript), Nancy Findley; Charles Phelps letters, Jeff Phelps; Henry Seage first and second diaries, Steve Roberts; Seage's third diary, John DeVinney; Silas Sadler letters and diary, Charles Doolittle diary, and C. Fox letters, a private collector; Irvin Miner diary, Robert Walkowiak; Noah Cressey letters, Lynn Bryant; George Millens diary, Glen McQueen; certain Harrison Jeffords letters (except where otherwise noted), from another collector who wished to remain anonymous; Edgar Noble diary, Thomas Spain; David Webster letters, Steve Bucher and Rose Miller; Albert Westgate letter, Kenneth Andrews.

Books, Articles, and Other Published Material

Adams, George W. *Doctors in Blue: The Medical History of the Union Army in the Civil War.* Dayton: Morningside Books, 1985.

Anderson, William M. *They Died to Make Men Free: A History of the 19th Michigan Infantry in the Civil War.* Dayton: Morningside Books, 1994.

Barrett, Orvey S. *The Old Fourth Michigan Infantry.* Detroit: W. S. Ostler, 1888.

Bertera, Martin, and Ken Oberholtzer. *The 4th Michigan Volunteer Infantry at Gettysburg: The Battle for the Wheatfield.* Dayton: Morningside Books, 1997.

Beyer, Walter F., and Oscar F. Keydel. *Deeds of Valor: How America's Heroes Won the Medal of Honor.* Vol. 1. Detroit: Perrien-Keydel, 1907.

Boies, Albert H. "Brave old Woodbury." *National Tribune* (Washington, D.C.), March 19, 1896.

———. "Malvern Hill." *National Tribune* (Washington, D.C.), February 13, 1896.

———. "The Spirit of Comradeship." *Confederate Veteran*, vol. 23, September 1915.

———. "War Memories." A series of six articles based on his Civil War diaries, *Adrian (Michigan) Daily Times,* March 20 and 27, April 3, 10, 17, and 24, 1886.

Burton, Brian K. *Extraordinary Circumstances: The Seven Days Battles.* Bloomington: Indiana University Press, 2001.

Busey, John W. *These Honored Dead: The Union Casualties at Gettysburg.* Hightstown, N.J.: Longstreet House, 1996.

Campbell, Robert H. "Pioneer Memories of the War Days of 1861–1865." *Michigan Pioneer and Historical Collections* (MPHC). Vol. 30. Lansing: Van Koop, Hallenbeck Crawford, 1906.

Carpenter, Jesse H. *The War for the Union 1861–1865: A Record of its Defenders Living and Dead from Steuben County, Indiana.* Angola, Ind.: R. H. Carpenter, 1888–89.

Carter, Robert G. *Four Brothers in Blue.* Norman: University of Oklahoma Press, 1999.

The Civil War CD-ROM. Guild Press of Indiana, 1996.

Coco, Gregory A. *Killed in Action: Eyewitness Accounts of the Last Moments of 100 Union Soldiers Who Died at Gettysburg*. Gettysburg: Thomas Publications, 1996.

———. *A Vast Sea of Misery: A History and Guide to the Union and Confederate Field Hospitals at Gettysburg, July 1–November 29, 1863*. Gettysburg: Thomas Publications, 1988.

Coddington, Edwin P. *The Gettysburg Campaign*. Dayton: Morningside Books, 1979.

Coxe, John. "The Battle of Gettysburg." *Confederate Veteran*, vol. 21, no. 9, September 1913.

Davenport, Alfred. *Camp and Field Life of the Fifth New York Volunteer Infantry*. New York: Dick & Fitzgerald, 1879.

Eisenschiml, Otto. *The Celebrated Case of Fitz John Porter*. New York: Bobbs-Merrill, 1950.

Ellis, Franklin. *History of Livingston County, Michigan*. Philadelphia: Everts & Abbot, 1880.

Ellis, Helen H. *Michigan in the Civil War—a Guide to Material in Detroit Newspapers 1861–1865*. Lansing: Michigan Civil War Centennial Observance Commission, 1965.

Ellis, William A., comp. and ed. *Norwich University, 1819–1911: Her History, Her Graduates, Her Roll of Honor*. Vol. 2. Montpelier: Capital City Press, 1911.

Foote, Shelby. *The Civil War: A Narrative*. New York: Random House, 1958.

Fox, William F. *Regimental Losses In The American Civil War*. Albany: Albany Publishing, 1889.

Guinn, James M. *Historical and Biographical Record of Southern California*. Chicago: Chapman Publishing Co., 1902.

James, Henry B. *Memories of the Civil War*. New Bedford, Mass.: F. E. James, 1898.

Jorgensen, Jay. *Gettysburg's Bloody Wheatfield*. Shippenburg, Pa.: White Mane Books, 2001.

Judson, Amos. *History of the 83rd Regiment Pennsylvania Volunteers*. Erie, Pa.: B.F.H. Lynn, 1865.

Lanman, Charles. *The Red Book of Michigan; a Civil, Military and Biographical History*. Detroit: E. B. Smith, 1871.

Lawson, Albert. *War Anecdotes and Incidents of Army Life: Reminiscences from Both Sides of the Conflict between North and South*. Cincinnati: E. H. Beasley, 1888.

Leake, Paul. *History of Detroit—a Chronicle of its Progress, its Industries, its Institutions, and the People of the Fair City of the Straits*. Chicago: Lewis Publication Co., 1912.

Mertz, Gregory A. "General Gouverneur K. Warren and the Fighting at Laurel Hill." *Blue & Gray*, vol. 21, no. 4, summer 2004.

Michigan Adjutant General. *Records of Service of Michigan Volunteers in the Civil War*. Vol. 4. Kalamazoo: Ihling Bros & Everard, 1905.

Millbrook, Minnie Dobbs. *A Study in Valor: Michigan Medal of Honor Winners in the Civil War*. Lansing: Michigan Civil War Centennial Observance Commission, 1966.

Monaghan, James (Jay). *Custer: The Life of General George Armstrong Custer*. Lincoln: University of Nebraska Press, 1971.

Owen, C. W. *The First Michigan Infantry—Three Months and Three Years*. Quincy, Mich.: Quincy Herald Print, no date.

Parker, Francis J. *The Story of the Thirty-second Regiment, Massachusetts Volunteer Infantry*. Boston: C. W. Calkins, 1880.

Parker, John L. *History of the 22nd Massachusetts Infantry*. 1887; Baltimore: Butternut and Blue, 1997.

Pfanz, Harry P. *Gettysburg: The Second Day*. Chapel Hill: University of North Carolina Press, 1987.

Pohanka, Brian. "George Yates, Captain of the Band Box Troop." *Greasy Grass* (Custer Battlefield, Historical & Museum Association), vol. 8, May 1992.

Powell, William H. *The Fifth Corps, Army of the Potomac*. New York: G. P. Putnam's Sons, 1896.

Regan, Timothy J. *The Lost Civil War Diaries: The Diaries of Corporal Timothy J. Regan*. Ed. David C. Nelson and Kenneth J. Pluskat. Victoria, B.C.: Trafford Publishing, 2003.

Richter, William L. *The Army in Texas during Reconstruction, 1865–1870*. College Station: Texas A&M University Press, 1987.

Robertson, John. *Michigan in the War*. Lansing: Michigan Adjutant General and W. S. George, 1880.

Scott, Robert Garth. *Forgotten Valor: The Memoirs, Journals, & Civil War Letters of Orlando B. Willcox*. Kent, Ohio: Kent State University Press, 1999.

Seage, Henry S. *History of Co. E, 4th Mich. Infantry, 1861–1864*. Lansing: Thompson & Van Buren, 1897.

Sears, Stephen W. *Chancellorsville*. New York: Houghton Mifflin, 1996.

———. *Gettysburg*. New York: Houghton Mifflin, 2003.

Supplement to the Official Records of the Union and Confederate Armies. 100 vols. Wilmington, N.C.: Broadfoot Publishing, 1996.

United States. Surgeon General's Office. *Medical and Surgical History of the War of the Rebellion, prepared under the direction of Surgeon General Joseph K. Barnes, United States Army*. 3 vols. in 6 parts. Washington, D.C.: Government Printing Office, 1870–88.

United States War Department. *The War of Rebellion: A Compilation of the Official Records of the Union and Confederate Armies*. 70 vols. in 128 parts. Washington, D.C.: Government Printing Office, 1880–1901.

Vreeland, Carl. "Letters from Civil War Battlefields." *Oregon (Portland) Journal*, in three parts, June 24, June 25, and June 26, 1964.

Wert, Jeffry D. *The Sword of Lincoln: The Army of the Potomac*. New York: Simon & Schuster, 2005.

Wiley, Bell I. *The Life of Billy Yank: The Common Soldier of the Union*. Indianapolis: Bobbs-Merrill, 1951.

Yager, Verdie. *Reflections on the Bean: History of the Hudson Area in Prose and Picture*. Brooklyn, Mich.: Exponent Press, 1983.

Yates, Annie Gibson Roberts. "Colonel George W. Yates." 1877. *Research & Review* (Little Big Horn Association), vol. 15, 1989.

Civil War Era Newspapers

Adrian Expositor; Adrian Watchtower; Michigan (Ann Arbor) Argus; Ann Arbor Journal; Cleveland Herald; Cleveland Plain Dealer; Detroit Advertiser; Detroit Advertiser & Tribune; Detroit Free Press; Detroit Tribune; Hillsdale Standard; Hudson Gazette; Jackson Eagle; Jonesville Independent; Lansing State Journal; Monroe Commercial; Monroe Monitor; New York Herald; Philadelphia Enquirer; Steuben (Angola, Ind.) Journal; Steuben (County, Ind.) Republican; Sturgis Journal; Tecumseh Herald; Toledo Blade; Williams County (Byran, Ohio) Leader.

Index

C

G

N

O

P

Q

R

Y

Z